To John Lukas :

Your books have stretched
my mind. Vielen Dank,

Klaus P. Fischer

America in White, Black, and Gray

America in White, Black, and Gray

The Stormy 1960s

Klaus P. Fischer

continuum

NEW YORK • LONDON

2006
The Continuum International Publishing Group Inc
80 Maiden Lane, New York, NY 10038

The Continuum International Publishing Group Inc
The Tower Building, 11 York Road, SE1 7NX

Grateful acknowledgment is made to Schroder Music Company for permission to quote from the song "Little Boxes," words and music by Malvina Reynolds, copyright 1962 Schroder Music Co. (ASCAP). Renewed 1990. Used by permission. All rights reserved.

Continuum Publishing is committed to preserving ancient forests and natural resources. We have elected to print this title on 30% postconsumer waste recycled paper. As a result, this book has saved:
12 trees
545 lbs of solid waste
4,247 gallons of water
8 million BTUs
1,023 lbs of greenhouse gases
Continuum is a member of Green Press Initiative, a nonprofit program dedicated to supporting publishers in their efforts to reduce their use of fiber obtained from endangered forests. For more information, go to www.greenpressinitiative.org.

Library of Congress Cataloging-in-Publication Data

Fischer, Klaus P., 1942-
    America in White, Black, and gray : the stormy 1960s / Klaus P. Fischer.
        p. cm.
    Includes bibliographical references and index.
    ISBN-13: 978-0-8264-1816-6 (hardcover : alk. paper)
    ISBN-10: 0-8264-1816-3 (hardcover : alk. paper)
    1. United States—History—1961-1969. 2. United States—Social conditions—1960-1980. 3. Social problems—United States—History—20th century. 4. United States—Politics and government—1961-1963. 5. United States—Politics and government—1963-1969. 6. Nineteen sixties. I. Title.
E841.F49 2006
973.923—dc22
                                                        2006007584

To Max

CONTENTS

ACKNOWLEDGMENTS

As I was writing this book and mentioning the topic to dozens of friends and acquaintances, I was amazed that just about everybody had weighty opinions about the 1960s, opinions that usually followed generational lines. My older friends in their sixties or seventies delivered strongly negative judgments, while boomers fondly recalled their youthful excesses, which, of course, they did not want their children to repeat. Most surprising, my students at Allan Hancock College and at Chapman University were generally disgusted by the antics of the radicals of the sixties. Could there be a real swing in student attitudes? If so, it would be something devoutly to be wished for. Politically, too, the reaction to the 1960s revealed either strong liberal or conservative positions.

In short, exposed to a gaggle of voices, I always found eager and useful sounding boards—so many, that I can only list those who have been exceptionally helpful. First and foremost, I would like to thank Leonard Marsak—mentor, friend, and gentle critic—whose historical insights and shrewd judgments proved invaluable. The same is true of Jeffrey Russell, who has the sharpest eye for historical detail I have ever encountered. His balanced judgments about many controversial issues relating to the 1960s caused me to reconsider or modify a number of hasty judgments and questionable explanations. I would also like to thank several friends and colleagues who proved helpful in a number of ways, notably Gary Bierly, Roger Hall, Roger Welt, all of Allan Hancock College. Thanks are also due to Daniel Patrick Brown and Bruce Garber of Moorpark College and Gilbert F. LaFreniere of Willamette University.

Finally, thanks to my wife, Ann, who helped me in typing extensive portions of the manuscript while also working full-time as a school psychologist. My editor at Continuum, Frank Oveis, was a fine and discerning critic and remarkably well informed about the 1960s. Whatever shortcomings the book might have are solely my own.

1

INTRODUCTION

1. A Voice from the Silent Generation

I belong to the "Silent Generation" that was born shortly before and during World War II, a generation that straddled the interwar generation, raised during the Great Depression and hardened by World War II, and the baby boom generation that was launched on the land like a torrent between 1946 and 1964. If I had been born in the United States, I would belong to this neglected and silent generation, which has been effectively drowned out by the baby boomers and perhaps overlooked by recent historical accounts. But then I am different anyway because I was born in Nazi Germany and raised during my formative years in war-shattered Europe. To make things even a bit more complicated, I was raised by my grandparents, whose values and beliefs were deeply rooted in the nineteenth century. My grandfather, who was born in 1878 in Bavaria, was a young man around the turn of the century; his value system as a professional apothecary was drawn from a wide variety of sources: modern science, homeopathic and herbalist traditions, neo-romantic philosophies, and what they used to call the muscular values appropriate to German males such as strength, discipline, hard work, loyalty, and love of country. Born in the Kaiserreich, he lived through two world wars, financial and economic depressions, bewildering technological changes, and unprecedented political chaos, which left his country devastated and humiliated. At the end of his life—he lived into his eighties—he had trouble understanding his world. The same can be said of my grandmother, a very pious Catholic who moved through life with deep-seated inhibitions and repressions. Married to a much older man—a distant relative, in fact—she sacrificed much of her youth in order to run a perfect household for a husband who was brought up to expect an immaculate home and a superb kitchen. Her life revolved around religion and food and not much in between.

My mother, who had been married to my father during the war in what is generally called a "shotgun marriage," divorced my father shortly after the war and paid little heed to me. A neurotic and self-centered woman, she went through a series of unstable relationships, most of them with American GIs, until she married one of them and moved to the United States in 1954. My grandparents, suspecting that my mother was ill-suited to raise a child, had succeeded in gaining custody of me and packed me off to an exclusive private boarding school located in a castle at Neubeuern near Rosenheim, a school at the time run by Count von Stauffenberg, a relative of the legendary Nazi resister who almost managed to blow up Hitler in July

1

of 1944. I do not look back fondly on my high school (Gymnasium) years in Neubeuern. The school was a dumping ground for the children of rich industrialists, social climbers, declassed aristocrats, or just tired parents who, like my grandparents, had difficulty in raising their children properly. My academic performance at this elite school was less than sterling, especially in math and Latin. I made up for my mediocre academic performance by shining in sports, especially gymnastics, track, soccer, and skiing. My grandfather, who carefully monitored my performance at Neubeuern and must have spent a fortune on my education, shuddered when he saw my grades but was thrilled every time I was chosen as student athlete of the year. In fairness to Neubeuern, the academic grounding I got there made it relatively easy for me to excel in the American school system. Moreover, since the school groomed its students to be future leaders, I acquired a strong sense of discipline and respect for authority that, despite internal resistance, has never left me.

Although I would not describe either my upbringing or education as excessively authoritarian, I still found it stifling and restrictive. My mother, who was fading in and out of my life, had in the meantime managed to persuade me that America was the land of golden opportunity, and that the time had come to join her in America. Compared to another year of dreary schoolwork, America appeared the perfect solution to what seemed to me to be a dead-end life as a student cooped up in a dank castle in Bavaria. My grandfather's death in 1958 made the decision to leave Germany much easier. One year later, in the fall of 1959, I arrived in Chandler, Arizona, light years away from my castle in Bavaria and woefully unprepared for what was to come next.

What happened to me next is what Alvin Toffler would later describe as culture shock. The contrast between Catholic Bavaria with its mountains, tidy villages, churches, and castles and the sun-drenched Arizona desert with its rodeo culture could not have been greater. Apart from the difference in language and climate, what struck me was the bigness and "newness" of everything around me, which suited me well because it made it easier to forget the old world from which I had escaped. There simply was no visible sign of anything old or traditional, except for the Indians who lived on the margin, out of sight and out of mind. The Anglos who had moved in droves to Arizona after the Second World War, displacing Indians and Mexicans, were also in a sense newcomers who had escaped the bad weather back East or run away from their own past. I would later learn that the American love of the new—neophilia as some have called it—combined with a tendency to escape from the past, is very much an American character trait. Along with a strong bias for change, innovation, willingness to experiment, and openness to unconventional ideas, this love of the new constitutes an important feature of American life and culture.

Arriving in Arizona with a heavy baggage of social conventions, I was amazed and taken aback by the folksy attitude of the people I met. I was especially delighted by the custom of accepting people for what they were rather than accepting or rejecting them on the basis of their social origins. This was especially true of my peers at school, who accepted me openly and generously despite the differences of culture and language. I am sure that some of them probably thought that I had come from a different planet, and my earnest and labored efforts to decode their slang or idiomatic expressions caused much laughter. I had made it a point to learn and listen first before venturing any opinions. This struck my schoolmates as a bit weird because they had been conditioned since childhood to believe that they were special and unique, empowered to voice opinions on the weightiest subjects imaginable. They would speak up with great force and determination, which was so different from what I was used to in Germany. A student in the German school system was told to shut up, study hard, and voice an opinion only if asked by the teacher. That I was learning to adapt to the American school system may be gauged from a remark by a friend in my high school yearbook who said, "I remember the first day you came into my Latin American class and every time I asked you a question you always said 'yes.' Now it seems as though you are always saying 'no.'" He added: "Actually, I'm really kidding," which he really wasn't. I had learned to speak up.

My high school classmates struck me as easy-going, uninhibited, and lucky. Most of the seniors and many juniors drove rather than walked to school; they openly showed affection for their girlfriends in school by holding hands, embracing, or walking arm in arm—a jarring sight to someone brought up in a much more straightlaced culture. On my first day in school I was amazed by all sorts of uninhibited behavior. Girls, for example, would preen themselves in class by powdering their faces, applying lipstick, doing their nails, or otherwise refurbishing themselves. Contrary to later sixties complaints, discipline was relatively light and informal. Academic requirements were, for the most part, equally relaxed. When I showed up at Chandler High School in September 1959 to register for the fall term, my guidance counselor, Mr. Turner, asked me what classes I wanted to take for electives. I had to ask him several times to explain this to me because students had no right to choose any of their classes where I came from. Since I had spent six years in the German high school (Gymnasium) system, Mr. Turner assumed that my math and science background far exceeded what Chandler High School could offer me. He, therefore, automatically waived all my math and science requirements, which pleased me no end. Unknown to me at the time, I had come in for the "Halo Effect," the stereotypical assumption that all Germans, like Einstein, must be mental giants in math or science.

Fortunately, I did not come in for the negative stereotype of the goose-stepping Nazi who was depicted in the American media as a fiendish enemy of everything that is decent and civilized. Not once did anyone ever try to stigmatize me personally for anything the Nazis might have done during World War II. My German background was never held against me and therefore did not cause social tensions, which is not to say that it did not cause many inner tensions in the sense that it made me acutely aware of the evils my homeland had perpetrated during the war. At the same time, America afforded me the opportunity and the resources to explore, honestly and objectively, what the Germans had done during the Nazi period. The subject of World War II was still fresh in everyone's mind when I arrived in the United States in 1959—so much so that it seemed as though Americans were refighting the war almost every day on television, in the movies, and in the pages of newspapers and magazines. The "Good War," in fact, was almost a national obsession, and it was triumphantly recounted in a host of self-congratulatory series on TV such as *Victory at Sea*, *Crusade in Europe*, *Crusade in the Pacific*, *Air Power*, *The West Point Story*, *The Silent Service*, etc. The cold war, which was still intense, strongly reinforced this American sense of triumphalism. Many Americans, no doubt, hoped that a strong infusion of jingoism would reduce the pervasive sense of anxiety about nuclear annihilation that was putting a wrinkle in an otherwise optimistic culture. Whether this national bluster actually decreased anxiety is debatable; but the aim was to give Americans the impression that any war, even nuclear war, was winnable by a victory culture that believed itself to be supreme and invincible.

Although I do remember a few nuclear air-raid drills while in high school, no one seems to have taken them too seriously. My peers, like probably most Americans, did not take many things too seriously. Their aim in life was to have a good time. Few social issues disturbed Americans in 1959. It was not until the mid 1960s that the climate of opinion began to shift dramatically, and that was largely the result of the civil rights movement and the Vietnam War. I remember entering a fairly placid America that was still being presided over by President Dwight D. Eisenhower, a now much undervalued president who served his country well and projected a strong show of confidence and trust. Eisenhower's America, however, was a predominantly white America—self-assured, smug, arrogant, above all, convinced of its inherent superiority over any other power on earth.

In retrospect, we know that this was make-believe rather than reality. Much about the 1950s was not what it seemed to be. It is, for example, an optical illusion to see the 1950s as conservative, dull, or uneventful. Social tensions and ethnic conflicts periodically erupted, but the country as a whole managed to maintain the cultural myths widely disseminated by its elite institutions, and that included the belief that the American free enterprise system had abolished the working class and would eventually equalize and harmonize all social problems. Few people of my age group, however, felt very deeply about social problems, and it was not until the mid 1960s that many middle-class college students claimed that they felt "oppressed" in America. Until that day, most members of my age group worried more about their personal lifestyles than they did about social justice or international relations. My friends were concerned about cars, girls, music, and other extracurricular activities; they were decidedly unconcerned about school, which they regarded as a terrible drag. What would happen after they finished high school—whether they would marry, go into the service, get a job, or go to college—was not a matter of urgent concern for most of them.

I was different from most of my American friends because I came from a different culture with different assumptions about a lot of things. At the same time, I worked very hard at being American, as I understood this at the time. Like most German-Americans I assimilated rapidly by mastering the English language and by identifying with American mores and manners. I had made a vow to become American for better or worse. As far as I was concerned, I would never go back to Germany other than as a visitor; anything else would have meant having to admit to my German relatives that I had failed to make it in America. So, unable to rely much on my mother, I had to make it on my own.

In the summer of 1960 I got my first introduction to the world when I went to work as a grocery "carry-out boy," braving the 110 degree heat, saving enough money to buy a car, and then heading for college in the fall of 1960. I discovered quickly that American higher education, for all its shortcomings, was a liberating and mind-extending experience. For one thing, I was pleasantly surprised to learn that with a bit of savings and help from my mother, a college education was definitely afford-able, not just for me but for anyone who was willing to make financial sacrifices and long-term commitments. American taxpayers in those days were far more generous than they are today in supporting a superb system of public schools and universities, both in Arizona and in most of the nation. Arizona State University, the campus I attended in the fall of 1960, was going through a remarkable expansion in order to accommodate the bulging baby-boom generation. From a small "Normal School," training teachers around the turn of the century, the campus had burgeoned into a massive complex of buildings that sprawled in all directions across the small town of Tempe, now a suburb of Phoenix.

Such freewheeling academic expansion, so typical of the 1960s, meant having to stand in long lines and attend large classes, especially on the lower division level. Reg-istering for classes, for example, required lining up along with hundreds of students in the blistering heat in front of the gymnasium, waiting to be admitted to the inner sanctum, where the school had transformed the gym into a vast trade show of classes, replete with departmental booths and class lists. The scorching sun notwithstanding, the registration process was actually very smooth and efficient—so much so, that the people at Disneyland would probably have been envious if they had watched it; for once being in the proper roped-in line, a student would circulate through the gym, sign up for classes, wind his way through additional rooms and annexes, get his pic-ture ID card taken, pay his tuition at various cash registers, and exit as a bona-fide stu-dent for the upcoming semester. I regarded the whole registration spectacle and other ingenious methods of mass processing students with a sense of awe and amusement rather than annoyance. In fact, unlike some students who then and later complained about feeling like tiny cogs in a massively indifferent machine, I have never felt alien-ated, isolated, or marginalized at any of the universities I attended. Moreover, I did not resent having to take a few large classes or having to submit myself to the rules or reg-ulations of the university. The multiversity of the 1960s was for me—and I suspect for most other students—a place of remarkable freedom and self-discovery. Professors were respected and they respected students. I remember most of my professors with great fondness. In those days, male professors still wore suits and bow ties, even in the hot desert sun. They were, for the most part, extremely well grounded in their disci-plines, serious about teaching their classes, and very generous in spending a lot of time with students outside the classroom.

A substantial number of my professors were veterans of World War II and had attended college on the GI Bill. They respected the values of education as well as the value of freedom that they had been fighting to protect. With few exceptions, they were open to new ideas, tolerant of student opinions, and rarely imposed doctrinaire views. I do not recall a single instance of a professor demanding that students conform to what we nowadays call "political correctness." Professors, of course, had strong convictions, but I was never exposed to any form of ideological correctness.

Coming from a far more authoritarian school system, where the Herr Professor walked on air and held his nose in the presence of the peons, I positively luxuriated in this atmosphere of academic openness and professional good will. Professors steered me to the right books and gave me plenty of opportunity to explore different topics. Library resources were excellent. In fact, my friends in Germany were often incredulous when I told them about the wide variety of books, articles, or documents I was able to procure on a host of subjects ranging from Nazi Germany, Communism, existential philosophy, to comparative literature—the fields that interested me most at the time. How ironic that I could inform myself better about the recent history of my own country in America than in Germany itself. I will always be grateful for the resources and generous help I received from the academic institutions I attended as a student or taught for as a teacher.

The notion of some sinister "multiversity," so popular among left-wing students in the 1960s, has been completely alien to me, which brings me to the subject of this book and why I am writing it. I have always considered the university a friendly and civilized institution; but that institution, like most others in America, has been radically transformed and, in my opinion, seriously undermined by the events of the 1960s. The politicization of the university, as everyone knows, began with the turbulent changes associated with the civil rights movement, the Vietnam War, and the rise of the New Left. I witnessed that turmoil at close hand at several institutions; I also had heated arguments with fellow students about social change, justice, and, of course, the Vietnam War, which affected us all. While identifying with progressive social change, especially the struggle over civil rights in the South, I found myself frequently on the opposite side of the cultural war because I saw no future in rejecting middle-class lifestyles in favor of radical or utopian panaceas. As a student of cultural history who had grown up in war-shattered Europe, I was dumbfounded whenever students would tell me with apparent sincerity that they felt "oppressed" in modern America. Their protests, safely mounted, of course, from the financially secure position of well-heeled middle-class backgrounds, struck me as so much eyewash. Nor was I much impressed by their leaders, who struck me as shallow, narcissistic, uninspiring, and distinctly juvenile. At the same time, I could not help but marvel at their sense of empowerment and how cocky they were in confronting not only the university but the whole "system," which usually turned out to be the unholy trinity of the government, the Pentagon, and the draft. I wondered where this self-assurance, self-empowerment, and self-assertion came from. What was the source of this moral certitude, which prompted many students to stand up to authority and defiantly deliver "non-negotiable" demands?

I witnessed a number of student protests throughout the 1960s, including the riot that occurred at Isla Vista next to the campus of the University of California in 1970, where students burned down a branch of the Bank of America. At the time of this and other riots I was completing my Ph.D. at the University of California. Hardly a week went by, it seemed, when the normal routine of university life was not disrupted by sit-ins, protests, demonstrations, and confrontations between student protesters and police. A stream of outside agitators exacerbated an already volatile situation. I can distinctly recall several incendiary speeches given on one occasion by Timothy Leary and William Kunstler, speeches that prompted student radicals to go on a rampage in Isla Vista, battling the police for two days. I was also caught in a violent confrontation between police and radical protesters on the campus of UC Santa Barbara, a confrontation that could serve as a key to my retrospective account of the 1960s and its sound and fury. I had just left the library, a place, incidentally, that was not frequented by radical students, and absent-mindedly strayed into the no-man's-land that separated a long row of screaming students and an equally long row of combat-ready policemen who were about to charge the students who were taunting them. Clutching my library books, I made a split-second decision not to be squashed like a bug between these two converging forces. I sprinted like a gazelle to the nearby administration building, where some kind-hearted lady, seeing me coming, flung open the door, let me in, and quickly slammed it shut. It was just in time because all hell then broke loose outside, with policemen charging the students with their guns and rubber truncheons.

This encounter with violence on a university campus made me wonder whether I was wasting my time being serious while others were insisting on being irrational. I asked myself whether I was the only one moving through a no-man's-land separated by two irrational sides or whether there were others who were revolted by the highly charged atmosphere of the time. I found out quickly that there were many students who resented these violent disruptions, but at the time voices of moderation and mature judgment were in very short supply. I recall being completely unable to identify with those who were polarizing the situation and I cursed both sides for their uncompromising positions and their willingness to wreck the university. It seemed to me at the time that what I had witnessed was an absurd melodrama, and that I should probably record it in a way that no one at the time was willing to see. My professional interests at the time, however, centered on the tragedy of my German heritage, not the strange antics of my newly adopted country. The stormy 1960s, however, have always been fresh on my mind, and I have read almost every account that has been published since. The works we have on the 1960s have been personally disappointing; they strike me as remarkably one-dimensional and politically biased. It is for this reason, together with my own need to recollect what has turned out to be my American heritage, that I offer a different perspective on the 1960s. It is to some degree very much an outsider's perspective, especially since it comes from someone who, at the time, was still traveling through the cultural and political landscape as a foreigner, marveling at this unfolding drama. On the other hand, it is also the perspective of someone who since that time has considered himself an insider with a stake in America. It may well be that such a vantage point has its advantage because I do not write to defend a parti pris. Since I was not a camp follower, left or right, in the 1960s, I am not a camp follower of historians who have colored that decade with either conservative or radical brushes. This angle of vision might just possibly offer a better perspective of what America was like before and after the 1960s and why.

2. The Way We Were: Before and After the 1960s

Older Americans who have fleeting memories of the 1950s can still recall the jarring contrasts of a decade that witnessed great economic growth and affluence side by side with cold war terror and anticommunist witch-hunts. Clashing images, periodically culled from old magazines or seen on television documentaries, tell us part of the story: Coca Cola and the H-bomb, McDonald's hamburgers and fallout shelters, Marilyn Monroe and Pat Nixon, Elvis Presley and Ed Sullivan, Rosa Parks and Ozzie and Harriet. The country tried to make up for time lost on war and economic hardship by following a path of unabashed consumerism. By the mid-fifties, Americans bought well over five million cars a year, and they threw away as many. Some fifty billion bottles of coke were consumed a year, thousands of highways constructed, motels and fast-food chains established. Consumption became a national religion. In the mid-fifties, a marketing consultant felt obliged to make an urgent plea for "enforced consumption" by saying that "our enormously productive economy ... demands that we make consumption our way of life, that we convert the buying and the use of goods into rituals, that we seek our spiritual satisfactions, our ego satisfactions, in consumption. . . . We need things consumed, burned up, worn out, replaced, and discarded at an ever increasing rate."[1]

Yet the culture of consumption concealed a reality most white Americans would rather not talk about too much in the 1950s, a reality in the form of poverty, racial inequality, bigotry, and conformity. Not even the 150 million tranquilizers that Americans consumed annually could conceal a certain inward dread and anxiety about that underworld. The psychic state of the nation was not what it appeared to be on the surface. Outwardly, American society seemed prim, proper, and almost neo-puritanical; it was a world of expanding capitalism in which the demand for conformity was shouted from corporate rooftops. A generation weaned on depression and war, redeemed by hard work and organizational teamwork, evinced a positive zeal for replicating in peacetime the military model that had worked so well in wartime. This zest for standardization could be seen everywhere: in the burgeoning suburbs with their Levittown tract houses, in the McDonaldized food industry across the nation, in streamlined entertainment on television, in the standardized tests and curricula in the nation's schoolrooms.

The term "nonconformist" became a byword for being "un-American." The McCarthy period, after all, had shown how one could mass-produce the standardized, 100-percent American: white, red-blooded, square, and patriotic. Even beauty, epitomized by the Miss America contests, was standardized in the ideal American beauty: white, middle class, svelte, and blond. Clairol hair products said it all: "if I have but one life to live, let me live it as a blond" because "blonds have more fun."

"The Girl" image that supposedly reflected the ideals and values of young women in America was really manufactured by the advertising industry. It was surely no accident that Miss America was crowned at Atlantic City or Miami Beach, places associated with leisure and consumption. As Harvey Cox has pointed out, "The Girl" is an idol who sanctifies a set of phony values and "compounds her noxiousness by maiming her victims in a Procrustean bed of uniformity."[2]

The same sort of cultural uniformity prevailed in the school system. Americans sent their children to school in yellow buses, and they expected the schools to enforce strict discipline. Unlike today, American public schools enforced strict dress codes on the assumption that slovenly dress encouraged undisciplined behavior. This meant no jeans for the boys, no pants or short skirts for the girls. Teenagers were supposed to look like adults; they were expected to be well dressed and well groomed. Girls wore hair that looked like mom's perm-pressed, beehive head, while boys wore crew cuts to make them look like miniature cadets practicing to be war heroes like their fathers. High school principals worried about kids chewing gum or getting out of hand at football games or dances. At high schools around the nation young people attended dances called "sock hops," which were great fun and later evoked much nostalgia in a TV series called *Happy Days*. Tom Mathews, recalling the period for *Newsweek* can still see "guys padding the hall in saddle shoes and humming Sh-Boom."[3] A nice girl was a virgin who didn't smoke cigarettes. No one heard of ideology because there were few issues that aroused political passions. "We were suspended closer to the Age of Sinatra than the Age of Aquarius," Mathews said, adding that the bad trips came later.[4]

At colleges, professors disparagingly called the young generation of students the Silent Generation because they were politically uninvolved, which may have been a reaction to McCarthyism and cold-war terror. No one, it seemed, wanted to go out on a limb and risk being redlined. Panty raids were the most daring things male college students did in the 1950s. Women went to college to find a man so that they could raise children and live the suburban life. Marriage and family life promised security and happiness in a rapidly expanding economy. In 1955 the two non-fiction best-sellers were Better Homes and Gardens' *Decorating Book* and Betty Crocker's *Cookbook*.[5]

Most Americans appeared relatively satisfied in the 1950s. In its July 4th, 1955 commentary, the editors of *Life* Magazine editorialized under the headline "Nobody is Mad with Nobody" that the nation was "up to its ears in domestic tranquility. Embroiled in no war, impeded by no major strikes, blessed by almost full employment, the U.S, was delighted with itself and almost nobody was mad with nobody."[6] Real Estate was cheap, interest rates low, and prices on most consumer goods were quite affordable. Gasoline was 17¢ a gallon, cheap enough to encourage Detroit to keep on building ever larger automotive dinosaurs that culminated in the greatest orgiastic indulgence, fins and all, called the 1959 Cadillac Eldorado. Ownership of cars was matched by ownership of homes. Three-bedroom tract homes ranged from $5,500 to $7,500 in the mid 1950s. A steak dinner was $1.50.

Popular culture and entertainment were, for the most part, bland and escapist.

Americans watched TV shows that stressed inoffensive entertainment and family values: the *Adventure of Ozzie and Harriet, Leave It to Beaver, The Donna Reed Show*, and *Father Knows Best*. They loved slapstick comedy by watching Jackie Gleason on the *Honeymooners*, Lucille Ball on *I Love Lucy*, and the old-time comedians, as sharp as ever, George Burns and Jack Benny. Army recruiters claimed that many young people joined the army because they thought army life resembled the zany world of Sergeant Bilko depicted on *The Phil Silvers Show*. Children watched the adventures of Spin and Marty, and Annette on the *Mickey Mouse Club*; they also eagerly followed the adventures of Superman as he saved the world in his "never-ending battle for truth, justice, and the American way."

Strict censorship kept vulgarity and risqué subjects from appearing on television and motion pictures screens. Chaste fiction was the expected ideal in the literary world, prompting some historians to call the 1950s neo-Victorian in outlook. Good triumphed over evil; real heroes stood proud and tall. They were also invariably white, ruggedly handsome, and brimming with self-confidence. By watching television or motion pictures one would not have known that there was another side, a darker underside, to American life in the form of ugly racism and grinding poverty. The image that America projected at home and abroad was that most Americans lived in posh mansions, wore fashionable clothes—three piece suits and ties for the men and elegant dresses, white gloves, and high-heel shoes for the women—and expressed themselves in articulate, even eloquent English. The tone was elevated and designed to reinforce high standards and expectations. Blasphemy was taboo and there could be no alternative to Judeo-Christian morality, the family, and monogamous heterosexual relationships. It was a white man's world in the literal sense of the word because white men dictated the tone and temper of the age. Women were seen as still belonging in the home, and minorities—blacks, Latinos, Indians, Asians—were relegated to distinctly subservient positions in the white establishment. It was a monocultural rather than a multicultural society, proclaiming a triumphalist message to the rest of the world.

In the twenty-first century Americans still send their children to the public schools on yellow school buses, but the schools are very different from what they were in 1950. School principals no longer worry about kids chewing gum in class or even wearing the sloppiest clothes—torn jeans, vulgar T-shirts, sneakers, or baseball caps—but whether they bring guns, knives, explosives, or other lethal weapons to school. Violence in schools has been mounting steadily in the last thirty years, culminating in a widely publicized massacre at Columbine High School outside Denver, where two demented students, intent upon killing every single student, descended on their school with explosives and assault weapons, murdered at will, left a veritable battlefield strewn with bodies of dead students, and then immolated themselves by committing suicide. In the permissive culture of today, teachers have difficulty maintaining discipline, let alone teaching serious subjects to students who have been weaned by television and the relentless message of self-indulgence and self-gratification it preaches. "Good morning, teacher," resounding across schoolrooms fifty years ago, has been replaced by yawns or disparaging epithets. Connie

Shepard, a former high school teacher in Orange County, California, quit her job after a six-foot, freckled-faced red-haired sixteen-year-old student screamed at her: "Shut the fuck up, you bitch."[7]

Such erosion in discipline over the past fifty years has been accompanied by an equally alarming drop in such basic subjects as reading, writing, and arithmetic. Students are routinely promoted from one grade to the next regardless of their academic performance, and just about everyone who attends class regularly graduates from high school. In some cases, widely publicized by reformers, high school graduates have been unable to read their own diplomas. Things are not that much better on the college level, where the grading of general core courses has been either seriously slackened or entirely eliminated by a new educational establishment often more interested in ideological indoctrination than rigorous scholarship. This new establishment consists of now graying baby boomers who are attempting to instill what Martin Gross has called a new "secular theocracy" of political correctness.[8] Their message is that America is tragically flawed and riven by injustice and exploitation. They see America in terms of distinct and antagonistic ethnic groups who have been victimized by white racism and need permanent therapeutic help and financial assistance. They have imposed a multicultural model on American education that stresses group identity and promotes favored status to historically victimized groups. Critics are marginalized, censored, or expelled from the ranks of educators. Some of our finest universities have promulgated "speech codes" and sexual harassment policies that spell out what students can or cannot do or utter. Words like multiculturalism, diversity, racism, and sexism are loosely bandied about by people who claim to celebrate and protect "minorities," which includes everyone except dominating white men, who have created all existing inequities. Who would have thought it possible in 1950 that a largely white cultural or educational establishment could engage in periodic bouts of collective self-loathing?

The new educational establishment has patronized young people by offering them a dumbed-down curriculum that is often simply a continuation of high school coursework. The official message is that everybody can finish college, and not just finish but finish with honors. Administrators and teachers have dumbed down the curriculum, inflated grades, eliminated vocational programs, and readjusted normed tests in order to make it appear that just about everyone is smart. This trend toward enforced academic egalitarianism surfaces periodically when we learn, for example, that 84 percent of recent Harvard seniors graduated with "honors."[9]

Although the cold war is over and communism has collapsed around the world, Americans feel no safer today than in 1950. Violence stalks the streets of our cities, the court system is on the verge of breaking down, millions of Americans are in prison, and terrorists pose a constant threat to our national security. With the economy booming in the year 2000, Americans are as well-off today than they were in 1950; yet few would claim today that "nobody is mad at nobody." Quite the contrary, we live in a culture of infantile complaint, as Robert Hughes has said, in which "Big Daddy is always to blame and the expansion of rights goes on without the other half of citizenship—attachment to duties and obligations."[10] The hallmarks of good citizenship such as voting, membership in clubs, volunteer work, and social service are fading rapidly. Trust in government and its good word has also been dissipated, and for good reasons: presidential misconduct, corruption in high office, misuse of government funds, empty slogans and unfulfilled promises, failure to protect military secrets, and foreign policy debacles. The measure of our dwindling trust in government and in each other is the mass production of lawyers, police, security guards, electronic surveillance systems, and the explosive growth of penitentiaries around the country.

All this may point to a significant generational change that involves the withdrawal from civic-mindedness to self-centered hedonism. Over the past fifty years Americans have tried to create a civilization that does not depend on delayed gratification of individual needs and pleasures but on their instant gratification. This culturally authorized permission to indulge freely without prior restraints has been especially remarkable in sexual mores and activities. Since the 1960s Americans have sharply separated recreational from procreational sex. There is no shame attached to premarital sex in most parts of the United States. Contraception is socially acceptable, censorship is less pervasive, interracial marriages are widely accepted, gays and lesbians march in parades to celebrate "gay pride," and abortion is legal.

Many people would call these things positive gains, but whatever they are, they must be measured against the costs that have been incurred in the form of sexually transmitted diseases, especially AIDS; the breakdown of the traditional family; the harm that has been done to children by irresponsible adults seeking only their own pleasures and by the degrading commodification of simulated sexuality on television, in the movies, and on the Internet. Americans of all ages can now easily access the most degrading and revolting spectacles. If in 1955, we turned on television, we would have seen uplifting and idealized versions of reality; but if we do it today, we are likely to see something far more disturbing than the bland or inoffensive fare offered in 1955. Surfing the television channels on July 16, 2000, the viewer would have run across a curious but intriguing message that was blinking on the screen, beckoning one to watch a segment of the *Jerry Springer Show* entitled: "Shocking Family Secrets." On closer inspection, the viewer would have heard a young man boasting to a large audience and to his brother who was on the stage with him that he had been sleeping with his grandmother. Everyone, including the brother, pretended to be shocked, but the cocky young man didn't see what the big deal was, brushing aside his brother's outrage, he said that he just wanted to find out if grandpa, now diseased, was right when he boasted that grandma was the greatest lay in town. After boos and hisses from the audience, the host called on Kitty, the grandmother, to come out and explain her part in the incestuous affairs. She did so amidst wild guffaws and gales of laughter from the audience, which showed its warm appreciation of the show's host and the amazing spectacle he was putting on with wild outbursts of "Jerry, Jerry, Jerry." This wonderful segment was then followed by further family scandals such as that of Rob, who was sleeping with his cousin but pretended to be upset because she, in turn, was sleeping with another cousin.

Although the *Jerry Springer Show,* now cancelled, is not representative of what one sees on television today, it was on the cutting edge of an avant-garde trend that celebrated degrading, vulgar, and deviant spectacles. Springer has had numerous and more respectable predecessors. The National Education Association (NEA), for example, funded $70,000 for a gallery show that featured Shawn Eichman's *Alchemy Cabinet*, which treated spectators to the joy of seeing a jar with bloody fetal remains from the artist's own abortion.[11] "Performance artist" John Fleck publicly urinates on a picture of Christ; Annie Sprinkle masturbates on stage with various sex toys and invites members of the audience to explore her private parts with a flashlight; Karen Finley smears her body with chocolate, burns the American flag, and chants "God is Dead."[12] Such aesthetic performances, according to avant-garde critics, should not be condemned because they make an important social statement that must be heard. Works of art cannot be labeled "wrong" in themselves; they are simply an expression of the needs and feelings of the artist. Decency is entirely in the eye of the beholder, and what may be shocking to one person could be creative to another. The worst moral or aesthetic sin is to be "judgmental." Even a song about gang rape and genital mutilation should not be condemned if it has an "infectious beat" and "vivid imagery."

In the fifty years between 1950 and 2000 American culture underwent more convulsive changes than in the whole period stretching from the end of the civil war to the 1950s. Some have regarded these changes as a breath of fresh air, a chimney sweeping of reactionary moral codes and repressive prohibitions. They embraced organizations such as COYOTE (Call Off Your Old Tired Ethics), luxuriated in their new freedom, and gave full vent to hedonistic pleasures without regard to any social consequences. Many people, however, still believe that a healthy culture should not give a forum to those who want to undermine its traditional values. They say that every time we fund or watch the work of artists or producers who hate America, celebrate loathsome losers as heroes, or grovel in violence and sado-masochistic themes, we implicitly strengthen their dark visions and become complicit partners in their subversive activities.

Just as Americans stood up to McCarthyism in the early 1950s, Americans have increasingly gone on record that they oppose the "airborne pollutants" of popular culture in today's society. They have expressed concern about the impact of violence and explicit sexual content on the nation's children, who are exposed to such things on television and in films, music, and video games. More than 90 percent of all programs offered during children's prime viewing hours are violent in nature. By the time the average teenager graduates from high school, he or she will have witnessed fifteen thousand murders on the tube.[13] Such a barrage of violent images, the critics point out, not only threatens to rob children of their normal childhood innocence but also distorts reality and undermines character growth. In their efforts to find scapegoats, they point to Hollywood, the entertainment industry, and perverted artists and performers. The popular entertainment industry and its performers respond by saying that they are merely giving people what they want, and that art is simply a mirror image of the collective unconscious. Thus, if art reflects violent images and obsessive preoccupation with deviant or aberrant ideas, it simply makes a statement about the actual state of our collective being. The response by upholders of tradition is to argue that the artists and producers are sick, while the rest of America is normal and decent. Madonna once pointed out that "the actors and singers and entertainers I know are emotional cripples. . . . Really healthy people aren't in this business, let's face it."[14] She should know, having made a career out of being a slut. Should we therefore heave out the Madonnas, porn stars, traffickers in violent entertainment and return to happier days when good always triumphed over evil and wholesome entertainment was the order of the day?

Whether such happy days ever existed, except in the nostalgic memories of those who are outraged by present discontents, has been questioned by most historians. While it may be true that we cannot take a flying leap back into some imaginary past, it is also true that an imaginary past has sometimes been a great impetus in shaping the future. In the climate of the current "cultural wars" about the future of American civilization, the past is constantly with us, and perhaps no other decade has been as decisive as the 1960s in shaping the world as it is today, for better or worse.

3. An Age of Protest

The period from 1960 to 1974—from the election of John F. Kennedy to the resignation of Richard Nixon—represents a profound shift in the axis of American culture, which until that time defined itself, rightly or wrongly, as a white middle-class culture with a strong commitment to Christian values, free-enterprise capitalism, the political values of the eighteenth century, and a unique sense of American exceptionalism.

These commitments to Western beliefs were not entirely subverted, but the protest movements of the stormy 1960s eroded the foundation on which these beliefs rested, thus unhinging American culture from its axial faiths and plunging the country into a chaos of contending styles from which it has never fully recovered. Largely as a result of the 1960s, America is a "cultureless" society today, a mere agglomeration of ideas and people loosely tied together by commercial relationships and a political-legal system, now much degraded, that has provided a measure of social stability but that may also prove incapable of carrying us safely over the growing internal divisions that are separating us from each other.

The meaning of the 1960s can be understood only by examining the intricate conflict between the mainstream corporate-technological culture and the various protest movements that challenged its dominating assumptions and modes of control. Four major protest movements emerged in the 1960s: the civil rights movement, the antiwar crusade, the New Left, and the youthful "counterculture." Although there was considerable cross-fertilization between them—whites marching shoulder to shoulder with blacks to end segregation in the South, Americans with a strong moral conscience joining young people to protest the war, ordinary college students and radical professors supporting various aspects of New Left ideology, and millions of disaffected, alienated, and just plain bored young people attaching themselves to the hippie way of life—the protest movements were quite distinct in their essential aims and group affiliations. The most successful protest movement was the civil rights movement because its cause was widely recognized by most Americans as just and also because its tactics of peaceful resistance and moral sincerity, initially exemplified by serious and honorable men, made a deep impression on American public opinion. Although the civil rights movement subsequently splintered and veered away from its integrationist objectives, it left a lasting legacy not only in the area of social justice but also in the field of radical tactics and moral persuasion.

The antiwar movement, which was the most amorphous in its social composition, drew heavily on the civil rights movement for its tactics and moral positions. The changing war in Vietnam determined its essential nature, scope, and intensity, which expanded and then contracted with the course of the war. With the end of the draft and America's humiliating withdrawal from the war, which resulted in a communist victory in Vietnam, the antiwar protest quickly fizzled and thus no longer represented a real threat to the dominant power structure. The New Left, which at one time had a strong beachhead in American colleges and universities but very little support outside the academy, fragmented in 1969 as a result of ideological vacuity, internal bickering, and incompetent leadership. Countercultural movements, on the other hand, represented a far more serious and lasting threat to the corporate establishment because, at one time or another, they comprised a sizable part of a whole generation of young people, collectively referred to as the baby boomers. Seventy-six million strong, this generation would systematically challenge and reject many of the values, beliefs, and mores of their elders. Generational conflict, of course, is an inherent element in historical change, but never before in history did this conflict reach the level of intensity that it did in the 1960s.[15]

The causes of these disruptive protests can be understood only in their historical context. As might be expected, historians do not agree on the exact meaning of this unusual decade in American history.[16] The conventional view, which is not overly illuminating, is that the protest movements, particularly the counterculture, were merely a symptom of underlying problems in American society, though there is considerable disagreement about the relative importance of such problems and the causes that produced them. Some historians stress the importance of the great demographic changes that occurred in the postwar period, especially those relating to the baby boomers, but they fail to explain precisely how that generation shaped the history of the 1960s. Other historians attribute the great protests of the 1960s to structural changes in the postwar economy, to the cold war, some recurring "righteousness fever" that erupts periodically in American history, generational conflict, and even the decline of American culture.

If there is disagreement over causes, the same is true over consequences. Conservatives such as George Will, Allan Bloom, Robert Bork, William F. Buckley, and Roger Kimball have condemned the 1960s as an unmitigated disaster for our civil culture. Their criticism focuses largely on the alleged poisonous effects of the sixties on morality and individual lifestyles. In the eyes of conservatives, private and public decency has seriously deteriorated as a result of the decline in shared moral norms, widespread crime and drug usage, welfare dependency, the politicization of education, the weakening of the nuclear family, divisive ethnic ideologies, feminism, sexual permissiveness, and the degradation of popular entertainment. Conservatives have particularly drawn attention to the collapse of Judeo-Christian morality and its replacement, either by accident or by design, by an all-pervasive form of moral relativism. They have also raised an alarm concerning the collapse of the nuclear family, which they attribute to the rise of feminism and the feminist belief that men and women should be treated interchangeably—something, they claim that, having never been tried in history and counter to biology, is bound to wreak havoc on family life, the workplace, and gender relationships.

Conservatives also argue that even the vaunted successes in civil rights that have been commonly attributed to the 1960s have been undermined by radical tactics that, in turn, have spawned new socially divisive civil rights issues. Specifically, they single out what they call false egalitarian doctrines prompted by sixties radicals who have tried and often succeeded in enlisting the federal government in redressing past inequalities by discriminating in favor of certain protected groups such as blacks, American Indians, Latinos, women, and so forth. Such legislative and judicial social engineering has been conducted under the broad label of affirmative action, the preferred liberal tactic of fixing the past. Robert Bork, among others, has indicted sixties radicals, many of them tenured at our major universities or serving in government institutions, for having subverted the Constitution by turning it into an instrument for the propagation of false egalitarian ideas. The Constitution, the conservatives insist, does not confer equal rights but rather the equal exercise of those rights that it specifically enumerates. By that argument, the Constitution should not be used as a blueprint of discovery leading to endless additions of new rights.

In response to this chorus of conservative accusations, the left replies that all of us today, for better or worse, stand on the moral high ground of the sixties. Both liberals and left-wing progressives believe that far more good than bad has come out of that troubled decade. The lives of women, minorities, and gays, they claim, have been immeasurably improved by the legislation and social changes of the 1960s. The range of individual freedom and self-expression was far greater than it had been in the conservative 1950s, a decade during which the range of permissible actions was extremely narrow and circumscribed. Leftist historians, including Todd Gitlin, Morris Dickstein, Edward P. Morgan, and David Pichaske, argue that the politics of protest and self-expression opened up America's political and cultural space to more people than ever before. As a result, life was made more decent for millions of people. Even the democratic vision, they hold, was immensely strengthened by the fact that individuals felt more empowered to participate directly in the political process. This included a new "politics of compassion," which the political left regards as the hallmark of democratic polity, a communitarian vision based on equality, moral politics, and personal empowerment.

Another beneficial outcome of the 1960s, according to its defenders, was the growth of the environmental movement and its holistic vision of Mother Earth. Protecting the environment from corporate greed and spoliation was one of the most lasting legacies of the 1960s. Finally, the war on poverty and the protection of those who cannot protect themselves very well—the elderly, the handicapped, and other marginalized groups—represents another great achievement of the 1960s.

Although all sides agree that the 1960s brought about sweeping changes, they do not agree on the origin, nature, and extent of these changes. Observers on both the right and the left tend to view the sixties through their own ideological lenses, prompting them to offer misleading judgments not only on specific issues but also on the overall significance of the 1960s within the stream of history. Particularly unclear is the question of how the stormy sixties fit into the broad stream of American or even Western history. Some historians have viewed the 1960s as one of those historical cataclysms comparable to the American, the French, or even the Russian Revolution; but since there was no political revolution in the 1960s, the analogy to 1776 or 1789 quickly breaks down. In what other sense, then, can we speak of revolution? The answer given by some writers such as Theodore Roszak or Charles Reich is that the 1960s revolution was not a political revolution but a revolution in consciousness.[17] These writers concentrate on the "subversive" values of countercultural radicals and their rejection of bourgeois culture, without, however, making it very clear whether this rejection had any lasting historical effect or was just an ephemeral rebellion by young people that was doomed by the aging process or the flexibility of the mainstream culture in absorbing and neutralizing the protest.

Hunting for historical antecedents, some historians have compared sixties protesters to early-nineteenth-century romantics, French bouzingos of the 1830s, Russian populists of the 1860s, German Wandervögel of the 1890s, or, going even further back in history, Gnostics and Manicheans in the late Roman Empire, heretical movements such as the Albigensians, Waldensians, Lollards in medieval times, and Anabaptists or other extreme sectarians of the Reformation.[18] Historical analogies are suggestive because they remind us, as Nathan Adler pointed out, that humans have only a limited repertoire of responding to recurring needs and crises, which confirms once more what the authors of the Bible knew long ago: there is nothing new under the sun.

What characterized the 1960s was a recurring romantic protest movement against a classical mainstream culture that had become too rigid and too unresponsive to the needs of many young people. Such protest movements, which Nathan Adler has called antinomian, reject not only all the lawful institutions of a society but also their established modes of knowing or consciousness.[19] Antinomian or gnostic groups in history claim to possess a personal and direct method of illumination that is superior to mainstream or institutional paths to the truth or to salvation. These movements usually develop in times of rapid social change or in response to wars, plagues, or famines. Their members are seized by apocalyptic anxieties and often fall under the influence of charismatic leaders who bypass regular political channels and appeal directly to the people in vivid phrases and slogans. Separating themselves from the social mainstream, antinomian groups renounce family, marriage, or occupations and form alternative, communal lifestyles that often involve sexual libertinism and radical changes in dress and manners.

Sensing the coming of a new world, antinomian groups systematically reject the prized things of this world, through either passive resistance or militant aggression. The goal is to provoke the established powers, to repudiate all the values they cherish. If antinomian groups have a political style, it is anarchistic in the sense that it involves a total rejection of the values of contemporary society, a hatred of authority, and a belief in revolutionary change.

Without overextending historical analogies, there is no doubt that the young protesters of the 1960s exhibited many traits associated with previous antinomian groups in history. Feeling betrayed by the established culture, the young turned to protest and alternative values. Just as a host of religious movements over the centuries protested against the Roman Catholic Church for not living up to its ideal of catholicity—that is, its claim to be broad and inclusive—the young felt that mainstream American culture failed to live up to its professed ideals of universal rights for all of its citizens. The difference between previous protest movements and those of the 1960s was not necessarily the scope of the protests nor their intensity but the broad involvement of so many young people and the threat the protests posed to the possibility of maintaining any common culture at all in the United States.

What were the causes of these great upheavals? They seem to fall into six specific categories:

1. Certain cultural contradictions (fault lines) in American society
2. The impact of the baby boom generation
3. Exceptional economic and demographic changes
4. The rise of a teenage subculture
5. Breakdown and failures in socializing and educating the young
6. Racial and ethnic conflicts at home and war abroad in Vietnam

In the following pages, I argue that the 1960s opened with small but clearly audible movements along these fault lines in American society. Pressures on the civil rights fault line erupted into the first earthquake, followed by the Vietnam War and the generational conflicts that had built up all along. John F. Kennedy was a major catalyst of change, and his tragic death ushered in five years of unprecedented turmoil in American society. During those five years (1963–68), the shock waves of civil rights, Vietnam, youth rebellions, and cultural wars reached such intensity that America seemed on the verge of social collapse.

In reconstructing the dramatic events of the 1960s, I therefore locate the decade's center of gravity in those five years that stretch from the assassination of John F. Kennedy in November 1963 to the election of Richard Nixon in 1968. It seems to me that these five years of the 1960s, like those of the French Revolution (1789–94), were accelerations of historical change, rich in drama, violent in nature, and pregnant with the future. Although I have tried to observe historical chronology throughout the book, the chapters on the two great "carrier movements" of the 1960s—civil rights and the Vietnam War—are designed to tell a continuous story, going beyond how Kennedy, Johnson, or Nixon dealt with civil rights or the Vietnam War.

Without overextending a metaphor taken from natural events, I argue that the nation survived these earthquakes and aftershocks because the American people could draw on two centuries of democratic experiences that allowed them to cope with these disasters and repair some of the damage through concessions and accommodations to various aggrieved constituencies. Democracy served as a pressure release, but the way in which American democracy had been weakened in the process prevented long-term solutions from being implemented. The greatest damage to American society, however, occurred not so much in the political arena as in the cultural domain. The problem was a biological one: seventy-six million pampered young people tried to break the generational ties that usually safeguard historical continuity. Their revolt was made possible by permissive parenting, affluent times, and excesses in the consumer and mass media culture. In chapters 8–11, I explore at length the consequences of these youthful rebellions and their impact, for better or worse, on American society. Since the generational pig (the boomers) is still being digested by the python (the social system), these observations, of course, must be taken as tentative, but they do provide, I believe, more than a glimpse into the foreseeable future.

2

FAULT LINES IN A
LAND OF PERFECTION

1. The Myth of a Perfect Beginning

America is the final form of Western self-expression, carrying within itself the best as well as the worst of the Old World out of which it was made. Forged from the cultural elements of the Old World, the genius of America has been to maintain a considerable degree of cultural diversity within the broad context of a national "American" identity or creed. As an immigration society undergoing constant change, America has always managed to redefine itself as a nation, but that redefinition has also been difficult because it involved a strong tug-of-war between two forces pulling in opposite directions, one toward cultural diversity and the other toward a unitary style in the nation's life and culture. A permanent synthesis has proved elusive because the nation continues to be a multiracial, multiethnic, and to some degree multilinguistic society. The motto *e pluribus unum*—out of many one—has never completely held true because the cultural differences that separated various ethnic groups often threatened to overshadow the nation's common center.

Yet throughout American history one could always detect a pulsating energy that had its source in a distinct national creed. Until now, this centripetal force has been able to overcome the various centrifugal forces pulling at the vital center; and while it is true that the melting pot never melted, America has always been able to call on its unifying political ideals and inherited traditions.

American culture, like the ancient Hellenistic culture, is syncretic in the sense that it is a fusion of different or opposing principles and practices, just as the Hellenistic was a union of Greek and Near Eastern traditions. Such pluralistic cultures, composed as they are out of divergent elements, are always subject to internal contradictions. American culture has not been immune from such contradictions, which, under strong stresses, have sometimes formed countercultural syndromes tearing at the seams of the cultural mainstream. At the center of American history stands the Civil War, a living monument to the internal fissures in American history. In the decades leading up to the 1960s some of these cultural fissures stemming from the Civil War continued to operate; others had been added during the Gilded Age, the Great Depression, and the two world wars. The national landscape was full of cultural fault lines: the failure to find a broad consensus by which a plurality of people could be integrated into the mainstream; the difficulty of reconciling lofty national creeds of equality and universal wealth and happiness with existing realities of widespread inequality and poverty; a tradition of legalized inequality and discrimination against nonwhite minorities, especially African Americans; a belief in the Puritan work ethic alongside hedonistic consumerism; intellectual modernism warring against the heart and soul of the American dream; and a weak political system capable only of makeshift compromises and economic concessions but not meaningful structural reforms in American society.

America or the New World is the dream of the Old World, a dream of escaping from a world of tyranny into a world of freedom and golden opportunities. For well over two hundred years America has been a paradise for Old World sinners, for it was here, if anywhere, that a person could forget the sins of his past and find redemption through the land and the spirit it evoked in the hearts of those who needed to be born again. Over the course of time, America became more than the material resources it offered to land-starved immigrants: it became a powerful beacon of hope to the world, sending out a series of messages that resonated with millions of people around the world. America's most inspiring ideal was the promise of freedom, and Americans still believe that they have been singled out by God to carry the torch of freedom throughout the world until all humanity is free. Unfortunately, Americans also believe that only they have conducted the world's first serious experiment in building a new nation on a utopian vision of human freedom, self-fulfillment, and happiness.

The founding fathers who gave political shape to these ideals have often been depicted as hardheaded realists who tempered their utopian visions with a strong Calvinist conviction that humans were inherently wicked and sinful, and that political perfection was, at best, a distant goal. Although this judgment is partly true, the fact remains that the founders were also utopian progressivists who projected an imaginary vision of perfection against an imperfect reality in hopes that their posterity would take the vision as a standard and strive to fulfill it.

The remarkable success of the founders in forging a new nation based on democratic principles, however, gave rise to a troublesome mythology that the American political system was made by demigods who instituted a perfect form of government. This static view of American perfectionism effectively threatened to arrest historical development toward future perfection because if America started with perfection, it had no place to go, except to degenerate and revert to the failures of the Old World.

From the moment the nation was founded, Americans divided over the meaning and implementation of freedom. Many Americans committed themselves to the belief that their form of government was and ought to be unchanging because it was perfect in itself. They insisted that the Constitution was cast in cement and had to be interpreted the same way in which a true believer interpreted the Bible—in a one-dimensional and fundamentalist manner. There were others, however, who saw the Constitution as a living document that could be adapted to changing times, yield new insights, and support new rights in response to different social circumstances. Despite these different approaches, both sides agreed that the Constitution represented an unchanging bedrock of government, and that modifications or amendments should be the extreme exception rather than the norm. This viewpoint was accepted almost from the inception of the new nation; for once the romance of the revolution was over, most Americans abandoned political radicalism in favor of conservative protectionism. Radicalism is based on the proposition that any form of government, should it fail to meet the needs of the people, must be replaced by another and perhaps even a different *form* of government. In America, however, the term radical always had to stop short of its real intention. Strictly speaking, the term radical means "going to the roots" or favoring extreme change in the institutions and traditions of a society, preferably through revolutionary violence. Since Americans have generally venerated their institutions as perfect, they saw no need to sweep them away, and certainly not through violent revolution.

The founders, of course, were far more subtle in their political thinking on the issue of social change than subsequent generations assumed. The founders did not believe that they had created a perfect form of government, but only a plan to make it possible, and they hoped that future generations would approximate the standards they set for them. Future generations of Americans, however, tended to see the accomplishments of the founders as a frozen rather than a living monument, a fossil set between the pages of a book or a document exhibited in a display case. Though born in revolution, they became the most unrevolutionary people and supported revolutions in other parts of the world only if they met the test of their own revolutionary experience. Since they believed that they were already blessed by political perfection, they often displayed condescending or self-righteous attitudes toward people who chose to govern themselves differently.

The obverse of these apparent shortcomings stemming from the idea of utopian progressivism is the American sense of righteousness and faith in the future. A strong commitment to axial beliefs has given the American people a sense of absolute certainty that their political institutions are superior to any others in the world. While this view has encouraged smug, self-righteous, and arrogant attitudes in the American people, it has also saved the United States from equally self-righteous revolutionaries who wanted to subvert its democratic form of government. The American sense of political exceptionalism, it has often been argued, has saved the country from the upheavals of revolution that have rocked the rest of the world in the twentieth century. The American political tradition has, therefore, been almost entirely pragmatic and reformist; it has aimed at rooting change in already existing traditions and institutions, bringing them as much in line with the ideal projections of the founding fathers. Even the radicals of the 1960s moved largely within the permissible framework of the American political tradition. Regardless of what their critics said of them, the majority of sixties radicals wanted to reform the alleged abuses of American society and bring the country in line with the ideals of 1776. Sixties radicals were greater utopian progressivists than the conservative protectionists who mistakenly labeled them un-American and un-democratic. Their vision of America was progressive because it aimed at greater social perfection. This progressive vision was rooted in the American experience, but so was its opposite—that perfection had already been achieved and needed to be protected against its detractors.

2. Immigration: More Pluribus Than Unum?

America's uniqueness stems not only from a shared belief in political perfection, either as an inherited patrimony or a future inevitability, but also in its commitment to serve as history's first genuine immigration society. This new immigration society would welcome the tired, poor, and huddled masses yearning to breathe free and transform them into a new American race. Out of the many diverse races of people around the world would then emerge one new and higher American race. America was to be the melting pot of the world, transforming the many into one distinct American type: a new democratic citizen committed to the blessings of life, liberty, and the pursuit of happiness.

The new American man, according to Hector St. John de Crevecoeur, a French immigrant and author of *Letters from an American Farmer,* was a person who "leaving behind him all his ancient prejudices and manners, receives new ones from the new mode of life he has embraced, the new government he obeys, and the new rank he holds. The American is a new man, who acts on new principles."[1] Crevecoeur and the people who founded the new nation believed that America could melt the different individuals of all nations into a new race of people who shared a unique national creed.

The national creed referred to by Crevecoeur was that of democratic self-government and the underlying principles that supported it: government by consent of the governed, individual liberty, broad civil rights, political checks and balances, and free enterprise. The spirit animating the new creed was the philosophy of the Enlightenment with its emphasis on reason, toleration, and the dignity and equality of all human beings. The Enlightenment creed, of course, was strongly Anglo-Saxon in nature because America's original settlers were predominantly from English-speaking countries, which explains why Americans speak English and why their nation's political institutions and traditions, though rooted in the culture of the West, exhibit a distinctly Anglo-Saxon coloration. The emerging white Anglo-Saxon culture, however, harbored within itself what were regarded as unassimilable groups, chiefly black slaves and recalcitrant Indians. Moreover, as wave upon wave of huddled masses hit the teeming shore of America, the ideal of a single national creed was sorely tested over time because the newcomers often tenaciously clung to their native folkways, customs, and religions. Yet assimilation to an emerging American way of life was generally accomplished within a few generations. Every major group of immigrants—Germans, Scandinavians, Italians, Irish, East European—at first encountered considerable hostility and discrimination by already established groups, especially by the original settlers, who saw themselves as the country's reigning political and cultural elite. Stratification by ethnic affiliation was a fact of American life, and the social slights and humiliations experienced by recent immigrants and their children has filled accounts that occupy many library shelves all over the United States.

Anti-immigration feelings were never far below the social surface in a society composed of immigrants, especially in hard times when the Know-Nothings and other anti-foreign groups excoriated foreigners and held them responsible for every social ill that had afflicted American society. All men are created equal was often amended to read in practice that all men are created equal except the Irish who do not need to apply for jobs, the Italians who are too dangerous to apply, the Poles who are too dumb to apply, and the Negroes who are too inferior to apply because they are only fit to be slaves. Xenophobia, or extreme fear of foreigners, has been a persistent theme in American history, but it has been largely amorphous and poorly organized. In 1856 the Know-Nothing Party, which had made anti-immigration its major objective, ran Millard Fillmore, a former president of the United States, for the highest office of the land. Fillmore lost, and so did nativism. Since that time no xenophobic party has emerged in America, though anti-foreign sentiment continued to surface periodically. Large numbers of immigrants not only continued to come to America but were eventually absorbed into the mainstream of American life. Assimilation was facilitated by three factors: the power of the national creed, the elasticity of the frontier in absorbing millions of settlers, and free-enterprise capitalism. Excepting Indians and blacks, what was important was not one's blood or origin but one's merit and one's bank account.

The Europeanization of the continent proceeded with breathtaking speed and against all obstacles. Metaphorically, it reminds us of the old world seeking the fountain of youth in the new world. Inheriting the family fortune, old world youngsters released their repressed energy and tried to carry out their dream of unlimited opportunities "from sea to shining sea," only to discover that growth happened too fast, that gains were left unconsolidated, divisions allowed to remain unhealed. The American house of cards almost collapsed with the civil war, but the union ultimately survived and America went on a binge of industrial expansion that was the envy of the world. Millions of new immigrants arrived to share in the American dream of freedom and unlimited opportunities. Yet the many did not become one; the melting pot did not melt. Too many groups were left out of the Anglo-Saxon, white, and Protestant mainstream, particularly those groups who bore the brunt of ethnic and racial discrimination such as blacks, Indians, Latinos, and Asians. It should be of more than passing interest that the playwright who invented the metaphor of the melting pot, Israel Zangwill, referred to the races of Europe when he invoked the image of the melting pot. It was the races of Europe, not blacks, Indians, or Asians that he saw going through the crucible of God's melting-pot:

> America is God's crucible, the Great Melting-Pot where all the races of Europe are melting and reforming. . . . Here you stand in your fifty groups, with your fifty languages. . . . and your fifty blood hatreds. A fig for your feuds and vendettas! Germans and Frenchmen, Jews and Russians—into the crucible with you all! God is making the American.[2]

When Theodore Roosevelt saw Israel Zangwill's play, he exclaimed afterwards from his box: "That's a great play, Mr. Zangwill, that's a great play."[3] The president was obviously carried away by the play's noble theme that the United States was the only nation on earth that could remold different nationalities into one unified people. Deep down, however, like many Americans, he harbored doubts that the process was all but guaranteed. In a very prescient remark, Roosevelt warned that "the one absolutely certain way of bringing this nation to ruin, of preventing all possibility of its continuing to be a nation at all would be to permit it to become a tangle of squabbling nationalities, an intricate knot of German-Americans, Scandinavian-Americans, English-Americans, each preserving its separate nationality."[4]

The urge toward ethnic separatism has been a perennial problem in American history, and living patterns in America's major cities attest to its remarkable resilience. At certain times in American history, ethnic conflicts have been endemic as various groups, often consisting of young people, waged war against each other in the larger cities, pitting micks against kikes against wops against spicks against polacks against niggers, etc.

America's solution to such potentially disruptive conflicts was to rely on a combination of mythology and hardheaded realism, to preach a gospel of universal equality and to practice a social policy of economic growth and expansion that it was hoped would eventually blur social or ethnic differences. The assumption behind this approach was that ties of wealth and well-being would transcend ties of race or class, and that America would eventually be able to empower the teeming millions and lift them out of poverty and ignorance. Thus, with everybody well-off, there would be no more conflict, the assumption being that all social, racial, or ethnic conflict is fueled by economic circumstances. Two twin myths had to be widely believed to make this approach even remotely successful. The first myth was that America was a land of unlimited opportunities in which anyone who was hard-working, thrifty, and innovative could rise from rags to riches, from log cabin to the White House. The second myth presupposed and reinforced the first: the move from rags to riches was possible only under a completely free enterprise system in which people were left alone to pursue their economic self-interest without government interference. Conflicts are good, provided that they are redirected from unproductive ideological concerns and channeled into competitive enterprise. Unless they disturb the peace and cause violence, individuals and groups ought to be left alone to pursue their economic self-interest. After all, the business of America is business, the channeling of collective energy into material affluence for the greatest number of people. This being achieved, everything else will take care of itself.

3. The Flaws of Consensus Liberalism

The philosophy that gave shape to these myths and popular longings was liberalism, an Anglo-American political style that derived from Protestant individualism, Lockean ideas of equating property rights with freedom, utilitarian doctrines of the human as a selfish being endowed with the rational capacity to maximize pleasures and minimize pains, and American pragmatism, which judged the value of human actions in terms of their usefulness or "cash value." Liberalism's essential aim has been to liberate people from traditional restraints, except those that restrained people who could not restrain themselves. It defined liberty essentially in a negative form as the absence of restrictions; but since its focus was almost entirely on the autonomous or liberated individual, whose will and appetite were supposed to reign supreme, liberalism gave relatively little thought to the question of how these liberated and self-seeking individuals could be integrated into a larger community with strong collective values that transcended mere individual preferences.

Liberalism opposed the traditional values that derived from preindustrial communities, values that focused on humans as social beings rooted in a strongly homogenized religious environment. Instead, it viewed people as autonomous beings who had the capacity to calculate their own self-interest and should be allowed to choose their own values. Following the Enlightenment faith in reason, liberals believed that reason and education could serve as substitutes for traditional religion, long-standing customary practices, and strong "law and order." In their estimation, liberated individuals would be their own source and sanction of morality; they would do the right thing because it was right and not because it was superimposed on them by God or community sanctions.

This was "classical liberalism," and it gave carte blanche to unrestrained self-expression, the absence of restrictions, and minimal government interference in the lives of individuals. It was the natural philosophy of venture capitalists and sturdy pioneers, but it lacked a strong moral and community-building spine. Some have even accused it of being a philosophy without a moral compass because of its inability to generate a moral philosophy out of an amoral model of selfishness and egoism. The liberal response has been to separate morality and politics, arguing that the aim of politics is not to produce virtuous citizens who find fulfillment in their community, but to liberate individuals from community restraints so that they can discover self-fulfillment through self-enrichment. Economics thus trumps morality, which is relegated to the private sphere or to what people do on Sunday.

As long as there was a strong ballast of moral control associated with traditional religion and community standards, liberalism appeared to do little damage and was, in fact, seen as a liberating force; but once the amount of usable moral energy was being depleted by liberal inroads, the traditional, morally integrated community was finished. In its place came the pluralistic society of competing interest groups, for it turned out that autonomous people could not fend for themselves alone in an expanding and complex industrial society. They combined for mutual protection and formed increasingly complex and powerful organizations. Having liberated individuals from traditional authorities, was the individual now to be subordinated to new authorities, finding self-fulfillment not as an individual but as a member of a large economic organization? It became clear that the rise of large-scale interest groups and corporate organizations made classical liberalism increasingly difficult, if not impossible.

Liberal democracy had come out of a small world of self-governing and autonomous communities that were only indirectly affected by government. As long as America did not have a national state, classical liberal democracy was possible. The rapid industrialization of America in the late nineteenth century, however, forced a reorganization of government, which until that time had been largely small-scale and inactive. In fact, compared to European governments, America had no real national government until the turn of the century. The federal government had limited itself to national security through the maintenance of a military, the conduct of foreign policy, and the collection of tariffs and taxes. This changed dramatically between 1890 and 1945. As a result of various reform movements that sprang up in response to the excesses of the industrialization of America, government became progressively involved in the affairs of individuals and organizations.

This caused a split in liberal ranks between those who held on to doctrines of rugged individualism and minimal government and those who favored a strong government that would take an active role in the economy and adjudicate between contending interest groups. Both sides, however, reconciled themselves to the fact that modern industrial America consisted of competing interest groups who must be allowed to pursue their interests freely, but who cannot be allowed to monopolize the market or unduly deprive individuals of their economic opportunities. The role of government was seen as refereeing the competing interests through monetary or material concessions. As long as groups did not barricade themselves behind rigid ideologies, compromise was always possible. Liberals believed that debilitating social conflicts could always be avoided by economic concessions or reasoned discussion. The state would serve as a referee sorting out various conflicts, hopefully in a neutral and mutually beneficial spirit.

These optimistic assumptions were based on a liberal belief that government in the United States could not be an instrument of special interests in a pluralist democracy. According to this notion, power in the United States was divided and scattered among a plurality of competing interests, making it difficult, if not impossible, for any single group to acquire a monopoly over the whole of government. Individuals and groups thus always had the opportunity to exercise some degree of power under a pluralist democracy. Liberal strategy, therefore, aimed at inclusion, or allowing competing interests to acquire a share of power, which in practice meant "a piece of the pie." Liberals adamantly rejected radical complaints that there was no plurality of diverse interest groups in industrial America but simply a set of interlocking corporate institutions that exercised sovereign power and disguised their oligarchic practices behind a smokescreen of empty democratic pieties. The sheer diversity and the ever-changing nature of economic power, liberals argued, precluded any one group in America from exercising a monopoly on power, and that included besides economic also political power.

Liberals believed that they had successfully worked out a model of interest group politics that reflected the socioeconomic realities of American society. The model stressed consensus and compromise. It assumed, despite liberal disclaimers, that the individual was insignificant and counted only as a member of a particular ethnic, religious, fraternal, political, or economic group. Each group, if formally organized and not favoring the overthrow of American democracy, had intrinsic legitimacy and was entitled to bring power to bear on the government to get what it wanted. The role of government is not to represent the individual but organized interest groups that claimed to represent individuals and their aspirations. Liberals thus no longer envisaged society as a community of equals but rather as a tangle of organized interests that had to be brought together by skillful cajoling, compromise and concessions. No one in America, liberals believed, ever gets the whole pie; one must settle for a share of the pie. This is because politics, like economics, reflected the rational self-interests of its members, who could be counted on to compromise in the basically open-minded and conciliatory political system that liberalism provides. Recognizing that there are a host of interests that have varying claims to preferential treatment, groups will naturally forgo certain aims in favor of "half a loaf." Groups that feel left out of the mainstream and claim that they have been unjustly treated in America must be patient, give shape to their grievances by organizing politically, and present their case to the American people. Since the American people are a good and generous people, they will sooner or later recognize legitimate grievances and redress them.

Much of liberalism was wishful thinking, but it was not malicious. It naively assumed that divergent interests would either be harmonized by some "hidden hand" (the market) or by some extraordinarily gifted liberal legislators who would rise above self-interest and usher in compromise leading to the "common good." Both assumptions rest on faith: the market, which is supposed to be left alone to work itself out, is a metaphysical abstraction, and a selfless elite is an impossibility under a psychological model that explicitly postulates the inherent selfishness of all human beings. But in addition to these troublesome flaws, there is also liberalism's dubious mythology that power in the United States is dispersed in such a way as to preclude monopolies of power from dominating the political system. A corollary of this mythology is the belief that everyone is either represented under American democracy or is capable of being represented. This involves the pretense that the nation's political diversity can be strained through a two party system that supposedly straddles the liberal center. How a system that deliberately excludes unorthodox ideas and the interests of minority groups could be representative was either conveniently glossed over or rationalized as a shortcoming that would eventually be remedied.

The fact is that the American political system, despite claiming to be pluralistic and diverse, is in reality a highly streamlined business system interested primarily in the politics of affluence with only marginal concerns for issues that lie outside the purview of the corporate world. This is not to deny the existence of political issues that transcend the bread and butter issues that are of concern to the American voter. American politics is a carnival of pseudo-events, mudslinging, clashing personalities, and often contentious issues, but it is rarely a genuine expression of populist sentiments. It is carefully choreographed by the two reigning parties and the organizations that bankroll their politicians. Choices are strictly circumscribed and limited to pseudo-alternatives that turn out to be indistinguishable.

The two major parties in the United States, the Republican and the Democratic parties, are simply two opposite sides of the same coin: modern liberalism. Both practice the politics of affluence and promote the idea that the good life is the goods life. The differences between them come down to emphasis and tactics. The Republican Party, the party of business, has historically pursued the policies of classical liberalism with its emphasis on unrestrained individual enterprise, small government, and free trade, while the Democratic Party, the party of labor, focused more on economic justice and looked to government to implement it. Both parties, however, are broadly committed to economic growth and the proposition that economic affluence promoted happiness and social tranquility. Both parties also believe that capitalism, properly shaped and managed, would eventually promote social justice and enhance the democratic way of life. If we exclude the extremist wings in both parties—reactionary businessmen or religious fundamentalists in the Republican Party and left-wing radicals in the Democratic Party—we find that, as a matter of principle as well as self-interest, both parties usually reject ideological zeal in favor of pragmatic compromise. They have tried to straddle the moderate political center, assuming, rightly or wrongly, that this is where the majority of the American voters could be found. Finally, both parties realized that politics in a modern mass society was quantitative and required a very broad appeal to the largest numbers of people, which meant second-guessing their interests, frustrations, discontents, and prejudices. The application of "social science" procedures to divine what the electorate felt at any given point was held to be increasingly important by both parties, for once having discovered what the majority of the voters really wanted, the next step consisted in giving them at least the illusion that, once elected, a party and its politicians would do their utmost to satisfy every whim of the voters. The two parties focused heavily on pursuing the politics of affluence, which consisted in promising their constituencies that they could bestow the greatest economic happiness on the greatest number of people.

The two major parties also harbored the three acceptable forms of liberalism in America: left-wing liberals, pragmatic liberals, and right-wing liberals. Left-wing liberals, sometimes also called left-wing "progressives" were sentimental and optimistic reformers who believed in the goodness of human nature and the perfectibility of the social order through government-sponsored welfare programs and income redistributions. They were secularists who rejected Christian beliefs in favor of various philosophical sentiments such as equality, progress, human solidarity, and international peace. Their home was among New York intellectuals, most of them from Jewish immigrant backgrounds. The *New Republic*, *The Nation*, and later *Kenyon Review* and *Partisan Review* were their chief literary forums. In the 1930s many of these progressives had been enthusiasts for the Soviet Union, believing that their hopes for a better future were being perfected in Stalin's workers' paradise; but since America had marginalized the Socialist and Communist parties to the periphery of the political spectrum, many progressives preferred to remain within the political fold of the Democratic Party, where they continued to agitate for "real" rather than just piecemeal reforms. In 1948, many of these left-wing progressives defected from the Democrats and followed Henry Wallace in forming a new Progressive Party consisting of disenchanted New Dealers, starry-eyed idealists, and Communist-fronters. In 1952 and 1956, they enthusiastically supported Adlai Stevenson for the presidency because they believed that he represented, as they did, the real social conscience of the Democratic Party.

The predominant liberals in the postwar period were the pragmatic liberals, sometimes called "consensus liberals" because of their claim that they were the only group that could forge a broad consensus from divergent views. Claiming to be more open-minded and flexible, pragmatic liberals saw themselves as superior mediators who could compromise, overcome rigid ideological positions, defuse extremist demands, and move the more reasonable opposition to a mutually beneficial solution. Pragmatic liberals believed that they occupied the "vital center" on the political spectrum.[5] The word "vital" was intended to imply democratic, reformist, and moderate, the very qualities, according to pragmatic liberals, that the majority of the American people supposedly exemplified.

Historians have described pragmatic liberalism as more of a mood than a consistent political philosophy, but that view is too narrow because those who considered themselves liberal in this sense—and that included at one time a sizable section of American academia as well as influential politicians in both parties—believed that they had "modernized" liberalism by rejecting the foibles of both the left and the right. In place of discredited ideologies and failed causes, pragmatic liberals claimed to offer a genuine alternative: moderate, centrist, tolerant, flexible, and realistic.

The term ideology became a byword for intellectual intolerance and was reserved for those who had given their hearts and minds to totalitarian doctrines. In 1959 Daniel Bell published a widely read book that announced in its title *The End of Ideology*, tacitly implying that liberalism was not an ideology but presumably a set of flexible doctrines that merely produced useful results and could be discarded in favor of new strategies when the old one no longer worked. It was politics reduced to pragmatic technique rather than principle. Everything else, liberals claimed, was just a regression to primitive forms of consciousness that required submission to unchanging faiths or absolutes. By contrast, liberals claimed a progressive thinking-cap that was impartial and self-correcting because it presumably followed scientific method.

Some liberals even claimed a direct link between liberalism and science, arguing that "liberalism can move forward, like science, because it embraces self-correcting principles which permit the correction of error . . . without an overthrow of the system that makes such correction possible."[6] The self-serving assumption behind this extraordinary claim was that liberals were somehow free of the taint of partisanship, fanaticism, and bias simply because they claimed to be using scientific procedures. Unencumbered by dogmatic principles, which a rigid faith always entails, they claimed to be impartial in the use of evidence. They would approach political issues with a neutral state of mind, collect evidence, frame hypotheses, and offer solutions in a bipartisan manner. In politics, as in science, truth, and fairness could only be found through the application of the correct (liberal) sort of thinking: skeptical, open-minded, receptive to different claims, fact conscious, and tentative. The good liberal should never say "I am sure," but "I am inclined to think that under present circumstances this opinion is probably the best."[7]

By claiming the moral high ground of self-correcting scientific expertise, pragmatic liberals succeeded in looking smartly up-to-date, especially in an age that was making a fetish out of science and technology. In other words, by donning the mantle of science, particularly "social science," liberals could invalidate the positions of their political adversaries, condemning them for being "paranoid," authoritarian, intolerant, dogmatic, and the like. Relying on various psychological studies, notably *The Authoritarian Personality* by Theodor Adorno and his collaborators, *The Nature of Prejudice* by Gordon Allport, and *Escape from Freedom* by Erich Fromm, liberals tried to establish correlations between types of politics and modes of thought, reaching the edifying conclusion that liberalism was conducive to "flexibility of mental structure," individualism, toleration, open-mindedness, whereas other political positions (conservatism, fascism, socialism, communism) fostered rigidity, collectivism, intolerance, and so forth. The liberal mentality thus declared itself healthy and wholesome, while denouncing its opposition as unhealthy, neurotic, and even psychopathic. The authors of the *Authoritarian Personality*, for example, managed to saddle the whole political right with authoritarianism, but absolved liberals from the same disease. Even Gordon Allport, the most judicious liberal researcher, held that whether the tolerant person is militant or pacifistic, he is very likely to be liberal in his political views. Prejudiced people, he held, are often more conservative,[8] a view that was also echoed by Richard Hofstadter in his widely used book *The Paranoid Style in American Politics*, in which the whole political right is tarnished with the same brush of paranoia, bigotry, and intolerance.[9]

This zeal in battling the dragon of totalitarianism by enlisting the aid of behavioral science appears at first quite uncharacteristic of supposedly dispassionate and open-minded liberals—uncharacteristic until one realizes that many pragmatic liberals had formerly been true believers in left-wing causes and had now transformed themselves into cold warriors. Their hard-nosed anticommunism was often a kind of expiation of youthful indiscretions, when they had romanticized Marxist utopias, admired the Soviet Union, joined popular front groups, and identified themselves with the suffering masses. Such attitudes gradually chilled in the postwar period when it became fully known what crimes Stalin and Hitler had perpetrated. With the horrors of Stalinist purges, Auschwitz, and the atom bomb fresh in everyone's mind, liberals began to reexamine their formerly optimistic views of human nature, turning for inspiration to neo-orthodox theology (Niebuhr, Tillich, Barth) and Freudian psychoanalysis.

The manifesto of this reexamination was Arthur Schlesinger's book *The Vital Center*, published in 1949. Schlesinger, who later served in the Kennedy administration, believed that pragmatic liberals were intellectually and strategically poised to hold the moderate center in American politics. He forcefully argued that the great ideologies on both the left and the right had failed in their promise of human liberation and needed to be replaced by more scientifically based strategies that aimed, not at ultimate secular redemption, but more modestly at piecemeal reform and social engineering. Similar views, besides Schlesinger's, were voiced by Daniel Bell, David Riesman, Sidney Hook, Richard Rovere, and John Kenneth Galbraith. The time had come, these men argued, to stop chasing after ideological rainbows and confront the hard realities of the postwar years: defending freedom against communist aggression and reforming rather than destroying capitalism. They told their former allies on the left to stop worrying about capitalism, which was here to stay.

This was precisely the message the establishment running the security state wanted to hear. The result was that many pragmatic liberals became increasingly sought after by the government, accepting positions as researchers, policy advisers, or paid agents of CIA front organizations. As establishment insiders, it was no accident that pragmatic liberals were becoming less critical of the injustices of American society. Their former kinship with the masses also dissipated, giving way to a kind of impatient and, to some extent, condescending elitism that condemned "mass man" as inherently prone to demagogic appeals and vulgar tastes. Pandering to the whims of the masses, many felt, would level the culture to the lowest common denominator.

In order to forestall the destructive potential to the public good that vulgar consumerism presented, pragmatic liberals focused on strategies that could make people's lives more meaningful and aesthetically enjoyable. Liberals urged people to rise above their own material self-interest by getting involved in political activities that promoted the common good. John Kenneth Galbraith and Arthur Schlesinger, for example, called for a renewal of the "public sector"—schools, parks, hospitals, slums, highways—on the grounds that all Americans would benefit from public services, warning that excessive preoccupation with personal consumption would eventually degrade the public sector and lower the quality of life for all Americans. Since they regarded national defense as part of the public sector, pragmatic liberals had no moral qualms in favoring massive spending on the growing security state, claiming that it would not only benefit the public sector but also assure steady employment.

Many young radicals of the 1960s who were weaned on this type of pragmatic liberalism would later denounce it, perhaps unfairly, as a sham and a pretense. They saw it as smug, elitist, and condescending, as an expression of corporate types and their allies in academia who had bargained away strong spinal principles in favor of economic security under a capitalist warfare state. Pragmatic liberalism seemed to be telling them: don't rock the boat, do what is socially expected, get good grades, score high on the SAT, graduate from the right university, and land that secure, lifetime job in a corporation that allows you to enjoy the good life. The message, spoken and unspoken, seemed timid, flabby, flat, false, and unheroic. Worst of all, it seemed to turn a blind eye to the inherent injustices in American society: poverty, racism, inequality, and institutional deception.

Right-wing liberals, often misleadingly labeled conservatives, were really classical liberals who championed unfettered free-enterprise capitalism. Most of them could be found in the Republican Party, which was often little more than the auxiliary of the business community. It would be a mistake, however, to see the business community in any sense as being monolithic in its organizational structure. Among its members, of course, could be found self-centered plutocrats who only thought in terms of money and profits, but one could also find liberal conservatives with a strong social conscience and sense of political responsibility like the Adamses,

Lodges, or Roosevelts—old families deeply rooted in American history who disliked the narrow class interests of the nouveaux riches and appealed to broad national interests. On the extreme liberal right, just as on the extreme liberal left, there were extremists who crossed the liberal line and advocated reactionary and authoritarian positions that smacked of fascism. These were the anti-Roosevelt and anti-New Dealers, strongly opposed to the social reforms of the 1930s, which they condemned as socialistic or communistic. Many of them were given to conspiratorial beliefs that the New Deal was inspired by a host of like-minded evildoers—communists, socialists, Jews, one-worlders—who wanted to undermine the American way of life. During the cold war they enthusiastically supported the House Select Committee on Un-American Activities and the witch-hunts inspired by Joseph P. McCarthy, the junior senator from Wisconsin, who inspired a concentrated assault on alleged communists in the federal government, the military, schools and universities, and the entertainment industry. Those who identified themselves with these postwar attacks on politically incorrect "Un-Americans," had no interest in remedying social or racial injustices at all; on the contrary, they supported various doctrines—Americanism, states' rights, rugged individualism, the Southern strategy, the moral bootstrap—that turned out to be thinly disguised prejudices against ethnic minorities.

Out of the various amorphous groupings on the liberal right wing, efforts were made to forge a genuine conservative movement with distinct philosophical tenets and practical approaches to implement them. The problem with American conservatism was that it lacked strong popular attraction and was limited for the most part to conservative liberals who lacked the sort of political principles that could help them either forge a broad coalition with the liberal center or, alternatively, aid them in coopting the liberal center and capturing a mass following. The Republican Party, which harbored an assortment of right-wing liberals, had been displaced from the political center since the Great Depression and only gained the White House in 1952 because it fielded an immensely popular candidate for president, Dwight D. Eisenhower, not because it straddled the political center with a new set of political doctrines. It was not until the election of Ronald Reagan that the Republican Party made a real bid to become a majority party of a more conservative nature. The 1960s were dominated by pragmatic liberals in the Democratic Party who set the terms of the social agenda, witnessed its breakdown under the impact of radical protests, and were ultimately routed from their stranglehold on American politics by an angry population that gave Richard Nixon and the Republican Party a chance to redefine the terms of the social debate.

The stage of the 1960s, then, was set by a liberal political framework that was pragmatic enough for change, if forced to change, willing enough to engage in social reform, if pressured into reform, but unwilling and, in fact, incapable of accommodating the rising demands on the extreme ends of the political spectrum. Liberal consensus in an age of mass protest is an exercise in political futility that generally gives rise to radical revolution or conservative counterrevolution. In America, however, it caused what can only be described as a state of prolonged disequilibrium in which old social and cultural divisions, far from being resolved, continued to coexist in a new and troublesome way. This is because the very framework of American politics was designed to avoid radical solutions, either in right- or left-wing form. But sometimes social problems require radical solutions, and to allow them to operate solely in a liberal framework means having to live with unresolved or cosmetically solved problems indefinitely.

The 1960s offer a case study in the failure of a weak political style that proved inadequate in resolving long-standing social and cultural problems. The radical solutions offered by the political left were decisively rejected, though many radical features trickled into the mainstream through liberal concessions or defaults; but if left-wing radical solutions failed to alter the liberal structure of American society, the same was true of the so-called conservative reaction that followed on the heels of various radical experiments of the 1960s. Both left and right were checkmated by the real driving force in American society—the corporate technocracy that had its own agenda in the form of economic growth and profits. It was the business system and the technology supporting it that controlled the real agenda America has been following for the past century.

Genuine radicalism as well as genuine conservatism are incompatible with how business is conducted in America because radicalism tends to promote violent change and conservatism opposes change. The business system prefers controlled change tailored to its economic interests; it prefers a weak political style that can be molded to its purpose, and that style is and always has been liberal: socially permissive, conciliatory, nonintrusive, and growth-oriented. The liberal style, especially in its pragmatic and right-wing form, is the most congenial style to the business community, for it allows the business community to conduct its business more freely than any other political style. As a result, the country has continued to prosper under its seductive embraces and powerful mystifications.

Paradoxically, the business system constantly plunges the country into uncharted regions because it has no essential moral and political direction. As it does so, it creates havoc on the political and cultural domain and then stymies both of them from resolving the resulting social problems. One of the salient points of this analysis of the 1960s is that the corporate technocracy really operates in an open-ended revolutionary setting because its economic agenda requires periodic and radical changes in the technologies that increasingly and almost exclusively promote economic growth and profits. These changes, however, are never planned, directed, or controlled because the political system has been deliberately weakened and gridlocked. It is as though the sorcerer's apprentice, unable to control the technology in the absence of his master, has gone amok, while the rest of us are standing helplessly by and allowing our lives to be controlled by the sorcerer's technology. This Faustian metaphor suggests that since the postwar years, if not before, all of us are being controlled by an amoral corporate machine that none of us, individually, nationally, or globally, is able to control. It may be that all of us are on a high-speeding, out-of-control train to the unknown, unable to get off.

What many observers of American history never seem to understand is that the dynamic force that propels American society is neither politics nor culture, but eco-

nomic development and the technology that undergirds it. Such a system can tolerate social divisions and cultural incoherence almost indefinitely—provided, of
course, that they do not interfere with its essential economic functioning. What this
has meant, however, is that the primacy of business over politics and culture has not
freed up sufficient energy to resolve long-standing and festering social problems. It
is safe to say that America's systemic social divisions will not be solved until the
American people radically change the dynamic that drives their civilization, an
unlikely and perhaps impossible occurrence.

4. Beacon or Crusader:
Splits in American Foreign Policy

How does a land of perfection that at the same time replenishes itself through immigration respond to other nations? Before World War I American foreign policy was
guided by a metaphorical association with "a beacon on the summit of mountains to
which all the inhabitants of the earth may turn their eyes, a genial and saving light
till time shall be lost in eternity, and this globe itself dissolves, nor leaving a wreck
behind."[10] These sentiments, expressed by John Adams in 1824, were widely shared
by many Americans who felt, and still do, that America is the last best hope of the
world because, as the poet Philip Freneau, put it:

> Here independent power shall hold sway
> And public virtue warm the patriot's breast
> No traces shall remain of tyranny
> And laws and patterns for the world beside
> Be here enacted first.
> A new Jerusalem sent down from heaven
> Shall grace our happy earth.[11]

The ideal of a shining beacon to the rest of the world could mean on the one hand
that America, by setting the highest democratic standard, simply wanted to serve as
a moral example to other countries; but it could mean on the other hand that, confident of its own perfection, it had a responsibility of becoming a crusader on behalf
of its moral principles. As long as the United States was a minor power, seeking to
avoid what George Washington called "entangling alliances," the noninterventionist
ideal of a moral beacon generally guided American diplomacy. In practice, this has
meant a combination of isolationism and firm assertion, as in the Monroe Doctrine,
that the United States would not tolerate foreign interference in the Western Hemisphere. The Monroe Doctrine specified that the United States would not tolerate any
further colonization of the Americas by any European power, that any European
interference in the Western Hemisphere would be regarded as an unfriendly act, and
that the United States, in turn, would avoid entanglements in European affairs. This
was a brilliant compromise between high-minded idealism and shrewd national self-
interest, for it allowed the United States to pursue its Manifest Destiny in the West-

ern Hemisphere and at the same time avoid entangling itself in the quagmire of European conflicts. By the end of the nineteenth century, however, rapid industrialization had propelled the United States to the rank of the most powerful economic nation in the world.

Imperial power caught up quickly with economic power. Following the Spanish–American War of 1898, the United States was well on its way to making a transition from an isolationist country to a major world power. The entrance of the United States into World War I in 1917 was another step in the direction of world power status; but it was at this point that America's "split-mindedness," as John Lukacs called it, began to manifest itself in the form of Wilsonian progressivism.[12] The notion of America as beacon gave way to America as international crusader on behalf of national self-determination, global markets, international justice, democratic freedoms, and the need for an international organization to keep the peace.[13] Behind Wilson's vision of the "New Freedom" was the certainty that God supported his belief that what was right for America was right for the world, and that, if necessary, America was entitled to teach countries in the Western Hemisphere, and later in Europe, how to elect good democratic leaders. Wilson's missionary fervor was not solely or even partially the result of his Presbyterian moralism, but it was contained in American perfectionism all along. Now that the United States was a major power, this perfectionism could be shaped into a practical policy of intervention, provided, of course, that it was backed up by resounding moral principles of a universalist nature. That this appeal to noble principles was often violated in practice by the most self-serving actions was either ignored or morally adjusted to fit the "progressive" mold.

Starting with Woodrow Wilson, there emerged a disconcerting habit in American foreign policy of imposing sweeping moral principles on international problems that defied subsumption under generalized rules. As George Kennan observed in his *Memoirs*, Americans have a "congenital aversion" to taking specific decisions on specific problems, but to seek "universal formulae or doctrines in which to clothe and justify particular actions."[14] At various times, this practice of projecting universal principles on specific events, often with the best of intentions, has resulted in rhetorically hollow, though propagandistically effective, declarations such as making the world safe for democracy, national self-determination, peace without victory, freedom of the seas, the right of people to choose their own form of government, freedom from fear and want, abandonment of force, and so forth.

Armed with such grandiose principles, American leaders have frequently hectored the rest of the world about adopting noble democratic ideals, while at the same time tolerating and even supporting the vilest dictatorships. This tendency to uphold incompatible ideas and practices has been described by George Orwell as "the power of holding two contradictory beliefs in one's mind simultaneously and accepting both of them."[15] Why Americans have been able to practice such split-mindedness is not entirely clear, though it undoubtedly can be traced to a general human short-circuit in thinking whenever moral principles clash with self-interest and need to be simultaneously upheld. The sort of split-mindedness that America has displayed in its foreign policy probably also derives from the essential incompatibility between democracy and imperial power. As to the American habit of persistent universalization, George Kennan has suggested that this most likely stems from the fact that the American people are used to a "government of laws," which means that in their view legitimacy derives from generalized norms of a legal nature rather than from executive discretion or delegated leadership.[16]

Whatever the reason for this split-mindedness and the need to bridge it through universal moral principles, the fact is that the American people have been deeply torn by the prospect of playing an imperial role in the world. Following World War II, however, the global position of the United States was such that a return to isolationism was unthinkable. The defeat of Nazi Germany and Japan, together with the sole possession by the United States of the atomic bomb in 1945, had made the United States a global superpower. This new role required a huge security state with its interlocking military and industrial conglomerates: the Pentagon, CIA, state department, defense department, business contractors, and so forth. During the cold war, United States military installations had been established all over the world in response to treaty obligations and contractual agreements with well over a hundred different governments. Politicians welcomed such globalization of U.S. military power and called for more. Section 9 of the Republican Party platform of 1956 called for the "establishment of American bases strategically dispersed all around the world."[17] To illustrate this almost exponential growth in American imperial power, consider the bureaucratic growth in the number of state department employees: in 1917 the state department employed 1,700 people; by 1956 that number had increased to 40,000.[18]

And yet there were many Americans, even in the highest positions of power, who expressed strong misgivings about the emergence of what President Eisenhower would later call the military-industrial complex. Critics viewed the rise of a massive military state, the proliferation of nuclear weapons, and the use of a global "containment" strategy with deep forebodings. They would rather have seen the United States beat its swords into ploughshares and earmark financial resources for domestic needs. Diverting precious resources from the civilian to the military sector was seen not only as unproductive but recklessly provocative because it threatened to enmesh the country in overseas conflicts that might well lead to a nuclear confrontation with the Soviet Union.

Such voices of alarm, however, were usually silenced by a steady chorus of sermonizing anticommunist politicians who were incapable of distinguishing a reified abstraction called communism from an actual nation called Russia that was engaged, just as was the United States, in a quest for imperial expansion. It was Winston Churchill who had warned the Western world that the real enemy in the postwar was not communism but the territorial aims of Russia. Being already in possession of Eastern Europe, the Russians were poised to overrun the rest of Europe, aided and abetted, it was feared, by communist subversives in western Europe. For the Russians, communism was a convenient smokescreen that hid brutal imperial designs. The loss of Europe to Russian totalitarianism would have struck a mortal blow to Western civilization. Churchill was right when he said that Europe was more important than Asia and that the real struggle with the Soviet Union was imperial or geopolitical rather than ideological. Containing Russia was therefore the right thing to do, but containing communism all over the world was the wrong thing to do. Ironically, misgivings about formulating a universal policy of "containment" were voiced by the author of that policy himself, George Kennan, who wanted to contain Russia rather than to battle the dragon of communism wherever it appeared around the world. Kennan, a professional diplomat, objected to Truman's formulation of the containment doctrine on the grounds that it amounted to an open-ended commitment to every country that asked for U.S. help in its real or imagined fight against "communism." President Truman's proclamation of the containment policy has been widely hailed as an act of brilliant statesmanship, but its open-ended and overly tendentious nature has not often been emphasized by historians. The Truman doctrine, in fact, underscores both the strength and the weakness in American foreign policy in general; it reveals once more the theme of split-mindedness in its simultaneous assertion of lofty idealism and generosity side by side with overweening arrogance and heavy-handedness. Did American policy makers on both sides of the political aisle really propose to give assistance to people yearning to be free if it was not the same democratic yearning felt by Americans? When President Truman pledged assistance to people yearning to be free, did he really mean the statement that immediately followed this heartfelt sentiment, namely, that the United States "must assist free peoples to work out their own destinies *in their own way*?"[19] (emphasis added) Neither the United States nor the Soviet Union had any intention of allowing people around the world to determine their own destinies if those destinies conflicted with the self-interests of either of the superpowers. It was on this point that Kennan expressed a more subtle and realistic position, and that was that American commitment should be flexible, while at the same time grounded in democratic principles. The scholar-diplomat argued that U.S. assistance to any country should be tailored to specific circumstances; it should be in the form of a helping hand rather than a heavy foot. In practice, what this implied was that assistance should always be predicated on a specific requirement, namely, "the willingness and ability of the threatened people to pick up and bear resolutely the overwhelming portion of the responsibility and effort in their own defense against both direct and indirect aggression—not just to sit back and hedge against the possibility that resistance might not be effective and leave the burden of the struggle to us."[20] If this sapient advice had been followed by American decision makers, the United States would have been spared the tragedy of Vietnam.

Kennan's advice on this or many other positions did not carry much weight because professional diplomats in the United States have usually played a very small role in foreign policy decisions. In a pluralistic society, where independent decision making is subject to a host of counterbalancing forces, the influence of professional diplomats has always been overshadowed by executive or congressional leadership. Both, in turn, have been subject to public mood or opinion, whose shifting natures have made consistent and principled decision-making very difficult. Although a loose consensus on foreign policy emerged during the cold war, it was not always clear what that consensus really was; and the uncertainty about that consensus stemmed from the fact that the United States did not have a highly developed sense of national purpose that consistently shaped the nature of its foreign policy. The profoundly different positions held by various political groups in the postwar period illustrates the dilemma.

There were three broad schools of thought on the conduct of American foreign policy, each reflecting its own underlying political philosophy: left liberalism, conservatism, and pragmatic liberalism. These positions loosely correspond to our previous division of American politics into left liberalism, libertarian or conservative liberalism, and pragmatic liberalism. Left liberals, who called themselves "progressives" had supported America's participation in World War II because they saw the war as a "people's war" that the United States and the Soviet Union had waged against fascism. Left liberals and socialists hoped that the United States and the Soviet Union would extend their wartime coalition into the postwar period so that international peace and justice could be secured. They supported the United Nations as the best instrument of bringing about world peace. In the immediate postwar period left liberal ideas were prominent in American academia and in certain highbrow journals such as the *New Republic, The Nation,* the *Atlantic Monthly,* and *Harper's.* When the Soviet–American partnership collapsed in 1945-46, left liberals blamed the United States for unduly provoking tensions between the superpowers, citing various misguided U.S. decisions such as keeping the Soviet Union in the dark on the development of the atomic bomb, delaying tactics in opening a "second front" during the war, terminating lend-lease, spurning Moscow's plea for a six billion dollar postwar loan, and distrusting Soviet intentions regarding various postwar settlements. Although these views were popular with American intellectuals on the left, they had minimal influence on U.S. decision makers or the public at large.

More popular in the immediate postwar period were the conservative nationalists rather than the progressive internationalists. Before World War II, most conservatives had been isolationists, but following the war they became vocal anticommunists who believed that the fruits of victory had been snatched from the United States by subversives at home and by communists abroad. They had no faith in the United Nations, the Russians, or even the western allies. Apart from setting off political or rhetorical fireworks, the conservatives lacked clearly defined foreign policy objectives. Their anticommunism was as much inner-directed as it was outer-directed because of a widespread belief during the cold war that the United States had been softened up on the home front by socialist subversives. Politicians like Senator Howard Taft, referred to by his followers as "Mr. Republican," had nursed a longstanding grievance against the New Deal, which they denounced as either communistic or a stepping stone toward Soviet collectivism. In order to prevent this inevitable slide into governmental tyranny, the conservatives planned to spend most of their political energies in the domestic arena, hoping to roll back New Deal centralism and thereby restore the Republican liberties of free enterprise, individual rights, and community control.

The pragmatic liberals distanced themselves from both the progressives and the conservatives, whose positions they believed to be either unrealistic or extreme.

Instead they insisted that they held the "vital center" in American politics. The left, they believed, had been totally unrealistic about human nature and the possibility of fulfilling ideological utopias. Their experience in World War II with totalitarianism on both the right (fascism) and the left (communism) had dampened their fervor for peaceful accommodations. In their view, communism was an international menace that had to be resisted at all costs. The cold war, they argued, was not the result of the treacherous deals made by Roosevelt at Yalta, as the conservatives had charged, nor by Washington provocations that had undermined United States–Soviet relations, as left liberals claimed, but by the simple fact that the Soviet Union was an expansionist power that could be stopped only through a combination of economic containment and military might. In the field of foreign policy, liberal pragmatists favored diplomatic realism rather than ideological wishful thinking. The aim of foreign policy makers should not be to perfect the world but to promote the vital interests of the United States.

The American people generally identified themselves with the more moderate and nuanced position of the pragmatists. During the McCarthy era, however, paranoia of communism shifted the public mood decisively in the direction of the conservative nationalists. It was during this time (1950–54) that the political left was widely distrusted by the American people, perhaps rightly so because left-liberal solutions to international problems would have had devastating consequences to the vital interests of the United States. The political left seems to have been oblivious to the totalitarian dangers of the Soviet Union, especially at a time when Joseph Stalin still tyrannized the Russian people as well as all those who were living under Soviet rule. The Soviet leaders were not peaceful internationalists who wanted to make the world safe for human brotherhood and equality; on the contrary, the Soviet leaders were true believers in communist ideology who planned to put the same totalitarian straitjacket on all of Europe that they had already forced on Eastern Europe. Many of those who called themselves progressives seriously underestimated the potential for evil that lay coiled at the very heart of Soviet communism. The American people seemed to have felt this truth in their bones, too, which explains the support they gave to the various measures undertaken by the United States to stop the aggressive designs of the Soviets, measures that included economic containment, the Marshall Plan, the establishment of NATO, the Berlin Airlift, and so forth.

Without fully comprehending it, however, the American people did not realize how these diplomatic, military, and economic strategies had shifted the whole axis of American foreign policy from a traditionally noninterventionist position to an active policy of global intervention. The Monroe Doctrine, as we recall, had generally kept the United States on a noninterventionist course. The Wilsonian experiment in making the world safe for democracy (1917–19) had been seen as an apparent, even tragic, misdirection. The cold war changed all this for the simple reason that the United States was the only superpower that could effectively resist totalitarian expansion either in Europe or elsewhere in the world. Since the British lion no longer roared, as William O'Neill pointed out, the American eagle had to scream or the Soviet bear would have descended on all of Europe.[21]

Inheriting the mantle of empire, however, was not a task that the majority of the American people welcomed, and the same was true of leading political groups. The conservatives were unwilling to take an active interventionist role, hoping somewhat unrealistically that countries threatened by communist subversion would somehow rid themselves of such dangers with minimal assistance by the United States. Although anticommunism was *de rigueur* among conservatives, it did not translate into a coherent foreign policy. What it did, however, was to fan a great deal of domestic paranoia about communist subversion in the government, academia, and the entertainment industry. If the conservatives were ambiguous about the nature of American foreign policy, the progressives—including especially the followers of Henry Wallace—tiptoed through the political landscape in search of the Wizard of Oz. In traveling on the yellow brick road of revolutionary socialism, they hoped to reach global peace, justice, equality, and human brotherhood. They assumed axiomatically that true revolutionary movements in the modern world had to be socialist in nature. Moreover, they assumed, almost as an act of faith, that socialism was compatible with democracy. The possibility that liberal democracy was compatible with capitalism, indeed entailed each other, was rejected out of hand by left liberals. Their faith in government-sponsored egalitarianism was so strong that it blinded them to the historical fact that government collectivism was an inherent enemy to human freedom.

With an eye to the 1960s, it would turn out that left-wing "progressivism" was yet another species of American perfectionism, a form of secular redemption that strongly appealed to left liberal intellectuals and innocent young people in search of a philosophy or meaning in life. Despite being well intentioned, progressives represented more than a nuisance in American politics, for their public protests would seriously paralyze American foreign policy in the 1960s. The reason for this was the powerful influence these left liberal ideas exercised on American higher education and on young people who faced the draft during the Vietnam War. At a time when the civil rights movement had aroused awareness of social inequality and the Vietnam War pricked the nation's moral conscience, many young people found refuge and solace in the growing peace movements that had mushroomed around the country.

With conservatives thundering away at subversive communists but lacking a clear-cut foreign policy, and left liberals preaching international peace and compromise with the Soviets, the field belonged to the "consensus liberals," who reluctantly shouldered the mantle of empire but only if their efforts could be publicly justified in the language of Wilsonian internationalism. As previously mentioned, the problem with "consensus liberalism" centered on its inconsistent assumptions about human nature, the power and scope of government, and the role of the United States in the world. Consensus liberals were unable to reconcile democratic idealism and hardheaded international *Realpolitik*. Yet transforming themselves into cold warriors, they had no trouble in supporting tinhorn dictators around the world as long as they pretended to be anticommunist and pro-Western. John Lukacs, as we have seen, regarded such inconsistent attitudes that affirmed mutually contradictory positions as split-mindedness. Examples of such split-mindedness could be found in abundance during the cold war in the form of noble rhetoric side by side with cynical interventionism in the Caribbean, Latin America, Africa, and Southeast Asia. It was as though Americans wanted to have their foreign policy cake and eat it too; they seemed to believe that ruthless power politics on the international scene could be conducted within the framework of a perfectly liberal democracy. This faith was an old one, reminiscent of Jefferson, who believed, as Robert Tucker and Daniel Hendrick pointed out, that "America could have it both ways—that it could enjoy the fruits of power without falling victim to the normal consequences of its exercise."[22] Perhaps this was like squaring the circle, because no imperial power in history has been able to conduct itself without moral blemishes in conquering, occupying, and governing other people. The ideal of "liberal empire" concocted by British statesmen and political pundits in the late nineteenth century could never quite hide its self-serving motives behind its noble or euphemistic slogans such as "mandates," "protectorates," "bearing the White Man's Burden," "national efficiency," and so forth.[23] Dictating to other people that imperial control was for their own good or their own protection has rarely redounded to the benefit of colonial people. By the late 1940s the British people realized that imperial power was compatible neither with the geopolitical reality of a small country nor with the steady growth of their parliamentary democracy. Churchill's exhortation in 1945 to the British people not to be cravenly afraid of being imperial no longer resonated with the British electorate.

The American people, too, sensed this incompatibility of imperial power with their own democratic traditions. John Lukacs was right that "in some ways Americans wanted to rule the world, and that in others they did not."[24] On the one hand they were proud to be the sole possessor of atomic weapons in 1945 and of having defeated Nazi Germany and Japan. They did not mind Americanizing the world through economic expansion or putting limits on Soviet power through containment, the Marshall Plan, and NATO. On the other hand, the American people were uneasy about the heavy cost involved in these global measures, afraid also of sticking their noses into other people's business and getting hurt in the process. Above all, there was widespread uncertainty, especially in intellectual circles, that the growth of a military-industrial complex would lead to the militarization of society and drain precious resources from social problems at home.

In an age of conservative conformity such as the 1950s these fears and doubts did not find a mass sounding board. The fault lines would not split wide open until the late 1960s, but by that time another quite unforeseen consequence of American foreign policy came to pass: the steady decline and moral influence of American power and prestige in the world. The single-minded pursuit of an ill-defined policy in Vietnam had steadily drained the moral and financial capital that America had accumulated in the immediate postwar period. This loss of power was undoubtedly the result of America's split-mindedness, which in turn probably stemmed from a long-standing chimera in its own perfection and omnipotence. At the same time, American society was also riven by internal contradictions pertaining to race relations, the Achilles heal of American society. In race relations, just as in foreign policy, Americans had subscribed to two mutually contradictory principles, namely, that racial segregation was compatible with democratic values of liberty, justice, and human equality. The notion that "separate but equal" was democratically defensible turned out to be a fallacy of historic proportions.

5. The Racist Blood-Knot in American History

Thomas Jefferson, the author of the Declaration of Independence and the most eloquent spokesman on behalf of enlightened doctrines that all men are created equal and endowed by their creator with inalienable rights to life, liberty, and the pursuit of happiness, was also a planter aristocrat who lived on a large Virginia estate at Monticello with eight family members, fourteen free craftsmen, and 118 enslaved African Americans. One of those 118 slaves was Sally Hemings, who along with her mother, Elizabeth, and five other siblings had been brought to Monticello by Jefferson's wife, Martha. Sally Hemings's grandmother, Elizabeth, had come to America as the mistress of a white sea captain named Hemings and had then become the property of John Wayles, Martha Jefferson's father. John Wayles made Elizabeth his mistress after the death of his third wife, and they had six children together, one of them being Sally Hemings. When Jefferson's wife died in 1782, he began a long love affair with Sally Hemings and fathered five children.[25]

What makes this story of an interracial affair so poignant in the history of the United States is not that whites enslaved blacks, stamped them as racially inferior, or used them for sexual pleasures but that one of the founding fathers of the Republic, the author of the Declaration of Independence and other lofty national documents, the Platonic personification of America, could actually love a slave and father her five children. Given the explosive nature of Jefferson's affair and the racist thinking that was common during and after his lifetime, it should not be surprising that historians, bent upon safeguarding his image, would cover up his interracial affair with Sally Hemings, despite the fact that his illicit relationship with Hemings was made public in the *Richmond Recorder* on September 1, 1802. James Thomson Callender, who made the accusations that "it is well known that the man, whom it delighteth the people to honor, keeps and for many years has kept, as his concubine, one of his slaves,"[26] was subsequently denounced as a scurrilous scandalmonger.

Seventy-one years later, in 1873, Sally Hemings's third son, Madison Hemings, gave a statement to an Ohio newspaperman providing a detailed account of his family tree that purported to show that he was the son of Thomas Jefferson and Sally Hemings. According to Hemings, Jefferson had taken Sally Hemings to Paris, where she became pregnant. Since French law recognized her as a free person, she expressed the desire to remain in France as a free person rather than return to America as a slave. Jefferson, however, persuaded her to return to Virginia and solemnly promised her that he would free all of her children when they reached the age of twenty-one. Shortly after her arrival, she gave birth to Jefferson's child but it lived only for a short time. She gave birth to four others, of whom Jefferson was the father; their names were Beverly, Harriet, Madison, and Eston.

Madison Hemings's story disappeared from public view until the 1950s, when it was rediscovered by historians. Interestingly enough, only Fawn Brodie gave the story serious credence in her book *Thomas Jefferson: An Intimate History* (1974). In order to maintain the consensus of a Platonic, sexless Jefferson who was too other-worldly to consort with women, and certainly not black women, historians dropped a veil of purity around the image they had constructed for Jefferson. The truth, now confirmed by DNA evidence, suggests that Jefferson did indeed father five children with Sally Hemings.

Black Americans, of course, had long known the truth about interracial affairs, namely, that white slave masters had routinely consorted with black women since the beginning of slavery. They were convinced that the Jefferson–Hemings liaison did take place. They knew Jefferson's heirs had borne the same blood stigma that had afflicted all of their black ancestors. No black person in American history was immune from the stigma of race, not even the heirs of the third president of the United States.

To illustrate how persistently this racial curse afflicted black people in America, it is instructive to skip another seventy years after Madison Hemings gave his account to an Ohio newspaperman. Shortly after World War II, one of Jefferson's putative descendants, Robert H. Cooley III, began to learn the facts of life under segregation in the South as a young boy when his mother took him shopping in Petersburg, Virginia. Before taking him downtown, she made him drink a lot of water so that he would be spared the humiliation of separate facilities in the segregated South. As they shopped, the young boy noticed signs that said "White" and "Colored." He turned on the colored fountain, tasted the water, but couldn't see any colored water, as the sign indicated. One day, he took a bus and sat down right behind the driver because he only had a short way to go. The driver snarled at him "you get back of the bus, boy." The boy's pleading that he was only going to go three stops made no difference. The driver insisted: "Boy, if you don't get in the back of the bus, I'm going to call the police."[27]

When Robert was twelve, he visited his grandparents' home in Pittsburgh, and it was here that his grandfather and two uncles told him their family secret that he was related to Thomas Jefferson. He was elated. But the excitement passed quickly when he realized that nothing had changed for him in the segregated South of the 1950s. He was still a second-rate citizen. "Gee Whiz," he said, "here I am the grandson of the President of the United States, the author of the Declaration of Independence, and I still can't do the things I'd like to do."[28] Even in 1964, when he was a law student at the University of Virginia, whites would walk away when he went to the law library and sat down at a table. And this at a university that had been founded by his ancestral grandfather.

Jefferson's liaison with Sally Hemings embodies one of the great flaws in American history, and the flaw is in the form of an apparent contradiction, as are so many of the other fault lines in the land of perfection. The contradiction is this: Jefferson, like many decent Americans, abhorred the idea of slavery, while at the same time owning slaves and trying to justify the practice by claiming that blacks were inferior to whites. He could, on the one hand, wax eloquent about the notion that all men are created equal and accuse George III for encouraging selling human beings, while on the other hand musing about the inherent inequality of black people. "I advance it . . . as a suspicion only," he said, "that the blacks, whether originally a distinct race, or made distinct by time and circumstances, are inferior to the whites in the endowments both of body and mind. . . . This unfortunate difference of color, and perhaps of faculty, is a powerful obstacle to the emancipation of these people."[29]

What, then, is to be done with black people in America? His heart opted for the Sally Hemings solution: miscegenation. The Romans, he pointed out, had already recognized that the emancipation from slavery merely required one effort—that the former slave mixed with his former masters. This is what Jefferson did with Sally Hemings, but it was too radical a solution to be entertained seriously in his own day. This is why the politician Jefferson followed his calculating mind. For us—referring to his own generation—emancipation means that "when freed, he [The black man] is to be removed beyond the reach of mixture."[30] Presumably, this meant repatriation to Africa, which would put blacks out of sexual reach for whites.

Jefferson, like most Americans of his generation, was deeply ambivalent about race and slavery. Despite his noble rhetoric about equality and human rights, he tolerated the most degrading sort of inequality in the form of black slavery; but if all men were created free and equal, as Jefferson had argued, how could one justify the perpetuation of inequality among such a sizable part of the American population? The men who framed the Constitution of the United States laid only the theoretical foundation for equality and human dignity; they were too concerned with the fragile state of the new republic to abolish slavery because that would have caused the southern states to bolt the new union. So the founders compromised in order to establish a "United States of America." Enlightened minds like Jefferson, Madison, Franklin, Adams, and Washington hoped that enlightened practices would catch up with enlightened ideas in future generations, rendering slavery as obsolete as it was immoral. Failing that eventuality, many looked to repatriation to Africa as the final solution to the black question.

The seed of tragedy, sown with the arrival of twenty black slaves in 1619 at Jamestown, thus bore fruit in the eighteenth century, survived the storms of the American Revolution, was transplanted in the nineteenth century to the western states, and reached its apex in the antebellum South. Behind the slavery issue, of course, resided powerful vested interests and ideological justifications. The new nation was a fragile house of state, weakened by deep-seated sectional and economic issues—North vs. South, agriculture vs. industry—that would erupt in civil war in 1860. These centrifugal forces split the nation into two hostile camps, and the arguments on both sides hardened into intransigence. At issue, among others, were four million chattel slaves who were regarded by their owners as private property who could be taken as slaves anywhere in the United States. The Constitution had placed no obstacles in the way of slavery or even its expansion because it accepted slavery as a local institution to be protected or prohibited by the wishes of the individual states.

As previously mentioned, America is a nation of immigrants that has tried to assimilate its foreign population into the mainstream, if not in one generation then certainly in two or three generations. Black slaves have always been the exception to this pattern because white America has had an irrational fear of blood pollution. Whites expected their children to look white, not black, Indian, or Latino. By rejecting cultural as well as racial assimilation, white Americans looked to other means of handling the growing black population under their control. They could emancipate their slaves from the institution of slavery, but this still left unresolved the social question regarding the role of black people in a white society. If blacks were to be emancipated, what should be done with them after emancipation? Should they be fully included in white society? Should they live a segregated existence on a coequal basis with whites? Should they be evacuated from all white territories and resettled on black reservations like the Indians? Should they be repatriated to Liberia or some other African territory?

When slavery came under increasing attack by enlightened whites, especially in the North, it was never full emancipation that the majority of the American people embraced as an alternative, but some form of segregation. Since the 1830s the term Jim Crow was used to describe segregationist approaches, both in the South and in the North. The term refers to segregation laws, instituted mostly by southern states, that aimed at excluding black people from the white community in any capacity other than one of subservience or inferiority. These laws excluded African Americans from all aspects of white life and culture, extending to churches, schools, housing, jobs, restaurants, public transportation, sports, hospitals, funeral homes, zoos, cemeteries, and so on.

The aim of segregation was to create two parallel and rarely intersecting ways of life: one for favored whites and the other for inferior blacks. Segregation was justified by elaborate racial doctrines that declared blacks to be biologically and therefore culturally inferior to whites and sternly warned against the mixing of the races on the grounds that it would weaken the white gene pool. A whole generation in the mid to late nineteenth century, including prominent educators, scientists, clergymen, politicians, and journalists, defended white supremacy by appealing to the Bible, Darwinian biology, the ideology of Anglo-Saxonism, and eugenic science.

C. Vann Woodward has shown that segregation grew up contemporaneously with slavery but was not caused by slavery.[31] This is because slavery made segregation impractical for economic and social reasons. Owning slaves meant supervising and caring for them, so that close interaction, including sexual relations, was unavoidable during the course of daily life in the South. The institution of slavery, in fact, made relations between the races much more intimate in the South than it did in areas where it was not practiced. In the South, where slavery was standard, segregation never meant separation but holding back black people in a perpetual state of servitude to white people. Although slavery was virtually eliminated in the North by 1830, this did not mean that blacks enjoyed a much greater degree of freedom than they did in the South. In the North, just as in the South, blacks were excluded from meaningful participation in northern life and culture. Alexis de Toqueville was surprised and shocked to encounter racism in those areas that had supposedly abolished slavery. He wrote in the early 1830s that slavery was in retreat but "the prejudice from which it arose is immovable. In that part of the Union where Negroes are no longer slaves, have they come closer to the whites?" He answered in the negative, arguing that "race prejudice seems stronger in those states that have abolished slavery than in those where it still exists, and nowhere is it more intolerant that in those states where slavery was never known."[32]

Even the Great Emancipator, Abraham Lincoln, realized that Negroes would never be accepted as equals by whites, saying in 1858, "I will say then that I am not, nor ever have been in favor of bringing about in any way the social and political equality of the white and black races [applause] . . . and I will say in addition to this that there is a physical difference between the black and white races which I believe will for ever forbid the two races living together on terms of social and political equality. And insomuch as they cannot live, while they do remain together there must be the position of superior and inferior, and as much as any man I am in favor of having the superior position assigned to the white race."[33]

This speech was made in proslavery southern Illinois, but that same year Lincoln also gave a rousing speech in Chicago affirming the equality of men, illustrating how even the most enlightened and decent white Americans were torn on the "race question." Jefferson or Lincoln, of course, must be seen in the context of their respective times, which in both cases favored a strong separatist and segregationist approach to racial relations. Some of the most influential spokesmen of Lincoln's age favored a white republic, and endorsed either segregation or repatriation of blacks to Africa. Repatriation, in fact, had been one of President James Monroe's pet projects for solving the problem of slavery. The plan involved setting up an American-sponsored colony in West Africa that was to be called Liberia. In 1824 the colony was founded and its capital city, Monrovia, was named in honor of President Monroe. Although a few thousand freed slaves did go to Liberia and ruled the country as an elite caste, the experiment of resettling what amounted to an alien group of black Americans among indigenous African tribes badly backfired by causing social conflicts that have continued in Liberia to this day. Most black Americans suspected that America, for all its terrible shortcomings, was still a better place than the Dark Continent, which for them was now but a distant memory. Yet the idea of Africa as an alternative to America has continued to preoccupy black people ever since Monroe conceived his repatriation scheme in the 1820s. Marcus Garvey, a West Indian immigrant would later try to revitalize the repatriation movement by promoting the resettlement of blacks in Africa; but his Universal Negro Improvement Association, other than instilling pride in being black, turned out to be a financial fiasco. Garvey's Black Star Line Steamship Company, intended to transport blacks to Africa, went bankrupt in 1923, and Garvey was convicted of fraud and imprisoned.

Repatriation, in other words, continued to be entertained by both blacks and whites throughout the history of the republic. The Great Emancipator Lincoln encouraged black people to emigrate to Africa at various times because he could not foresee any other lasting solution to the racial question. Most of his biographers, of course, have ignored his white prejudice in order to maintain the Lincolnesque illusion of unblemished idealism. This has been done either through willful omission or the practice of selective quotation. Lincoln's hagiographers have often made it a practice to cite passages of Lincoln's speeches or writings that heighten the "halo effect," while ignoring those that do not—even if it occurs in the course of a single speech. A troublesome example was Lincoln's speech of 1854 in Peoria that referred to slavery as a "monstrous injustice"; but in the course of the same speech Lincoln also indicated that he would prefer to see the black slaves, once freed, sent to Liberia, to their own native land.[34]

This conviction, which Lincoln maintained as president, does not make him a racist pure and simple, as some recent historians have argued, but it does indicate how even the most enlightened white man recoiled from the notion of racial equality in white America.[35] Lincoln was not a racial egalitarian—few people were in the 1860s—but neither was he a racist oppressor. The truth is that he glimpsed the moral untenability of racial thinking without being able to free himself from its seductive allure or its political effectiveness. We cannot expect Lincoln to jump out of his time; nor can we judge him by the standards of ours without distorting history.

Although racial equality became a preferred civil war aim on the part of Lincoln and the North, victory did not bring racial equality for either southern or northern African Americans. The South was devastated, psychologically traumatized and occupied by union troops until 1877. African Americans had been legally emancipated, but once the South was released from military occupation the gains that had been made by black people during those twelve years of "Reconstruction" were gradually lost as the South capitulated to racism and segregation. The South reverted to the evils of racism primarily because the North relaxed its opposition to segregationist practices, which, in turn, reflected the North's own ambivalence on the racial question.

A series of United States Supreme Court decisions between 1873 and 1898 confirm this steady relaxation of anti-racial and anti-discriminatory policies, culminating in the infamous *Plessy v. Ferguson* decision in which the Supreme Court declared that "legislation is powerless to eradicate racial instincts" and laid down the rule of "separate but equal" as a justification for racial segregation. Two years later, in 1898, the Court sanctioned racism by approving the Mississippi plan for depriving blacks of the franchise. Other southern states quickly followed suit in stripping African Americans of the right to vote. This consisted in erecting barriers to voting that involved property or literacy qualifications, barriers that were coming down on most advanced industrial nations in the Western world. Southern states devised ingenious voting qualifications that allowed whites to slip through literacy restrictions by means of special "grandfather" or "good character" clauses. Just to make sure that no black man would ever exercise his right to vote, special "poll taxes" were initiated, and as a further safeguard, for it was conceivable that a black man could learn to read, acquire property, and pay his poll tax, special white primaries automatically excluded blacks from exercising their right to vote.[36]

In order to enforce this ironclad system of racial discrimination and exclusion, southern states resorted to outright intimidation and police terror. Law enforcement officials were generally recruited from lower-class whites with strong racist predilections. Beyond the law but often working hand in glove with it were the Ku Klux Klan and the favorite pastime of white bigots—lynching innocent black people.

Starting in the 1890s race relations in America, North as well as South, steadily deteriorated, despite the fact that the country was passing through an age of reform associated with movements such as populism and progressivism. Jim Crow laws started raining down on helpless African Americans, beginning with separate places on railroad cars and waiting rooms in railway stations. Next came segregation on steamboats and streetcars. Signs reading "Whites Only" began to proliferate throughout the South, many of them posted over entrances and exits to theaters, boarding houses, toilets, water fountains, waiting rooms, and ticket windows. A lot of ingenuity, as C. Vann Woodward tells us, went into separating the races at popular sports events and amusements. It goes without saying that blacks could not play on white teams throughout the nation. Cities instituted residential segregation and imposed harsh penalties for violating the rules. Curfews kept African Americans off the streets after 10:00 P.M. in numerous southern cities.

Jim Crow laws sometimes went to ridiculous extremes: in Alabama African Americans were prohibited from playing checkers with whites, while Mississippi insisted that black people could be transported only in white taxi cabs. Lawmakers in Florida and North Carolina made sure that white students would never touch textbooks that had previously been used by black students. New Orleans segregated its prostitutes, and Oklahoma its telephone booths.[37]

The North was not much better than the South, often exhibiting parallel lines of prejudice and discrimination. Nor did World War I, in which 360,000 blacks participated in noncombatant positions, alleviate the plight of black people in America. In fact, a wave of racial violence swept across the United States in 1919, much of it connected with the prevailing xenophobia relating to Bolsheviks and other revolutionaries in the immediate postwar period. This mounting hysteria over subversive foreigners also reinvigorated the Ku Klux Klan, which increased its membership by five million, not only in the Deep South but also in other parts of the country. In the wake of this mounting tide of racial intolerance, many states tightened their rules concerning racial relations, especially in sports and recreational activities. Although the 1930s witnessed a slight relaxation in racial intolerance, little progress was made in promoting civil rights for African Americans.

The crusade for black civil rights that had once fueled the abolitionist movement, however, had never been forgotten or abandoned by either victims or perpetrators. For many enlightened white people, the rise of Nazi Germany with its vicious racial doctrines highlighted America's own shortcomings in denying civil rights to blacks. In the meantime, black people were doing their best to break the shackles of apartheid. In 1909 the National Association for the Advancement of Colored People (NAACP) was founded for the purpose of promoting civil rights for African Americans, particularly through litigation and expanding educational opportunities. Other organizations that promoted civil rights for black people were the National Urban League and the Commission on Interracial Cooperation. The Harlem Renaissance, a black literary and artistic movement, attracted widespread attention to black creativity in music and the fine arts. The increasing popularity of jazz, a unique African American contribution to American culture, also brought the races closer together. Intellectuals and well-meaning philanthropists, many influenced by the social gospel movement, began to agitate for black civil rights. By the time the United States found itself at war with Nazi Germany, a national awareness was beginning to form that African Americans could not be kept in perpetual servitude at a time when the country had committed itself to destroy the racial hatred that fueled Nazi Germany.

This awareness of the existence of a fundamental social evil in American society was also brought about by great demographic changes relating to the migration of black people from the South to the industrial northern states (Ohio, Illinois, Pennsylvania, New York, Michigan) between 1930 and 1950. It is commonly recognized that urbanization has meant greater freedom and opportunity for black people. On the political level this turned out to be a real boon to the Democratic Party because blacks flocked to the Democrats rather than the Republicans in the North, which was a real reversal for the Republican Party, the party of Abraham Lincoln and emancipation. In an ironic turnabout, the party of white supremacy, the Democratic Party, became on the national level the champion of black civil rights just as it had become the voice for greater opportunity for other minorities under Franklin Roosevelt. This historic reversal of black allegiance to the two national parties would mean that white liberals in the Democratic Party would spearhead the second reconstruction in race relations. The Republican Party missed a great moral opportunity when it divested itself of black support, and it compounded that mistake by trying to forge alliances with disaffected white supremacy leaders in the South. The South, of course, was still predominantly Democratic by the beginning of the 1960s, but by the end of the sixties southern whites had defected to the Republican Party as a result of the Democrat-sponsored civil rights movement.

Despite the fact that millions of blacks supported President Roosevelt, his administration did very little in the area of civil rights, being too preoccupied with the Depression and World War II. The emphasis during the war was on unity rather than division, and black leaders generally voiced little criticism of the government out of fear that public protest could be interpreted as undermining the war effort. In World War II, just as in World War I, blacks still served as noncombatants, and the vast majority of the units in all of the fighting forces remained strictly segregated. Blacks drew strength in cheering for individual black accomplishments, especially in sports and entertainment: Jackie Robinson crossing the color line in Major League Baseball; Joe Louis finally knocking out Hitler's white hope, Max Schmeling; Louis Armstrong thrilling white fans. In the end, such pride was always offset by the reality of discrimination: even the best black performers still could not sleep in the same hotel rooms as their white counterparts.

The postwar period ushered in what has often been called the Second Reconstruction, which, it was hoped, would fulfill the unrealized goals of the First Reconstruction that followed the Civil War. Unlike his predecessor, President Harry S. Truman moved far more decisively on civil rights by creating a Committee on Civil

Rights, which produced an uncompromising report calling for the elimination of segregation. In 1948 Truman issued an executive order to integrate the armed forces, an order that, interestingly enough, was kept from the press by the military. Resistance to full integration in the military finally broke down during the Korean War because casualties seriously depleted white fighting ranks, forcing unit commanders to replace white casualties with fresh African American troops.

In the end, neither Truman nor his successor, Dwight D. Eisenhower, assumed real leadership in galvanizing public opinion against racial injustices or bringing enough pressure to bear on Congress to pass civil rights legislation. Real leadership in the civil rights struggle came from the judiciary, particularly the Supreme Court of the United States. One of the chief issues that preoccupied the Court in the early 1950s was the pretense of die-hard segregationists that the school system in the South, which was strictly segregated, was separate but also equal. Meager resources had been invested by public authorities in black education, which was universally substandard. Even if "separate but equal" had been attempted honestly, the task of maintaining parallel and equal school systems was impractical and financially unfeasible. Dedicated and able attorneys working for the NAACP, notably Thurgood Marshall, challenged the constitutionality of the separate-but-equal provisions of *Plessy v. Ferguson* in one of the most important Court cases: *Oliver Brown et al. v. Board of Education of Topeka, Kansas*. The judgment was delivered by the new Supreme Court Justice Earl Warren, former governor of California, who delivered the final judgment in favor of the plaintiff. The doctrine of "separate but equal," the Court declared, has no place in public education; the plaintiffs, the Court held, had been deprived of the equal protection of the laws guaranteed by the Fourteenth Amendment to the Constitution.

The South was stunned. A period of quiet restraint followed the 1954 Supreme Court decision because the Court did not issue the decree to implement the decision until May 1955. As soon as the decree came down, the South responded with cries of "segregation forever." Mississippi stepped forward first in defiance; other southern states followed. Panic seized many parts of the South by the beginning of 1956. The Court decision was a mortal blow to a whole way of life that had characterized the South for two centuries. Citizens councils, aimed at defying the end of segregation in the public schools, sprouted all over the South. Blacks, now equally aroused to push their goals to end all segregation, not just school segregation, responded with economic boycotts, the most famous being the Montgomery bus boycott that had been called after Rosa Parks, a black seamstress, was arrested when she refused to go to the back of the bus and give up her seat to a standing white man. The civil rights movement was gathering critical momentum, just as it was producing, in its first assimilationist phase, a series of superb leaders, notably Martin Luther King, Bayard Rustin, James Farmer, and Ralph Abernathy.

The late 1950s saw massive white resistance to ending segregation in the South. Southern leaders, egged on by Harry F. Byrd of Virginia, claimed that state authorities possessed the right of "interposition," which allowed them to override alleged violations of the Constitution by the United States Supreme Court. This was a warmed up pre–Civil War argument, made by "nullifiers," that the Supreme Court possessed no power to decide matters that concerned purely state issues such as education. In such cases, Byrd and others contended, the federal government had no right to dictate to state authorities what they should or should not do. Under a new emerging label of "states' rights," the old argument, widely endorsed by both conservatives who feared the tyranny of the federal government and by die-hard segregationists who wanted blacks marginalized as an underprivileged minority, the South attempted to reinvigorate the claim that the states had framed the Constitution and could therefore reject acts of the federal government that intruded on matters reserved to the states. What followed was a flood of pro-segregationist measures by Alabama, Georgia, Mississippi, South Carolina, and Virginia.

The Eisenhower administration was taken aback and refused to act decisively for several years. Ike even had second thoughts about having appointed Earl Warren to the Supreme Court, confessing that it was "the biggest damnfool decision I ever made." The Democrats were no better, counseling "time and patience," in the words of Eisenhower's opponent, Adlai Stevenson. The country was not in a radical mood, having just weathered the repressive McCarthy years. An atmosphere of fear, however, began to permeate the southern states. The NAACP was virtually driven underground. Arkansas elected a self-proclaimed segregationist, Orval E. Faubus, as governor, and other states followed suit. In 1957 Faubus called out National Guardsmen to prevent nine blacks from attending the all-white Central High School in Little Rock. On court order, he withdrew the guard; but when the black students tried to attend, they were greeted by a hysterical mob that showered them with racial epithets: "Niggers, keep away from our school. Go back to the jungle."[38] When it became clear that white hysteria had reached such a level of intensity that the safety of the black students could not be guaranteed, President Eisenhower acted decisively, federalizing the Arkansas National Guard and sending a thousand reliable troops of the 101st Airborne Division to Little Rock. With fixed bayonets, the paratroopers dispersed the mob and made sure that the black students entered Central High School. The spectacle of U.S. paratroopers escorting nine black students to class was both chilling and humiliating to a nation that fancied itself a leader of the free world. The South, however, dug in its heels: Faubus became a regional hero, as did later George Wallace and Ross Barnett. Faubus continued to defy the courts and was overwhelmingly reelected for a third term. Southern resisters had persuaded themselves that recent troubles had really been caused by "outside agitators," and that southern Negroes were content and happy. As the 1960s opened, southern illusions were quickly lifted. In C. Vann Woodward's judgment, 1960 was the year of "massive awakening for the Negroes of the South."[39]

3

THE PIG IN THE PYTHON

A Generation of Vipers?

1. Baby Boomers and Their Parents

Just four months after World War II ended, the first of the "baby boomer" babies, Kathleen Casey, was born in Philadelphia at one second after midnight on January 1, 1946.[1] Kathleen Casey was the first of a wave of babies that inundated America in the postwar period. Demographers predicted that the upsurge would wane after a few years, assuming that young American couples would make up for their wartime postponement of having children in about two years. They were completely wrong. Few observers of this remarkable increase in population in the 1940s had any idea that America was undergoing an exceptional biological phenomenon that would have profound cultural implications. In fact, in addition to economic changes, it was the baby boom that triggered some of the disruptive changes of the late 1960s. Between 1946 and 1964, seventy-six million Americans were born and launched on a society whose institutions proved inadequate to acculturate them without serious social problems. Demographers use the metaphor of the "pig in the python" to describe the shape of the baby boom generation. It became increasingly obvious from the moment that historians looked at this astonishing phenomenon that it would be difficult to absorb this bulge without considerable discomfort, and that a country awash in young people could expect serious disruptions in its traditional way of life. So many young people meant, in the first place, that there would be too many people fighting for space, recognition, self-fulfillment, and happiness. Given the fact that there were so many baby boomers, it followed that they would have to stand in longer lines, fight for space in overcrowded schools or colleges, and compete for jobs in a marketplace that was not expanding rapidly enough to accommodate them, especially after the inclusion of women, who were also demanding equal access to economic opportunities.

Another salient characteristic, in addition to their large numbers, was the self-image that characterized the baby boomers. Reared in affluence and generally indulged as precious and special by their parents, the baby boomers expected to inherit a world of ever-growing prosperity that would allow them to fulfill their innermost longings. It is safe to say that no generation in American history saw itself so "empowered" or entitled to special consideration as the boomers. Landon Jones, who examined this generation at length, tells us that the special features associated with the boomers included their large numbers, longer but not necessarily better education; expectation of affluence; feeling of specialness; longing for authenticity; demand for new values and different lifestyles; different attitudes about marriage and divorce; a greater number of ambitious women; inability to delay gratification; and shorter attention spans.[2]

Generations define themselves by both what they accept and what they reject from the previous generation. A generation is defined by its common experiences, the same decisive influences, and similar historical problems. As José Ortega y Gasset has pointed out, three generations are alive and active at the same time: the young, the mature working adults, and the old. They experience their time as contemporaries; but they are not coevals because they live together in three very different periods of life.[3] Ortega used an imaginative metaphor to depict the difference between generations. Picture, if you will, a generation as a caravan within which a person moves as a prisoner but also voluntarily. From time to time he sees another caravan pass with a strange and curious profile—the other generation.[4] Although all of us are "fatefully inscribed within a certain group having its own age and style of life," each generation carries the previous one in itself even while rejecting some of its beliefs. This was true of the baby boomers as well, although they appeared to reject most of the beliefs of their elders. Immersed as they have been in a kind of collective narcissism that prompts them to talk endlessly about themselves, they have managed to drown out the world of their parents and grandparents. Yet we need to recapture that world and its beliefs if we are to understand not only the boomers but also the world they are creating for us today.

The parents of the baby boomers were decisively shaped by two major historical forces: the Great Depression and World War II. The war cured the depression and set the stage for a remarkable postwar boom, enabling the parents of the baby boomers to enjoy a high standard of living that their children would subsequently take for granted. Since most fathers had gone to war—fifteen million served in the armed forces—they had assimilated a distinctly militaristic attitude that encouraged habits of obedience, discipline, and respect for authority. Men returned from the war eager to create a tidy and standardized world, both at home and in the workplace. Just having defeated a stubborn enemy around the world, men also returned with a euphoric sense of empowerment that seemed to validate the American belief in some special dispensation from the laws of historical tragedy. The American creed that everything was possible as long as one set one's mind to it seemed triumphantly vindicated.

Since their lives had been uprooted by economic depression and war, the parents of the baby boomers longed for stability, routine, and safety. They put down roots in those islands of institutional safety called Levittowns, suburban tract houses that looked much alike, row upon row and ringed by manicured lawns. These were the little boxes on the hillside, little boxes made of ticky-tacky, little boxes all the same, as Malvina Reynolds would later call them. Here baby boom parents settled down to live the good life, which they understood to be the goods life—risk free, affluent, and happy.

To support the good life as the goods life required continued commitment to the Protestant work ethic. The key to material success, baby boom parents believed, was hard work, delay of gratification, and discipline. Baby boom parents admired free enterprise, but they generally shied away from the rugged individualism that earlier generations had supported. The Great Depression had taught them, and the war reinforced it, that safety and security resided in collective organizations that were scientifically planned and operated. Baby boom parents were children of FDR and the New Deal; they believed in scientific management, pragmatism, and the virtues of behavioral science. Samuel Beers, a one-time speechwriter for FDR and later a professor of government at Harvard, said that "Roosevelt taught us that in both spheres, domestic and foreign, government is the solution."[5]

The wartime model of management, based on these principles, would also characterize many peacetime organizations. Its focus was on group activity and coordination, emphasis on hierarchy, and subordination of the individual to company demands. The cultural role model of the 1950s was the "Organization Man"[6] and the good consumer—men and women who willingly adapted themselves to the world of corporate capitalism.

Baby boom parents believed in meritocracy rather than equality. Most of them had supreme confidence in the essential goodness and integrity of American institutions and the people who represented them. If dishonesty or corruption existed, baby boom parents rarely blamed the system or the establishment but instead the people who were corrupt. If an organization seemed to violate the canon of American values, baby boom parents generally turned a blind eye to injustice or reacted defensively either by ignoring it or rationalizing it as an aberration. Many also split or compartmentalized their lives, embracing inconsistent attitudes at home and in the workplace.

These attitudes, of course, were by no means symmetrical or consistent. A strong sense of individualism continued to operate in the private sphere. It was primarily in the public domain that baby boom parents sought shelter under a collective corporate umbrella, which increasingly turned out to be that interconnected maze of companies that made up the warfare state and the security state. In the private sphere they developed a curiously isolated and separate style of existence that Philip Slater described in his book *The Pursuit of Loneliness*. Despite their belief in organizational planning and teamwork, baby boom parents preferred to retreat into suburban loneliness in which deeper bonds and civic life began to erode and family life itself became splintered.

In recent years, the parents of the baby boomers have been celebrated in a number of works as the "greatest generation" in American history, an appellation that mostly centers on their sacrifices in the Second World War.[7] Such overblown assessments can be safely attributed to the historical shortspan of our time and the use of exaggerated claims that are by now almost *de rigueur* in our mass media culture. The World War II generation, of course, had many things to be proud of, particularly the courageous way it dealt with economic hardship and with the threat posed by both fascism and communism. When it came to raising children, however, the World War II generation did not do very well in socializing and educating the younger generation. They gave too freely and permissively without demanding the same commitment to discipline and hard work that they had internalized from previous generations. They often neglected their children, fobbed them off with money or material goods, and failed to provide them with firm discipline. The "greatest generation any society has ever produced," as Tom Brokaw claims, was certainly not perceived as so great by others in the 1930s. In fact, it was being described at the time as the "Lost Generation" that lacked a moral anchor and was given to lawless, violent, and promiscuous behavior. Depression-era children were condemned as moral delinquents who posed a serious threat to the future of the United States. A *Harper's* magazine article in 1936 saw the whole Lost Generation as "rotting before our eyes"; and one prominent journalist, tracking the Lost Generation in a major study, went so far as to say that young people were in a state "rapidly approaching a psychosis."[8] A common perception at the time was that young people were sunk in depravity by using illicit drugs, engaging in promiscuous sex, and resorting to criminal acts of various types. As Mike Males reminds us, the older generation usually believes that "today's youth" is always the worst, a misconception that is easily corrected by a balanced historical perspective.[9] The Depression-era generation was neither the worst nor the best generation in history, but it was a generation uniquely tested by historical adversities. Contrary to the fears of its elders, it met these challenges successfully because it had internalized the traditional American virtues of thrift, hard work, and delay of gratification. Unfortunately, it was not strong enough in successfully transmitting its values and attitudes to the new generation, a failure that haunts us to this very day.

2. The American Horn of Plenty: Paradox and Portent

Economic changes had a great deal to do with these developments. Beginning about 1950 the American economy surged into high gear and kept expanding for the next twenty years. As a result of this economic boom, the size of the middle class, defined in the 1950s as households earning between $3,000 and $10,000 a year, doubled from pre-Depression days and included close to 60 percent of the American people by the mid 1950s. Probably close to 90 percent owned television sets and 60 percent owned their own homes. Women were also beneficiaries of the boom, filling many jobs that the economic surge had created. Interestingly enough, the conservative culture of the 1950s, emphasizing political consensus and traditional family life, still glorified the role of women as mothers and homemakers, giving rise to acute psychological and social tensions because many mothers had to split themselves between being mothers and workers in the corporate world. It was in response to these conflicting demands and pressures that the radical feminist movement later challenged the patriarchal tradition of Western civilization.

Looking back on this remarkable postwar boom, which is unlikely to repeat itself, we now know what made it possible: a world war that ended the Depression, a cold war that helped expand the economy at high levels, and cheap energy that helped fuel the corporate machinery and turned the wheels of commerce. It was the national mobilization of human and natural resources necessary to fight World War II that put an end to the Great Depression. The cold war against communism, which followed on the heels of World War II, bolstered economic growth, especially in defense-related industries. Ironically, the strength of the U.S. economy owed much to the Soviets, a dirty little secret that was not widely recognized by most Americans, though Professor Sumner H. Slichter of Harvard pointed out as early as 1949, "In the absence of a cold war the demand for goods by the Government would be many billions of dollars less than it now is, and expenditures of both industry and Government on technological research would be hundreds of millions less than they are now. So we may thank the Russians for helping to make capitalism in the United States work better than ever."[10]

The trick now was to find the economic master key by which growth could be indefinitely continued. Politicians and economists in the postwar era thought they had discovered the magical formula in Keynesian "growth liberalism." John Maynard Keynes had argued that the uneven economic performance of Western economies was not an act of God or of Nature but false decision making by government. The wealth of a nation, according to Keynes, was primarily measured by a people's entrepreneurial energy, by its present accomplishments and expanding income levels. A high degree of income in the hands of individuals and groups encourages investments, production, and consumption, while also leading to prosperity. Unlike most traditional economists, who preached the virtues of thrift, savings, and self-denial, Keynes was a strong believer in spending and consuming, the more the better. One of Keynes's heretical claims was that savings, unless invested and freely circulating through the economy, could be a real obstacle to growth. The more money handed around the better, even if that pushes up the rate of inflation. A nation's continued growth depends on business investments and innovation, but it also depends, especially when markets have been satisfied or closed up, on the active role governments are playing in the economy. Keynes believed that government had a role in "priming the pump" by investing in socially useful enterprises such as the building and construction of roads, dams, airfields, public housing, harbors, museums, and so forth. If business did not invest sufficiently, Keynes believed, the government should take up the slack, as Franklin Roosevelt had done with the New Deal in the 1930s. Keynes, however, was not a socialist who believed that government should permanently regulate or even socialize the means of production. He believed in managed capitalism, and so did the liberals in the Democratic Party including John F. Kennedy, who followed his economic prescriptions. Keynesian economics played a vital role in what some historians have referred to as the postwar liberal consensus, which stressed government intervention through spending, even deficit spending, and monetary policies aimed at manipulating rates of interest and the money supply in order to control fluctuations in the economy.

Liberals believed that they had discovered not only the key to economic growth and the prevention of future depressions but also, *pari passu*, a method of solving social problems. Wealth tends to level and equalize; it is a universal healer of social injustices, provided, of course, that a benevolent government, staffed by scientifically trained experts, serves as a wise helmsman or ombudsman. According to Charles S. Maier, the "American organizing idea for the postwar economic world [was] the politics of productivity," a set of ideas and practices by which the liberal establishment hoped to eliminate class conflict through economic growth and affluence.[11] Throughout the postwar period (1945–1960) and beyond, most Americans, except the radicals of the 1960s, shared this growth ethic and its corollary that affluence is a universal healer that strengthens the family, helps fight and defeat communism, avoids class conflicts, lifts people out of poverty, increases social mobility, and leads to individual fulfillment and happiness. And it was not just the American people who believed this, but also people around the world who envied and tried to emulate the affluent American way of life—at least as it was projected abroad by American mass media.

The politics of affluence, however, did not solve all, or even most, human needs, especially spiritual needs. Yet in focusing on the paradox of affluence, the coexistence of wealth and poverty, the pressure it put on the traditional family, the social tensions it released on society in the 1960s, we can begin to see the unfolding of the social fault lines of the 1960s. In the first place, the explosive growth of the American economy in the postwar period caused significant demographic and geographic changes. As previously mentioned, the historic shift of population from country to city to suburbs continued at a rapid pace. Between 1945 and 1960 an average of thirty million people a year changed their place of residence. The new mobility benefited some sections of the country much more than others. Americans were especially attracted to the Sun Belt, comprising the fifteen states that describe a sort of crescent stretching from Virginia through Florida, Texas, Arizona, and California. Compared to the northeast Frost Belt, which declined in population, this Sun Belt nearly doubled in population. In the 1950s California alone accounted for one-fifth of the entire national growth in population, and by 1963 it had become the nation's most populous state. The press even began to talk about the southwest as a new frontier, for it was not just people who migrated there but also federal dollars. By contrast, both the Frost Belt and the Rust Belt with its deteriorating industrial structure began to feel like poor cousins in the American economy. From a political perspective, the migration to the southwest and west carried with it important clout. If the White House and its occupant are any indication of the future, these changes in demographics do not augur well for the northeast or the Rust Belt, for every president elected since 1964 has come from the southwest or west—Johnson, Nixon, Carter, Reagan, Clinton, and the two Bushes.

Most of the new migrating Americans, except blacks, eventually settled in the suburbs, a pattern that was encouraged by government policies. Both the Federal Housing Authority (FHA) and the Veterans Administration provided generous loans that enabled millions of Americans to afford inexpensive tract homes ($7,900 for a two-bedroom Levittown model) at low interest rates (4.5 percent fixed for thirty years).

Tax deductions for interest payments on home mortgages also provided incentives for buying rather than renting a home. Given these facts, it should not be surprising that the construction industry boomed in the postwar decades and it was American technological ingenuity that met the rising need for housing with a revolutionary method in home construction. The Levitt brothers of New York, who built family homes on Long Island, revolutionized home construction by erecting hundreds of houses in a single project. Working from standardized plans, highly specialized crews would descend on the building site and lay the foundations, while other crews would follow according to a scheduled timetable, raising factory-assembled framing modules, putting on roofs, stringing wires, installing plumbing, and finishing walls, windows, and doors. The first of these 17,000 homes built on Long Island housed 82,000 people; and although architectural critics, notably Lewis Mumford, denounced these tract homes as cookie cutters for bland people in bland houses, leading bland lives, the basic Levittown design and method became standard all over the country.[12] What critics of this suburban phenomenon failed to realize, aesthetic judgments aside, was that most Americans enjoyed living in new houses, however monochrome; and they did not mind moving like nomads all over the country. Above all, critics of tract housing, for the most part, did not realize that suburbanization signaled a radical shift in the way Americans had traditionally lived their lives in cities, small towns, or on the land. John Lukacs has pointed out that this development was unprecedented in the nation's history because it put an end to urban middle-class life and culture as it had been known for about a hundred years (1865–1965).[13] The habit of movement and migration, of course, was nothing new in American history, contributing to the American sense of rootlessness as well as autonomy, but what was new was the sheer scale of migration that World War II had unleashed and that corporate America and government encouraged.

The idea of "home" and rootedness in a particular community became meaningless when the average American household moved every four years. The same was true of ownership, whether of home or of land, with the result that Americans changed their attachment from place or land to real estate values that could be measured in dollars and cents rather than in love of hearth and home. Suburbanization and its allure to mobile middle-class whites had other, equally momentous consequences: the steady deterioration of central cities, often attributed to "white flight." This development of, course, did not begin in the 1960s but dated back to the turn of the twentieth century, especially when wealthier people wanted to enjoy city life while at the same time living in the suburban country. The revolution in transportation, especially the automobile industry, made this mode of living increasingly popular and affordable for many people. Government policies encouraged rather than inhibited these trends. Two landmark bills, the Federal Highway Act of 1916 and the Interstate Highway Act of 1956, financed the highways that enabled middle-class whites to flee the cities, taking away tax revenues these cities needed to maintain and expand their infrastructure: buildings, roads, libraries, water and sewage, public transportation, energy supply, law enforcement, and social services. Well-meaning government mortgages and loan programs, some dating back to the New Deal, had unintended and deleterious consequences for Americans living in inner cities, espe-cially in a form of discrimination called "redlining." This consisted in labeling whole inner city neighborhoods, particularly black neighborhoods, "credit risks" making them essentially off limits to middle-class buyers and condemning them to neglect because no one wanted to invest in their growth and development.[14] The GI Bill and the FHA encouraged suburban construction but not inner-city investments. Segre-gated public housing programs that concentrated the poor in deteriorating inner cities added to the problem of urban decay. The suburbs grew ten times faster than the city, and these suburbs were overwhelmingly white in population. There were no blacks in the Levittown development, primarily because whites did not want blacks as neighbors and also because, as the Levitt brothers put it, "We can solve a housing problem, or we can try to solve a racial problem but we cannot combine the two."[15]

The horn of plenty, as it turned out, was not benefiting non-white Americans, concealing economic and racial fault lines that would erupt in the 1960s. During World War II and after, millions of blacks migrated from the South to the North, ending up in deteriorating central cities such as St. Louis, Chicago, Detroit, Philadel-phia, Cleveland, Newark, New York, and Boston. William O'Neill has pointed out that this migration also meant a migration of poverty from rural to urban sections of the country. In 1930 half of America's poor lived on farms; in 1960 only 15 per-cent of the poor came from rural areas, while 55 percent came from urban centers.[16] The boom in housing construction bypassed poor blacks, whether they lived in rural or urban areas. By the 1960s inner cities, long neglected by city hall, state, or federal authorities, were a powder keg ready to explode, but one would not have known this by the illusory atmosphere of domestic tranquility of the 1950s. National attention was focused on the politics of affluence, on consumerism, middle-class family life, sports, and socially undisturbing entertainment. If there was a wrinkle in this other-wise monochrome white America, it expressed itself from time to time in a kind of siege mentality in the suburbs. In fact, one could argue that the dream of suburbia was at once an escape from and a new fortress against menacing forces at home as well as abroad.

Suburbia could stand as a metaphor of American security in the cold war, for it was in these thousands of tidy, well-manicured communities that Americans erected several walls of security to ward off real or perceived threats. In the first place, the suburb was widely seen as the place where a family-centered culture could be estab-lished as the backbone of Americanism as well as a bulwark against communism. As to the nature of the family, security required continuity or the maintenance of the monogamous family with its focus on domesticity and the preservation of tradi-tional gender roles that made the husband the breadwinner and the wife the home-maker. Elaine May has called this arrangement the domestic containment policy, the counterpart to America's foreign policy, which was designed to "contain" the spread of communism.[17] According to this domestic containment ideology, home owner-ship in suburbia, a traditional monogamous marriage—including traditional roles for women—and child-centered family patterns were all seen as important strategies in the national arsenal of fortress America.

In the home, it was the husband who controlled economic power. Father was supposed to know best, though Mom was regarded as his domestic partner and often a wiser and more sensitive sidekick. The double standard generally characterized matters of sexuality. Although premarital sex was widely regarded as undermining healthy sexual relations in marriage, the culture provided a lot of slack to young men for "sowing their wild oats," while strictly forbidding it for women—a double standard that would later rile feminists in the 1960s. The pressure on women to get married in the conservative fifties was intense. Magazines, books, and television programs constantly hectored young women to get married, offering helpful advice on "How to catch a husband" or "How to snare a male," but often warning that this should be done so cleverly that the man would be snared without knowing what hit him. In short, men should be pursued with bait rather than a net.[18] Dating was culturally encouraged, provided that young couples did not step over the line—that is, going beyond "petting" to sexual intercourse. A girl's reputation was considered destroyed if she was known to be sexually active. Americans called such damaged women "fast girls," "hot tomales," "loose girls," or "hussies." *Cosmopolitan* magazine warned young teenage girls that premarital sex not only sullied a woman's reputation but could also prevent them from being married at all. "The sex act," the magazine said, "was often painful and not pleasurable at all . . . Therefore if you have sexual intercourse at an early age you may be frightened and disgusted by it—and never marry."[19]

At the heart of this containment ideology was the cult of the child. The future of America belonged to children, and the way in which they were raised determined how that future was going to be shaped. The more children the better; they were good for the nation, filled a void for unfulfilled couples, and were "cheaper by the dozen," a saying popularized by the book of that title by Frank Gilbreth Jr. and Ernestine Gilbreth Carey. For women, babies were a biological means of self-empowerment, a way of asserting their role as mothers; but at the same time, babies also gave men a badge of masculinity, reinforcing the role of the paternal father figure. Young couples in the postwar period were inundated by a deluge of advice by "scientific" experts—psychologists, sociologists, anthropologists, pediatricians, and social workers—who offered the latest and most successful strategies for raising children, achieving sexual gratification, optimizing social adjustment, and so forth.

Brick by brick, over a fifteen-year period (1945–1960), Americans tried to construct a wall of security on all fronts, consisting of the ideal of suburbia, the traditional monogamous family, home ownership, sexual containment, Americanism, and anticommunism. The national mantra was spending and consuming, made possible by unusual economic growth in the postwar years. During the war, federal budgets had risen from $9 billion in 1939 to $100 billion in 1945, raising the gross national product (GNP) from $91 billion to $166 billion.[20] Although much of this revenue was spent on war requirements, a lot ended up in the hands of Americans in the form of savings because consumer goods were scarce, which forced Americans to practice self-denial and self-discipline. Following the war, however, the American people went on a binge of spending and burned most of the $140 billion they had saved during the lean war years. The urge to spend was sanctioned by Keynesian economists and their allies in government; it was also constantly hammered into the brains of Americans by advertising and aggressive salesmanship—so aggressive, in fact, that the sphere of privacy was constantly shrinking under the steady bombardment by television, radio, magazine, newspaper, telephone, and door-to-door sales.

In seeking answers to the disruptive changes of the 1960s, postwar economic developments played a major role; in turn, they caused significant demographic changes relating to the growth of suburbia, increased mobility, the migration of black people from the South to the North, and the rise of the Sun Belt to economic prominence. While there may not be a direct causal link between economic growth and fertility rates, there is an obvious correlation. Seventy-six million baby boomers did not drop on America out of a blue sky; they were the product of 15 million GIs returning from the war and exceptionally affluent times which made children affordable. How they were brought up, educated—or, alternatively, pampered and miseducated—would shape significant developments in the 1960s and beyond. In retrospect, Steve Gillon was right when he said that the boomers reshaped an earlier culture around their own single cohort, but this judgment has to be modified by remembering John Huizinga's well-known observation that "every political and cultural question in America is an economic one"—that is to say, the business of America is business.[21] In short, baby boomers were as much shaped by the growth and consumer ethic as they tried to shape the system. Gillon himself acknowledged this fact when he observed that as they moved through their life cycle, marketers and manufacturers moved with them.[22]

An important factor in the acculturation of the baby boomers was the fact that many of them were brought up in new suburban communities by parents who were cut off from traditional family networks. This was one of the results of a highly mobile workforce settling in remote suburban communities in which the social infrastructure of family and friends was often lacking. Young couples were, therefore, thrown to their own devices, having to create new social relationships in place of the old. Wondering what to do, especially when it came to raising their children, they often turned to the new "experts." This accounts for the fact that self-help books, most notably Dr. Benjamin Spock's *The Common Sense Book of Baby and Child Care* (1945) became so popular; experts served as substitute parents, teaching millions of amateurs who could not call on parents or grandparents, aunts or uncles, and ask them how to bring up babies. It was these economic changes and their impact on American family life that would produce those acute generational problems that erupted in the 1960s. The behavior of the baby boomers, for example, was a result of these changes, especially those directly related to the socialization process. It is safe to say that a real breakdown in the millennia-old process of socialization took place in the postwar period. The way in which young people were brought up and initiated into the mainstream of American society began to veer away sharply and perhaps decisively from traditional patterns.

The Duke of Windsor, not generally known for profound insights, had it right when he said that Americans obey their children wonderfully well. Deference to children, not unknown before World War II, became a new fetish in the postwar period. It arose in part from American faith in the future and the inevitable progress toward happiness that children would inherit and enjoy, but it also arose from parental guilt in not spending enough time with children, from permissive child-rearing strategies, and from mass-media pandering to young people and their needs.

This increasing worship and pandering to the young cannot be blamed on Dr. Spock, a now much maligned but actually commonsense baby doctor who believed in stern discipline and offered excellent advice in his work on child-rearing. Rather, the gradual breakdown of traditional family life must be blamed on disruptive economic patterns as well as ideological rationalizations that invested extraordinary expectations in children and assumed them to be inherently superior and wise.

Pandering to children and indulging their ego gratifications is unlikely to result in a robust, disciplined, and self-reliant generation of young adults. It is safe to say that the baby boomers were the most pampered generation in history. Most of them were conditioned by both parents and teachers to believe that they were special and unique, empowered to voice opinions on the weightiest subjects imaginable. They were told that their opinion or their vote really counted and that they should speak up against tyranny and injustice wherever they appeared in the world, which, their parents believed, was unlikely to occur in America because America, despite minor social flaws, was already perfect or moving toward perfection. It took some time for the baby boomers to see through the platitudes and official myths that were handed to them by parents and their leaders. In the 1950s their egocentricity was largely directed toward personal gratifications and social amusements. It was still the make-believe world of Ozzie and Harriet.

By virtue of their large numbers, the baby boomers tended to cluster in their own age groups. Moreover, since they did not extensively interact with their parents or their grandparents, they were less acculturated in the traditional mores and beliefs of American society. They increasingly fed on each other's juvenile attitudes and perceptions of the world, which often proved stubbornly resistant to parental and educational correction. This was made all the more difficult by the fact that the older generation, especially in the educational establishment, often pandered to baby boomers' demands. The classic example of shameful pandering to the demands of the baby boomers occurred in the wake of the many university protests of the 1960s, notably the one at Columbia University, where the intellectuals spinelessly buckled to student thugs and then proceeded to praise them as "the best informed, the best generation in this country . . . the cleverest and the most serious and decent."[23] *Time* magazine declared 1964 the "Year of the Kid," and in 1966 the same magazine proclaimed the under-25 generation as the "Man of the Year."

3. The Emergence of a Teenage Subculture

It did not take the consumer and advertising elite very long to realize that this large number of young people, clustering in their own company, could be readily shaped and exploited. It was in this way that a distinct teenage subculture, with its own mores, beliefs, and weaknesses, came into being. Whatever young people wanted or desired was accepted and reinforced by the consumer culture, provided, of course, that young people paid for the objects of their desires. This was no problem in the postwar period because children and young adults had more money to burn than any of their counterparts in American history. Discretionary spending by teenagers increased from $2.50 a week in 1944 to $10 a week in 1958. In 1958 the seventeen million American teenagers spent 9.5 billion dollars of their own money, quite apart from what their parents spent on them. The *New Yorker* magazine estimated that this was twice the national liquor bill and nine times the annual amount of Hollywood box-office receipts.[24]

A significant sector of the American economy catered exclusively to children and young adults, producing a wide variety of fad items: comic books, miniature soldiers, Barbie dolls, Hula Hoops, Davy Crockett caps, television cartoons, and above all, popular music in the form of rock 'n' roll. Popular music was becoming almost entirely devoted to juvenile themes. In Joseph Conlin's judgment, America became more like a teenage society with increasingly childish conceptions of reality.[25] In 1944 a new magazine, entitled *Seventeen*, was launched; it was the first magazine that exclusively catered to teenage tastes. But the man who first glimpsed the possibility of exploiting a mass market for teenagers was Eugene Gilbert, a young teenage entrepreneur from Chicago who identified himself with the bobby-soxer generation and their unique tastes. Working as a shoe clerk, he noticed that few teenagers shopped for shoes, despite the fact that the store was well stocked with shoes for teenagers. He managed to persuade the shoe store owner to pitch his advertising directly to teenagers, the result being that sales increased dramatically. Like the people who published the magazine *Seventeen*, Gilbert realized that teenagers themselves were the key to the marketing of teenage goods.[26] He founded his own market research company and hired teenagers to interview other teenagers, a shrewd move because it proved his hunch that teenagers would talk more freely to their own peers than they would to adults. Armed with research information gleaned from thousands of interviews with teenagers, Gilbert then sent out seductive messages to various companies that read:

> You want copy that talks to the guys and gals in their own language? We can write it for you! You want fresh ideas, groovy stuff? We can turn it out. . . . Our consultant board undoubtedly consists of the best-informed teenagers in their respective schools. Their knowledge plus our statistical information is definitely a terrific combo![27]

Before long, Gilbert had lined up some very well-to-do clients, including Esso gas, the magazine *Seventeen*, Simplicity dress patterns, Hollywood V-ette Vassarette brassieres, Mars candy, Hires soft drinks, Van Heusen shirts, Wide World Photos, the American Newspaper Association, and Royal typewriters. The Associated Press (AP) purchased Gilbert's weekly column of teenage opinion called "What Young People Think," which ran in three hundred newspapers. In 1947, Gilbert took his operation to New York, was celebrated as a boy wonder, and received prominent mention in

Newsweek, the *New Yorker*, *Harper's* magazine, and other publications. When he took his operation to London, however, nothing happened, because teenagers in Britain and elsewhere did not have enough money and freedom to be commercially interesting—at least not yet.

The fact that teenagers represented a new merchandizing frontier in the United States presupposed, in addition to growing economic affluence, important cultural changes that revolved around greater parental permissiveness. Journalists, child psychologists, sociologists, and historians were well aware that teenagers were becoming too independent and therefore a potential source of trouble. Giving young people too much money and freedom, it was held, could well undermine parental authority and result in rebellious, subversive, and criminal behavior. Even during the conservative fifties there was mounting public concern over out-of-control teenagers. Some blamed progressive education for undermining discipline by stressing self-expression or self-esteem and degrading educational standards by overemphasizing extracurricular activities. The schools, critics charged, were turning into places where young people socialized rather than learned. Other critics singled out the influence of psychological theories that seemed to excuse bad behavior rather than correct it. Freudians, for example, seemed to be saying that the child's bad behavior was not his fault because it was prompted by unconscious forces over which the child had little control. The solution was not to punish the child but to understand the underlying forces that prompted the child to behave in a certain way. Sensitivity, understanding, and love rather than harsh punishment were therefore the answer to youthful misbehavior. Still others blamed the culture of affluence, claiming that self-indulgence and lack of responsibility had infected parents and children alike and turned traditional cultural patterns of discipline, hard work, and unselfish love upside down.

The world of teenagers and the world of adults, however, seemed increasingly to belong to two different species, especially in the postwar years when a distinct teenage subculture with attendant dress, behavior, and styles of leisure could be identified. In the 1950s television mobilized teenagers even more successfully by catering to their needs and exploiting their weaknesses.

Yet the medium that became the real conduit of juvenile tastes was music. It was through music, as David Halberstam reminds us, that "a new generation of Americans was breaking away from the habits of its parents."[28] Halberstam notes that there was nothing the parents could do. Their kids had the money and the inexpensive appliances to listen to the music they wanted, and no amount of preaching by their parents could budge them from listening to Elvis Presley and the music he played—rock 'n' roll.

It was probably a musical event that signaled the arrival of a distinct teenage subculture, and that was the record "Rock Around the Clock" by Bill Haley in 1954. Being an obscure country and western singer in his thirties and sporting an unattractive spit curl that seemed plastered to his forehead, Haley gave little indication of becoming a teenage idol. The song "Rock Around the Clock," written by James Myers, was actually side B of a single called "Thirteen Women," which was designed to make Haley famous. Although "Rock Around the Clock" was a minor hit, it quickly fizzled and threatened to fade into obscurity had it not become the theme song for the motion picture *Blackboard Jungle*, a B movie about an idealistic teacher in an urban high school who turned his back once too often on his class and got beaten up by young thugs after interrupting the rape of a female teacher.

Blackboard Jungle was one of Hollywood's earliest attempts, later repeated ad infinitum, at depicting authority figures, especially teachers, as authoritarian bullies, old fogeys, and irritating killjoys. Yet such motion pictures and the music that accompanied them resonated with young teenagers who saw themselves oppressed by domineering parents and teachers. "Rock Around the Clock" became an international hit, selling sixteen million copies and prompting teenage audiences, aroused by its provocative lyrics, to go on rampages in America and Europe. After a "Rock Around the Clock" showing, young "Teddy Boys" (juvenile rebels) in Britain rampaged through the South London streets for several hours, overturning cars and smashing windows. Similar violence connected to the song erupted in West Germany, Italy, and France.

Quite apart from being a red-letter day for selling records to teenagers, "Rock Around the Clock" also represented a musical dividing line between young baby boomers and their older siblings who had grown up listening to various white vocalists such as Frank Sinatra, Dean Martin, Perry Como, Rosemary Clooney, and Pattie Page. It was a dividing line between mostly white and sentimental music and a far more vibrant, sexually charged and protesting music with strong African American coloration. The conduit, as shown later, was Elvis Presley, the "king of rock 'n' roll and musical pied piper of a whole generation of young people. As Landon Jones observed, the baby boomers were the rock 'n' roll audience:

> Rock was the sound track in the movie version of their lives. They discovered it, danced to it, romanced to it, and someday will presumably be buried to it. The music consolidated their group identity, bridging the emotions they all felt inside with peers who felt the same way.[29]

At the time "Rock Around the Clock" made number one on the charts of hit records in 1955, Hollywood discovered, or rather rediscovered, a recurring adolescent archetype and mass merchandized it to a the growing teenage market: it was the heroic theme of the innocent and misunderstood young rebel at odds with his uncomprehending adult world. The rebel was James Dean. Although the James Dean cult belongs more properly to the 1950s, it served as a prefiguration of mass-media-sponsored celebrity worship, in this case the mass adoration of the misunderstood young rebel whose genius was tragically cut short by cruel fate. In an increasingly secularized culture, the fallen hero was bound to be drawn from those areas of modern life that people had chosen to endow with a special kind of glamour: entertainment, sports, or politics.

In a deeper psychological sense, the adoration of the hero, whether he was a knight in shining armor, a saint ill used by the world, or a romantic rebel, represents a recurring archetype in world history. The James Dean cult was in many ways a recrudescence of the Young Werther cult of the early nineteenth century, except that Dean was dressed in T-shirt, leather jacket, and jeans rather than blue velvet jacket, yellow vest, and riding boots. In both cases, we find a young man thrust into a world he did not make and discovering that it did not conform to his youthful longings and desires. Though blessed with great talent and a romantic heart, the hero is slighted by an uncomprehending and straightlaced world that seeks nothing more than to stifle his rebellious spirit and force him to conform to its smug bourgeois values. The cruel denouement occurs when the hero finds himself rejected by the only romantic love of his life—the sister-madonna-faced Lotte or Pier Angeli—and either commits suicide or takes such inordinate risks behind the wheel of his Porsche that he eventually kills himself on a California highway.

The psychological dynamics of impossible love, of thwarted ambition, misunderstood needs, or great talent cut short represent a recurring theme in human life; and when these dynamics manifest themselves in the lives of adolescents, whose inexperience often makes them especially vulnerable, they call for patience, sensitivity, and understanding on the part of the adult world. Such understanding of adolescent rebellion, however, is usually the exception rather than the norm because adults tend to be threatened by youthful rebellion and seek to marginalize, ridicule, or quash it before it gets out of hand—that is, before it seriously challenges the guiding assumptions of the adult world.

The James Dean story, either in real life or on film, was the harbinger of teenage rebellion in American society. It was a story in manners and dress as well as in morals or political expression. The James Dean uniform consisted of cowboy boots, blue jeans, T-shirt, and leather jacket, all of it worn in a deliberately sloppy manner. Dean's persona, irresistible to both boys and girls, featured a handsome yet rugged face that expressed youthful vulnerability and sexual magnetism. The rebel's unruly mane and long sideburns suggested defiance and nonconformity to the military crew cuts then in fashion. The Dean persona was not complete, of course, without the ubiquitous cigarette that invariably dangled from the hero's pursed lips as he posed either on a motorcycle or in a sports car.

As to the cultural message behind the James Dean phenomenon, the theme is by now familiar to everyone. Our hero is always at odds with his parents and he must forge his own way in the world. He savors a multitude of experiences: a brief spell at UCLA, where he discovers a talent for acting; work on a refrigeration truck; stevadore on a tugboat; ship's boy on a yacht. He milks cows, tends to chickens, drives a tractor, raises a bull, plays star basketball, studies yoga and the clarinet, and in general learns something about everything. His life is a race against boredom; it is motion, preferably on a motorcycle or in a Porsche race car. The hero's overweening ambition eventually propels him into fame, first on broadway and then on the silver screen; yet, despite the fame and glamour, his inner life remains spiritually unfulfilled. His longing for the impossible love and the perfect thrill must necessarily fail in a world of chains and incomprehending middle-class midgets. In response, the hero milks the system for all the money it is worth while at the same time demanding to live "totally"—that is, demanding the right to pursue total self-expression and self-fulfillment. Invariably, this lifestyle implies risking death over and over again. In Dean's first motion picture, *Rebel without a Cause*, the rebellious hero not only clashes against the stupidity of parents and adult authorities but also against his own peers. He has to prove his virility by passing the "chicken test," which consists in racing his juvenile competitor to the edge of a cliff and shouting "chicken" if his rival jumps out of the car before he does. Happily, he survives the test by jumping out of the car before it plunges into the abyss, unhappily his peers blame him for the death of his rival, who plunged to his death when his belt gets caught in the car's door handle, preventing him from jumping out.

Dean's life and work was a great rejection, a rebellion against the smug bourgeois world of the postwar fifties. At first that rebellion was limited to a few artistic outsiders—James Dean, Marlon Brando, Elvis Presley, Hipsters, and Beats. It took place against a background of middle-class conservatism and cold war rhetoric. The 1950s, it has been said, lived on ideological pretensions by claiming that the postwar world was harmonious and happy. By pretending that the country was purring with contentment and that "Nobody was Mad with Nobody," as *Life* Magazine insisted in 1955, the country showed little patience with youthful rebellion and provided few outlets for it. Yet James Dean showed the way to the future in his rejection of parental authority, his defiance of adult tastes and values, and his insistence on total self-fulfillment. His tragic death in a car accident in 1955 assured his cult standing. There was something archetypal and romantic about the young hero driving his Porsche into the sunset and into oblivion on a California highway. His obsession with speed became the symbol of the young generation; it was also the modern substitute for the absolute. As Edgar Morin put it,

> Motorized speed is not only one of the modern signs of the quest for the absolute, but corresponds to the need for risk and self-affirmation in everyday life. Anyone behind a wheel feels like a god, . . . self-intoxicated, ready to strike other drivers with thunderbolts, terrorize mortals (pedestrians), and hand down the law in the form of insults to all who do not recognize his *absolute priority*.[30]

Finally, Dean was greater in death than he would ever have been in life. Like Elvis Presley and John F. Kennedy, Dean died a young man, forever cherished by his adoring followers as a heroic and unblemished young man. Being young, which is what America loves about itself, means being forever vital and creative. Death fulfills the destiny of every mythological figure; and in the eyes of many Americans, especially young Americans, James Dean or Presley or JFK never really died.

James Dean, of course, was only one of several emerging celebrity rebels. Another was the defiant, mercurial, and brilliant actor Marlon Brando, who had been Dean's role model. Unlike Dean, whose love of risk had pushed him over the edge, Brando went on to a long and distinguished career, maturing in his roles as he grew older. In the fifties Brando, along with Humphrey Bogart, Allan Ladd, Robert Mitchum, and William Holden, popularized the persona of Camus' rebel, the existential hero who plays by his own rules and prefers to live on the sharp edge, taunting authority figures and sticking up for the underdog. In the late 1940s and early 1950s, Hollywood had become enchanted by *film noir*, which depicted the raw but vital life of the underground, the downstairs world where crooks, criminals, drug addicts, hookers, outsiders, and mad artists mingled, rubbed each other raw and occasionally threw off real sparks of creativity. It was this world that a group of poets and writers began to glorify in the mid-fifties. They were called the Beats and they would serve as the vanguard of 1960s protests.

On May 21, 1957, the San Francisco police raided the City Lights Bookstore, arrested its owner, Lawrence Ferlinghetti, and seized copies of a book of poetry by Allen Ginsberg entitled *Howl and other Poems*. The book, along with other questionable works, was declared "obscene and indecent" because it glorified protest against corporate America and celebrated personal freedom through drugs and sexual activity, including especially homosexual love. Ginsberg's works energized the radical fringe of bohemians who had already spiritually seceded from the white middle-class mainstream they so thoroughly despised. Ginsberg was a troubled young man whose Jewish nonconformist nature, along with his homosexuality, made him a lifelong opponent of conventional society. At Columbia University, where he majored in English, he was repeatedly in trouble with the administration over his misbehavior in the dorms and was suspended. He then moved into the off-campus apartment of Joan Adams, a married Barnard student. It was in this setting of bohemian conviviality that Ginsberg developed a network of like-minded outsiders with passionate literary and artistic aspirations, notably Jack Kerouac, a ruggedly handsome and athletic on-and-off-again student, and William Burroughs, a tall, emaciated-looking but intensely intellectual figure with a baggage of drug addiction and wasted opportunities behind him. Kerouac was itching to escape from the straitjacket of his strict Roman Catholic upbringing and experience life in the raw. Burroughs, son of a wealthy businessman whose paternal grandfather had invented the adding machine, had graduated from Harvard with a degree in English and then moved to New York, where he spent more time as a bartender, factory worker, advertising copy writer, garbage collector, and even exterminator than he did as a writer. The army discharged him during World War II because of his "nut house" record.[31] Burroughs was a wastrel and a scoundrel who was morbidly fascinated by low life, which he subsequently lionized in novels like *Junkie* (1953) and *Naked Lunch* (1959). At the time he met Ginsberg and Kerouac, he was living off a small trust fund from his wealthy parents, which allowed him to go slumming in the seedier parts of New York. It was through Burroughs and his underground contacts, notably the Times Square hustler Herbert Huncke, called "the Creep" by the police, that the two former Columbia students got their serious introduction to the criminal underworld. Kerouac later claimed that it was through Huncke that he heard the word Beat, by which Huncke meant down and out but which for Kerouac implied a more exalted way of life associated with bohemian night life: jazz, drugs, sex, and cool conversation. Black bebop and hipster life was like mana from heaven for Ginsberg, Burroughs, and Kerouac, a release from straightlaced guilt-ridden Jewish, Protestant, and Catholic traditions. The Creep, according to Jill Jenner, became a kind of crucial figure, a sort of Vergilian guide to the lower depths for these white males.[32] Eventually, Huncke the Creep went to jail and Burroughs was arrested for writing false narcotic prescriptions. Soon after being bailed out of jail by his family, Burroughs then married Joan Adams and moved to Texas for a cooling-off period. A misogynist and drug addict, Burroughs had no real love for or commitment to Joan Adams or her child. He later accidentally killed her in Mexico by playing William Tell but missing the water glass on Joan's head and pumping a bullet into her head instead.

In the absence of Burroughs and Huncke, Ginsberg and Kerouac needed and found another hustler in Neal Cassady, a frenetic charmer and car thief from Denver. Cassady was Kerouac's Vergil to the roads, highways, and seedier byways of America, his subterranean guide to the heaven that was painted as hell for conventional Americans. Kerouac clearly had Cassady in mind when he wrote in his famous novel *On the Road* (1953) that the only people who interested him were "the mad ones, the ones who are mad to live, mad to talk, mad to be saved, desirous of everything at the same time, the ones who never yawn or say a commonplace thing, but burn, burn, burn like fabulous yellow roman candles, exploding like spiders across the stars and in the middle you see the blue centerlight pop and everybody goes 'Awww!'"[33] Kerouac was soon off with Cassady crisscrossing the country on his legendary quest for self-discovery. Today *On the Road* still evokes vivid images of adolescent adventures in the 1950s, of getting one's kicks on Route 66—events that actually contained some deeper meaning beyond the colorful descriptions of wacky characters on the move. The notion of movement, of course, was a metaphor for modern America; and thus, the book captures a glimpse of this whirling, buzzing confusion as it was experienced by a few white drop-outs from corporate America.

What did the road teach Kerouac and his motley crew of adventurers? In a moment of self-reflection the author wondered what all this motion was about, for having been eight thousand miles on the road he was right back in Times Square, right in the middle of rush hour, watching "the absolute madness and fantastic hoorair of New York with its millions and millions hustling ever for a buck among themselves." Is this all there is? In answer to this gnawing existential question, which is never explicitly raised in the book, Kerouac has one epiphany that he draws on repeatedly: the meaning of life is to live it as passionately and intensely as possible, to grab and exploit every opportunity that comes along—spontaneously and without regard for consequences. This is what Dean Moriarty (Neal Cassady) was all about; he was excited and hungry for life. This is also what another hero of the book was about, Old Bull Lee, a teacher who had traveled the world once too often, met too many bizarre people, devoured the works of Spengler and the Marquis de Sade, and stayed in expensive hotels and hung around foul-smelling pissoirs. Old Bull Lee was high on life, high on sex, inviting Kerouac and his cronies to try out his Orgon accumulator, the Reichian sex cabinet that supposedly trapped vibrating atmospheric atoms charged with sexual energy, enabling the user to achieve prodigious orgasms.[34] Where could one learn about such characters and experiences if one did not take to the road? And here is the key to an otherwise rambling book: the road *is* life in America; take it and you will be redeemed.[35] Unlike the more hopeful hippies of the 1960s, who took to the roads in droves, Kerouac did not believe that the road led to any final goal or destination. There was no political vision in Kerouac, Burroughs, or even Ginsberg. Their politics spanned the whole spectrum, from Kerouac's political indifference to Burroughs's reactionary rantings and Ginsberg's romantic anarchism.

In their own lives many of the Beats remained marginal outsiders who nursed their alienation from the mainstream by becoming professional social invalids. Without a deeper moral or religious compass, they would later move through middle and old age with regrets, resentments, and self-loathing, proving that a road without a destination is a road to nowhere. While not traveling on the road, Kerouac, it turned out, lived with his mother and later returned to his Roman Catholic faith. He drank himself to death at the age of forty-seven. Ginsberg moved to Berkeley, California, and embarked on his own tangled odyssey of self-discovery. His genius for self-promotion and turning up at prominent countercultural events of the 1960s brought him fame and notoriety. The flower children of the 1960s venerated him as a sage, hanging on his every word or mantra. In the youthful counterculture he was even seen as the greatest poet since William Blake, an iconographic status that made many look the other way when it came to his sordid personal life. As to Neal Cassady, alias Dean Moriarty, he died of a drug overdose, discovered on a lonely railroad track in Mexico, sun-scorched and dehydrated, but mumbling faintly, "64,928," a reference to the number of railroad ties he had counted before dying.[36]

The significance of Beat subculture for the 1960s was its cult of the alienated rebel, whether it was James Dean in *Rebel without a Cause*, Marlon Brando in *Wild One*, Kerouac's *On the Road*, Burroughs's *Naked Lunch*, or Ginsberg's *Howl*. In each of these cases, the youthful rebel, torn by psychological conflicts, projects his *angst* on conventional middle-class society, which refuses to ratify his narcissistic and often plainly deviant needs. By looking at the Beats we can already see a clear outline of the adolescent tsunami of the 1960s, including the endless demands of liberation from all conventional manners and standards. The fortress of neo-Victorian morality of the 1950s was clearly being softened up by these beatnik moles, eating both its healthy and its rotten roots. To use an analogy from biology, social systems are like ecosystems whose natural rhythms can be disrupted by unnatural stresses. Within social ecosystems some of the major causes of disintegration can be found in the breakdown of limits on appetite, desires, and self-satisfaction. In preaching a gospel of total liberation from social control, in placing their naked egos ahead of the need for educating children, sacrificing themselves for one's country, pledging loyalty to collective values, the Beats showed the way for millions of boomers of how middle-class fortress America could be brought down.

One of the most dangerous messages of the Beats was not just their glorification of the rebel, which can be culturally creative, but their flirtation with psychopathically deranged criminals. This manifested itself, for example, in Norman Mailer's paean to the "hipster" and his lifestyle of sexual promiscuity, drugs, and violence. In an essay written for *Dissent* in 1957, "White Negro," Mailer took as his social role model the white racial stereotype of how blacks allegedly lived their lives without silly white Puritanical restraints. Black men and women were superior sexual animals, less inhibited and more sensuous and exotic. Their dark sexual urges always bordered on vulgarity, for this is what good sex is all about. Mailer had a particular fondness for the carefree, hustling black male who followed his own code of ethics, unencumbered by family ties or obligations. One is thus either hip or a "White Negro" or one is square, "trapped in the totalitarian tissues of American society,"[37] a deplorable example of bifurcation and misjudgment of American social life. Yet Mailer pushed this enchantment with hipsters beyond the limits of moral sanity when he went on to defend psychopathic killers as necessary elements in decomposing a rotten social system.

In the pages of the *Village Voice*, which he helped found in 1955, Mailer covered the hip scene in Greenwich Village, New York, and inveighed against conformist America. A prolific writer, he is, in retrospect, a trailblazer to the radical sixties and its many dissonant voices and attitudes, not least of which was the chic habit of living immoral lifestyles and posing as a paragon of political virtue. The only hip morality, Mailer suggested, was to do what one felt like whenever and wherever it is possible. Since no one could foretell consequences of actions, one might as well act on pure impulse or feelings. That one could choose moral principles rooted in religious values did not exist in Mailer's moral consciousness; when it came to personal morality the novelist was simply tone-deaf. This was not true of his liberal political views, which he advertised at every opportunity, claiming that he was the existential writer, half noble physician and half seer showing the way to a better world, a world having rid itself of cannibals (self-devouring warmongers) and Christians (phony do-gooders, conformists, and hypocrites).

Mailer yearned for a romantic hero who could bridge the sharp divide of American society, giving satisfaction to its Dionysian underground while at the same time moving gracefully though the Apollonian upper levels of middle-class America. In 1960 the novelist attended the Democratic National Convention in Los Angeles and had a premonition that John F. Kennedy might just possibly be the man who fit the bill. Eisenhower, Mailer suggested, had only embodied half the needs of the nation, "the needs of the timid, the petrified, the sanctimonious, and the sluggish." Would Kennedy satisfy the "untapped, ferocious, lonely and romantic desires, that concentration of ecstasy and violence which is the dream life of the nation?"[38] Mailer felt that there was a good possibility that Kennedy could become a kind of hipster president, and that underneath that suave façade, which he displayed to the public, there was probably a hipster superman trying to get out. If this was the case, the novelist hoped, then the real vital spirit of America could be resuscitated. Perhaps Kennedy was the superhero who had come to "supermarket America" and was ready to dismantle it. For Mailer, the Beats, and the young protesters of the 1960s the supermarket was a symbol of everything that was wrong with corporate America; for Mailer it represented the spirit of homogeneous uniformity, psychoanalyzed people, packaged commodities, and interchangeable, geographically unrecognizable tract homes. Little did Mailer know in 1960 that his hope of violent turbulence was shortly to be fulfilled and that John F. Kennedy would be one of its chief catalysts.

4

JOHN F. KENNEDY AND
THE CAMELOT IMAGE

1. Kennedy the Man and the Leader:
Image and Reality

On Wednesday July 24, 1963 a young Arkansas teenager belonging to the American Legion Boys Nation Program, Bill Clinton, visited the White House along with a dozen other young delegates. In the Rose Garden of the White House young Clinton excitedly listened to a brief address by the president, who complimented the young men's work, especially their support for civil rights. The president then shook hands with several young men, including Bill Clinton. A photo of the famous handshake symbolically prefigures the passing of the presidential torch from one generation (Kennedy) to another (Clinton). The picture freezes the excitement and awe on the young man's face.[1] The same excitement would have undoubtedly been expressed by millions of other men or women had they been in Clinton's place. Few other presidents in the twentieth century were able to establish such a close emotional rapport with young people as John F. Kennedy. The president's charisma gave young Americans renewed hope in the American dream that everything was possible and achievable in America: wiping out poverty, ending war, and attaining social justice.

We have numerous testimonials showing just how deeply Kennedy affected both young and older Americans. Those young Americans who joined the Peace Corps or served in the armed forces believed that Kennedy had given them new hope that their individual efforts would make a difference in moving the nation in a progressive direction. Bill and Susan Montfort, for example joined the Peace Corps because they were stirred by Kennedy's appeal to unselfish service for their country, "the idea of giving, not getting."[2] Philip Caputo said that he, like so many young soldiers, had "been seduced into uniform by Kennedy's challenge to ask what you can do for your country and by the missionary idealism that he had awakened in us."[3] The man who photographed the tragic moment when Kennedy was assassinated, Abraham Zapruder, was there in Dallas that day, according to his son, because he loved the president.[4] Even the man who shot Lee Harvey Oswald, the president's assassin, claimed that he did it because he loved Kennedy and wanted to redress a wrong in the universe.

Despite his brief presidency, Kennedy served as a real catalyst of change; he was the nation's first "cool president": suave, sophisticated, unconventional and risk-taking. For young people, he was a political James Dean, a hero with a thousand faces. He moved young people emotionally, especially with the noble sentiments he evoked and ultimately with the tragic way he was felled by an assassin's bullet.

Historians have suggested that generations could be distinguished by the impressions they receive around the age of seventeen, which would be the year 1963 for the advanced guard of baby boomers.[5] In that year, John F. Kennedy was assassinated, an event that etched itself into the collective memory of those who were old enough to experience it. What followed the death of the president was the inflation of the Camelot image that had already been nurtured during Kennedy's presidency. The illusion of an eventual restoration of Camelot by the legitimate heir to the throne, Robert F. Kennedy, was, of course, assiduously cultivated by ardent Kennedy followers, but the dream (and Robert Kennedy) did not survive the turbulent changes of the 1960s. The horror and the loss experienced by most Americans on November 22, 1963, however, marked the beginning of a national cultural division that has continued to this day. For young Americans, the year 1963 would turn out to be a seminal event in the nation's history.

John F. Kennedy was one of the driving forces of change in the 1960s because he provided the psychological impetus that reawakened the American myth that motion toward moral and political perfection was America's inherent destiny. Speaking in the loftiest rhetoric, he urged Americans: "ask not what your country can do for you—ask what you can do for your country." It was January 21, 1961, Inauguration Day, when John F. Kennedy spoke these words. On that day millions of Americans could watch a remarkable historical contrast on their television sets, for here on the same podium were two men representing different generations: the elderly Dwight D. Eisenhower, the outgoing president representing the conservative 1950s, and the youthful and vibrant Kennedy, the incoming president representing the radical 1960s. Speaking in the crisp winter cold without an overcoat or hat, the young president made specific reference to the fact that the torch had been passed to a younger generation of Americans. As he did so, the camera periodically panned over to the heavily clad Eisenhower, visibly freezing in the brisk winter cold. As Thomas Reeves has pointed out, it was a visual metaphor of two contrasting men and periods.[6] It was also something else few people noticed at the time: the triumph of image over substance, for Kennedy was, as I shall argue, a media product whereas Eisenhower was a man of substance and character. Since the election of John F. Kennedy, American life and politics have been increasingly colored by visual images. People pay more attention to the cultivated and changeable exterior than to the moral interior in assessing their candidates for high office. As Reeves observes, we follow psychologists in preferring the term "personality" rather than "character" because character is an old-fashioned moral term that suggests the existence of objective standards of ethics that someone has internalized and that have helped him shape his character.[7] Personality, on the other hand, is the superficial and often outward persona that we display to the world, changing it as it suits us. Personality describes the bearing and behavior of a person, whereas character describes the deeper existential level of values, beliefs, emotional stability, and intellectual depth. It is Reeves's contention that Kennedy did not have good character, though he certainly had a sparkling personality. Character is a function of good upbringing, which requires the inculcation rather than the mere mimicking of moral virtues.

John F. Kennedy was the scion of a large and wealthy family of Irish Catholics. His father, Joseph P. Kennedy, had made the family's fortune in banking and finance, mostly in stock and real estate speculation. He ruled the family like a monarch and taught his children, four boys and five girls, to be fiercely competitive and socially active. Winning was everything and losing was the worst sin. Their mother withdrew into her religion or her own social interests and avoided intimacy with her children, and the tone in the family was definitely set by the domineering father who was intent on establishing a family dynasty on the backs of his children.

The dynamics of family life that would mold many of the Kennedy children, including John Kennedy, revolved around this interplay of a domineering father and a submissive, inconsistently imperious, and often emotionally ineffective mother. Kennedy later said of his emotionally distant mother: "my mother was either at a Paris fashion house or else on her knees in some church. She was never there when we really needed her. . . . My mother never really held me and hugged me. Never. Never!"[8] The large Kennedy family was always a beehive of activity marked by competitive games and social amusements. However, there was the odd person out: Rosemary, who was mentally retarded and simply did not fit the Kennedy image of fierce competition, wit, and social grace. A lobotomy, old Kennedy reasoned, would surely take care of the problem, but the surgery failed tragically and rendered the girl permanently disabled. Rosemary was discreetly tucked away in a mental asylum, out of sight and out of mind. Her father never mentioned her again; in his eyes she was a loser.

Since the Kennedy patriarch himself never achieved his real ambition to become president of the United States and was fobbed off with minor posts (head of the Securities and Exchange Commission, chairman of the Maritime Commission, ambassador to Britain) by FDR, who needed but disliked him, he labored mightily to groom his own sons for the job. Initially, the patriarch concentrated on his oldest son Joe Junior and then, after Joe's death in a plane accident in World War II, on his second oldest son, John Fitzgerald. The trouble was that Jack, a charming, handsome, and sickly child, showed little serious interest in politics; his aim in life was to have a good time and chase as many women as he could, an area where his philandering father had already set a dubious example.

The deeper one gets immersed in Kennedy literature, the more appalling the recognition that Jack Kennedy's life was molded, every step along the way, by his calculating father. It is not that the son enjoyed being soft wax in his father's hands, but that he genuinely believed that he had little choice in resisting his father and the corrupting money he held over his head. He stoically confessed at one point, "I guess Dad has decided he's going to be the ventriloquist, so that leaves me the role of the dummy."[9] The father, as it would turn out, bankrolled his campaigns, hired ghostwriters to help him publish his speeches, articles, and books, and discreetly helped him cover up his many indiscretions with women of ill-repute.

Does this imply, then, that Kennedy had no inner substance whatsoever? By no means. Young Kennedy had genuine abilities of his own and gradually realized that, with his father's influence and money, he could write his own script in the world of politics. He had always enjoyed the world revolving around him, even more so now that his family was solidly behind him in his quest for the highest office in the land. He turned into an overweeningly ambitious and talented politician who immensely enjoyed stage-managing everything around him. Kennedy saw politics as a theatrical spectacle that could succeed only with good acting and superb stage sets. The glamour surrounding motion pictures and movie stars had always been a Kennedy preoccupation. Joseph Kennedy himself had entered the movie business in 1926, bankrolling various films and chasing starlets, showgirls, and movie stars, including Gloria Swanson. The son inherited this fondness for the glitz and glamour of Hollywood, and if he could not be an actor on the screen perhaps he could be an actor on an even larger political stage, using all the theatrical trappings of film to make his role credible to a national audience.

From the moment John Kennedy entered the public arena in 1947 as a Massachusetts congressman, his father spared no expense in helping him manufacture a public personality in the form of a serious, high-minded, and deeply intellectual young man who was blessed by a special kind of talent and charisma that would eventually sweep him into the highest office of the land. Already while Jack was a senior at Harvard, his father made sure that his senior thesis was rewritten by professional writers and subsequently published as a popular book, entitled *Why England Slept*. The book was a Book-of-the-Month Club selection and appeared on several best-seller lists. Kennedy's Pulitzer Prize–winning study *Profiles in Courage* was largely crafted by a team of professional writers, notably Theodore Sorensen.[10] In fact, it was Sorensen, a very gifted young writer with a knack for memorable phrases, who became Kennedy's speechwriter and personal conduit to the intellectual community. No effort was spared to win over liberal intellectuals such as James MacGregor Burns, who wrote a flattering biography of John F. Kennedy; the economist John Kenneth Galbraith; the historian Arthur Schlesinger, who was besotted with the Kennedys; Theodore White, who wrote a sentimental and extremely partisan account of the 1960s campaign; Arthur Goldberg; Joseph Rauh; and many others. Writers ghosted articles under Kennedy's name during the presidential campaign and had them published in *Life* or *Look* magazines, the *Progressive*, and *Georgetown Law Review*.[11]

An important element in the public Kennedy persona was the war hero story that Joseph Kennedy had confabulated as early as the late 1940s, but that turned out to be so persuasive to the public that it was steadily embellished and ultimately turned into a motion picture, entitled *PT 109*. Recent research has shown that the war hero image did not conform to reality, and that, if anything, young Kennedy may have been negligent in his duty as an officer and personally responsible for the sinking of *PT 109*.[12]

The Kennedy image, as it was being constructed in the 1950s would not be complete if it had not been for the glamour and beauty that his wife Jacqueline (Jackie) Kennedy brought to the campaign. Old Kennedy could not have wished for a better wife for his son. Jacqueline Bouvier was not only beautiful and highly intelligent, but she also came from a well-established, if not overly well-to-do, family of genteel patricians. She would later mightily contribute to the Camelot legend. The marriage itself was one of convenience: Jacqueline was a beautiful stage set who could give Jack the social and cultural graces he lacked. Since Jack was a shameless philanderer, sleeping with hundreds of women ranging from famous actresses (Gene Tierney, Marilyn Monroe, Marlene Dietrich, Jayne Mansfield, Angie Dickinson, etc.) to a Mafia mistress (Judith Campbell Exner) and just plain prostitutes, his father purportedly had to intervene on numerous occasions to save the marriage, offering Jackie a million dollars so that the marriage could continue.[13]

All this, of course, was hidden from the American people. In public, Jack and Jackie, as they were affectionately called, were a superb pair: he had the political talent and she had the refined style. The public was seduced by the glamour that emanated from the White House, which became a media machine in its own right replete with public relations experts, academic trimmers, slick speechwriters, and damage control managers.[14]

Of course, not all observers of the Kennedy phenomenon were taken in by the image. Even within Democratic ranks there were people who had serious misgivings. Former President Truman thought that Kennedy was woefully unprepared for the highest office in the land, and so did Eleanor Roosevelt, who thought him immature and lacking in strong convictions. His running mate, Lyndon Johnson, had even fewer illusions about the man he would serve:

> It was the goddamnest thing, here was a young whippersnapper, malaria-ridden and yallah, sickly, sickly. He never said a word of importance in the Senate and never did a thing. But somehow, with his books and Pulitzer Prizes, he managed to create the image of himself as a shining intellectual, a youthful leader who could change the face of the country.[15]

Johnson's allusion to Kennedy's health was well taken, for the evidence strongly supports the fact that young Kennedy was something of a medical miracle. All of his life, he was afflicted by a host of illnesses, some of them so serious that we can only marvel at his resilient ability to perform any public duty at all. He had a congenital back problem, exacerbated by his wartime experiences, that constantly caused him agonizing pain and, at one point, almost cost his life after an unsuccessful back operation. He also suffered from partial deafness in his right ear, frequent stomach problems that forced him to stick to a very bland diet, and recurring bouts of venereal disease due to his many sexual escapades. But Kennedy's most serious illness, which was never revealed to the American people, was Addison's syndrome, a failure of the adrenal glands to produce a sufficient quantity of hormones, which was fatal until the discovery of synthetic substances containing hormone-like activity. In 1949 the Mayo Clinic discovered that cortisone, taken daily either by injection or tablets, allowed Addison's patients to live a normal life, although the medication had a number of side-effects such as skin coloration that looked like a permanent tan, thickening hair, and increased sexual desire. Kennedy lived on pills. Just as Hitler had his Dr. Morell, the pill pusher who made the German leader dependent on a variety of powerful medications, Kennedy had Dr. Max Jacobson, aptly dubbed Dr. Feelgood by his patients because he freely injected amphetamines laced with steroids, animal cells, and other goodies. Dr. Feelgood, an escapee from Hitler's Germany, became an important person in Kennedy's life, freely dispensing dangerous medication that made his patient overly dependent, if not addicted, to amphetamines and painkillers.

Yet part of Kennedy's strength was that he rose above these pains and disabilities and managed to project an image of vigor, youth, and excitement. Although spending more than half of most days in bed, he concealed his low energy by producing the illusion of being constantly on the move and therefore being able to move the country again after a supposed decade of conservative inaction. His impatience, love of sportsmanship, passion for winning, and noble rhetoric were infectious to all those he touched, and that included a whole generation of young Americans. Would America have gone to the moon without his strong advocacy for the space program? Would young people have felt such a strong passion for political involvement without his leadership?

The set of beliefs that made up Kennedy's New Frontier program had a powerful psychological impact, especially on young people who were looking for unselfish goals. Despite their self-indulgent habits, many baby boomers did believe in the noble things they had heard in civics classes about justice, equality, honesty, and integrity. They admired what they saw in Frank Capra movies. A totally cynical generation would have been less self-righteously critical or angry when confronted with the facts of racial injustice, political corruption, or foreign policy blunders. Any account of the 1960s that leaves out the genuine idealism that characterized the youthful protest movements of that decade would distort what really happened.

2. The Kennedy Administration: The Best and the Brightest?

Sargent Shriver, Kennedy's brother-in-law and the director of the Peace Corps, recalled that John F. Kennedy used the phrase "the best and the brightest" to describe the sort of people he wanted in his administration.[16] As he began to assemble his team, Kennedy instinctively and almost exclusively tapped the talents of what Richard Nixon would later disparagingly refer to as the eastern establishment, which consisted of the scions of elite eastern families whose sons and daughters had attended exclusive prep schools and then gone on to attend the best Ivy League universities. Many of these favored sons and daughters of the eastern establishment had gone to serve in the State Department, the Pentagon, or those government agencies that dealt with foreign affairs and defense. Critics at the time charged, perhaps not unjustifiably, that members of the elite establishment, Democrats as well as Republicans, recruited others from their own class—that is, from Ivy League schools and great banking or law firms of New York or Boston. Members of this elite circle knew each other through family connections, school, and social occasions. Among the more gold-plated figures of this group were Robert Lovett, James Forrestal, Douglas Dillon, Allen Dulles, Dean Acheson, George Ball, and Averell Harriman.

Kennedy believed in the mystique of this establishment, which in turn supplied him with the names of candidates who would give his administration a special kind of legitimacy and luster. Since commoners rarely occupy the seats of the mighty, even in a democracy, it should not be surprising that the members of the establishment spoke the language of the American business community. In their politics they were opposed to both left- and right-wing extremism, rejecting anticapitalism as well as right-wing McCarthyism. They favored consensus in foreign policy, and that meant the containment of communism whenever it threatened to subvert pro-Western or noncommunist governments.

From a psychological point of view, Kennedy preferred tough-minded risk-takers, fiercely competitive and socially acceptable. He took an immediate liking to interesting, witty, and charming men and women. One of his greatest dreads had always been boredom, and that included a positive dislike of dull and unimaginative people. Kennedy also displayed a marked preference for pragmatists who did not mind changing their position if circumstances demanded flexibility. This is one of the reasons why Adlai Stevenson always remained an outsider in the Kennedy administration; he was too rigidly principled, pedantic, and reserved, quite apart from the fact that he did not support Kennedy for his party's nomination in 1960. Besides hard-nosed realists and high achievers, Kennedy looked for war heroes, for people whose mettle had been tested under fire and the hardship that combat imposed on soldiers.

Many of the "best and the brightest" were Harvard educated, like the president himself, liberal, reform-minded, and fiercely competitive. The president's cabinet, in fact, was a coalition of thoughtful pragmatists who shrouded themselves in the mantle of virtuous idealism. It was also a relatively young cabinet, including the president's own thirty-five-year-old brother as attorney general. Besides his own brother, Kennedy's cabinet included Robert McNamara, a dynamic Ford Motors executive and business expert as Secretary of Defense; Dean Rusk, of the Rockefeller Foundation as Secretary of State; Douglas Dillon, scion of a wealthy Wall Street banking family and Undersecretary of State under the Eisenhower administration as Secretary of the Treasury; Luther Hodges, governor of North Carolina as Secretary of Commerce; Arthur Goldberg, of the AFL-CIO, as Secretary of Labor; Stewart Udall, an Arizona Democrat, as Secretary of the Interior; and Abraham Ribicoff, governor of Connecticut, as Secretary of Health, Education, and Welfare. Some of these appointees were Democratic insiders, representing particular interest groups in the Democratic Party, while others (McNamara, Dillon) were liberal Republicans. The "best and the brightest," of course, also included a host of special assistants, aides, department heads, and military experts. The most notable among those were Pierre Salinger, the president's colorful and capable Press Secretary; Theodore Sorensen; the president's sounding board and speechwriter; the brothers McGeorge and William Bundy, who served as White House National Security Chief and Assistant Secretary of State respectively; Walt Rostow, MIT economist and economic advisor;

General Maxwell Taylor, Kennedy's trusted military aide; and Arthur Schlesinger, the well-known Harvard historian who served as policy aide and liaison to the liberal community. The roll of Kennedy men, for there was not a single prominent woman among them, except in secretarial positions like the one held by Kennedy's long-time private secretary, Evelyn Lincoln, would not be complete without the names of the "Irish Mafia," the men who doted on Kennedy and carried out his every whim: Kenneth O'Donnell, Dave Powers, and Larry O'Brien.

The characteristic quality that defined the men of Kennedy's inner circle was tough-minded pragmatism. Following their charismatic leader, these men made a fetish of energy and style; they projected a confident image of technological and managerial know-how. McNamara was paradigmatic of this impatient and often arrogant style. A business whiz with a Harvard MBA, he had left the presidency of Ford Motor Company to apply his statistical mind to defense. McNamara was in many ways a kind of Dickensian Mr. Thomas Gradgrind who reduces all human expressions to purely technical equations or manipulations. To McNamara and his colleagues, all social problems could be reduced to formal analysis by technical experts, translated into social policy, and implemented by capable managers. If a problem could not be submitted to scientific analysis with appropriate technical resolution, it was not a problem but an illusion. All social conflicts or frictions are essentially a breakdown in communication between competing groups and can always be resolved by rational dialogue, compromise, and mutual concession. Leadership, as the Kennedy pragmatists saw it, was the use of conciliatory management techniques by proven experts with the right academic credentials. As Kennedy put it quite succinctly: "The central domestic problems of our time are not basic clashes of philosophy or ideology, but ways and means of reaching common goals—to research for sophisticated solutions to complex and obstinate issues."[17] In short, political or socioeconomic issues are basically administrative, executive, and managerial. The raison d'etre of leadership is action and management. "Some critics today worry that our democratic, free societies are becoming overmanaged," observed McNamara, adding, "I would argue that the exact opposite is true. As paradoxical as it may sound, the real threat to democracy comes, not from overmanagement, but from undermanagement."[18]

The image of Camelot was later used by Kennedy supporters to describe the hope and vision that guided his administration. The imagery showed a vibrant, handsome president and his beautiful young wife, surrounded by a host of passionate crusaders who were eager to help the president in revitalizing a stagnant nation and to lead it to a New Frontier of domestic equality and international peace. The Kennedys were shrewd politicians who realized that public image was of paramount importance in American life and culture. The new president knew that his political success would have been impossible without the use of mass media, especially television. He placed particular importance on carefully choreographed press conferences, working very closely with media-savvy press secretary Pierre Salinger. Nothing was left to chance as Salinger primed the telegenic president for a press conference. Questions and answers were carefully rehearsed and favorite reporters often received planted questions. Not surprisingly, the president performed brilliantly: he appeared suave, sophisticated, witty, and knowledgeable. One historian of his presidency observed that he often sold himself better than he did his views. In judging his public performance, Pierre Salinger later correctly observed that "except for Franklin D. Roosevelt, no president of the modern era has been more expert in public relations than JFK."[19]

The Kennedys had long forged close ties with newspaper journalists and editors such as Ben Bradlee, a prominent liberal journalist; Arthur Krock, another veteran newspaperman; Roland Evans, a well-known syndicated columnist; Hugh Sidey, a Time-Life correspondent; Charles Bartlett, a reporter and Washington correspondent for the *Chattanooga Times*; and Joseph and Stewart Alsop, both newspapermen, friends, and family relations. The Kennedys spoke their language and enlisted them in their various campaigns and public policies. Furthermore, the new president allowed reporters, photographers, and television people unprecedented access to the White House. In February 1962, after having initiated a restoration of the White House, the American people got a personal tour through the White House conducted by the first lady, who charmed them with her high-pitched and seductive voice and good looks. Charming pictures of little John, the president's young boy, showed the cute child responding to daddy's clapping hands like a lap dog or hiding in the kneehole under the president's desk. Other pictures showed young Caroline riding her little pony. Kennedy also permitted television cameras to follow him on his daily rounds, but the cameras, of course, were switched off when the president frolicked behind the scenes in what could hardly be described as a wholesome family way. It was Kennedy's conviction, reinforced especially after reading a biography of the life of young Melbourne, the British prime minister, that the private lives of the elites were strictly off limits to the ordinary run of people, and that what prominent leaders did behind closed doors, no matter how objectionable to common tastes or morals, was nobody's business.[20] The press almost universally supported this right to personal privacy by presidents and congressional leaders throughout the sixties.

In this ongoing effort at image construction, the Kennedys also encouraged the official view that the new administration, compared to the pedestrian Eisenhower administration, was highly refined and cultured. Accordingly, the president, strongly supported by his wife, sponsored poetry readings, chamber music, and art exhibits in the White House. The president himself did not read much poetry, nor could he distinguish between a Renoir and a Cezanne. When Red Fay, one of his trusted friends and assistants, asked the president who the painters were that the president was pointing out, his boss said: "My God, if you have to ask a question like that, do it in a whisper. . . . We're trying to give this administration a semblance of class."[21] The president had no ear for music, no interest in opera, dozed off at symphony concerts, and was bored by ballet. It was Jackie who loved art and music. The only music, she said, that the president really appreciated was "Hail to the Chief." By all accounts, the president read widely but not deeply. He read many newspapers, loved spy movies, and talked incessantly about politics, with some sports, mostly baseball and football, sandwiched in-between.

Much of this, of course, was cinematic illusion, but it resonated strongly with the American people. Yet, behind the glittering façade of noble idealism, exhorting the American people to kill the dragon of communism and reclaim the magical kingdom, resided arrogant assumptions about American exceptionalism. The Kennedy men believed that they were graced by some special dispensation, and they managed to spellbind a sizable number of the American people into believing that a certain amount of omnipotence had attached itself to the administration and its leader. For years, the Kennedy propaganda machine, lavishly bankrolled by its patriarch, Joseph P. Kennedy, had molded the American people into believing that the president was more than just an ordinary man. Even James MacGregor Burns, the Harvard political scientist who had written a highly favorable biography of John F. Kennedy, was somewhat irritated by the hyperbole of the Kennedy mystique:

> He is not only the handsomest, the best dressed, the most articulate, and graceful as a gazelle. He is omniscient; he swallows and digests whole books in minutes; his eye seizes instantly on the crucial point of a long memorandum; he confounds experts with superior knowledge of their field. He is omnipresent; no sleepy staff member can be sure that he will not telephone—or pop in; every hostess at a party can hope that he will; he has no need of Ike's staff apparatus; he is more than a boss, more than a fox. He's superman![22]

What was the reality of John F. Kennedy's one thousand days in office? On the domestic front, Kennedy's impatient attitude encountered a massive immovable object in the form of a decidedly conservative Congress that seemed in no mood to pass his New Frontier program. In 1961 and again in 1962 Congress rejected his proposal for medical care for the elderly and for expanded federal aid to education. Congress also voted down his proposal for a new cabinet post for urban affairs. His tax reforms were greatly watered down by Congress and his request for an income tax cut, aimed at stimulating the economy, was also rejected by Congress.

The source of opposition to Kennedy's domestic reform resided in the House of Representatives, which was dominated by conservative southern Democrats and equally conservative Republicans, the two often forming a solid block in opposing liberal reforms. Although the 1962 congressional elections netted a few seats for the Democrats, the new Congress was no more amenable to Kennedy's programs than the old one. When the president was assassinated in November of 1963, Congress had not passed a single piece of legislation that he had proposed at the beginning of that year.

The president's most important legislative success was the Trade Expansion Act of 1962, which gave him extensive powers to cut tariffs, while at the same time providing federal aid to businesses that were adversely affected by foreign competition. Kennedy's abandonment of protectionism was widely hailed as a positive step in providing the means of increasing the rate of economic growth through the expansion of exports. In return for permitting imports from the booming Common Market countries and from Japan, the president hoped that the United States would, in turn, secure broader markets abroad for its own exports.

The sluggishness of the economy was due in part to the hostility of the business community and its lack of confidence in the Kennedy administration. Business had been suspicious of Democratic administrations since Franklin Roosevelt, and Kennedy did little to allay these doubts. In 1962 he contemplated raising taxes in order to maintain a balanced budget and low inflation. This required price stability, especially in the steel industry. In January 1962 he met with Roger Blough, chairman of U.S. Steel, Dave MacDonald, the head of the steelworkers, and labor secretary Goldberg. The two sides, business and labor, agreed to work out a mutually beneficial contract that would be noninflationary in nature. In April, however, the steel companies announced a 3.5 percent hike in prices. Kennedy was livid with rage because he felt betrayed and humiliated by Blough, who had assured him in January that steel prices would not be raised. "You double-crossed me," he told Blough; and to Ken O'Donnell he vented his anger by shouting: "He [Blough] fucked me. They fucked us and we've got to try to fuck them. My father told me business men were all pricks, but I didn't really believe he was right until now.... God I hate the bastards."[23] The Kennedy machine then proceeded to make life uncomfortable for the steel magnates. Excoriated in the press, threatened by Internal Revenue audits and by administration announcements that the federal government would shift contracts to smaller steel companies, Blough and other steel magnates caved in and repealed their price increases. Kennedy was by nature a negotiator, but if pushed against the wall, with his reputation on the line, he was willing to use whatever means available to get his way. Although his handling of the steel crisis was highly popular, big business was infuriated, referring to Kennedy's tactics as "fascistic."

Kennedy's record on civil rights, discussed in a separate chapter, was not impressive for the same reason that his social legislation fell short of its goal: southern Democrats, who were staunch segregationists, joined forces with equally recalcitrant Republicans and succeeded in blocking any civil rights legislation. It was not until 1963, after intense unrest and violence in the South, that Kennedy became emotionally committed to the cause of civil rights. He had not mentioned a word about black civil rights in his inaugural address, which rang out with bold statements about extending freedom around the world. Kennedy did establish a Commission on Equal Employment Opportunity (CEEO) aimed at eliminating discrimination in federal employment, asking Lyndon Johnson to chair the committee. His special advisor on civil rights, Harris Wofford, wanted to push Kennedy to take bolder steps on civil rights, and so did Martin Luther King Jr., who increasingly felt that the president had no real moral passion for civil rights.[24]

In retrospect, Kennedy misjudged the dynamism of the civil rights movement. He simply did not want to become too deeply entangled in the turmoil of civil rights, partly because he feared losing the South to the Republicans, partly because his real interest was in foreign policy. He could also read polls. Gallup polls had shown that 64 percent of the American people disapproved of the actions of Freedom Riders, while only 24 percent approved.[25] In 1962 another Gallup poll revealed that only 6 percent of respondents mentioned racial problems when asked: "What do you think is the most important problem facing the country?[26] The president had no personal experience with black Americans; he simply did not move in their circles. His belated civil rights speech of June 11, 1962, though heart-felt and sincere, did not carry any but moral weight. As to the famous March on Washington, the Kennedys were more concerned about the possibility of violence than they were about throwing their enthusiastic weight behind it. The president did not find it important enough to attend the event; nor did he trust Martin Luther King Jr., as shown by his willingness to allow the FBI to wiretap him.

The discrepancy between the president's idealistic pronouncements and his actual behavior was evident also in most of his foreign policy involvements. On the one hand there were noble pronouncements for public consumption, and on the other secretive and covert operations behind the scenes. Latin America was one of many examples. Very early in his administration, the president launched the Alliance for Progress, a long-range program of economic aid and development designed to combat the conditions of poverty that contributed to the spread of communism in the Western Hemisphere. The United States extended loans, grants, and technical help to Latin American nations hoping that this would lead to land reform, social progress, and democracy. Unfortunately, decades of having propped up militaristic regimes militated against the Alliance for Progress. Military juntas in countries such as the Dominican Republic actively stymied progress toward social reform by overthrowing constitutional governments. Many Latin American leaders saw the Alliance for Progress as a money-lending scheme that looked generous but was basically condescending American self-interest. As Robert Dallek has pointed out, it was difficult for Kennedy to square the idea of national self-determination in Latin America with the reality of secret American interventions in Cuba, Brazil, British Guiana, Peru, Haiti, the Dominican Republic, and every other country that appeared to drift to the political left.

In the meantime, the Kennedy administration faced brushfires in other parts of the world: the Congo, Laos, Vietnam, Berlin, and the Middle East. In looking at this period, one cannot help but gain the impression that Kennedy was always reacting to crises—to the point that, in Dallek's judgment, he appeared more like a "crisis manager" than a proactive leader.[27] Inheriting a growing quagmire in Vietnam, Kennedy pursued a weak policy of "half-in-half-out" in Vietnam, unable to extricate himself but also unwilling to make a decisive commitment. Having inherited a corrupt regime, headed by Diem, he boosted it along until it became obvious that a regime change was needed in order to avert a complete disaster. Yet the way in which Diem and his brother were murdered with American connivance in the fall of 1963 did not bring credit to his administration. At the time of his assassination, the United States had over sixteen thousand military personnel in Vietnam, when it had only been a few hundred at the time of Kennedy's inauguration. Nor was the picture much better in neighboring Laos, a country that had also suffered from communist subversion for some time. By the terms of the Geneva Accords, a neutral government had been formed under the leadership of Prince Souvanna Phouma; but North Vietnamese troops, still stationed in Laos, kept supplying and supporting the communist Pathet Lao. In response, Kennedy approved a secret CIA-sponsored counterinsurgency program, involving thirty-six thousand opium-growing Hmong and other tribal warriors who were supported by a thousand Thai "volunteers" paid by the CIA. Air America, owned by the CIA, conducted secret bombing operations. This secret war went on for years without any congressional oversight or knowledge. As Thomas Reeves put it, this secret operation was "illegal, immoral, dangerous, and a far cry from the idealism so often expressed in the president's formal speeches."[28]

In June 1961 Kennedy embarked on his first overseas trip to Europe, including a visit to Paris and Vienna to meet Charles de Gaulle and Nikita Khrushchev respectively. Making the trip with excruciating back pain, the president won the celebrity contest in both Paris and Vienna, but lost the political clash of wills with Khrushchev. Next to the fashionable and handsome Kennedys, Nikita Khrushchev and his dumpy-looking wife appeared like two deprived Siberian peasants. In private, however, the young president received a steady pummeling by the feisty Khrushchev, who tongue-lashed him, baited him, and unnerved him badly. "I never met a man like this," a dejected Kennedy later told Hugh Sidey; "I talked about how a nuclear exchange would kill seventy million people in ten minutes and he just looked at me as if to say, 'so what?' My impression was that he just didn't give a damn if it came to that."[29] The shrewd Ukrainian peasant, of course, did not want nuclear war; he was out to test the inexperienced Kennedy, whose overly moderate and reasonable tone annoyed him no end. Khrushchev did not give an inch at Vienna; he rejected a ban on nuclear testing in the atmosphere, denounced American imperialism, and threatened to stop the hemorrhaging of the East German population, who were leaving their communist prison through the remaining escape hatch of Berlin.

On August 13, 1961, Khrushchev made good on his threat to close the Berlin escape hatch, having made it clear to his inner circle that "Berlin is the testicle of the West. Every time I want the West to scream, I squeeze on Berlin."[30] Working closely with Walter Ulbricht, the East German leader, the communists built a concrete wall that ran straight through the middle of Berlin, sealing off the communist eastern sector of the city from the western sector controlled by the three Western powers of the United States, Britain, and France. By so doing, the communists effectively stopped the exodus of East German refugees, who had simply gone to Berlin, the capital of the German Democratic Republic (DDR), and then crossed over to West Berlin and freedom. For the next twenty-seven years, East Germany was walled in by concrete and barbed wire, and its citizens had to endure a dreary life under a stagnant and repressive regime. As in April, the Kennedy administration was caught flat-footed and inactive. The wall was clearly a violation of postwar occupation policies, but Kennedy did not want to risk a war with Russia.

3. Eyeball to Eyeball:
The World at the Nuclear Brink

Facing a sluggish economy, an unresponsive Congress, and an unfriendly business community, Kennedy looked to foreign affairs to redeem his faltering administration. His performance, however, was as uneven in foreign policy as it was uninspiring on the domestic front. In fact, the Kennedy-Khrushchev game of "nuclear chicken" brought the world to the brink of annihilation.

The year 1961 was largely a failure in foreign policy for the Kennedy administration. The president had hardly moved into the White House, when the feisty and belligerent Khrushchev, delivered an aggressive speech in Moscow in which he pledged that the Soviet Union would support wars of liberation against colonial powers. The Soviet premier was clearly testing Kennedy's resolve, suspecting that under that handsome façade the American president was probably a pushover. In this estimate he was not alone, for cold-hearted and cynical observers in America had made the same judgment, including former president Eisenhower, who referred to Kennedy as "Little Boy Blue."[31]

The first test of Kennedy's resolve came in April 1961 when the young president reluctantly backed a CIA plan, prepared during the Eisenhower administration, to topple Fidel Castro's regime in Cuba. The plan called for invading Cuba with anti-communist Cuban exiles in hopes of igniting a popular uprising on the island. On April 17, about twelve hundred ill-prepared fighters landed at Cuba's Bay of Pigs, a thinly inhabited and swampy area on the south coast of Cuba, hoping to push inland within a few days. As the chief American adviser told the insurgents, "you will go straight ahead, you will put your hands out, turn left, and go straight into Havana."[32] The president, however, had decided against direct U.S. involvement, which meant that once the invaders were on the beaches they were on their own. There would be no U.S. Air Force supporting them by air or Marines backing them by land. Stranded and abandoned, the invaders were quickly smashed by Castro's forces. Kennedy had suffered a humiliating defeat, which exposed the poor decision making that had prompted the ill-fated operation.[33] Moreover, this covert operation contravened both international law and American agreements with Latin American countries that prohibited such subversive operations. To his credit, Kennedy took full responsibility and publicly shrugged his shoulder by citing an ancient Chinese proverb that victory has a hundred fathers and defeat is an orphan. Schlesinger, who had warned the president against the invasion, admitted sadly but correctly that the "gay expectations of the Hundred Days were irrevocably over, the hour of euphoria past."[34]

The Bay of Pigs operation, meant to topple Castro from power, actually strengthened the dictator's control over Cuba. During the next eighteen months Castro forged closer and closer ties with the Soviet Union, for having been invaded once, the dictator knew that he would face another attack sooner or later. In the meantime, Kennedy regrouped and redoubled his efforts to get rid of Castro. The Kennedys, in fact, began to obsess about Castro and the alleged threat he represented to the United States. Scores of CIA plots were hatched to assassinate Castro, some of them verging on the pathetic such as dusting his shoes with powder that would cause his beard to fall out or planting chemicals in his cigars that would produce temporary disorientation. At least eight assassination attempts on Castro's life, some of them involving the Mafia, were initiated. All failed. The Kennedys continued their vendetta, authorizing a secret CIA project entitled Operation Mongoose to topple Castro from power.

Kennedy's most serious crisis, and perhaps the gravest crisis in American history, came in October 1962. How closely the Cuban dictator had enmeshed himself with the Soviets became clear in the summer and fall of 1962 when American intelligence began reporting that the Russians were supplying the Cubans with massive economic and military aid. In early October aerial photographs, taken by American spy planes, revealed that the Russians were secretly installing nuclear missile facilities in Cuba. The Soviet leader had taken an enormous risk in coming to the aid of Cuba, a risk motivated partly by a desire to support a communist ally and partly to shift the nuclear balance in favor of the Soviet Union.[35] Khrushchev's plan was to sneak over sixty missiles into Cuba; forty-two of them being medium-range (1,100 miles) and twenty-four long-range missiles (2,200 miles). This effort was to be carried out by twenty-two thousand Russian troops and technical experts, working closely with the Cubans. Khrushchev knew that an operation of this size could not be concealed from the Americans indefinitely, but he hoped that full disclosure would not have to be made until the missiles were fully operational, making the program a *fait accompli*. In the meantime, the wily Soviet premier publicly admitted that the Russians were providing military assistance to Cuba, but lied about concealing medium-range surface-to-air missiles that were being installed in Cuba.

The truth, unknown to Kennedy, was that already by mid-October of 1961, nine tactical missiles, equipped with nuclear warheads and possessing a reach of thirty miles, had already been installed. Moreover, the local Soviet commander had been authorized to use them at his own discretion. Kennedy was blissfully ignorant of the fact that an American invasion of Cuba would have been repelled and annihilated with nuclear weapons.

What now began to unfold was probably one of the most perilous crises in world history: two superpowers, armed to the teeth with weapons of mass destruction, challenging each other over the balance of terror. The prospect of facing nuclear missiles ninety miles off the continental United States was a nightmare come true for most Americans; but what many Americans did not know was that U.S. missiles, stationed in Europe and in Turkey, had long been pointing straight at Russia, some of them positioned within less than a hundred miles of Soviet territory. With this being said, Khrushchev's gamble to raise the stakes in this contest of "nuclear chicken" was reckless in the extreme.

Once being fully briefed on the nature of the crisis, Kennedy decided that the Soviet missiles had to be removed from Cuba. Various options were discussed: air strikes followed by an invasion; the demilitarization of Cuba by UN mandate; the closing of Guantanamo and/or the withdrawal of U.S. missiles from Turkey in exchange for Soviet dismantling of missiles in Cuba; or an embargo of the island of Cuba. Kennedy chose the embargo. The president went on television on October 22 and declared a naval quarantine, demanding the immediate removal of already installed missiles and threatening to stop, search, and turn back any Soviet ship carrying offensive weapons to Cuba. By all accounts, Kennedy deftly managed the crisis by going to the American people and putting most of his cards on the table, except those he needed to trump his treacherous adversary. In the eyes of the world,

Khrushchev stood revealed as not only a liar but a menace to world peace. This became especially apparent at a dramatic UN session when Ambassador Stevenson made his Russian counterpart, Valerian Zorin, squirm publicly as he tried to defend a web of Soviet lies.

On October 24, Soviet ships approached the quarantine line, stopped, and turned back. Other Soviet ships, not carrying war material, agreed to be searched. On October 25, Kennedy contacted the Soviet premier again and asked him to remove the missiles. Khrushchev agreed but demanded, in return, that the United States pledge not to invade Cuba and remove its Jupiter missiles from Turkey. Kennedy agreed to both demands, and it was on that basis that Khrushchev removed the Soviet missiles from Cuba. The American people, however, were not informed about Khrushchev's conditions, only that the Soviet premier, faced by American resolve, had blinked first and had withdrawn with his tail between his legs.

Kennedy's actions were widely hailed as a great victory, and the president was delighted with himself. "I cut his balls off," he confided to an aide.[36] In retrospect, Kennedy handled the crisis with great aplomb and avoided a horrible catastrophe. His bargain with Khrushchev, however, had some unintended consequences. Not only did Kennedy remove American missiles from Turkey, but he also allowed nearly forty-five thousand Soviet troops and advisers to remain in Cuba, where they would subsequently train a highly mobile Cuban army of communist mercenaries fighting anti-Western forces in Latin America, Asia, and Africa. Kennedy also assured the Soviet premier that he would discourage any efforts by Cuban exiles in America to invade Cuba, which many anti-Castro Cubans saw as a sellout.

4. The Trauma of November 22, 1963, and Its Aftermath

In November 1963, concerned about the prospects of his reelection in 1964, Kennedy planned trips to Florida and Texas. Unlike the deep southern states, which would probably be lost to the Democrats in 1964 because of Kennedy's commitment to civil rights, Florida and Texas were crucial electoral states that could not be taken for granted by the Democrats. On November 18, Kennedy visited Tampa and three days later he headed for Fort Worth and Dallas. Neither Texas governor John Connally nor Lyndon Johnson thought that the Texas trip was worth making, but Kennedy forged ahead for two reasons: raising funds from wealthy Texas donors and mending a political rift that had opened up in the Democratic Party in Texas between Connally conservatives and liberals led by Senator Ralph Yarborough.[37] There was a sense of impending danger about this trip. When Adlai Stevenson had gone to Dallas in October to give a speech commemorating United Nations Day, he had been harassed, spat upon, and hit on the head with a sign by right-wing extremists. Kennedy was well aware of the existence of small vocal right-wing groups in Dallas who hated his liberal administration. One such group of Kennedy haters in Dallas, members of the John Birch Society, flooded the city with leaflets and placed a full-page advertisement in the November 22 edition of the *Dallas Morning News*, accusing Kennedy of being an agent of international communism. When Kennedy showed the black-bordered advertisement to his wife he said "We're heading into nut country today. But Jackie, if somebody wants to shoot me from a window with a rifle, nobody can stop it, so why worry about it?"[38]

On November 16, 1963, the *Dallas Times Herald* published the exact route of the president's motorcade, which would proceed from Love Field airport into the heart of Dallas for a presidential luncheon at the Trade Mart.[39] The route would take the president along Main Street, then turn right on Houston Street, followed by a left turn onto Elm Street, which led through Dealey Plaza, a public square that was bordered on the right by the Texas School Book Depository. The map of the exact route of the presidential motorcade indicated that the cars would pass directly in front of the Book Depository building, giving a potential assassin a clear view of his target. The weather on November 22 was excellent, so that the Kennedy advance team saw no need to protect the president from possible rain by putting a bubbletop on his Lincoln convertible. The presidential limousine would, therefore, be an easy target. Neither the Dallas police nor the president's security team had carried out a thorough inspection of the route, though an FBI agent, James Hosty, had been monitoring the activities of a communist and pro-Castro activist called Lee Harvey Oswald. Although Hosty had visited Oswald and learned about his job at the Texas School Book Depository building, the FBI agent failed to act decisively on his information. Furthermore, Hosty was told by his superiors in the FBI to destroy a note Oswald had given him, warning the FBI to stop bothering his family. Some historians suspect that the destruction of Oswald's handwritten note and the subsequent firing of Hosty might have been part of an FBI coverup.[40]

Who was Lee Harvey Oswald, the man who killed the president of the United States?[41] In both appearance and demeanor Oswald was the exact opposite of Kennedy: he was a small, balding, deeply insecure loser who had a long trail of failures behind him. Born in 1939 in New Orleans, he was raised in Fort Worth, Texas, in a very unstable family environment. His mother, Marguerite, was a domineering and neurotic woman who failed at being a wife, mother, and provider. Lee Harvey was her son from a second marriage to Robert Edward Lee Oswald, who died before Lee Harvey was born. Her third marriage to Edwin Ekdahl, who brazenly cheated on her, was also a failure. The mother's instabilities, along with her frequent changes of work and location, made it difficult for her to provide adequately for her children— John Edward Pic, the oldest from her first marriage, Robert Jr., and Lee Harvey. At one time all three had been placed in an orphanage. Lee Harvey never settled for very long in any community, being packed off to various different places—Fort Worth, New York, and New Orleans, among others. There is every indication that Lee Harvey was a troubled child with a violent temper, a sullen disposition, and a rebellious attitude toward authority. Though not unintelligent, he did poorly in school because the family never settled long enough in one location. While living in the Bronx in 1952, Lee was cited for chronic truancy and remanded to Youth House for three weeks of psychiatric evaluation—the first of several interventions by school, social workers, and later military psychiatrists looking into Lee Harvey's unstable and self-defeating behavior. It was in his early teens that Lee was attracted to communist literature, probably finding in it a source by which he could bolster his developing antisocial attitudes. His attraction to communism, however, was not deep enough to prevent him from signing up for the Marine Corps in 1956, having previously dropped out of high school. His older brother Robert had already volunteered for the Marine Corps, showing Lee that this was one way of making a new start and getting away from his domineering mother.

Lee Harvey Oswald was not a good Marine. Given his rebellious nature, it was not surprising that he had difficulty in conforming to Marine discipline. He was twice court-martialed for carrying an unregistered firearm and speaking disrespectfully to his superior officers. His fellow Marines remembered him as a defiant loner with a chip on his shoulder, alternatively picking fights or keeping to himself. The Corps trained him as an aviation electronics operator, working in a radar unit monitoring airplanes. Although he performed satisfactorily and was sent to Japan and the Philippines, his personality caused serious concern, especially after he accidentally shot himself in the arm with a .22 caliber Derringer he had purchased without permission. This led to a court martial, demotion in rank (from corporal to private), three weeks of hard labor, and a fine of fifty dollars. The gun incident is important for several reasons: it shows his fascination with guns, his careless manner, and his defiant attitude of bypassing authority. As to his marksmanship, which would become such a contested topic of debate after the assassination of the president, Marine records show clearly that Oswald was a good shot, performing above average on his sharpshooter's test.

After the self-inflicted gun injury, Oswald soon wore out his welcome in the Marine Corps, feeling unjustly picked on by his fellow Marines and his superior officers. In September 1959, he left the service and, without telling his family, said good-bye to the United States. On October 16 he arrived in Moscow, checked into the Hotel Berlin and then announced that he wanted to renounce his U.S. citizenship. Since Oswald was a furtive, secretive, and sly man who enjoyed deceiving and covering up his tracks, it is difficult to explain what motivated him to take such a rash act. His diary, which is highly suspect and doctored up after many of the events he described had long transpired, offers only pieces of the puzzle. Apparently, Oswald had uncritically accepted communist propaganda that the Soviet Union, not the United States, was the land of the future, that the millions of people who were heading to the United States were going in the wrong direction and that he, Lee Harvey Oswald, was marching in the right direction. When U.S. officials and news media got wind of this unusual defection of a former Marine, they pricked up their ears and tried to find out more. Oswald, however, remained tight-lipped, only giving out minimal information, always insisting that his actions were guided by moral and political conscience rather than ulterior motives.

Since the fall of communism we now know that the Soviets were equally puzzled by Oswald's defection, wondering whether he was a CIA plant. The evidence suggests that, after intensive interrogation by the KGB, especially by a later defector called Yuri

Nosenko, the Soviets at first were not certain whether they were dealing with a loser or possibly a spy, but one way or the other they felt it best to discourage him from remaining in Russia. When Oswald tried to commit suicide, the Soviets relented and gave him permission to stay. They even found him a good job and an apartment in Minsk, where he would work for the next two years as a technician in a radio and television factory. While in Minsk, he attracted a small circle of friends, including Marina Prusakova, a pretty and vivacious young woman, whom he married in 1961. Despite the indulgent treatment he received at the hands of the Russians, Oswald discovered that the workers' paradise was not what he thought it was cracked up to be, subsequently writing in his diary, "I am starting to reconsider my desire about staying. The work is drab. The money I get has nowhere to be spent. No nightclubs or bowling alleys. No places of recreation except the trade union dances. I have had enough."[42] Whether this and other entries were written after the fact, possibly to construct a rationale for a defector who had become disillusioned, is open to debate.

The most likely reason for Oswald's return to the United States was his inability to create a permanent home anywhere because he simply did not know what that meant, being a perpetually restless and deeply unhappy man. In 1962 Oswald returned to the United States with his wife, Marina, and his four-month-old daughter, June. Between June 14, 1962, when Oswald arrived in Fort Worth, and November 22, 1963, when the president was assassinated, Oswald's movements followed the same erratic pattern of his past life. He moved in with his brother Robert and then with his mother, who was living in Fort Worth at the time; he also looked for work in Dallas. Marina and Marguerite did not get on well at all in the small apartment they shared; they quarreled frequently and distrusted each other. Oswald then moved Marina into a decrepit apartment where things deteriorated even further. The reclusive Oswalds attracted attention from two quite different groups: local Russian émigrés, including a shadowy figure called George de Mohrenschildt, and agents of the FBI. Although FBI agents interviewed Oswald on several occasions, they reported that he had nothing to do with the local communist party and probably presented no danger to the community.

In retrospect this was a fatal misjudgment, because Oswald may have left the Soviet Union but he still had the communist bee in his bonnet. Dumping his wife and children with kind-hearted Russian émigrés and their friends, Oswald eventually found work in Dallas, first at a typesetting firm and then at the Texas School Book Depository building. His movements became more and more furtive and elusive, giving later conspiracy buffs endless ammunition to construct possible connections between Oswald and the Cubans, Russians, the Mafia, right-wing extremists and even Lyndon Johnson. No matter how hard historians have tried to put together his activities in some logical sequence, they have always come up against missing links and unanswerable questions. This problem of Oswald's enigmatic behavior prompted one assassination scholar to compare Lee Harvey Oswald to a Rubik's Cube, for "no sooner does a side start to take shape than another side becomes distorted."[43]

What we do know is that Oswald's fascination with guns, his hunger for intrigue, and his communist convictions were stronger than his love or concern for his family. Records show that only six months after his return to the United States Oswald ordered a .38 caliber Smith and Wesson revolver by mail, followed two months later by a mail order purchase of a 6.5 mm Mannlicher-Carcano Italian military rifle with a four power (4x) scope—the same rifle found on the sixth floor of the Texas School Book Depository Building after the assassination. In late March 1963 Marina snapped the infamous photo showing Lee, all draped in black, proudly holding his rifle with his left hand and exposing his revolver on his right waist in a holster, a pose reminiscent of gunslingers or patriotic Minute Men. We have persuasive evidence that barely two weeks after this photo was taken, Oswald fired a shot at retired General Edwin Walker, whose right-wing views he despised. The general, who had been sitting on a desk in his dining room, was saved because the bullet was deflected by a wire screen in the window and a wooden frame across the middle of the double window. Still, the bullet zipped through Walker's hair, barely missing his skull.[44] Marina, who found out about the attempted assassination, decided to remain silent, morbidly afraid of both her husband and the authorities. Oswald's behavior then became even more bizarre. He left Dallas for New Orleans, living briefly with his aunt, Lillian Murret. While in New Orleans he became involved in the Fair Play for Cuba Committee, standing on street corners and passing out FPCC handbills. He even appeared on a radio and television program contentiously arguing that the United States was committing a crime against innocent Cuba. His cameo appearances once more brought him to the attention of the FBI and local law enforcement agencies, but he was always able to talk himself out of real trouble. In September, Oswald took a bus to Mexico City, trying to obtain a visa to Cuba, but both the Cuban and Soviet officials put him off so long that he left Mexico in early October, checking in at the Dallas YMCA. Two weeks later, on October 16, he started working at the Texas School Book Depository. Just four days later, Marina gave birth to another baby girl, Audrey Marina Rachel Oswald. Baby or not, Oswald was now on a collision course with his country's heart and soul—the presidency of the United States.

We can only speculate what led Oswald to make his fatal decision to kill the president of the United States. Whatever it was—an ideological deed or a desire for immortality, perhaps a twisted need to prove by killing the most powerful man in the world that he was not a loser—Oswald seems to have acted rather quickly and opportunistically, possibly making his decision only after hearing about the president's visit to Dallas and seeing the map of the proposed presidential route in the *Dallas Times Herald*. On November 22, Oswald left his boarding house in Dallas, wrapped his 6.5 mm Mannlicher-Carcano rifle with some brown paper, and headed to the sixth floor sniper's nest at the Texas School Book Depository building, overlooking Dealey Plaza and Elm Street. Except for boxes of books, the sixth floor was empty when Oswald positioned himself at the far left-end window, using several cardboard boxes as a waist-high support for his rifle.[45] The site provided the assassin with a bird's-eye view of the presidential motorcade; and when the president's Lincoln convertible came into the sight of Oswald's four-power telescope at 12:30, the assassin managed to get off three shots in rapid succession. The first shot missed the presidential limousine and hit a curb. The second shot hit the president in the neck and sliced through his trachea, exiting through the front. That same bullet then struck Governor John Connally, who was sitting on a jump seat in front of the president. Neither the president nor Governor Connally would have been fatally wounded by this bullet. It was the third bullet that turned out to be fatal to the president, striking him in the back of the head and spraying the interior and exterior of the car with blood, brain tissue, and bone fragments. If the President had not been held rigidly erect by a back brace, the third bullet might have missed him because the force of the second bullet would have pushed him forward and downward into the limousine.

Abraham Zapruder, a Jewish refugee from Russia who loved Kennedy, filmed the gruesome scene in living color, capturing the look of horror on Jackie Kennedy's face, her impulsive and pitiful effort to get out of the limousine by crawling her way onto the trunk while Secret Service men scrambled to secure themselves on the jump steps of the convertible. The whole motorcade then shifted into high speed to get to Parkland Hospital. It was a scene of utter confusion and panic that would later etch itself in the national psyche forever. The president died at Parkland Hospital at 1:00 P.M. Just two hours later, fearing a conspiracy, Lyndon Johnson was sworn in as the new president on Air Force One, flanked by Judge Sarah Hughes of the U.S. District Court in Dallas, who read the oath of office to him, by Jackie Kennedy, still wearing her blood-stained pink dress, by Lady Bird Johnson, and by assorted aides.

In the meantime, Oswald had managed to leave the Depository in just three minutes after he had shot the president. He boarded a bus; but when it became hopelessly tangled up in traffic, he hailed a cab and directed the driver to take him to the 700 block of North Beckley, just a few blocks from his apartment. He then fetched his pistol and put on a jacket to conceal it. After leaving his apartment, Oswald walked off briskly to find another bus, but was spotted by Dallas patrolman J. D. Tippit, who had a suspicion that the man he stopped fit the police description of the suspected assassin. When Tippit got out of his patrol car, Oswald shot and killed him. Oswald was now in full flight from two killings. An eyewitness reported him sneaking into the Texas Theater, which was just then playing a war film entitled *Cry of Battle*, starring Van Heflin. Police quickly swarmed into the theater and overwhelmed Oswald, who allegedly said: "It's all over." When he resisted arrest, taking a swing at an officer, he was wrestled to the ground, screaming "Don't hit me any more!" and "This is police brutality!"[46] He was then booked into the Dallas Police Headquarters, where he was formally charged with the murder of officer J. D. Tippit.

When asked whether he had killed the president, Oswald gave evasive answers and deflected questions by claiming that he was a victim of police brutality—the sort of behavior that was characteristic of his petty, sly, and defiant personality. While these events were transpiring in Dallas, Air Force One, now carrying both the dead body of the president and the recently sworn in President Johnson, was winging its way to Andrews Air Force Base outside Washington, arriving about 6:00 P.M. (EST). By this time, the American people were riveted to their television screens, many of them following the blow-by-blow account of the tragedy by listening to the veteran news reporter Walter Cronkite, who had announced the death of the president earlier in the day. The nation got a visual shock in seeing the traumatized first lady, still wearing the pink dress that was soaked with her husband's blood—she reportedly said "Let them see what they've done . . . I want them to see."[47] People could also see the distraught brother, the attorney general, escorting his sister-in-law and staring at his brother's casket as it was lifted from Air Force One. The new president, in a short statement, told the American people that he would do his best in carrying on, that he shared the deep sorrow the Kennedy family was going through; and he asked the American people and God for their support.

When the fingerprints found on the rifle that had killed the president were identified as those of Lee Harvey Oswald, he was formally charged at 1:30 A.M. the next morning with having assassinated John F. Kennedy. Despite repeated interrogations, Oswald was as unrepentant as ever, playing an evasive game with the police that yielded little new information. On Sunday, November 24, at about 11:21 the nation got another shock when a nightclub owner with Mafia connections, Jack Ruby, walked into the basement of the Dallas Police Headquarters and joined a small group of television cameramen, reporters, and police who were waiting for Oswald as he was about to be transferred to a larger county facility. The television cameras recorded the sequence of unfolding events, showing Oswald and security men emerging from the elevator and making their way to the waiting police van. The camera showed a man with a dark suit and hat approach Oswald and his police entourage, pulling out a handgun and firing a shot into Oswald's abdomen, yelling: "You killed my president, you rat."[48] Wrestled to the ground, the assassin's assassin told the police "I am Jack Ruby. You all know me."[49] This was a reference to the fact that, as a Dallas strip joint owner, Ruby was indeed well known by the police.

The assassination of a popular president followed by the assassination of the assassin, followed by a magnificently orchestrated state funeral, overloaded the sensory nerves of the American people. There was numbness, paranoia, and, above all, a desperate need to know what had really happened. Had the president been killed by a lone assassin? Was he the victim of a vast conspiracy at the highest level of government? Were the Cubans responsible? Was it the CIA, the Mafia, the KGB? Following the assassination of Oswald, most Americans had a sinking feeling that the president was brought down by a dastardly conspiracy, and who could blame them? After all, Oswald was an American traitor, a Marine who had defected to the Soviet Union, who even after his return had engaged in subversive activities and left behind him a tantalizing trail of unexplained clues. And there was Ruby, a fast-talking and erratic tough with a long string of business failures behind him. Ruby was a dim bulb, but he fancied himself a mobster wanna-be along the lines of the Chicago mafiosi he had served as a runner while living there.[50] What had happened in Dallas struck many Americans as reminiscent of political life in a banana republic, and the new Johnson administration, therefore, made it one of the first official acts to examine the Kennedy assassination, if only to lay to rest the mounting rumors about the strange events in Dallas.

Accordingly, on November 29, 1963, the president issued Executive Order 11130, establishing a fact-finding panel entitled The President's Commission on the Assassination of President John F. Kennedy. Headed by Supreme Court Chief Justice Earl Warren, the commission included solid and trusted members of the Washington establishment, including the director of the CIA Allen Dulles and prominent congressmen and senators such as Gerald Ford, Richard Russell, John Sherman Cooper, and Hale Boggs. The commission soon found itself under considerable pressure by the president, who was facing a general election in 1964 and wanted a timely resolution confirming what he thought was obvious—namely, that Oswald was the lone assassin and that Ruby was the lone assassin of Oswald. Although the committee was supported by a staff of legal counsels and staff members, it chose not to serve as a real investigative body conducting it own inquiries. Instead, it relied largely on FBI and CIA agency information; but in view of what had happened in Dallas, it was clear that these agencies had been napping or covering up sensitive information. This was especially true of Hoover's FBI, which had been remiss, if not derelict, in its duty to keep a better watch on Oswald and his connections. Despite Allen Dulles's presence on the commission, the CIA was practically of no use to the investigation. As with the FBI, there were too many skeletons rattling in CIA closets, especially its ongoing covert activities against Fidel Castro. Both agencies, therefore, were afraid of embarrassing disclosures. They did not want any publicity or humiliating stains on their reputations.

The president's brother Robert neither involved himself in the commission's work nor later challenged any of its conclusions. Known to be a real pitbull who never shunned an opportunity to get even, Kennedy's silence and noninvolvement are more than puzzling, if not downright incomprehensible.[51] The attorney general, of course, was grief-stricken, but this does not explain his inactivity. It is likely that Kennedy was as much his brother's keeper in death as he was in life, if not more so. He knew very well that there were at least four groups who wanted the president dead: the mob, Jimmy Hoffa and the teamster leadership, disgruntled Cuban exiles who felt abandoned after the Bay of Pigs, and die-hard segregationists. It must have been particularly disturbing to know that his own vendetta against Hoffa, combined with the Kennedys' long-drawn-out battle with organized crime, might be responsible for the November 22 tragedy. Robert Kennedy was hated by the mob and Hoffa; he had also managed Operation Mongoose, the CIA operation to assassinate Fidel Castro. Moreover, Robert Kennedy knew every sordid detail about his brother's connection to the Mafia boss Sam Giancana, with whom he shared a mistress, Judith Exner.

The Warren Commission never seriously explored CIA or mafia involvement in the assassination, an omission that would lead to endless speculation by the critics. Although numerous witnesses were called and their testimonies filled twenty-six volumes in the final report, these reams of documents revealed no startling new evidence and did not fully support the commission's uncompromising judgments that neither Oswald nor Ruby had any accomplices. Perhaps it was asking too much for the government to investigate itself, but then the commission had made a big show of independence and objectivity. In 1964 few people thought of bringing in an outside independent commission with full power of investigating sources inside and outside the government. The Warren Commission did not possess this discretion, being the instrument of Lyndon Johnson and the White House; its members were politicians who had other obligations and could not devote full time to the work of the commission. They delegated investigative procedures to the FBI or CIA and did not call in outside forensic experts. They commissioned an artist, who never saw the autopsy photos, to draw a rough sketch of JFK's neck and head injuries. In fairness to the commission, it was the Kennedy family that refused to release the gruesome autopsy pictures, thereby causing much needless speculation. If an autopsy had been held in Dallas, which is what Texas law required, decades of convoluted arguments about Kennedy's body, including his missing brain, could have been avoided. The Kennedy men, however, hustled the president's body out of Parkland Hospital over the vocal protests of hospital officials. Secret Service agents drew their weapons and removed the bronze coffin from Texas jurisdiction.[52]

In retrospect, it was perhaps expecting too much for the commission to bring in a definitive report. There were too many loose ends—so many, in fact, that a whole conspiracy industry developed over the next decades. As of this writing most of the loose ends have been pursued and examined, the most puzzling being the "magic one-bullet" theory set forth by the Warren Commission. The commission claimed, and subsequent empirical tests have supported, that the second bullet fired by Oswald sliced through the president's neck, hit Governor Connally in the right armpit and traveled through his wrist lodging itself in his left thigh. Despite a barrage of sarcastic criticisms of this "bastard bullet" theory, it is still a better explanation than the endless claims that Kennedy was fatally wounded from the front by a shooter from behind a retaining wall on the "grassy knoll" at Dealey Plaza.

The Warren Commission, for all its obvious shortcomings, provided the best available explanation: Oswald was the lone shooter who killed the president and Ruby was the lone shooter who killed Oswald. Chief Justice Warren believed that his commission had found the uncontestable truth, telling the *New York Times,* "if I were still a district attorney and the Oswald case came into my jurisdiction, given the same amount of evidence I could have gotten a conviction in two days and never heard about the case again."[53] If the chief justice of the United States believed that Lee Harvey Oswald was the sole assassin of the president of the United States, why didn't the American people believe it? Therein lies a history in itself, a complex story of conspiracy buffs, idiot savants quibbling over technicalities, mass media scavengers, and the hard fact that the majority of the American people simply could not believe that a young, charismatic president could have been felled by so insignificant a loser as Lee Harvey Oswald.

No sooner had the Warren Commission published its findings than the critics started to gnaw at its conclusions. The air was rife with conspiracy theories, and it quickly became obvious that the Warren Commission had not laid any of them to rest. Less than two years after the Warren Commission delivered its findings, two major books questioned the integrity of the commission's research. One book, a best-seller, was Mark Lane's *Rush to Judgment*, the other, a more scholarly work was Edward J. Epstein's *Inquest: The Warren Commission and the Establishment of the Truth*. Both works essentially accused the Warren Commission of fitting facts and information into a preconceived political mold; both claimed that there were too many loose ends, especially revolving around the single-bullet theory. The commission, these critics said, had deliberately foreclosed investigation into alternative explanations.

Lane and Epstein were only two of a dozen persistent critics of the Warren Commission who continued to raise serious questions that threatened to undermine public confidence in the official version of the truth. In fact, the atmosphere surrounding the topic of Kennedy's tragic death became lurid and unwholesome. Hardly a week went by when magazines, newspapers, television, or radio did not feature some "new" information about Oswald, Castro, the CIA, the FBI, or right-wing nuts in Dallas (the city's reputation was sullied for years). In response to endlessly circulating speculations, the Kennedy family decided to counter the ongoing rumors by commissioning William Manchester, a well-known journalist who had already written a positive biography of the president, to write a fair and well-balanced account of the president's death. The publicity surrounding the writing and publication of the Manchester book resembled a soap opera. The somewhat shy and retiring Manchester, who was also a severely wounded combat soldier of World War II, alternatively waged battles with the Kennedys, who were concerned about certain unflattering passages in the book that showed Lyndon Johnson as a vulgar and cynical politician, and news-hungry reporters, who seemed to be more interested in matters of necrophilia than the truth. When the book, entitled *Death of a President*, came out in 1967, it settled nothing—at least with the critics, for Manchester essentially ratified the Warren Commission's findings that Oswald was the lone assassin. In February 1967, the district attorney of New Orleans, Jim Garrison, announced that he and his staff had solved the Kennedy assassination case, and that he would try the key individuals who were involved in it. Shortly afterwards, he arrested Clay Shaw, a local retired businessman and civic leader. The much publicized trial, extensively covered and criticized by the major media, turned out to be a three-ring circus and revealed Garrison as a flamboyant, quirky, and mentally unstable prosecutor. The trial attracted just about every assassination buff, left-wing activist, foreign reporter, and mass-media pundit.[54] In the end, Garrison came up empty. The jury unanimously cleared Clay Shaw of any connection with the assassination. But the more Garrison was criticized by the media and the experts, the more he was supported by what would become a loud chorus of antiestablishment critics who trusted no one, including especially the government of the United States.

Conspiracy books and theories continued to wax and wane over the next decade, trying to alert the American people to what they believed to be the existence of a vast conspiracy that had allegedly brought down a popular president. As will be shown presently, the Kennedy family and its influential supporters had created the Camelot mythology, and as long as the American people were spellbound by it, the insatiable appetite for knowing more about the hero and his death continued unabated. In

1974, public interest in the assassination was ignited again when a transcript of the Warren Commission, hitherto withheld, revealed that the commission had discussed the possibility that Oswald might have been an FBI informant. Conferences on the assassination were held in New York and Boston, galvanizing public interest in convening another congressional investigation. In March 1975 Geraldo Rivera aired the Zapruder film for the first time on ABC's *Goodnight America*. One month later, Virginia congressman Thomas Downing, who believed that Kennedy's death was the result of a conspiracy, introduced a resolution (House Resolution 1540) recommending that the assassination of the president be reinvestigated. In 1976 Congress set up a commission, chaired by Downing, that was charged with reopening the case. After nearly three years of careful work and spending $5.8 million, the committee prepared a long final draft that essentially confirmed the Warren Commission's conclusions that Kennedy's wounds came from Oswald's rifle, but it left the door open for the possibility of a conspiracy. Just about the time the report was to be published, the commission was confronted with the sensational report of two "acoustics experts" who claimed that the open microphone of a Dallas motorcycle policeman in the area, proved with "95 percent accuracy" that a fourth shot was fired from the grassy knoll. We now know that the dictabelt containing the alleged sound of a fourth shot yields no such conclusion, but to Downing's commission it was persuasive enough to postpone publishing the six-hundred-page report in favor of a nine-page preliminary summary highlighting the flawed acoustics report. This, of course, emboldened the conspiracy buffs, as did the commission's suspicions that, while the mob as a whole was not involved in the assassination, individual mobsters were possibly implicated. The commission even named suspected organized crime figures such as Jimmy Hoffa, Santo Trafficante, and Carlos Marcello. It was bad enough for a government commission to name suspects without any proof whatsoever, but worse to legitimize the bogus claims of conspiracy advocates.

Despite a renewed spate of books that came out in the wake of the commission's final report, no compelling evidence has surfaced invalidating its essential findings. In fact, a 1998 PBS *Frontline* investigation reexamined a film of the presidential motorcade taken by Robert Hughes from the corner of Main and Houston streets, which shows movement by a person in the sixth floor corner window of the Texas School Book Depository.[55] What more is needed than showing that someone was moving in the sniper's nest moments before Kennedy was shot, finding the rifle with Oswald's prints on it, and recovering three spent cartridges? Apparently the best available evidence is never the best conceivable, or alternatively, does not fit the Procrustean bed of conspiracy ideology. As Gerald Posner put it, "fake audio tapes, doctored pictures, bogus interpretations of existing records, and false confessions continue to plague the JFK case."[56] Upon close examination, those who have pitched these conspiracy theories turn out to be disenchanted critics of American society who stubbornly cling to the belief that Kennedy might have been a real social redeemer, a caped crusader taking on the dark, sinister forces that were undermining American society—the fascist military, corrupt corporations, Mafiosi, and CIA spies. The comedian Mort Sahl, who became personally consumed by the assassina-

tion, lost his sharp wit by endlessly hectoring his audiences about the web of deceptions spun by right-wing forces and flabby liberals (Social Democrats, as he called
them). The same was true of the left-wing reporter Mark Lane, the "gadfly" of the
Warren Commission, who whipped up public alarm by charging that there had been
complicity and cover-up at the highest level of government. Lane was followed by
numerous mass media scavengers, not least of which was the Hollywood director
Oliver Stone, who strung together preselected visual images in his widely viewed
movie *JFK* (1991) suggesting that Kennedy was murdered by a right-wing, CIA-
supported conspiracy. During the course of this pretentious piece of propaganda,
Stone even tried to portray Jim Garrison as a heroic prosecutor, courageously battling organized crime, government cover-ups, and ignorant media insiders. To suggest at that late date that Garrison was anything but a complete fraud is to invite
ridicule among serious scholars.[57] Unfortunately, most people get their information
from movies or television programs, and they compound the problem by assuming
that objective truth is validated by being "seen." As a student pointed out to this
author, "If you saw the documentary *JFK* you would change your mind about the
assassination." So much for thirty-five years of teaching historical methods and his-
toriographical procedures!

As with the assassination of Abraham Lincoln, some die-hard conspiracy buffs are
still looking for the smoking gun in the Kennedy assassination, conveniently forgetting that we have the smoking gun, that it belonged to Lee Harvey Oswald, and that
no compelling evidence has surfaced to show that Oswald was part of a conspiracy.
Some years ago, Gerald Posner wrote a meticulously researched and crisply written
study entitled *Case Closed*, which summarized and reanalyzed all previous findings
and came up with the same conclusion the Warren Commission had reached in
1964: the lone Oswald shot Kennedy and the lone Ruby shot Oswald. Given the
ongoing fascination with Kennedy's death, which often far exceeds interest in his
actual presidency, the conspiracy industry will never consider the Kennedy case a
closed book; but with this being understood, we need to heed Posner when he said
that Oswald was the only assassin, for "to say otherwise is to absolve a man with
blood on his hands and to mock the President he killed."[58]

5. JFK: The Legacy

For three days in November 1963 (November 23-25) the American people were huddled around their television sets watching a wake and a funeral worthy of a king.
Who can forget the images of the president's coffin as it lay in state at the Capital
Rotunda; the picture of little John John, the president's three-year-old son saluting
the American flag on top of his father's casket; the funeral procession in which the
coffin would be drawn by the same gun caisson that had carried Franklin Roosevelt;
the riderless horse that followed the coffin; and the burial at Arlington National
Cemetery. The world was paying homage as well, for the funeral was attended by 220
representatives from 102 nations, including such foreign dignitaries as Charles de

Gaulle, Emperor Haile Selassie of Ethiopia, President Eamon de Valera of Ireland, Prince Philip of Great Britain, Chancellor Ludwig Erhard of West Germany.

The funeral was the beginning of an extraordinary outpouring of sympathy, grief, and adulation for the fallen President. Although Jackie Kennedy was emotionally distraught, she was also outwardly serene and, as it would turn out, determined to build her husband's legacy, to make sure that the American people did not forget what they had lost.[59] Jackie Kennedy was supported in the creation of what would turn out to be the Camelot legend by a host of Kennedy intimates—Theodore Sorensen, Arthur Schlesinger, Paul Fay, Hugh Sidey, Ken O'Donnell, and Dave Powers, among others—who reinforced the notion that Kennedy had been an unblemished hero who belonged to the pantheon of great presidents such as Washington, Jefferson, Lincoln, and Franklin Roosevelt. As Thomas Reeves pointed out, the Kennedy assassination unleashed "a literature of adulation, the likes of which the nation had not experienced since the death of Lincoln."[60] The legend that the young president had been a superhuman hero was promoted in endless books, articles, carefully selected photographs and films, reissues of his books and speeches, and so forth. Americans thought they had lost their romantic hero with a thousand faces, and they would measure all his successors, especially poor Lyndon Johnson, by the glamorous cinematic image they had of John F. Kennedy.

What was at work behind this collective need to believe in the great hero who would make a difference was a primitive myth-making consciousness that was deeply embedded in the human psyche in general and the American psyche in particular. But there was something more troubling about this reversion to mythic thinking: it was the manufacture of political imagery. In George Bernard Shaw's play *Man and Superman*, John Tanner captured the essence of modern political systems, left or right, democratic or totalitarian, when he proclaimed that "the art of government is the organization of idolatry,"[61] by which he meant lifting human beings into godlike creatures who are all-powerful, all-knowing, and all-wise. Modern political leaders, especially those who have been blessed with good looks, charm, stage presence, and the gift of gab, have known this truth almost instinctively because power does not just come out of the barrel of a gun. The German sociologist Max Weber, in distinguishing between the substance and style of political leadership coined the term "charisma" to refer to the persuasive style and emotional appeal of a successful leader. In a democratic context, it has become indispensable for a politician to connect emotionally with the audience, to evoke passions and formulate bold visions for the future.

Romantic hero worship is deeply rooted in the Western tradition, as Thomas Carlyle noted over a hundred years ago when he insisted that hero worship was the ultimate and final creed of mankind.[62] What he meant was that humans appear to have some primeval metaphysical need to reach beyond the self to some hero, a Man-God who embodies supernatural strengths and for that reason is worthy to lead the people and to be worshiped by them. What the modern desiccated age required, Carlyle believed, was some collective recrudescence of the romantic hero who would shape inchoate social forces in his own image. Kennedy, like Carlyle, also possessed a passion for heroism and the mythic past. His romantic view of history undoubtedly came from his Irish roots and from his fondness for the biographical approach to history. For the Irish, history is the collective biography of great leaders and their heroic deeds. The Emerald Isle, as everyone knows, has been one of the world's great treasure troves of magical tales. Until the mid-twentieth century, Ireland was relatively untouched by the rationalistic forces of modernity, retaining a pre-urban, religious, and even archaic way of life that many Irish immigrants brought with them to America.

The Kennedys retained a fierce sense of clannishness that was common among the Irish in America. For one thing, ethnic self-identity served as a wall of security against hostile anti-Irish and anti-Catholic prejudices. In another way, Irish clannishness supported a family structure that was intensely male-oriented; it was a world of male bravado, banter, and storytelling, the taller the tale the better. Among the Kennedys, according to Thomas Meier, this clannishness expressed itself in a family blood bond that was rarely breached on a deep level by any outsider. Kennedy, however, would enlarge the band to include those he considered "brothers," not just flesh-and-blood siblings, but those who pledged loyalty to each other and to their hero, the president. One of President Kennedy's favorite lines from Shakespeare was spoken by a young prince leading his men into battle on St. Crispin's Day: "We few, we happy few, we band of brothers;/For he to-day that sheds his blood with me,/ Shall be my brother."[63]

Behind this tradition of hero worship and bands of brothers, which the Kennedys so admired, was the belief that one man, the hero, could make not just a difference but a monumental difference. John F. Kennedy projected and democratized this mythology, persuading ordinary Americans, especially young Americans, that every single one of them could make a big difference in changing the world. Roger Hilsman, Kennedy's Assistant Secretary of State for Eastern Affairs, expressed this mythology perfectly when he said after Kennedy's death that "we thought that the world could be changed . . . we thought one man could make a difference."[64] Kennedy was convinced that he was that man, that he could "serve notice to the world" because the torch of freedom had been passed to a new, vibrant, and exceptional generation of Americans. This was a dangerous delusion on several accounts. In the first place, it elevated American exceptionalism to the level of the absolute and the role of the hero to that of a demigod. It also encouraged personalizing power and subordinating institutions to the will of "the best and the brightest." As Garry Wills has pointed out, "Charisma, the *uniquely* personal power, delegitimates institutions."[65] This personal use of power by Kennedy has been noticed by several historians who agree that Kennedy "thought in terms of people rather than structure or organization," of New Frontiersmen pulling the country into the future.[66]

Kennedy and his frontiersmen were fond of sneering at the stodgy Eisenhower management style with its focus on committee work, staff meetings, and traditional channels of governmental agencies. Theodore Sorensen proudly remembered that staff meetings were rarely held. The president, he recalled, "abandoned the practice of the Cabinet's and the National Security Council's making group decisions like corporate boards of directors. He abolished the practice of White House staff meetings and weekly Cabinet meetings. He abolished the pyramid structure of the White House staff. . . . He abolished several dozen interdepartmental committees which specialized in group recommendations on outmoded problems. . . . He paid little attention to organization charts and chains of command which diluted and distributed his authority."[67] The last sentence captures the essential Kennedy style of personal and inspirational leadership, unencumbered by layers of bureaucracy, lodged squarely in the hands of the president. In the words of Richard Reeves, "Kennedy did not think of himself as being on top of a chart; rather he wanted to be in the center, the center of all action."[68]

It is amazing that those who later complained about an "imperial presidency" were so taken by this personal style of government. The "best and the brightest" fluttered to the center of power like moths to the flame; they basked in the sunshine of Kennedy's presence. Garry Wills compared them to a small band of like-minded men, in conferences that were "flexible, secret, and hard-hitting," believing that they could save the sluggish democracy despite itself.[69] What these Kennedy insiders— McNamara, Taylor, Bundy, Sorensen, Schlesinger, Hilsman, and Robert Kennedy— enjoyed so much about their positions was to be in the company of the charismatic president and to be considered by him part of the band of brothers. As such, they formed a tight bond, often insulated from criticism and following their leader from one crisis to another. As previously shown, Kennedy was not only a risk-taker but also a man who thrived on motion and crisis. The same was true of most of his intimates, for those who stood for conservative patience never made it into the inner circle. Sorensen took great pleasure in recounting the crises of the administration, counting no fewer than sixteen during the president's first eighteen months in office. David Halberstam captured the atmosphere of the Kennedy team perfectly when he referred to them as crisis-mentality men who had come to Washington as movers and shakers, "linked to one another rather than to the country; in their minds they became responsible for the country but not responsive to it."[70]

In assessing Kennedy's legacy, two questions have to be kept in mind: What was his impact on American history? And what influence did he exert on the 1960s? As to the first question, a consensus has developed among historians that his tenure in office was too brief to have made a major difference, either in domestic or international affairs. Historians have referred to his career as an "unfinished life," à la Schubert's *Unfinished Symphony*. Camelot historians, faced by the darker side of their hero, have tried to burnish his image by falling back on a series of clichés: Kennedy, they insist, was a late bloomer who showed great capacity for growth through experiences. He "enjoyed" power and exercised it with caution and grace. His admirers are also fond of using an analogy from existential philosophy, comparing Kennedy to the existential hero who authenticates himself through action and hardship. If he had lived, we are told, the country would have taken a different, less violent, turn. Kennedy would have disengaged the United States from Vietnam, thus preventing the social explosions of the 1960s.[71]

All of this is wishful thinking based on partisanship and unprovable speculations.

More specifically, what did Kennedy accomplish in office other than projecting powerful images? What piece of legislation stands out? What was real rather than visionary about the New Frontier? Kennedy's supporters usually cite the space program and the Peace Corps as examples of his two enduring successes. Although there is no doubt that his strong support for the space program assured its later successes, especially the moon landing in July 1969, Kennedy's backing of the space program was born not of noble idealism but of cold war necessity. Shortly after being sworn into office in January 1961, the Soviets put their first man, Yuri Gagarin, into orbit, prompting a frenzied conference in the White House during which Kennedy asked: "Is there any place where we can catch them [the Russians]? Can we put a man on the moon before them? . . . If somebody can just tell me how to catch up?"[72] This, of course, contrasts quite sharply with the noble public relations statement he delivered saying, "I believe this nation should commit itself to achieving the goal, before this decade is out, of landing a man on the moon and returning him safely to earth. No single space project in this period will be more impressive to mankind." The prospect of beating the Russians to the moon appealed to Kennedy's competitive nature, which he universalized to fit the New Frontier spirit of risk-taking, motion, adventure, sacrifice, and so on. To Eisenhower, the moon landing was nothing more than an expensive "stunt" that deflected from other priorities; to Kennedy, however, it was a call to arms. Accordingly, in May 1961 he committed the United States to the Apollo Space Program. Starting in 1963, following the assembly of the necessary framework for such an ambitious undertaking, the government spent five billion dollars a year on the Apollo Program, which turned out to be a spectacular public relations triumph, just as Kennedy had predicted. On July 20, 1969, the world watched Apollo 11 land Neil Armstrong and Edwin "Buzz" Aldrin on the moon, afterwards being congratulated by president Richard Nixon.

Was the moon landing worth forty billion dollars? Only a few prominent critics raised their voices in the 1960s, perhaps challenging Kennedy and the liberal frontiersmen in their assumptions that the United States could go to the moon, defeat communism around the world, declare war on poverty, and pay any price or bear any burden necessary to . . . ? The assumption of unlimited financial resources and committing them to grandiose projects all at the same time was Kennedy's signature on the American archetype of exceptionalism.

This was true also of the Peace Corps, though it involved a much lesser financial cost. Termed the most enduring program of the Kennedy administration and financed for decades by both parties, the idea behind it seemed a noble one: sending college-educated young Americans to primarily underdeveloped countries and providing the energy and know-how to put these countries on a sound economic (capitalist) and political (democratic) basis. At its peak in 1966 the Peace Corps had sixteen thousand volunteers in close to sixty countries around the world. The program resonated strongly with idealistic college students who wanted to save the world from poverty and political oppression. Behind the noble rhetoric of Kennedy, who was forever hectoring young people to make sacrifices for their country, the Peace Corps was just one of Kennedy's cold war projects to win the *war* against communism. The Peace Corps was not a program born out of an idealism that was as pure as the driven snow. Along with counterinsurgency, the Alliance for Progress, the space race, and "action diplomacy," it was only one arrow in the Kennedy quiver. Furthermore, the Peace Corps was not a real passion for Kennedy, who loved combat as much as he said he loved peace. His interest in the Green Berets, the counterinsurgency force he helped develop, was far greater than his interest in the Peace Corps. Kennedy loved James Bond more than he did Gandhi; in fact, he strongly identified with Ian Fleming's Bond—the suave, cool, and manipulative secret agent "with a license to kill." Just like Bond, Kennedy saw himself as an action hero fighting the forces of evil, and along the way consuming women like martinis: shaken but not stirred.

The Peace Corps was an outcome of the cold war and the idealism of the early 1960s. By the 1970s, it was a declining program because young people had become disenchanted with government and foreign countries saw it as a cynical instrument of American imperialism. Few critics were honest enough to criticize the Peace Corps by asking a more probing question: Why would American leaders exhort culturally and linguistically unprepared young people to go to faraway and often hostile places around the world? Did they seriously think that this would make up for their own shortcomings and bunglings in Europe, Africa, Asia, and Latin America? As a graduate student, I asked these questions and was usually ignored. Did John F. Kennedy, in tapping the vein of youthful idealism, place unrealistic burdens on the shoulders of young people?

The man who thrived on risks and change and prided himself on controlling events turned out to be controlled and overwhelmed by events himself—so much so that at the time of his death he had a long string of failures behind him. It started with the disaster of the Bay of Pigs, which exposed the inadequacies of a bloated security system, moved on to a disastrous meeting with Khrushchev in Vienna, the Berlin crisis, the temporary collapse of arms control, criticism of the Alliance for Progress, and the ever-deeper involvement in Vietnam. The Cuban missile crisis only appeared to be an exception because the public was deceived about the concessions Kennedy had made to the Russians, concessions that would have serious consequences for the future.

What ultimately remained of the brief Kennedy presidency was a certain image and mood, which turned out to be more important to the 1960s than Kennedy's actual accomplishments. Kennedy strongly reinforced the perception, certainly in liberal circles, that the Eisenhower administration had been stagnant, conservative, and unresponsive to change. Kennedy succeeded in persuading a sizable number of Americans, especially young people, that they had a responsibility to get the country moving again, presumably in the direction of the New Frontier, the metaphor for liberal activism. Although Kennedy himself was what we would call today a liberal conservative, he raised enormous expectations for sweeping liberal reforms that would transform the country. And to help him in this task of social reconstruction, he assembled a new brain trust, "the best and the brightest," consisting of inflated intellectuals puffed up with an arrogant sense of self-importance. This brain trust dragged the country into a decade of crisis and an unwinnable war that would cost 58,000 lives and seriously tarnish the good name of the United States.

In retrospect, the image that the New Frontiersmen tried to pin on the Eisenhower administration was false. The American people had trusted President Eisenhower, as indicated by almost every public poll in the 1950s and 1960s. Moreover, public confidence in the institutions of government was very high during the Eisenhower years. It was the Kennedy-Johnson administrations, followed by the disastrous Nixon presidency, that produced the crisis of confidence in the integrity and honesty of government that still haunts us today. Kennedy contributed to this crisis by elevating image over substance and in the long run seriously tarnishing his public image through his reckless personal life. Only a very split and unintegrated man could project an image so much at odds with his real behavior. Most Americans in the 1960s were convinced that Kennedy was a faithful husband, dignified public servant, good Catholic, brilliant intellectual, and the picture of good health. That he was witty, charming, and capable of many acts of genuine kindness cannot be denied, but the nation was deceived by not seeing the darker side of Camelot—the fact that the president was a lascivious satyr, an unfaithful husband, a reckless risk-taker, callous and insensitive to those he disliked, an ineffective legislative leader, and a very unhealthy man. That such things were not publicly known illustrates the triumph of style over substance. Kennedy was a product of public relations, and, like Marilyn Monroe, James Dean, Marlon Brando, the president epitomizes America's love affair with images. Garry Wills has called Kennedy's presidency the Appearances Presidency rather than the Imperial Presidency,[73] though Kennedy undoubtedly aspired to embellish the office with the kind of pomp and circumstance he admired in British royalty. It says something about his political skills that he managed to convey the impression of style, vigor, youth, and idealism throughout his political career, and it also says something about the hunger of the American people for celebrity icons that the Kennedy image is still largely intact with many Americans. This author, too, would have probably gone to the ends of the earth for Kennedy in the 1960s if the charismatic president had asked him, but being much older now, he likes to believe that, knowing what his parents and grandparents in Germany did in following another charismatic leader into the abyss, he would have avoided blind allegiance to any putative hero.

5

SEARCHING FOR THE PROMISED LAND

Black Civil Rights

1. Sit-down Protests in the South

At the time of the Montgomery bus boycott the Reverend Martin Luther King Jr. expressed what was on the minds of most black Americans when he said that there comes a time when people get tired:

> We are here this evening to say to those who have mistreated us so long that we are tired—tired of being segregated and humiliated, tired of being kicked about by the brutal feet of oppression. We have no alternative but to protest. For many years we have shown amazing patience. We have sometimes given our white brothers the feeling that we even liked the way we were being treated. But we have come here tonight to be saved from that patience that makes us patient with anything less than freedom and justice.[1]

Rosa Parks was tired, Martin Luther King was tired, and so were millions of black people who had endured racial injustice for so long. The times were ripe for change as the conservative Eisenhower administration gave way to the impatient activism displayed by John F. Kennedy and his New Frontiersmen. Representing African Americans was Martin Luther King Jr. and a new generation of black leaders who wanted to articulate black grievances and shape them into a moral crusade so compelling that only bigots could stand up and say that they opposed racial equality.[2] King and his supporters of the Southern Christian Leadership Conference (SCLC), the civil rights organization that sprang from the Montgomery bus boycott, had chosen mass protest to confront white racism. It was clear to King, as the bus boycott and other protests had shown, that such public protests would evoke violent responses by southern segregationists and their willing helpers in local law enforcement agencies. Black protesters could expect to be cursed, spat upon, beaten, jailed, and even killed. King believed that such white reactions were likely to backfire when exposed to the scrutiny of the nation as a whole. A national audience, he believed, was more likely to identify with orderly protesters who had taken a vow to conduct themselves in a nonviolent manner. King wanted white people viscerally involved in this moral crusade; he wanted them to "see" racial bigotry and hatred in action, for it was only when people were confronted with evil directly that they were likely to act against it.

Americans had developed a thick skin of moral insensitivity to black suffering, countless ways of "not seeing" it because it was across the railroad track, on the other side of town, in the black slum, in the South—in short, not in the white backyard. King and his followers knew that if they really wanted to end segregation they would have to break down the wall that whites had constructed to keep black people out of the American mainstream. What gave King and his followers the moral high ground was his appeal to the religious conscience of Americans. King himself came from a Protestant evangelical background that appealed to both the head and the heart, focused on oratorical style, and attempted to energize both social life and work with Christian faith. Named after the great German protester, Martin Luther, King came from an upper-middle-class family from Atlanta. His father, Martin Luther King Sr., was one of the leading black Baptist ministers of Atlanta who was widely respected for his oratory and his diplomatic skills. After graduating from Morehouse College, a small black college on the west side of downtown Atlanta that catered primarily to middle-class blacks, King attended a white liberal, but racially mixed, seminary near Philadelphia called Crozer Seminary. While at Crozer, he discovered the works of Walter Rauschenbusch, who had been one of the leaders of the social gospel movement at the turn of the century and had served as pastor of Hell's Kitchen, one of the worst slums in New York City. Rauschenbusch had argued that Christianity had to be relevant to people's lives and that meant that Christians had to involve themselves in social work on behalf of the poor and the needy. King admired Rauschenbusch's optimism and the power of Christian love to transform the world until he read the neo-orthodox theologian Reinhold Niebuhr, who saw evil as a permanent feature of life that would always block man's perfectionist desires in an essentially immoral, secular culture. The desire for social justice, Niebuhr taught, would always be stymied by the disproportionate nature of political and economic power in any society. Since the relationship between groups was based on power, it was naïve to preach a gospel of love to the powerful. In a secular and materialistic society the powerful were unlikely to share or give up their wealth and power. Niebuhr made King think deeply about his optimistic view of the world, the nature of social inequality, and the capitalist system that promoted selfishness and greed.[3] It was also Niebuhr who recommended that American blacks use the pacifist tactics of the Indian leader Gandhi. Niebuhr realized that the use of nonviolent protests would be difficult because southerners had convinced themselves that Christian principles were compatible with racial oppression. King planned to checkmate by nonviolence those who believed that they could indulge in evil while at the same time claiming that they were good Christians. As long as the civil rights movement clung to nonviolent practices that were rooted in compassionate Christian principles, it would maintain the moral high ground in the eyes of the American people; but as soon as it adopted violent tactics and promoted separatist ideologies, it lost national support.

This is why the leadership of King and his followers was so crucial in the movement, for King was rooted in the southern evangelical tradition; he used the church as the primary instrument for promoting black emancipation. The church was indispensable to success because it provided moral authority by serving as the conscience of the movement; it acted as a grapevine, making it possible to spread the word; it offered a convenient and well-known place for meetings, strategy sessions, and fundraisers; and finally, it supplied the leadership that gave direction to the movement.[4] When Martin Luther King graduated with a Ph.D. from Boston University and headed south with his new wife, Coretta, he had no inkling of the task that would shortly be thrust on him. As a twenty-five-year-old pastor of the Dexter Avenue Baptist Church in Montgomery he looked forward to leading a fairly tranquil congregation of middle-class blacks, but the reality of the city's vicious racism forced him to take an active role in civil rights that would draw him into the Montgomery bus boycott and then into the larger maelstrom: leadership of the Southern Christian Leadership Conference, national spokesman for black civil rights, and finally, martyrdom.

Behind Martin Luther King came a whole new generation of black college students who were as impatient as their white counterparts to promote social justice.[5] The character and outlook of many of these young people had been shaped by their churches and youth organizations. Unlike their elders, who counseled patience and perseverance, they were more inclined to take direct action. The "sit-in" movement, by which black students demonstrated their opposition to racial discrimination by basically sitting in segregated restaurants or theaters, originated with black college students in the South. In February 1960, four black students from North Carolina Agricultural and Technical College sat down at the five-and-dime lunch counter in Greensboro and demanded to be served.[6] The waitress, as expected, refused to seat them: "I'm sorry, we don't serve colored in here." The students politely flashed a receipt of items they had bought elsewhere in the store, which contradicted the waitress line that the store did not serve colored people. The manager tried to be friendly saying, "Fellas, you know this is just not the way we do business."[7] The students persisted in their "passive demand for service" and just sat there until the store closed. Soon white customers, who checked to see what the commotion was all about were shocked, snarling: "Nasty, dirty niggers, you know you don't belong here at the lunch counter," while others were supportive: "Ah, you should have done it ten years ago. It's a good thing I think you're doing." A black dishwasher, who apparently had internalized white racism by mimicking it, accused the students of jeopardizing his own job: "That's why we can't get any place today, because of people like you, rabble-rousers, troublemakers. . . . This counter is reserved for white people, it always has been, and you are well aware of that, so why don't you go on out and stop making trouble?"[8] But making trouble with racial injustice was the only way of stopping it, especially once the momentum of protest had begun to stir people into taking action. Numerous sit-ins followed and spread to neighboring Durham, Winston-Salem, and beyond.

On April 15, 1960, three hundred students from fifty-eight colleges met at Shaw University in Raleigh, North Carolina, and created the Student Nonviolent Coordinating Committee (SNCC). The meeting at Shaw University had been arranged by Ella Baker, the executive director of the Atlanta chapter of the Southern Christian Leadership Conference, in hopes of coordinating civil rights strategy and of involving students in the movement on a more organized basis. Little did Martin Luther

King and other members of SCLC suspect in 1960 that the students in SNCC would eventually march to their own drummer and derail the movement from its nonviolent track. The original goal of SNCC was to mobilize protesters and force direct confrontations with segregationists rather than rely upon traditional methods of lengthy court proceedings or token concessions by the white power structure.

The sit-in movement along with the Freedom Riders, who went South by bus, was designed to breach the wall of segregation and to expose the lie behind which the south had barricaded itself—namely, that a separate life for blacks was equal, either in the South or anywhere else in the nation. Although these challenges to white racial supremacy caused savage reprisals from dyed-in-the-wool segregationists, who struck back at black activists and their supporters with everything in their arsenal, the black movement remained nonviolent. The chants and the lyrics of that period made this quite clear: "Keep Your Eyes on the Prize," "I'm Gonna Sit at the Welcome Table," "Deep in my heart, I do believe that we shall overcome some day." Moreover, black and white solidarity for those who believed in racial equality was widely celebrated, as voices rang out: "Black and white together" and "We shall overcome."

2. Freedom Rides

In March 1961, the new director of CORE (Congress of Racial Equality), James Farmer, decided to send "Freedom Riders" into the South by bus in order to test whether the southern states were complying with a recent Supreme Court decision (*Boynton v. Virginia*) that extended a 1946 prohibition against segregation in vehicles engaged in interstate travel, to include all transportation terminals. Farmer's strategy was to force confrontations with southern segregationists in hopes that such provocations would force the federal judiciary to intervene.[9] In April, CORE officially announced that it would provoke civil disobedience by using peaceful Gandhian methods. On May 4, 1961, two interracial groups, including James Farmer, left Washington D.C. on two buses, a Greyhound and a Trailways. Ugly incidents involving racial epithets, scuffles, and arrests occurred at various terminals in Virginia, the Carolinas, and Georgia; but it was not until Freedom Riders entered the Deep South that serious trouble began. At Anniston, Alabama, an angry mob surrounded the Greyhound bus and attacked it with blackjacks, iron bars, clubs, and tire chains. With its windows smashed and tires slashed, the bus made it a few miles outside Anniston, where it was attacked again by members of the mob who had followed the bus in automobiles. Someone threw an incendiary bomb into the bus that almost asphyxiated the Freedom Riders, who barely escaped with their lives. Almost simultaneously the Trailways bus arrived at Anniston. Eight whites jumped on the bus and demanded that the blacks move to the back of the bus. When they refused, violence ensued. Two white Freedom Riders, James Peck and Walter Bergman, were badly beaten, with Bergman suffering permanent brain damage. Police Commissioner T. Eugene "Bull" Connor had promised the KKK some unmolested time to attack the freedom fighters, and this is exactly what these white thugs did as they assaulted the Freedom Riders at will. Alabama Governor John Patterson called the Freedom Riders a bunch of troublemakers and advised them to get out of Alabama. Finding themselves stranded and isolated, the Freedom Riders boarded a special flight to New Orleans arranged by the Justice Department. The CORE-sponsored Freedom Ride was temporarily discontinued.

SNCC continued where CORE left off, organizing a new Freedom Ride from Nashville to Birmingham. As soon as the bus reached the outskirts of Birmingham, Connor's police escorted the bus to the terminal and promptly arrested the Freedom Riders by putting them into "protective custody." The next day, Connor drove the volunteers 150 miles to the Tennessee-Alabama line, hoping that he had seen the last of them. The student volunteers, however, managed to get right back to Birmingham, where they were joined by additional volunteers from Atlanta and Nashville. On May 20, the bus left Birmingham without incident, but when it pulled into the terminal at Montgomery, all hell broke lose. "Get those niggers," a woman screamed, egging on a crowd of nearly one hundred enraged segregationists who fell on the helpless protesters with lead pipes and baseball clubs. John Lewis was knocked to the ground with a soda crate and suffered a concussion.[10] James Zwerg, a white exchange student from the University of Wisconsin who was attending Fisk University, was trampled into the hot tar of the pavement and smashed in the face with a suitcase; and while one assailant held his dazed head between his knees, other members in the mob took turns punching Zwerg and smashing in his teeth. White adults held children on their shoulders so that they could enjoy the spectacle, cheering encouragingly "kill the nigger-loving son of bitch."[11] Not a single policeman was in sight, though John Doar of the Civil Rights Commission of the Justice Department, who was watching the violence while being on the phone to Washington, managed to give a blow-by-blow account of the affair to his superiors.

Those superiors had been monitoring the progress of the Freedom Riders with increasing alarm; they feared that black militants might enmesh the federal government too deeply in black civil rights. John F. Kennedy had campaigned as a champion of civil rights in 1960, but once in office his pragmatic instincts led him to search for a middle ground, a position that would appease blacks without alienating white southerners. The South, however, was politically dominated by conservative Democrats who still believed in white supremacy and states' rights. In Congress, especially in the House of Representatives, conservative Democrats often joined with Republicans in opposing liberal legislation, and it looked as though the progressive New Frontier legislation might be permanently bottled up in committees dominated by this political bloc in Congress.

Kennedy, therefore, wanted to move cautiously and slowly on civil rights; he did not want to be pushed precipitously into bold action that might be regretted later on. Violent actions in the South that involved the federal government raised the whole thorny issue of law enforcement, which was largely a matter of local rather than federal authority.[12] Americans had traditionally opposed a federal police force because they believed that such a force raised the specter of totalitarianism and was incompatible with the Constitution. Law and order were therefore local matters; and in the

South, law enforcement often resided in the hands of die-hard segregationists. There were many racist police officials and justices in the South who swore to resist integration until hell froze over. Of the eight district judges Kennedy appointed, four willfully obstructed the efforts of the Justice Department to enforce the law.[13]

Kennedy's chief law enforcement officer, of course, was his own brother, Robert Kennedy, who seemed to be more interested in busting organized crime than he was in promoting the cause of black protesters in the South. In addition to fighting a kind of personal crusade against organized crime, the attorney general also saw himself as his brother's keeper, anxiously monitoring Jack's reckless sexual indiscretions, which included an affair with Judith Exner, the mistress of Mafia Boss Sam Giancana. The director of the FBI, J. Edgar Hoover, had assiduously collected a bulging file on Kennedy's indiscretions, as he had on other influential politicians, and he dangled that file, like a sword of Damocles, right over the heads of the Kennedys, threatening to drop it if they interfered in the internal affairs of the FBI. Hoover had been less than energetic either in fighting organized crime or monitoring civil rights violations. As the civil rights movement gathered speed, Hoover was more concerned about alleged communist infiltration in civil rights disturbances than he was in enforcing the law and protecting the lives of civil rights demonstrators. In fairness to Hoover, it must be mentioned that he despised the Ku Klux Klan, which he saw as a threat to the nation's democratic institutions. He prosecuted the Imperial Kleagle, Edward Y. Clarke, on charges of white slavery, wiretapped the phone of the well-known Klansman Bobby Shelton, and sent hundreds of agents into the Deep South in order to infiltrate the Klan. In Hoover's eyes Klansmen were like "water moccasins, rattlesnakes and red-necked sheriffs," a group of "sadistic, vicious white trash."[14]

In understanding the role of the federal government in the civil rights movement, it is crucial to keep in mind the tug-of-war between the FBI director, with his rigid and self-serving code of law enforcement, the attorney general, fighting different battles on different fronts, and the president's reckless private life, which threatened periodically to get in the way of the law. Hoover was a man of the past with his own pedantic and authoritarian habits. He had a visceral hatred of Martin Luther King and seemed to be more offended by his sexual peccadillos than by his civil rights activities. Hoover also suspected that King was either a communist or consorted with known communists, alerting the attorney general that one of King's advisors, Stanley Levison, was one such communist.[15] When President Kennedy told King to sever his relationship with Levison, King at first obliged but later changed his mind. Hoover then persuaded the president to wiretap King. What followed was an ongoing campaign by the FBI to discredit King as a man and a moral leader.

Neither Hoover nor the Kennedys could stop King from encouraging further civil rights demonstrations. On May 21, 1961, King flew to Montgomery to support the resumption of Freedom Rides. On that evening close to twelve hundred people crowded into Ralph Abernathy's First Baptist Church, where the Montgomery Improvement Association had sponsored a peaceful demonstration. Across from the church a huge mob of whites had assembled to harass and threaten the black rally. Violence quickly broke out when white segregationists beat up blacks who were standing in front of the church and even broke into the church to start fights. Stones, bottles, stench bombs, and firebombs were thrown into the church, causing pandemonium. Federal marshals eventually restored a measure of order by forming a police line around the church. The governor of Alabama reinforced the police marshals with state troopers and National Guard units, declaring a "qualified martial rule."

The Kennedys wanted a "cooling off" period, but the civil rights leaders rejected that on the grounds that they had been cooling off for a hundred years. CORE, SLCC, and SNCC all agreed to resume Freedom Rides and established a committee for that purpose. On May 24, a Trailways bus full of bruised veterans of the early ride left Montgomery for Jackson, Mississippi. Behind the scenes, the Kennedys made a deal with Mississippi senator James Eastland that specified that in return for no police violence the federal government would not contest the arrest of the Freedom Riders by state authorities. This is exactly what happened. The Freedom Riders were promptly arrested, but as hundreds of Freedom Riders continued to violate the law, refused to pay their fines, and willingly went to jail, the federal government had to act if its mandate about nondiscrimination in interstate facilities was to have any legitimacy. On September 22, 1961, the Interstate Commerce Commission announced that interstate carriers and terminals had to display signs that clearly stated that seating was to be conducted without regard to race, color, creed, or national origin. By the end of 1962 CORE announced that the battle of interstate travel had been won.

The Freedom Riders exposed southern racism on a nationwide basis; they also emboldened the more militant black civil rights advocates, especially in CORE and SNCC, to broaden their attacks on segregation in the South. At the same time, the Freedom Rides also exposed the lukewarm attitude of the Kennedy administration and its fear that such protests could lead to political defections by white southern Democrats. The administration, ever conscious of the importance of image, was also concerned about world opinion, for what was happening in the South was undermining the nation's image of a peaceful, just, and democratic society.

3. Voter Registration

As the freedom rides wound down, acrimonious discussions broke out among the various civil rights organizations about the future course of the movement, particularly about the tactics civil rights activists should choose in pursuing full equality for black people. On June 16, 1961, Robert Kennedy met with leaders of CORE, SCLC, and SNCC and strongly urged them to abandon potentially violent demonstrations in favor of registering black voters on the grounds that voter registration was the key to change in the South. The debate about civil rights strategy was particularly bitter among the ranks of SNCC. One group, led by Marion Barry and Diane Nash, favored continuation of provocative demonstrations, while another group, spearheaded by the "three Charlies"—Jones, McDew, and Sherrod—believed that registering blacks to vote was the more democratic and therefore the more effective means of empowering blacks, especially since such methods had the support of the federal government. The rift between the two factions in SNCC was patched up by James Farmer, who was elected by the students to serve as SNCC's executive director. Farmer strongly believed that the civil rights movement had to rely on both direct action and voter registration, and he accepted a proposal by Ella Baker that SNCC should be organized into two branches: one dealing with direct action projects and the other with voter registration. CORE proceeded to follow SNCC's strategic reorientation, accepting James Farmer's avowal that direct actions and voter registration were not mutually exclusive. Shortly thereafter, the major civil rights organizations joined in a new Voter Education Project (VEP), funded by private and corporate donations.

The voter registration drive was jump-started by Robert Moses in rural southwest Mississippi. Moses was a well-educated and talented organizer who worked against great odds and with indomitable courage in registering disenfranchised blacks in the Delta counties of southwest Mississippi. What he did there and how he did it would inspire similar registration drives in 1962–63.[16]

Supported by southern law enforcement agencies, southern segregationists systematically stymied the efforts of black activists who wanted to enfranchise blacks. The federal government, which could have made a difference, was hesitant to interfere in the internal affairs of southern states. Only in Mississippi did the federal government involve itself directly, when James Meredith, a black student, was prevented from matriculating at the University of Mississippi in 1962. When Governor Ross Barnett defied a federal court order to admit Meredith to the university, President Kennedy dispatched hundreds of federal marshals to Ole Miss to assure his admission.

A similar show of federal force was not forthcoming in Albany, Georgia, where civil rights activists launched a comprehensive two-pronged attack on white racism that involved voter registration and direct actions (demonstrations, sit-ins, boycotts). The Kennedy administration adopted a hands-off policy, justifying its inaction by claiming that a cooling-off period would benefit the moderate Democrat Carl Sanders in his gubernatorial chances against more die-hard segregationists of the stripe of Ross Barnett. Essentially handed carte blanche approval to deal with black protesters, the local police chief, Laurie Pritchard, conducted mass arrests, while at the same time avoiding ugly incidents involving white mobs. The national media commended Pritchard's actions as skilled police work, and even Martin Luther King's arrest failed to arouse much national concern. The collapse of the Albany movement emboldened southern segregationists in meeting black militancy with skillful policing, all the while trying to avoid negative publicity. However, vicious white violence combined with arbitrary police actions continued over the next five years throughout the South and in other parts of the nation. Despite impressive civil rights gains on the national level, race relations increasingly deteriorated. "We've got to have a crisis to bargain with," remarked a subdued civil rights leader who believed that the movement was flagging and needed a national *cause célèbre* to stir the federal government into action on behalf of civil rights reform.[17]

Martin Luther King agreed with this sentiment and chose the citadel of racial bigotry Birmingham, Alabama, as the site of the next major confrontation. It was in Birmingham that Sheriff "Bull" Connor had already made his reputation as a dyed-in-the-wool segregationist who intimidated not only the black citizens of Birmingham but also moderate whites who were willing to negotiate with black leaders. "Bull" Connor did more than just bully; he flagrantly defied federal mandates to desegregate bus terminal facilities by twice arresting the terminal manager for complying with federal regulations. On April 3, 1963, King launched the opening salvo of protest by leading a march through the city. Surprisingly, Connor kept a low profile and merely paraded his attack dogs to show King just who was in charge. Shortly after a week of peaceful demonstrations, King was served with an injunction against further demonstrations. Announcing to reporters that "we have reached the point of no return" and adding that he was willing to go to jail to defy a bad law that was designed to perpetuate tyranny under the guise of "law and order," King defied the injunction and was promptly arrested and imprisoned for three days. While in jail, King learned that eight Albany clergymen had made a public statement condemning the demonstrations and urging civil rights leaders to press their claims for justice in the courts. King could not allow this statement to go unanswered. Writing on scraps of paper with a pen smuggled into his cell by a trusted follower, King wrote one of his most moving declarations on civil rights. In his "Letter from Birmingham Jail" King made it clear why he was in Birmingham:

> I am in Birmingham because injustice is here. Just as the eighth century prophets left their little villages and carried their "thus saith the Lord" far beyond the boundaries of their home town, and just as the Apostle Paul left his little village of Tarsus and carried the gospel of Jesus Christ to practically every hamlet and city of the Greco-Roman world, I too am compelled to carry the gospel of freedom beyond my particular home. I cannot sit idly by in Atlanta and not be concerned about what happened in Birmingham. Injustice anywhere is a threat to justice everywhere. We are caught in an inescapable network of mutuality tied in a single garment of destiny. Never again can we afford to live with the narrow, provincial "outsider agitator" idea. Anyone who lives inside the United States can never be considered an outsider anywhere in this country.[18]

King then forcefully outlined the strategy civil rights leaders should follow in their nonviolent demonstrations against injustice. They should first gather the facts whether injustice existed, then try to negotiate, purify themselves spiritually, and finally turn to direct action. Since the Birmingham authorities had failed to negotiate in any meaningful sense, King argued that the city left the movement no choice but to engage in direct action. He explained that "non-violent action seeks to create such a crisis and establish such creative tension that a community that has constantly refused to negotiate is forced to confront the issue."[19] He compared this process to a Socratic dialogue, which equally tries to create tension in the mind so that individuals could rise from the bondage of myths and half truths to the realm of objective truth.

King also brushed aside the criticism that he was breaking the law, arguing that there were two types of law—just and unjust. A just law, he held, was a man-made code that squared with the moral law or the law of God, while an unjust law was a code that a majority inflicted on a minority that was not binding on itself and that the minority had no part in formulating. Citing Saint Augustine and Saint Thomas Aquinas, King appealed to natural law grounded in divine authority, holding that an unjust law was no law at all, and that people had a moral responsibility to disobey such unjust laws.

When King emerged from jail, he found that the demonstrations had ebbed. As the number of adults was dwindling, King agreed with a suggestion from James Bevel, who had joined SCLC after participating in the Nashville sit-ins, that teenagers and children should be used in peaceful demonstrations. Bull Connor now badly overplayed his hand by turning high-pressure water hoses on both adults and children, leaving many of them dazed and bloodied in the streets. Wielding nightsticks and electrified cattle prods, Connor's goons dispersed the marchers; but far from pacifying the demonstrators, these violent police actions resulted in equally violent reprisals by erstwhile peaceful demonstrators. Young blacks showered the police with a hail of bricks, stones, and bottles. This, of course, only encouraged Connor's forces to retaliate at will. The Reverend Fred Shuttlesworth, who went into the black quarter in order to calm nerves, was lifted off the ground by the jets of a high-pressure water hose and thrown against the wall of the Sixteenth Street Church with such force that he had to be carried off unconscious in an ambulance.

Birmingham whites, feeling the heat from Washington, eventually decided that such violent disruptions were taking their toll on the economic lifeline of the city and had to be brought to an end. The merchants of the city concluded an agreement with King and the SCLC that, in return for halting demonstrations, the city would desegregate and make genuine efforts to employ blacks in Birmingham. Moreover, SCLC succeeded in having hundreds of imprisoned demonstrators released on bond. Before returning to Atlanta, King pleaded for peace and reconciliation, but that plea fell on deaf ears; for neither blacks nor whites in Birmingham were fully satisfied with the biracial accord. The staunch pro-segregation governor of Alabama, George Wallace, immediately disavowed the Birmingham accord. Connor's policemen then menaced the city's black quarters by patrolling the streets with sawed-off shotguns, and the police chief called on white citizens to boycott those stores that had agreed to desegregate. Violence flared up again when two dynamite explosions wrecked the home of the Reverend A. D. King, Martin Luther King's brother, and blew out a section of the Gaston Motel, where King and the SCLC had established their headquarters. Enraged blacks, seeking revenge, pelted police and fire fighters with stones and bottles. "Kill Whitey" was replacing nonviolent protests. The period of the submissive African American was clearly over. Many black protesters had discovered that mass social disruptions frightened the white establishment and might just galvanize the federal government into taking positive steps on behalf of the protesters. In response to the Birmingham violence, the Kennedy administration ordered three thousand army troops near Birmingham and prepared to call out the Alabama National Guard. Although the bombings stopped and the biracial agreement was formally ratified, Birmingham continued to seethe with racial tensions well into the fall of 1963.

The cumulative impact of well over two and a half years of protests, was finally capturing the full attention of the Kennedy administration, especially after the Cuban missile crisis had subsided in late 1962. It was the attorney general, Robert Kennedy, who was undergoing a gradual change of heart on civil rights, and, in turn, prompted his brother, the president, to take more resolute actions. On May 24, 1963, the attorney general met with a group of prominent blacks who had been assembled by the novelist James Baldwin. The idea behind the meeting, which was to consist of a broad spectrum of prominent black spokesmen other than conventional civil rights leaders like King or Wilkins, was to find out what was on the minds of ordinary blacks. Besides Baldwin, the conference was attended by Lena Horne, Harry Belafonte, the playwright Lorraine Hansberry, the psychologist Kenneth Clark, and assorted activists. The meeting began on the wrong foot, when Jerome Smith, a young Freedom Rider, addressed the startled group and told them that the prospect of being in the same room with the attorney general nauseated him; he then proceeded to shock Kennedy even more by saying that he would not fight for his country as long as blacks were treated as second-class citizens. The atmosphere continued to chill as the attorney general was forced to submit to lengthy accounts of black suffering and bitter complaints of government inaction. The meeting was a sobering education for the young liberal attorney general, who began to suspect that a more active civil rights approach was required to support the moral and legal demands for black justice, now more urgent than ever before.[20]

On June 11, 1963, the Kennedy administration was confronted with another southern defiance when Governor George Wallace of Alabama threatened to prevent two black students from matriculating at the University of Alabama. Announcing that he would draw a line in the dust, Wallace bellowed out to a crowd of cheering supporters: "I draw the line in the dust . . . and I say, Segregation now! Segregation tomorrow! Segregation forever!"[21] The president could not let this defiant challenge go unanswered; he, too, had to draw a line in the sand, warning Wallace and all other segregationists that their time was over. On the evening of June 11, Kennedy addressed the American people on television and gave one of his finest speeches on civil rights. The president told the American people that racial discrimination had to be confronted not only as a legal issue but also as a moral issue. The time had passed, he said, when America's racial injustices could be met by "repressive police action," but only by the efforts of Congress, state and local governments, and private citizens, working together in order to assure that all Americans received equal rights and opportunities. Appealing to the moral conscience of white Americans, he said:

> If an American, because his skin is dark, cannot eat lunch in a restaurant open to the public; if he cannot send his children to the best public school available; if he cannot vote for the public officials who represent him; if, in short, he cannot enjoy the full and free life, which all of us want, then who among us would be content to have the color of his skin changed and stand in his place?[22]

Counsels of patience and delay were no longer possible, Kennedy told the American people; the time to act forcefully was at hand. He promised to send Congress a civil rights proposal that would commit this country to the proposition that "race has no place in American life or law." The address was a shining moment for the president, who had searched his own conscience for some time, undoubtedly asking himself how much longer he could subordinate the moral issues that drove civil rights to the political exigencies of appeasing southern segregationists. He had finally chosen sides, and so did many honest and decent Americans. But Kennedy's forceful moral stand did not still racial hatreds. Just four hours after his address, Medgar Evers, the NAACP field secretary in Mississippi, was driving home late at night in Jackson, Mississippi. His wife Myrtie had kept the children up because they wanted to know what their father thought of the president's speech, which they had listened to earlier in the evening. When Evers walked up to the house a sniper shot him in the back. He bled to death in front of his wife and children.

In order to speed up the momentum gained by Kennedy's civil rights speech and the civil rights proposal winding its way through Congress, movement leaders, galvanized by A. Philip Randolph, planned a massive rally in the nation's capital. Randolph, who conceived the idea of a mass rally, was a veteran of the civil rights movement. As head of the Brotherhood of Sleeping Car Porters, he had played a prominent role in the movement, proposing a march on Washington in 1941 that compelled Franklin Roosevelt to desegregate the defense industry. His aide, Bayard Rustin, was a skillful organizer who also had a proven track record in the movement. Although Rustin organized the march on Washington, he stayed largely in the background because of his checkered past in the communist party and his arrest on moral charges as a homosexual. Rustin had traveled a long road as a civil rights advocate that led from a Quaker upbringing, a short stint in the communist party, prison as a conscientious objector during World War II, to Gandhian advocate of nonviolent protest. Both Randolph and Rustin believed that the march on Washington should be peaceful and welcome both black and white supporters of civil rights.

The Kennedys at first opposed the march but finally approved it as long as it remained peaceful and supportive of the administration's efforts on behalf of civil rights. Anxious to maintain a liberal consensus, the leaders of the march felt obliged to muzzle potentially militant activists who could discredit the peaceful rally. John Lewis, who had questioned the alliance with white liberals and even the value of the proposed civil rights bill itself, had to be persuaded to subordinate his militancy to the greater good of civil rights unity. That unity was already very fragile in the summer of 1963. The radicals in CORE and SNCC were moving toward more extreme positions, and to the left of these widely recognized civil rights groups was the militant and separatist group called the Nation of Islam. Malcolm X, the sharp-tongued voice of "Black Muslims," had gone to Washington to mock the march; but when he encountered a strong sense of black unity, he temporarily bit his vituperative tongue and watched the spectacle from the sidelines.

On August 28, 1963, a hot and sunny day, 250,000 people from all across America, black and white, gathered under the Lincoln Memorial to voice their support for freedom, equal opportunities, and jobs. Although there was a profusion of speakers, the rally was also an interracial—perhaps one of the last mass-integrated—celebration of racial equality.[23] People clasped hands as Joan Baez sang "We Shall Overcome"; they sang along with Peter, Paul, and Mary who asked "How many times must a man look up before he can see the sky," and the crowd fell silent when Bob Dylan sang a ballad in memory of the recently murdered Medgar Evers. Odetta sang "I'm on My Way," containing the memorable line: "If they ask you who you are, tell them you're a child of God." The performances on stage also included Josh White, whose career as a folksinger dated back to the 1920s when Rustin had been one of his sidemen; Bernice Johnson, a singer who had given up opera in favor of music derived from Africa; Rutha Harris, another gifted singer who had switched from opera to singing freedom songs; Marian Anderson, who sang "He's Got the Whole World in His Hands;" and the ever-popular and charismatic Mahalia Jackson, singing "I Been Buked and I Been Scorned."

A host of celebrities, politicians, religious leaders of all faiths, union officials, and plain ordinary Americans, all came together, if only for a brief moment, to express their faith in the American Dream. The closing address, given by Martin Luther King, would forever stay in the memories not only of those who experienced it directly but also those who saw it on television or listened to it on the radio. King gave a carefully crafted speech on the plight of black people in America, highlighting the fact that since the Emancipation Proclamation the condition of black people had not changed very much. He insisted, however, on the ripeness of time in the struggle for freedom, calling upon the "veterans of creative suffering" to make real the promises of democracy, racial justice, and equal opportunities. King was about to sit down, when Mahalia Jackson called out from behind him: "Tell them about your Dream, Martin!"[24] King set aside his notes and in a moment of spontaneous inspiration and religious fervor, he shared his dream with America:

> I have a dream that one day this nation will rise up and live out the true meaning of its creed: "We hold these truths to be self-evident—that all men are created equal." I have a dream that one day on the red hills of Georgia the sons of former slaves and the sons of former slaveholders will be able to sit down together at the table of brotherhood. I have a dream that one day even the State of Mississippi, a desert state sweltering with the heat of injustice and oppression, will be transformed into an oasis of freedom and justice. I have a dream that my four little children will one day live in a nation where they will not be judged by the color of their skin but by the content of their character. I have a dream today when we let freedom ring, when we let it ring from every village and every hamlet, from every state and every city, we will be able to speed up that day when all of God's children, black men and white men, Jews and Gentiles, Protestants and Catholics, will be able to join hands and sing in the words of the old Negro Spiritual, "Free at Last! Free at Last! Thank God Almighty, we are free at last."[25]

In the fall of 1963 Martin Luther King's dream was punctured repeatedly by mindless violence in the South. In September, a bomb exploded at the Sixteenth Street Baptist Church in Birmingham, a city referred to by blacks as "Bombingham," and took the lives of four black girls in the basement of the church just as they were changing into their choir robes. Dozens of other children were injured.[26] These senseless killings underscored the vicious racism that still operated in the South, but the violence also swung national opinion in favor of black civil rights. On November 22, Kennedy was assassinated, yet another act of senseless violence. The Kennedy assassination, along with the good will the civil rights movement had accumulated, stirred widespread sympathy for the civil rights proposal that the late president had submitted to Congress. But it was Lyndon Johnson's legislative skills that assured that the civil rights bill of 1964 was signed into law on July 2, 1964. The historic Civil Rights Act committed the federal government in the fight against racial injustice by prohibiting discrimination in places of public accommodation, banning discrimination by employers and unions, and, ending the long-standing practice of treating women as second-class citizens, outlawing discrimination based on either race or sex. In order to put teeth into these provisions, the federal government was authorized to withhold funds to public programs that practiced discrimination by employers. The act also called for the establishment of an Equal Employment Opportunity Commission, a Community Relations Service, and financial as well as technical support to communities seeking to desegregate their schools.

It is important to realize that this civil rights act came a century after the Civil War, and that it took mass upheavals, a supportive presidency, and a determined liberal bloc in Congress, including liberal Republicans, to become the law of the land. The question now was whether the liberal bloc in Congress, working closely with the Johnson administration, would continue to press for further reforms demanded by the country's civil rights leaders. The answer would depend on the nature of black demands and expectations, the political and moral persuasion of black leaders, and the ability of the liberal leaders in Congress to convince white Americans that the "Second Reconstruction" had to move far beyond a simple Civil Rights Act. The black movement itself was beginning to fracture in 1964 as serious internecine conflicts between its various branches—SCLC, SNCC, CORE, NAACP—made a united front increasingly difficult. Voter registration was still an unfinished goal in 1964; and though all civil rights groups agreed to concentrate on this objective, they disagreed about tactics. The leadership in SNCC was pressing for more radical approaches after numerous violent encounters with white segregationists in the South. Beyond merely attaining the franchise, radical civil rights activists began to embrace a more revolutionary agenda aimed at changing the social and economic structure of American society rather than being content to participate in it. Others, like Martin Luther King, still concentrated on realistic and attainable objectives such as voter registration, decent jobs and housing, school desegregation, and an end to police brutality. The civil rights movement was clearly approaching a fork in the road: one road might lead to a radical "Marshall Plan" for black people, while the other might lead to further piecemeal advances, incremental perhaps but nevertheless progressive, leading black people eventually to full integration. Fissures in the movement prompted black activists to embrace too many goals and strategies, some of them increasingly at odds with each other, thereby not only fracturing the movement but also inviting a white backlash that would bring the "Second Reconstruction" to an abrupt end.

After the March on Washington, SNCC and CORE members went south to register blacks to vote. Robert Moses, who had attempted to organize disenfranchised blacks in Mississippi since 1961, was convinced that enfranchising blacks was the key to political success. In 1964, blacks constituted 42 percent of the total population of Mississippi, a fact that told Moses that significant changes could be made if blacks elected their own people to public office. Joining forces with several racial advancement groups that had been loosely tied to the Council of Federated Organizations (COFO), Moses conducted what he called Freedom Elections, selecting a slate of candidates for governor and lieutenant governor. Although the state did not recognize the Freedom Elections, Moses was proven right in his claim that blacks would turn out in great numbers at the polls if given an opportunity. This is why SNCC, which Moses represented, CORE, and COFO pooled all of their resources for Freedom Summer, a program designed to register blacks to vote in Mississippi. Allard Lowenstein, a white liberal activist, persuaded Moses to recruit white college students for the project in order to highlight national attention by showing that black and white students shared the same goals and ideals. Lowenstein was able to recruit over a hundred students from Yale, Stanford, and Berkeley. SNCC members were skeptical of the presence of white students from elite universities, and tension quickly developed. Some black members came from poor and uneducated backgrounds and resented the superior attitudes of their white counterparts. As the project gradually got off the ground, the level of white violence rose dramatically. The Ku Klux Klan bombed the headquarters of SNCC, CORE, and COFO. Black churches associated with the Mississippi Freedom Summer went up in flames. Numerous black people were assaulted and several murdered. Then on June 20, 1964, three civil rights fighters—Michael Schwerner, Andrew Goodman, and James Chaney—left Meridian, Mississippi, to investigate a church burning in Neshoba County. They never made it; their badly burned car was found just outside Philadelphia, Mississippi. For over two weeks, the nation's attention was riveted on the terror-plagued state of Mississippi. Lyndon Johnson authorized an FBI manhunt, augmented by four hundred sailors, near Philadelphia. In early August, with sailors dredging nearby waters in a swampy area, they found the bodies of the three murdered civil rights fighters buried near an earthen dam. The three young men, it turned out, had been arrested by Philadelphia's deputy Sheriff, Cecil Price, who then arranged to have them released just long enough for several members of the Ku Klux Klan to kidnap them and take them to a deserted road where other Klan members were waiting for them. Chaney, who was black, was savagely beaten before being shot. The Klansmen mockingly said to the two white civil rights fighters "So you wanted to come to Mississippi? Well, now we're gonna let you stay here. We're not even gonna run you out. We're gonna let you stay here with us." They chanted in unison: "Ashes to ashes, dust to dust, if you'd stayed where you belonged, you wouldn't be here with us."[27] Then they dispatched the two white civil rights leaders, Schwerner and Goodman. The Klansmen then buried the three bodies with a bulldozer.

The three summer months of June, July, and August can only be described as a nightmare for the civil rights movement. In addition to the murdered civil rights fighters, several others were also killed, assaulted, or seriously injured. While most of the white students headed back to the safety and comfort of their homes, the three civil rights organizations managed to carry on courageously and elected sixty-eight delegates to the Democratic Convention in Atlantic City. Since the regular party organization in Mississippi excluded blacks from voting and holding office, this alternative slate of largely black delegates challenged the regular lily white delegation and demanded to be seated as the legitimate delegation from Mississippi. This left Lyndon Johnson and the leaders of the Democratic Party in a real pickle. For some time now, Johnson had made it known to black people that their home was in the Democratic Party and that he strongly supported full black participation in the democratic process. The Mississippi Democratic Freedom Party was led by Fannie Lou Hamer, a sharecropper's daughter, who said enthusiastically that she believed with all her heart in the victory of the delegation. Hamer was a remarkable woman with an arresting background. Just a few years before her appearance at the Democratic Convention, she had been sterilized without her knowledge by Mississippi health authorities. In a stunning testimony to the credential committee, she also revealed that she had been savagely beaten by the Winona police in 1963 after trying to register to vote. She and her husband had also been fired from their jobs for the same reason. Hamer's enthusiasm, however, quickly dissipated when it became obvious, after harried and secretive negotiations behind the scenes, that the Democratic leadership would refuse to seat the delegation.[28] Lyndon Johnson was not about to sacrifice the South in the upcoming election against Goldwater. Johnson let Hubert Humphrey, his designated vice president, perform the dirty work, letting him know that his slot on the ticket depended on his handling of the crisis. The best the Democratic leadership was willing to offer the Freedom Delegation was a lame compromise by which two members of the delegation would be seated and the rest could stay as "honored guests." The Mississippi Democratic Freedom Party turned the offer down flat, calling it a "sellout" and accusing the liberal Democrats of being false friends. Robert Moses and many other civil rights activists who had organized the Mississippi voter registration drive felt betrayed. SNCC never again put its trust in liberals or the national government. Johnson, of course, did not need the South to win the election; as it would turn out, he lost the Deep South to Goldwater, but won all other states except Arizona. In a moral but pyrrhic victory, the Mississippi Freedom Party delegates occupied the seats reserved for the regular delegates who, with the exception of three members, had bolted the convention.

Although Lyndon Johnson for once earned the title "Landslide Lyndon," for he swamped Goldwater in the 1964 election, his main focus for the immediate future was not civil rights but Great Society legislation. He was still angry about the aggressive behavior of Mississippi Freedom Party delegates at the convention in Atlantic City and was increasingly suspicious and jealous of Martin Luther King, especially after King received the Nobel Peace Prize and was named Man of the Year by *Time* Magazine. Hoover continued whispering into the president's ear that King was "the most notorious liar in the country,"[29] and that the SCLC was infiltrated by communists. As for King, his immediate goal was to agitate for black voter registration in the

South, concentrating once more on Selma, Alabama, where white resistance was strongest. In January 1965, shortly after receiving the Nobel Prize, King conducted daily marches on the Dallas County courthouse, which were largely peaceful and nonviolent because Sheriff James Clark was very careful in not provoking the demonstrators. In nearby Marion, however, a civil rights demonstrator, Jimmie Lee Jackson, was killed by Alabama state troopers. The death of Jackson provided the impetus to a proposal by SNCC and SCLC leaders that a mass march should be conducted from Selma to the state capitol in Montgomery, culminating in the presentation of a list of grievances to the governor.

When Governor Wallace got wind of the proposed march, he ordered an immediate ban. King wanted to postpone the march until a federal judge had voided the governor's ban, but he was unable to restrain the marchers who set off on their journey on March 7. The marchers got as far as the Edmund Pettus Bridge, the main pathway out of Selma, where Sheriff Clark's deputies, reinforced by state troopers, were waiting and spoiling for a fight. As so many times before, the nation was treated to another assault against peaceful marchers. Attacking the demonstrators from front and sides, state troopers, followed by Sheriff Clark's deputies on horseback giving the rebel yell, charged the protesters, swinging bullwhips, chains, cattle prods, and rubber tubing wrapped in barbed wire. Few demonstrators held their ground under this onslaught, except John Lewis, who was beaten to the ground and suffered another skull fracture.[30] Dazed and disoriented by savage blows and the effects of tear gas, the protesters fled in panic.

Having instigated the march, King was torn whether he should desist or urge his troops once more into the breach. The message from Washington, however, was not encouraging. President Johnson insisted that the march was illegal and should not be resumed. King was now caught between the passions of his followers, especially the younger activists, and the liberal establishment in Washington, which did not want to see a repeat of "Bloody Sunday." A compromise was finally worked out between King and Washington by which the marchers would cross the Pettus Bridge, stop when commanded to do so by state troopers, worship briefly, and then return to Selma. The problem with this agreement was that King, who did not want to lose face with the protesters, did not share it with his followers, so that when he ordered the marchers to return after having crossed the bridge and prayed, many people in the crowd were stunned, feeling betrayed and abandoned.

The abrupt termination of the Selma to Montgomery march drove further divisions into the civil rights movement. SNCC had made its opposition to King's strategies quite clear for some time, criticizing him for his nonviolent tactics and his tendency to hug the national limelight after SNCC activists had done the hard organizational work and laid the groundwork that made many of the mass protests possible. The failed march on the capital, however, prompted President Johnson to request a voting rights bill from Congress on March 15, 1965. In his address to a joint session of Congress, Johnson made reference to the recent violence in Selma and promised that his proposed voter registration bill would fully enfranchise blacks and put an end to the crippling legacy of bigotry and injustice in America. Only six days after the failed march on Montgomery, King resumed his plan to march, by whatever means, to the state capital to present a list of grievances to the governor. "Walk together, children, don't you get weary, and it will lead us to the Promised Land," King told his followers. Protected by the federalized Alabama National Guard, a large crowd made the long fifty-mile march to Montgomery, arriving at the grounds of the capitol on March 25. King spoke eloquently to the large interracial crowd, pointedly asking, "How long will it take?" He answered, "Not long, because you will reap what you sow. How long? Not long, because the arm of the moral universe is long but it bends toward justice. How long? Not long. Because mine eyes have seen the glory of the coming of the Lord."[31]

On August 3, 1965, the House of Representatives passed a voting rights bill by a large majority, and the next day the Senate followed suit. The Voting Rights Act prohibited states from enacting or maintaining restrictions that would prevent eligible voters from registering and casting their votes. Federal officers were authorized to overrule local registrars if there was compelling reason to suspect racial discrimination. Federal intervention could also be triggered in those counties in which fewer than fifty percent of black voters had cast ballots in the last presidential election. The act put real clout into the hands of black voters. By the end of the decade two-thirds of the eligible black voters were registered in the South.

The Voting Rights Act coincided with a host of legislation passed by Congress in 1965 under the liberal banners of the Great Society. Some historians have argued that the drive toward black equality would not have been possible without the support of liberal-minded reformers. How long would the tenuous relationship between white liberals and black civil rights advocates continue to operate on a level of mutual support? The answer, as it would turn out, was only as long as the civil rights movement remained within the peaceful framework of incremental reform envisioned by white liberals. By 1965, however, more radical voices in the black movement were challenging Martin Luther King's peaceful and integrationist approach, countering it with strident demands for black power, revolution, and separatism.

An ominous sign that the civil rights movement might become derailed from its largely peaceful track came shortly after the passage of the Voting Rights Act. On the evening of August 11, a highway patrolman stopped a black man for speeding in Los Angeles and arrested him for drunken driving. The arrest brought out a small crowd, which, in turn, brought more officers on the scene. A pattern of baiting the police, followed by police overreaction—a pattern that would repeat itself over the next few years in other cities—began to develop. A bystander was mistakenly struck by the police with a billy club. A young black woman was dragged into the middle of the street for allegedly spitting at the police. After the police left, an agitated black crowd hurled stones at passing white motorists and set cars on fire. The police delayed its response and further inflamed the people on the street. The next evening, violence flared up again, followed by window smashing, looting, and arson. On the morning of the third day, August 13, a huge crowd gathered in the business district of Watts, a black section of Los Angeles, and began looting.[32] Police delays emboldened the looters, who now fanned out into other areas. Around noon, firebombing began, and it became clear that the rioters wanted to assault whites and drive them out of the ghetto. The police asked for reinforcement from the National Guard and, making liberal use of their fire power, the combined forces descended on Watts and ruthlessly restored order. Over four thousand people were arrested, a sizable part of Watts had gone up in flames, and thirty-four people were dead. Approximately thirty-five million dollars in damage had been inflicted.

The Watts riot was followed only one day later by another black ghetto uprising on the west side of Chicago, and a few days later by racial violence in Springfield, Massachusetts. The summer of 1966 brought further racial violence in Chicago, Cleveland, Dayton, Milwaukee, and San Francisco; but the most destructive wave of racial violence swept over a hundred American cities in the summer of 1967. The worst occurred in Newark, New Jersey, where the black ghetto erupted in a virtual civil war against the lily white and corrupt city administration. Hardly a day seemed to go by without some racial disturbance in America's urban communities. Television cameras showed blacks rioting, vandalizing property, and venting their rage on "Whitey." Slogans like "Kill whitey," "Burn Baby Burn," "Black Power," "Long Live Malcolm X," were replacing earlier slogans of "We Shall Overcome," "Black and White Together," "Keep Your Eyes on the Prize," or "I'm Gonna Sit at the Welcome Table."

What accounts for this drastic change of attitude? The Kerner Commission, a National Advisory Commission on Civil Disorders appointed by Lyndon Johnson in 1967, later reported that these civil disorders were caused by white racism, creating the conditions—poverty, unemployment, slum housing, and poor education—that made black violence inevitable:

> This is our conclusion: Our nation is moving toward two societies, one black, one white—separate and unequal.... What white Americans have never fully understood—but what the Negro can never forget—is that white society is deeply implicated in the ghetto. White institutions created it, white institutions maintain it, and white society condones it.[33]

The commission also argued that the success and notoriety of black demonstrations in the South strongly resonated with urban blacks in the North and elsewhere in the nation. The Kerner report made reference to "rising expectations" that were set in motion by black demonstrations in the South. The commission recommended the creation of two million jobs over the next three years, massive school desegregation, 600,000 new housing units, and a guaranteed annual income. These unrealistic proposals, made under obvious crisis conditions, were politically naive, coming as they did at a time of rising expenditures on the Vietnam War. Some historians have criticized the Kerner report as a classic case of white liberal guilt because it solely ascribed the blame of the riots to "white racism," without also focusing on the choices and behaviors of the rioters.[34] The Kerner report also made no mention of Johnson's civil rights efforts, nor any accomplishments that the war on poverty had made in improving the condition of black people. The report's ideological message was actually quite clear to careful readers because it made explicit reference to the fact that it was designed to educate whites and not blacks.[35]

For many black activists the Kerner Commission seemed to validate disruptive protests as legitimate responses to poverty. In other words, if instigating crises through mass demonstrations brings about change and concessions from white authority, why not stage them in America's urban ghettos? But in the judgment of most white Americans, there was a difference between a demonstration and a riot. When Martin Luther King took his movement to Chicago in 1966 under the banner of the "Chicago Freedom Movement," he used peaceful methods to try to compel the city to take meaningful steps to solve urban decay, unemployment, and housing discrimination. His failure to accomplish these objectives peacefully played right into the hands of radical activists intoxicated by their own rhetoric of black power and violent revolution. King was tragically caught between white backlash and black radicalism, losing control over the direction of the civil rights movement and sinking into increasing despair.

The sense that nonviolent protests were futile was widely shared by members of SNCC and CORE, especially after yet another violent assault on a peaceful marcher, James Meredith, who had set out on a peaceful march from Memphis, Tennessee, to Jackson, Mississippi. As soon as Meredith, who had broken the color bar at the University of Mississippi, entered the state of Mississippi, he was shot by a Klansman and seriously injured. This incident, one in a long line of violent assaults on peaceful protesters, was the straw that broke the camel's back for many civil rights activists, who determined that from now on different and more radical tactics had to be employed to break the yoke of oppression.

4. Black Nationalism

By 1965 black people had attained legal and constitutional rights that had formerly been enjoyed only by whites. The older civil rights leaders wanted to bring African Americans under the protection of the Constitution as coequal partners with whites. Barriers to integration had toppled between 1961 and 1965, but there was a sense among the younger and more radical black activists that the civil rights movement, to maintain its momentum, had to go beyond legal equality to economic justice, the development of racial pride, and even separation from the white community. By pushing beyond equality and integration, the movement, in Harvard Sitkoff's judgment, "created aspirations it could not fulfill and developed a new sense of racial pride that verged on being black racism."[36]

The integrationist ideal expressed in Martin Luther King's "I Have a Dream" speech gave way to visions of black power or black nationalism. The key was race. Radical African Americans saw themselves primarily as African rather than American; their self-definition was racial, ethnic, and, in a vaguer sense, nationalistic. They did not want to participate equally in the American dream but wanted to live in a separate but equal community of blacks. Perceiving themselves to be a different race of people that would never be accepted as equals in white America, they demanded to live an independent and separate existence in America.

Malcolm X and the Nation of Islam defined themselves as members of a different ancestral blood community, and so did radical activists in CORE and SNCC.[37] But how did these radical activists propose to live their own separate existence in America? The more extreme nationalists called for either reparations and exclusive black territories, ethnically cleansed of white people, or they demanded relocation to Africa. These solutions, of course, were politically impossible because the United States was unwilling and unable to divest itself of sovereign territory, nor were African states willing to accept sizable numbers of Americanized black people. If such extreme demands were impossible, was some political separatism even conceivable in America? This consisted in envisioning a kind of Huguenot solution of self-governing and culturally self-sufficient black communities within the United States. Many Black Panthers favored such more or less hermetically sealed black communities. It did not occur to them, however, that separatism was inconsistent with the nation's heritage of assimilation and integration. Calls for separation, coming on the heals of decades of demands for integration, were politically self-defeating, quite apart from seriously weakening the civil rights movement. In addition, the emphasis on black nationalism and black self-identity encouraged strident attitudes that undermined the moral high ground the movement had enjoyed until the mid-sixties. It was also a siren song, as David Burner pointed out, enticing black people to look first to their black skin rather than to their individual resources in improving their lives.[38]

The focus on black power and pride was not in itself unhealthy because it restored pride and stimulated self-discovery leading to self-growth. From a cultural point of view, this emphasis on being black led to the cultivation of lifestyles and forms of expression that were more congenial to black people, styles that did not mimic white preferences. Hair straightening and skin bleaching gave way to natural or curly "Afro" hairstyles, and "soul food" and "soul music" were more expressive of black tastes. It also became increasingly fashionable for blacks to convert to Islam and to abandon Christian in favor of Arabic names, as did the boxer Cassius Clay, who called himself Muhammad Ali, joined the Nation of Islam, a black separatist church, and refused to be inducted into the U.S. Army.

One of the most radical voices of black separatism was Malcolm Little, better known as Malcolm X (1925–1965), who was the most eloquent in preaching the gospel of black nationalism. Tall, agile, handsome, highly intelligent, and light-skinned, Malcolm X rose from obscure and asocial conditions to become a serious contender for black leadership in America. Malcolm X was born in Omaha, Nebraska, in 1925 to the Reverend Earl Little, a militant follower of black nationalism associated with Marcus Garvey. Malcolm claimed that his light black skin was due to the fact that his grandmother, who came from the British West Indies, was raped by a white man. He later confessed that he hated "every drop of that white rapist's blood"[39] that was in him—a very revealing remark about his own racial hatred of whites. Malcolm's childhood experience centered on his father's pastoral activities and the harassment the family was exposed to as a result of his father's crusading activities on behalf of Marcus Garvey's Universal Negro Improvement Association. The family moved to Lansing, Michigan, largely to get away from the white racism of Omaha; but conditions were no better but were, in fact, worse, in Lansing than they had been in Omaha. In 1931 the Reverend Little was allegedly attacked by angry whites, thrown under the wheels of a streetcar, and crushed. Malcolm X later claimed that his mother, cheated out of her husband's insurance policy because the death was listed as a suicide, was unable to take care of her seven children at the height of the Depression and had to be hospitalized in a mental institution. The children became "wards of the state" and were placed in foster homes. After a period of truancy and petty theft, Malcolm ended up in reform school and gradually straightened out. Being bright and inquisitive, he received good grades and was even elected class president by his white peers in seventh grade. In his autobiography he downplayed this honor by claiming that it was probably due to his overeagerness to be whiter than whitey; but that pretense, he said, was deflated once and for all, when his English teacher, Mr. Ostrowski, advised him to forget about becoming a lawyer and settle for carpentry. "Don't misunderstand me, now," Mr. Ostrowski allegedly said, "we all here like you, you know that . . . but you've got to be realistic about being a nigger. A lawyer—that's no realistic goal for a nigger. You need to think about something you *can* be. You're good with your hands—making things, why don't you plan on carpentry."[40] This condescending remark apparently made Malcolm change inside, drawing away from white people and gradually hating them.

With his hopes for an academic career foreclosed, Malcolm left school after the eighth grade and moved to Harlem and later to Boston. By his own admission, he now received an education in street-smarts, selling reefers, running numbers, pimping, and generally living the life of a hipster. He also discovered or rediscovered his African roots, which made him despise the white man. Thinking that he was ever so much more clever than straight white or black people, he quickly overplayed his hand as a hustler and ended up in prison for attempted burglary.

Prison changed Malcolm. He took stock of his wasted life, read voraciously and widely, and thought deeply about the meaning of life as a black man in America. While in prison, he corresponded with Elijah Muhammad, the leader of the Nation of Islam; Malcolm converted and changed his name from Malcolm Little to Malcolm X, the X standing for his unknown black family in Africa.[41] The leader of the Lost Nation of Islam, Elijah Muhammad, taught a gospel of black redemption that he had allegedly learned from an Arab merchant, Wali Farad, who called himself the Mahdi, or the expected one. According to Farad and Muhammad, white "blue-eyed devils" had imposed Christianity on black people in order to make them submissive to whites. In the beginning all humans were born black until a black devil called Yakub genetically created "a bleached-out, White race of people" on the island of Patmos. Over time, these white blue-eyed devils seized power through wealth and deceit. The Jews who were liberated by Moses were also white devils; their claim to be God's chosen people was as absurd as the Christian belief that Jesus was the son of God. Whites have always enslaved and exploited black people, but after six thousand years of oppression their reign on earth will end. Until then, Black Muslims must keep their faith with Allah, purify themselves spiritually, and prepare for the time when Allah will destroy white civilization and restore the black race to its rightful and superior place in the world.

This message of black supremacy resonated with Malcolm X, who dedicated the rest of his life after leaving prison to spreading the gospel according to Elijah Muhammad. He became Elijah's most ardent follower and faithful mouthpiece. By the time Malcolm X joined the Nation of Islam, popularly called the Black Muslims, the movement had already gained a foothold in the ghettos of Chicago, where it originally recruited its following. Those who joined the movement renounced liquor, drugs, tobacco, idleness, sexual promiscuity, and certain foods such as pork, fried chicken, black-eyed peas, and collard greens. Elijah Muhammad laid particular stress on hard work and commercial enterprise as indispensable prerequisites to black success and autonomy.

Before long, Malcolm X became an ambitious speechmaker and proselytizer second to none. His message was one of uncompromising black nationalism and hatred for all white people. The idea of integration, he preached, was an illusion, and Martin Luther King, who was proclaiming it, was nothing more than an Uncle Tom. The March on Washington, which Malcolm X observed at close range, was the "farce on Washington." As Malcolm put it, "No *sane* black man really wants integration! No *sane* white man really wants integration! No sane black man really believes that the white man ever will give the black man anything more than token integration. No! The honorable Elijah Muhammad teaches that for the black man in America the only solution is complete *separation* from the white man!"[42]

One hate-drenched message after another rolled from the lips of this intoxicated true believer, causing alarm and consternation not only in the white community but also among the traditional leadership of the civil rights movement. Malcolm X mocked the siren song of "We shall overcome some day" and found the spectacle of black civil rights leaders marching arm in arm with their white oppressors positively revolting. But Malcolm X was too bright to believe Elijah Muhammad's doctrine in the manner of a simplistic and obedient follower indefinitely. In March 1964 he broke with the Nation of Islam primarily because he had outgrown its overly cautious and passive approach to black oppression, but also because he discovered that Elijah Muhammad was not the pure prophet Malcolm thought he was. Launching out on his own, Malcolm drifted, searched for new approaches, and slightly tempered his rabid anti-white hatred. A trip to Mecca, where he encountered Muslims of all sorts of different racial groups, seems to have prompted a belated epiphany that some white people might actually be good people. He came back from Mecca less strident but as uncertain as ever as to how black Americans should organize themselves in white America. His new Organization for Afro-American Unity still stressed separation, but few black Americans were drawn to it. Moreover, the followers of the Nation of Islam viewed Malcolm X as an apostate who deserved to be killed. Fear of assassination haunted Malcolm X, and on February 21, 1965, three Black Muslims did in fact kill him at a rally in Harlem. Transfigured by martyrdom, his followers would make a maudlin cult to their fallen hero. This was especially true of the young black civil rights activists, who would embrace his gospel of black nationalism.

Malcolm X's followers and admirers in the civil rights movement were Stokely Carmichael (Kwame Toure), H. "Rap" Brown (Jamil Abdullah Al-Amin), LeRoi Jones (Amiri Baraka), Eldridge Cleaver, Huey Newton, and Bobby Seale. Whether they belonged to the Nation of Islam, SNCC, CORE, or the Black Panthers, these radical activists were united in their hatred of white America, which they condemned as racist and oppressive. No longer content to demonstrate peacefully, they advocated striking back at their oppressors. This turn toward black power, gradually building up after endless bloody encounters with white bigots, developed in 1965 and 1966. SNCC is a case in point. The original members of SNCC, black and white, were reform liberals who believed in racial integration, nonviolence, a supportive federal government, and the possibility and desirability of joining the middle class. Stokely Carmichael, who took over the leadership of SNCC in 1966, purged whites from the organization, abandoned nonviolence, and preached a strident form of Pan-Africanism.

Born in Trinidad in 1941, Carmichael came to America in 1962, living in Harlem. A bright and precocious student, he did well at the prestigious Bronx High School of Science. While in high school, he read communist literature and joined the Young Socialists. After completing high school, he attended the predominantly black Howard University, where he got involved in a student affiliate of SNCC. In 1961, he joined the Freedom Riders and was arrested in Jackson, Mississippi, and sentenced to spend time at the notoriously harsh Parchman Prison. His prison experience, combined with the violence he encountered in his subsequent activities in registering blacks in Mississippi and Alabama, convinced Carmichael that nonviolent protest was ineffective and should be abandoned in favor of "black power." The term "black power" was proclaimed by Carmichael after being released from prison at Greenwood, Mississippi, when he addressed a crowd of black activists and said:

This is the twenty-seventh time I have been arrested—and I ain't going to jail no more! ... The only way we gonna stop them white men from whippin' us is to take over. We been saying freedom for six years and we ain't got nothin'. What we gonna start saying now is Black Power![43]

Exhorting the crowd to chant "black power," the cry went up again and again for black power, whatever that meant. As a psychological slogan, the term would resonate over the next years. After Carmichael successfully helped registering black voters in Lowndes County, Alabama, he also founded an African American Party, the County Freedom Organization, which took as its symbol a black panther. The symbol of the black panther, originally associated with the Lowndes Black Panther Party, was used by Huey Newton and Bobby Seale. In 1966, as previously mentioned, Stokely Carmichael became chairman of SNCC and promptly expelled all whites from its ranks. He then baited white America by unleashing incendiary but also colorful slogans that threatened revolution and urban guerrilla war. Carmichael was more of a celebrity hound and flamboyant poser than a creditable revolutionary. He had no clue how SNCC could translate its incendiary slogans into political practice, which was just as well because it would have meant certain defeat in a country that widely rejected his Mau Mauing tactics. Even within the civil rights movement there was little support for Carmichael's ineffectual bravado and blustering. In 1966 a poll revealed that black Americans strongly favored integration rather than black separatism, and that King outpolled Carmichael among black rank-and-file voters by a ratio of 88 percent to 19 percent. Carmichael spent his brief tenure as chairman of SNCC grandstanding, speechifying, and traveling on a pilgrimage to Havana, Cuba, where he hobnobbed with Fidel Castro and proclaimed his support for third world revolution against American oppression:

> We share with you a common struggle, it becomes increasingly clear; we have a common enemy. Our enemy is white Western imperialist society. Our struggle is to overthrow this system that feeds itself and expands itself through the economic and cultural exploitation of non-white, non-Western peoples—of the Third World.[44]

Carmichael resigned his chairmanship in SNCC in 1967, briefly joined the Black Panther Party, and left the United States for Guinea, where he died in 1998. The man who took over the moribund SNCC organization after Carmichael was H. "Rap" Brown, known as "Rap" because of his ability to rap or communicate with his black brothers on the streets. His contribution to radical theory, as Joseph Conlin put it, was the slogan "Burn, Baby Burn!"[45] Brown, like Carmichael before him, advocated black guerrilla warfare in the ghettos of America. After inciting riots in Dayton, East St. Louis, and Cambridge, Maryland, he was arrested and jailed. Released on bail, he was rearrested for carrying a gun across state lines and was sentenced to five years in prison. While appealing his conviction, he violated parole again by traveling to California and giving incendiary speeches. The 1968 Civil Rights Act had a provision in it called the "Rap Brown Amendment," which referred to his recent violation and specified that it was illegal to cross state lines and incite a riot. Brown's trouble with the law continued over many years. In 1971 he was captured after a shoot-out during a burglary and sentenced to prison in 1973. While in prison, he converted to the Nation of Islam and took the name Jamil Abdullah Amin. After his release in 1976, he opened a grocery store in Atlanta and assumed leadership of the Community Mosque. His troubles with the law continued despite his apparent devout life as a Black Muslim. In 1995 he was arrested on assault and weapons possession charges and in 2000 he was arrested for murder.

With such sterling leadership, it should not be surprising that SNCC gradually faded from the civil rights movement. The same was true of CORE under the leadership of Floyd McKissick, who had replaced James Farmer. Casting out whites and championing black nationalism, CORE steadily lost members and funding.

The most feared black group, however, was the Black Panther Party, founded in Oakland, California, in October 1966 by Huey Newton and Bobby Seale. Oakland born and bred, Huey Newton was a product of the ghetto; he was strong, street-smart, and angry. Teaming up with Bobby Seale, another enraged product of ghetto life, the two wrote a ten-point program for the Black Panther Party, including such demands as black self-determination, decent housing, an end to police brutality, educational opportunities, peace and justice. All of these demands sounded eminently liberal, except the demand for exemptions from military service, an Afro-centric educational curriculum that exposed white oppression, the release of all black prisoners from American prisons, all black juries trying blacks, and territory exclusively reserved for black people. Having drafted a party program, the two men then opened an office in Oakland in January 1967, with Newton serving as minister of defense and *Führer*. The party recruited primarily street thugs from the Oakland ghetto and delighted in confronting the hated white establishment, especially its police "pigs." Inasmuch as the Panthers had an ideology, it was derived from Frantz Fanon's book *Wretched of the Earth* and a smattering of communist doctrines.

Joseph Conlin's judgment that the Panthers were street-gang thugs masquerading under the cover of black nationalism and "black is beautiful" is essentially correct. Before he plunged into radical politics, Newton was known on the streets of Oakland as a "bad-ass motherfucker." He was also a drug addict and most likely a murderer. On the other hand, Newton was not without a certain flair for the flamboyant or the-atrical, making sure that Panthers wore combat jackets, jackboots, raised their clenched fists and shouted "Black Power" or "Power to the People." In Oakland, and subsequently other cities, the Panthers formed armed patrols monitoring the behav-ior of the white police in the ghetto, ostensibly to prevent them from brutalizing black people. The bravado of the Panthers was widely applauded by ghetto residents and by white radical and liberal sympathizers. In fact, an unhealthy symbiosis devel-oped in the late 1960s between some white liberals and the Panthers. The conduit between the Panthers and their white sympathizers was Eldridge Cleaver, a serial rapist who had spent time in San Quentin, was released in 1966, and joined the Black Panthers. While in prison, Cleaver had written a series of autobiographical accounts of his wasted life, his struggle with his own self-identity, and his hatred of White America. His writings came to the attention of the editor of *Ramparts*, a radical left-wing journal, who was so impressed by what he read that he passed it on to several influential literati such as the novelist Norman Mailer and the literary critic Leslie Fiedler. With such major names behind him, Cleaver's autobiographical rantings were published in 1968, under the title *Soul On Ice*. The book was a radical provoca-tion. It indicted white people for robbing black people of their real identity and mak-ing them slaves of an oppressive capitalist system. Cleaver also indicted whites for robbing black men of their manhood, which in his mind justified his rapes of white women as an insurrectionary act: "I felt I was getting revenge. From the site of the act of rape, consternation spreads outwardly in concentric circles. I wanted to send waves of consternation throughout the white race."[46]

Consternation he certainly spread among the white race, except sympathetic lib-erals and fellow comrades on the radical left. *Soul On Ice* became a best-seller, was widely assigned in college courses, and is still in print today. In his introduction to *Soul On Ice*, the critic Maxwell Geismar praised the book as a "heroic work of con-temporary fiction that "rakes our favorite prejudices with the savage claws of his [Cleaver's] prose."[47] The book, according to Geismar, is full of hidden depths, secret kinds of sexual mysticism, and wonderful ironic descriptions; Geismar even found a kind of "adolescent innocence," the innocence of genius, in Cleaver's insurrectionary rape ideology.[48] The *New York Times Book Review* referred to *Soul On Ice* as "a collection of essays straight out of Dante's *Inferno;* the *Nation* called it "beautifully written, brilliant"; the *New York Review of Books* found rare honesty and even gentleness in it; the *New York Times* declared it one of the ten best books of the year; and Yale professor Richard Gilman, outdoing everyone in smarmy adulation, praised the book as unsparing, tough, lyrical, and quite beyond the comprehension of white literary standards because the "Negro doesn't feel the way whites do, nor does he think like whites."[49]

This extraordinary outpouring of liberal white guilt, as shameless as it was embarrassing, has been immortalized by Tom Wolfe in *Radical Chic,* in which he lampooned the avant-garde literati and its enchantment with uncouth barbarians coming out of the cold and hobnobbing with the cultural elite.[50] There is nothing new here, of course, because one need only turn back the pages of history to those delightful tea parties given by Munich society matrons, inviting the *Führer* and his entourage—brownshirts, whips, revolvers, and all—to a bit of tea, schnapps, and pastries. Wolfe's account of the composer Leonard Bernstein hosting a soiree for the Panthers in New York is reminiscent of Carola Hoffman, known as Hitler Mutti (mommy) inviting the *Führer* to tea. Born of a combination of guilt, suspended critical faculties, and enervated instincts, such acts of swooning over revolutionaries tell us a great deal about the chaotic sixties. The Panthers, of course, basking in such adoration by misguided white admirers, milked it for all it was worth.

The reality, however, was more disturbing. Bloody shoot-outs with the police were the direct outcome of the ideology of "armed revolt." FBI director J. Edgar Hoover declared the Panthers outlaws, had them infiltrated, watched, wiretapped, and harassed. In 1967 Huey Newton was sentenced to fifteen years for killing an Oakland police officer, whose gun appeared to have gone off accidentally in a scuffle. Coming after notorious Black Panther demonstrations in the state capitol, during which armed Panthers invaded the California chamber, state authorities had lost all patience with the Panthers. Newton was sentenced for manslaughter in May 1970, but was subsequently released. Two prominent Panthers, Fred Hampton and Mark Clark, were killed in a shoot-out with police in Chicago in December 1969. Although the Panthers changed tactics from armed revolt to community organizing, ghetto social work and nonviolent protest, the long arm of the law continued to dog them. Internal divisions of the movement further weakened the Panthers. The more than thirty chapters nationwide had always acted independently. The Oakland chapter, for example, acted independently from the Black Panther Party headquartered in Los Angeles; in 1968 the Los Angeles branch merged with SNCC to form LA-SNCC. Angela Davis, a prominent student of the radical professor Herbert Marcuse, had joined LA-SNCC, then the Oakland Branch, and then the Communist Party. Her shifting allegiances, ideological squabbles and run-ins with the law are fairly typical of black activism in the late 1960s. By 1972 the Black Panther movement had splintered beyond repair after a dispute between Huey Newton and Eldridge Cleaver. Cleaver fled the country to escape the IRS, Newton went to UC Santa Cruz, where he received a Ph.D. in social philosophy from the department of "Consciousness" studies; Seale founded the Peace and Freedom Party, was unsuccessfully indicted for murder in 1971, and failed in his bid for mayor of Oakland in 1973. The surreal life of sixties radicals would not be complete without tracing their bizarre futures. Newton did not take advantage of his Ph.D. but repeatedly clashed with the law on weapons charges and embezzlement of public funds. In 1989 he was killed on the streets of Oakland as a result of a drug dispute. Cleaver converted to Christianity and founded Eldridge Cleaver Crusaders; he also patented a new design for men's trousers that had no zippers but a pouch and tube for the testicles and penis so that the male organ could be liberated. In the 1980s, Cleaver joined the Church of the Reverend Sun Myung Moon, discovered that God dwelled in man's sperm, and then became a Mormon. In his obituary, the *New York Times* noted, in addition to his bizarre metamorphoses already mentioned, that Cleaver, finally, *even* became a Republican.

5. The End of the Second Reconstruction

Nothing could have been more calculated in losing white support of civil rights than the threats and insults black radicals hurled at white people in America. By using race as the major criterion of self-identity, these black nationalists not only lost support among white liberals, but they also played right into the hands of white segregationists. Many whites blamed black radicals for the racial riots that had turned major cities into war-torn battlefields. By 1968 white America was in an ugly mood, unwilling to make further concessions to African Americans, especially when the demands were backed up by threats of civic disorders. Lyndon Johnson, who had done so much for civil rights, felt personally insulted by the ingratitude of the black community and its moderate leaders for being unable to stem the violence. He told Joseph Califano, his aide for domestic affairs, that he was afraid that "Negroes will end up pissing in the aisles of the Senate," and making fools of themselves, the . . . way they did after the Civil War and during Reconstruction. He was worried, Califano remembered, that just as government was moving to help them, "the Negroes will once again take unwise actions out of frustration, impatience, and anger." He feared that the riots would make it more difficult to pass Great Society legislation and would threaten the gains the administration had already made.[51] Johnson had always distrusted King before, but when the civil rights leader continued to accuse his administration of not doing enough for black civil rights, the president was infuriated.

Johnson did not fully realize that the civil rights movement, which had plunged the nation into a social crisis, was itself in a state of crisis by 1966. Why this should have been so has been much debated by historians. As a "resident alien" and graduate student at the time, I was much impressed by the gains black people had made between 1960 and 1965; and in retrospect, these gains were real enough. Racial discrimination was definitely receding, black income levels were rising, and black people had been fully enfranchised and brought under the protection of the Constitution. Yet it was precisely these gains that raised further expectations of even swifter progress, which the liberal establishment was unable to satisfy. All too many black people, especially young radicals, were drawn into the vortex of 1960s protest and swept away by unrealistic expectations of instant redemption. In the case of black people this centered on the expectation that two hundred years of slavery, discrimination, and economic inequality could be solved by government legislation within a decade, if not sooner. Such expectations made everyday inequality feel even worse. Black radicals asked why Washington did not do something immediately about persisting patterns of poverty, discrimination, racial stereotyping, and police brutality?

Neither the federal government nor the civil rights community knew how to proceed on civil rights issues after 1965, and in what direction. By 1968 the black civil rights movement had reached a complete impasse on how to proceed. Radicals in SNCC, CORE, and the Black Panthers acted like bantam roosters crowing incendiary slogans, thereby infuriating whites and splintering the movement itself. As previously shown, civil rights organizations had never successfully coordinated their goals and strategies. The Southern Christian Leadership Conference was never well managed either, being held together by King's charisma, oratorical skills, and growing international reputation. In 1964, King had received the Nobel Prize and *Time* magazine made him Man of the Year, but to black radicals, these honors made him a white establishment figure and therefore irrelevant to the revolution.

By 1967–68 King was caught in a crossfire of white reaction and black revolutionary fervor, uncertain how to proceed. He was dogged by the FBI, distrusted by the president, and steadily losing support from liberals, including Jewish liberals, who were outraged by black radical antisemitism. When King mounted the Chicago Freedom Movement, aimed at improving housing conditions and employment in Chicago, he crashed against the hard rocks of Mayor Daley's political machine. Although King and Daley reached a "Summit Agreement," Daley made only empty promises that were not subject to any enforcement whatsoever. A Gallup poll at the time showed that King was no longer one of the ten most admired men in America.[52] Spied upon by the FBI's COINTELPRO, a program designed to infiltrate communist organizations and hate groups, unable to bring together squabbling black civil rights groups, King was a distraught man who no longer expected that the promised land was just around the corner. He had clearly taken on too much, and he felt increasingly isolated and depressed. It is at this point that he began to commit serious tactical errors.

In order to parry the threat from the civil rights left, particularly SNCC and CORE, King began to attack capitalism and demanded a nationwide redistribution of wealth from the rich to the poor. He also called on the Johnson administration to end the war in Vietnam because it was immoral and disproportionately fought by poor minorities, especially African Americans. In December 1967, King dropped another bombshell by announcing a Poor People's march on the nation's capital, threatening to "cripple the operations of an oppressing society." Hundreds of thousands, he promised, would descend on Washington, camp out in the Mall, and refuse to leave until the government gave in to the protesters' demands. The demands included, among other things, a thirty-billion-dollar antipoverty appropriation, a guaranteed annual income, construction funding for 500,000 units of low income housing, and government support of full employment for all Americans.[53] President Johnson was adamantly opposed to the march on several grounds. In the first place, the spectacle of a quarter of a million poor people marching on the capital threatened to undermine his war on poverty, which he had proclaimed to be a great success. Second, Johnson felt intimidated by King's belligerent rhetoric and his open threat to cause civil disorder if his demands were not met. SCLC had made it clear that government refusal of or inaction on its demands would be met by national boycotts of major industries. There was also a third reason why the president regarded King's campaign as unacceptable, and that reason was Vietnam. By 1967 the United States government was spending twenty-four billion dollars annually on the Vietnam War, and there was no end in sight. King was asking the government to spend more money on poverty than what was being spent on Vietnam; he asked, in effect, that poverty appropriations be increased by 300 percent. Why King would have put forward such an unrealistic proposal is not entirely clear, but some of the reasons can be found in the hyper-inflated expectations of the late 1960s, the internal conflicts in the civil rights movement, and King's misreading of the Kerner report, which he thought to be a further liberal mandate for civil rights reform.

Although King often expressed fears of a coming backlash, he seriously misread the political barometer. Having been driven by a sense of urgency for over a decade, sensing that further concessions could still be wrung from white America, King simply could not stop; he had to push on, no matter what. The march on the capital was set for April 22, the day when Congress planned to reconvene. King had premonitions of impending doom, frequently talking about his own coming death. The end came on April 4, 1968, when King was gunned down by an assassin, James Earl Ray, in Memphis, Tennessee. King had gone to Memphis to support a garbage workers' strike, but the peaceful march he hoped to lead turned into a riot, forcing the civil rights leader to withdraw from the march. King was unaware that he had been stalked by a white racist, James Earl Ray, who was probably a hired assassin. King's death touched off an orgy of urban violence across the country as black Americans vented their rage on the streets of America. It was not a good testimonial for the fallen leader, who had counseled nonviolent actions to the very end. The night before his death, King had said that he had been to the mountain top, seen the promised land, but that he might not make it there with his black brothers. He proved to be tragically right.[54]

With King's death the Second Reconstruction came to an end. The March on Washington went ahead as planned, but it turned out to be a miserable failure. Ralph Abernathy, a good man but an ineffectual leader, soldiered on in King's place. In May the marchers constructed a ramshackle shantytown just off the Mall near the Lincoln Memorial, in Washington D.C. Bad weather, inadequate facilities, and crime tore into this makeshift facility, forcing the police to close it down on June 22, 1968. The nation hardly noticed; it had its fill of protests, demonstrations, and riots.

Civil rights organizations fell on hard times after King's death. The Southern

Christian Leadership Conference carried on into the 1970s with greatly reduced funds and much weaker leadership, first under Reverend Ralph Abernathy, and then under a series of even weaker men who transformed SCLC into an interracial civil rights advocacy group. CORE marginalized itself with its strident demands of separatism and faded from the scene in the late 1970s. SNCC completely disintegrated in the early 1970s, a victim of its own delusions of grandeur. The Black Panthers, as previously mentioned, embarked on a similar road to destruction. Of all the civil rights organizations of the 1960s only the National Association for the Advancement of Colored People (NAACP) and the Urban League survived and even flourished in the wake of the stormy 1960s. Both opted for the politics of realism rather than revolution, concentrating on bread-and-butter issues for black people and on legal solutions to the problems still plaguing them such as unemployment and racial discrimination.

The black civil rights movement was like a rolling stone that set in motion other national protests: antiwar demonstrations, student protests, the feminist movement, hippie power, gay power, brown power, red power, among others. It furnished the rhetorical slogans and the tactics of protest: sit-downs, marches, demonstrations, occupations of land and buildings, boycotts, and so forth. Until 1965, the civil rights movement, being largely nonviolent, held the moral high ground, but the emergence of black nationalism undermined that foundation and caused a white backlash that brought the Second Reconstruction to an end. The civil rights movement had reached a fork in the road: one path led to further violence and black separatism, the other to consolidation of rights achieved and progressive reforms yet unattained. Under the pressure of white backlash and incremental progress, black civil rights leaders chose the second path, hoping that the promised land might yet be reached peacefully.

6

LIBERALISM AT HIGH TIDE
UNDER LYNDON JOHNSON

1. A Texan in the White House

The contrast between handsome and suave Kennedy and burly Lyndon Johnson could not have been greater. Cinematically, it was a crude contrast: Johnson was ebullient, flesh-pressing, hard-drinking, homespun, and profane, while Kennedy was urbane, witty, and sophisticated. Johnson came from west Texas and graduated from San Marcos College, while Kennedy came from Boston and graduated from Harvard. It took the nation quite some time to adjust to the new and insecure president. Johnson was well aware of his own insecurities, which he usually covered up with a veneer of bluster, ingratiating solicitude, downright intimidation, and breathtaking exuberance. The new president was physically intimidating: 6'3" tall, a huge angular head, a massive nose, and big floppy ears that, according to one historian, made him look like an angry African elephant.[1] Beneath the rough exterior, however, perched an insecure ego. Kennedy had once reminded Ken O'Donnell, his personal aide, that in handling Johnson "you are dealing with a very insecure, sensitive man with a huge ego."[2]

Where did this insecurity and big ego come from? It came from Johnson's obscure social background in Stonewall, on the banks of the Pedernales River, which was situated in Blanco County, Texas. His father, a small-time farmer and trader in cattle and real estate, was a hard-drinking and shiftless man with a fondness for tall tales and grand political ambitions. His mother, Rebekah Baines, came from a well-to-do family with social pretensions. She had attended Baylor University and saw herself as a cultured and romantic southern lady with literary ambitions. She expected that her son Lyndon would become a cultivated and sophisticated gentleman. Rebekah's marriage was not a happy one, and it may well be true that she saw in Lyndon a kind of delegate who could carry out a mission she had failed to achieve in her own life. In Lyndon, she probably saw a substitute for a dead father, an unsuccessful marriage, and a failed career. She also gave her son conditional love, rewarding him with love when he met her expectations and withdrawing it when he did not. As Doris Kearns pointed out, love alternatively given and taken away would become a pattern in Lyndon Johnson's own relationships. It was called the "Johnson freeze-out."[3] Rebekah Johnson was dreamy, romantic, and bookish; by contrast, Sam Johnson was earthy and practical. The son overidealized his mother but was more eager to resemble his

father. Although Sam Johnson served in the Texas state legislature, he never succeeded in Rebekah's eyes; she saw him for what he was: a small-time farmer and a bitter disappointment as a husband.

Out of this parental dynamic emerged the split Johnsonian persona, characterized
by admiration for cowboy folklore, exaggerated manliness, love of politics, but also
a desire for sophistication and grace that his mother expected and the rough-hewn
Texas culture prohibited. All of his life Johnson at once had an aversion to men of
culture as well as a concealed respect for them. The test of manliness for Johnson was
shooting animals, driving cars recklessly, and boozing hard. He would later delight
in putting down "cultured" people by acting in a deliberately uncouth manner, using
foul language and crude gestures, humiliating subordinates by discussing issues
while he was sitting on the toilet, and even displaying his sexual organs for shock
effect.[4]

By the time we see him at San Marcos College we can already glimpse the traits of
the future politician. He was active in student government, edited the student newspaper, became a prize-winning debater, and attached himself to people with
power—the president, college officials, and professors. Two other Johnsonian habits
were also on display during his college years: doing people grand favors and expecting to collect on them later on and a meddlesome tendency to control or order about
people "for their own good." After graduating from San Marcos College, Johnson
went briefly into teaching elementary school before going to work for a young congressman, Richard Kleberg, whom he followed to Washington in the winter of 1931.
It was the height of the Great Depression, yet Johnson's spirits were high. Like the
constituents he represented, Johnson believed in the American dream of wealth and
success, a dream he would cling to tenaciously and that would tide him over future
hardships and safeguard the belief that every American could succeed in life through
hard work, treating people generously and courteously, and living a clean life. Since
Kleberg often neglected his congressional duties, Johnson basically managed the
day-to-day affairs of the congressman's office. For Johnson, Washington was a new
world, a learning experience that would never leave him. He diligently studied everything there was to know about government, including things that were not mentioned in the textbooks—that is, what was going on behind the scenes—the gossips,
rumors, scandals, skeletons in the closet, and so forth. He quickly mastered how
Congress actually functioned and generally made himself useful to his party. He also
looked to people who could be useful to him such as Sam Rayburn and Wright Pat-
man, two Texas congressmen who had served with his father in the Texas legislature.
During the four years Johnson worked for Kleberg, he developed a taste for power
that would never leave him. His aim was set: to become a Washington insider and
remain at the center of power for the rest of his life. In 1934, while still an aide to Kleberg, he married Claudia Taylor, a cheerful and loyal companion who would suffer
his many marital indiscretions with remarkable Christian forbearance. Given his
voracious appetites, it should not be surprising that Johnson frequently strayed
throughout his marriage. He carried on a long love affair with Madeleine Brown, a
woman from Dallas who bore him a son. He also had numerous casual liaisons with

various women, including a sexual tryst with a secretary in the Oval Office.[5] His wife, whom he affectionately called Lady Bird, silently and stoically endured Johnson's philandering and even tried to justify his indiscretions after he had died by telling a television producer, "You have to understand, my husband loved people—all people. And half the people in the world are women. You don't think I could have kept my husband away from half the people."[6]

In 1935 Franklin Roosevelt appointed Johnson director of the Texas branch of the National Youth Alliance (NYA), a New Deal organization designed to provide jobs for young people. He used this position as a springboard to promote his own political prospects. In April 1937 he was elected to fill a congressional vacancy that had opened up with the death of Texas congressman James Buchanan. He was subsequently reelected to five successive Congresses, serving in the House from 1937 until 1949. In 1941 Johnson ran unsuccessfully for the Senate against the incumbent governor "Pappy" (Wilbert L.) O'Daniel, and that same year, just five days after the Japanese attacked Pearl Harbor, he became the first congressman to enlist in the armed forces. Johnson spent less than a year in the navy because Roosevelt issued an executive order that specified that elected officials should serve in the capital rather than in the trenches. In 1948, Johnson ran again for the Senate and beat former governor Coke Stevenson in a runoff primary by a mere eighty-seven votes. The small margin of victory earned Johnson the title "Landslide Lyndon" by those who suspected that he had stolen the election. An investigation into the disputed election by a federal court was abruptly halted by Johnson's brilliant legal ally Abe Fortas, who subsequently played a major role in Johnson's political career. Johnson's shenanigans in the 1948 senatorial election, according to Robert A. Caro, the most meticulous Johnson biographer, "violated even the notably loose boundaries of Texas politics."[7] The tactics he employed during the campaign were utterly cynical and unscrupulous; they revealed, in Robert Caro's judgment, that Johnson's "morality was the morality of the ballot box, a morality in which nothing matters but victory, . . . a morality that was amorality."[8]

The scandal associated with Johnson's 1948 senatorial victory was not the first nor would it be the last scandal in Lyndon Johnson's rise to power. For some time, Johnson had financed his campaigns and had raised money for the Democrats by allying himself with Brown & Root, a Texas contracting firm. In return for campaign funds, Johnson arranged lucrative government contracts for Brown & Root. In 1942 the IRS investigated both Johnson and the Texas company and discovered not only that fraudulent methods of campaign funding had been used but also that the company itself had been evading taxes to the tune of over one million dollars. In 1944 the federal investigation was halted as a result of Roosevelt's personal intervention. Although a small fine was imposed on the company, no trial was held and no one went to prison.[9] Johnson's personal wealth, based originally on his acquisition of an Austin radio station, KTBC, was periodically questioned, but he always insisted that he had bought the station for Lady Bird, and that she had expanded the growing Johnson commercial ventures. While Senate leader, Johnson also aroused suspicion by the dubious dealings of his personal protégé, Bobby Baker, who used his connections with Johnson to obtain defense contracts for his own vending-machine company. The accusations swirling around this scandal in 1963 were so serious that President Kennedy considered dropping Johnson from the Democratic ticket. Once in office, however, Johnson called upon Abe Fortas, later Supreme Court Justice, and Clark Clifford, a long-time Democrat insider, to cover up the scandal. Baker was indicted and went to prison in 1971. The career of another Johnson aide, Walter Jenkins, also ended in disgrace when it was discovered that he had made homosexual advances to a young man in the Washington YMCA men's room. Johnson himself always evaded exposure by being able to call on influential lawyers or politicians who owed him a debt and protected him from serious public scandal. Some of these men such as Sam Ervin, Herman Tallmadge, and Daniel Inouye would later hound Richard Nixon and drive him out of office.

Once elected to the Senate, Johnson quickly became a major leader. Throughout the 1940s and 1950s, power in the Senate was exercised by an informal coalition of conservative Republicans and equally conservative Democrats, whose loose working partnership dated back to Roosevelt's expansion of big government, particularly his unsuccessful attempt to pack the Supreme Court. Key committee chairmanships were dominated by members of this informal coalition. The most important figure and the one who taught Johnson most about the nature and dynamics of the Senate was Richard Russell of Georgia, a courteous, quiet, and unassuming southerner with strong pro-segregationist leanings. Another mentor of Johnson was Sam Rayburn, Speaker of the House, fellow Texan, and the man who had persuaded Roosevelt to appoint Johnson as a director of the National Youth Administration. Like an eel, Johnson slid through the inner sanctum of the Senate, learning, adapting, and simply always being there when it counted. Those who saw Lyndon Johnson operate in the Senate in the 1950s would never forget him; he was a dynamo, appearing everywhere—on the Senate floor, in the cloakrooms, caucuses, corridors, and always dealing, cajoling, negotiating, and generally getting things done. The famous "Johnson treatment" consisted in Johnson's invading a man's private space, looking down on him and going nose-to-nose, all the while backslapping, flesh-pressing, and arm-twisting.

In 1953 Johnson became Senate Minority Leader and positioned himself as the leading voice in the Democratic Party. Always on the move, pockets bulging with slips of paper containing useful information, he buttonholed people, pumping them for information or trying to talk them into joining his camp. What he wanted from his followers was absolute loyalty: "I don't want loyalty. I want *loyalty*. I want him to kiss my ass in Macy's window at high noon and tell me it smells like roses. I want his pecker in my pocket."[10] Not even a heart attack in 1955 slowed him down, and Democrats expected him to run for the presidency in 1960. If the Senate had chosen the new president, Johnson would clearly have been the top choice, but he had two major liabilities as a presidential candidate: he lacked charisma and he was a southerner. Kennedy had to choose him as his vice-presidential candidate because he needed to carry Texas and the South, and that is precisely what Johnson did for Kennedy, helping him carry Texas and six other southern states.

Kennedy tried to keep Johnson busy with the trappings of power and periodic minor assignments, but Johnson knew he would always be a marginal outsider in the glittering Kennedy administration. At the time of Kennedy's assassination he was a forgotten man, later describing the vice presidency as "filled with trips around the world, chauffeurs, men saluting, people clapping, chairmanships of councils, but in the end it is nothing. I detested every minute of it."[11]

Following the assassination of John F. Kennedy, Johnson sincerely tried to heal the political and psychological traumas the nation had experienced since November 23, 1963. He told the nation that he would carry out the promises of Kennedy's liberal New Frontier program. He also appointed a commission to investigate the nature and scope of the Kennedy assassination, appointing Earl Warren, the chief justice, to preside over its proceedings and selecting what he regarded as unimpeachable leaders as members of the committee—Allen Dulles, CIA director; John McCloy, a former U.S. high commissioner of Germany; Senator Richard Russell; Republican Senators John Sherman Cooper and Gerald Ford; and Democratic Congressman Hale Boggs. Having moved in a highly charged political atmosphere of intrigue, suspicion, and manipulation, Johnson was obsessed with fears and insecurities about his role as an accidental and unelected president. Although he was a better prepared leader than Kennedy had been, Johnson realized that in the eyes of most Americans he simply did not fit the Camelot image the Kennedys had publicly cultivated. Robert Kennedy, the late president's brother, did not make it any easier on Lyndon Johnson. Bad blood had existed between them for some time, and the next few years only led to further deteriorations in their relationship. In the eyes of Robert Kennedy and other Camelot insiders, Johnson was a usurper, no matter how hard he tried to carry out the fallen martyr's cause. Johnson knew that this was a cross he would have to bear, confessing "I took an oath, I became President. But for millions of Americans I was still illegitimate, a naked man with no presidential covering, a pretender on the throne, and illegal usurper."[12] In 1966 *MacBird,* a dark political satire by Barbara Garson, even insinuated, among other things, that Johnson plotted the murder of John F. Kennedy. This play, though not without its humorous barbs, was a typical 1960s provocation and illustrates how difficult it was for Johnson to forge his own identity and clear himself of the usurper accusation.

In his autobiography, Johnson also admitted that he had a liability as a southerner, seriously doubting whether a southern politician could unite the nation. He pointed out that the metropolitan press of the Eastern seaboard would never find a southerner acceptable as a president. His reference to the Eastern seaboard press was well taken, for Johnson, like Nixon after him, was mercilessly attacked by liberals in the press. Johnson had to submit himself to what he called "endless articles about my style, my clothes, my manners, my accent, and my family," adding that, in addition to these things, there was something else at work—"a deep-seated and far-reaching attitude—a disdain for the south that seems to be woven into the fabric of Northern experience."[13]

Reelection in his own right, perhaps by large mandate, was the obvious cure for Johnson's political condition. Several indicators proved favorable in 1964. After the trauma of November 22, 1963, the country was in a receptive mood for national unity and social reform. The new president skillfully exploited this mood and used his political talents to pass the Kennedy legacy: tax cuts, civil rights legislation, federal aid to education, Medicare, and antipoverty programs. Last but not least, the president's political opponents virtually conceded defeat by picking a conservative Don Quixote who seemed to be tilting at windmills. That man was Barry Goldwater, the Arizona senator whose conservative vision of America did not resonate with the American people in 1964.

The two mainstream parties, having to accommodate a variety of special interests, were, and continue to be, periodically vulnerable to ideologically driven agendas promoted by zealous advocates. Aided by the divisions or indifference of the mainstream membership, these ideological zealots sometimes succeeded in pressing their own stamp on a party. This happened to the Republicans in 1964, and it would happen to the Democrats in 1972. In 1964 the Grand Old Party (GOP), the party of Lincoln and emancipation, was captured by disenchanted conservatives who nominated Barry Goldwater, a political maverick without a strong power base, as their party standard-bearer.[14] Goldwater was a physically attractive and straight-shooting senator from the Valley of the Sun in Phoenix, Arizona. There was nothing complicated about the Arizona senator, as there was about the troubled, torn, and deeply ambiguous Lyndon Johnson. Goldwater was an old-fashioned rugged individualist who believed in the traditional American virtues of family, hard work, and loyalty to country. Not known as an overly demonstrative person, Goldwater did have three very strong passions that he injected into most of his campaign speeches: love of country, hatred of communism, and passionate advocacy for small government. At the San Francisco Cow Palace in July 1964 the Goldwater forces easily steamrolled over a weak opposition by the traditional Eastern Republican establishment that tried, alternatively and vainly, to promote the candidacies of Nelson Rockefeller and William Scranton. In a Chautauqua atmosphere, the Goldwater delegates, most of them affluent middle-class whites, cheered as Goldwater denounced big government liberalism and those who were soft on communism. The delegates were especially jubilant when Goldwater brushed aside mass media critiques that he was an extremist, reminding the convention that "extremism in defense of liberty is no vice," and that "moderation in the pursuit of justice is no virtue." His critics pretended to be shocked by Goldwater's rhetorical outbursts and warned that he was speaking an alien language suggestive of ultra-rightist movements in Europe. This was clearly bafflegab, but it eventually accomplished its aim of painting Goldwater as a dangerous, erratic cowboy who was shooting constantly from the hip and therefore could not be entrusted with responsible leadership. In 1964 the liberal press brilliantly typecast Goldwater as a dangerous and muddled candidate.

In retrospect, Goldwater was simply a man out of season, a conservative nationalist in an age that still looked to centralized planning and government entitlement programs as a means to the collective good life. Philosophically, Goldwater offered the country a real choice, not an echo, as one of his campaign slogans proclaimed.

This meant simply that he opposed everything Lyndon Johnson wanted to sell the American people: big government spending, civil rights legislation, a nuclear test ban treaty, high benefits for the unemployed, a higher minimum wage, Medicare, and so on. Goldwater spoke for white middle-class interests, especially the newly rich of the southwest and the western states. These upwardly mobile, professional, and business groups of the Sun Belt resented government handouts to the poor and the under-privileged because such programs raised the specter of higher and higher taxes and socialist income redistributions. Many of Goldwater's supporters were not "mean-spirited" or war-mongers, as they were labeled by their liberal opponents at the time, but genuinely concerned about the role and function of government in people's lives. In the highly charged political climate of 1964, however, the Goldwaterites were writ-ten off the books as antediluvian reactionaries who wanted to drag the nation back into the period of unregulated capitalism. Goldwater made things worse during the campaign by delighting his opponents with ill-advised remarks about selling the Tennessee Valley Authority, getting rid of Social Security, and nuking the commu-nists.

With the nation's press whipping up fear of Goldwater, all that Johnson had to do was to act and sound presidential. In Atlantic City, the Democrats presented a show of unity that was marred only by the Mississippi Freedom Party trying unsuc-cessfully to be seated in place of the segregationist, lily-white delegation. Johnson was the cat's meow in Atlantic City, personally stage-managing the convention and arranging every detail. Even the "excitement" over his running mate was carefully scripted, as were the restraints put on Robert Kennedy, who was given an inconve-nient time slot to deliver a eulogy to his dead brother. Just having turned fifty-six, the president marked the occasion of his birthday by publicly cutting a huge cake in the convention hall that *Time* magazine said "seemed to be big enough to have and to eat too."[15] With ego overflowing and confidence brimming, the president flung himself into the 1964 campaign against Barry Goldwater. The Democrats succeeded in caricaturing Goldwater as a man from a bygone era—the bitter cold war and the values of preindustrial America. They also depicted Goldwater as a trigger-happy cowboy bent on unleashing nuclear war on the world. The most shameless political commercial ever used in a presidential campaign showed a little girl picking petals from a daisy in a field, with the voice-over giving the countdown: "Ten, nine, eight, . . . three, two, one," then showing a nuclear explosion and the ominous mushroom cloud, the voice-over warning: "These are the stakes. To make a world in which all of God's children can live or go into the dark. We must either love each other or we must die. The stakes are too high for you to stay home." Fade out: Vote for President Johnson on November 3.[16]

As the campaign of 1964 drew to a close, a Johnson victory was all but inevitable. Goldwater could only count on his own hard-core conservative followers; everyone else, as it turned out—farmers, urbanites, ethnic minorities, the poor, the elderly, moderate Republicans—voted for Lyndon Johnson. The result was a landslide vic-tory for Johnson, the most spectacular victory since FDR defeated Alf Landon in 1936. Johnson captured 43,126,506 popular votes (61.1 percent) as opposed to Goldwater's 27,176,799 (38.5 percent) votes. The margin of victory was as large in the Electoral College, with Johnson defeating Goldwater by a margin of 486 to 52. Goldwater carried only Arizona, his home state, and five southern states. Ironically, sixteen years later Ronald Reagan would sweep to an equally impressive victory on a conservative platform loosely similar to the one that had crushed Goldwater in 1964. Such would be the stunning reversal of what appeared to be a lasting liberal consensus following Johnson's landslide victory. As it would turn out, the liberal apogee lasted only four years, but few observers could have known this after Johnson's impressive victory.

The future for liberal reform now seemed all but assured. The three branches of government were solidly in Democratic hands, and so was the Supreme Court under the leadership of Earl Warren. In order to bolster his liberal support in the Supreme Court, Johnson appointed his friend and partner Abe Fortas to the Court, thus assuring himself of a "mole" who could keep him abreast of current thinking in the Court. The Court was in his pocket and two-thirds of both houses of Congress were also on his side. The times were ripe for liberal reform. Even so, Johnson favored an aggressive approach in his dealings with Congress. The only successful way of dealing with Congress, he believed, was to develop almost incestuous relationships with the legislative body. A president, in his judgment, had to know individual legislators better than he knew himself; and then, on the basis of this intimate knowledge, he had to "build a system that stretched from the cradle to the grave, from the moment a bill is introduced to the moment it is officially enrolled as the law of the land."[17] Johnson was himself the best liaison with Congress.[18]

When Johnson gave his aides the green light to forge ahead full steam on the road to the Great Society, he consciously wanted to close the liberal circle of reform that his great mentor Franklin Roosevelt had begun in 1933. Like FDR, Johnson was a liberal pragmatist rather than a doctrinaire radical. Having served in the legislative branch of government most of his adult life, he understood that politics was the art of the possible, that it was based on negotiation and compromise. He believed strongly in the philosophy of consensus, which meant building bridges to the opposition because the other side has legitimate interests in a democracy. A parliamentary system, Johnson felt, could not work if the two major parties embraced rigid principles because that would make it difficult, if not impossible, to forge alliances and involve the other side of the aisle in meaningful negotiations so that laws could be based on mutual consensus. Politicians with rigid or doctrinaire principles could not be expected to reason together and do the people's business. As far as he was concerned, Johnson said before he became president, "I am a free man, a Senator, and a Democrat, in that order. I am also a liberal, a conservative, a Texan, a taxpayer, a rancher, a businessman, a consumer, a parent, a voter, and not as young as I used to be nor as old as I expect to be—and I am all of these things in no fixed order. . . . At the heart of my own beliefs is a rebellion against this very process of classifying, labeling and filing Americans under headings."[19]

2. The Great Society

In his first inaugural address to Congress and the nation in January 1964, Lyndon Johnson had pledged that his administration would wage an "unconditional war on poverty in America," adding that "we shall not rest until the war is won."[20] This preoccupation with poverty was at once personal and political: as a young man Johnson had experienced considerable hardship, making him receptive to Franklin Roosevelt's New Deal and the Democratic Party, which had made itself the standard-bearer of the poor and the dispossessed. There was a strong and committed group in the Democratic Party, consisting of bureaucrats who had come to power during the Kennedy years, who believed that poverty could be eliminated in their lifetime in America. Several influential books of the late 1950s and early 1960s had drawn attention to systemic poverty amidst the nation's affluence. One was John Kenneth Galbraith's work *Affluent Society* (1958), which drew a striking contrast between the nation's wealth and affluence and the existence of public squalor. According to Galbraith, both the nation's urban landscape and its rural countryside were plagued by pockets of poverty, squalor, and neglect. But the book that influenced policy-makers most, including John F. Kennedy, was Michael Harrington's *The Other America* (1962), a poignant and disturbing look at American's invisible poor, who had been overlooked and ignored by affluent white America.

The American people had been of two minds about poverty since the founding of the nation: they had inherited a moral tradition, deeply rooted in Puritanism, that identified two types of poor people in America: the deserving and the undeserving poor. The deserving poor were those who could not work because they were sick, crippled, or unemployed as a result of circumstances beyond their control. The undeserving poor were lazy, irresponsible, and parasitic people who had deliberately made bad choices. Members of the second group were called bums, idlers, ne'er-do-wells, gadabouts, hobos, trash, and the like. The deserving poor were entitled to society's help and protection without incurring too much social blame, while the undeserving poor deserved to be thoroughly stigmatized and humiliated whenever they asked for public help. Until the New Deal, the federal government played a relatively minor role in taking care of the nation's poor. Responsibility for the poor was held to be the function of the family, philanthropic groups, and local authorities. Unlike Europe, which had an extensive network of government welfare programs, Americans had been reluctant to subsidize the poor through government-controlled welfare. The key difference between Europe and America had been the steadily expanding economy in America and the abundant resources on which it was based. Given the fact that affluence was the general norm rather than the exception, the American people viewed poverty as a personal failing and saw no reason to marshal federal resources to combat it. The Depression, however, began to shift this negative perception, especially among liberal and left-wing social critics. Social activists like Michael Harrington viewed poverty as circumstantial rather than personal, blaming unrestrained capitalism and advocating government intervention to alleviate suffering. Oscar Lewis, in his study of Mexican-American families, *Children of Sanchez* (1961), used the term "culture of poverty" to argue that poverty was a socially transmitted handicap, a behavioral flaw that was rooted in drug abuse, violent crime, family dysfunctions, and social discrimination.

As heirs to the New Deal, Democrats put themselves squarely in charge of Johnson's crusade to eliminate poverty in America; they embraced the poor, especially minorities, as their natural constituency. In waging "war on poverty," both Kennedy and Johnson relied on a new and committed group of social scientists turned social advocates. Armed with the tools and techniques of social science, these planners and policy specialists would provide the organizational strategies to implement Johnson's Great Society programs. One of the most prominent academics was Daniel Patrick Moynihan, a Harvard sociologist; another was Robert Lampman, an authority on income distribution who had written a book on how poverty in America could be measured. What probably jump-started the war on poverty were the rising expectations released by the civil rights movement and the synergistic efforts of liberal reformers and a committed president who not only wanted to fulfill Kennedy's legacy but also put his own stamp on the liberal reform movement.

The American people were in a generous mood throughout the first half of the 1960s. Once Johnson had implemented Kennedy's proposals for personal and corporate tax cuts, the economy went into high gear. Inflation was low until 1968 and employment higher than ever before. On May 22, 1964, Lyndon Johnson unveiled the details of the Great Society during a commencement ceremony at the University of Michigan. Having broken the legislative deadlock in Congress through a combination of skillful legislative work and personal cajoling and bullying, Johnson shepherded an unprecedented number of bills through the 89th Congress, a torrent of legislation that had been equaled only by his role model and mentor Franklin Roosevelt. Historians have seen Johnson's Great Society as essentially a continuation of FDR's New Deal, though Ronald Reagan would later insist that the key to his own success was attacking the Great Society and defending the New Deal.[21] Reagan's criticism referred to Johnson's unrestrained use of deficit spending, the proliferation of government bureaucracies, and the poorly designed and insufficiently administered programs of the Great Society. It is true, of course, that Johnson relied far more heavily on deficit spending than Roosevelt had, but the economy in the 1960s, unlike that of the 1930s, was booming and unemployment was at a historic low. By 1965 the tax cut had boosted the gross national product by twenty-five billion dollars. This, in turn, produced a federal surplus and pushed unemployment to a historic low of 3.9 percent. By the end of fiscal 1965 the economy had achieved an annual growth rate over the previous five years of 5 percent without inflation.[22] Arguments persist over the merits and effectiveness of Johnson's Great Society programs, but their demise was due to the costly war in Vietnam and the nation's eventual lack of support for massive federal welfare spending.

After Lyndon Johnson launched the war on poverty with such great fanfare in his State of the Union address in January 1964, he gathered around him the most energetic and idealistic activists since the brain trust of Franklin Roosevelt. Yet for all of his grandiosity and "pie in the sky promises," Lyndon Johnson was always, first and foremost, a politician with a strong sense of the art of the possible. In fact, he told his entourage of liberal reformers that they had a window of opportunity that might close within just a few years. He was right. In 1964 Johnson had a united country behind him. Extraordinarily affluent times, an outpouring of support for John F. Kennedy's New Frontier legacy, control of all three branches of government—all of these gave Johnson a huge boost for his reform measures.

There was something peculiarly American about waging a "war on poverty," especially in times of affluence. In trying to explain this unusual phenomenon, most historians have been well off the mark, postulating theories based on ideology or faulty causal reasoning. Affluent times made spending on poverty possible, but did not cause it. The cold war did not cause the war on poverty either. Lyndon Johnson did not use the war on poverty as a ploy to buy off or co-opt black protest, an argument made by radical leftists. Poverty programs were conceived early on in the Kennedy administration, long before black militants threatened to burn down the country. Poverty programs were motivated by a combination of liberal concern for neglected and forgotten Americans and deep-seated guilt feelings about having tolerated racial prejudices against black people. Within the reform camp it was liberal intellectuals who had a real fire in the belly in the 1960s. Scholarly interest in how poverty could be studied, measured, and remedied did not seriously begin until the late 1950s. Robert Lampman, an economist at the University of Wisconsin, compiled a bibliography of poverty at that time that filled less than two pages; in 1970 Dorothy Campbell Tompkins published another that came to 442 double-column pages with 8,338 entries.[23] Clearly, intellectuals, especially those on the left, had created a cottage industry that even now shows few signs of lessening in the academic world. The 1960s produced a professional class of social redeemers who claimed to be speaking for the poor and who formulated ambitious programs to lift them out of poverty through massive government spending. These poverty crusaders found in Lyndon Johnson the man who could fulfill their social utopias. The president had personal experience with poverty, and he initially lent a willing ear to the reformers, except those who favored socialist redistribution schemes. "The poverty program that [Walter] Heller described," Johnson later said, "was my kind of undertaking." He told Heller: "Go ahead. Give it the highest priority. Push ahead full tilt."[24] Johnson not only supported Heller's suggestions but also wanted the program to be "big and bold and hit the nation with real impact."[25] The president's enthusiasm for the crusade against poverty was infectious, attracting a swarm of liberal idealists to Washington like bees to the sweetest flowers. At one time or another the most prominent liberal academics, journalists, attorneys, and social activists flocked to Washington, notably John Kenneth Galbraith, Daniel Patrick Moynihan, Walter Heller, Arthur Schlesinger, Eric Goldman, Lester Thurow, Kermit Gordon, George Reedy, Bill Moyers, David Hackett, Robert Lampman, Lloyd Ohlin, Richard Goodwin, Joseph Califano, Richard Boone, and many others.

Some social redeemers were imbued with a strong animus against capitalism and a corresponding fondness for centralized planning and income redistribution. They wanted to shift income from the middle class to the poor, even promising a "guaranteed annual income" for everyone. Just how they envisioned such a socialist redistribution they dared not advertise to the American people, though a team of New York radicals, Frances Fox Piven and Richard Cloward, made no bones in the 1970s that they wanted to rub raw the sores of discontent through revolutionary tactics such as lawsuits, boycotts, demonstrations, and even urban warfare.[26]

Lyndon Johnson and most liberals would have none of this. The administration carefully avoided slogans suggestive of class warfare. Johnson was a liberal, not a radical; he strongly believed that his antipoverty programs would be fairly painless to middle-class taxpayers because they would be financed entirely from expanding revenues generated by existing tax rates.[27] The president may have experienced poverty in his youth, but he was proud of having pulled himself up by his own bootstraps— the widely accepted method rooted in American Puritanism. Johnson believed in giving a hand up rather than a handout, in providing opportunities to be productive rather than for doing no work.[28] Johnson put particular stock in education as a passport to economic success, and he took his message of hope to the road. Like a whirlwind he visited the country's poor areas, touting his Great Society programs. In his memoirs, *The Vantage Point*, Johnson recounts a visit to an impoverished area in eastern Kentucky and the discussion he had with a man named Tom Fletcher, who lived with his wife and eight children in a tar-papered shack, trying to support his family on $400 a year. Fletcher told the president that his two oldest children had already dropped out of school, and he feared the same would happen to the others. Stunned by the man's grinding poverty, Johnson promised him that he would provide the hand up the Fletchers of this country needed: "I want to keep these kids in school," he told Fletcher, adding in his memoirs that "my determination was reinforced that day to use the powers of the Presidency to the fullest extent I could, to persuade America to help all its Tom Fletchers."[29]

This episode reveals a flash of genuine empathy and willingness to help; but at the same time it also captures the typical LBJ braggadocio that many Americans would distrust as hollow. Johnson did have generosity, social conscience, and magnanimous impulses; he was also deceitful, insecure, and vulgar. As to Tom Fletcher, why did the man have eight children he could not support? Why did two of his children quit a free, publicly financed school? Why did Mr. Fletcher stay in an economically depressed area? Was it true that there were thirty-five million Fletchers in America? Was this a crisis of Depression-scale proportion? That such questions were not even raised tells us a great deal about LBJ and other liberals who were beating the drums announcing a "war on poverty" with a poverty "Czar" warning the nation that there was an urgent crisis that had to be solved within a decade. The way in which Johnson and the liberals magnified the threat, raised expectations, and poured money into this crusade, while at the same time fighting a costly war abroad, would pave the way for an inevitable day of reckoning. Critics wondered what made these liberal activists think that they could succeed when every generation in the past had failed? Johnson impatiently waved off such questions by saying "I'm sick of all the people who talk about the things we can't do. Hell, we're the richest country in the world, the most powerful. We can do it all. . . . We can do it if we believe it."[30]

Johnson's statement was a typical expression of American exceptionalism, left, right, or center. It gives us an answer to the question of why the social reformers actually believed that they could eliminate poverty in their lifetimes. To them America could do anything it set its mind to: eliminating poverty, defeating communism, landing a man on the moon, providing a guaranteed annual income to everyone, housing for the homeless, pensions for the retired, a pollution-free environment, international peace, and much more.[31] In this sense Johnsonian reform zeal was a continuation of the periodic moral crusades in American history mentioned in chapter 2. The resulting letdown in the late 1960s was particularly painful, coming as it did after such high expectations. In trying to change every social problem at home and simultaneously changing the world in America's own image was to toy with disaster, to move from hubris to the fall.

At the heart of Lyndon Johnson's Great Society programs was the war on poverty. To wage it, the president relied on the new Office of Economic Opportunity under the direction of Sargent Shriver, John F. Kennedy's brother-in-law. In August 1964 Congress passed the Economic Opportunity Act, which authorized a billion dollars to retrain the poor. The new opportunity act contained a number of different programs to accomplish this mission. Title I, the Job Corps, established centers that would train young people for both basic and advanced skills, while at the same time setting up Neighborhood Programs. Title II, the Community Action Program, envisioned active participation by the poor in the decision-making process of training young people in marketable skills. Other titles involved rural loans, small business development centers, and VISTA (Volunteers in Service to America), a kind of domestic Peace Corps. Shriver and his staff also used funds to offer legal services to the poor and designed an innovative program, entitled Head Start, to provide enough educational skills to preschool children so that they would start on an equal footing with their more advantaged peers before entering elementary school.

One of the most controversial features of the new Economic Opportunity Act revolved around Shriver's Community Action Programs, which were designed to put greater control into the hands of the local poor for whom the programs were designed. The idea behind it, sound in theory but often misapplied in practice, was to bypass Washington bureaucrats in favor of local agencies that were presumably better informed about what was needed on the local level. In practice, the direct flow of federal funds often ended up in the hands of local radicals or downright hustlers, who misappropriated federal funds before they could trickle down to the poor who really needed them. Shriver believed in "maximum feasible participation" by the poor, but this proved to be difficult because the poor had little practice in "participatory democracy."[32]

Some historians have argued that if there was any real radical element in the antipoverty programs it resided in these Community Action Programs because they represented a real threat to social stability. Johnson was vaguely aware of potential trouble from what he called "kooks and sociologists,"[33] but he did not realize that the

Office of Economic Opportunity (OEO) was infiltrated by radicals who saw his opportunity programs as a means of implementing Saul Alinsky's strategy of "rubbing raw the sores of discontent."[34] Since the Community Action Programs called for "maximum feasible participation" by the poor for whom the programs were intended in any particular area, the door was open for radical activists to mobilize community discontent and wage class warfare.

In October 1964 Congress allocated $300 million for community action, which set off a wild scramble by local communities all over the country to get as much of a share of these federal dollars as they could. OEO officials, sensing that federal funds would probably be misused by local mayors or city councils, insisted that the poor had to be organized and included in the decision-making process. If a community could not prove genuine participation by the poor, there would be no federal funding. Within hardly a year of the creation of CAP, 415 community action groups had sprouted over the length and breadth of America's urban landscape.[35] In February 1965, OEO issued guidelines that spelled out that mayors could not pack community action boards with carefully handpicked cronies who would do the bidding of the city mayors rather than represent the needs of the poor. A month later, Richard Boone, head of CAP planning and policy, issued more precise guidelines in a manual entitled *Community Action Workbook*, in which he proposed that the poor be empowered with the help of trained activists, which opened the door to elite radicals using the "system" under the guise of "grassroots democracy." It looked as though government officials themselves planned to remold local communities over the heads of democratically elected mayors and city councils.

It goes without saying that the mayors, especially big city mayors like Richard Daley of Chicago, Sam Yorty of Los Angeles, and John Shelley of San Francisco, denounced these government policies as not only usurping the democratic process but as radical tactics that could instigate serious class warfare in the United States. The mayors vigorously pressured the Johnson administration to change course and shift control of the CAP to local rather than federal supervision. The American public was generally unaware of the seriousness of these political battles, for they involved more than just a power struggle between federal and local authorities. Behind the fight over money was the emergence of a radical elite that wanted to change corporate America. In the end, the liberal politicians killed these Community Action Programs because they threatened their own middle-class power base. Before this happened, however, considerable social turmoil was caused by radical demagogues who used CAP as a weapon to "rub raw the sores of discontent."

A sampling of the CAP in practice illustrates the point. In Harlem, New York, the urban landscape was disfigured by thugs who used Mau-Mau tactics to exact their pound of flesh from "whitey." The term "Mau-Mau" was named after the black militant rebels of Kenya, who used terroristic methods to gain independence from white British control. In the United States, Mau-Mau tactics were far less violent, yet they too relied on the threat of force to achieve their ends. In practice, Mau-Mauing by black nationalists involved mobilizing a gang of "black brothers," descending on welfare agencies, and "shaking down" officials by cussing them out, screaming at them, banging on tables, and threatening violence if black demands were not met. Fred Siegel has called this form of intimidation the "riot ideology" by which "violence and the threat of violence were leveraged into both a personal style for street kids and a political agenda based on threat and intimidation."[36]

In Harlem, liberal activists had set up "Project Uplift" designed to keep idle teenagers from burning down the black community. The program, however, was so badly managed that marauding gangs, who had never done any serious work, descended on the Project Uplift office and threatened to burn it down if they did not receive their paychecks. The intimidated agency was forced to hire a local security firm to protect itself against its own clients. Project Uplift overspent its budget and had to be bailed out repeatedly by the Office of Economic Opportunity. OEO not only continued to subsidize Project Uplift but even increased its funding, some of which supported the Black Arts Theatre, a brainchild of the black nationalist LeRoi Jones. The activist spent $100,000 on the Black Arts Theatre and hired 242 people to help him stage a succession of "guerrilla theatre" plays that blended black racism with radical Marxism.[37]

Mau-Mauing occurred in several other cities. In San Francisco militant blacks preached hatred against whites by organizing demonstrations against Mayor John F. Shelley because he had paid insufficient heed to "maximum feasible participation" by the poor (local activists) in the Community Action Program. In the wake of the Watts riots, the beleaguered Shelley completely capitulated to the militants, who then reorganized community action boards with poor people and then proceeded to run the program with complete autonomy. What followed was a binge of spending by self-serving activists who were more interested in feathering their own nests than lifting anyone out of poverty in the predominantly black neighborhoods of the Western Addition and Hunter's Point. At one point the leader of the dissidents on Hunter's Point, Charles Sizemore, who was closely associated with black militants who were Mau-Mauing San Francisco State College, descended on Mayor Shelley's office with thirty thugs and demanded that the mayor restore cuts in the summer youth program. If the mayor did not come up with the money, Sizemore threatened, "this goddamn town's gonna blow."[38] The mayor capitulated, as did the CAP board, when, at the end of summer, it coughed up an additional unfunded $30,000 under threats of violence.

Problems with federal funding for poverty programs, not all of them Community Action Programs, were endemic in the 1960s. In Chicago, local antipoverty officials discovered that youth gangs, notably the Blackstone Rangers and the Eastside Disciples, were actually running an OEO program. In Cleveland, federal money was siphoned off by the "Reverend Black Muslim," Ahmed Evans and his disciples, who, like Charles Sizemore, believed that when one stole from the white man one was simply dealing with real politics. The Reverend Ahmed Evans used federal dollars to underwrite his favorite "New Libya" project, preparing his disciples for the final days and a showdown with the white man.[39] In Oakland, which had a festering ghetto about to erupt in 1966, the federal government allocated $23 million to prevent a riot and create jobs. Bypassing the mayor, who had asked to control the "employment project," federal officials proceeded to run it on their own and mismanaged the troubled project between 1966 and 1969. According to a *Los Angeles Times* article in March 1969, the federal project had spent the $23 million and created a total of twenty new jobs.[40] Where did the money go? In Oakland, as in many other places, the money was spent on political patronage and paid sinecures—in short, old fashioned graft.

Community Action Programs, of course, were only one branch of the Great Society tree, though clearly the most twisted and deformed branch. They were mismanaged by inexperienced activists or just plain hustlers, who conducted their business right under the noses of government officials. The Office of Economic Opportunity, which was run out of the executive branch of government, proved difficult to control by congressional oversight. It was almost impossible for congressmen or senators to keep up with the sheer size of the burgeoning programs and how they were managed, let alone whether they met their intended goals. According to a Brandeis University study of twenty Community Action Programs in cities ranging in population from 50,000 to 800,000, most of the programs used strategies to coopt the poor rather than to empower them; and such community services that they actually provided often merely duplicated services already supplied by municipal authorities.[41] Another study, conducted by Barss, Reitzel, and Associates, a think tank in Massachusetts, found that Community Action Programs provided few benefits to the poor and made very little difference.[42]

In addition to Community Action Programs, there were also Job Corps programs, rural and urban loan programs, and VISTA—Volunteers in Service to America. The Job Corps, loosely patterned after the New Deal's Civilian Conservation Corps, was intended to provide job training for young people in camp settings. Since the program recruited school dropouts, some of whom had criminal records, the camps were often plagued by rowdy behavior, drug abuse, sex scandals, and crime. Although the program produced modest results in the employment of marginal young men and women, it fell far short of the optimistic expectations that Sargent Shriver had aroused in its participants. Shriver soldiered on bravely even after Johnson had lost interest in the New Opportunities Programs, believing that, given the right funding, poverty could be wiped out within ten years. Johnson, of course, would spend more time, energy, and resources on the Vietnam War than he would on the war on poverty, though he continued to insist that the country could wage the two wars simultaneously.

In addition to the programs conducted under the aegis of Shriver's agency, there were numerous other Great Society programs. In 1964 Congress passed the National Defense Education Act, which offered federal support for the teaching of the sciences and the humanities as well. One year later, two additional education bills were passed: the Elementary and Secondary Education Act and the Higher Education Act, the former appropriating over one billion dollars for improving education on the primary and secondary level, while the latter provided scholarship funds for the first time for college students. The important innovation of these new laws was that they extended educational funding to private as well as public schools because the government insisted that it was aiding students rather than schools.

The jewel in the crown of Great Society programs was undoubtedly Medicare for the elderly. The idea of a government-funded program to provide medical care for the American people was first suggested by Franklin Roosevelt, but organized opposition by the American Medical Association and by the nation's insurance carriers had always prevented passage of a Medicare bill. Although Johnson was unable to pass a national health care bill for all Americans, he was able to pass such a bill for American seniors. With his liberal majority in both Houses of Congress and gaining the support of Wilbur Mills, the powerful chairman of the House Ways and Means Committee, Johnson was able to pass the landmark Medicare bill in 1965. The act covered most medical and hospital costs for elderly Americans over the age of sixty-five, except for a small annual deductible. Medicare also provided medical care for the poor who paid payroll taxes. As an extension to Medicare, Congress added Medicaid, a program of health care for those on welfare, regardless of age. Both Medicare and Medicaid were to be run by the Social Security Administration, the former being a federal program and the latter a joint federal and state program. Making concessions to physicians, who had strongly opposed a government operated health system, the sponsors of Medicare allowed physicians to charge Medicare patients customary fees rather than dictating fees to the physicians. Medical specialists such as radiologists, anesthesiologists, or pathologists were to be paid separately rather than be included in hospital reimbursements. Both of these concessions were bound to drive up medical costs, as was subsequently proven because medical practitioners did not mind bilking the government as much as they could get away with. Lyndon Johnson was undoubtedly correct when he said that "no longer will older Americans be denied the healing miracles of modern medicine. No longer will illness crush and destroy [their] savings."[43] What Johnson could not foresee was the unprecedented rise in health care costs that was partly prompted by Medicare and Medicaid and the bureaucratic mismanagement of the system by federal and state authorities.

Generous federal spending was also applied to Aid for Dependent Children, including food stamps to recipients of AFDC. The number of Americans on AFDC rose steadily throughout the sixties—from 4.3 percent in 1965 to 8.5 percent in 1970.[44] In 1965 about six hundred thousand people received food stamps; ten years later, more than seventeen million received food stamps.

The Great Society programs were aimed at making life not just healthier but also more "beautiful" for all Americans. A host of consumer protection measures were passed during the five years of Johnson's presidency. These measures included provisions for clean air and water, product safety, mine safety, highway safety and beautification, and child safety. A new law established the National Endowment for the Arts and the National Endowment for the Humanities, dispensing federal funds to artists, writers, scholars, and musicians. The Corporation for Public Broadcasting and the Kennedy Center also received increased funding to raise the general level of knowledge and aesthetic appreciation.

Such massive government involvement in the lives of the American people required an equally massive expansion of government departments, bureaucrats, and regulatory agencies. In order to meet these new government needs, Johnson had

Congress approve two new cabinet offices—Transportation and Housing and Urban Development (HUD). He appointed Robert C. Weaver, a black American, as Secretary of Housing and Urban Development. The Housing Act of 1968 provided federal funds for affordable housing, but this government program, designed for poor Americans, benefited middle-class families more than it did poor families.

Lyndon Johnson's war on poverty is still the subject of intense scholarly debate and scrutiny, which generally revolves around several interrelated issues: Why was it fought and by whom? What is poverty and how could it be measured? And did the programs of the war on poverty actually lift the poor out of poverty and raise their standard of living? As to the first question, Daniel Patrick Moynihan provided the best answer when he confessed that "the war on poverty was not declared at the behest of the poor: it was declared in their interest by persons confident in their own judgment in such matters."[45] Moynihan should know, for he was one of the intellectual activists who was part of the planning and implementation of the war on poverty. Very early on in the Johnson administration, Moynihan published a controversial study entitled *The Negro Family: The Case for National Action*, in which he called for a strengthening of the beleaguered black family through job opportunities. Although the report did not seriously question the assumption that job opportunities would be accompanied by improvement in family structure, Moynihan's work raised concern about certain peculiarly black family dysfunctions such as high rates of illegitimacy, single-mother households, high unemployment rates, and welfare dependency. Moynihan's study attributed some of the pathologies to the bad choices poor black people made in America's inner cities. Even the slightest hint that poverty might be related to the actions of the poor themselves was denounced by liberals as insensitive, uncaring, and racist, which were exactly the charges leveled at Moynihan's report. The liberal elites were outraged that one of their own would question the axiomatic belief of welfare liberalism that the poor were pure victims of circumstances beyond their control: exploitive market conditions and substandard living conditions related to it. Moynihan implicitly questioned the deterministic model that victims were not responsible for their condition, for as an urban researcher he was well aware that inner-city pathologies ranging from alarming delinquency and crime rates to drug offenses and irresponsible sexual behaviors could not be entirely ascribed to socioeconomic circumstances. Moynihan was one of the first to break ranks with orthodox liberals on this issue, but he strongly continued to adhere to the belief and practice of providing equal opportunities for the poor, black or white; what he adamantly opposed, which he spelled out in further detail in his book *Maximum Feasible Misunderstanding* was the practice of welfare dependency as a way of life. His figures indicated a rising tide of welfare dependency in inner-city ghettos, especially in Aid for Dependent Children (AFDC) caseloads. African American children, later followed by some other ethnic minority children, were not raised in normally functioning homes, for by the late 1960s over 70 percent of black children were recipients of AFDC benefits. This meant that such children were born as welfare children and were supported by the government rather than by their families.

Moynihan was not the only one who questioned the well-meaning but faulty assumptions liberals had made about the causes of poverty and their behavioral corollaries. In July 1966 James Coleman published a far-ranging report on educational opportunities in the United States and found that school funding, buildings, curricula, and teachers were not directly responsible for promoting learning among students. Coleman's extensive study, based on tests administered to 567,000 students, surveys of 70,000 school principals, information gathered from 4,000 schools, revealed that "per pupil expenditures, books in the library and a host of other facilities and curricula measures show virtually no relation to their achievement of the social environment of the school, if the educational background of the students and teachers is held in constant."[46] Coleman threw cold water on liberal dogma when he stated that "schools bring little influence to bear on a child's achievement that is independent of his background and general social content." In short, it was in the home that education was either cherished or ignored, encouraged or neglected. If educational achievement and upward mobility were not prized at home, school by itself was bound to make little difference. By saying this, the Coleman report had put in question one of the chief strategies of the war on poverty, which was to improve educational opportunities through massive government spending.

Both Moynihan and Coleman belonged to the liberal activists of the 1960s who inspired the war on poverty and similar government projects, though both began to break ranks with their more orthodox compatriots. In other words, an elite group of liberal activists inspired the war on poverty, claimed that they were speaking for the poor, and knew how to remedy the problem. Before remedying the problem, however, the poverty experts had to define what it meant to be poor. This task fell to the President's Council of Economic Advisors, chaired by Walter Heller. The planners avoided qualitative factors relating to how poor people perceived their economic condition; they also avoided the question whether poverty might not be an intractable problem. In the context of American society, very few people suffered from absolute deprivation such as the absence of food, clothing, and shelter. Instead, the council concentrated on a "decent standard of living" and assumed that this inherently subjective term could be measured by income distribution. In the minds of liberal reformers a decent standard of living for a family of four required an annual income of at least $3,000. By American standards that sort of minimal income would provide a family with a home, car, TV set, refrigerator, bathtub, heating, food, and clothing. Most Americans, of course, already had those material possessions, but those who did not, Johnson believed, should be given a "hand up" by the federal government. To Lyndon Johnson and his reformers, poverty was a condition of relative deprivation that could be remedied by the federal government working closely with state and local government agencies.

One of the problems encountered by the Johnson team was that the social reformers had drawn an arbitrary line for measuring poverty. If a $3,000 income or less meant being poor in 1964, the expanding economy by itself would lift a substantial number of poor people out of poverty. Economic growth by itself would raise income levels, thus making government intervention unnecessary except for those living in absolute deprivation. The reformers countered this argument by insisting that, deeply entrenched in American society, there existed what became known as "structural poverty" of the sort that could only be changed through massive government aid. This thesis had been promoted by Michael Harrington in his book *The Other America* (1962) and was widely accepted despite Harrington's ideologically motivated interpretation of the evidence. Harrington and his followers assumed that the United States entered the 1960s with a growing number of poor people, possibly as many as fifty million, or more than a third of the population.[47] This was false. The economy, as previously shown, was steadily expanding in the postwar period. The gross national product had risen from $181.8 billion in 1929 to $282.3 billion in 1947; by 1960 the GNP had further increased by 56 percent to $439.9 billion.[48] Changes in the GNP have a strong inverse relation to change in poverty, so that poverty decreases as the GNP increases.[49] This was as true of the 1960s as it had been throughout the postwar period, which witnessed a steady decline not an increase in poverty. The question most frequently raised in this connection has been how much Lyndon Johnson's poverty program actually reduced poverty. In his memoirs Johnson proudly claimed that when he left office in 1968, government figures revealed that of the 35 million people trapped in poverty in 1964, 12.5 million had been lifted out of poverty, a reduction of almost 30 percent in just over four years.[50] Johnson did not prove that this reduction was the result of his antipoverty programs, nor could he prove it given the fact that, compared to other government spending, relatively little was spent on antipoverty programs. There is very little empirical evidence that Johnson's antipoverty programs were working at all, partly because their goals were vaguely defined or unmeasurable and partly because they were poorly administered. Income inequality, which had been the measure of poverty, was not reduced, and the reason why it was not was Johnson's modest goal of increasing opportunities with existing taxes and expanding revenue. Johnsonian liberals never envisioned a radical reorganization of society by means of income redistribution from the rich to the poor. They simply spent surplus revenues that had accumulated in affluent times, hoping that such seed money, going into various antipoverty programs, would provide greater economic opportunities for the poor to get off the dole rather than to stay on it.

It is an ongoing theme of this analysis of the 1960s that liberals had benevolent intentions without ever taking into account their unintended consequences. For politicians like Lyndon Johnson, the war on poverty was what is commonly called a "win-win" proposition: it was virtuous, relatively cheap as compared to the Vietnam War, and impossible to judge while it was unfolding. If the economy kept expanding, the president did not have to be defensive about spending money on the poor, especially since it did not involve increased taxes on the rich or on the middle class. He could also attribute the decrease in the poverty line to the effectiveness of his Great Society programs rather than to the expanding economy. Either way, he had kept his promise to the poor and reassured his middle-class base.

The unintended consequences of Johnsonian liberalism—overspending on domestic programs and cold war programs—was steady inflation, balance of payment deficits, welfare dependency, a bloated regulatory bureaucracy, the weakening of the dollar and the decline of U.S. economic power in the world. As to whether any of Johnson's Great Society, especially its antipoverty programs, did any good in the long run has been fought out largely on partisan lines, with liberals supporting the Great Society programs, while conservatives condemn them as wasteful, unproductive, and misconceived. Radicals on the left, of course, criticized the Great Society programs from the beginning, claiming that they did not go far enough in the direction of socialist redistribution schemes and high taxes on U.S. property owners. A consensus among many historians, including reform liberals, however, suggests that the Great Society was a failure for several reasons.[51] In the first place, the goals were unrealistic, even for a rich and affluent country like the United States. Just as it is impossible to pray oneself out of poverty, one cannot spend oneself out of it. In the second place the Great Society programs were poorly administered by its planners, many of whom were intellectuals without administrative experience. Moynihan was not far off the mark when he said that "the men of whom the nation had a right to expect better, did inexcusably sloppy work."[52] Politicians and administrators, he observed, played God with other people's lives as well as their money. The government simply did not know what it was doing other than formulating untested programs, allocating funds, and hoping for the best. One of the unpardonable sins of social scientists was to set policies rather than measure outcomes in an objective manner.[53] Moynihan also sarcastically mentioned that social scientists not only claimed to love poor people but that they got along very well with rich ones too, especially when they went searching for funds. What was wrong with so many liberal activists, according to Moynihan, was their presumption of superior empathy with the problems of the downtrodden.[54] One could add that for many social activists and reformers, there were motives involved that transcended pure altruism. Most of the financial benefits of Great Society programs were reaped by left-liberal poverty workers and planners rather than by the poor for whom the programs were intended. The real beneficiaries, according to Allen Matusow, were middle-class professionals such as doctors, lawyers, teachers, social workers, builders, and bankers who provided a variety of services to the poor.[55]

A third reason for the failure of Great Society programs was the cost being incurred during the 1960s by the Vietnam War. In 1976 Robert Warren Stevens estimated that the total cost of the Vietnam War, including budgeting and indirect costs, amounted to a staggering $882 billion.[56] In 1964 when Johnson proclaimed his war on poverty, the administration allocated less than a billion dollars to the war on poverty; by contrast, the Vietnam War was consuming five times as much money. Between 1965 and 1967, the cost of the Vietnam War rose from $5 billion to over $26 billion.[57] Whatever forward momentum the Great Society programs enjoyed between 1964 and 1965 was stopped with escalation of the Vietnam War. Moreover, Johnson and McNamara, the two architects of escalation, were also the instigators of the great surge in inflation that began in 1966, concealing the truth from both Congress and the American people and taking countermeasures when it was too late.[58] In a moment of rare candor Johnson told Califano, his domestic legislation coordinator, "I'm fearful we are overpromised, overextended, and overenthusiastic."[59]

Although it is fashionable to overemphasize race if one is liberal or radical and to dismiss it if one is conservative, the failure of antipoverty programs must take race into account for two significant reasons. First, most Americans associated poverty with poor people living in economically deprived areas such as Appalachia and other parts of rural America. The people who lived in these parts of the country were largely white; they were the sort of people John F. Kennedy had met in West Virginia, when he had his first face-to-face encounter with people living in grinding poverty. Inner-city blacks were of little concern to white Americans, except for social workers or radical activists. One could even make the argument that the topic of poverty itself was relatively unimportant to the majority of white Americans. A 1964 Gallup poll posed the question: "Will poverty ever be done away with in this country?" Only 9 percent of the respondents thought that poverty could be eliminated, while 83 percent said that it could not.[60] Starting in 1965, the majority of the American people associated ghetto blacks with rioters and looters, an impression reinforced over the next three years by television images of blacks burning down buildings and leaving stores with everything that was not nailed down. Such images had a devastating impact on white middle-class America. Following the passage of civil rights legislation, which most white people outside the South supported, white Americans lost patience with black demands, especially those rolling off the lips of radical black agitators—Stokely Carmichael, H. Rap Brown, LeRoi Jones, Eldridge Cleaver, and Huey Newton, among others. Black nationalism, combined with New Left radicalism, shifted public perceptions against Great Society programs in general and color-blind compassion in particular. Just how much this shift of perception can be attributed to racism is difficult to say, for in fairness to white middle-class sensibilities, their reactions to black behavior had often little to do with race but more to do with the violence and lawlessness of the rioters. As previously mentioned, racial issues did not motivate the Johnson-Kennedy Great Society, but they did play a role in the shifting perceptions of white Americans in the wake of urban riots.

Race played another role in the war on poverty, a role clearly foreseen by Moynihan. One of the more devastating unintended consequences of liberal reforms was that they subsidized poverty through flawed government welfare policies. Before 1965, economic dependency on government welfare had decreased by one third from what it had been a decade before. After 1968 welfare dependency steadily increased. Charles Murray has shown that the number of people living in poverty—using government measures of income distribution—steadily increased between 1968 and 1980.[61] During that same time, welfare programs quadrupled. Murray argued that the poor lost ground not because of the Vietnam War, shifts in demographics, Watergate, or racism, but because of flawed social policies that essentially subsidized poverty. In other words what made the poor continue to be poor were the very programs designed to lift them out of poverty.[62] The liberal welfare state, for example, undermined the black family by subsidizing unwed pregnancies and single-mother households. Housing programs in the form of high-rise apartment buildings turned out to be an unmitigated disaster, for these "projects" destroyed traditional black neighborhoods and created new and even more malignant slums. Crime, teenage pregnancy, sexually transmitted diseases, and drug dependency were more virulent in inner-city ghettos than in the rest of the nation, which is saying a lot given the permissive environment of the 1960s.

The argument that poverty programs failed because they were ineffective is a half truth when considering the 1960s. They failed for other reasons, as have been indicated—overspending on Vietnam, mismanagement, corruption, racial issues, and unrealistic expectations. Murray's argument that government expenditures on the poor were misconceived, misdirected, and ineffective is a true but insufficient reason for the failure of the Great Society. The failure lies in a multiplicity of factors, not least of which was the split-minded conception of Johnson's whole enterprise. Johnson declared war but chose to fight another one which he obviously found more important. As Irwin Unger put it, "Johnson the hawk poisoned Johnson the liberal";[63] and even if the liberal Johnson had won the upper hand, he still would have been obliged to maneuver within the permissible limits of reforms acceptable to the middle class, and that meant steering clear of radical changes in the structure of American society. The result was a flurry of legislation, social spending, and inflated rhetoric that did not substantially change income distributions and made just a slight dent in the poverty rate between 1964 and 1968 (from roughly 18 to 13 percent). Although the Great Society programs were launched on a high moral plane, Johnsonian liberals had no idea about unintended consequences, nor raised serious questions about the social responsibility a society should expect from those who are recipients of welfare generosity. In the view of the critics, the Great Society may have been a generous revolution but it was also one that the majority of the American people came to regret because it failed to achieve its intended goals.

3. Liberal Justice: The Warren Court

In the 1960s American motorists sometimes passed huge billboards that announced: "Save Our Republic: Impeach Earl Warren." These signs, put up by the right-wing John Birch Society, expressed the belief that the liberal Earl Warren Court, espousing un-American doctrines, was destroying the American Republic. Most Americans, of course, rejected that paranoid view, but few doubted the importance and the power wielded by the Court, beginning with its controversial decision in *Brown v. Board of Education* (1954) and ending in *Roe v. Wade* (1973). What made the Warren Court so menacing to conservative Americans was its unabashed liberal activism. As will be recalled, it was the judicial branch of the American government that took the lead in civil rights for black Americans, and throughout the 1960s the Court consistently pushed for the expansion of civil rights for all Americans.[64]

The Warren Court's interpretation of the Constitution was loose constructionist; it viewed the Constitution as an evolving document subject to reinterpretation if warranted by "changing circumstances." The Court did not believe that it was possible under all circumstances to defer to the intentions of the framers of the Constitution, particularly since the founders had viewed liberty in a negative sense as the absence of restrictions rather than in a positive sense as enumerations of additional rights that needed to be discovered and extended to a greater number of individuals or groups. The civil rights movement tested the Court's "living constitution" position to the limits of feasible extension of rights compatible with social stability. Although the Court initiated a revolution in race relations by giving real constitutional substance to equal protection laws, it did not, contrary to its extreme critics, encourage democracy on the streets or protect criminals from prosecution. Even as liberal a justice as Arthur J. Goldberg wrote that "the rights of free speech and assembly" do not protect marchers "in the middle of Times Square at rush hour."[65] And Justice Hugo Black, who moved to a far more conservative position in the mid-1960s challenged the majority which had overturned breach-of-peace convictions against protesters by saying that "it is high time to challenge the assumption in which too many people have too long acquiesced that groups that think they have been mistreated have a constitutional right to use the public's streets, buildings, and property to protest whatever, wherever they want without regard to whom such conduct may disturb . . . But I say once more that the crowd moved by noble ideas today can become the mob ruled by passion and greed and violence tomorrow."[66]

The Court's judicial activism was not simply due to the strong leadership wielded by Earl Warren, who had been appointed by President Eisenhower, but the presence of a majority of liberal advocates such as William O. Douglas, John Harlan, Hugo Black, and Potter Stewart. The Court's philosophy was contained in the doctrine of "preferred freedoms," which held that the Court had a responsibility in reviewing legislation to see whether it abridged civil rights or civil liberties. This view dated back to 1938, when Harlan Stone in *U.S. v. Caroline Products Company,* had made reference to this doctrine in a footnote to his decision in the case.[67] Stone urged the Court to scrutinize legislation by federal or state legislators for any civil liberties violations. His colleague Hugo Black enunciated a related doctrine of "incorporation" that held that the Fourteenth Amendment to the Constitution not only placed restrictions on the authority of the federal government but also incorporated all the states under the same provision. The long cherished principle of "judicial restraint," practiced by previous justices such as Oliver Wendell Holmes and Louis Brandeis, began to give way to a far more active Court under Earl Warren. *Brown v. Board of Education* was the first Court decision that signaled this change in the high Court toward judicial activism.

It took some ten years for the other two branches of government to catch up with the liberal decisions of the Supreme Court on civil rights and civil liberties. By the time both the Kennedy and Johnson administrations had fully committed themselves to civil rights, all three branches of government were in full harmony with the spirit of liberal activism. The Supreme Court would strike down southern ordinances and state laws against disturbances of the peace when used as an instrument of repressing civil rights protests. It also struck down segregation laws in private facilities such as restaurants, hotels, or department stores. The Court also prohibited fornication laws that had prevented cohabitation between whites and blacks because, as Justice Stewart put it, "I cannot conceive of a valid legislative purpose under our

Constitution for a state law which makes the color of a person's skin the test of whether his conduct is a criminal offence."[68]

In 1965 the Supreme Court was again several months ahead of the federal government when it struck down a Mississippi tradition of preventing African Americans from voting. The federal government followed suit with the Voting Rights Act, promising to enforce this interpretation of the Constitution. Liberal activists then directed their attention to school segregation, first in the South and later in the North. In *Griffin v. Prince Edward County, Virginia* (1964), the Court declared that black children had been denied due process and equal educational opportunities as a result of the county closing its public schools, converting them into private schools, and giving parents tax credits for attending such "state-accredited" schools. The Court also conferred broad powers on district courts to enforce desegregation, including the power to override duly elected local school boards. This intrusion by the federal Court and its proxies, the district courts, in the educational affairs of local schools was widely denounced as arbitrary and undemocratic, later causing much bitterness in Court-mandated busing schemes throughout the nation. In *Green v. School Board of New Kent County* (1968), the Supreme Court rejected the theory and practice of "freedom of choice" that states had used to maintain a dual system of education, thus making it easier to use forced busing to achieve full integration.

Liberal judicial activism was evident in other areas of American life and culture. In *Engel v. Vitale* (1962), the Court outlawed prayer in public schools on the grounds that such state-sanctioned prayers, even if "denominationally neutral," violated the constitutional prohibition against laws respecting an establishment of religion. In subsequent cases, the majority of the justices, except Stewart, reaffirmed this position that no state could require prayers, recitations from the Bible, or even the Lord's Prayer. In 1965 the Court struck down a Connecticut law prohibiting the dissemination of birth control information and the use of contraceptive devices. Justice Douglas, who wrote the majority opinion in *Griswold v. Connecticut* (1965), argued that restricting knowledge was a violation of the First Amendment and that the First Amendment also contained "a penumbra where privacy is protected from government intrusion."[69] Waxing eloquent if vague, Douglas suggested that specific guarantees in the Bill of Rights might also have "penumbras formed by emanations from those guarantees." In other words, by divining the intentions of the founders, which, of course, meant going far beyond the letter of the law to "penumbras" and "emanations" one might be able to discern a veritable gold mine of liberal rights that had hitherto resided in that gray marginal portion of that opaque body called the Constitution. In a concurring opinion, Arthur Goldberg, joined by Earl Warren and William Brennan, actually called for "the creation of a whole body of extra-constitutional rights."[70] Such was the natural culmination of Anglo-American liberalism, for John Locke had already insisted in the seventeenth century that the function of government was not only to safeguard man's natural rights but also to *expand* them. Presumably, additional natural rights could be found in penumbras and emanations. Of course, who could say that rights previously taken for granted, such as the right to private property, could actually be found in penumbras or emanations? The Constitution, as Justice Black pointed out, did not mention the "right to private property," nor did it mention "zones of privacy," as Justice Douglas had assumed.

The privacy doctrine that liberal justices claimed could be found in "zones of privacy" implied by the First, Third, Fourth, Fifth, and Ninth Amendments, was ultimately transformed into a right to personal dignity, autonomy, and the right over one's own body. As everyone knows, this became the principal argument in *Roe v. Wade* (1973), which held that a woman had complete autonomy (privacy) over her own body. It followed that restrictive abortion statutes were therefore unconstitutional because they denied women the right to choose, a violation of the due process clause of the Fourteenth Amendment. *Roe v. Wade* was an outcome of the civil rights movement and its extension to groups who claimed to have been systematically discriminated against by judicial, legislative, and customary practices. Although it legalized abortion, it raised a host of related constitutional issues, not least of which was the question whether the unborn fetus had a "right to life."

The Court's liberal activism was nothing short of revolutionary in a related field that concerned personal lifestyles and social expressions—human sexuality. Starting in 1952 with a decision in *Roth v. United States* and culminating in *Miller v. California* in 1973, the Court gutted most traditional obscenity laws relating to sexual behavior and expressions. Part of the problem was the Court's inability to define obscenity; and whenever the Court tried to nail down the term, the decisions became vaguer and more elusive. In *Roth v. United States*, Justice Brennan, who formulated the decision for the majority, reaffirmed the longstanding view that obscenity was not protected by the First Amendment; but in trying to define obscenity he offered the most permissive definition to date. According to Brennan, material was not obscene unless in was "utterly without redeeming social importance."[71] Sex and obscenity, the judge declared, were not synonymous:

> The portrayal of sex, e.g., in art, literature and scientific works, is not itself sufficient reason to deny material the constitutional protection of freedom of speech and press. Sex, a great and mysterious motive force in human life, has indisputably been subject of absorbing interest to mankind through the ages; it is one of the vital problems of human interest and public concern.[72]

So what was the test of obscenity? Brennan put the matter as follows: material is obscene if the work "taken as a whole" and applying community standards, appears to the prurient interest of the average person. The term "average person" begged the question since the Court had no idea what average meant, but that it meant "adult" was sufficiently clear, thus excluding children. Prurient interest was obviously in the eye of the beholder, as evidenced by Justice Stewart's memorable statement referring to hardcore pornography: "I know it when I see it."[73]

The Court's definition contained enough loopholes through which pornographers could slide in their efforts to merchandise sexual materials. At the time Brennan delivered his judgment, the range of sexually permissive materials was still relatively narrow, centering on risqué novels such as D. H. Lawrence's *Lady Chatterley's Lover* or Henry Miller's *Tropic of Cancer*, together with erotic magazines such as

Playboy or sexually revealing scenes in films. This was to change dramatically during the 1960s.

The Court fiddled with the problem of obscenity throughout the 1960s without committing itself to either an unequivocally legal or a strong moral position. In 1973 the Court, now headed by Chief Justice Warren Burger, revisited the issue of obscenity in *Miller v. California.* Trying to narrow the scope of obscenity, the Court found that material could be regarded as obscene only if it appealed to the prurient interest of the average person, violated contemporary community standards, depicted patently offensive sexual conduct, and lacked serious literary, artistic, political, or scientific value.[74] These narrow definitions, however, were still so vague that most material, as was subsequently proven, would find its way into the public domain with minimal restrictions by law enforcement agencies.

If the Court's leaning was decidedly libertarian on individual rights, it was egalitarian on socioeconomic issues. It interfered, for example, in legislative redistricting by states because segregationists had used redistricting in order to marginalize black voters, as in Alabama, where the city of Tuskegee had redrawn the city's boundaries in such a way as to exclude black voters. Electoral redistricting had always been the prerogative of state authorities, but the justices held in *Gomillion v. Lightfoot* (1960) that legislative acts may become unlawful if they are designed to accomplish an unlawful end. Similarly, in *Baker v. Carr* (1962) the Court supported the federal district court in Tennessee, compelling redistricting in order to achieve equitable reapportionment that represented shifts in demographic patterns. These decisions caused a political as well as a legal firestorm because they clearly overstepped the Court's proper judicial powers. Even Justice Frankfurter, a liberal justice, complained that the Court was ignoring past precedents limiting its powers in political matters. By abandoning its traditional practice of avoiding political entanglements, Frankfurter argued, the Court might be losing the moral authority it held in the eyes of the American people.[75] The Constitution had provided for a federal form of government rather than a centralized administrative state; it had given the states broad latitudes in many areas, including reapportionment that took into account geographical factors such as redistricting in favor of rural areas. Overvaluing the votes of rural districts, the Court held, violated the due process clause of the Fourteenth Amendment.

Probably one of the most resented set of decisions by the Court, especially by law enforcement officials, was the Court's consistent willingness to protect the rights of the accused while neglecting the rights of victims. The Court's concern about the rights of defendants, especially poor or non-white defendants, must be seen in the context of the police brutality that had been widespread in American society. Giving a suspect "the third degree" commonly meant beatings, sleep deprivation, hours of interrogation, trickery, and similar brutal methods of forcing confessions. Earl Warren believed that such interrogation tactics were not only inconsistent with constitutional rights of individuals but also unnecessary, provided the police had followed sound investigative procedures. The chief justice was also motivated by strong egalitarian convictions that every individual, rich or poor, black or white, must be treated equally under the law. That same egalitarianism also motivated most of the other judges, who shared the chief's concern for the underdog and for those who had been mistreated by law enforcement officials. On the other hand, neither Warren nor the other justices believed in coddling criminals or letting them go free on mere technicalities. Warren's own father had been murdered and no one had ever been arrested for the crime. Furthermore, the chief had been a tough but fair Alameda County prosecutor and California attorney general.[76] This being said, the Court pursued a radical egalitarian approach that would politicize the Supreme Court for decades to come. Abandoning the principal of "original intent" by which to judge legal issues, the Court substituted "changing historical circumstances" as an ad hoc approach. Behind the concept of "changing historical circumstances," however, resided a bedrock belief, and that was the liberal faith in socioeconomic determinism. In regard to crime, that belief held, as Warren put it, "that crime is inseparably connected with factors such as poverty, degradation, sordid social conditions, and weakening of home ties, low standards of law enforcement and the lack of education."[77]

The case that produced a firestorm of opposition to the Court in this regard was *Miranda v. Arizona* (1966), requiring police officers to warn suspects of their constitutional rights. For some time the Court had attempted to move the nation's diverse and often conflicting criminal procedures in the direction of centralized and uniformly administered legal system. As in civil rights cases, the Court claimed the power to overrule state standards, thus driving another nail in the coffin of states' rights. The Phoenix police had located a 1953 Packard belonging to a woman who had been raped and kidnapped. The car was parked in front of Ernesto Miranda's home. Shortly afterwards the victim identified Miranda in a police lineup; and after just two hours of vigorous interrogation, Miranda signed a confession. Miranda's background was full of red flags: he had been arrested for rape before, had numerous arrests for being a Peeping Tom, and had received a dishonorable discharge from the military. A psychiatrist had labeled him a "sociopathic personality" stemming from rampant sexual fantasies. To the judges, however, his limited knowledge of English and his deprived background weighed heavier on their legal consciences than his criminal history. Neither before nor during his interrogation was Miranda ever advised of his right to an attorney. His signed confession was subsequently overturned by the Court because it violated his constitutional rights. Until the Miranda case, state courts had judged the admissibility of confessions by the standard of "voluntariness" standard—that is, whether the confession had been voluntary rather than coerced. Miranda had not been abused; the police even gave him a sandwich and allowed him to get a good night's sleep. The Warren Court, however, insisted that police officials had violated Miranda's constitutional rights. In a 5–4 decision, with Clark, Harlan, White, and Stewart in dissent, the Court held that Fifth Amendment rights against self-incrimination existed outside formal court proceedings, that suspects could not be compelled to confess under threatening interrogation procedures, and that suspects must be given the now familiar Miranda warning:

> You have the right to remain silent; anything you say can and will be used against you. You have the right to talk to a lawyer before being questioned and to have him present

when you are being questioned; and if you cannot afford a lawyer one will be provided for you before any questioning, if you so desire.[78]

Although many law enforcement officials around the nation predicted that the sky would fall in with this decision, the routine police business went on much as before. In some widely publicized cases, defendants were released because Miranda rules had been violated, but the widely feared release of thousands of murderers did not take place. Warren was actually quite taken aback by this outcry and repeatedly reminded critics that the ruling did not outlaw confessions or police interrogations, provided that they were conducted within the framework of his ruling. Nevertheless, Miranda bashing continued to be common and found its way most prominently into public consciousness in Clint Eastwood's *Dirty Harry* movies, showing serial killers beating the rap again and again until Dirty Harry took the law into his own hands.

In assessing the Warren Court, historians have delivered sharply opposing verdicts, with conservatives condemning the Court's decisions as constituting an unmitigated social catastrophe and liberals praising them as enhancing civil rights and liberties. On one point, however, both are in agreement: the Court was the most liberal and activist Court in American history; and as such, it has exercised a profound influence on American life and culture. What has been often overlooked, however, is that while the Court's aims were liberal, its consequences often undermined its libertarian intentions. By weakening the power of local authorities, for example, the Court unwittingly strengthened the role of the federal government and its inherent tendency to impose bureaucratic centralism on all intermediate institutions such as the family, local schools, fraternal organizations, municipalities, state legislatures, business groups, and so forth. In this respect the Court was profoundly split-minded, fluctuating in its decision making between egalitarian motives, which usually enhanced state power, and radical individualism, which undermined strong community control.

On racial issues the Court generally followed a consistent egalitarian doctrine, extending the equal rights protection clause of the Fourteenth Amendment to previously excluded minorities. The Court's *Brown v. Board of Education* decision, intended to end segregation against blacks, set a precedent for extending the same protection to other groups that claimed to have been systematically discriminated against in the past: religious minorities, political protesters, aliens, ethnic minorities, prisoners, criminal defendants, and so forth. Over the next decade, the practice of legally legitimizing group rights rather than individual rights would become a common judicial tool for rectifying alleged past injustices. This explains the Court's willingness to follow the federal government's imposition of "affirmative action" programs in hiring "minorities," which set off intense and often convoluted arguments about who was a member of a minority group and whether skin color should be the primary determinant. In practice, these programs undermined the concept of equality under the law because they gave arbitrary preference to governmentally "protected" groups—African Americans, Latinos, Indians, but curiously also women, a group that was hardly a minority.

When it came to personal lifestyles, especially the whole range of sexual expressions, the Court was radically libertarian, discovering all sorts of specific rights hitherto unknown. Obscenity statutes tumbled like tenpins as the Court steadily extended the zone of privacy and permissible expression. As will be recalled, in *Griswold v. Connecticut*, the Court invented the constitutional right to privacy, which provided the legal justification of numerous lifestyle choices including birth control, abortion, and no-holds-barred sexual activities, all of them with the liberal proviso, of course, "as long as no one gets hurt."

What, then, was the Court's baseline for judging cases that contained important social consequences? The answer is the prevailing mood for democratic (liberal) change, which in the 1960s fluctuated between egalitarian and libertarian tendencies. One thing can be stated with some degree of certainty: the majority of the judges in the Warren Court followed "loose constructionism." They saw themselves as liberal activists, and they have been rightly credited for taking the lead in the noblest American undertaking of the twentieth century: rectifying the legal inequalities that had been imposed on black people. This courageous undertaking bolstered the Supreme Court's image as a shining beacon of equality, but it also empowered the Court with a degree of authority rarely seen in the past. Beginning with the Warren Court, the judicial branch of the government began to grow in power and influence that were never envisioned by the founders, and over time, the Court began to infringe on the legislative branches of government, thus exceeding its constitutional mandate. By claiming the power to identify and "enumerate" additional rights not mentioned in the Constitution (Ninth Amendment), the justices seemed to forget that it was not their mandate to add rights to the Constitution. It was the people, or the states, not nine unelected justices holding their offices for life, who were empowered by the Constitution to enumerate rights. But once the practice of judicial activism had been set in motion, it proved difficult to contain it except by politicizing the appointments to the Supreme Court and other federal courts. The prevailing winds of one day, however, blow differently the next, as do the whims of politicians and political parties. The Court bends, too, but far more slowly, since it is an unelected body. Sitting presidents, having learned to appreciate the powers inherent in the Supreme Court, are eager to make appointments to the Court that reflect their own political leanings. As a result of the polarizations of the 1960s, the Supreme Court has become the fulcrum of ultimate decision making, mandating social programs, deciding issues of life and death, brokering disputed elections, involving itself in national security issues, and generally becoming the last court of appeal on just about every dispute. Rather than regaining their constitutional mandates of power, both the executive and legislative branches have attempted to politicize the Court by promoting judicial candidates who reflect the political thinking of one party or another. Appointments to the Supreme Court now have to pass the right liberal or conservative litmus test, with ugly and even degrading rituals attending such appointments. It was the Warren Court that shifted the constitutional balance in favor of the Supreme Court and led to these unintended consequence.

4. From Great Society to Sick Society

Between 1965 and 1968 the Vietnam War was dwarfing all other national issues at the expense of domestic social programs. Lyndon Johnson was impaling himself on the horns of a dilemma: as a firm believer in American triumphalism he had waged two wars simultaneously: a war on poverty and a war on communism. He saw no contradiction in spending profusely on both because he believed that the American horn of plenty would never be exhausted. Guns and butter were mutually attainable goals; they were to bring about the Great Society. Since 1964 this political wheeler-dealer had orchestrated a brilliant campaign of government advocacy on behalf of the poor, the elderly, the handicapped, minorities, students, and farmers. Not since FDR's New Deal had so many bills sailed through Congress in an orgy of deficit spending. Billions were spent on the war on poverty, on Medicare for the elderly, on education, inner city and urban development, and the like. Hundreds of government programs were unleashed to support Johnson's liberal agenda. The majority of the American people supported these measures, still looking to centralized planning and government welfare policies for the collective social good. When Barry Goldwater offered an alternative choice in the form of limited government, local control, and individual responsibility, he was soundly beaten in 1964. Yet, even in 1964 there was a growing sector of the American electorate that resented big government spending, high taxes, centralized planning, and costly welfare programs. They increasingly asked what constitutional principle justified the massive income transfers that the Johnson administration was not only taking for granted but institutionalizing as a permanent feature of social policy. The answer justifying this great shift in welfare policy was a moral rather than a constitutional one. The reason why welfare spending had to be massive and permanent, Johnson and his supporters had argued, was due to the existence of deep-seated "structural poverty" in American society. The Johnson administration accepted this axiomatic faith that the social system was inherently unjust, absolved individuals from being responsible, and recommended sweeping changes in government spending on the war on poverty, changes that stopped short of income redistributions and higher taxes. This was particularly relevant to the future of black people in America. If black people were poor, it was the result of institutional racism, as the Kerner Commission on Civil Disorders explained after race riots had inundated America's cities in the 1960s. Whether black or white poverty was the issue, the only acceptable causal explanations were deterministic and invariably seen as stemming from structural poverty, racism, the economy, or changes in demographics. That poverty might be an inherent and permanent condition in human life or that it could also have something to do with the responsible actions of the poor was too heretical to be seriously entertained because it ran counter to America's exceptionalism and to the liberal credo that poverty, injustice, and vice are the result of environmental conditions rather than the actions of responsible human beings.

Yet America's horn of plenty was not self-replenishing. As the next chapter will show, starting in 1967 the Vietnam War alone was imposing over $20 billion a year on a weakening economy, and increased welfare spending (from $37 billion in 1965 to $104 billion in 1972) pushed the economy close to the breaking point.[79] Race riots, combined with massive protests against the war, pushed American society itself to the brink of collapse. The Great Society had become the "sick society," as Senator J. William Fulbright observed in late 1967. Only six months later, Johnson would announce, "I shall not seek, and I will not accept, the nomination of my party for another term as your president." His own party was in shambles, as both Senators Eugene McCarthy and Robert F. Kennedy led an internal opposition against Johnson's policy in Vietnam. The stage was set for the most divisive year in American politics in the twentieth century—1968. When it was all over, Martin Luther King and Robert F. Kennedy had been assassinated, race riots had erupted in more than one hundred cities, the Chicago police had rioted against protesters during the Democratic Convention, and Richard Nixon had captured the presidency and ushered in a conservative reaction under the banner of "law and order."

The liberal consensus was shattered. It had taken close to a decade to explode the belief that poverty, war, and most social problems could be solved through massive government intervention in the economy and in the lives of its citizens. Four interconnected beliefs, which had formed the basis of the postwar consensus, were in shambles in 1968. The first had been the deeply held belief that the American ethics of growth fostered egalitarianism and was therefore a revolutionary force worthy of being exported throughout the world. The second was the assumption that capitalism equalizes social conditions and thus resolves social conflict. The third was the claim that capitalism had abolished class distinctions and had lifted the majority of the American people into the well-to-do middle class. The fourth belief was that the capitalist horn of plenty would eventually put an end to divisive ideologies and social differences and usher in a Great Society of abundance, domestic tranquility, and collective security.

It did not happen, and the reason why it did not was that the American people, especially the well-to-do, did not want to pay a prohibitive price that might undermine a corporate system that generated more wealth than any other known economic system in the world. The left liberal utopia would have required massive tax increases and government redistributions, none of which the American people wanted. Working Americans still had a healthy distrust of radical activists, militant unions, community action programs, and the federal government; they preferred to make it on their own without becoming recipients of government largess. As Godfrey Hodgson pointed out, most Americans still believed that they could win the lottery; they did not hate the rich, but merely envied them and hoped to join their ranks.[80]

In the meantime, the war continued for another six years, America's divisions hardened, and confidence in American institutions appeared undermined beyond repair. This was particularly true of the presidency, an institution that Americans had trusted implicitly; but that trust was spent after repeated lies and deceptions from American presidents, mostly notably Richard Nixon, who disgraced his office through a series of high crimes and misdemeanors in the Watergate scandal and was forced to resign from office in 1974, the first American president to do so.

The cumulative impact of a decade of protest and social division led to a kind of national nervous breakdown. One manifestation of that nervous breakdown was a widespread feeling on the part of many Americans that they were living not in one but in several different realities. People felt that they were living in surrealistic times in which the extreme was the norm. To almost everything there appeared to be a parallel reality. Opposed to middle-class life, there emerged hippie communes and experimentation in bizarre "alternative lifestyles." Official mainstream journalism was countered by underground journalism (*Ramparts, Berkeley Barb, Rolling Stone, Village Voice, Psychedelic Review*). The official university was challenged by the "open" university, replete with courses in witchcraft, demonology, I Ching, Zen, herstory, vampirism, and erotic literature. The established Christian religions were challenged by an influx of Eastern religions and a revival of pagan ideas and practices. Mainstream music was countered by folk and rock 'n' roll. And social conventions stressing marriage and family values were trumped by the "open" marriage, creative divorce, communalism, and polymorphic perversion.

What led to these symptoms of national decay were four large-scale crises: the Vietnam War; a resulting economic downturn; the collapse of the liberal consensus in 1968; and deeply divisive countercultural movements. The major cause of America's mounting social problems was the Vietnam War, for along with civil rights protests, the nation's longest war provided the impetus for much of the turmoil of the late 1960s and early 1970s.

7

VIETNAM AND PROTEST

1. Approaching a Quagmire

On September 29, 1972, a rainy Friday, a young twenty-seven-year-old artist and two friends planned to board the ferryboat *M.V. Islander* at Woods Hole, Massachusetts, to collect some of the artist's belonging at Martha's Vineyard. Before embarking, they stopped by at a tavern across the street from the ferry. It was there that they saw Robert McNamara, the former Secretary of Defense, standing at the bar talking to a man with whom he planned to cross the Vineyard Sound.

The young artist had been drinking a little more than usual that day, which might explain his willingness to act on what would turn out to be a spontaneous rage to kill the architect of the Vietnam War. The young artist was a nice Catholic kid from Worcester who was trying to become a painter. He had gone to art school at the height of the Vietnam War and did his best to avoid the draft. This was not a simple decision because two of his brothers had already gone to Vietnam, one of them later becoming a general. His mother's brother had been an admiral in World War II and received the Congressional Medal of Honor. Whether these family ghosts had anything to do with his decision to turn on McNamara is probably doubtful; but what is not beyond doubt is that some pent-up rage against the war was triggered when he saw McNamara that day. What the young man despised in McNamara was shared by many young men of his generation: the secretary's supercilious and self-confident air and how he conveyed it to the American people in clipped sentences that bristled with statistics. Seeing him that evening, the young man later recalled, evoked memory flashes of the secretary's conferences, of one in particular during which someone asked him whether any bombs were hitting villagers in Vietnam. Standing there with his wooden pointer and his eyeglasses reflecting weird polygons of light, the flippant response was that bombs don't always fall were they are supposed to fall.[1]

As the ferry crossed the Vineyard Sound, the young artist at first just wanted to confront McNamara on Vietnam, but as he observed the secretary in the lunchroom of the ferry's top deck, he changed his mind about merely shouting at McNamara's face: "Here he was, starting out his long privileged weekend on the Vineyard, stretched out against the counter like that, talking loud, laughing, obviously enjoying himself a great deal. It was as if he owned the lousy steamship authority or something."[2] It was then that he decided to throw McNamara overboard. On the ruse that there was a telephone call for the secretary, he lured McNamara out on deck where the phone was supposedly located. They were about a mile or two out of Woods

Hole. It was very dark. The two men were right on the edge of the ferry with only a four foot railing with a metal grate in it running to the floor of the deck protecting passengers from falling into the sea. The young man jumped at McNamara and tried to push him overboard:

> I was scared as hell but I think I was pretty calm, too. I didn't say a word, you know, here's to Rolling Thunder, sir, or this one's for the Gulf of Tonkin, you lying sack of crap. Nope, nothing like that. I just grabbed him. I got him by the belt and his shirt collar, right below his throat. I had him over, too. He was halfway over the side. He would have gone, another couple of seconds. He was just kind of hanging there in the dark, clawing for the railing. I remember he screamed, "Oh, my God, no." I'm pretty sure his glasses came off.[3]

What saved McNamara was that he somehow managed to get his fingers interlocked into the metal grillwork of the ship's railing, holding on for dear life until several passengers, who noticed what was going on, restrained the young man and stopped him from completing his assault. "He was amazingly strong, I give him that," said the young artist later; but he angrily brushed aside the subsequent rumor that he had done what he did to prevent McNamara and other wealthy landowners from buying property at Jungle Beach, on the south side of Martha's Vineyard, in order to stop the nude swimming that was going on there.[4] He also resented stories that circulated about McNamara, the tough Colorado mountain climber, overpowering a crazed hippie half his age. The young painter said that he regretted having done it, but in the context of the sixties what he did made sense.

As for McNamara, he was badly shaken but decided not to press charges, so no police report was ever filed. Opinion on the island was split, with some regarding the assault on McNamara as a mad act, others applauding it as the right thing to do to a warmonger. Years later, when the artist, now fairly well-to-do, returned to Martha's Vineyard, he encountered McNamara in a restaurant at Edgartown. The two exchanged brief knowing glances across an obvious generational divide.

Over no other event or subject, except perhaps music and personal lifestyles, was there such a generational gap between the GI generation and the baby boomers as there was over Vietnam. The war was conducted by the World War II generation, and the young were expected to fall in line and fight against communist aggression and to protect the American way of life. This, incidentally, included McNamara's own son, Craig, who defied his father over Vietnam by avoiding the draft, taking part in antiwar demonstrations, dropping out of Stanford, and eventually leaving the country to look for a simpler way of life in South America.[5]

America's involvement in the Vietnam War, directly and indirectly, lasted for three decades, starting with the postwar period in 1945 when the French decided to reestablish their colonial empire in Indochina. On September 2, 1945, shortly after the Japanese surrendered to the United States, the leader of the anti-Japanese Vietminh guerrilla forces, Ho Chi Minh, addressed a cheering crowd in Hanoi and proclaimed the independence of Vietnam. During his address, Ho Chi Minh appealed on several occasions to Thomas Jefferson and the Declaration of Independence, saying,

All men are created equal. They are endowed by their Creator with certain inalienable Rights; among these are Life, Liberty, and the pursuit of Happiness. This immortal statement was made in the Declaration of Independence of the United States of America in 1776. In a broader sense, this means: All the peoples on the earth are equal from birth, all the peoples have a right to live, to be happy and free.[6]

On the reviewing stand with Ho Chi Minh were American army officers, United States airplanes flew over Hanoi, and a Vietnam band struck up "The Star-Spangled Banner." How ironic that the new leaders of the Democratic Republic of Vietnam, who had drawn such a close association to the American revolution and its democratic ideals, should soon find themselves so hopelessly enmeshed with America in one of the longest and bloodiest wars of the twentieth century.[7]

The reasons for this tragedy are long and varied, residing in the apocalyptic climate of the cold war, in France's inability to regain its colonial empire during an age of decolonization, in America's missionary spirit to save the world from international communism, and in the equally fervent crusade of Soviet and Chinese communists to save the world from capitalism. Ho Chi Minh was a nationalistic communist who wanted to chart an independent course for Vietnam that steered free of foreign entanglements in an increasingly bipolar world. His *nomme de guerre* was actually Nguyen Ai Quoc or Nguyen the Patriot, one of the many aliases of this mysterious and in many ways inscrutable leader.[8] What is known with some certainty is that he was the son of a central Vietnam civil servant who worked for the French colonial service, and that he shipped out of Saigon as a young cabin boy on a French liner in 1912. After four years at sea, with stops in Boston and New York, Ho Chi Minh settled down in Paris, working as a photographic retoucher. He also joined the French communist party as one of its founding members. In 1919 he made a brief cameo appearance at the Paris Peace Conference, where he unsuccessfully made a plea on behalf of the Vietnamese people for national self-determination. His movements thereafter are somewhat obscure because he decided to become an itinerant revolutionary, who established important links with like-minded revolutionaries in Russia and China. While traveling in China under the name of Mr. Ling, a Chinese businessman, he established contacts with Chou En-lai, Chiang Kai-shek, and assorted generals, diplomats, and journalists. In 1945 the American OSS recruited Ho Chi Minh as an agent charged with gathering intelligence information about the Japanese in Indochina. The OSS also provided substantial financial support for the establishment of a guerrilla force, the Vietminh, whose mission was to wage war on the Japanese in Vietnam.

After Ho Chi Minh's forces drove the French out of Vietnam, Ho Chi Minh found little support from either the democratic West or the communist world in supporting his crusade of getting rid of Western colonial control and forging an independent Republic of Vietnam. William J. Duiker has shown that Ho Chi Minh did not have much support from either China or the Soviet Union in the immediate postwar period (1945–55), which only confirmed him in his strong conviction that his people were waging a war of national liberation that, in the final analysis, had to be won by the Vietnamese people themselves.[9] After the proclamation of the Democratic

Republic of Vietnam on September 2, 1945, Ho Chi Minh saw himself as the legitimate leader of the Vietnamese people. By that time, he was not only an experienced revolutionary organizer but also an intellectual of considerable merit, a man who could draw on decades of travel, political connections, and extensive study and reading. He also had a flair for creating or encouraging a certain leadership mystique that portrayed him as "Uncle Ho" (Bac Ho). This was the image of the quirky, worldly wise poet-politician who dressed in khaki and sandals, lived frugally in a tiny house behind the presidential palace and could be seen walking every day through the green shade of the acacia trees. Although this was a communist revolutionary invention, it served its propagandistic purposes, especially with gullible Americans on the left who preferred to see Ho Chi Minh as "Uncle Ho" and LBJ as a vulgar and predatory Texas Cowboy. The reality was that Ho Chi Minh was a determined, tenacious, and ruthless leader who had two strong passions: love of country and a belief in communism. Modest in his personal needs and incorruptible in his principles, he never lost sight of liberating Vietnam from foreign control and transforming it into a model communist society.

Given the rising tensions between East and West, Ho Chi Minh's goal of charting an independent course for Vietnam that steered clear of foreign entanglements proved to be impossible and unrealistic. Already in 1947, the United States formulated its containment policy aimed at curbing an expansionist Soviet Union by way of a globe-girdling strategy of military, economic, and political commitments to all nations opposing communism. After the Soviet Union exploded its first atomic bomb and China became communist in 1949, the United States became even more fiercely anticommunist and was, therefore, less and less willing to support any nationalistic, anticolonial movement that might be supported by either Moscow or Peking. Ho Chi Minh's dream of an independent Vietnam would therefore have to wait for another day. Because of rising anticommunism in the United States, the Truman administration abandoned Roosevelt's decision to prevent France from regaining Indochina. After the French returned to Vietnam, they encountered serious opposition from the Vietminh, who refused to allow the French to resume their prewar control. Negotiations between the French and Vietminh forces quickly fell apart. In November 1946 a French cruiser shelled Haiphong, killing six thousand civilians; and while this event was transpiring, French troops were pouring into southern Vietnam with transportation, equipment, and uniforms supplied courtesy of Uncle Sam. The first stage of the Vietnam War had begun. After attacking a French garrison in Hanoi, Ho Chi Minh's forces withdrew into the country and prepared for a prolonged guerrilla war against the French.[10] That war came to an end when the French forces were decisively defeated by General Giap at Dienbienphu in 1954.

On May 7, 1954, the French formally surrendered to the Vietminh communists after being defeated at Dienbienphu. France abandoned the north and tried to salvage as much as possible below the seventeenth parallel. By the terms of the Geneva Conference, which followed the defeat at Dienbienphu, Vietnam was divided along the seventeenth parallel pending a final political settlement that was to to be reached by all parties as a result of national elections. The United States was just an "interested" party to these proceedings and promised "to refrain from the threat or use of force to disturb them."[11] The division of Vietnam into north and south was to be purely temporary, with neither side being allowed to join a military alliance. Following national elections, scheduled for the summer of 1956 and supervised by an international commission composed of Canada, Poland, and India, the country was to be reunified.[12]

In the context of the bifurcated thinking of the cold war, United States policy was to build up South Vietnam as a bulwark against communism, just as Moscow and Peking encouraged Ho Chi Minh in spearheading a communist government that would eventually control all of Vietnam. The binary logic of cold war reality renders absurd the notion that either side wanted "free" elections in Vietnam. The truth is that each cold war side waged the Vietnam War by proxy, backing the most promising candidate to do its bidding. In retrospect, the communists chose wisely, the United States chose badly. The Eisenhower administration backed the former emperor Bao Dai and his prime minister, Ngo Dinh Diem. There was nothing remotely democratic about this new South Vietnamese government, but the United States was not so much interested at the time whether a government was democratic as long as it was not communist and supported the United States. The Bao Dai regime, which most Americans could not distinguish from Bo Diddly, was little more than an "oriental despotism with a French accent,"[13] but that was enough for it to qualify for $100 million in U.S. foreign aid.

In the meantime, the division of the country into a communist North and a Western-sponsored South led to extreme political, social, and economic instability. Hundreds of thousands of refugees, most of them persecuted Catholics, fled from the North to the South with support from the American navy. The South Vietnamese army was little more than a rabble. Communist Vietminh forces had pockets of control in the Mekong Delta. Assessing United States prospects in this politically torn country, Secretary of Defense Charles E. Wilson advised Eisenhower to get out of South Vietnam as soon as possible, warning that he could see nothing but "grief in store for us if we remained in that area."[14]

On October 23, 1955, Diem defeated Bao Dai in a rigged referendum and became chief of state. Three days later he proclaimed the Republic of Vietnam, with himself as president. Diem was a strong nationalist and anticommunist.[15] His father, a Roman Catholic, had been an official at the imperial court. Under restored French rule, Diem had served as Minister of the Interior. Diem was more of a scholarly recluse than a leader. A staunch Catholic, he had been befriended by Cardinal Spellman, who made it possible for him to attend Maryknoll Seminary in the United States between 1951 and 1953. His fervent appeals for an independent non-communist Vietnam attracted the attention of prominent U.S. politicians, especially such Democratic senators as John F. Kennedy and Mike Mansfield. Though a man of principle, Diem was also rigid and inflexible, seeing the world in sharp opposites of good and evil. He was also an elitist who had little understanding of the needs of the Vietnamese people. Facing certain collapse in May 1955, the Diem regime survived largely through U.S. assistance. With firm U.S. backing, Diem blocked the elections that were supposed to be held by the terms of the Geneva Accords in the summer of 1956.

By the late 1950s there were fifteen hundred American advisors in Vietnam, most of them training the South Vietnam Army and paying the salaries of its soldiers to the tune of $85 million per year. A Command and General Staff College for senior officers had also been established. The chief organization charged with overseeing this military mission was called MAAG, or Military Assistance and Advisory Group, headquartered in Saigon. Its mission was to fight an essentially conventional war.[16] Little was done to promote democracy or to introduce economic development on the village level. Diem wanted personal power; he distrusted popular rule and majority opinion. His political role model, as quaint as it was obsolete, was the nineteenth-century emperor Minh Mang, who was hailed at the time as a progressive because he convened an assembly of mandarins to approve his royal decrees. Diem also shamelessly practiced nepotism: three of his brothers were appointed to a cabinet of six. They completely dominated the legislature, with Diem carefully handpicking its members. As to democratic legitimacy, it can be argued that the emerging South Vietnamese government had little support from the majority of the citizens it presumed to represent. Almost from the moment of its inception, the South Vietnamese government was a U.S. creation, not because it represented the majority of the Vietnamese people but because the United States could use this government to oppose communism. Unlike the North Vietnamese government, which had strong support in the countryside as an insurgency movement, the South Vietnamese government never captured the hearts and minds of its people. President Kennedy had it right when he said that "in the final analysis, it is their [the Vietnamese] war. They are the ones who have to win it or lose it. We can help them, we can give them equipment, we can send our men out there as advisers, but they have to win it, the people of Vietnam, against the communists."[17] What Kennedy missed was the fact that communism was, at best, a peripheral issue. The core issue involved in the Vietnamese war was national liberation from colonial control—French and then American. By making it an American war, as Michael Walzer has argued, the United States waged this war for American purposes, in someone else's country.[18]

Related to this issue of American involvement in Vietnam's internal struggle is the question whether the insurgency movement against the South Vietnamese government was inspired by communist aggression, orchestrated in Hanoi, or whether it stemmed from indigenous roots in the South in response to Diem's oppressive regime. William Duiker's argument that insurgency was a genuine revolt in the South but organized and directed from the North is overly simplistic.[19] As Lewis R. Ward has shown, the Vietnam War consisted of two disparate but interlinked conflicts—an insurgency and an invasion, but the two conflicts had one manager: the politburo in Hanoi.[20] The Hanoi regime was no better than Diem's autocratic regime, especially in its treatment of dissidents (Catholics, Buddhists, landowners, middle-class professionals), many of whom either fled to the South or were exterminated. It has been estimated that Hanoi eliminated somewhere between three thousand and fifteen thousand dissidents.[21] Both the North and South Vietnamese governments were oppressive in their own different ways: in the North, Ho Chi Minh's communists imposed a dictatorial, one-party state that wiped out dissidents, stripped peasants and others of their land and properties in so-called land-reforms (always a communist euphemism for state sponsored confiscation), and imprisoned others in forced labor camps; in the South a minority Catholic clique, backed by military force and U.S. aid, resorted to repression in order to fend off communist guerrillas, factious sects, and gangsters.[22]

Between 1957 and 1959 Diem's government mounted major offenses against communists in the South. These anticommunist policies were devastatingly effective. In response, the North authorized a resumption of armed struggle: "Group 559" constructed special infiltration routes into South Vietnam via the Ho Chi Minh trail, while another group (Group 759) was organized to send men and supplies to the South by sea. In December of 1960 the Hanoi leadership founded the National Liberation Front (NLF) for South Vietnam. Shortly afterwards, communist guerrillas increased their attacks on South Vietnamese officials, assassinating over three thousand between 1958 and 1959, and launching military operations against South Vietnamese controlled villages and on overexposed South Vietnam forces. The term Vietcong, which meant Vietnam communist, was applied to the guerrillas by the Diem regime. In order to counteract communist subversion, Diem launched an ill-fated "Agroville" program that relocated peasants in areas where the army could provide for their security from communist attacks. The peasants, however, deeply resented being removed from their land and homes. Diem's program, like the later "strategic hamlet" program, failed because it was never intended to help poor peasants but to secure the countryside against communist infiltration. Uprooted from their ancestral lands, peasants would find themselves in unfamiliar surroundings, harassed by either Vietcong guerrillas or by corrupt Saigon officials.

In the meantime, the U.S. military shifted its tactics from conventional warfare to counterinsurgency because it became increasingly obvious that guerrilla tactics could not be countered by purely conventional military means. As the Eisenhower administration came to an end, the problems in Laos seemed far more important than the one in Vietnam. In Laos, as in Vietnam, the American-sponsored regime tried to stop the communist Pathet Lao. Eisenhower felt that Laos might be the "cork in the bottle" whose removal might threaten all of Southeast Asia. In retrospect, the logic behind this sort of thinking was a fallacious variety of the "slippery slope" or "domino effect." The fallacy behind this assumption is the belief that a proposed course of action would lead, by a series of steps, to an undesirable or even catastrophic outcome. The fallacy holds that once we take that first fateful step we shall find ourselves inevitably slipping down the slippery slope. Actions are necessarily connected, like links in a chain, so that the occurrence of one action will lead to the next, and so on, to the bitter end. As Bob Hope, returning from Vietnam, told reporters: "Everybody I talked to there [Vietnam] wants to know why they can't go in and finish it, and don't let anybody kid you about why we're there. . . . If we weren't, those Commies would have the whole thing, and it wouldn't be long until we'd be looking off the coast of Santa Monica."[23] This was Bob Hope's version of the famous domino theory, the belief held by postwar administrations that the United States was locked in mortal combat with international communism, and that the victory of communism in one country would set in motion a ripple effect that would inevitably infect neighboring countries. Thus, if the United States did not draw a line in the sand and stop communism dead in its tracks in Vietnam, the falling Vietnam domino would topple all the others, leading to the fall of Cambodia, Thailand, Laos, the Philippines, New Zealand, Australia, Hawaii, and so on.

President Eisenhower was one of the first to articulate this theory publicly after the French lost at Dienbienphu, saying: "You have a row of dominoes set up, you knock over the first one, and what will happen to the last one is the certainty that it will go over very quickly. So you could have the beginning of a disintegration that would have the most profound consequences."[24] The same faulty metaphor was repeated by Kennedy, Johnson, and Nixon. Asked whether he believed in the domino theory, Kennedy said in an interview with NBC News:

Mr. Brinkley: Mr. President, have you had any reason to doubt this so-called "domino theory," that if South Viet-Nam falls, the rest of Southeast Asia will go behind it?

The President: No, I believe it. I believe it. I think that the struggle is close enough. China is so large, looms so high just beyond the frontiers, that if South Viet-Nam went, it would not only give them an improved geographic position for a guerrilla assault on Malaya but would also give the impression that the wave of the future in Southeast Asia was China and the Communists. So I believe it.[25]

The U.S. press was no more prescient in defending this dubious theory. The *New York Times*, for example, editorialized that southeast Asian nations such as Laos, Cambodia, Burma, Thailand, Malaysia, and Indonesia would be endangered if Vietnam fell. The *Times* opined that in that event the security of the United States would be seriously jeopardized throughout the western Pacific, threatening India and unleashing almost unstoppable revolutionary movements by the Red Chinese and by communists around the world.[26]

Historical hindsight shows that indigenous nationalistic movements with Marxist convictions in one country did not spread "like a virus" to other countries, nor was communism, as assumed by Washington policy makers, a monolithic movement without specific national or cultural variations. It is striking how American policy makers strapped themselves into the mental straitjacket that the domino theory implied. Equally striking is the fact that most American policy makers were also ill-informed about the history, geography, and culture of the Far East. Few realized how insuperable the obstacles were when it came to an extensive military, political, and economic involvement in the internal affairs of Indochina.[27]

2. Paying Any Price and Bearing Any Burden

The Kennedy era (1961–63) promised more American involvement in Vietnam. Kennedy's "best and brightest" essentially continued previous American commitments, but with the greater degree of ideological fervor so characteristic of the New Frontiersmen.[28] In his Inaugural Address the newly elected president told the nation and the world that the United States would "pay any price, bear any burden, meet any hardship, support any friend, oppose any foe to assure the survival and success of liberty."[29] Although Kennedy was not an inflexible cold warrior, he considered Vietnam the cornerstone of the Free World in Southeast Asia, just as he considered Berlin the bulwark against communism in Europe. The Kennedy administration viewed communist guerrilla warfare as an international disease, to be combated by every possible means: counterinsurgency, massive foreign aid, and far-flung intelligence operations. Kennedy and his advisers were global activists who wanted to check the communist threat wherever it reared its head. The result was that Kennedy plunged more deeply into the Vietnam morass than his predecessor. He was also poorly informed about Diem's regime, which was on the verge of collapse by the time his administration took power.

In January 1961, the feisty and belligerent Soviet premier, Nikita Khrushchev, made a militant speech promising Soviet support for wars of national liberation. The Kennedy administration saw this as a virtual declaration of war.[30] The frontiersmen, circling the wagons around the White House, were gripped by a veritable siege mentality, made all the more menacing by far more serious trouble spots in places such as Laos, Cuba, and Berlin. Fortunately, a settlement was negotiated in Laos. At the same time, special forces were sent to train the South Vietnamese in counterinsurgency methods. Vice president Lyndon Johnson was dispatched to Vietnam to give personal assurance to the South Vietnamese that America would not permit the country to fall into the hands of the communists. After calling Diem the Winston Churchill of Vietnam, he recommended additional American aid to South Vietnam. At the same time, the CIA initiated a secret war in Laos, arming nine thousand Hmong tribesmen for action against the Ho Chi Minh trail.

In October 1961, President Kennedy sent Walt Rostow and General Maxwell Taylor on a fact-finding mission to Vietnam; their recommendation was to increase American military involvement, especially through the use of the newly created Green Berets, an elite counterinsurgency force. Both Rostow and Taylor believed that the situation in Vietnam was deteriorating, and therefore required an expansion of U.S. military power. A "Limited Partnership" with the South Vietnam government, consisting of eight thousand U.S. combat troops, was proposed. This increase in manpower was intended to be a logistical force of engineers, medical groups, and military advisers. In retrospect, it was still a token commitment, a kind of "half-in, half out" measure, as the historian Richard Herring called it.[31] Averell Harriman, Assistant Secretary of State for Eastern affairs (1961–63), doubted that the repressive Diem regime could last. Chester Bowles, Undersecretary of State and a critic of U.S. involvement in Vietnam, warned that the United States was "headed full blast up a dead end street."[32] President Kennedy, who was deeply enmeshed with the Soviets in cold war conflicts all over the world, felt that he had to flex his muscles toward "that son-of-a-bitch Khrushchev." In private, however, he was dubious about an all-out commitment to Vietnam and refused to send troops. He was willing to support a limited commitment consisting of aid and advisers. He may have glimpsed that the "new partnership" might tie the United States ever more tightly to the South Vietnamese government; but such doubts were assuaged by a strong confidence, born of American exceptionalism, that the United States knew what was good for Vietnam.

Combining an aggressive brand of missionary zeal and technological know-how, U.S. policy planners envisioned relocating South Vietnam peasants into "strategic hamlets," really armed stockades, thus isolating the guerrillas from their food chain and recruiting base in the South. The aim was to use aggressive insurgency methods, borrowed from the British experience in Malaya, and to reduce communist guerrilla forces to "hungry, marauding bands of outlaws."[33] Some criticized this approach as a mere updated version of Diem's failed "agroville" program of the late 1950s, while others claimed that it was a heavy military investment that was kept secret from the American people. As it would turn out, the strategic hamlet program did not serve the people it was ostensibly designed to help: the peasants of South Vietnam. Instead, it was deliberately used by the Diem regime in order to extend its control and power over the countryside. In most cases, peasants were forcibly resettled into new hamlets that turned out to be far removed from their nearest markets, leaving their inhabitants isolated, unprotected, and susceptible to Vietcong infiltrators. It goes without saying that many South Vietnamese peasants became Vietcong sympathizers not because they identified with communism but because they resented the South Vietnamese government for its heavy-handed, coercive methods, for its lack of military protection, and for its unreasonable expectation that the new hamlets and farmlands would be productive and profitable. Ironically, Ngo Dinh Nhu's chief lieutenant, who helped him carry out the strategic hamlet program, was Colonel Pham Ngoc Thao, a secret communist functionary.[34]

Side by side with the strategic hamlet approach, the United States replaced the Military Assistance Advisory Group (MAAG) with a new organization called Military Assistance Command, Vietnam (MACV), headed by General Paul Harkins, later known for his optimistic and misleading reports. The number of U.S. advisers jumped from 3,205 in December 1961 to more than 9,000 by the end of 1962.[35] Interestingly enough, information about this increase in U.S. advisers was withheld from the American people. Greater American military presence and advice did not translate into victories against the communists. In fact, throughout 1962 the Army of the Republic of South Vietnam (ARVN) launched a series of offenses that were unsuccessful.

The unpopular and corrupt nature of the Diem regime, combined with the strong rapport the communists were forging with ordinary peasants, explains why the guerrillas continued to recruit insurgents. In the meantime, the United States command waged what some have called technowar, as its helicopters "rattle-assed" around the country looking for guerrillas.[36] By the end of 1962 the insurgents had mobilized three hundred thousand members. Being involved in an internal civil war in an Asian country, most Americans had difficulty in distinguishing who was an insurgent, who was a peasant, and who was a friendly official. U.S. troops often gunned down innocent civilians; and in their eagerness to find technological solutions to human complexities, used napalm and defoliants to flush out real or imagined guerrillas, degrading the environment and its food chain.

As American intervention deepened, it became embarrassingly obvious to the Kennedy administration that President Diem's South Vietnamese government was unrepresentative, undemocratic, corrupt, and oppressive. Diem himself retreated into isolation, letting his sinister younger brother Ngo Dinh Nhu take care of everyday government business. Nhu's wife, Madame Ngo Dinh Nhu, also called the Dragon Lady, was just as bad. A Catholic in a Buddhist country, she appeared imperious, haughty, and intemperate. The whole government appeared little better than a narrow family oligarchy, aloof from the people and thoroughly corrupt. Several able U.S. reporters, among them David Halberstam of the *New York Times*, Neil Sheehan of UPI, and Malcolm Browne of the Associated Press, quickly exposed such corruption in the South Vietnamese government and reported that such a regime was not worth supporting.[37]

In response to mounting criticism by both the press and members of Congress, President Kennedy sent yet another team to Vietnam on a fact-finding mission. The product of this mission was the Hilsman-Forrestal report of early 1963, which tried to strike a balance between official optimism and harsh criticism of the United States by journalists such as Halberstam and Sheehan. President Kennedy, however, still had no clear-cut plan or vision of how this evolving war could be ended.[38]

In May 1963 a religious crisis rocked South Vietnam when Diem's troops fired on a crowd at Hue protesting the ban on displaying multicolored flags on the anniversary of Buddha's 2527th birthday. On June 13, 1963 an elderly Buddhist monk publicly doused himself with gasoline and burned himself alive in front of a large crowd at a major Saigon intersection. The monk's self-immolation, pictures of which were quickly splattered over the front pages of the world's press, triggered a popular uproar in South Vietnam. Workers, students, and antigovernment activists joined in opposition to the unpopular Diem regime. Discontent even spread to the army. The Dragon Lady, Madame Nhu, dismissed the incident and similar immolations as "barbecues" and offered to furnish gasoline and matches for more suicides. Diem's opponents in Washington now realized that they had a serious crisis on their hands in Vietnam, and that perhaps a regime change was in order. South Vietnamese generals opened secret negotiations with the United States about toppling Diem. President Kennedy, inundated by conflicting accounts and divisions within his own administration over toppling Diem exclaimed at one point: "My God! My government's coming apart";[39] and adding in greater anger at another point, the president said: "This shit has got to stop"[40] By the end of August the United States was committed to a coup.

In the now familiar pattern of U.S. response to the Vietnamese crisis, another fact-finding team was dispatched, consisting of General Taylor and Secretary of Defense McNamara. Henry Cabot Lodge, the United States ambassador, who had replaced Frederick Nolting, was authorized to inform the secret plotters that while not wishing to encourage a plot, the United States would not thwart a change of government! The main concern in the Kennedy administration, as Stanley Karnow has rightly pointed out, was pragmatic rather than ethical—that is, whether the plot would work rather than whether it was morally defensible.[41] On September 2, 1963, Duong Van Minh and other generals struck and murdered Diem and his brother Nhu. There was a collective sigh of relief in Washington, but only six weeks later John F. Kennedy himself was assassinated in Dallas. A military junta, consisting of twelve army officers, assumed power in South Vietnam, only to isolate itself at military headquarters near Saigon's Tan Son Nhut Airport. The new junta did little to stem the decline.

3. Hot Damn Vietnam: LBJ and the War

Following the assassination of John F. Kennedy on November 22, 1963, the war in Vietnam would take a sharply different turn under his successor, Lyndon Johnson. The new president had inherited a civil war in Vietnam that was dictated by the us-versus-them logic of the cold war. Between November 1963 and July 1965, Johnson transformed a limited commitment to an open-ended one by significantly escalating the war and Americanizing it.[42] By the end of 1963 there were fifteen thousand American military advisers in South Vietnam; two years later their number had reached two hundred thousand. The shadow of an expanding war in Vietnam considerably darkened with the intrusion of Johnson's volatile and explosive personality. Johnson liked to strut on a big stage and put on a big show, but he rarely acted brutally or with malicious intentions. Whether out of insecurity or well-intentioned motives or both, he wanted to fulfill the promises and hopes of New Deal liberalism, which consisted in making the government a close partner in the lives of the American people. In practice, this meant government-sponsored financial and contractual aid to private industries carrying out government policies (defense, research, education, public health, transportation), broad welfare programs, and an ever-increasing number of regulatory agencies to implement such a broad-scale involvement of the government in the lives of the American people. Lyndon Johnson's role in this enterprise equalled, if not surpassed, that of Franklin Roosevelt, for he brought decades of political experience and boundless energy to this project. Although he had a voracious appetite for power and a gift for manipulating, browbeating, and intimidating people, Johnson possessed two unselfish, if perhaps misguided, convictions: that the American way of life, as he understood it, was superior to any other way of life on earth and that he could help to perfect it, even on a global scale. Like most politicians of his generation, Democrat as well as Republican, Johnson did not believe in rewarding aggression, especially communist aggression. He was particularly paranoid about being "soft on communism," hating to be upstaged on this issue by right-wing Republicans. He wanted to make sure that Ho Chi Minh was not going to take over South Vietnam under his watch, privately saying that "I am not going to lose Vietnam. I am not going to be the President who let Southeast Asia go the way China went."[43] His deep-seated ethnocentrism, however, prevented him from understanding what he was up against in Southeast Asia, a part of the world that he tended to see in narrow American, if not

Texan, perspective. This also involved a serious misunderstanding of Ho Chi Minh's fanatical resolve. Tragically, Johnson also underestimated the resolve of the American people and how far they were willing to follow him into an ever-deeper entanglement into what would soon turn out to be a hopeless stalemate.

When Lyndon Johnson became president after the tragic death of John F. Kennedy, he assumed that he could bargain with Ho Chi Minh in the same way that he had so successfully bargained with his political opposition in Congress. He thought that it was simply a matter of sitting down with old Ho, negotiating, making concessions, and reaching a mutually satisfactory compromise. But Ho Chi Minh was a communist fanatic, not a democratic politician; he did not believe that all differences could be settled by economic concessions or peaceful arbitration of political differences. Ho Chi Minh was a revolutionary communist who wanted the United States out of Vietnam and Vietnam transformed into a communist state. It took Lyndon Johnson some time to grasp this point. In 1965, he still thought that he could buy off Ho Chi Minh by offering to develop the economic resources of the Mekong Delta, reminiscent of Roosevelt's development of the hydroelectric resources of the Tennessee Valley in the 1930s.[44] "Old Ho can't turn me down, old Ho can't turn me down," Johnson repeated after making the offer.[45] Old Ho, of course, wanted the United States to withdraw completely from Vietnam. As this gradually began to sink in on a stunned Johnson, who by instinct and temperament was no warmonger, he started tightening the vise on Ho Chi Minh by incrementally expanding the war and hoping that this would get his adversary to the conference table. When this did not do the trick, the infuriated Johnson unleashed more and more bombs on his adversary. The result was that communist resolve grew stronger rather than weaker, while Johnson's determination grew weaker rather than stronger. Domestic opposition to the war added to Johnson's increasing uncertainty that the Vietnam War could be won under the conditions he had chosen to fight it. Johnson's will and that of the American people eventually buckled: the enemy had a stronger commitment to its cause and to the belief in the righteousness of that cause. This is why Vietnam, after decades of bloody conflict, would fall to the stronger believer.

In response to this U.S. escalation of the war in South Vietnam, the North Vietnamese Central Committee ordered the National Liberation Front (NLF) to step up political agitation and infiltration. The United States, in turn, pledged to match communist buildups by increasing its aid to South Vietnam. The United States declared that its central objective was to assist the people and government of South Vietnam to win the war against "the externally directed and supported *communist conspiracy*" (italics mine).[46] In January 1964 a group of army officers, headed by General Nguyen Khanh, overthrew the divided junta. Ambassador Lodge felt that one-man rule was probably better than a divided junta. The Khanh government, however, was much weaker than the Diem regime had ever been. It also faced staggering social problems and was badly led by a sleazy leader who "strutted and swaggered like a character in a Chinese opera."[47] In addition to the daunting social problems, which remained unaddressed, Khanh squabbled with his generals and suffered humiliating setbacks against the Vietcong in the Mekong Delta.[48]

Lyndon Johnson at first employed "more of the same" in 1964. He appointed General William Westmoreland, a capable paratrooper and veteran of World War II and Korea, to replace the ineffectual and ever-optimistic Harkins. Taylor replaced Lodge as ambassador. Then on August 2, 1964, an ominous event took place in the Tonkin Gulf. The destroyer *USS Maddox*, conducting electronic espionage off the coast of North Vietnam, encountered a group of North Vietnam torpedo boats and fired on them. South Vietnam gunboats had bombarded the island of Hon Me the previous evening. It is assumed that the North Vietnam torpedo boats suspected that the *USS Maddox* was supporting the South Vietnamese gunboats. The torpedo boats launched their torpedoes and were driven off by the *Maddox* and by fighters from the carrier *Ticonderoga*. Lyndon Johnson was enraged by what he assumed to be communist aggression and sent the destroyer *C. Turner Joy* to support the *Maddox*. On August 4, the two U.S. destroyers reported being under attack, but neither visual sighting nor radar blips confirmed the presence of enemy gunboats. The U.S. government and the press, however, reported that enemy gunboats had fired on the two U.S. destroyers.[49] Johnson decided to strike back with a "firm, swift retaliatory air strike" against North Vietnam torpedo boat bases. Although Secretary of Defense Robert McNamara reportedly said he was not certain who fired first on whom, he nevertheless fully supported the raid.[50] Lyndon Johnson then secured the Gulf of Tonkin Resolution from Congress, authorizing him to "take all necessary measures to repel any armed attacks against the forces of the United States and to prevent further aggression."[51] Ernest Gruening, a Democrat from Alaska, and one of only two senators to oppose the declaration, called it a "predated declaration of war."[52] J. William Fulbright, senator from Arkansas and chairman of the Foreign Relations Committee, concerned more about possible reactions from right-wing Republicans than about giving Lyndon Johnson a blank check to conduct the war, shepherded the resolution through the Senate. Lyndon Johnson's firm response and his deft political handling of the crisis gave him broad public support. According to a Harris poll, his popular approval skyrocketed from 42 to 72 percent overnight.[53]

In the meantime, Johnson deceived the public that he was seeking no wider war in Vietnam. The situation in Vietnam, however, further deteriorated. Khanh was losing control and resigned on August 1964. Following a period of coups and countercoups, a civilian government was formed under Phan Huy Quat, only to be toppled in May 1965 by Air Marshal Nguyen Cao Ky and General Nguyen Van Thieu. In October 1964 Khrushchev fell from power and China exploded its first atomic bomb.

Inside South Vietnam the situation worsened. The fifth government since Diem's fall took office in February 1965. Despite massive U.S. aid, the South Vietnamese army was disintegrating. Government corruption was rampant. General Westmoreland recommended and received the fifty thousand combat and supply forces he had requested for the summer of 1965. By late July 1965 Lyndon Johnson set the course from which he would not deviate for the next three years: that of steadily deploying new forces, conducting air strikes, and infusing massive financial aid into South Vietnam. While doing so, he not only refused to level with the American people but deliberately misled them into believing that America was only waging a "limited" war. Ambassador Lodge pointedly asked him: "How do you send young men there in great numbers without telling why?"[54]—a good question that cried out for an honest explanation. Yet no national emergency was announced, no declaration of war delivered. Lyndon Johnson thought he could inflict sufficient pain on the enemy so that he would stop fighting and negotiate. "I'm going up old Ho Chi Minh's leg an inch at a time," he told Senator George McGovern.[55] The truth was that Johnson, a political pragmatist and wheeler-dealer, was plainly baffled by the determination and single-mindedness of Ho Chi Minh. Having spent a lifetime as a parliamentary negotiator, manipulator, and compromiser, he neither understood the nature of his rigid ideological adversary nor the Vietnam people he pretended to save for democracy. Johnson's ethnocentric blind spot was shared to a large extent by many of his political advisers, who were equally innocent of the language and culture of Vietnam and Southeast Asia.

Crawling up Ho Chi Minh's leg a step at a time hardly seemed an appropriate strategy of winning the war. Critics of the war saw it as no more than childish tit-for-tat with the lives of young Americans. And Ho Chi Minh definitely had the manpower and support from China and the Soviet Union to match such incremental escalation. The policy of seeking to do what would be "enough, but not too much," was self-defeating since no one knew what was enough. Johnson seriously underestimated Ho Chi Minh and his determination to liberate and unify all of Vietnam under communist control. It was clear that Ho Chi Minh was not awed by the power of the United States. A U.S. journalist had it all wrong when he said aboard the aircraft carrier *Ranger*: "They just ought to show this ship to the Vietcong—that would make them give up."[56] The mere application of technological might, it turned out, did not turn the trick. By 1967 the United States would have nearly half a million troops in Vietnam and there was no end in sight.

On February 24, 1965, the U.S. military command unleashed operation Rolling Thunder, which concentrated on military bases, supply depots, and infiltration routes into South Vietnam. Unlike earlier operations such as Flaming Dart, which were mostly retaliatory, Rolling Thunder was a continuous bombing operation that would go on for years. On March 8, 1965, Marines in full battle gear came ashore at Danang, the first U.S. combat troops to land on the Asian mainland since the Korean War. This crucial event, barely noticed in the United States, was a real turning point in the Americanization of the Vietnam War.[57] In early 1966 air strikes shifted to North Vietnam's industrial and transportation systems. But there were precious few promising targets, since North Vietnam was a preindustrial country and its people moved about largely on bicycles. Some cities were heavily damaged, forcing the communists to locate their command posts underground. It is estimated that the communists dug thirty thousand miles of tunnels.[58] American war planners apparently had no idea of what "ant labor" could accomplish in Southeast Asia. By the mid-1960s the North Vietnamese were also getting substantial aid from both Russia and China. Ho Chi Minh was thankful that 320,000 Chinese engineers and artillery troops built roads and installed anti-aircraft batteries; he also accepted massive arms from the Soviets. At the same time, he refused to bind himself to either power, exploiting their differences and reserving the final right to make decisions for himself. The charge that Ho Chi Minh was a puppet of the Chinese or the Soviets cannot be maintained.

By 1967 the United States was spending profusely and reaping few benefits. A typical B-52 sortie cost $30,000. Air operations between 1965 and 1967 amounted to a total of $1.7 billion. Between 1965 and 1968 the United States lost 950 aircraft over Vietnam. The "search and destroy" missions searched more than they destroyed; many of them, as critics contended, were "ass-rattling" in the jungle. Support from allies such as Australia or South Korea was, at best, token or symbolic. General Westmoreland was a capable logistical planner who could supervise men and facilities, but he had little understanding of the kind of war he was fighting. He mistakenly believed, as did his commander-in-chief, that he could fight a sophisticated technological war with communist guerrillas on foreign and inhospitable terrain. But it did no good to exploit the technological possibilities of the latest gadgets in dense jungle terrain. Did those eager technological geeks really believe that portal raid units could actually pick up the odor of human urine, that herbicides such as Agent Orange could defoliate the jungle, or that napalm would wreak havoc on friend and foe alike? Did they not foresee that such weapons of mass destruction would destroy one-half of South Vietnam's timberlands, quite apart from causing horrendous health problems for everyone for decades to come? The mentality of the men who conducted the Vietnam war, military and civilian, was singularly one-dimensional: more men, more bombs, more shells, more napalm. They covered the sky with B-52s, helicopters, and aircraft of all sizes and exotic types. One aircraft, a converted DC-3 transport, was outfitted with dozens of machine guns called "Puff the Magic Dragon" that could fire eighteen thousand rounds per minute. Bombs and rockets of all sorts proliferated. One rocket, the "Walley," an air-to-surface missile, could be operated and guided to its target by a fighter pilot who watched its trajectory on a screen.[59] All in all, the United States dropped three times as many bombs on Vietnam as it had dropped on Europe, Asia, and Africa in World War II.[60]

The enemy countered this flashy display of lethal technology with ambushes and hit-and-run operations. Few set-battles were waged in which one side or the other gained or lost territory for any period of time. Only along the demilitarized zone did the two sides pound each other with artillery reminiscent of World War I fighting. In early 1967 the United States unleashed operation Cedar Falls, sending thirty thousand U.S. troops against the Iron Triangle, an NLF stronghold just north of Saigon. American intervention on that scale bought some time for the demoralized and inefficient South Vietnamese army, but it did not bring the war to a close.

Instead, U.S. war planners became increasingly obsessed by "body counts" of dead Vietcong on the assumption that favorable "kill ratios" would eventually do the trick. "Our mission," Philip Caputo recalled, "was not to win terrain or seize positions, but simply to kill: to kill communists and to kill as many of them as possible. Stack 'em like cordwood. Victory was a high body count, defeat a low kill-ratio, war a matter of arithmetic." The pressure on unit commanders to produce enemy corpses was intense, and they in turn communicated it to their troops.[61] Since it was difficult to distinguish civilians from combatants, the rule of thumb, according to Philip Caputo, was this: "If it's dead and Vietnamese, it's VC."[62] Hanoi, however, had no trouble replacing its losses and matching each American escalation with fresh military troops of its own. Given the limitations it had set for itself, namely, that of fighting a limited war, the United States could gain no more than a stalemate, and even that was doubtful in view of the deteriorating political situation in South Vietnam and antiwar protests on the home front.

General Ky surprised everyone by surviving in office for more than six months, but few expected him to hold on much longer. At a Honolulu meeting with President Johnson in February 1966, he promised reform in return for more U.S. aid. The Buddhists renewed their agitation, calling for the end to foreign domination. It was a virtual civil war within an insurrection.[63] The term "pacification" became a favorite slogan for victory. Using NLF tactics, the pacification plan called for fifty-nine-man teams, trained in propaganda and social services, to go into villages, live with people, and carry out reform, thus undermining and co-opting the guerrillas. The corrupt Saigon bureaucracy and poor coordination between Americans and Vietnamese made it difficult to carry out this ambitious plan. The Revolutionary Development (RD) teams were constantly stymied by local authorities, who saw them as a threat to their own autonomy. They were also undermined by ARVN units who extorted taxes and fees from villagers and stole chickens and pigs.

Efforts to write a democratic constitution and hold free elections also proved difficult in a country that lacked democratic traditions. The September 1967 elections were not as corrupt as they were made out to be at the time. General Nguyen Van Thieu and Ky were elected by 35 percent of the vote, with Thieu becoming president and Ky vice president. Thieu and Ky, it was becoming obvious, were simply figureheads, for behind them were the Americans. The whole war, in fact, was being Americanized. This was especially true of the home front in South Vietnam. The United States flooded the country with goods, turning Saigon and other cities into corrupt boomtowns where everything was for sale. Vietnamese children wore Batman T-shirts, and seedy bars and whorehouses mushroomed. Wild spending unhinged the economy, driving up prices as much as 170 percent between 1965 and 1967. The flood of U.S. goods also destroyed native industries. Crime and corruption flourished.

In addition, South Vietnam was overrun with refugees, many of whom had fled from the communists but many of whom were also landless peasants who were supposed to have been "resettled" by the pacification project. A large number of people became rootless and impoverished, which made them a fertile breeding ground for fifth columnists. Relations between Americans and the South Vietnamese, though still correct and often friendly, became more tense and embittered. "My time in Vietnam," said one GI, "is the memory of ignorance. I didn't know the language. I knew nothing about the village community."[64] Many Vietnamese regarded the presence of American troops as an occupation rather than a potential source of liberation.

In the meantime, the wily and aging Ho Chi Minh figured that America would tire of the war and adamantly refused to negotiate. Johnson, for his part, was willing to stop the bombings only if Hanoi deescalated and withdrew its troops from the South. The NLF was not to be included in any future negotiations because that would be, as Hubert Humphrey said, "like putting the fox in a chicken coop."[65]

By the mid-1960s the faraway war in Vietnam that was supposed to be just a limited war was coming home to roost. In fact, it was in America that Ho Chi Minh won the war, not on the battlefield in Vietnam. The war aroused more opposition at home than any other war in American history. Between 1965 and the end of the war, America was inundated by antiwar protests, some of which brought well over one hundred thousand people unto the streets of America, undermining morale and plunging the country and its citizens into turmoil and bitter recrimination on all sides. What accounts for this profusion of protest and dissent in the late 1960s?

4. Hell No, We Won't Go

Dissent and conformity are necessary elements in a democracy, alternating according to the degree of social change that a society is facing. Throughout its history, the United States has harbored a variety of dissident groups that were profoundly opposed to the mainstream culture. Excepting those relatively small groups or individuals who hated America in the sense that they opposed its democracy or economic way of life, most protesters have opposed the mainstream culture for failing to live up to their perception of the American dream of liberty, equality, the pursuit of happiness, and universal peace. Whenever irreconcilable issues such as slavery, war, economic depression, or political reform threatened to tear apart the national fabric, various diverse groups of dissidents converged and coalesced to form an adversary culture that challenged the mainstream. The 1960s witnessed the reemergence of such an adversary culture; its origins stemmed from generational conflicts, the civil rights movement, and the war in Vietnam.

Given the existence of a powerful strain of moral perfectionism in American history, one would expect that lofty ideals of perfectibility would clash with the existence of imperfections that have always existed in real historical societies. Most Americans have been conditioned to believe in either the reality of present political perfection or in its eventual attainment. Imperfections in the form of corruption, betrayal, and failed hopes or aspirations have therefore been more deeply felt in America than they have in societies where failure and imperfections were accepted as a natural condition of life. For Italians, French, or Germans, who can look back on a long and checkered past filled with many inconclusive national triumphs, failures, tragedies, opportunities missed and turning points unattained, the desire to perfect social life has been of far less importance than it has to Americans. This explains, in large part, America's obsession with equal opportunities, perfect fairness, universal peace and justice, the elimination of all pain and suffering and the like.

American perfectionism derives from two broad sources: the Puritan heritage and the doctrines of the Enlightenment. Among adversary types one usually encounters left-wing liberals with strong egalitarian tendencies, religious pacifists, isolationists, and various nonconformist critics. Adam Garfinkle, who has traced the origin and development of adversarial groups in American history, has argued that the various streams of adversarial culture in the twentieth century reflect the secularization of the religious impulse.[66] In regard to antiwar sentiments, which in turn reflect an anti-establishment ethos within American political culture, one can identify three major streams—all of them converging in the 1960s: religious pacifism, liberal peace activism, and radical socialism.

Religious pacifism, which has surfaced periodically in American history, gathered serious momentum with the rise of America as an imperial power and its subsequent participation in World War I. Although religious pacifism originated in Puritan New England and Quaker Philadelphia, it spread with the expansion of the country, usually linking with similar Protestant denominations such as Quakers, Baptists, Methodists, and Congregationalists. In 1917, when the United States entered World War I, the Quakers established the American Friends Service Committee (AFSC), dedicated to the resistance and abolition of war. Liberal pacifism was a secular reform movement that originated between 1865 and 1914, the post–Civil War period and the outbreak of World War I. It had close ties to abolitionism and the rise of the women's movement in the late nineteenth century. The rise of imperialism greatly strengthened the movement. Many populist and progressive reformers squarely opposed imperialistic entanglements. The Anti-Imperialist League, formed in 1895, was made up of a coalition of intellectuals (Mark Twain, William James), labor leaders, clergymen, educators, lawyers, and even white supremacists, black activists, and industrialists. During the populist-progressive era (1890–1914) no fewer than forty-five peace groups were founded, among them the American Association for International Conciliation, the Carnegie Endowment for International Peace, the League to Enforce Peace, the World Peace Foundation, and the Women's International League for Peace and Freedom.

The peace movement was also strongly influenced by international socialism and communism. In 1905, Upton Sinclair, the novelist and social critic, founded the Intercollegiate Socialist Society, a forerunner of the radical Student Union of the 1930s and the Students for a Democratic Society of the 1960s. All of these movements, especially the socialist peace movement, established links with organized labor, which made them a force to be reckoned with in American society. During the interwar period (1919–1939), antiwar sentiment and isolationism were widespread, whether inspired by religious or political motives. A man like A. J. Muste, for example, combined protestant pacifist convictions with radical socialist doctrines, believing that turning the other cheek was perfectly compatible with proletarian class solidarity. The Catholics were not too far behind the Protestants in pacifistic and socialistic doctrines. In 1933 Dorothy Day and Peter Maurin formed the Catholic Worker, houses of charities feeding the poor, along with a journal by that name whose object it was to join together the beliefs of St. Francis of Assisi and the ideals of the Industrial Workers of the World—the Wobblies.

During the Second World War appeasement, pacifism, and antiwar sentiments moved off the radar screen, but they reappeared in various shapes and forms during the cold war. A great deal of antiwar sentiment in the postwar period centered on nuclear disarmament. In 1957, a number of left-liberal intellectuals and activists such as Lawrence Scott, Norman Cousins, Clarence Pickett, and Benjamin Spock founded SANE, or the Committee for a Sane Nuclear Policy. In 1963 the Kennedy administration established the ACDA, or Arms Control and Disarmament Agency, staffing it with mainstream liberals rather than left-liberal anti-bomb activists. The new agency, headed by John J. McCloy, was supposed to wage a peace race rather than an arms race, a phrase coined by Columbia University sociologist Seymour Melman, but it did little to stop or even to restrain the largest buildup of strategic nuclear missiles in the atomic age.[67] Left-liberal anti-bomb activists had to search outside the government to find a congenial home, joining SANE, and Turn Toward Peace, founded by Muste and Linus Pauling, among others; and the Institute for Policy Studies (IPS), a brain child of Marcus Ruskin, who had previously served in the ACDA.

Although radical groups had been protesting U.S. imperialism throughout the 1950s, their influence on government policy or public opinion was negligible. Before 1965 public demonstrations against the Vietnam War were small and rare; but when the war became an American war, with more and more young men being sent to Vietnam, opposition began to gather force. The main focal points of antiwar resistance came from the universities, particularly from America's elite institutions such as Harvard, Yale, Princeton, Columbia, Brown, Michigan, Cornell, and Berkeley.[68] Although academics benefited from billions of dollars in government-sponsored research and students enjoyed deferments from military service, the intellectual climate of opinion on America's campuses was overwhelmingly liberal and antimilitary. There was a pervasive terror-rage among the students about the draft, which was a real Sword of Damocles that could easily fall on students' heads in case Uncle Sam decided to suspend deferments owing to manpower needs.[69]

By the mid-1960s, radical organizers saw U.S. campuses as a fertile market for recruiting followers and using them as spearheads of radical opposition not only against the war in Vietnam but against corporate America as well. Three distinct groups could be discerned at many politicized American institutions of higher learning: professional organizers, usually from Students for a Democratic Society (SDS) and various pacifist groups; local radicals and their supporters among the faculty; and large numbers of students and hangers-on who enjoyed going to mass rallies, listening to live music, chanting slogans, and generally feeling virtuous and heroic about love and peace.[70] College campuses, of course, were only one segment in the larger adversary culture in America. Antiwar protesters could be found among three groups: liberals and left liberals, who generally rallied around SANE, ADA (Americans for Democratic Action), and Clergy and Laity Concerned about the War; radical leftists who either affiliated themselves with the New Left (SDS) or with traditional socialist groups such as the Socialist Workers Party (SWP) and its campus affiliate the Young Socialist Alliance (YSA); and a host of pacifist groups who opposed war on either religious or philosophical grounds. Liberals, of course, were the establishment in the 1960s, but there were considerable defections from the mainstream "vital center" the longer and bloodier the war became. This would cause a major split in the Democratic Party when left liberals defected from the liberal mainstream over the conduct of the war and forged various makeshift alliances with the radical left. In 1968 the Democratic Party was so badly divided that it lost the election to Richard Nixon, redefining itself as a socialist and pacifist party and then losing even more overwhelmingly in 1972 than in 1968.

Followers of the radical left perceived their country as a corporate fascist nation, maliciously spelling Amerika with the German "k" in order to evoke a fascist or Nazi association. They saw the Vietnam War as yet another imperialist venture to oppress third-world countries, exploiting their resources, and propping up fascist dictators to do their bidding. The left was much given to abstract theorizing, a great deal of which was derived from German philosophy and from German left-wing writers such as Herbert Marcuse, Theodor Adorno, Walter Benjamin, Erich Fromm, Wilhelm Reich, and others. Conceptualizing the world through Marxian and Freudian categories, leftist thinkers and those who used their slogans were especially fond of reifying the *system* or the *establishment*, terms used to denote a host of sinister institutions that allegedly oppressed, exploited, and alienated the majority of the American people. In hindsight, this was a false intellectual perception: it may have been that certain intellectuals or students felt themselves oppressed in modern America, but the same could not be said of the American people as a whole, who by every objective indicator, were proud to be Americans and generally felt that they were living the good life in America. The left-wing literati, on the other hand, felt themselves to be tiny cogs caught in an inhumane and oppressive machine that had to be ended rather than mended. In their minds, the system was a cancer that could not be treated with Band-Aids but had to be destroyed by revolutionary means. Neither the means nor the ends, however, were ever clearly spelled out by leftist radicals because, apart from vague utopian visions and revolutionary rhetoric, the movement lacked a strong core of realistic values. Some have even argued that the New Left, as opposed to the disciplined old Marxian left, deconstructed its own belief system by following two agendas that were inherently at odds: on the one hand, they favored an uprising on behalf of the ideals of liberal humanism against a soulless system, while on the other they called liberal humanism a deception that rested on false Western-style notions such as democracy, rationality, objectivity, and the autonomy of the individual.[71]

Pacifists were far less given to such overarching theories about the evils of finance capitalism. Their religious traditions favored the reform and purification of individual souls as a prerequisite to social reform. Those who tended to follow their hardcore utopian convictions, as Reinhold Niebuhr called them, favored aggressive and confrontive street demonstrations, while the soft-utopians counseled more restrained and nonviolent approaches. Like the radical left, pacifists lacked a coherent social ideology, splintered into different groups that clustered around well-known personalities (A. J. Muste, the brothers Dan and Philip Berrigan, David Dellinger, Dr. Benjamin Spock), failed to forge strong ties to other antiwar protesters, and were habitually reactive in their responses to the war.

Until 1966, these heterogeneous antiwar movements were still middle-class and aimed at reform rather than revolution.[72] Many protesters felt betrayed by Lyndon Johnson's lies that he was not seeking a wider war while at the same time escalating the war without a clear-cut solution of how he proposed to win it. Most protesters wanted an end to the bombing and an immediate negotiated settlement that included the Vietcong. When Johnson continued to play the same game of hide and seek, ambush and retaliation with the Vietcong, the antiwar movement, and even the nation as a whole, became increasingly alarmed. Protests on a nationwide basis began in the spring of 1965 when twenty-five thousand protesters under the sponsorship of SDS marched on Washington, the largest peace march in American history until that time. The march received unprecedented press coverage and resulted in a steady growth of membership for SDS to over fifty chapters and several hundred members. The march on Washington, on the other hand, revealed future problems for the peace movement. Liberals and moderate socialists (Norman Thomas and H. Stuart Hughes) boycotted the march because SDS refused to bar the communists from participating in it, thus revealing what would turn out to be growing fissures between moderates and radicals. SDS compounded this growing division by opting for a policy of revolutionary confrontation, though it was not very clear then or even later just what course such revolutionary resistance should take. Presumably, it was to destroy corporate capitalism, but what was to take its place remained a much debated question. This was precisely the problem with SDS, namely, that it was led by students (a necessarily temporary stage in life) and that these students lacked a coherent national organization. Curiously, this weakness was of their own choosing because the leaders of the SDS, notably Tom Hayden and Al Haber, favored a decentralized approach that allowed individual chapters to set their own agendas and remain open to diverse ideological views.[73]

In May 1965 the "teach-in" movement swept through American academia. It started at the University of Michigan, where professors from various academic specialties taught an all-night symposium on the conflict in Vietnam to well over three thousand students. From the Michigan campus the teach-in then spread to other campuses nationwide. On May 15 a national teach-in, sponsored by the Inter-University Committee for a Public Hearing on Vietnam, was held in Washington, D.C. The administration had promised to send McGeorge Bundy, but Johnson's National Security Adviser was too busy tending to a crisis in the Dominican Republic to show up for the scheduled national debate that had been arranged by faculty members in cooperation with various antiwar groups. The debate, beamed out by radio and television, was conducted on a fairly sophisticated academic level, pitting several pro-administration scholars (Zbigniew Brzezinski, Walt Rostow, Arthur Schlesinger) against their critics (Hans Morgenthau, Bernard Fall, and Seymour Melman).

One week after the national teach-in over one hundred thousand people, organized by the Vietnam Day Committee, gathered at the University of California at Berkeley to protest the war. The Vietnam Day Committee was the brainchild of several quirky gadflies, notably Jerry Rubin and mathematics professor Stephen Smale, who planned to organize a mass rally designed to be half carnival and half serious, featuring a variety of antiwar celebrities.[74] The group invited many prominent dissenters, not all of whom attended. Bertrand Russell sent a note of support, while Jean-Paul Sartre not only declined to attend but strongly criticized the planned event on the grounds that those who were putting it together were marginal outsiders without strong political connections. Norman Mailer, however, attended the event, as did Dr. Benjamin Spock, I. F. Stone, Yale historian Staughton Lynd, and Norman Thomas. The event itself was a media happening, as Jerry Rubin, who had dropped out of Berkeley, had intended it to be. Rubin envisioned the revolution as "theater-in-the-streets," a non-violent carnival featuring serious speakers but also comedians, mime artists, and singers.[75] Rubin and the Vietnam Day Committee placed their faith in "participatory democracy," by which they meant getting as many people together, finding out what was on their minds, and where they wanted to go, the assumption being that shared consensus would always emerge because people instinctively knew where they wanted to go. The importance was to empower people to express themselves freely and publicly without having their choices or decisions dictated from above by rigid leadership or party authority. Rubin and other members of the New Left seemed to believe that authority, structure, doctrine, and discipline undermined democracy and were therefore elitist, a byword of everything that was wrong with American society. In practice, however, "expressive politics" or "participatory democracy" as practiced by the New Left was little more than gaudy theater without much substance, evoking widespread hostility and criticism by the majority of the American people.

Such tactics, of course, were strongly condemned by the more disciplined and better organized cadres of the old left, which criticized the New Left leaders for confusing style with substance and predicting that the peace movement would hopelessly fragment itself. Left radicals could all agree on ending the war and changing corporate capitalism, but they neither wanted or knew how to forge a single mass movement, with singular means and ends. This incoherence became quite clear from the beginning of the peace movement. After the national teach-in and the Vietnam Day, no real consensus had emerged, other than engaging in a variety of spontaneously organized acts of civil disobedience: burning draft cards, taunting the police, holding rallies, and marching on despised symbols of oppression (military bases, the Pentagon, government buildings, despised corporate headquarters, and even university administrations). The hope was that such public acts would raise the consciousness of those who opposed not only the war but the very structure and value system of mainstream America. There was a growing consensus against the war, but rather than building that, the left agenda promoted more and more radical ideas about American culture that alienated many war resisters and undermined the movement.

In July 1965 the Vietnam Day Committee staged a protest in Oakland, California, aimed at stopping the trains that brought draftees to the Oakland Army Terminal. Protesters distributed leaflets to the draftees and lectured them on the criminal nature of the war, insinuating that anyone who joined the army was complicit in a criminal enterprise. The protests were to be crowned by a march on Oakland from Berkeley. In a highly charged atmosphere, the protesters marched down Telegraph

Avenue, and as they approached the city line of Oakland, where battle-ready highway patrol and Alameda county sheriffs were waiting to stop them, the unwieldy crowd faced a divide in the road with no return: to the left lay Oakland and martyrdom, to the right Berkeley and ignominious defeat, and to the rear were angry Hell's Angels waiting to attack them. Although the crowd screamed: "left, left, left," their leaders overruled participatory democracy and called for a retreat.[76] The Oakland debacle effectively discredited the Vietnam Day Committee, and what remained of it with the departure of those who had counseled caution was highjacked by the extreme left. Rubin looked for greener pastures and wilder antics, while Professor Smale redis-covered mathematics. Staging ever more radical stunts did not help the peace move-ment, and neither did the infiltration of the peace movement by histrionic celebrities who embarked on peace-finding missions to communist countries. One of the first of these self-destructive tactics occurred in the same month that the Vietnam Day Committee tried to march on Oakland. A delegation of what Lenin had called "use-ful idiots," the Women's Strike for Peace, journeyed to Jakarta to meet their alleged counterparts from North Vietnam and the Vietcong. The American delegation was led by Cora Weiss, an heiress of the Helena Rubinstein cosmetic fortune. This meet-ing was a portent of things to come: future trips by American protesters to Hanoi, Moscow, Havana, and other communist capitals. The protesters felt morally invigo-rated and heroic; they rarely suspected that they might be useful conduits for com-munist propaganda and disinformation.

Although the majority of the American people still supported the war between 1965 and 1967, and "campus kooks" provided useful bogeys for politicians, the American media's coverage of the war and the protests that were launched against it brought about a definite swing in the national mood. It must be remembered that "news coverage" before 1960 had been a minor blip on the nation's TV screens, lim-ited before 1963 to merely fifteen minutes of evening news by the major broadcast-ing companies such as CBS, NBC, and ABC. After September 2, 1963, when Walter Cronkite expanded his evening news program from fifteen to thirty minutes, the major news networks greatly expanded their coverage of newsworthy stories, and those inevitably included action-packed, violent, or sensational stories. On the American side, news coverage of the war, including correspondents following the troops into battle, was more extensive and intensive than in any other war in history, and it was generally of high quality. The same could not be said for the communist side, which operated in a closed-circuit totalitarian mold and made no pretense at objectivity and truth. Being an impatient people, inclined toward the "quick fix," Americans did not take very long to discover that media accounts of the war and offi-cial Washington optimism did not harmonize. By mid-1967 the media elite was clearly abandoning its earlier support of the war, and many correspondents sympa-thized with the antiwar movements.

Opposition to the war steadily increased throughout the course of 1966. In March the second NCCENV International Day of Protest attracted fifty thousand protest-ers to New York and smaller numbers to other cities throughout the United States. Two radical activists, Allard Lowenstein and Curtis Gans, started the "dump the

Johnson" movement within the Democratic Party. Congressional opposition to the war also gathered force. William Fulbright, who had earlier supported Johnson in getting the Gulf of Tonkin Resolution passed by the Senate, now began to develop serious reservations about the war and, as chairman of the Senate's powerful Foreign Relations Committee, held critical hearings on the conduct of the Vietnam War. There were also defections among Johnson's closest advisers by men who began to have second thoughts about the war. Whenever Bill Moyers, personal assistant to the president, came to see Johnson, he was greeted with the ritualistic comment: "here comes mister 'stop the bombing.'" McGeorge Bundy and Robert McNamara, too, began to distance themselves from the president's position and ultimately left the administration. To make matters worse, the Democrats lost forty-seven seats in the House of Representatives in 1966. Finally, the "Wise Men," a group of powerful statesmen and policy experts whom the president trusted (Dean Acheson, Clark Clifford, Allen Dulles) also voiced grave doubts and eventually told the president in no uncertain terms that the war was not winnable and recommended a bombing pause and negotiations with North Vietnam.

Johnson could not ignore these political insiders because they could threaten to undermine the liberal consensus he had tried to build following the assassination of John F. Kennedy and the landslide victory in the election of 1964. On the domestic front, the president was hailed as a legislative genius for the Civil Rights Act of 1964 and for the passage of a host of Great Society programs; but favorable public support was unlikely to continue as long as the war in Vietnam overshadowed his well-earned acclaim in the area of domestic accomplishments. By 1965 even major civil rights leaders such as Martin Luther King sharply criticized the president's handling of the Vietnam War. King represented the moderate or integrationist wing of the civil rights movement; even stronger criticism emanated from the far more radical wing of the civil rights movement. Radical black activists such as Stokely Carmichael, H. Rap Brown, Eldridge Cleaver and the Black Panthers, and Malcolm X of the Nation of Islam proclaimed a belligerent nationalistic and separatist message. Within SNCC, radical hotheads called for urban guerrilla war in "Amerika," claiming that black America, just like Vietnam, was white occupied territory waiting to be liberated. These radical notions came from Frantz Fanon, a Caribbean-French psychiatrist and social critic who had written an inflammatory political tract entitled *Wretched of the Earth* (1963), which denounced white colonialism and called for a worldwide revolution against Western civilization.

Claiming to represent black America, SNCC pushed for guerrilla war behind enemy lines in "Amerika." One SNCC song made this quite clear, sending a chilling message to white middle-class America:

Hell, No, No! I Ain't Gonna Go! I ain't goin' to Vietnam.
I ain't burning my brothers to serve the man.
I ain't goin' to Vietnam.
The Vietcong's just like I am.[77]

The refrain called the U.S. army the Ku Klux Klan. White radicals were enamored with such black posturing, and many literati glamorized such inflammatory black rhetoric as heroic and inspiring. Some hoped to use the most radical part of the black movement as a battering ram to bring down corporate America, "letting a nigger pull the trigger," as the saying had it. Black radicals, however, did not make common cause with white radicals, making it known in no uncertain terms that they did not need honkeys to run their own revolutionary movement. At a National Conference for a "New Politics," held at Palmer House in Chicago in 1967 over the Labor Day weekend, the black delegates, who menaced the meeting with their loud voices and weapons, made it quite clear that whites were unable to think and feel like blacks, and that they did not want their racial discontent highjacked by white militants, who had their own ideological agendas. When Martin Luther King delivered the keynote speech, black militants repeatedly interrupted him with chants of "kill whitey, kill whitey." The militant black delegates, who represented only less than one-fifth of the delegates, then proceeded to make thirteen demands, including 50 percent representation on all committees, condemnation of U.S. support of imperialistic Zionism in the Middle East, and nationwide efforts to cleanse white communities of their "savage and beastlike" character.[78] Dripping with guilt and morally tongue-lashed, the white delegates caved in to the intimidation of the black radicals, but many slunk away uneasy about the possibility of ever finding common ground with militant blacks.

The Palmer conference was a prelude to "Stop the Draft Week" in October 1967, to be followed by a march on the Pentagon. The nation's college campuses teemed with protests against the draft, and on October 15, radical students organized a "Stop the Draft Week." Most of the protests were in the form of peaceful demonstrations and acts of civil disobedience such as publicly burning draft cards, which carried a $10,000 fine and five years of imprisonment. Many students opposed the war on moral and strategic grounds, believing that it was the wrong war in the wrong place, and that its assumed threat to the United States was an illusion. The prospect of being sent to the jungle in a remote part of the world for no apparent reason was generally intolerable to many students, who had so far enjoyed a sheltered and privileged life in American society. At the same time, American college students were acutely aware of the fact that going to college sheltered them from the draft, provided, of course, that they kept going to school and maintained a C grade point average. They also knew that their peers outside the academic umbrella—and that included most minorities and working-class Americans of draft age (18–30)—would bear the brunt of the fighting. Since students were not, for the most part, cynical time-servers, they compensated for their privileged status by turning their opposition to the war into a moral crusade against war itself. Although there was much insincerity and naivete in this attitude, there was also a great deal of honest moral objection to the obscenity of industrial mass killing inherent in twentieth-century warfare. During "Stop the Draft Week" (October 16–23), some radical students already went beyond protest to active resistance and street violence. In Oakland, for example, radicals attacked the local draft board with bricks, bottles, and metal bars. At several campuses emotionally overwrought students clashed with local police forces.

The students received considerable support from liberal and leftist professors and well-known national literary figures. In September, the Institute for Policy Studies had drafted a resolution, entitled "A Call to Resist Illegitimate Authority," that was signed by 158 prominent members of the left and published by the *New York Review of Books*. Several clergymen who had signed the resolution promised sanctuary to draft resisters in their churches and synagogues.

The high point of protest in 1967 occurred on October 21–22 with the March on the Pentagon. The march on the Pentagon, which attracted over one hundred thousand protesters, was organized by the National Mobilization Committee to End the War in Vietnam (MOBE). Since the march attracted a numbers of different groups, the organizers of the march let each group pursue its own tactics, although there was an overall "plan" that involved three stages: a rally at the Lincoln Memorial; a march on the Pentagon followed by a peaceful rally; and a second rally at the Pentagon, accompanied by civil disobedience for those who wanted it. As the protesters converged on Washington, it became clear that this was not a monolithic protest because it consisted of a very broad spectrum of opponents to the war in Vietnam, ranging from high-minded literary figures such as Norman Mailer, Robert Lowell, Dwight MacDonald, Noam Chomsky, Paul Goodman, to prominent clergymen, middle-class professionals, working people, students, black activists, and an array of colorful street people and hippies. The march also ranged from the solemn to the pathetic. Serious speeches were delivered about why America was in Vietnam and should have never been there. The highmindedness, however was quickly dissipated by theatrical antics and scatological remarks. John Lewis of SNCC asked for a moment of silence in memory of Che Guevara, while David Dellinger seized the microphone and announced the end of peaceful opposition to the war in Vietnam. A small group of flower children walked up to the bayonet wielding soldiers who guarded the Pentagon and stuck flowers into their rifle barrels. Scores of witches surrounded the Pentagon and shouted magical incantations to the spirit world in a vain effort to levitate the building and purge it of its evil spirits. Scuffles and violence occurred when militants tried to break through the police lines to enter building. Among those who tried to break through the police lines was the novelist Norman Mailer, who later recounted his experiences in a spirited book, *The Armies of the Night*. Mailer, who was dressed like a banker in a pinstripe suit, vest, and maroon and blue regimental tie, was set upon by marshals, who refrained from billy-clubbing him only because he said: "Take your hands off me, can't you see? I'm not resisting arrest."[79] Mailer was then jailed, along with some eight hundred protesters, including Dellinger and Chomsky.

The March on the Pentagon was grand theater, but it changed nothing in the short run. The more radical protesters, frustrated by the government's apparent lack of concern, came away from the event more convinced than ever that peaceful methods of protest were ineffectual and that future protests had to be even more confrontational, disruptive, and revolutionary. What the protesters, living for the moment and expecting immediate change, did not realize was that the government was losing its credibility over Vietnam. Those protesters who did realize how the political winds were blowing, took it as a positive sign that the times were riper for revolution. The protests had stirred a national debate, and there were clear-cut signs that the Johnson administration was losing that debate. The national debate over Vietnam also brought two new terms into common usage: "hawks" and "doves," supporters and opponents of the war. From a broad political point of view, hawks tended to be right-wing Republicans and conservative Democrats, while the doves spanned a spectrum of pacifists, academics, students, and left-wing activists. Among the protesters, as we have seen, were some prominent individuals such as Dr. Benjamin Spock, the baby doctor who had taught the GI generation how to bring up their progeny; the boxer Cassius Clay, who refused to be inducted into the army and changed his name to Mohammed Ali; the SDS leader Tom Hayden and his future wife, the actress Jane Fonda; Dr. Martin Luther King; and prominent politicians like J. William Fulbright, Eugene McCarthy, Mike Mansfield, and George McGovern; and media celebrities of various kinds.

By the fall of 1967 the antiwar protesters had gained the moral high ground by denouncing the lethal technological war America was waging on a much smaller enemy. Many claimed that America was committing war crimes, and the philosopher Bertrand Russell convened a war crimes tribunal in Stockholm to try the Americans under the same indictments the Allied powers had used to judge the Nazis at Nuremberg in 1946. National televised hearings were convened by Fulbright, war protesters conducted "lie-ins" in front of troop trains and disrupted draft boards. Critics raised questions then and later whether all these protests encouraged Hanoi to stay the course. Judging from postwar accounts by the communist leadership, there is no doubt that Hanoi was heartened by the antiwar protests, but there is every indication that Hanoi would have continued fighting no matter what. As to reactions by the American people in the fall of 1967, polls reveal that Johnson was losing steadily in the polls, but there is also evidence to show that many Americans were getting sick and tired of the protests and the protesters. Many Americans, at that stage of the war, seemed to be more revolted by the hippies than by the Vietcong.[80]

Lyndon Johnson's credibility gap, however, widened. Mutual recriminations were the order of the day. With no end in sight for the war, with race riots erupting in many cities and young people refusing to support the war, the nation seemed to be on the verge of a nervous breakdown.[81] Even within the administration critics began to appear. One was Bill Moyers, Johnson's personal assistant, another was George Ball, who resigned from the State Department; even McNamara, one of the chief architects of the Vietnam War, began to develop growing doubts. Ruminating on the conflict, McNamara conceded that "the picture of the world's greatest super-power killing or seriously injuring 1,000 non-combatants a week, while trying to pound a tiny, backward nation into submission on an issue whose merits are hotly disputed, is not a pretty one."[82] By the summer of 1967 Lyndon Johnson was a troubled man. "Bomb, bomb, bomb, that's all you know" he complained to his generals; and the infuriated president added: "Well, I want to know why there's nothing else. You generals have all been educated at taxpayer's expense, and you're not giving me any ideas and any solutions for this damn little piss-ant country."[83] He lost confidence in everyone, including McNamara, who finally resigned to accept an appointment to head the World Bank. Johnson tried to steer an impossible middle ground between the military "bomb them into the Stone Age" crowd and the "get the hell out of Vietnam" camp. The result was war by improvisation that defied military logic and, worse for Lyndon Johnson, political logic as well. Johnson became increasingly withdrawn and paranoid, belittling the "Nervous Nellies" or naysayers in his administration and blaming the protesters for undermining the war. He authorized the CIA to spy on assumed traitors, an activity specifically forbidden under CIA's original charter. The program was code-named CHAOS and called for the compilation of files on more than seven thousand Americans.[84] At the same time Johnson unleashed a propaganda blitzkrieg to shore up popular support. It didn't do much good. The impetus for change came from a the "Wise Men," who told the president in no uncertain terms that the war was unwinnable.

Then on January 30, 1968, came the Tet Offensive, launched by the communists to coincide with the beginning of Tet, the lunar year and the most festive of Vietnam holidays.[85] The Vietcong infiltrated more than a hundred cities and towns, including Saigon, in an audacious, go-for-broke strike against South Vietnam. The communists planned to carry the war into South Vietnam's urban areas, to demoralize their enemies, and to gain the upper hand in any peace negotiations. Wherever they went, they acted with unprecedented brutality, slaughtering government officials and other "class enemies" such as teachers, lawyers, doctors, businessmen, and missionaries. In Hue, teams of Vietcong murderers, armed with lists of names, rounded up three thousand people and killed them in cold blood, either by shooting them or clubbing them to death.[86] It is interesting to note that these communist atrocities were not widely reported in the U.S. press, which was then preoccupied with the American massacre at My Lai, a small pro-Vietcong hamlet where Lieutenant William Calley and his platoon murdered more than two hundred men, women, and children.

In the end, the Vietcong invaders were repelled by combined U.S. and South Vietnamese forces, but the bold Vietcong invasion had put the lie to years of false propaganda that the war was as good as won. Not only had the guerrillas unleashed a coordinated attack all over the country, they also besieged the U.S. embassy in Saigon. The American public, watching one of their citadels under attack by the Vietcong, could hardly believe what they saw on their television screens. Although the communist offensive was a military defeat for the communists, it was at the same time an overwhelming psychological victory for Hanoi.

"What the hell is going on?" asked Walter Cronkite during the Tet Offensive: "I thought we were winning the war?"[87] Many Americans shared his anger, particularly after years of upbeat messages from the White House that victory in Vietnam was just around the corner. Lyndon Johnson's credibility gap had widened beyond repair. Jarring images of U.S. military bungling could be seen almost every day on the nation's television screens. Several pictures were particularly jarring: one showed a young officer explaining that his troops had to "destroy the town to save it," while another featured a brutal pictures of the Saigon police chief executing a young NLF captive by shooting him in cold blood—the picture forever freezing the moment when the bullet shattered the young man's head.[88]

The military, however, knew only one strategy: escalate the war, send more troops, and drop more bombs. Westmoreland's insatiable demand for more of the same began to prompt criticism from within the administration, especially from Clark Clifford and others who were recommending a shift in strategy. Instead of more search-and-destroy missions, Pentagon civilians urged greater tactical concentration on securing the population and on forcing the South Vietnamese Army (ARVN) to take a greater role in the fighting. Johnson also focused on halting the bombing and sending out feelers for negotiation.

On the home front, Walter Cronkite's public assessment signaled a real change in public opinion, and Lyndon Johnson later admitted as much when he said that he knew he was losing the support of the American people after the venerable reporter came back from his fact-finding mission to Vietnam and reported on February 7, 1968, that "to say that we are close to victory today is to believe, in the face of evidence, the optimists who have been wrong in the past. To suggest that we are on the edge of defeat is to yield to unreasonable pessimism. To say that we are mired in a stalemate seems the only reasonable, yet unsatisfactory conclusion."[89] That opinion was now shared by the majority of the American people, and its effects were in the form of widespread disillusionment. By mid-March of 1968 this sense of disillusionment found its way into the primary campaigns. Senator Eugene McCarthy of Wisconsin, an outspoken critic of the war, won 42 percent of the vote in the New Hampshire primary, which was widely interpreted as a defeat for Lyndon Johnson. McCarthy's boost in the campaign, in turn, galvanized Robert F. Kennedy into challenging the president for the nomination of his party in 1968.

Seen against a background of antiwar protests and hostile media criticism, these startling political developments began to turn the American people against a long-term commitment to South Vietnam. Westmoreland later charged that North Vietnam won not on the battlefield but in the American media, a judgment that is, at best, a half-truth. The United States was losing the battle for the hearts and minds at home because its leadership had chosen to wage stalemate on the battlefield. If Lyndon Johnson had accepted Westmoreland's suggestion for further massive commitments, the United States would have had to spend $10 billion more on the war in 1969. The country was already facing a $19.8 billion budget deficit, widening imbalances in international trade accounts, and a run on the nation's gold supplies.[90] It would have meant a major tax increase and cuts in domestic programs, driving a stake into the heart of Johnson's Great Society.

This is why Lyndon Johnson rejected Westmoreland's proposal for more troops. On March 31, 1968, he told the nation in a televised speech that he would reduce the bombing to the area just north of the demilitarized zone and look for a negotiated settlement. Then he dramatically announced, "I shall not seek, and I will not accept, the nomination of my party for another term as your President."[91] The president had recognized the futility of fighting this war indefinitely; he had crucified his administration on the war in Vietnam.

If Johnson had a strategy at this point it was "fighting while negotiating." The hawks—Rusk, Rostow, Ambassador Ellsworth Bunker, and the military—wanted to continue fighting without making significant concessions. Clifford and Harriman, on the other hand, wanted extrication as soon as possible. The battle between these two forces raged throughout 1968.

Sensing that the United States was about to throw in the towel, Hanoi finally agreed to talk at Paris. Formal negotiations began on May 13, 1968, and immediately deadlocked. In the meantime, the administration pursued a foreign policy in Vietnam by increasing bombing raids and seeking to solidify its South Vietnam base through pacification and Vietnamization. It was hoped that such signals of resolve would bring the North Vietnamese back to the table for serious negotiations. Hastily launched crash programs in Vietnam, coming on the heels of years of neglect and corruption, achieved little. Moreover, domestic problems in South Vietnam intensified. Ky and Thieu bickered constantly and the Buddhists remained alienated. In America, campus unrest mounted, culminating in several campus riots, notably at Columbia University.

In October 1968 Lyndon Johnson announced a bombing halt that neither brought peace nor helped Hubert Humphrey's faltering campaign for the presidency against Richard Nixon, a known hardliner on the war. In Paris, there was bickering over the size and shape of the conference table. The year 1968 ended in military and diplomatic deadlock.

5. Nixon's War and Defeat in Vietnam

Richard Nixon, the new president, brought in a fresh foreign policy team that was led by Henry Kissinger. The new Nixon men pledged not to make the same old mistakes, yet their policies were more of the same, except under new slogans.[92] Nixon, like his predecessor, believed that he could build up an independent, noncommunist Vietnam. The results, as Richard Herring has pointed out, was to plunge the nation into six more years of bloody warfare in Indochina, mounting social unrest at home, and a peace settlement that was neither honorable nor lasting. During the election campaign, Nixon had periodically hinted that he had a "secret plan" to end the Vietnam War, but history has shown that he had none, other than trying to threaten the North Vietnamese with annihilation. Nixon called this tactic the "Madman Theory," telling Bob Haldeman, his personal assistant, that:

> I want the North Vietnamese to believe that I've reached the point where I might do anything to stop the war. We'll just slip the word to them that "for God's sake, you know Nixon is obsessed about Communists. We can't restrain him when he's angry—and he has his hand on the nuclear button"—and Ho Chi Minh himself will be in Paris in two days begging for peace.[93]

The buzzwords under Nixon were "Peace with Honor," "Vietnamization," "Silent Majority," and so on. Like the "best and the brightest," Nixon's people shared a penchant for secrecy and a burning desire for power. Unlike the previous Washington "insiders" of the Democratic establishment, Nixon brought with him loners and outsiders like himself who shunned bureaucracies and formal procedures in favor of bold ideas and quickly improvised plans. Among them was the brilliant and highly ambitious Henry Kissinger, a former Harvard professor and German-Jewish exile from Nazism, whose knowledge of foreign policy was based on extensive scholarship and years of experience in a variety of diplomatic posts. Nixon first picked Kissinger as his security advisor, working out of the White House with a staff of like-minded, hard-boiled realists who often worked outside regular bureaucratic channels, including the State Department. In one way this arrangement favored innovation, but in another it resulted in secretive decision making and bungled operations. The language alternated between noble-sounding rhetoric, so typical of Nixon, and the most cynical abuses of power. Both Nixon and Kissinger knew that the war was tearing the country apart, but they also feared that a precipitous withdrawal from Vietnam—cutting one's losses, so to speak—could have devastating consequences for the prestige and power of the United States. Envisioning a New World Order based on American primacy, Nixon could not countenance withdrawal from Vietnam without first building up a solid and democratic nation there. He believed that the United States could force North Vietnam to negotiate on terms that the North Vietnamese had already rejected under Lyndon Johnson.

As a first step, the Nixon administration proposed that both sides withdraw their military forces from South Vietnam and restore the demilitarized zone as a boundary between north and south. In order to show that he was serious, Nixon ordered intensive bombing of North Vietnam sanctuaries in neutral Cambodia. Beginning in March 1969 and continuing over the next fifteen months, 3,630 B-52 raids were flown over Cambodia. The operation, carried out in total secrecy in order to avoid rekindling antiwar protests, was tastelessly called Menu, with individual components referred to as Breakfast, Lunch, Snack, and Dessert. For public relations purposes, Nixon matched his military escalation with announcements that he would be reducing American forces in South Vietnam. Not surprisingly, Hanoi rejected his peace plans as a farce and told the Americans that they would sit in Paris "until the chairs rot."[94] On the domestic front, the Cambodian operation not only served to revitalize the war protests, for the *New York Times* revealed the bombing in May, but it also led to those widespread abuses of executive authority (wiretapping, burglary, etc.) that ended in Watergate. Nixon was now embarked on that fatal encounter with his domestic "enemies" on the left that would involve him in a merry-go-round of recriminations, deceptions, lies, and plain illegalities.

In July 1969, Nixon unleashed a "go-for-broke" strategy to end the war by savagely bombing North Vietnam. The operation, code-named Duck-Hook, failed to achieve its purpose. On September 2, 1969, Ho Chi Minh died of heart failure at the age of seventy-nine; his successors—Le Duan, Pham Van Dong, and Vo Nguyen Giap—pledged to carry on the struggle until all the aggressors had been removed from Vietnam. Hanoi's standard line did not change: the United States must withdraw all of its troops and abandon the Thieu regime. Nixon again improvised by falling back on the Vietnamization policy he had inherited from Lyndon Johnson. He warned the American people that a pullout would result in a "blood bath" in South Vietnam. Bypassing the liberal media and hostile opponents on the nation's campuses, Nixon appealed directly to what he called the "great silent majority" (November 3, 1969). He stated dramatically that "North Vietnam cannot humiliate the United States, only Americans can do that."[95] It was a clever political strategy that put his opponents on the defensive because Nixon had appealed to patriotic Americans to support an honorable peace involving minimal American sacrifice. Nixon's appeal to the American people was a great success. Even before his broadcast on November 3, a national poll revealed that 71 percent of the American people overwhelmingly approved his approach to the Vietnamese war[96] Nevertheless, Nixon's liberal and radical opponents responded by organizing peace demonstrations on October 15 and November 15, 1969. In contrast to the previously violent protests, the moratoriums were serious and peaceful, culminating in Washington's March of Death when protesters carried candles from Arlington National Cemetery to the Capitol, placing signs bearing the names of GI's killed in Vietnam in wooden coffins.

Nixon, however, stayed the course, even though few anywhere seemed to know what that course really was. Presumably, it meant fighting while negotiating and putting South Vietnam on a firm political, economic, and military basis. General Abrams, who had replaced Westmoreland, was undoubtedly correct when he referred to this Vietnamization strategy as a "slow surrender." The South Vietnamese, who had not been consulted, referred to it as a "U.S. Dollar and Vietnamese Blood Sharing Plan." Others denounced Vietnamization as a fig leaf to cover United States betrayal.[97]

When Nixon took office in January 1969, U.S. forces in Vietnam numbered 850,000. The new administration increased this force to one million, turning over vast quantities of military weapons and supplies to South Vietnam. Plans for Vietnamization were now termed "Accelerated Pacification Campaigns." Regular forces were assigned to secure villages, conduct village elections, and train officials in "civic responsibility," American style. By early 1970 the Nixon administration claimed to have made significant gains. Yet long-term progress was still slow. Through the Phoenix program, the National Liberation Front (NLF) infrastructure was damaged but not destroyed. The South Vietnamese government was still autocratic, undemocratic, and corrupt. The Army of the Republic of Vietnam (ARVN) appeared formidable in numbers and weapons but was actually a hollow house of cards. The practice of "ghosting" or keeping dead soldiers on the payroll so that their pay could be pocketed was very extensive: it ran as high as 20 percent. Desertion rates were also high, and there was a shortage of qualified, competent, and honest officers.

By the spring of 1970 Nixon's inconsistent strategies had only succeeded in confusing the American people. In March 1970 he announced a phased withdrawal of 150,000 troops over the next year. In the same month Cambodia's neutralist Prince Sihanouk was overthrown by a pro-American clique headed by Prime Minister Lon Nol. Nixon denied direct involvement in the coup, though Lon Nol surely knew that the United States would welcome it. Kissinger later argued that the United States only belatedly came to Lon Nol's aid when it became obvious that North Vietnam wanted to destroy him. A change of government in Cambodia now muted criticisms that the United States was violating Cambodian neutrality in its efforts to wipe out North

Vietnamese sanctuaries there. Nixon told the American people that he decided to send U.S. troops into Cambodia because he believed that it would buy time for Vietnamization. It was a bold and controversial move. On April 30, 1970, he told a stunned nation that he was committing troops to Cambodia, having just previously assured the American people that he wanted to extricate the United States from further entanglements in Southeast Asia. He justified this provocative step by accusing Hanoi of aggression and insisting that the United States was a great power that could not be bullied by communist regimes: "If when the chips are down, the world's most powerful nation acts like a pitiful helpless giant, the forces of totalitarianism and anarchy will threaten free nations throughout the world."[98]

Nixon, of course, was right in arguing that North Vietnam had violated Cambodian neutrality all along. Yet what happened now made things worse for Cambodia. Chased out of their sanctuaries, the North Vietnamese spread out throughout Cambodia, lent support to the Khmer Rouge insurgents who were fighting Lon Nol, and plunged the country into a genocidal civil war.[99] Although the United States supported Lon Nol, he was little more than a weak pawn to help salvage a failed policy in Vietnam.

The domestic reaction to the Cambodian invasion resembled the violent protests of the late 1960s. After Nixon referred to protesters as "bums," demonstrations erupted across the nation's campuses. At Kent State University four students were killed in angry confrontations with National Guardsmen and police. There were also serious congressional reactions. The Senate terminated the Gulf of Tonkin Resolution and cut off all funds for American military operations in Cambodia after June 30, 1970. Nixon responded with icy contempt and bellicose rhetoric, thinking that these would muzzle his critics. By the terms of the Huston Plan, Nixon threatened to initiate far-reaching attacks on individual freedom and privacy, authorizing intelligence agencies to conduct surveillance activities against opponents of the war. The plan even endorsed burglarizing the homes of suspected opponents of the government. Although the plan was not implemented by the FBI and other agencies, some of the tactics it recommended were subsequently used to trace down the links that allegedly connected radicals to communist countries.[100] Nixon eventually rode out the storm and withdrew American troops from Cambodia. His risky strategy, however, had only exacerbated the Vietnam problem. Cambodia fell to Pol Pot and his deranged communist killers, who eventually massacred close to two million of their own people. The war in Vietnam continued, and so did Nixon's war on the home front. Nixon had made it clear to his inner circle that war had to be declared on his domestic enemies and that that would include the use of secret and unconstitutional methods of the sort that would eventually lead to his resignation. A virtual "siege mentality" set in at the White House.

In the meantime, deadlock and dissension were the order of the day on the diplomatic front, although secret talks between Kissinger and Le Duc Tho had intermittently taken place in Paris since February of 1970. After two years of fighting and dissembling, Nixon's position was worse than Lyndon Johnson's. Nixon, however, kept one promise: he steadily reduced the number of troops stationed in Vietnam, leaving 175,000 of whom only 75,000 were combat ready. Then, in February 1971, he approved a major ground operation into Laos to destroy North Vietnam sanctuaries. While the operation was going on, General Giap attacked two South Vietnamese divisions that had crossed the border with 36,000 North Vietnamese troops that were well supplied with the latest Soviet tanks. The Army of South Vietnam took a terrible beating, suffered high casualty rates, and retreated back into South Vietnam. War protest continued at home and overseas. In early 1971 Vietnam Veterans Against the War conducted an investigation of United States war crimes in Indochina. In April, a group of disenchanted veterans, one of them being John Kerry, future senator from Massachusetts, descended on the nation's capital with faded uniforms adorned with combat ribbons and peace symbols. They testified to their own involvement and knowledge of war crimes and acrimoniously tossed away their medals. Several days later, thirty thousand members of the "May Day Tribe," a radical left-wing group led by Rennie Davis that supported the communist struggle against the United States in Vietnam, invaded the capital with the avowed intention of shutting down the government; they staged "lie-ins" on bridges and major intersections. The nation was getting a "reality dose" of what it was really like in Vietnam. After a long and much publicized trial, Lieutenant William Calley was court-martialed on March 29, 1971, for at least twenty-two murders of innocent men, women, and children who were massacred in the village of My Lai in 1968.[101]

As soon as the My Lai trial ended, the nation was reminded of additional Vietnam-related scandals. On June 13, 1971, the *New York Times* published the "Pentagon Papers," a collection of secret Vietnam War documents that had been filched from the Pentagon by Daniel Ellsberg, a defense department official who had served in Vietnam. The documents were arranged in such a way as to reveal that bureaucratic planners and decision-makers were both deceiving and self-deceived. The documents confirmed what critics had been saying for years, namely, that the Kennedy-Johnson administrations had deliberately misled the American people about their intentions in Vietnam.[102] Nixon, in turn, became more paranoid than ever about government leaks, which he believed threatened the security of the American people. He sought an injunction from the Supreme Court prohibiting the publication of the Pentagon Papers. He lost that battle when the Supreme Court authorized publication. The enraged Nixon then ordered the creation of a clandestine group of "plumbers" to plug leaks within the government, instructing them to use any means to discredit Ellsberg. They tried to do so by breaking into the office of Ellsberg's psychiatrist and stealing his medical file. Later, they broke into the offices of the National Democratic Party at their Watergate headquarters in Washington, D.C., setting in motion a chain of events that would lead to Nixon's resignation in August 1974.

While these protests were sowing deep divisions into the political fabric, it should not be surprising that such dissensions also found their way into the armed forces. Morale in the armed forces, especially in Vietnam, seriously deteriorated. Discipline in the ranks often broke down and drug usage increased. "Fragging" (killing) officers reached unprecedented proportions. More than two hundred incidents of fragging were reported in 1970 alone. In the same year it was estimated that sixty-five thousand servicemen were using drugs and forty thousand were hooked on heroin. Racial conflicts also abounded in the armed services.

In May 1971 Kissinger presented a comprehensive peace plan, only to have it rejected by the North Vietnamese because it committed the United States to the Thieu regime. Thieu had won a contested election that was widely denounced as corrupt. In February 1972, the wily Nixon played one of his deftest cards when he travelled to Beijing on a diplomatic mission aimed at detente with China. The trip was designed, in part, to drive a wedge between an increasingly security-conscious China and an aggressive Soviet Union. It was well known that Mao Tse Tung did not relish the massive buildup of Soviet forces on his northern and western frontiers, nor did he entirely approve of North Vietnam's independent approach to the war. Mao wanted an end to the war, and he communicated this position through his able and convincing foreign minister Zhou Enlai. As if to underscore its independent position in the war, North Vietnam launched a massive invasion of the South in March of 1972. By that time the United States had only 95,000 forces left to defend South Vietnam. In the first stage of the campaign, the communist invasion was a great success. Spearheaded by Soviet tanks and 120,000 North Vietnamese forces, the invaders penetrated into the Central Highlands, but Nixon was not about to buckle. He responded by directing massive B-52 raids across the DM2: "the bastards have never been bombed like they're going to be bombed this time," he said. Interestingly enough, both Congress and the public rallied around the president's move. Nixon's poll ratings shot up dramatically.

Nixon's decisive actions probably averted defeat in South Vietnam, but the war was still a stalemate. Moreover, the North Vietnamese offensive starkly revealed the weakness in training and willpower of the South Vietnamese army, which had enjoyed a 5:1 numerical superiority over the invading communist army. The Saigon government had about one million men under arms, and the United States had equipped that army with some of the finest military equipment in the world. After ten years of training, the South Vietnamese army could still not operate on its own. Nixon proved to be right when he said that "all the air power in the world will not save Saigon if the South Vietnamese aren't able to hold on the ground."[103]

Following the failed North Vietnamese invasion and the reelection of Nixon in November 1972, North Vietnam and the United Stated slowly inched toward a compromise. The United States agreed to allow North Vietnamese troops to stay in the South after a cease-fire and agreed to establish a tripartite electoral commission charged with arranging a settlement after the cease-fire had gone into effect. This commission was to be composed of the Saigon regime, the Provisional Revolutionary Government, and the Neutralists. Within sixty days after a cease-fire, the United States would withdraw its remaining troops, the North Vietnamese would return all POWs, and a political settlement would then be arranged by the tripartite National Council of Reconciliation and Concord.

Kissinger thought that Thieu would be pleased with the settlement he had reached in Paris without Thieu's participation. In this he was sadly mistaken. The infuriated Thieu and his government regarded the Paris agreement as a *fait accompli* that confirmed their worst suspicions of their vacillating, fair-weather American friends. In the end, Nixon supported Thieu, and Kissinger's peace plan broke down. Kissinger continued to spar with his counterpart, Le Duc Tho, but in the end, the two men decided to call it quits and resolve the issue by force.

Nixon's only hope to save face in Vietnam was to pump massive aid into South Vietnam in the form of over a billion dollars in military hardware. On paper, the infusion of such massive military hardware made South Vietnam one of the largest armed forces in the world.[104] Nixon followed this up by resuming massive bombing. In January 1973 peace talks resumed in Paris. Although the atmosphere was grim, both sides wanted a settlement. The final agreement, signed in Paris on January 27, 1973, was much like the October settlement, except for a few cosmetic changes. This time, Nixon imposed the agreement on Thieu, sweetening the pot by "absolutely" guaranteeing U.S. intervention if North Vietnam violated the terms of the agreement.

This was hardly "Peace with Honor," though it allowed the United States to extricate itself without being completely humiliated. It also secured the return of most POWs. North Vietnamese troops remained in the South. The Provisional Revolutionary Government (PRG) was given political status. The political future of South Vietnam was to be handled later, hopefully by political means. The 1973 agreement existed only on paper and not on the battlefield, where both sides still jockeyed for position. As South Vietnam quickly lost ground to a much more determined North Vietnam, American war-weariness, combined with the Watergate scandals, made it difficult to support the South Vietnamese government, mired as ever in inefficiency and corruption. After Nixon's resignation, Congress drastically cut back aid to South Vietnam. In the spring of 1975 the North staged its final invasion. Amid scenes of utter chaos, the United States evacuated its remaining personnel and walked away from a situation that could sustain no further sacrifice or commitments. It was a stunning loss, the first one in American history. All of Vietnam was now unified under communist control, the very goal that the United States had sought to prevent and for which 58,000 Americans had given their lives.

6. The End of Victory Culture?

After the collapse of the South Vietnamese government, President Gerald Ford issued the following official communique: "The Government of the Republic of Vietnam has surrendered. Prior to its surrender, we have withdrawn our Mission from Vietnam. Vietnam has been a wrenching experience for this nation. . . . History must be the final judge of that which we have done or left undone, in Vietnam and elsewhere. Let us calmly await its verdict."[105] History itself, of course, does not judge, but historians do, and they do so from hindsight and from their own ideological perspectives. It should not be surprising, therefore, that defeat in Vietnam spawned a flood of contentious books about the war and why it ended so ignominiously, quite apart from the question of what it did to the nation's pride and optimism. Despite the many differences historians have held on the conduct or meaning of the war, there is at least one common agreement, and that is that the war was an unmitigated disaster for everyone concerned. Most historians today argue that the war, as it was being waged, was unwinnable for at least three reasons.

In the first place, the American cause for fighting a land war in Southeast Asia was never clearly spelled out to the American people. Presumably, it was to help the democratic government of South Vietnam in staving off a communist inspired takeover of the South. The distinction between "North" and "South" Vietnam, however, was largely linguistic, as was the pretense that the South was democratic or freedom-loving and therefore worth defending. After more than ten years of watching the sordid spectacle of corruption, coups, and countercoups in South Vietnam, most Americans gradually saw no reason why they should prop up a corrupt Vietnamese regime with the lives of young Americans.

In the second place, the leadership of the United States fought a political rather than a military war; its aim was not the defeat of enemy troops in the field, but the application of just enough pressure on the enemy so that he would either give up or negotiate for peace. Since the enemy could match American efforts in both manpower and materiel, this strategy implied a lengthy war of attrition and a battle of will rather than of armor. American war planners fooled themselves into believing that they could bring Ho Chi Minh to heel by using lethal technology and by fighting a "limited" war, matching the enemy's escalation of conflict with an opposite and equal reaction of violence. But the threshold of pain for Americans was appreciably lower than that of the enemy, a tenacious and brutal foe bent on sacrificing millions of lives in order to accomplish his objective. Americans were an affluent and spoiled people who had no stomach for a bloody war that threatened to devour its young people. The communists, on the other hand, were ready to "pay any price and bear any burden" to achieve victory. The strategy of escalating a limited war was, therefore, ignorant in purpose and, as it would turn out, incompetent in its application; and in order to defend it, the Johnson and Nixon administrations necessarily had to resort to Orwellian doublespeak—namely, that defeat was really victory, that destruction of entire villages was just "rooting out the infrastructure," that the use of lethal chemicals was designed to "defoliate" the jungle to detect guerrillas, that massive and enforced relocations were necessary in order to "pacify" the country, and that carpet bombing a poor preindustrial country was simply "protective retaliation."

In the third place, the United States lost the war because it was fighting too many crusades simultaneously, and from a position not of strength but of weakness. American leaders were imbued with a false sense of supremacy and invincibility; they assumed that America was godlike and capable of waging anticommunist crusades around the world, while at the same time ending poverty, racism, and injustice on the home front. Lyndon Johnson exemplified this hubris, for he believed that the American way of life could be perfected at home and simultaneously exported abroad, by persuasion or by force. But Johnson had the cart before the horse: the United States was undergoing wrenching social changes over a multitude of domestic imperfections and injustices. In other words, the country was internally divided and therefore hardly in a position to take on the role of the world's policeman. No country, not even the United States, can wage a multitude of crusades simultaneously: fighting wars, containing communism around the world, ending poverty, achieving racial equality, going to the moon, and rehabilitating everyone who has been ill treated by the world. At the time that Johnson escalated the war, the country was deeply divided along generational, ethnic, class, and religious lines, hardly the best time to embark on a land war in Southeast Asia. Martin Luther King caught this incongruity of fighting a faraway conflict at a time of internal racial unrest when he said that "we are taking the black young men who had been crippled by our society and sending them eight thousand miles to guarantee liberties in Southeast Asia which they had not found in Southwest Georgia and East Harlem."[106] "The best and the brightest" did not send their sons to Vietnam, making sure that they were preserved from harm by a class-ridden "selective service" umbrella; they sent the sons of working-class or ethnic minorities into combat; and when these young men returned, their college "betters" called them suckers or baby killers. In the end, the war exacerbated and inflamed class, ethnic, and racial tensions at home, poisoning the lives of a generation of Vietnam veterans. John Kerry had it right when he testified before the Senate Foreign Relations Committee by saying "the country doesn't know it yet but it has created a monster, a monster in the form of millions of young men who have been taught to deal and to trade in violence . . . , men who have returned with a sense of anger and betrayal which no one has yet grasped."[107]

This sense of anger and betrayal, of course, is not new in history, for young men have often returned to a nation in turmoil after a lost war. The Germans come to mind after two lost wars, having to make sense out of defeat. After World War I the Germans refused to accept the reality of defeat and blamed it on subversives at home, on a multitude of amorphous forces that had conspired to prevent victory by stabbing the army in the back. After a period of denial, there were also advocates of the "stab-in-the-back" mythology in America, mostly among the leaders of the military, right-wing conservatives, or simply ordinary Americans who had been taught that America never loses a war. The military, in seeking scapegoats, blamed the media for having undermined the war effort and poisoned morale at home. General Douglas Kinnard gave a questionnaire to 173 army generals who had commanded in Vietnam and asked them about the role of the media in the Vietnam War. The response showed that 67 percent of the respondents felt that the media had conducted a "psychological warfare campaign against the United States policies in Vietnam that could not have been better done by the enemy."[108] The generals unanimously condemned the press for its war coverage and for aiding and abetting the enemy.

The generals, of course, were not alone. The Vietnam War hatched more than one aggrieved constituency. Everybody was mad at somebody. The generals hated the media, the media despised the military, the protesters despised the "system," blacks despised "whitey," Hispanics hated "gringos," women were inflamed against "male chauvinists," the Nixon men turned against the "effete snobs" of the eastern establishment, radicals denounced "corporate capitalism," conservatives yelled at "flaming liberals," liberals barked at "right-wing" bigots, and so on.

The Vietnam War, combined with the contentious civil rights conflicts, changed the national mood for decades to come. Defeat in Vietnam spelled the end of victory culture, of brimming optimism and brash ideas of saving the world. What, after all, did America have to show after two decades in Vietnam? More than 58,000 Americans had died, untold devastation had been inflicted on a poor country, billions of dollars had been poured into a bottomless pit, and many of those who returned were psychologically scarred for life. Few had believed that America was fighting for democracy in Vietnam or was safeguarding the world order from evil communists. As Michael Herr reported: "Hearts and Minds, Peoples of the Republic, tumbling dominoes, maintaining the equilibrium of the Dingdong by containing the ever encroaching Doodah; you could also hear the other, some young soldier speaking in all bloody innocence, saying, 'All that's just a *load* man. We're here to kill gooks. Period!'"[109] To most soldiers, unfamiliar with Vietnam's culture and terrain, it had been a matter of simple survival, which meant killing the enemy. But since the line that separated friend from foe was often fuzzy, it proved impossible to identify a communist gook from the average run-of-the-mill Asian gook. When in doubt, it was sometimes safer to kill every gook. This was often called the "Mere Gook rule" or "If it's dead it's Vietcong."

Vietnam thus had unintended moral consequences for a generation of young Americans, most of whom came from blue-collar or minority backgrounds. Many of them were robbed of their innocence and idealism. Privileged college students referred to Vietnam soldiers as "suckers," mocked their simplistic idealism about America, and then sneered at them when they returned by calling them baby killers. Many of the young men who had gone to Vietnam did so as delegates of victory culture. As in World War II, the GIs saw warfare as a competitive sport and as a means to validate their manliness. Philip Caputo tells us that he joined the Marines because of the legendary exploits of its warriors. He wrote that those who did not live through the early sixties may find it hard to grasp what these years were really like, the kind of pride and overpowering self-assurance that shaped his generation. Under the spell of the Kennedy mystique, the young men sallied forth to save the world for democracy. Caputo pointed out that "war is always attractive to young men who know nothing about it, but we had also been seduced into uniform by Kennedy's challenge to 'ask what you can do for your country' and by missionary idealism he had awakened in us."[110] Caputo believed himself to be John Wayne: "Already I saw myself charging up some distant beachhead, like John Wayne in *Sands of Iwo Jima*, and then coming home a suntanned warrior with medals on my chest."[111] The reality was entirely different: there was no straight path from the Halls of Montezuma to the Shores of Tripoli, no beaches at Normandy, or landings at Guadalcanal; there were no decisive battles, nor was there a winnable objective. Instead, it was "a monotonous succession of ambushes and dogfights." Beyond adding more corpses, none of the endless encounters with the enemy achieved anything. As far as the soldiers were concerned, their mission was not to win terrain or seize positions, but simply to kill as many real or assumed communists as possible. Thus, if the war planners had any objective, it turned out to be the body count.

It is important to ponder this military strategy and its impact on the troops and on the nation's moral conscience. "With respect to the word 'win' one of the Pentagon war planners said, "this, I think, means that we succeed in demonstrating to the Vietcong that they cannot win."[112] General Westmoreland defined winning in the same basic ambivalent sense when he said that it meant convincing the Vietcong that they are unable to win. Ambassador Lodge used a more Skinnerian approach by suggesting that we do not have to destroy Ho Chi Minh but simply "to change his behavior."[113] An American journalist, intoxicated by America's technological power, as previously noted, believed that the North Vietnam leaders would give up after being invited to see one of the magnificent American aircraft carriers. Failing that, many thought that by waging a brutal war of attrition on the North Vietnamese, it would become clear to them eventually that they could not resist the sheer technological might of the United States. As previously shown, this was the techno-war mentality of higher body counts, kill ratios, war by machine calculation.

The mentality involved here is the virtue of industrial mass killing that was perfected in two world wars in the twentieth century. It is also the mentality that fueled the Holocaust, the sort of bureaucratic thinking that strips the enemy of all human qualities and treats him like a disposable waste product that can be converted into an asset on the statistical ledger. To the war planners, who were far removed from battlefield reality, the body count was just a statistical abstraction; but to the killers in the field it became a brutalizing experience that gave the lie to the illusion that this kind of combat was noble and uplifting. If killing has no larger objective beyond killing itself, then the act of killing becomes its own *raison d'être*. This can only mean that a soldier fights only to kill and is therefore only a killer. The remorseless logic of such evil seems to have escaped the war planners, who had retreated into their own Orwellian cocoon of euphemistic rationalizations. As Robert J. Lifton has pointed out, the phenomenon of the body count is "the perfect symbol of America's descent into evil" because it managed

> to distill the essence of the American numbing, brutalization, and illusion into a grotesque technicalization: there is something to count, a statistic for accomplishment. I know of no greater corruption than this phenomenon: the amount of killing—any killing—becomes the total measure of achievement. And concerning this measure, one lies, to others as well as to oneself, about why, who, what, and how many one kills.[114]

Besides brutalizing the men who fought in Vietnam, the war also left deep intergenerational scars because the burden of fighting was not shared equally. In a deeper sense, the Vietnam War laid bare not only the conflict between generations and in the generation of the young itself, but between different views of reality. To most young Americans, especially those who protested on university campuses, cold war reality was surreal and meaningless; the same reaction, however, was also experienced by many Vietnam soldiers who had difficulty understanding the official version of what they were supposed to be doing in the rice paddies of Southeast Asia. Both the protesters at home and the soldiers overseas were fighting their own war, sometimes at cross purposes, sometimes in the same key; and their war was not necessarily against the communists or even against the establishment. Behind the frustrations and protests of young people, which the war definitely exposed, was the need for direction, clarity, and honesty that the country's leadership, political and military, miserably failed to supply, for at every turn young people felt that they were being manipulated, lied to, and misled. Both the political and military leaders undermined America's civic religion by lying and setting bad examples. Is it therefore any wonder that many soldiers who returned from this meaningless war lost all sense of meaning, as did one veteran who said: "When I went to Vietnam, I believed in Jesus Christ and John Wayne. After Vietnam, both went down the tubes. It don't mean nothin.'"[115]

The poet Robert Bly pointed out that the Vietnam War seriously eroded male confidence because the older generation failed in transmitting the culture of honest male camaraderie that had prevailed in World War II when there had been a certain feeling of trust all up and down the line. This was not true of the Vietnam War. The older men did not maintain a sense of decorum that is always frayed but always essential in wartime; they allowed and often encouraged the foulest language and behavior. As Bly suggested, "the older men led the way to the whorehouses and made no attempt to preserve the continuity between civilian life for the young males. It was a violation of trust."[116] Unit commanders, as previously mentioned, also pressured soldiers to report and even lie about body counts. The military leadership also exercised bad judgment by instituting one-year field-term rotations, which undermined unit cohesion because soldiers were constantly rotated in and out of their units, making it difficult to maintain a sense of cameraderie and esprit d'corps. Even the language used by the older generation, as we have seen, was Orwellian in its mendacity. As Robert Bly suggested, "when older men betray younger men, and lie to them, in government and the field, what happens then to male values? What happens to a society in which the males do not trust each other?"[117] The answer is the society that war and protest has produced.

8

THE CRISIS OF 1968

The Fall of Liberalism

1. A Speculative Stampede on Gold

On March 31, 1968, Lyndon Johnson announced that he was not running for reelection, a political event that would wreck not only the Democratic Party but the liberal consensus that the Democrats had forged in the 1960s. Few Americans at the time realized that an equally significant crisis was unfolding in the economic domain—a monetary crisis that had been gripping global financial markets since November 1967. In March 1968 officials at Fort Knox, Kentucky, where the nation's gold supplies were kept, loaded an estimated $500 million worth of gold bars on a heavily armed convoy. The shipment of gold ingots was then placed aboard a transport plane at a nearby Air Force base. The precious cargo next made its way to the Bank of England; it was inspected, loaded onto Swiss and British planes, and finally ended up in Swiss bank vaults. *Time* magazine reported on March 22 that these gold transfers were setting off "a frenetic speculative stampede" that could threaten the financial system of the Western world. What was behind this crisis and how did it presage the economic downturn of the American economy?

The gold crisis was preceded by chronic balance of payment deficits that had been growing since the Kennedy administration. Foreign markets for U.S. goods were starting to decline as a result of the resurgent economies of Europe and Japan. Furthermore, profuse spending on the Vietnam War and social spending, together with growth-inducing tax cuts, were seriously overstraining U.S. financial institutions, producing an acute economic crisis in 1968. The gold crisis of March 1968 was the latest herald of bad economic news.

The currencies of international financial markets were based on the soundness of the U.S. dollar and the gold supply that backed it up. This arrangement went back to the Bretton Woods Conference in 1944, which established the International Monetary Fund (IMF) and the World Bank. The purpose of Bretton Woods was to secure a stable international monetary system that would prohibit discriminatory currency practices and exchange restrictions. Using the U.S. dollar as a standard, currency exchange rates were pegged to gold at $35 an ounce. The United States committed itself to exchange gold for dollars at the rate of $35 per ounce upon demand of foreign governments.[1] Therein lay the rub. With billions of dollars in balance of payment deficits and a shrinking gold supply, how long could the United States secure the $35-per-ounce-of-gold commitment? As it would turn out, that commitment was challenged by two apparently different parties: international gold speculators (Middle Eastern sheiks, oil interests, Latin American businessmen, affluent Asian speculators) and by foreign governments, particularly France under the leadership of Charles de Gaulle. As early as 1965 the French president had mounted his first attack on the special status of the "Anglo-Saxon" dollar and pound in the international financial system. In 1967 de Gaulle and his allies struck again, first at the pound and then at the dollar, forcing devaluation of the pound from $2.80 to $ 2.40. The French president was well aware of the fact that major international monetary players had accumulated over $30 million that could be redeemed through gold. Given the worsening U.S. balance of deficits, profuse spending on Vietnam and domestic programs, and the ever-shrinking gold reserves, would the United States be able to redeem these dollars if France and its allies decided to unload their dollars and demand prompt payment in gold at $35 an ounce?

In March 1968 France decided to do just that, triggering an international monetary crisis that called for quick action by the United States and other Gold Pool nations such as Britain, Switzerland, Italy, Belgium, West Germany, and Holland. Queen Elizabeth declared a "bank holiday" in foreign exchange trading, which shut off the gold dealing in Britain and soon afterwards in other countries as well. Only the Paris Bourse remained open. The United States then called an international conference at the Federal Reserve Board in Washington to resolve the monetary crisis. The participants agreed on a "two-tier" system for gold transactions, according to which the federal government would continue to sell gold at $35 per ounce to central banks in the pool but private speculators would have to conduct their transactions in the private or free market. The agreement, in other words, established an official market and a private market, the former for central banking purposes at the $35–per-ounce-of-gold rate and the latter following the free market of supply and demand. The gold pool players also agreed to establish a new system of international reserves that was based on currency rather than gold. The world's leading bankers were given Special Drawing Rights (SDR) in the form of paper (currency) gold in order to meet the liquidity needs of expanding world markets.

Although the Washington conference averted the impending collapse of the old global financial system, it also exposed the serious problems in the U.S. economy. The Vietnam War had aggravated the balance of payment deficits, triggering a round of inflation that threatened to undermine the economic expansion of the postwar period.[2] In his January 1967 budget message to Congress, Johnson had already called for a 6–percent temporary surcharge on corporate and individual income taxes, but the president's proposal was stymied by Wilbur Mills, the powerful Democratic chairman of the House Ways and Means Committee, which served as a clearing house of approval of all fiscal proposals. Mills was a Democrat, but he judged Johnson to be a dangerous spendthrift who would keep on spending unless restrained by Congress. In October 1967 Mills temporarily tabled Johnson's proposal for a tax surcharge on the grounds that it would trigger a recession. Mills knew that Congress was reluctant to increase taxes, and he could also read the polls showing a steady decline in Johnson's popularity. The president, in fact, was reaching the moment of truth that had been deferred for some time: he had to choose between guns and butter. He chose guns, despite the fact that race riots were tearing apart the nation and undermining morale on the home front. Instead of cutting his losses in an unwinnable war and redirecting funds thus saved for domestic needs, the president stubbornly stayed the course in Vietnam. In Robert Dallek's view, the war was becoming a "personal test of his judgment, of his wisdom in expanding the conflict in the first place."[3]

In the meantime, the budget deficit got worse. Budget analysts estimated that the 1968 deficit would be $19.8 billion, most of it directly attributable to the Vietnam War and the Great Society.[4] During the first three months of 1968 intense congressional battles raged over the deficit and how it could be contained, let alone substantially reduced. In March, William McChesney Martin Jr., chairman of the Federal Reserve Board, told a Detroit audience that "it is time to stop pussyfooting and get our accounts in order. It is time to stop talking of guns and butter. We must face up to the fact that this is a war economy."[5] Wilbur Mills was coming to a similar conclusion, changing his mind on tax increases. Working with like-minded conservative Democrats and Republicans in the House, Mills was now ready for raising taxes and cutting expenditures. After considerable haggling, an agreement was reached in June that called for a $10 billion surcharge and a $6 billion cut in spending. Johnson and his Great Society boosters were beginning to recognize that there were economic limits to their appetites and that those limits, in turn, would exact a severe political price. The Revenue and Expenditure Act of 1968 was imposing some discipline on domestic spending, and by doing so, took the winds out of the sail of economic growth and expansion. Johnson's Great Society was now but a distant dream. Growth liberalism had come a cropper, and some even predicted that the American Century, based on free enterprise capitalism, might also be at an end.

The gold crisis may have ended by the summer of 1968 but the economic conditions that had fueled it continued to weaken the U.S. economy. The year 1968 signaled the end of the postwar boom, bringing in its wake economic stagnation and continuing inflation, a phenomenon that economic historians would later call "stagflation." Although this did not manifest itself fully until the fall of Vietnam (1975), the symptoms were evident in 1968. By waging a costly war in Vietnam, while at the same time spending profusely on domestic programs, Lyndon Johnson had succeeded in overstraining the economy to the breaking point, and in doing so, he paid the ultimate political price: the ruin of his own political career and the collapse of the liberal coalition he had so carefully put together in 1964. In little over three years Johnson had fallen from the great heights of political popularity to the depths of political ruin. Here was a towering man who had so craved the approval and love of the American people that he was willing to buy their love through government largess; yet the more he gave the less people seemed to like him. Asking a White House group at one point, "Why don't people like me," one honest guest replied "Mr. President, you are not a very likeable man."[6] Johnson's tragedy resided in a combination of grandiose promises and deceitful dodges to extricate himself from having to deliver the goods. In the end, the good politician in him also failed, for he allowed himself to be outflanked by liberal intellectuals who painted him as a crude usurper of Camelot, by left-wing radicals who sneered at his social programs and called him a warmonger, by ungrateful black militants, by aroused Republicans, and by opportunistic dissidents within the Democratic Party. The man who had sought the love of the American people was thoroughly despised by so many of them in the spring of 1968. It was Lyndon Johnson who did himself in by pursuing an American version of "guns and butter." As Irving Bernstein put it, "he acted as though he could have both, while everyone, himself included, knew that he could not."[7] Johnson's course of action met reality in the form of economic crisis, followed by a political crisis that spelled the end of consensus liberalism. Here was a strong connection between the gold crisis, Vietnam, inflation, and the Great Society. The history of the sixties, as the economic historian Robert Collins has shown, was not entirely written on the turbulent streets of America.[8]

2. Losing the Streets: The Crisis of Law and Order

Following the assassination of Martin Luther King Jr. on April 4, 1968, race riots erupted in 172 American cities, causing 43 deaths, 3,500 injuries, and 27,000 arrests.[9] Some of these civil disorders were spontaneous reactions to the assassination of King; others were incited by black militants, notably Stokely Carmichael, who inflamed an angry crowd in Washington D.C. by urging blacks to "go home and get your guns. When the white man comes he is coming to kill you. I don't want any black blood in the street. Go home and get you a gun and then come back because I got me a gun."[10] In Washington D.C. the police were unable to contain the violence and called on the White House to send in the army. The president was caught in a terrible dilemma: if he did not call in the army, the looting and arson would threaten the very seat of government; on the other hand, if he called in federal troops he would be sending a clear signal to the nation that his administration was unable to control lawlessness in its own backyard. At 4:00 P.M. on April 5, looting had come within two blocks of the White House. Looking out of the windows of the White House, Johnson could see black smoke from burning buildings fill the sky over the capital. Johnson later recalled that, while watching this sad spectacle, he was overcome by a "sick feeling" wondering, "as every American must have wondered, what we were coming to."[11] By 5:00 P.M. that afternoon troops with fixed bayonets surrounded the White House and soldiers patrolled the city, securing the west steps of the capitol by setting up a machine gun post.

The arrival in the capital of 14,000 troops joining the 2,800 Metropolitan Police Department officers evoked widespread feelings of both shame and anger across the nation. More and more Americans believed that the president had failed to exercise strong leadership and that he had lost control over events at home and abroad. Historical hindsight confirms this view, for Johnson's liberal administration had impaled itself on the war in Vietnam and the war on the streets of America. In the eyes of many Americans, the president was losing the three wars he had declared since 1964: the Vietnam War, the war on poverty, and the war on crime. It was street crime and civil unrest that would bring down the liberal house Johnson had built.

As to street crime, the statistics tell us part of the story. Before the 1960s homicide rates had steadily decreased from 9.7 per hundred thousand population in 1933 to 4.7 per hundred thousand population in 1961. Between 1961 and 1974 the homicide rate moved sharply upward, reaching a peak of 10.2 in 1974. In the period stretching from 1960 to 1978 reported robberies more than tripled, automobile thefts doubled, and burglaries nearly tripled.[12] In New York City robberies rose from 6,600 in 1962 to 78,000 in 1972, a staggering increase of 1082 percent.[13] No wonder that street crime was at the center of white middle-class concern, as poll after poll in 1968 clearly indicated. On January 26, 1968, *Time* magazine opined that law and order, along with the Vietnam War, constituted the major election issue in the upcoming November general elections. One month later, the Gallup poll reported that the majority of the American people identified crime and lawlessness as the major domestic issue. According to Thomas and Mary Edsall, the authors of *Chain Reaction: The Impact of Race, Rights, and Taxes on American Politics* (1991), it was the steep rise in crime and urban protests (civil rights, racial riots, student protests, antiwar demonstrations) that turned white urban voters against Johnson's Great Society.[14] Although the two authors exaggerate the influence of racism among white urban ethnics, there can be no doubt that the social excesses of the 1960s turned the traditional white ethnic core against the liberals in 1968. There had been a festering white discontent in major cities since World War II, some of it undoubtedly racial, but also centered on security and safety issues. Working-class whites owning homes in inner-city neighborhoods were afraid of encroaching slums and declining property values, blaming blacks and Johnson's Great Society programs for having caused the problem.

In 1964 Barry Goldwater had made law and order a centerpiece of his presidential campaign and Governor George Wallace of Alabama had shocked the Democrats when he garnered 33 percent of the vote in the Wisconsin Democratic primary campaign. More explicitly racial in his campaign than Goldwater, Wallace had linked not just southern but also northern fears of integration with fear of crime; he had shown the way to a future motherlode for the Republican Party.[15] It was Nixon who realized that a law and order campaign could be waged by gliding over racial issues and focusing attention on fear of lawlessness rather than its causes. And fear there was in 1968—fear of black militants, fear of violent antiwar protesters, foul-mouthed, long-haired hippies, supercilious liberals, opinionated academics, and so forth. A Chicago policeman gave voice to white working-class fears and anger of protesters of all stripes "pissing on the flag," calling police officers "pigs" and ridiculing traditional American values:

> The way we saw it—well, I'll only speak for myself here—is that the whole country was going to hell faster than you can wipe your nose. We had shit to clean up every night— and nobody writes about that—human garbage with a mouth. And the press, they just

wrote everything that these bastards said—and the biggest words that they used against us was "police brutality." My *ass* it was. We were not the ones breaking windows and throwing bottles and tying up traffic and making it so that an honest man could not make a living because they were disrupting things all over the damn place. And what were we to do about all the other crimes that were taking place? We were thinly spread, overworked, stressed out—and when things weren't fixed right, or at least the way people thought they should have been, we took hell in our own neighborhoods; boy do I know it. We got friggin hell.[16]

In response to mounting criticisms of the administration's handling of civil disturbances, the addled president and his advisors were caught off guard, reacting to rather than anticipating violent events. Despite his rough exterior, Johnson was squeamish about the use of force against civilians. Deep down, he believed that the riots were rooted in socioeconomic conditions, and that the war on poverty would eventually remedy the violence. The war on poverty, according to Johnson and the liberals, was also a war on crime, a linkage that would come to haunt both of them in 1968. As it turned out, far from reducing crime, the war on poverty was actually accompanied by an increase in crime. Although a few riots had occurred before 1965, they were relatively small and easily contained. Sixteen days after Johnson signed the Civil Rights Act of 1964, riots broke out in Harlem and Rochester. Liberals explained these racial disturbances by arguing that they were caused by the "rising expectations" on the part of oppressed inner-city blacks, recommending more social programs to remove the "root causes" of rebellion. In 1965 the Watts riot, which spawned a host of serious uprisings in the late 1960s, was also explained in a similar vein. The Voting Rights Act, passed just five days before the Watts ghetto blew up, was seen by liberals as a step in the right direction of empowering black people so that, in addition to more social programs, they would eventually control their own destinies in urban America.

In the meantime, the Johnson administration banked on more social programs and further studies of street crimes by scholarly experts. Studies of juvenile delinquency and crime had been conducted since the early Kennedy administration; they had been conducted with great fanfare but had accomplished very little in practice. In 1964 Nicholas Katzenbach, the assistant attorney general, suggested convening a committee to study street crime and "rioting by Negroes." Headed by Harvard law professor James Vorenberg, the committee conducted a far-ranging investigation; but before the committee had even reached its findings, the president already raised excessive expectations by telling the members of the committee that "today we have taken a pledge not only to reduce crime but to banish it."[17] The committee's final report made no such promises; instead it made over two hundred recommendations dealing with law enforcement, the courts, and correctional facilities, holding out reasonable hopes that these recommendations, if followed, would reduce crime rather than end it. Johnson did not want to hear about complexities; he wanted quick fixes.

The first clear-cut signal that the Democrats were on the wrong side of the law and order issue came in 1966 when Ronald Reagan defeated Pat Brown for the governorship of California. A former actor, president of the Screen Actors Guild, and public relations spokesman for General Electric, Reagan and his media-savvy advisors had orchestrated a brilliant campaign that tapped deep into the veins of discontent among white middle-class Californians, especially those living in the more affluent suburbs of Orange County. Reagan saw student protests, crimes and urban riots as a moral rather than an economic problem, denouncing violent protesters and rioters as either dupes of radical ideology or as avowed subversives who were breaking the law under the guise of civil rights. Rather than raising false expectations among African Americans with promises of federal spending, Reagan proposed cuts in welfare spending, swift punishment for lawbreakers and economic incentives for moving the poor from welfare to workfare. Reagan denounced Great Society programs because they rewarded people for *not* working, for making them permanent wards of the government. In 1966 Reagan's anti-government message found far greater resonance with white middle-class voters than it did when Goldwater proclaimed it in 1964. In a speech to students at the University of Southern California, Reagan said that "for every ounce of federal help we get, we surrender an ounce of freedom," adding that the "Great Society grows greater every day—greater in cost, greater in inefficiency and greater in waste."[18] Fourteen years later, Reagan would carry this message to the rest of the country and into the White House.

Californians were clearly showing signs of frustration with liberal social policies; they increasingly believed that conservative critics had a point when they linked liberal social spending with the decline in law and order. And it was not just Californians who were changing their minds about the liberal project and associating it with permissiveness and crime. In November 1966, the same month Reagan was elected governor of California, the voters of New York, the most liberal city in the United States, turned down a revised police board that would have been fully authorized to investigate alleged reports of police brutality under the aegis of civilian control. It was a stunning defeat for the liberals who had praised the measure as a progressive civil rights issue. The voters saw the revised board as yet another measure to stifle strong law enforcement. White ethnics in Brooklyn, especially Catholic workers, regarded the issue of crime as a no-brainer. As far as they were concerned, the civil rights of lawbreakers came with definite civil restrictions when it came to streets of New York, where muggings, murder, and mayhem were becoming the order of the day. Just how unsafe the streets of New York had become was brought home two years before by the brutal murder of Kitty Genovese.

In the early morning hours of March 13, 1964, Catherine "Kitty" Genovese, a twenty-eight-year-old bar manager from Queens, parked her red Fiat in a parking space adjacent to the Long Island rail station in Kew Gardens. She got out of her car and walked the last thirty yards toward her apartment building; but when she saw a suspicious-looking man standing in her path, she headed rapidly toward a nearby intersection, where a police call box was located. The man she had spotted, however, caught up with her and stabbed her several times. Kitty, as she was affectionately called by her friends and family, screamed repeatedly, "Oh my God, he stabbed me. Please help me."[19] Lights went on in nearby buildings and people peered out to see what the commotion was all about. One man shouted down from a window: "Hey, let that girl alone."[20] The attacker then left and windows closed. As Kitty staggered toward her apartment, however, the attacker returned and stabbed her again. Kitty cried out in agony: "I'm dying!" Windows opened and closed. No one came to her rescue, nor bothered to call the police. The attacker thereupon got into his car and drove away, only to change his mind because, as he later confessed, "I came back because I knew I'd not finished what I set out to do."[21]

In the meantime, Kitty Genovese, barely alive, dragged herself to the rear of her apartment building, but finding the door locked she crawled along the wall of the building until she reached the hallway of 82–62 Austin Street, collapsing in the hallway leading to the second floor. The attacker, following the trail of blood, caught up with her. He coldly raped her, took her money, a mere $49, and finished her off with his knife. It was not until 3:50 A.M. that a neighbor called the police, although thirty-eight of Kitty's neighbors had watched at least one of the assaults on her. The killer, Winston Moseley, a twenty-nine-year-old business machine operator who was married and had three children, confessed to the crime a week later, telling the police that he had killed two other women and raped many more. Claiming that he had "an uncontrollable urge to kill," Moseley unsuccessfully pleaded innocent by virtue of insanity and was convicted of first degree murder and sentenced to death. While awaiting execution on death row at Sing Sing, his death sentence was commuted to life imprisonment on a legal technicality. In 1968 Moseley escaped while being taken from prison to a Buffalo hospital for minor surgery; he overpowered the guard, took his gun, and held five people hostage, raping one woman hostage in the presence of her husband. The FBI finally closed in on him and persuaded him to surrender. Returned to prison, Moseley play-acted the role of victim, allegedly apologized to the Genovese family "for the inconvenience I caused,"[22] finished a B.A. degree in prison, and continued to appeal for an early parole, claiming that prison had transformed him into a vastly difference and reformed human being. The appeal was denied.

If there was one grisly homicide that stood out and etched itself on the national conscience during the 1960s it was the slaying of Kitty Genovese. In an editorial of March 20, 1964, the *New York Times* contended that "seldom has *The Times* published a more horrifying story than its account of how 38 respectable law-abiding middle class Queen's citizens watched a killer stalk his young woman victim . . . without one of them making a call to the Police Department that might have saved her life."[23] The thirty-eight witnesses, of course, offered various predictable excuses: they were afraid to get involved, thought it was just a domestic quarrel, feared for their own safety, believed that someone else must have called the police, and so forth. One witness said that she did not call because her English was too poor. Psychiatrists, sociologists, politicians, and pundits of all sorts weighed in and tried to sanitize the tragedy by reducing it to abstract theories of "urban alienation," "bad Samaritanism," "television violence," "the bystander effect," and so on. Whatever the cause, the "Kitty Genovese Syndrome" as it became known, haunted law-abiding Americans, especially those who lived in large cities. It set off a national debate about street crime that did not abate in the 1960s. Liberals counseled understanding, treatment, and rehabilitation, while conservatives recommended law and order and swift punishment. By the late 1960s liberals were losing the argument on street crime, especially the underlying assumption behind it that the root cause of crime could be found in poverty, racism, and urban slums.

Liberals were also losing at the polls. In the 1966 midterm elections the Democrats lost forty-seven seats in the House, three seats in the Senate, and eight governorships—all of this attributable to civil disorders, welfare spending, street crime, and the Vietnam War. In 1967, as previously mentioned, riots broke out in over a hundred cities across the nation. The images of black looters and arsonists shocked white America to such an extent that many whites began to lose confidence in the effectiveness of antipoverty programs and even civil rights legislation. There is no doubt that by the beginning of 1968 many Americans had lost faith in liberalism and in the Democratic Party as its custodian.

The White House itself was gripped by a kind of siege mentality during the fall of 1967. A confidential report circulating through the administration during the fall, entitled "Thinking the Unthinkable," painted several apocalyptic scenarios according to which the nation might become a garrison state in which blacks and whites would be strictly segregated, the former taking control of inner cities and the latter of the suburbs.[24] According to the report, the United Nations would move from New York to Paris, Reagan Republicans would take over the suburbs, the Democratic Party would lose its majority, and the country would hopelessly balkanize itself. The report, however, also painted more optimistic possibilities such as the development of model cities, the emergence of a prosperous black middle class, and greater ethnic integration.

In the summer of 1967 race riots ignited in cities all over the United States. Two of the worst occurred in Newark and Detroit. Newark, as previously mentioned, was run by a corrupt Democratic machine, and the city's ghetto was one of the worst in the nation. By contrast, the Motor City had been touted as a model of racial progress, a city that had a prosperous black middle class. Moreover, as subsequent statistics revealed, 83 percent of the rioters were employed, half of them being members of the United Auto Workers union.[25] Liberals tried to correct the negative perceptions white Americans had absorbed while watching television images of black looters by arguing that the riots gave blacks political self-consciousness and self-esteem, a collective sense that they could force change on the white establishment. More money, they said, was the answer. And herein lay the liberal problem: whether out of guilt or generosity or both, liberals seemed to believe that African Americans, unlike immigrant groups, were a unique class of Americans who should be given a social pass, even for bad behavior, which could be excused by reference to poverty or racism. As Fred Siegel put it, "like those third-world nations that had chosen to pursue a non-western path to prosperity, American blacks were to be given their due and offered an honored place in American life without having to make the long journey up the social ladder by gradually accumulating the skills needed for economic success."[26] Deep down in their bones most Americans could not accept such ideas because they clashed with their fundamental beliefs in self-reliance and hard work as the means to success. This is why the majority of the American people were strongly opposed to affirmative action programs, set-asides for "protected minorities," quotas, and so forth.

The race riots in Watts, Harlem, Newark, Detroit, and other cities raised the thorny issue of law enforcement, which resided in the hands of local city or state authorities. When and under what circumstances was it proper for the federal government to come to the assistance of local authorities? The Detroit crisis brought this issue into sharp relief. Governor George Romney of Michigan had called out the National Guard in order to help the Detroit police department to contain the riot; but when these forces proved insufficient to stop the violence, Romney called on the federal government to quell the insurrection. To do so, however, Romney had to issue a formal request to Washington that a state of insurrection existed in Detroit, and that the state of Michigan was unable to put it down. Johnson was reluctant to intervene because dispatching the army into the motor capital of the world would undermine his claim that Great Society programs were working and that, consequently, race relations were improving. In other words, sending crack paratroopers into one of the largest cities in America to restore law and order was a potential public relations nightmare. As Harry McPherson, Johnson's special counsel and speechwriter, so aptly put it: "we talk about the multitude of good programs going into the cities, and yet there are riots, which suggests that the programs are no good, or the Negroes past saving."[27]

Although Johnson continued to believe that his Great Society programs were working, if just given enough time and money, and that black people were definitely worth saving, an increasing number of white Americans were beginning to doubt that liberal solutions were working. By 1968 the liberals were in retreat. It was the conservatives who would successfully tap into white middle-class discontent and frame the national debate in the language of "law and order." Conservatives also assuaged white guilt by arguing that white racism did not cause inner-city riots; it was the rioters who caused the riots. In taking issue with the Kerner report, which had blamed white racism for black violence, Sam Ervin, a conservative Democrat from North Carolina, said that "when all is said, the President's Commission reaches the insupportable conclusion that everybody in the United States except the rioters are responsible for the riots," adding that the recommendations of the Kerner Commission called for unacceptable "ransom legislation."[28] What the press called Johnson's "credibility gap" was widening beyond his ability to close it. The president was losing all the "wars" he had declared: Vietnam, poverty, and street crime. Vietnam was turning into a bottomless pit, blacks were rioting in America's major cities, and crime was out of control. Sending additional troops to Vietnam and paratroopers into American cities was not the best way of "winning hearts and minds." As previously mentioned, Johnson was not a war-monger, and he had grave misgivings about using federal troops or relying on counterintelligence tactics to put down civil disorders. His critics rarely gave him the benefit of the doubt, painting him as a failed leader sticking stubbornly to failed programs. That such accusations would have been made by the Republicans goes without saying, but that prominent members of his own party were ready to undermine his presidency was one of the major reasons for the rout of the liberals in 1968.

3. The "Dump Johnson" Movement

In the summer of 1967 two left liberal activists, Allard Lowenstein and Curtis Gans, conceived a plan to bring down Lyndon Johnson by finding a strong Democratic candidate who could effectively oppose the president for renomination by his own party. The scheme had the looks and sounds of a palace revolution, a daring party coup to remove an increasingly unpopular leader. Both Lowenstein and Gans were veterans of the civil rights struggles of the early 1960s; they were also inveterate idealists who had made it their mission to redeem America's democratic tradition. Lowenstein had been a protégé of the late Eleanor Roosevelt, who saw in the young man a social progressive after her own heart. As a student, Lowenstein had been active in a host of liberal activities, notably the National Student Association, which elected him president in 1951. Although Lowenstein moved in socialist circles and was mentored by Norman Thomas and Irving Howe, he was not a communist. But when he discovered that the National Student Association was backed by CIA money, and that Johnson was leading the nation into disaster in Vietnam, he became a determined opponent of the administration and looked for ways and means to change its leadership.

Lowenstein's comrade-in-arms was Curtis Gans, a charter member of the Students for a Democratic Society (SDS), who wanted to transform the Democratic Party from a cold war party into a peace and social welfare party. On August 15, 1967, Gans formally launched the "Dump Johnson" movement at a NSA convention at the University of Maryland. The two activists also opened a "Dump Johnson" office in Washington D.C. in order to attract followers from dissidents in the Democratic Party who were willing to oppose Lyndon Johnson.

One month after the "Dump Johnson" movement had been launched, Lowenstein paid a visit to Hickory Hill, Robert Kennedy's home in McLean, Virginia, to discuss the possibility that Kennedy might challenge the president in 1968. Present at the meeting were the historian Arthur Schlesinger Jr., James Loeb, the publisher and former ambassador to Peru, Adam Walinsky, a Kennedy aide, and Jack Newfield, a young reporter who had accompanied Lowenstein. Schlesinger opposed Kennedy's involvement in the presidential race on the grounds that it would be a doomed effort, a view shared by Kennedy himself, who added that he was afraid that "people would say that I was splitting the party out of ambition and envy. No one would believe that I was doing it because of how I felt about Vietnam and poor people."[29] Although Kennedy thought that Lowenstein was doing the right thing, that Johnson was a "coward and a quitter" and therefore vulnerable in 1968, at this stage in the game, Kennedy was too shrewd to offer himself as a sacrificial lamb, a role that he wanted someone else to play before plunging into the fray. As he put it to the assembled group that night, "I think that someone else will have to be the first one to run. It can't be me because of my relationship with Johnson. And his feeling toward me has more to do with my brother than me."[30]

Kennedy's allusion to Johnson and his brother was well taken, but not in the sense that Kennedy seems to have understood it. Johnson and Robert Kennedy had developed a visceral dislike of each other that can be traced back to the time of the Democratic Convention of 1960 when the Kennedys began to develop second thoughts about picking Johnson as vice president on the Democratic ticket. On this occasion, as on so many others, John Kennedy used his brother as a foil to test the waters, letting him take the blame if the Kennedy position failed to work, and accepting the credit if it succeeded. Robert Kennedy's direct and sometimes abrasive style came in handy on numerous occasions, but it also earned him a reputation for being ruthless, vindictive, rude, and intolerant. Being his brother's crisis manager, Robert Kennedy often resorted to heavy-handed tactics, and he did it so well that the halo never disappeared from his brother's head. From the moment his brother died, however, Robert Kennedy was on his own, though the halo effect continued to provide some umbrage for the heir apparent. With Johnson in power, the shoe was now on the other foot, for it was now Kennedy who felt the sting of jealousy, slights, and vindictive behavior meted out by the insecure Lyndon Johnson. The unhealthy relationship between Robert Kennedy and Lyndon Johnson has been extensively explored by historians, and for good reason. Johnson had a monkey on his back throughout his presidency, and that was Robert Kennedy, who, in turn, walked in the company of his dead brother's ghost. Neither Johnson nor Robert Kennedy could rid themselves of the Kennedy mystique, for both believed in it.

As previously mentioned, Johnson was haunted by the Kennedy mystique because it prevented him from being himself—a rough Texan with brilliant political talents who wanted to feel secure with who he was and not to have to look over his shoulder pretending to be anyone else. As for his part, Robert Kennedy could not let go of the mystique either, because he felt a responsibility to be a better keeper of his brother's legacy than he had been of his brother's political career while he was alive. The reality was that the younger brother was a man quite different from his older brother. Robert was a far more intense and single-minded man than John, a perfectionist and something of a moral bully, qualities he probably acquired as a result of a sterner religious upbringing than any of his siblings. Whatever goals he pursued in life—prosecuting communists as an aide to Senator McCarthy, shaking down mobsters, indicting corrupt union officials like Jimmy Hoffa, or waging battles on behalf of poor people—Robert Kennedy enshrouded them with high moral, even religious purpose, reinforcing his strong sense of rectitude. While his brother often paid lip service to moral causes, Robert Kennedy believed in them. It was not until the 1968 presidential campaign that Kennedy really found his stride as a crusading activist and social reformer. Whatever Robert Kennedy did or said was immediately noticed by the insecure and increasingly paranoid Johnson, who suspected a Kennedy rat. Their relationship deteriorated steadily into name calling and sly insinuations. Johnson was convinced, and for good reasons, that Kennedy wanted to run for the presidency himself and reclaim his brother's legacy.

If Robert Kennedy, after testing the political waters did not think that it was in his interest to challenge the president for the nomination of the Democratic Party, was there someone else who did? It so happened that there was someone who had been waiting in the wings for some time to challenge Lyndon Johnson. His name was Eugene McCarthy, senator from Minnesota. According to McCarthy's account of the events under review, he had postponed announcing his political plans for 1968 until he could determine what Kennedy planned to do, claiming that he still thought in 1967 that Kennedy could make the strongest challenge.[31] After concluding that Kennedy would not enter the primaries, McCarthy announced his intention on November 30, 1967, to challenge Johnson in the 1968 Democratic primaries. At that time, his chances for success looked hopeless. Few people except antiwar activists knew who McCarthy was; and when his name came up, more people than not confused him with Joseph McCarthy, the anticommunist crusader of the 1950s. Even among rank-and-file Democrats, Lyndon Johnson outpolled McCarthy in a popularity contest by three to one.[32] Who was this bold challenger of a sitting president?

Eugene McCarthy was born in the small agricultural town of Watkins, Minnesota, in 1916. He was the son of an Irish-American father and a German-American mother. This mixed parentage, some historians have argued, shaped his contradictory character, for Eugene absorbed his father's gruff, caustic, and hot-tempered manners while at the same time learning to subordinate them to a certain reserve, patience, and gentleness he had inherited from his mother. Although both his father and mother were good Catholics, Eugene was more strongly influenced by his mother's intense passion for religion, which would guide him throughout his career. Educated in Catholic schools, first at St. Anthony's in Watkins, a school run by German nuns, and then at St. John's Preparatory in nearby Collegeville, which was run by Benedictine monks, McCarthy appeared destined for a life in the church. In 1932 McCarthy entered St. John's University, which was attached to the Preparatory School. When McCarthy entered St. John's, the university was changing from a small parochial college ministering primarily to German Catholic immigrants to a strong center of Catholic intellectual thought in the midwest.[33] It is safe to say that the intellectual rigor McCarthy found at St. John's, combined with its strong emphasis on spiritual devotion, was the most important influence on his life. Perhaps the most significant feature of his Catholic education, apart from his delight in the purity of Thomistic philosophy, was the missionary zeal the Benedictines had instilled in him for social justice and compassion for the poor. Influenced heavily by Dorothy Day (1897–1980), founder of the Catholic Worker movement and lifelong peace and social reform activist, McCarthy strongly believed that the church had an obligation to participate in social reform while at the same time stemming the tide of secular materialism by strongly rechristianizing American institutions and traditions.

After graduating from St. John's in 1935, McCarthy spent the next five years as an high school English teacher and school principal in the two tiny Minnesota towns of Tintah and Kimball, followed by an assignment in Mandan, North Dakota. It was in Mandan that he met his future wife, Abigail Quigley, who also taught in Mandan. Although McCarthy proposed to her, they decided to postpone marriage plans because of financial difficulties and traditional attitudes that frowned on a wife working alongside her husband as a teacher. In 1940 McCarthy was invited by his alma mater to teach courses in education and economics. Hardly a year later, and after considerable soul-searching, McCarthy decided to enter the novitiate at St. John's and became Brother Conan. It may have been partly the recognition that he was unsuited for a monastic existence, partly the feelings he still held for Abigail that caused him to leave the novitiate; and after just a month of seminary training in Milwaukee, McCarthy gave up plans for a religious vocation, returned to Watkins, and resumed his relationship with Abigail, marrying her in 1945. Although McCarthy left the monastery, the monastery, according to his biographer, never left him.[34] Exempt from the military during World War II because of a physical disability, McCarthy spent the war years working for the War Department deciphering Japanese codes for the Signal Corps. He got into politics after meeting Hubert Humphrey, who was then mayor of Minneapolis. Allying himself with the popular and liberal Humphrey in fighting the left-leaning influences on the Democratic Farm Labor Party, McCarthy gained important political experiences and then ran successfully for Congress in 1948. The people of Minnesota reelected him five times to the House of Representatives, where he established a reputation as the brightest of the young liberals.[35] In 1958 McCarthy won election to the Senate, taking his place next to Hubert Humphrey, by then the senior senator from Minnesota. Although winning easily, as he did in his congressional campaigns, McCarthy's political style was less than inspiring, especially for those who worked for him. He was by nature a loner, listening to his own drummer, and he struck people as too professional and withdrawn. Furthermore, he hated giving speeches, ignored advice, and sloughed off criticisms either with intellectual put-downs or obscure witticisms. Yet his suave manners and earnest opinions always carried weight with his constituents, who saw in him a man of spiritual depth and ethical probity.

While in the Senate, McCarthy formed a close relationship with other liberal Catholic senators such as Philip Hart of Michigan, Edmund Muskie of Maine, Mike Mansfield of Montana, and later, Edward Kennedy of Massachusetts. All of them had made their compromise with power and patronage; all of them had also come under the wheeling-and-dealing influence of Lyndon Johnson, whom they both admired and resented. In 1960, McCarthy supported Humphrey for the Democratic nomination, partly because Humphrey was an old friend and colleague and partly because he regarded Kennedy as a "spoiled rich kid" who did not deserve to be president. His standing during the Kennedy administration was, therefore, not very good, especially since McCarthy continued to do his best in annoying the Kennedys as much as possible. His fortunes subsequently improved during the Johnson administration, but his maverick personality would always put him at odds with the powers-that-be sooner or later. Johnson seriously toyed with the idea of picking McCarthy for his vice-presidential running mate in 1964, but his vainglorious nature moved him eventually to pick the more pliable Humphrey. McCarthy never forgave Johnson for choosing Humphrey, nor Humphrey for accepting the post. When McCarthy heard that Johnson had wanted to announce the name of his running mate with the unsuspecting Hubert and himself on the rostrum with Johnson, he said "What a sadistic son of a bitch."[36] As to Humphrey, McCarthy increasingly mocked his hollow rhetoric and his meek subservience to Johnson.

But what really turned McCarthy against Johnson was the Vietnam War. As a member of the Foreign Relations Committee, McCarthy had initially supported the administration in the Gulf of Tonkin Resolution, but he gradually changed his mind when the war turned out to be a hopeless stalemate. He also began to challenge what he called "the gradual usurpation of power"[37] by the executive branch of government, the overextension of U.S. power in the world, and the covert activities of the CIA. By 1967 the stage was set for McCarthy to assume the mantle of a crusading maverick challenging the liberal establishment of which he had been a quixotic insider since 1948.

In his November 30 announcement that he planned to challenge Lyndon Johnson in 1948, McCarthy spoke of a "deepening moral crisis" in America and promised a revitalized approach to politics that would offer an alternative to radicalism. He said that he was hopeful that his challenge would "alleviate the sense of political hopelessness and restore to many people belief in the processes of American government . . . and counter the growing sense of alienation from politics which is currently reflected in the tendency to withdraw in either frustration or cynicism, to talk of non-participation and to make threats of support for a third party or fourth party or other irregular political movements."[38] McCarthy's reference to third or fourth parties as "irregular" attests to his intrinsic conservatism—the belief that constituted traditions, institutions, and customary practices must be protected against radical change. His opposition to the war and his liberal stand on social issues blinded many of his followers, especially young college students, to the fact that their candidate was really a Burkean reform conservative rather than a radical populist. Nevertheless, his bold move to oppose the president in 1968 was received by many young and mostly nonradical students with great enthusiasm.

Idealistic college students, pacifists, and Stevensonian Democrats were about all McCarthy had to work with in November 1967. Although there was no shortage of funding, much of it coming from affluent New York liberals, McCarthy started out with a ramshackle organization that was rich in enthusiasm and short on organizational talent. McCarthy picked Blair Clark, general manager of CBS News, who barely knew his candidate, as his campaign manager. Clark got the distinct impression that his boss did not want to run a real campaign but preferred to run around the country like Peter the Hermit without any organization whatsoever.[39] Unlike Peter the Hermit, however, McCarthy lacked both the oratorical skills and the rapport with the peasants that would have inspired his followers to join his crusade to the holy land. In fact, McCarthy's political performance was, to say the least, underwhelming: he hated mingling with people and disliked giving phony speeches; and when he did speak, he was so flat and dull that one reporter described his speechmaking as being nearest to that of Calvin Coolidge. Even his announcement that he was running for the presidency struck one reporter as remarkably uninspiring: "He wore a gray suit. His hair was gray, his eyes were gray, and his face seemed to have grayness to it. He was all gray, like some sort of essence."[40] Indeed, his candidacy appeared headed into a gray melancholy waste until the Tet Offensive in January 1968 gave his campaign a tremendous boost.

The Tet Offensive, as previously mentioned, changed the perception that most Americans had about the Vietnam War. Although the offensive was a military failure for the North Vietnamese, the American public saw it as a defeat for the whole American war effort. Public support for the war dropped dramatically. In February Johnson's overall popular standing in the polls dropped to 41 percent, with 42 percent being negative. On his handling of the Vietnam War, 35 percent expressed support, 50 percent registered disapproval.[41] Johnson's unpopularity greatly invigorated the moribund McCarthy campaign, especially in New Hampshire, the first state in which McCarthy planned to challenge the president. It was in New Hampshire that the McCarthy staff managed to ignite a grassroots student campaign to change direction on Vietnam. Lowenstein and other McCarthy campaign organizers recruited thousands of college students to conduct a door-to-door campaign in New Hampshire, insisting that the young activists look "clean for Gene," that is, cut their hair, shave their beards, wear no jeans or miniskirts, and avoid the trappings of countercultural slovenliness. The Children's Crusade, as reporters called it, was a great success. On March 12, the voters thoroughly humiliated the president by giving McCarthy 42 percent and 24 delegates. Johnson, a write-in candidate, won by gaining 49 percent of the vote, but his victory was a Pyrrhic one, for the voters of New Hampshire had shown just how vulnerable the president was with the Democratic, let alone the Republican, electorate.

Although Johnson did not panic, McCarthy's showing in New Hampshire clearly unnerved him. What really worried the president was not what McCarthy would do, for he lacked the ability to put together a wide coalition of electoral groups, but what Robert Kennedy might do after Johnson's poor showing in New Hampshire. Johnson had good reason to fret about Kennedy, who was reassessing his political position. Polls in mid-March revealed that the Democrats preferred Kennedy over Johnson by a margin of 44 to 41 percent; by contrast Democrats preferred Johnson over McCarthy by a large margin of 59 to 29 percent.

During the week following the New Hampshire primary three prominent Democrats—Johnson, McCarthy, and Kennedy—played cruel mind games at each other's expense and that of the nation. The Kennedy camp approached the Johnson people and suggested that the two sides reconsider an earlier proposal to convene a special Vietnam Commission to review American policy in Vietnam. Kennedy and Sorensen met with Clark Clifford, the new Secretary of Defense who had replaced McNamara, and made a proposal that Kennedy would not run for the presidency if Johnson publicly admitted that the Vietnam involvement had been an error and that he would appoint an independent commission to come up with alternative policies. The proposal was absurd, for it would have meant the president's loss of control over foreign policy. One White House aide called the proposal "the damnest piece of political blackmail"[42] he had ever heard. When Johnson turned him down flat Kennedy was ready to announce his candidacy. Johnson despised and feared

Kennedy, calling him a runt and a little shitass. Kennedy returned the favor, mocking Johnson's vulgarity and dismissively referred to him as a war-crazed cowpuncher. McCarthy, for his part, disdained both Johnson and Kennedy. The relationship between these three insufferable egos made any compromise between them impossible, splitting the party into McCarthy, Kennedy, and Johnson constituencies.

On March 17 Robert Kennedy stepped behind the lectern at the Senate Caucus Room, where his brother had announced his candidacy for the presidency in 1960, and threw his own hat into the ring, saying somewhat disingenuously: "I do not run for the presidency merely to oppose any man but to propose new policies. I run because I am convinced that this country is in a perilous course and because I have such strong feelings about what must be done, and I feel that I am obligated to do all that I can."[43] Having said that, Kennedy then flew to New York to march in the annual St. Patrick's Day Parade.

When Lyndon Johnson heard about "the runt's" decision to run for the presidency, he was beside himself, later telling Doris Kearns that his worst nightmare had come true:

> I felt that I was being chased on all sides by a gigantic stampede coming at me from all directions. On one side, the American people were stampeding me to do something about Vietnam. On the other side, the inflationary economy was booming out of control. Up ahead were dozens of danger signs pointing to another summer of riots in the cities. I was being forced over the edge by rioting blacks, demonstrating students, marching welfare mothers, squawking professors, and hysterical reporters. And then the final straw. The thing I feared from the first day of my Presidency was actually coming true. Robert Kennedy had openly announced his intention to reclaim the throne in the memory of his brother.[44]

There was also Johnson's health, which his wife, Lady Bird, feared would not be able to withstand another four years. Johnson had suffered a serious heart attack in 1955; he had also been hospitalized on several occasions during his term of office for a severe respiratory infection, a gall bladder and kidney stone removal, and throat surgery on a benign polyp. Given his family history, with no one on his father's side living beyond sixty-five years of age, Johnson believed that he would probably not survive a second term. He died in 1973 on his ranch in Texas. A stressful second term would have killed him much earlier. This being said, it was Kennedy's entrance into the race that pushed him over the edge. On March 31, 1968, he took himself out of the race, stating unequivocally that he would not seek and would not accept the nomination of his party for another term as his party's candidate for the presidency.

In the meantime, Kennedy and McCarthy were slugging it out on the hustings. Kennedy's belated entry into the race confirmed for many the suspicion of his enemies that the senator from New York was a ruthless opportunist. This is certainly how McCarthy saw it, accusing Kennedy of having broken a personal promise that he would stay out of the campaign. There had been no such promise, but even if there had, as Arthur Schlesinger Jr. pointed out, priority in entering competition hardly conferred the moral right to be the only liberal candidate.[45] It did not really matter, because by that time both candidates so thoroughly despised each other that they were prepared to give their support to Hubert Humphrey in case they lost in the primaries.[46] Both candidates were competing for similar constituencies—the college-age population and the progressive wing of the Democratic Party. Where Kennedy definitely held the edge was with poor minorities, especially poor blacks and Latinos. It was these groups that Kennedy touched far more intimately than the somewhat standoffish McCarthy, for as soon as Kennedy had announced his entry into the campaign, he took his message to the streets in one of the most frenetic populist crusades in the postwar period.

While the Democrats were attacking each other, the nation continued to plunge from one crisis to another, now more serious than ever because the country was led by a weakened president who was also a lame duck. On April 4, 1968, Martin Luther King Jr. was assassinated in Memphis, setting in motion race riots across the nation. Campaigning for his first primary in Indiana, Robert Kennedy courageously broke the news of King's death to a large black crowd in the heart of the Indianapolis ghetto. Speaking from the heart and from personal experience of unbearable grief, Kennedy said:

> I have bad news for you, for all of our citizens, and people who love peace all over the world, and that is that Martin Luther King was shot and killed tonight. Martin Luther King dedicated his life to love and to justice for his fellow human beings, and he died because of that effort. . . . For those of you who are black and are tempted to be filled with hatred . . . against all white people, I can only say that I feel in my own heart the same kind of feeling I had when I had a member of my family killed, but he was killed by a white man. . . . What we need in the United States is not division; what we need . . . is not violence or lawlessness, but love and wisdom and compassion toward one another . . . whether they be white or they be black. . . . So I shall ask you tonight to return home, to say a prayer for the family of Martin Luther King, that's true, but more importantly to say a prayer for our own country, which all of us love. . . .[47]

Despite some chants of "Black Power," the crowd dispersed peacefully, but not so in the rest of the country, where riots and arson broke out in over a hundred cities. These civil disorders, together with mounting student insurgencies on the nation's campuses, played themselves out against a backdrop of menacing international crises: student rebellions in France, Britain, Italy, West Germany; Soviet tanks rumbling into Czechoslovakia to put an end to the brief experiment with democracy under Alexander Dubcek; the seizure of the U.S. intelligence ship *Pueblo* by North Korea; the My Lai massacre; and the politicized Olympic Games in Mexico City, among others. The political air was highly charged with revolutionary expectations and uneasy forebodings of doom and gloom. In America, talks of a Great Society changed to debates about the decline of American society. With the country appearing to be a rudderless ship whose captain was preparing to abandon it, the majority party was in disarray, as Johnson's contenders were fighting bitter intramural battles. To make matters worse, on April 17, Vice President Hubert Humphrey announced his candidacy for the presidency. While his two opponents competed in the primaries, the vice president methodically collected delegate support from party leaders, who controlled 60 percent of the delegates in 1968.[48] The vice president, who could sometimes be self-defeatingly obtuse, promised the American people the "politics of joy," a political blooper of the first order, coming as it did at a time of crisis and violence. Yet Humphrey was also a shrewd politician who knew how to gain support from the most important constituency in the Democratic Party—labor union leaders and blue-collar workers, the vast majority of whom were white.

In the spring of 1968, Hubert Humphrey was deeply uncertain about winning the Democratic nomination, let alone of gaining the White House. Despite his happy warrior façade, playing the unruffled happy liberal, Humphrey was really a harried and torn man. Like the president he served, he was a New Deal liberal and a fervent believer in government activism on behalf of America's neglected, forgotten, and oppressed groups: African Americans in both the South and the nation's urban slums, impoverished farmers, blue-collar workers, struggling to keep above water as a result of foreign competition and corporate cutbacks. His background explained most of his political attitudes. He was born in 1911 in Wallace, South Dakota, a tiny agricultural town of a few hundred souls. His father was a pharmacist and a dyed-in-the-wool Democrat of the William Jennings Bryan and Robert La Follette tradition of "Prairie Populism." The son inherited not only the father's politics but his gift of gab, which at one time even moved Lyndon Johnson to remark that "Hubert has the greatest coordination of mind and tongue of anybody I know."[49] There was another important quality Humphrey inherited from his father and that was his sense of loyalty to family and employer. While studying at the University of Minnesota, that sense of loyalty compelled Humphrey to return to the family store in Huron, South Dakota, giving five years of his life to keep the family business from sliding into bankruptcy. The Depression further molded Humphrey's view of the world and prompted him to pursue a political career. His master's degree thesis at Louisiana State University was apparently so excessively laudatory to FDR and the New Deal that his original thesis adviser, who fortunately for Humphrey left for Harvard to complete his own graduate degree, criticized the work as overly partisan. Humphrey got his M.A. degree but not before being seriously rattled during his orals when one professor said: "Hubert, I've decided I'm going to fail you on this examination." When the dumbfounded Humphrey asked why, the professor replied, "Well, if we give you a degree, you'll just as likely as not end up a college professor and if we flunk you right now, you are more likely to go back to Minnesota and run for the United States Senate, and you'll amount to something."[50]

Whether Humphrey would have amounted to anything in academia is debatable, but that he was a natural for salesmanship and politics is beyond doubt, as shown by his subsequent political successes: mayor of Minneapolis, senator, presidential candidate in 1960, and Lyndon Johnson's vice president in 1964. H.H.H., as he was often referred to, was a thoroughly decent man without a mean bone in his body, but he was also annoyingly glib and superficial. Though never at a loss for words, his rhetoric was sometimes almost ludicrously platitudinous, giving rise to frequent quips that Humphrey's mental interior was mostly hot air. In a particularly telling and unkind characterization of him by Mayra Mannes, "Hubert the Happy":

Goes yackety, yackety,
Yackey, yackety, yack.
If anyone tells him for God's sake to knot it,
He cheerfully yacketys back.

If he stopped yacking, he couldn't go anywhere,
Poor little Hubert, he couldn't go anywhere—
That's why he always goes
Hoppity, yackety,
Hoppity
Yackety
Yack.[51]

The reference to Hubert the Happy was in part an allusion to the vice president's inappropriate and unfortunate remark that his run for the presidency was designed to promote the "politics of joy." Coming on the heels of urban riots, antiwar protests, and the assassination of Martin Luther King Jr., the press naturally pounced on Humphrey for coining such a ridiculous slogan.[52] As subsequent events would reveal, there was precious little joy and much agony in Humphrey's bid to capture the presidency. In addition to facing the charismatic Kennedy and the aloof and cerebral Eugene McCarthy, Humphrey was stymied every step along the way by a mean-spirited Lyndon Johnson who delighted in ridiculing and even degrading his vice president. After announcing his decision not to run for reelection, Johnson spent much of his time either sulking or jealously clinging to his power without much concern for his vice president or the future of his party. This, of course, is not how he subsequently portrayed his final months in the White House, claiming that in his continuing search for peace he wanted the presidency out of politics.[53] This was plain nonsense. Johnson had never really thought much of Humphrey, whom he liked but did not admire or respect. After having his "pecker in his pocket," Humphrey's political usefulness was over. Although the vice president had sterling credentials on social issues, having written a book entitled *War on Poverty*, he played a minor role in Johnson's antipoverty decisions; and as the president became obsessed with the Vietnam War and issues relating to national security, he completely shut out Humphrey from executive decision making, probably suspecting the vice president's garrulous tongue might jeopardize national security. One historian even claimed that Johnson's treatment of his vice president was not just malicious but positively sadistic.[54] Johnson did not encourage Humphrey to run in his place, refused to help, and even blocked some necessary funding that he could have made available to the vice president's campaign. One gains the distinct impression from the available evidence that Johnson was such a self-absorbed and petty man that only one thing was important to him after March 31—his legacy. The rest was spitefulness, the primary recipients being his Democratic rivals, particularly Robert Kennedy, whom he deeply despised, but also poor Hubert, whom he regarded as a silly nuisance. McCarthy was beneath contempt. Deep down, Johnson was probably more closely attuned to the manipulative talents of Richard Nixon, whom he considered his equal in the fine art of Machiavellian politics and therefore, a worthier successor.

Yet the vice president was an astute politician in his own right. He also had a strong constituency in the Democratic Party. Traditional party regulars, representing the old labor union core of the party, were overwhelmingly pro-Humphrey. They regarded McCarthy as a marginal candidate and feared Kennedy as a reform-minded idealist who might just possibly break up the stranglehold of party bosses and replace them with young crusading policy wonks. In 1968 the party regulars still controlled the vast majority of convention votes. Primaries were largely popularity contests.

In 1968 the Democrats had a nominating system that followed the "unit rule," according to which all votes in a state delegation were given to the candidate who received a majority of delegate votes. The system was widely criticized, especially by liberal reformers, because it denied any representation to the minority. The majority in the southern states had used this process to lock out racial minorities and reform-minded liberals. Although the unit rule seemed to violate the idea of fairness, it made for party cohesion and unity when it came to supporting strong nominees or platforms. Later, when the Democrats abandoned the unit rule, opting for a proportional system of representation following the convention of 1968, they gave too much power and influence to minority groups, splintering the party and ending up with various weak nominees such as George McGovern, Walter Mondale, Michael Dukakis, Al Gore, and John Kerry. In 1968 the primaries were inconsistently conducted in different states, some using a proportional system of representation, others a "winner take all" approach. Candidates could gain a substantial number of votes by running in the primaries, but these delegates, for the most part, were not legally obligated to vote for a primary winner. In 1968 a candidate who had won all the primaries was not necessarily assured of the nomination. Party regulars, however, carefully watched how candidates were performing in the primaries, which explains why the McCarthy and Kennedy camps were desperately trying to impress party regulars. Humphrey's strategy was to let the McCarthy and Kennedy campaigns wear each other out. There is even some evidence that Humphrey or his backers gave considerable financial support to the McCarthy campaign in order to derail the Kennedy train that was picking up speed in April.[55]

Although McCarthy won in Wisconsin, out-polling Johnson, who was still on the ballot, by 56 percent to 35 percent, Kennedy had not had time to get on the ballot in that state. In the first major confrontation between McCarthy and Kennedy in Indiana, it became quite apparent which of the two candidates had the greater appeal. The cerebral McCarthy said all the right things Democratic voters wanted to hear on the war and on civil rights, but his delivery lacked any real passion. Robert Kennedy was just the opposite: he connected emotionally with the voters by giving impassioned speeches, engaging his audience, even allowing ecstatic followers to touch him to the point of tearing at his clothes, his hair, and making his hands bleed. As Kennedy found his stride, some began to look at him as a reincarnated John

Kennedy, a political redeemer who would heal the country's deep divisions. Those who watched the Kennedy campaign up close, as this author did in 1968, wondered whether the ruthless "bad Bobby" had given way to the "good Bobby"; in other words, had Kennedy gone through an existential transformation or was all this talk about a "new Kennedy" just like a "new Nixon" so much empty rhetoric by his campaign managers? Was Arthur Schlesinger right when he referred to Kennedy as a real tribune of the people, a tribune analogous to Tiberius or Gaius Gracchus, the two Roman Republican leaders who came from patrician backgrounds and yet served the marginalized underclass?[56] Although it is doubtful that the nation saw a "new Kennedy" in 1968—a leopard does not change its spots—there is evidence that the trauma of his brother's death and the search for his own identity produced profound changes in his self-perception and in his views of the world. Too much can be made of his followers' claims that he opened himself up to Greek tragedy or existential philosophy, surrounded himself with notable literary figures, and turned himself into a genuine populist with a radical program of national regeneration. In the end, Kennedy was a Kennedy, a believer in the Kennedy mythology and in his mandate to carry the torch for his fallen brother. With this being said, Robert Kennedy was still an unusual and impressive politician, a candidate who was remarkably receptive to new ideas and to different constituencies. Moreover, he was that rare politician who was courageous enough to tell people, especially privileged people, what they did not want to hear but what they should hear.[57] His empathy for marginalized Americans—blacks, Latinos, the poor in general—was entirely sincere, perhaps to the point of being a consuming passion, comparable to his passion to take on communists, gangsters, Lyndon Johnson, or corrupt union leaders. His campaign increasingly resembled a populist crusade verging on demagoguery. It also veered steadily to the left, and this is where the crusader would have defeated the politician in him, for it was unrealistic to win the presidency in 1968 with only a core support from minorities.

On May 7, Kennedy scored a big victory in Indiana, receiving 42.3 percent of the Democratic votes, followed by 30.7 percent for Governor Roger Branigin. McCarthy came in a distant third with 27 percent. A week later, Kennedy also decisively defeated McCarthy in Nebraska, building up enough steam to carry him successfully through the rest of the primaries. A pall of despair hung over the McCarthy campaign, which appeared rudderless and in complete disarray. McCarthy made things worse by not stepping up to the plate and acting decisively. His handlers wondered whether he had what it takes to assume leadership on a national basis. Those advisers who had been with him from the beginning of the campaign began to dislike him by the time it was all over. As one of them put it, "He screwed us. We gave him a lot. . . . He owed us more than he gave us."[58]

Surprisingly, McCarthy appeared to be redeemed in Oregon, where he outpolled Kennedy by a margin of 45 percent to 39 percent. This was the first time a Kennedy had lost an election, but the senator from New York did not let the defeat undermine his fierce determination to win. Kennedy attributed the defeat to Oregon's overwhelming white middle-class electorate, saying, "This ain't my group."[59] The regular working-class Democrats were also not Kennedy's group. The Teamsters, the largest union in Oregon, still remembered Kennedy's vendetta against Jimmy Hoffa and the indictment of Portland's mayor, Terry Schrunk, for his involvement in union racketeering. Schrunk had been acquitted for his involvement with the Teamsters and was still mayor of Portland, the largest city in Oregon.

The golden state of California, with its "winner take all" primary was a make-or-break event for the Kennedy campaign. Since California was one of the most diverse states in the union, containing large numbers of minorities, Kennedy's chances of success were far better in California than in Oregon. The Kennedy campaign was more intense than ever, as the candidate took to the road and competed for votes all over the state. The candidate embarked on a whistle-stop tour from Fresno to Sacramento, campaigned in inner cities of Los Angeles and San Francisco, met with prominent blacks, Latinos, antiwar protesters, and regular Democrats. Wherever he went people hailed him as a social redeemer who would set everything right: ending the war, bringing blacks and whites together, speaking the language of the young, caring for the poor, and so forth. There was a distinct air of political revivalism about this campaign and the frantic pace that defined it. The candidate spoke about a "new politics" without being overly clear about what was so new about his policies that deviated significantly from Johnson's Great Society. Kennedy spoke vaguely, but in a language that resonated with young radicals, about more power to the people, transferring power to local communities, which pleased left liberals. At the same time, he talked about civic responsibility and the inherent limitations of federal spending to solve all social problems, a message that resonated with conservative Democrats. It appeared that Kennedy was the man for all seasons. Some saw him, as Garry Wills observed, as a kind of genteel rebel, even a substitute Ho Chi Minh, Mao Tse Tung, Fidel Castro, or Che Guevara.[60] Yet others saw him as a republican tribune of the people, still others as a law-and-order man, for had he not gone after mobsters and corrupt union officials? Blacks and Latinos saw him as that rare white politician who understood their problems and was willing to address them. These amorphous feelings never congealed, nor did they translate into a coherent electoral strategy. Many liberal historians are convinced that, had Kennedy lived, he would have crafted such a broad electoral coalition, defeated Humphrey and then Nixon, and healed the nation. This, of course, is wishful thinking, but what can be taken from the 1968 campaign is this: of all the candidates running that year, Robert Kennedy was the most promising, for he had high intelligence, energy, compassion, and a deep commitment to public service.

But once more, an assassin deprived the nation of such a promising politician. After winning the California primary, defeating McCarthy by a margin of 46.4 percent to 41.8 percent, Kennedy was shot by Sirhan Bishara Sirhan, a young Palestinian immigrant, at the Ambassador Hotel in Los Angeles on June 4th. Shortly after Kennedy had given a victory speech in the ballroom of the Ambassador Hotel, telling his jubilant followers, "and now it's on to Chicago and let's win there," he left the hall by taking his entourage through the kitchen. It was here that Sirhan, who had vowed to kill Kennedy for his pro-Israeli views, was waiting for him. At 12:15 on the morning of June 5, Sirhan stopped behind Kennedy, lifted his .22 caliber revolver, screamed "Kennedy you sonofabitch," and fired a bullet into his head. Mortally wounded, Kennedy collapsed on the pantry floor as blood drained from the wound in the back of his head. Sirhan kept firing, eight bullets in all, wounding several other people in the crowded kitchen—until at length, he was pinned against a stainless steel serving table and disarmed by hotel staffers and Kennedy bodyguards.

History had repeated itself. In juxtaposing images from November 22, 1963, and June 5, 1968, the *Newsweek* headline said it all: "Once Again . . . Once Again."[61] People throughout the nation were stunned; many prayed for Kennedy as he was undergoing surgery at Good Samaritan Hospital in Los Angeles. At 1:44 A.M. on June 6, 1968, Robert Kennedy died of his head wounds. What followed was another sad and solemn funeral that evoked memories of recent assassinations, especially Martin Luther King Jr. and John F. Kennedy. "I hate this country," said Jackie Kennedy, "I despise America and I don't want my children to live here anymore. If they're killing Kennedys, my kids are number one targets."[62] She made good on that promise by marrying Aristotle Onassis, the Greek shipping tycoon, and leaving the country. Although Jackie Kennedy's feelings were not shared by most Americans, there were many people, especially young Kennedy and McCarthy followers, who shared the former first lady's views of America. If we add to this group of alienated reform idealists the many left-wing radicals in SNCC, the Black Nationalists, and associated militants who had hated America all along, we can begin to understand the emergence of a permanent reservoir of deep disenchantment, if not hatred, with American society that still haunts us today. The assassination of Robert Kennedy seemed like the final blow that killed all the high expectations of the 1960s. It was as though something had taken the air out of the inflated American balloon. A Kennedy aide, Jack Newfield, captured the mood of young idealists perfectly when he said:

> Now I realized what makes our generation unique, what defines us apart from those who came before the hopeful winter of 1961, and those who came after the murderous spring of 1968. We are the first generation that learned from experience, in our innocent twenties, that things were not really getting better, that we shall *not* overcome. We felt, by the time we reached thirty, that we had already glimpsed the most compassionate leaders our nation could produce, and they had all been assassinated. And from this time forward, things would get worse: our best political leaders were part of memory now, not hope.[63]

4. Thunder from the Right

Jack Newfield was right about things getting worse, wrong about his generation being the first to have experienced such traumatic events, and doubly wrong about the Kennedys being the best compassionate leaders the nation could produce. Ever since Goldwater had run on a law-and-order platform, conservatives on the political right had been thundering against expensive government-sponsored compassion that extracted no obligation from its recipients. They also inveighed against judicial activism, which seemed to encourage the endless expansion of rights without corresponding responsibilities and restraints. The political right opposed the rights revolution partly on philosophical grounds, claiming that it exceeded the intent of the Constitution, partly on racial grounds. In the South, the civil rights revolution meant an attack on white domination. Southern politicians may have used appeals to "states' rights," but what they were really opposing was the extension of civil rights to black people.

One such southern politician who spoke not only for his confederate rebels but also for many working-class whites elsewhere in the nation was George Corley Wallace, who ran as a third-party candidate in 1968.[64] As will be recalled, Wallace was the segregationist governor of Alabama who had stood in the doorway of the University of Alabama trying to keep James Meredith, a black student, from enrolling at the university. By southern standards, Wallace had been a democratic populist somewhat comparable to Louisiana's "Kingfish" Huey Long of the 1930s, except that Wallace did not extend his social compassion for "plain folks" to black people. Wallace was as close to a self-made man as one could find in 1968. He was born in Clio, Alabama, the son of a struggling farmer who grew corn and cotton and raised cattle and hogs. George worked his way through the University of Alabama and finished a law degree there. In 1942 he joined the Army Air Corps, eventually becoming a flight engineer on a B-29 bomber in the South Pacific. After the war Wallace entered politics in his native state of Alabama, serving four terms in the state legislature. In 1958 he lost his bid for the governorship because of his moderately liberal views on racial issues, vowing never to be "out-niggered" again. Promising the voters "Segregation now, segregation tomorrow, segregation forever," Wallace was elected governor in 1963 and promptly defied government mandates to integrate the university.

By 1964 Wallace had become a hero to southerners, and he took his states' rights campaign nationwide, running surprisingly well in the Democratic primaries in 1964. Since term limits in 1966 prevented him from reelection, he made arrangements for his wife, Lurleen, a former dime store clerk, to succeed him as Governor of Alabama—one of the most reprehensible acts of incestuous politics in American history. Although Lurleen sat in the governor's chair, the real power was exercised by George Wallace himself. His wife, however, was suffering from terminal cancer and she died in 1968. Shortly after her death Wallace declared himself a presidential candidate for the American Party, which was essentially the party of Wallace. He promised the voters a victory in Vietnam and a restoration of law and order at home.

Wallace had been a boxer in his younger years and he approached the 1968 campaign as a boxer, head bobbing, arms swinging, and hitting hard at his opponents. His favorite targets were long-haired hippies, student demonstrators, and pointy-headed intellectuals. On the hustings, Wallace could really work his audiences, consisting mostly of angry white urban workers who resented Great Society liberals because they had neglected them in favor of minorities and the poor. When Wallace told these audiences that liberals were hypocrites, "over educated, ivory tower folks with pointed heads looking down their noses at us," he hit a responsive chord. Ordinary working-class Americans had enough of four years of Democratic spending, high taxes, street crime, and a war that disproportionately took the lives of their own sons. Wallace impressed these people with his folksy yet aggressive manners and his no-holds-barred attacks on student protesters, Washington bureaucrats, communists, and sissy liberals.

Both Democrats and Republicans were concerned about the possibility that Wallace might take away enough votes from their core constituencies that the election could end up a stalemate, with Wallace holding the keys to the kingdom. Indeed, Wallace managed to get on the ballot in all fifty states, which was a remarkable feat since his campaign did not seriously get under way until June of 1968. The "spoiler from the south," as *Life* magazine called him, planned to take away enough electoral votes from the two mainstream parties to force the election into the House of Representatives, playing the kingmaker and squeezing major concessions from the party he decided to support. This "southern strategy" might just possibly have worked for Wallace had it not been for the successful preemptive moves by both the Republicans and the Democrats and by the strategic errors Wallace committed in the choice of his running mate, General Curtis LeMay. Once Humphrey recovered from the disastrous convention in Chicago, party regulars, especially the unions, united behind him and mounted a major attack on Wallace. Richard Nixon parried the Wallace threat by promoting the spoiler's message in a more coded and moderate language, but also by appealing to Strom Thurmond to spread the word that a vote for Wallace was basically a wasted vote.

Wallace was quick off the mark, but his appeal gradually waned once his opponents had him in their sights and took aim at his liabilities. As it turned out, Wallace's major mistake was to pick the wrong running mate, the reactionary General Curtis LeMay. The general had been a much celebrated "bomber man" in both the European and Pacific theaters of war. He was a stereotypical, cigar-chomping, no-nonsense soldier of the old school who believed that air power was a decisive factor in military success. The filmmaker Stanley Kubrick parodied LeMay as the buff, humorless, and morally tone deaf General Buck Turgidson, played by George C. Scott in the dark satire *Dr. Strangelove*. When Wallace called on LeMay to join his campaign, the general was in semiretirement, playing golf, socializing with fellow retired military officers, and serving as spokesman for an electronics company. The general soon made Wallace look even more menacing than he really was, talking freely about his fondness for nuclear weapons. One way to win the Vietnam War, the general had already advised, was "to bomb North Vietnam back into the Stone Age." Nuclear weapons, the general suggested, caused far less harm than people assumed. The nation should get over its "phobia" about nuclear weapons. Despite the fact that over twenty atomic bombs had been exploded on the Bikini Atoll, the devastation, he claimed, had been slight. As the general put it to a startled group of reporters, "the fish are all back in the lagoon; the coconut trees are growing coconuts; the guava bushes have fruits on them; the birds are back. As a matter of fact, everything is about the same except the land crabs. They get minerals through the soil, and I guess through their shell, and the land crabs were a little "hot" and there's a little doubt about whether you should eat a land crab or not."[65] Such amiable banter about the harmlessness of atomic weapons, which had tarnished Goldwater in 1964, did not endear the Wallace-LeMay team to the majority of the American people. Wallace began to slip in the polls after Labor Day. In the end, it was Richard Nixon rather than Humphrey who really outmaneuvered the spoiler from the south.

The resurrection of Richard Nixon from political obscurity was one of the most remarkable events of the 1968 presidential campaign.[66] After Nixon's narrow defeat by John F. Kennedy in 1960, and his humiliating defeat by Pat Brown for the governorship of California in 1962, it appeared as though "tricky Dick," as he was called by his political foes, had finally retired from politics. In a short press conference following his defeat by Brown, he snarled at reporters whom he accused of partisanship: "One last thing. The last play. I leave you gentlemen now, you will now write it. You will interpret it. That's your right. But as I leave you I want you to know—just think how much you're going to be missing. You won't have Nixon to kick around any more, because, gentlemen, this is my last press conference. . . . Thank you gentlemen, and good day."[67]

Such an undignified and resentful exit was characteristic of a man who had risen from obscurity and kicked around his political rivals since the late 1940s. Nixon was born in Yorba Linda, California in 1913, the son of a struggling rancher and proprietor of a service station and grocery store in East Whittier. Richard's mother was a devout Quaker who had persuaded her husband, a Methodist, to convert to the Quaker religion. Nixon's home was characterized by extreme religious devotion and strong discipline. Frank Nixon was a self-made, extremely independent and hottempered Irishman, while Hannah Nixon was a quiet, withdrawn, but very strongwilled woman who disarmed her husband's shifting moods and argumentative nature. Nixon's home was a loving but not an emotionally intimate one; it was also a relatively poor one. When Nixon was born, the small house his father had bought had no electricity or running water. As an obedient child, Nixon worked hard for everything and it did not come easy; but by dint of hard work, he tried to meet his mother's expectations of Christian self-improvement. Garry Wills, in a very perceptive psychological portrait of Nixon, has shown that Nixon's peculiar personality was a blend of an earnest Quaker upbringing and the shallow boosterism prevailing in small towns all over America, especially Southern California. This was the mental universe he inherited from his father; and despite his world travels, Richard Nixon carried it with him all of his life. Wills describes that view as a kind of Californianized mixture of old fashioned, straitlaced morality and the get-ahead-at-any cost business spirit of commercial America.[68] Was Nixon, then, the product of religious earnestness and the "hiss and puff of self-improvement" taught by Dale Carnegie and Norman Vincent Peale? Such psychological descriptions too often try to define a developing personality through rigid labeling, but at the same time they do capture aspects of a person's mental furniture and behavior. Nixon was in many ways one of the most elusive figures in American politics: an introvert in an extrovert profession, a self-made man who harbored conflicting impulses, attitudes, and beliefs. Enormously competitive, he had difficulties in making the first cut, yet picking himself up after every failure and trying again. He worked his way through Whittier College and then Duke University School of Law, staying on track, working hard, feeling insecure and barely getting by on his modest scholarship. For some time he lived in a small twelve-foot tool shed in a woods near the Duke campus. After graduating from Duke, Nixon went back to Whittier to practice law and he married Patricia Ryan, a young schoolteacher who came from a very poor, dysfunctional Irish-German family. Their marriage was a more loving one than John Kennedy's. Pat Nixon was a bright, patient, and somewhat rigid person who had difficulty in showing her feelings. There is a very revealing portrait of her by Gloria Steinem, who interviewed her during Nixon's campaign in 1968. This curious encounter also shows us the sharp contrast of the Depression generation and the baby boomers represented by Steinem, the new emancipated woman of the 1960s. When Steinem asked Pat Nixon who her role models had been and what dreams she had dreamed when she was young, Pat shot back that such things never entered her mind, because, as she put it, "I had to go to work. I haven't just sat back and thought of myself or my ideas or what I wanted to do . . . I've kept working. I don't have any time to worry about who I admire or who I identify with. I never had it easy. I'm not at all like you . . . all those people who had it easy."[69] Her husband did not have it easy either, nor did the marriage they had together.

When World War II broke out, Nixon was working as a junior lawyer for the Office of Price Administration in Washington, which he left after being accepted to the Navy Officer Candidate School at Quonset Point, Rhode Island. He spent over three years in the navy serving as a ground navigation officer in the South Pacific. The career paths of young Nixon and Kennedy now began to converge, for both served honorably in the navy; both also entered politics as young congressmen in 1947, the difference being that young Kennedy had big money and influence behind him while young Nixon did not. Backed by the local Republican Party in Whittier, Nixon waged a bitter campaign against the Democratic incumbent Jerry Voorhis, whom he maligned as being "soft on communism," a favorite tactic of Nixon's dirty campaigning. In fact, Nixon was a hard-hitting, single-minded campaigner who never hesitated to go for the jugular, though often and successfully disguising his personal attacks behind smokescreens of pious and patriotic rhetoric.

Once in Congress, Nixon managed to get himself appointed to three prominent House committees, the most important being the House Committee on Un-American Activities (HUAC), which he used as a springboard to national prominence. In its ongoing efforts to uncover communists, especially in government, HUAC hearings revealed that Elizabeth Bentley, referred to by the press as the Red Spy Queen, had been a courier for a communist spy ring inside the U.S. government. Bentley identified several people as communist agents, including Harry Dexter White, an Assistant Secretary of the Treasury under Roosevelt and Truman. The uncorroborated Bentley story led to an intensive investigation, headed by Nixon, that involved a former communist and later senior editor of *Time* magazine, Whittaker Chambers, who revealed an even more senior member of the State Department who was also a spy. The spy's name, who subsequently perjured himself under oath, was Alger Hiss, an impeccably upper-class liberal who had served in several government departments and at the time of his trial was president of the Carnegie Endowment for International Peace. Nixon and his team of investigative sleuths stripped his facade of respectability and revealed him as a consummate liar. In that case, they were right, for archival evidence from the former Soviet Union confirms that Hiss was a spy and a liar. Nixon's career was completely transformed; in the eyes of most Americans, except the liberal establishment, he was a national hero, a spy-catcher who uncovered sneaky communists ensconced in the highest places. Liberals, however, never forgave Nixon for his strident anticommunism and his attack on Hiss, whom they fiercely insisted was unjustly convicted. Since most liberals, including especially John Kennedy, were staunch anticommunists themselves, this liberal bias against Nixon was, to say the least, a case of well-deserved sour grapes. Many liberals persuaded themselves that Hiss had been the victim of a witch-hunt, and that Nixon had used the anticommunist phobia as a means of furthering his own career. Nixon may have been a political opportunist, but so were many of those who accused him of it. Much has been made of Nixon's mudslinging during his campaign for the Senate in 1950. His opponent was Helen Gahagan Douglas, a former stage and film star and a prominent Hollywood left-winger. Douglas was a self-righteous and supercilious poser who was highly unpopular among her own fellow Democrats, many of whom referred to her as the "Red Gulch."[70] Her flamboyant and progressive views, however, endeared her to the liberal intelligentsia, who created the yarn that Nixon had destroyed not only her political career but her innocent reputation. This is, at best, a half truth, for Douglas was widely disliked by Democrats and Republicans alike. John Kennedy, in fact, slipped Nixon an envelope containing a thousand dollar bill for his campaign against Douglas.

In 1951, after election to the Senate, Nixon met one of the trustees of the Carnegie Foundation who had been following the Hiss case very closely, telling Nixon: "The thing that most impressed me was that you not only got Hiss, but you got him fairly."[71] The trustee was General Dwight D. Eisenhower, who obviously saw in young Nixon certain talents that would later persuade him to pick him as his vice presidential running mate. Nixon served Eisenhower well, but Eisenhower did not serve Nixon well. Very early on in the campaign for the presidency in 1952, a scandal swirled around Nixon that he was using a political slush fund for his own private use. Eisenhower toyed with the idea of dropping Nixon from the ticket, but changed his mind when Nixon went on television and forcefully denied these allegations, melodramatically ending his defense in front of the cameras saying that he was not a quitter, that he had never misused funds, and that the only gift he had ever accepted was a little cocker spaniel dog that his youngest daughter named Checkers. The speech was vintage Nixon: puffed-up earnestness, corny sentimentality, transparent appeals to "common Americans," and sly innuendos against his opponents. Subsequently called the "Checkers' Speech," Nixon's appeal was enormously popular with the public and with Eisenhower, who kept him on the ticket.

During their eight years in office together, Eisenhower maintained a cool and very formal relationship with Nixon. Ike considered Nixon an intellectual lightweight; he also seemed to think that Nixon had not grown very much in office, for when asked in 1960 what Nixon had achieved in office, he said that he would have to think about it and then possibly come up with a few things.[72] Ike, of course, conveniently forgot that Nixon had filled in well during his heart attack, but it was clear that he did not believe that Nixon possessed real leadership abilities, never sure of his own leadership abilities in the sense that he was confident enough in his own strength to meet an opponent fairly and squarely. He could never leave well enough alone, constantly hitting below the belt and indignantly denying that he had done so. In Adlai Stevenson's judgment, "Nixonland" was a land of "slander and scare, a land of sly innuendo, the poison pen, the anonymous phone call, and hustling, pushing, shoving: the land of the smash and grab and anything to win."[73] Coming from a sore loser, this judgment, of course, is overdrawn, but only slightly so. Underneath the façade of moral rectitude, Nixon oozed insincerity; he also raised political platitudes to a fine art, sometimes so fine that they actually sounded profound and moving. And then there was the Nixon scowl, the fact that lent itself perfectly to the cartoonist's delight in distortion. Nixon had a pear face that Daumier would have liked; its hairline formed a widow's peak and the nose in profile looked like a ski-jump. His enemies fastened on his jerky, machine like movements, comparing him to a "fuzzy looking guy who appeared like somebody hung him in a closet overnight."[74] He did not project vigor or charisma either. Compared to Kennedy, he appeared old and grey, "and old man's idea of a young man." If all this is true, then why did Nixon dominate public life in America for well over a quarter of a century? One tentative answer might be that Nixon had a political genius for exploiting fear and insecurities, and of mobilizing them against his opponents.[75] His estimation of the public mood and his assessment of his opponents' strengths and weaknesses was as incisive as it was accurate. There was also his dogged tenacity and discipline that left him only when confronted with his public wrongdoing in the Watergate affair; but up to that point, Nixon never quit, even when his liberal foes had already written his political obituary.

After losing in 1960 and 1962, Nixon picked himself up again, soldiering on for various Republican candidates, hiring media-savvy advisers, and listening to the bitter complaints of ordinary Americans about the social excesses of the Great Society, the war, and the sins of the young generation. Thus, after assessing his Republican opposition, which he judged to be weak and ineffective, Nixon announced his candidacy for the Republican presidential nomination in January of 1968. At first, Nixon's only serious opponent was Governor George Romney of Michigan, who represented the liberal wing of the Republican Party. Romney, however, was a political naïf, and he quickly managed to undermine his chances by making unguarded statements, the most damaging being that in 1965, while visiting Vietnam, he had been subjected to "the greatest brainwashing that anybody can get"—a reference to the briefing he had received from optimistic military hawks in Saigon. The press showered him with derisive comments, best summed up by the *Detroit News*, which noted that "to be brainwashed you first must have a brain."[76]

Nixon breezed through the primaries largely unopposed, though Rockefeller and Reagan were lying in wait for him at the time the Republican convention approached in early August. Both Rockefeller and Reagan committed serious blunders that would help Nixon. Rockefeller waffled constantly, saying that he was definitely not a candidate and then changing his mind by declaring that he was. Reagan was unsuccessful in trying to cut into Nixon's southern support through the intervention of Strom Thurmond and Charles Reed of Mississippi, the head of the state delegation whom Reagan had ignored when Reed asked for his support in 1964. In the Republican primaries, and later in the national campaign, Nixon presented himself as a law-and-order man who would restore domestic tranquility and end the war in Vietnam. The mantle of law and order was a perfect fit for Nixon. He was the right man for a period of reaction, expressing the deep resentment of white middle-class Americans who were sick and tired of the social chaos the liberals had unleashed on society. How wrong *Time* magazine had been in 1962 when it contended that "barring a miracle, Nixon's public career has ended."[77] Instead, like a political Lazarus, he had risen from political death.

5. Miami, Chicago, and the Election of 1968

The Republicans held their convention in Miami Beach, the subtropical offshore island across the Bay from Miami, which was just as well because a race riot had erupted in Miami during the convention week. Safely removed from the racial and antiwar protests, the location should have provided the setting for merriment and relaxation, but *Newsweek* was right when it referred to the convention as a joyless affair.[78] The Grand Old Party looked like the Bland Old Party, nominating an old familiar politician under the guise of a "New Nixon." The "stop Nixon" movement was too little and too late. Both Rockefeller and Reagan, the two Johnnies-come-lately, miscalculated by assuming that Nixon's delegate count was not strong enough for a first ballot victory, so that if they could prevent him from getting the needed votes, his candidacy would probably crumble on a second ballot count. Nixon knew even before going to Miami that he had 687 first ballot votes, 20 more than he needed for the nomination. Despite some anxious moments, his southern strategy turned the trick and not just in Miami but later in the general election. For his running mate, Nixon chose Governor Spiro Agnew of Maryland, a Republican in a predominantly Democratic state and a region in the country that straddled the North and the South. Agnew, son of a Greek immigrant called Anagnostopoulos, was a self-made man who had come up the hard way, grateful for the system that made it possible and embracing the values of individualism, thrift, and hard work. Although he had been mildly liberal, defeating a race-baiting southern Democrat in 1966, he developed serious misgivings about the liberal persuasion after race riots erupted in Maryland, especially Baltimore, following the assassination of Martin Luther King Jr. He took the riots as a personal insult, called out the National Guard and asked for federal troops to restore law and order. Moreover, he called a meeting of black leaders and gave them such a tongue-lashing that many walked out on him. Thereafter, he became a stern law-and-order man, which commended him to Nixon, as did his imposing six-foot-two-inch presence and his glib and aggressive tongue. In reality, Agnew was a chinless wonder, a flamboyant flash in the pan who would be nonthreatening to Nixon and would bring "balance" to the ticket. The Nixon people, as it would turn out, did not bother to look closely at Agnew's background; if they had, they would have discovered that the Maryland governor had been involved in illegal kickbacks on government contracts. In 1973 he resigned the vice presidency while under threat of prosecution for bribery and tax evasion. In 1968, however, Agnew was useful to Nixon as a good frontman, a corporate role model, and an aggressive campaigner giving bombastic speeches.

Nixon's real weapon in keeping the South in line was Strom Thurmond, the former "Dixiecrat" turned Republican who was the only southern Republican leader who could persuade enough southerners to defect to the GOP. In return for Thurmond's support, Nixon promised that he would appoint conservative judges to the Supreme Court, oppose bussing to achieve racial desegregation, and increase defense spending.[79] Nixon's promise to appoint conservative judges was especially important to Thurmond, who was one of the strongest opponents in the Senate to Johnson's proposed appointment of the liberal Abe Fortas to the post of Chief Justice of the Supreme Court. Earl Warren had told President Johnson that he planned to retire but wanted to make sure that his seat would be filled by a like-minded liberal; he was also disturbed by the prospect that Nixon, whom he despised, would replace him with someone who did not share his judicial philosophy.[80] The Fortas affair turned out to be an embarrassing fiasco for Johnson, but Nixon's position greatly reassured Thurmond and other southern Republicans who had come to see the Supreme Court as a major abettor of street crime and cultural permissiveness.

When it was show-and-tell time, Nixon had enough delegate votes to carry him over the top on August 7, receiving 692 votes to 277 for Rockefeller and 182 for Reagan. As planned, he had over twenty-five votes to spare. Nixon's subsequent acceptance speech was a model of public relations and a herald of his message to the "forgotten Americans," the non-shouters, the non-demonstrators—that is, the vast majority of law-abiding Americans. At a time of national chaos, Nixon's message in Miami struck a responsive cord all over America. Appealing to these ordinary Americans whom he later called the "Silent Majority," Nixon posed a question and answered it for them:

> And this great group of Americans—the forgotten Americans and others—know that the great question Americans must answer by their votes in November is this: whether we will continue for four more years the policies of the last five years. And this is the answer, and this is my answer to that question: When the strongest nation in the world can be tied up for four years in a war in Vietnam with no end in sight, when the richest nation in the world can't manage its own economy, when the nation with the greatest tradition of the rule of law is plagued by unprecedented lawlessness, when a nation that has been known for a century for equality of opportunity is torn by unprecedented racial violence, and when the President of the United States cannot travel abroad or to any major city at home without fear of hostile demonstration—then its time for new leadership for the United States of America.[81]

Nixon, of course, was right about all these things, but his solutions were in the form of vague promises, a practice he had perfected in his own long standing political version of "rubbing raw the sores of discontent" without truly healing them. And yet, this is precisely what he promised the nation: the New Nixon would be a uniter, a healer, rather than a divider. In 1968 and again in 1972 the American people accepted the New Nixon but only because their faith in Democrats had been seriously shaken by four years of social turmoil. The Republicans left Miami unified and ready to do battle with a Democratic Party that was about the tear itself apart.

Compared to the staid Republican convention in Miami, the Democratic convention in Chicago resembled a slow, agonizing death rattle for the Democrats. The assassination of Robert Kennedy had left his followers heartbroken and rudderless, for there was no other candidate who could take his place. Neither McCarthy nor Humphrey was an acceptable alternative to their fallen leader, and it was not until Senator George McGovern entered the race on August 10 that the Kennedy loyalists had someone they could rally behind. McGovern was a left liberal who had strongly opposed the war in Vietnam; he also had definite ideas about reorganizing the Democratic Party by eliminating the unit rule, attracting minorities into the party fold, and reducing the power of traditional party bosses. Although McCarthy was instrumental in revamping the way in which the party nominated its candidates, the left-liberal McGovern wing of the party had to wait until 1972 before leading the next Democratic ticket. In 1968 McGovern was a Johnny-come-lately. Even if he had hammered out a strong coalition with the McCarthy faction, he would not have beaten Humphrey. Like Nixon, who went into Miami with enough votes for the nomination, Humphrey was headed to Chicago with enough delegates in his pocket to put him over the top.

What Humphrey suspected but could not foresee was that he was headed into a viper's nest. In August 1968 Chicago was a disaster waiting to happen. Mayor Daley, an old-fashioned Democratic machine politician, had persuaded the Democratic leadership that Chicago would be an ideal location to renominate Lyndon Johnson. Daley had even picked August 27, Lyndon Johnson's birthday, as the day the president was expected to be renominated. Johnson never went to Chicago and those who did regretted that they did. Chicago was just recovering from the devastating race riot that hit the city after Martin Luther King Jr. was assassinated, and the mayor was determined to prevent a repeat of the violence by every means available, even if that required a "shoot to kill" approach in handling rioters. Through his police intelligence units Daley had received information that the city would be inundated by tens of thousands of protesters bent upon disrupting the convention. His response was to turn the city into "Fort Daley," a solid fortress of police, national guard units, and army troops in reserve. Vowing that "no-one is going to take over the streets," Daley beefed up the police on the streets to 11,900 and had them work twelve-hour shifts, augmenting this core force with 5,649 Illinois National Guardsmen, 1,000 FBI agents, and assorted military intelligence officers.[82] The Chicago boss also ordered the construction of a cyclone fence topped with barbed wire, to be ringed around the amphitheater, the site of the convention. Since the city was going through a transportation strike, the delegates were to be bused to the convention site, escorted along the way by police motor cycles, unmarked cars, and helicopters from the air scanning the routes for potential disturbances. Once the delegates arrived they had to wear special badges in order to be admitted to the convention hall; and just to be on the safe side, Daley could count on 7,500 army troops waiting at nearby bases and air-fields.[83] Specially trained police intelligence agents were ready to infiltrate the ranks of the protesters and immediately report any sign of trouble.

Why did Daley amass such a huge force? In the first place, a group of young anar-chists, the Yippies, led by Abbie Hoffman and Jerry Rubin, had long signaled their intention to upend Chicago, Mayor Daley, and the Democratic Convention. Their goal was to turn the whole event into a joke, exposing Daley and the Democrats as authoritarian war-mongers. As will be shown in the next chapter, half of this was seri-ous and half of it was a put-on. But it was not just the Yippies but also numerous other protesters who converged on Chicago in August 1968, including radical students from SDS, antiwar protesters, radical anarchists, and civic-minded Americans who wanted to register their grievances with the Democratic administration. As the Chicago melo-drama unfolded, four distinct groups interacted and enacted a surreal spectacle of conflict and violence: long-haired Yippies and hippies, revolutionary-minded activists (Hayden, Davis, Dellinger), the Chicago police force, and the sensation-hungry press. The majority of the protesters, hippies and radicals, had come to Chicago not merely to protest but to disrupt the convention. Mayor Daley and his police were in an equally confrontational mood. Both sides spoiled for a fight. The news media, already angry with Daley's restrictions on unlimited access to "newswor-thy" sources, increasingly sided with the protesters and depicted them as innocent vic-tims of Daley's out-of-control police force, which the press compared to Nazi storm troopers. The commission that later investigated the events of August 25–29, the Walker Commission, referred to the action of the Chicago police force as a "police riot" but only mildly criticized the actions of the protesters. Daley tried unsuccessfully to counter the Walker Report with his own official report and with a filmed version based on that report called *What Trees Do They Plant*. In the eyes of the news media and later historical accounts, it was Daley and the Chicago police force who were responsible for the violence. This one-sided account has largely persisted among his-torians, who have viewed the battle of Chicago as a conflict between the countercul-ture boomer generation and the conservative reaction of the older generation. This simplistic version, pitting young idealists—the press often called them "our kids"—against the spiteful, resentful, and bigoted cops, has been repeated ad nauseam in his-torical accounts, documentaries, and self-congratulatory retrospectives by sixties radicals, many of whom have monopolized historical narrative to suit their own biases. This distortion is unlikely to survive intact as younger historians review the Chicago convention more objectively. It was not until the 1980s that voices other than the protesters and their willing allies in the press were allowed to be heard. The histo-rian David Farber, who grew up in Chicago, was the first to provide a more even-handed account of the 1968 Democratic Convention, letting his readers see the event from three major perspectives—that of the hippies, that of the antiwar protesters, and that of Mayor Daley's police force.[84] The tone of the book, however, clearly indicates that Farber sides with the protesters, whose narrative voices predominate and are cast in a far more favorable light than the voices of average policemen. Two recent books—*Battleground Chicago* by Frank Kusch (2004) and *Law and Order* by Michael W. Flamm (2005)—have provided additional and more nuanced documentation on the role of the police in 1968. It was not just in Chicago but all over the nation that the police were exposed to unprecedented provocation and abuse. Having said that, the Chicago police buckled under these provocations and, on several occasions, ran amock and attacked the innocent and the guilty alike. Mayor Daley made a dreadful error in judgment by ordering curfews and by refusing permits to thousands of protesters to sleep in the parks of Chicago. On the Sunday before the convention was scheduled to begin, the police cleared Lincoln Park, located in the northern part of the city along Lake Michigan. This set off the first violent confrontation, to be repeated throughout the following week. Protesters showered the police with obscene epithets, rocks, and bottles. The police, swinging their billy clubs, chased the protesters out of the park, beating up innocent bystanders including ten newsmen. This set the stage for similar, even more violent encounters between the protesters, convening either in Lincoln Park, the staging ground for the hippies, or Grant Park, where the more serious political protesters—Tom Hayden, Rennie Davis, and David Dellinger—launched their operations. From one day to the next, the level of violence escalated. Attracted to conflict like moths to the flame, newscasters found more drama on the streets than they did on the convention floor, giving the nation a spectacle without context. Television networks showed out-of-control policemen charging protesters without showing why they did so. Images became reality. NBC News put together a particularly misleading montage juxtaposing the violent police actions on the streets of Chicago with Soviet tanks rolling into Prague putting down the peaceful democratic government of Alexander Dubcek. Other images showed a smiling Mayor Daley on the convention floor juxtaposed against Chicago policemen clubbing young protesters, which gave viewers the impression that Daley was celebrating the violence. *Newsweek* reported that the police "went on a sustained rampage unprecedented outside the most unreconstructive boondocks of Dixie."[85] The same view was echoed by *Time* magazine, contending that the Chicago police caused a "sanctioned mayhem" and contravened every acceptable code of professional police discipline.[86] The marchers were depicted by the news media as young courageous idealists, as "our children," who had come to Chicago to engage in democratic protest. Tom Wicker of the *New York Times* said that "these were our children in the streets and the Chicago police beat them up."[87] After Dan Rather of CBS was roughed up on the convention floor, Walter Cronkite called Daley's security agents a bunch of thugs.

These polarizing images were a refraction of a biased press that took its own perceptions of reality and refused to submit them to critical scrutiny. Just how far the media was out of the mainstream of public opinion became clear when polls and feedback by viewers revealed that the majority of the American people supported the police rather than the protesters. This came as a particular shock to Walter Cronkite, the dean of the establishment press, when CBS received a flood of letter that were eleven-to-one in favor of the police. The *New York Times* reported that a nationwide poll overwhelmingly supported the police.[88]

On August 27, the day the convention was scheduled to nominate the Democratic candidate for president, the house fell in on the Democrats. In the afternoon, party regulars voted down a peace plank that had been introduced by the antiwar faction of McCarthy and Kennedy followers. Outside the convention hall antiwar protesters had assembled in Grant Park for the only peace rally the police had authorized. Within a short period of time, skirmishes between the protesters and the police turned the peace rally into a battlefield. When a young protester climbed the flagpole near the band shell and began to lower the American flag with the crowd chanting: "Tear down the flag," the police arrested him. This infuriated the crowd. Chants of "Pigs! Pigs! Kill the Pigs!" greeted the police, as did bricks, cans, eggs, tomatoes, and balloons filled with paint and urine. The police responded with billy clubs, mace, and tear gas. But even greater violence occurred near Grant Park, at the Conrad Hilton Hotel, where the McCarthy, Humphrey, and McGovern people had their headquarters. As the nomination began inside the ampitheater, thousands of angry protesters who had assembled in front of the Hilton were viciously attacked by the police. Swinging billy clubs, the police beat people indiscriminately, fired off tear gas canisters and shoved people through restaurant windows. Looking down on the street violence from his fifteenth-floor campaign suite, McCarthy likened it to Nazi Germany. The policemen often viewed the protesters as hippies gone wild. "It was scary to get close to these kids," said one policeman, "their faces were flushed; their eyes were glassy. They looked at you but it was as if they were looking right through you— and up close, you could smell the dope on them."[89] Officers made few distinctions between peaceful protesters and drugged out anarchists. They exploded with rage to provocations such as "Fuck the pigs," "Who's fucking your wife this afternoon, pig?" "Mother Fuckers," "Shitheads," "Ho Ho Ho Chi Minh," "Pig, pig, oink, sooo-ee." The police response was: "Get the bastards," "Kill the commies," "Kill, Kill, Kill."

Lance Morrow, a *Time* magazine reporter, correctly summed up the extreme polarizations acted out in Chicago when he said,

> In front of the Hilton, on Michigan Avenue, two sides of America ground against each other like tectonic plates. Each side cartooned and ridiculed the other so brutally that by now the two seemed to belong almost to two different species. The 60's had a genius for excess and caricature, on one side the love-it-or-leave it proud Middle American.... On the other side, the countercultural young, either flower children or revolutionaries, and their fellow traveling adult allies in the antiwar movement, the Eugene McCarthy uprising against the LBJ people whose hatred of the war in Vietnam led them into every greater alienation from society and its figures of authority![90]

While police battled protesters and body odor and tear gas, and the constant smell from the stockyards and slaughterhouses provided an unpleasant backdrop, the convention proceeded through a predictable nomination ritual. Delegates inside the hall were stunned when they saw the violent images on various television screens of what was going on outside the hall. Abraham Ribicoff, who was onstage nominating McGovern, took note of these outside street battles, departed from his speech, and remarked that "with McGovern, we wouldn't have Gestapo tactics on the streets of Chicago."[91] Mayor Daley, who sat directly in front of Ribicoff, rose to his feet, shook a fist, and screamed a racial epithet under his cupped hand—a remark later translated by lip readers as "Fuck you, you Jew son of a bitch, you lousy motherfucker, go home."[92] Ribicoff replied with a smile, "How hard it is to accept the truth. How hard it is."

Humphrey was the winning loser that night, choosing Edmund Muskie of Maine as his running mate. Humphrey won on the first ballot with a delegate count of 1,761, to 601 for McCarthy and 146 for McGovern. Humphrey had not competed in a single primary. The McCarthy followers, unable to accept the fact that all of their work had been in vain, erupted in cries of "Fourth Party, Fourth Party," but there was not going to be a fourth party in 1968 for the simple reason that McCarthy was not interested and McGovern was too much of a Democratic loyalist.

The Democratic Party went limping into the fall elections, and it did so with two northern liberals from small states. Humphrey was still beholden to Lyndon Johnson and had no campaign organization to speak of. Larry O'Brien, his campaign manager, told him after the Chicago fiasco, "Look, I'm going to work my tail off for you, but as your manager I have to say to you—right now, you're dead."[93] The polls confirmed it. The Gallup poll showed Humphrey fifteen points behind Nixon and only seven points ahead of Wallace.[94] It was not just lack of money or organization that dogged the Humphrey campaign, but the defection of significant groups within the Democratic coalition Franklin Roosevelt had put together. Elite liberals had steadily ignored white middle-class interests, called law-and-order advocates "racists," and made the concerns of the poor and racial minorities a national imperative. Lower-middle-class ethnics of Italian, Polish, Irish, and Greek descent, the blue-collar workers, and Catholic voters began to abandon the Democratic Party. They saw the liberal state as a coercive administrative and judicial state that was disregarding the will of the majority. They resented the imposition of policies they did not want: favoring minorities, endorsing group rights, expensive welfare programs, higher taxes, and so forth. Most devastating for the Democratic Party, however, was the loss of the whole South. When Lyndon Johnson signed the Civil Rights Act of 1964, he told Bill Moyers, "I think we just delivered the South to the Republican Party for a long time to come." This proved to be the case; it also explains Nixon's "southern strategy" and the historic electoral shift of the South from the Democrats to the Republicans.

By contrast with the Democrats, Nixon and the Republicans had both the money and the organization to mount an effective national campaign. The Nixon team boasted some experienced and talented people, including Frank Shakespeare, a former CBS executive; Raymond Price, a former editorial writer for the *New York Herald Tribune*; Harry Treleaven, an executive of Fuller & Smith & Ross Advertising in New York; Roger Ailes, executive producer of the *Mike Douglas Show*; Robert "Bob" Haldeman, a Seattle advertising executive; Len Garment, one of Nixon's law partners; and Patrick Buchanan, a young talented speechwriter. Team Nixon crafted one of the slickest media-savvy campaigns since John F. Kennedy had run for the presidency in 1960. The inner workings of the Nixon campaign have been skillfully recounted by Joe McGinniss, a Philadelphia journalist who followed the campaign throughout the country and wrote a book about his experiences entitled *The Selling of the President*

(1969). Determined not to commit the same mistakes that he made in his 1960 campaign, in which he had visited every state, Nixon devised a "two-track approach," using some tried-and-true spontaneous campaigning—giving speeches, holding rallies, handshaking, baby-kissing, and so forth—but focusing primarily on carefully scripted appearances that would leave nothing to chance. The latter strategy meant insulating the candidate from embarrassing, off-the-cuff remarks and hostile crowds of reporters or demonstrators. Nixon had been done in by television in 1960, and he was determined to master that medium and use it to his advantage.

The first step for team Nixon was to change the image that had been attached to their candidate portraying him as a sore loser, a grumpy old man, and a deeply divisive figure. The image of a "New Nixon" had to be created if their man had any chance of succeeding in 1968. The task of accomplishing this feat was assigned to a group of young men who were more attuned to the political uses of television, who knew that voters responded more favorably to images rather than to substantive arguments, and did so on an emotional rather than a cerebral basis. One of Nixon's advisors put this quite succinctly when he pointed out that rational arguments would "only be effective if we can get people to make the *emotional* leap, or what theologians call [the] leap of faith."[95] Reiterating Marshall McLuhan's dictum that the medium is the message, he added: "*We have to be very clear at this point: that the response is to the image, not to the man. . . .* It's not what's *there* that counts, it's what's projected—and carrying it one step further, it's not what *he* projects but rather what the voter receives. It's not the man we have to change but rather the *received impression*. And this impression depends more on the medium and its use than it does on the candidate himself."[96] Thus there was no need for a real "New Nixon," just a successful change of imagery that convinced voters that there was, in fact, a "New Nixon."

This is where the second track became imperative. Nixon's team of image makers, making broad use of television commercials and self-serving "infomercials," had to cover the nation's airwaves with a veritable blitzkrieg of advertisements that would convince the American voter that Nixon had really changed, that he represented ordinary America, and that he, unlike all the other candidates, could truly bring Americans together again.

If procedurally the Nixon campaign centered on image construction, substantively it aimed at capturing the great middle of ordinary Americans who were neither left-wing protesters nor right-wing reactionaries. This included blue-collar ethnics, affluent suburbanites, disenchanted Democrats of the South and Southwest, and old Yankee Republicans of New England. The deep South, Nixon realized, was probably lost to Wallace, but it was well worth going after the border states of Virginia, North Carolina, Kentucky, Tennessee, Missouri, and Oklahoma. If he could make substantial inroads into the South and the traditional Democratic coalition going back to FDR and the New Deal, Nixon believed that he had a good chance of capturing the presidency. This belief was shared by a sharp young adviser on his team, Kevin Phillips, who actually foresaw an emerging conservative realignment in American politics. Phillips, a Harvard Law School graduate, predicted that the liberal ascendancy in American politics dating back to the New Deal was about to change under the impact of the divisive social disruptions of the 1960s. Middle-class Americans, he forcefully argued, were sick and tired of radical protesters, welfare chiselers, scruffy hippies, insolent minorities, and an endless war in Vietnam. According to Phillips, white southerners would defect from the Democratic coalition and so would blue-collar suburbanites and Catholics. Looking at subsequent erosions of the traditional Democratic coalition, Kevin Phillips's predictions published in his 1969 book *The Emerging Republican Majority* would turn out to be remarkably prescient.

The Humphrey campaign did not gain any real traction until late September, when the vice president, trying to distance himself from Johnson, announced in a Salt Lake City speech that as president, he would stop the bombing over North Vietnam. The prospect of peace, Nixon realized, would benefit the Democrats more than it would the Republicans and what now unfolded was worthy of the best spy thrillers. Afraid that the Democrats would pull out a last "Hail Mary" play by stopping the bombing and persuading the South Vietnamese to join the Paris Peace talks, the Nixon campaign established contact with Anna Chennault, the Chinese-born widow of General Chennault, commander of the famous World War II Flying Tigers squadron. Chennault had important contacts in the South Vietnamese government, including President Nguyen Van Thieu; she was also a Republican activist who strongly supported Richard Nixon. Through a South Vietnamese conduit, Chennault urged President Thieu to object to Johnson's planned bombing halt, making it clear that the South Vietnamese would get a better deal from Nixon than they would from a lame duck U.S. president. Johnson got wind of these Republican machinations and used some "dirty tricks" of his own, wiretapping Chennault. One of Johnson's White House aides warned that Chennault might pose difficulties, saying that "she lives at Watergate—a huge apartment . . . she is constantly seeing Republicans—the risk of discovery is high."[97] As Robert Dallek sardonically pointed out, "the White House should have passed the memo along to Nixon and John Mitchell for future reference."[98] Nixon also got privileged information from Henry Kissinger, who had close contacts in both Washington and Paris. Historians claim that Kissinger's double dealing was the professor's desire to improve his job prospects in a future Nixon administration.

With hindsight, it now appears that both Johnson and Nixon engaged in dirty tricks, but effectively checkmated each other because neither could publicly admit to his secret double-dealing. The victim was clearly Hubert Humphrey. The full details of all the dirty tricks that took place behind the scenes of the election of 1968 are still unknown because the intelligence information obtained by the Johnson administration remains classified.[99] Nixon was too crafty to expose himself, probably relying on Spiro Agnew to handle the Anna Chennault channel to the South Vietnamese government. Although Johnson did call a bombing halt on October 31, President Thieu turned down the U.S. offer to participate in the Paris peace talks two days later. Humphrey gained in the polls, but not enough. On November 5, Richard Nixon was elected by a small margin of 499,704 popular votes out of 73 million cast, but his margin was substantially larger in the Electoral College, where he beat Humphrey by a margin of 301 to 191. Humphrey was a graceful loser. Although he had toyed with the idea of blowing the whistle on the Chennault story, he recognized that it would be interpreted as a last-minute act of desperation, quite apart from revealing Lyndon Johnson's wiretapping of Chennault and the Republican campaign.[100] So Humphrey said nothing and lost the campaign. Nixon may have won the campaign, but the Chennault affair, as Lewis Gould has pointed out, revealed the seeds of Watergate, for Nixon's handling of the affair shows clearly, if only retrospectively, the lengths to which he was willing to go to win.[101] His dark shadow would disfigure the American political landscape for the next six years and beyond.

9

A YOUNG GENERATION
IN REVOLT

1. America Awash in Rebellious Young People

In the post–World War II era, young people emerged as a distinct economic and cultural group, partly because of their large numbers and partly because of their growing influence on the cultural mainstream. Young people did not shape the course of public policy in the 1960s, but they played a significant role in protesting against racial injustice, the war in Vietnam, traditional social mores, and economic inequality. It should be understood that here the term *young* refers primarily to college students rather than young working Americans. If any segment of the young attempted to shape or alter the course of events during the 1960s, it was college students; they were the most vocal and strident, clamoring to be noticed and to be heard by older Americans. Their massive numbers, sense of empowerment, and frustration produced a shrill chorus of protest that, in retrospect, was all out of proportion to its importance to the nation's public affairs.[1]

In 1946 there were roughly two million college students in America; in 1970 their numbers had quadrupled to eight million. Many of these students came from white upper middle-class backgrounds. It would be a serious mistake, however, to assume that the majority of college students identified themselves with either the New Left or the right (Young Americans for Freedom [YAF]). In fact, probably only 3 percent of college students identified themselves with the New Left or other radical groups. Of the twenty-five thousand students enrolled at the University of California at Berkeley, no more than fifty could be considered hard-core radicals or revolutionaries. The same was true of other universities where militancy was particularly strong—Brown, Cornell, Columbia, Harvard, Yale, Princeton, and Michigan.

Student radicalism was especially intense at prestigious universities and at the larger "multiversities," where overcrowding was often a serious problem. Although many young people protested against a number of perceived injustices ranging from *in loco parentis* rules, civil rights violations, the Vietnam War, required ROTC training, to the draft, the most committed protesters came from the ranks of America's elites, from affluent white and professional parents who had brought up their children on the basis of child-centered, liberal, and democratic values. On the political left, many students came from Jewish families that had instilled in their children a strong sense of critical thinking and a commitment to social justice.[2] Furthermore,

Jewish parents had often inherited socialist traditions from Europe, together with a strong suspicion and dislike of authority. Jewish students, brought up to respect the importance of ideas, would play a leading role in radical causes. Although only 3 percent of the U.S. population was Jewish, 10 percent of the college population was Jewish. About 23 percent of youth from Jewish families identified themselves with the New Left, while only 4 percent of Protestant students and 2 percent of Catholic students supported the New Left. A significant number of New Left radicals were "red-diaper" babies—that is, children of Jewish communist or socialist parents. The major leaders of SDS and other left-wing groups came from Jewish parents with radical connections—Stanley Rothman, S. Robert Lichter, Steven Cohen, Ronald Radosh, Richard Flacks, Rennie Davis, Jackie Goldberg, Jerry Rubin, Mark Rudd, Abbie Hoffman, David Horowitz, Jane Alpert, Todd Gitlin.[3] Although a high percentage of New Left students came from Jewish backgrounds, the majority of Jewish students did not join SDS. Most Jewish activists were not practicing Jews but had rejected their Jewish religious heritage as counterrevolutionary. Such secularized Jews tended to view Judaism, especially in its Zionist form, as an obsolete messianic faith and often sympathized with the Palestinians as an oppressed people.

On the political right, young people who associated with groups like Young Americans for Freedom and other conservative associations generally came from white upper-middle-class Protestant parents who had professional or business backgrounds. Numerically, conservative students found themselves in the minority among the student population of the 1960s. Most students identified themselves as liberal or progressive; but frightened by the war and intimidated by the draft, they shifted slightly left of center and were thus susceptible to the revolutionary left. What is significant, however, is that the children of America's elites expressed themselves in strident anti-American terms that, at times, seemed to some Americans as plainly un-American and treasonable.

If there is one movement in the sixties that brought young people from all sections of society together, if just briefly, it was the countercultural movement with its vibrant rock 'n' roll music, psychedelic drugs, and alternative lifestyles. It was this movement rather than the New Left or the New Right that had the most radical impact on the nation's cultural domain.

The intellectual development of young radicals generally began with a sense that America's institutions—government, business, the military, and universities—were flawed and needed to be reformed, and then proceeded to a recognition that these institutions were evil and had to be overthrown. Only a few committed radicals made this transition from constitutionally acceptable protest to democratically unacceptable terrorism. But all of them brought a strong degree of idealism and energy to the program of changing America. What young radical students usually lacked was the knowledge, maturity, and discipline to translate their ideals into practice. By themselves, of course, students have never been able to change social, let alone educational, conditions. This is why, in Lewis Feuer's view, youth movements in general have attached themselves to a "carrier" movement of major social dimensions associated with suffering peasants, oppressed workers, nationalist causes, racial injustices, or anticolonial protests.[4] The intensity of student protests in the 1960s was largely the result of two great carrier movements on which young people super-imposed their idealism and readiness for self-sacrifice—the civil rights movement and the antiwar movement.

A great deal has been written about the positive aspects of youthful participation in major social movements, but there is, as Feuer reminds us, another side to youthful enthusiasm, and that is its inherent immaturity and even irrationality. It could even be argued that student movements have deflected political carrier movements into irrational or self-defeating directions, as was subsequently shown by the young hotheads in SNCC, the Black Panthers, SDS, and the Weathermen. Feuer argues that student movements are "born of vague, undefined emotions which seek for some issue, some cause, to which to attach themselves"; they are a "complex of urges—altruism, idealism, revolt, self-sacrifice, and self-destruction."[5] In this sense, they are not only a sign of generational problems but also "a sign of a sickness, a malady in society."

In modern times, student movements have been largely middle class in nature, displaying a strong preference for populism and identifying with some lowly and oppressed class or group.[6] From a psychological point of view, this symbiosis with the underdog may have its roots in the trauma of adolescence and the conflict it releases between bookish dreams and the adult demand to renounce them in favor of "reality" or the practical world. A real youth movement can only exist when a sizable and important element of young people finds itself at odds with an older generation as "a counterforce to be denounced as disrespectful, rebellious and revolutionary."[7]

The United States did not have a major student movement until the 1960s, because past intergenerational conflicts were rarely intense or widespread and also because educational institutions were far less authoritarian than they were in Europe. The faculty in Europe was generally conservative, and in Germany even reactionary, so that professors resisted all efforts at reform, as Friedrich Heer put it, "with the ferocity of a cornered rabbit."[8] In America, the 1960s shattered the "social equilibrium," which Feuer defined as a situation "when no generation feels that its energies and intelligence are being frustrated by the others, when no generation feels that solely because of its years is it being deprived of its proper place in society, and when no generation feels that it is being compelled to bear an undue portion of society's burden."[9]

In the 1960s there was a high level of intergenerational frustration, made all the more intense by the rising expectations of young people. Young Americans were generally pampered, undisciplined, and immature. This was the result not only of weak parenting but also of changing educational standards. A new generation of young Americans had been brought up without knowing very much about the world, about science, geography, and history—a generation, as Roland Stromberg put it, that "knew not Josef" (Stalin) and, we might add, knew little about World War II, Hitler, or the Holocaust.[10] In large part, this was because American public schools, especially on the college level, moved away from teaching demanding history, philosophy, or literature courses and began to focus more on making academic subjects "relevant" and personally fulfilling. In the humanities, ideologically driven agendas began to appear, many of them denouncing middle-class values as socially exploitive and psychologically repressive.

What happened in American education was similar to what was happening in the cultural domain—the rapid triumph of egalitarian over elitist tendencies, even among the nation's premier universities. The need and desires of masses of people began to overrule the more restricted or refined tastes of a small cultural minority. The dilemma can be illustrated by what happened in 1947, the year the Educational Testing Service, the brainchild of Harvard's James Bryant Conant and Henry Chauncey, was founded for the purpose of identifying the brightest students by means of standardized testing, requiring the already widely used Scholastic Aptitude Test (SAT).[11] The idea behind this goal was to find a better way of choosing a natural elite than the traditional one based on money or social status. Conant believed that the people deserved to be ruled by the most talented rather than the most well-heeled, and that standardized testing could identify raw intelligence and thus enable the brightest to attend the nation's elite institutions of higher education. He envisioned a new meritocracy derived from the best brains of all social classes.

Conant's ideal, however, ran counter to the egalitarian sentiments of the American people, particularly the belief that anyone who tried hard enough could succeed in education or business or anything one set one's mind to. It also clashed with an inherent anti-intellectual tradition in American culture that was suspicious of anyone who claimed to be better or pretended to know more than anyone else. Furthermore, Conant and his generation, weaned on ambitious principles of "social science," made a fundamental miscalculation that "raw intelligence" could be measured and then used as a basis of predicting success in college or life. Although the SAT became a permanent fixture in American higher education, it failed both as a predictor of success in college and as a gatekeeper to weed out unprepared students from attending college. Grades were judged to be as important as test scores, and they proved to be infinitely elastic as higher education expanded, new colleges were built, and masses of students were admitted. The GI Bill, which awarded generous payments to veterans for the purpose of attending school, was another cause of adding millions to the already enrolled number of college students. In the postwar decade over eight million GIs went to school, most of them to trade or technical schools but one-third to schools of higher education. By 1969 higher education was the largest mass industry in the country; one-half of the white male population of college age was enrolled in higher education. SAT scores, as it would turn out, were used only as one indicator of success by the vast majority of colleges and universities in the country.

It goes without saying that Gresham's law was bound to operate in the academic sphere just as it operated in the financial sphere: bad quality was driving out good quality; high standards suffered with the influx of many unprepared and intellectually unqualified young people. In retrospect, the SAT scores were reliable enough to confirm this picture of educational deterioration in the entrance requirements, for starting in 1963 the scores on both the verbal and mathematical sections of the SAT steadily declined as a result of enrolling unqualified students.[12] Huge numbers of young people were going to college and expecting to benefit economically and socially in the same way that the few talented students, who had attended schools in the past, had benefited from their educational experiences. Neither genetics nor the facts of economic life supported this assumption. College administrators, who had a stake in the new mass production system, were able to conceal this reality from the majority of the American people, perpetuating the myth that a college education was not only possible for all Americans but inevitably resulted in economic affluence and personal fulfillment. In order to safeguard the myth from exposure, college administrators pandered to student demands, watered down the curriculum, sanctioned inflated grades and easy course requirements, and devalued vocational education.

Yet the students were not grateful to the educational system. They felt themselves processed like a herd of cattle at the larger "multiversities"; they also claimed that they felt bored and alienated. All too many students expected fun and educational success at a minimal personal sacrifice; and while the schools increasingly obliged, it never seemed quite enough. Student dissatisfaction often turned to protest, and protest discovered its own philosophical or sociological language, a language that had already been shaped in the European academy a generation ago.

Mass education thus produced a sizable number of radical students and young professors who formed a new intellectual proletariat that denounced American institutions as unjust, reactionary, and repressive. This was the New Left, less organized and disciplined than the Old Left, but nonetheless equally opposed to the mainstream of American life and culture. The home of the New Left was the university, where a small core of militant students and professors tried with some success to galvanize the majority in the academy to work for radical change in the institutions and traditions of American society.[13]

The new radicals were not blue-collar workers chafing under the oppression of their capitalist employers but young college students from middle-class homes who were still being financially supported by their parents. Motivated either by a sense of guilt or by radical doctrines gleaned from Karl Marx, C. Wright Mills, Herbert Marcuse, and a growing stream of modernist critiques of bourgeois civilization, the students pretended to reject the outward trappings of affluence—expensive cars, jewelry, or clothes—and defiantly opted for genteel poverty and its trappings— cheap "pads," rundown cars, long hair, workmen's overalls, second-hand clothes, and defiantly resentful attitudes. Authority for these students was suspect on principle because it was repressive and exploitive. No discrimination was made between illegitimate and legitimate authority. All forms of hierarchy and elitism were equally suspect, which was bad news for the university, an institution whose *raison d'être* was based on high achievement, merit, and elitism. Radicals preferred equality and the absence of restrictions on ego gratification, embracing the motto: "it is forbidden to forbid," except, of course, when it involved views that came from the repressive mainstream.

Radical students also assaulted the whole classical and rationalistic frame of mind associated with Western civilization, preferring intuitive and subjective modes of thought over objective or analytical styles of thinking. They insisted on being alienated and regarded the university, especially the large "multiversity," as an oppressive authoritarian system. Drawing on the Beat movement of the 1950s, radical political doctrines, and the various uninhibited forms of self-expression embodied in folk music, rock 'n' roll, and drug use, the political avant-garde ensconced at colleges and universities tried to use the university as a staging ground for social and political change. Feeling "oppressed" in modern America, radical students tried to galvanize other segments of society into lobbying for radical change.

2. The New Left and Student Militancy in the 1960s

In October 1960 the sociologist C. Wright Mills wrote what would turn out to be a prophetic essay, in which he drew attention to a new kind of radicalism, which he called the "New Left." As distinguished from the "Old Left," which had become cautious and trade unionist, the New Left, Mills pointed out, had found a vibrant and intellectually fresh home among a new cultural elite of radical students and their more politically engaged professors.[14] Mills found hope for the future in those students who were protesting against the activities of the House Committee on Un-American Activities (HUAC) and participating in the civil rights movement. At the time Mills wrote his essay, the groundwork was actually being laid for a new student left movement that saw itself as the "voice, conscience, and goad of its generation."[15]

The Students for a Democratic Society (SDS) grew out of the youth wing of the League of Industrial Democracy (LID), a socialist organization founded in 1905 by Jack London and Upton Sinclair. The student branch of LID, known as SLID, was chartered in 1921 and became SDS in 1960, when it was invigorated by Al Haber and Tom Hayden, two students at the University of Michigan.

In 1960 Haber organized a Conference on Human Rights at the University of Michigan, which attracted hundreds of students from mostly mid-western universities. In view of the civil rights sit-ins that were being conducted at the time throughout the South, the students were primarily interested in discussing various confrontational tactics that might be employed to stop racial discrimination. Two years later, at another student conference held at Port Huron, Michigan, SDS students reached a consensus that their upbringing and education had poorly prepared them for the real world. Far from having been taught what the world was really like, the students claimed that they had been deceived about America's self-image as a free, equal, and democratic nation. The reality, the students insisted, was a country and a world steeped in oppression, inequality, cold war terror, racial bigotry, and middle-class hypocrisy. The students called for an end to war, unilateral disarmament, reduction in military spending, full equality for African Americans, an end to poverty, and participatory democracy. Tom Hayden, who drafted SDS's mission, a document called the Port Huron Statement, gave voice to the movement's hopes and aspirations for a better world, one that was to be founded on the yet unfulfilled promises of American freedom and equality:

> We regard men as infinitely precious and possessed of unfulfilled capacities for reason, freedom, and love. In affirming these principles we are aware of countering perhaps the

dominant conceptions of man in the twentieth century: that he is a thing to be manipulated, and that he is inherently incapable of directing his own affairs. We oppose the
depersonalization that reduces human beings to the status of things—if anything, the
brutalities of the twentieth century teach that means and ends are intimately related,
that vague appeals to "posterity" cannot justify the mutilations of the present. . . . Men
have unrealized potential for self-evaluation, self-direction, and creativity. It is this
potential that we regard as crucial and to which we appeal, not to the human poten-
tiality for violence, unreason, and submission to authority.[16]

The Port Huron Statement committed SDS to a new kind of radical activism that
was to be launched by students from America's major universities. Hayden, who
served as president of SDS from 1962 to 1963, saw the university as a catalyst of radical change in America. At the time of the Port Huron meeting, Hayden was a twenty-
three-year-old junior and reporter on the University of Michigan student newspaper.
Although he came from a Catholic background, Hayden had always been somewhat
of a rebel and an advocate for social change. In 1960 he joined SNCC and spent time
in the south helping black people in their campaign for voter registration. Hayden
was a dedicated leader but an inefficient and undisciplined organizer. Like most radical students he possessed a surfeit of rhetoric and a lack of consistent action. During his tenure, SDS had little to show but lofty rhetoric.

Although SDS rhetoric consisted of little more than glittering generalities, Hayden and the original leaders such as Al Haber, Carl Oglesby, Richard Flacks, Todd
Gitlin, and Carl Davidson, clearly distanced themselves from the old socialist or
communist left that had placed so much focus on ideological purity, discipline, and
party centralism. New Left members usually called themselves "democratic socialists," by which they meant that all power ultimately originated from and should flow
back to the people. By "all power to the people" SDS leaders meant "participatory
democracy," though it was never quite clear what that referred to in practice. Presumably it meant that ordinary people, wherever they lived or worked, should determine their own destiny rather than have their lives shaped behind their backs by an
exploitive capitalist system and its political lackeys in government. Inasmuch as SDS
had an ideology, it consisted of a smattering of socialist doctrine culled from Marx,
C. Wright Mills, Albert Camus, Herbert Marcuse, Frantz Fanon and anarchist or syndicalist tracts. From these sources, the students stitched together a makeshift and not
always consistent ideology aimed at what they felt to be capitalist exploitation, both
at home and abroad.

Capitalism, the students believed, was so inherently flawed that it would probably
collapse in their lifetime; their task was to prepare the way for it. Following Marx's
doctrine of the ever-increasing impoverishment of the proletariat, they expected
conditions to deteriorate until a revolutionary situation had been reached—the
famous Marxian "death knell" of capitalism. But precisely who were the exploited in
America? Were they workers, African Americans, the poor, or perhaps the students
themselves? Should American society be reconstructed to fit a student model of
political rectitude? It was undoubtedly true that poverty was a reality in America, but
the country's economy was more robust than it had been in almost a hundred years.

It was not the case that American society, except for black people, was riddled with intolerable inequalities, and it was certainly false that the U.S. economy was headed toward catastrophe. This is not to deny that there were structural inequalities in American life, and that something had to be done to alleviate them; but SDS leaders sitting on their high moral horses had little to offer but incendiary slogans. It was reform liberals in both parties who actually did the hard political work that led to civil rights reform and positive social legislation on behalf of those groups who had been left out of the economic mainstream. Far from building bridges to the working population that, like Marx, they knew only in the abstract, SDS activists failed miserably in forging alliances with either workers or the liberal community. Carl Oglesby and other SDS leaders dismissively referred to liberals as "corporate liberals," a species deserving of the deepest contempt because they were supposedly beholden to "corporate" or business interests.

The only way SDS actually established a presence in working-class communities was by sponsoring the Economic Research and Action Project (ERAP) in northern cities aimed at organizing the poor;[17] but since these efforts often bypassed established political channels, as shown in chapter 5, they accomplished little in the end. It may have been commendable and even meritorious to drop out of college and live among the poor, but SDS leaders lacked the organizational tools to move the poor from welfare to workforce. Rather than work through President Johnson's agencies that administered the war on poverty programs, SDS tried to operate what would turn out to be poorly coordinated and poorly administered programs in the slums of Baltimore, Cleveland, Chicago, Louisville, Newark, and Philadelphia. Lacking discipline and staying power, many SDS activists spent little more than a few months in poor communities, thus hampering a program that would have required years of hardship and dedication. Their activities, in fact, were often downright harmful because the students knew only one thing well—how to stage demonstrations and disruptions. They formed rent strikes, attacked welfare practices, and picketed city hall.[18] It also dawned on some SDS activists that hands-on social work had never been the original purpose of SDS, which was, after all, a student organization rather than a social-work force. However well meaning, what could pampered students from affluent backgrounds actually do for the poor? The suspicion could be raised that the poor were seen by the students as a means of bringing about the social changes desired less by the poor than by the students themselves. If this was in fact the case, students were more interested in radicalizing the poor than in actually helping them escape from poverty. Most ERAP programs folded quickly because they were poorly managed, inadequately funded, and insufficiently appreciated by the poor.

SDS was clearly operating in a vacuum. There was no strong tradition of radical socialism in America. Workers believed in capitalism and during the cold war associated all forms of socialism with totalitarian communism. Unlike Europe, where socialism had deep roots in trade union movements and political parties, America lacked a strong socialist or communist tradition that could have seriously challenged the established political system. Even during the Great Depression, neither the socialist party of Eugene Debs nor the Communist Party USA (CPUSA), though well organized and disciplined, ever posed a real danger to the two mainstream democratic parties. From its inception, therefore, SDS faced insurmountable obstacles in the American system. What made campus radicals think that they had a serious chance of redefining America's political future when they had no power in the economic domain?

The answer, of course, was youthful exuberance and the illusion of power that accompanied the short-term popularity of SDS between 1965 and 1968. That popularity was primarily the result of the unpopularity of the Vietnam War among college students. SDS leaders were misled into believing that their popular mandate from many students meant that students endorsed their radical ideology and that they could, therefore, politicize the university and use it as a battering ram to storm the citadel of corporate power. The reality, as it would turn out, was that there were only a few scattered radical groups in American academia, chiefly at some of the major universities such as Michigan, Wisconsin, Chicago, Cornell, Columbia, Brown, and Berkeley. But those radicals talked largely to each other and to a few radical professors, most of them belonging to the junior ranks of the faculty. Their publications—*Rampart, Studies on the Left, Dissent, Commentary, The Progressive*— were read by only the very few who were initiated into the conceptual universe of Marx, Freud, or literary criticism. In William O'Neill's shrewd judgment, the New Left "had no past, no present to speak of, no constituency, just hope and enthusiasm."[19] It may have had a short historical momentum, creating the illusion rather than the substance of change, especially in the absence of a major class to which its energies were supposed to be directed.

Youth, of course, is not a class but just a temporary stage of life, before a living has to be made. It is, in Erik H. Erikson's sense, a kind of moratorium or holding stage of life during which, hopefully, ideals can be formed and subsequently tested by experience. O'Neill has argued convincingly that SDS was aided by a certain historical momentum provided by the Vietnam War.[20] The war, together with the defiance of university authorities, gave the radical student movement a certain broad appeal that hid, at least for a few years, the essential hollowness of its ideology. Between 1963 and 1969 SDS ignited fires on many campuses.

3. The Catalyst: The Free Speech Movement at Berkeley

It started at the University of California at Berkeley in 1964, where the Free Speech movement erupted in response to the university's ill-conceived policy of excluding political activities from the campus.[21] That policy dated back to the 1930s when the university tried to prevent a communist-influenced student movement from gaining momentum on the campus, using the alleged threat of radicalism as an excuse to ban all political activities from the campus. Prewar Berkeley, the flagship of a still small university system—the others being UCLA, the agricultural school at Davis, and the small liberal arts college at Santa Barbara—was a provincial campus located in a predominantly conservative city. Its president, Robert Gordon Sproul, was an accountant who had saved the university's financial fortunes in the 1930s and then built one of the finest schools in the nation. Berkeley had welcomed émigré scholars fleeing fascism and attracted some of the most brilliant scientists, some of whom would play a leading role in the development of the atomic bomb. During the postwar period, Berkeley, like so many universities throughout the nation, experienced explosive growth in both student enrollments and public funding. In 1952, President Sproul created the new position of Chancellor at Berkeley, and he appointed Clark Kerr, a professor of industrial relations, a liberal democrat, and strong faculty advocate, to that position. As it would turn out, Sproul represented the old conservative Berkeley, Kerr the new liberal and corporate university. After Sproul retired in 1958, Kerr became president and set about charting a different course for the university. About the same time, the Berkeley city government changed from a conservative to a liberal controlled coalition.

Clark Kerr was the model of a liberal-minded bureaucrat: reasonable, quiet, diplomatic, and cerebral. He brought to the post both a preference for peaceful arbitration of policy differences that he inherited from his Quaker upbringing and a fondness for statistics that he owed to his education in behavioral science. Coalition building and consensus were his great strengths, while principled and determined leadership were his great weaknesses. In 1963 Kerr published the book that epitomized his vision for Berkeley and similar institutions throughout the nation. The university, according to Kerr, was to be an academic handmaiden to the corporate world; it was to train and furnish the technicians for corporate America. The title of the book, *The Uses of the University,* revealed its utilitarian theme, namely, that the primary function of a university should be socially useful and productive. Kerr both envisioned and worked for a close partnership between government and university, the former supplying funds and the latter furnishing corporate leaders and innovative ideas. Professors were to be judged by productive output in the form of articles, books, and government grants, while students were to be responsible and career oriented. Teaching, especially on the undergraduate level, was to be subordinated to research. Kerr's corporate vision was widely shared by his like-minded counterparts at other universities. In fact, the bald, bespectacled and owlish-looking Kerr represented an emerging type frequently encountered in corporate America following World War II. Unlike robber barons or fiercely independent business tycoons of an earlier era, Kerr's types represented the softer side of industrial America; they were custodial liberals, technocrats, public relations experts, or media savvy managers. Spending most of their time in corporate offices, conference rooms, or on business trips, such corporate leaders managed employees or students largely by remote control. It was not until the enraged students at Berkeley actually threatened to wreck his institution that Kerr emerged from his self-imposed isolation. Until that time he maintained such a low profile as to be virtually invisible, often working out of his home high in the hills above the campus where he managed a vast flow of paperwork with great aplomb. On campus, however, he was the invisible leader, prompting one administrator to remark: "There is no Clark Kerr."[22] As an indication of just how woefully isolated and uninformed Kerr was about the students under his charge, he made what would turn out to be the most ludicrous prediction about the young generation, saying "employers will love this generation. They are going to be easy to handle. There aren't going to be any riots."[23]

It should, therefore, not be surprising that in Clark Kerr obnoxious students found their perfect whipping post. The same would later be true of James Perkins of Cornell, Grayson Kirk of Columbia, Kingman Brewster of Yale, and others. In fairness to these men, it should be mentioned that they were confronted with massive numbers of unruly students and larger social forces over which they had little control. By the time he left office, Kerr was presiding over what he called a large "multiversity," consisting of nine campuses and over one hundred thousand students. The students at Berkeley, as at so many other campuses, came from privileged upper-middle-class parents; they resented the idea that the university acted like a surrogate parent, expecting them to adhere to strict rules of decorum, dress codes, and curfews. The struggle against such *in loco parentis* restrictions in the 1960s at Berkeley and elsewhere in the nation was unique in the history of higher education for its sheer intensity and disruptive nature. Previous generations had reluctantly put up with codes of etiquette, civility, and restraints. The baby boomers were different. Many students of the 1960s regarded all restrictions to free speech and the freedom to express one's personal preferences as intolerable and smacking of fascism. Students felt stifled by too many rules, not least of which were those that went beyond academic control and aimed at overmanaging their personal lives. The university, of course, had always been a kind of temporary caretaker of young people before they entered into society and earned a living. It had and always will house too many unprepared and immature young people who are full of energy and curiosity. What made the 1960s so different was the fact that never before had there been so many students at so many colleges at the same time, segregated from the mainstream society of work and responsibility.

Not surprisingly, traditional efforts to overregulate students and to prevent them from expressing political views, especially in a democratic society, were doomed to failure. The trouble at Berkeley started when the administration banned the card tables students had set up at the corner of Bancroft and Telegraph to solicit funds for political causes. Although the tables were outside campus property, the administration believed that the sight of unkempt and bearded radicals marred the image of a respectable academic institution. There was also considerable pressure from local conservatives, especially from William Knowland, former U.S. senator and owner of the *Oakland Tribune*, to do something about radical students. The ban turned out to be a dreadful mistake. Coming shortly after the beginning of the fall term and without having been discussed with student representatives, the ban was immediately defied by student activists, some of whom had recently been involved in civil rights protests in the South. Throughout September 1964 students and administrators played push and shove, with the students steadily escalating the conflict. From disseminating literature on a strip of sidewalk just in front of Sather Gate, the main campus gate, the student activists moved their tables to Sproul Plaza inside the campus; and when the administration tried to disband them, the students conducted demonstrations and sit-ins. On October 1, Jack Weinberg, a graduate student in mathematics and a veteran of Mississippi Freedom Summer, set up a table full of political literature and was arrested by a police officer for distributing political literature on campus property. Weinberg's supporters surrounded the police car and prevented the officers from taking him away by employing the sit-in tactics of the civil rights movement. Over a hundred students simply sat down and held the police at bay, using the roof of the police car as a podium to denounce the baffled and vacillating authorities. Apart from sitting in the back of the police car for thirty-two hours and later stating "Don't trust anyone over thirty," Weinberg played a minor role in the events that subsequently unfolded. The real leader of what would become known as the Free Speech movement (FSM) emerged during this sit-down when a tall, lanky and intense philosophy student, Mario Savio, took off his shoes, mounted the police car, and fired up the crowd with incendiary rhetoric. The battle was now joined: the self-righteous Savio steadily forced Clark Kerr and a divided Berkeley administration, headed by the ineffectual chancellor Edward Strong, into a tug-of-war that would lead to a humiliating defeat for the university.

Mario Savio was an angry and defiant young man who came from Catholic Italian-American working-class background. He had attended Queens College in New York and transferred to Berkeley when his parents decided to relocate to California. In the summer of 1964, Savio served in the civil rights movement in McComb, Mississippi, teaching black children. His experiences in the South strongly influenced his actions at Berkeley, for in his mind the students at Berkeley were essentially waging the same civil rights struggles as blacks were in the South. The comparison, of course, was spurious because Berkeley students had little, if anything, in common with oppressed black people in the South. Nor was Savio's inflammatory rhetoric any more accurate when he compared Berkeley administrators to Nazis and policemen to war criminals like Adolf Eichmann. The young philosophy student, weaned on Marxian doctrines of alienation, even went so far as to denounce the university as a "knowledge factory" so odious that students were justified in bringing its operations to a standstill:

> There is a time when the operation of the machine becomes so odious, makes you so sick at heart, that you can't take part; you can't even passively take part, and you've got to put your bodies upon the gears and upon the wheels, upon the levers, upon all the apparatus and you've got to make it stop and you've got to indicate to the people who run it, to the people who own it, that unless you're free, the machine will be prevented from working at all.[24]

Savio's overwrought rhetoric was quite off the mark. Clark Kerr was not a faceless fascist functionary but a mild left liberal with strong Quaker convictions. He was always negotiating between extremes for half a loaf, but the students always wanted the whole loaf. If Kerr was well meaning, he was also a dithering academic—all brains and no balls, as Savio maliciously remarked. One is tempted to follow Freud in arguing that what was at the heart of the conflict between Kerr the university surrogate father and Savio the radical son was a struggle for power with definite sexual overtones. Perhaps the same can be said of radical sons at other schools who wanted to cut off the balls of their fathers and assume control. The boomers envied their fathers for having had balls in fighting World War II; they were sick and tired of hearing about the glorious exploits at Iwo Jima or the beaches of Normandy. As Savio put it, "I'm tired of reading history. Now I want to make it."[25]

If Berkeley administrators had possessed a sense of humor and understood the needs and motivations of their students better than they knew their own careerist self-interests, they could have easily diffused the crisis. More enlightened judgment, backed up by firm discipline, could have prevented the crisis that quickly got out of control, spread to other institutions, and left American institutions of higher learning in a much weaker position than they had been before. The students, as it would turn out, played a cat-and-mouse game with the administration and unfolded a pattern of provocations that would be repeated elsewhere. The game was essentially as follows: students staged mass protests over some alleged grievance, administrators alternately overreacted or called for compromise; then both sides, pressured by irate politicians or extreme radicals, made reasonable compromise impossible. The small extremist minority among the students would try to create violent incidents in the hopes of radicalizing the majority. The administration often fell into the trap, overreacted with inappropriate, sometimes harsh measures, and eventually gave in to student demands.

The Berkeley Free Speech movement saw all of these steps in action. Although the faculty eventually voted to place no restrictions on free speech or student advocacy, the more militant students, forever trying to enmesh the majority of students, always discovered new grievances, putting steady pressure on increasingly addled administrators. In retrospect, there is much to be learned from the Berkeley case. The vast majority of Berkeley students were not radical at all; only a small minority of about fifty students were hard-core radicals—that is, communists, New Left socialists, or anarchists.[26] Savio had been a member of both SNCC and the Young People's Socialist League; Jackie Goldberg, a red-diaper baby, was an active communist, and so was her brother Art Goldberg, who described himself as a "Commiejewbeatnik"; Bettina Aptheker, daughter of the communist theoretician Herbert Aptheker, proposed a plan for the Free Speech movement that was based on communist popular front organizations of the 1930s; Sydney Stapleton was active in the local Young Socialist Alliance, a Trotskyite organization; Suzanne Goldberg, who married Mario Savio, was a New Left radical; Barbara Garson, who became famous for her political satire *MacBird* in which she accused Lyndon Johnson of the assassination of John F. Kennedy, was a member of the Young Socialist Alliance; Michael Rossman, a mathematics graduate student came from an Old Left family and called himself a red-diaper baby.

The left-wing orientation of the core FSM leaders was widely known; even Clark Kerr, in a much criticized public comment, referred to the FSM leaders as "Red."[27] This smacked of McCarthy red-baiting, but the political right in the 1960s was still paranoid about communist influences in American academia and elsewhere. The Berkeley radicals, however, were not Old Leftists, but more independent-minded "New Leftists," who saw themselves as democratic socialists with a humanistic vision.

Except for Savio, their most important leaders were the children of Jewish parents who had themselves been active politically in the prewar period. They had been reared in families where education was highly prized and social issues were eagerly debated. The fact that they spoke up, challenged authority, and argued contentiously, actually commended them to their professors, who saw in them hope for the future. Given their interest in social change, it is not surprising that most radical students majored in liberal arts or social sciences. Of the 733 student protesters who were arrested in the December 1964 Berkeley sit-in, none majored in business; most of them studied English, history, and philosophy.[28]

By the time of the Berkeley upheavals these radical students generally encountered a friendly and congenial home in humanities or social science departments. As a result of a far more diverse student population in the postwar period, there was a real change of the guard in academia. The old conservative, white, Anglo-Saxon and Protestant professors were gradually losing control to a more ethnically and ideologically diverse group of committed activists. For every faculty member who retired in 1966, Kenneth Heineman pointed out, five young, mostly radicalized professors replaced them.[29] At Berkeley and other elite universities many professors sympathized with student grievances, particularly the antiwar crusade. One of the most significant changes in higher education was, therefore, a decided political shift to the left and a corresponding effort to redefine the role of the university in American life and culture. The Berkeley upheavals signaled the death knell for the traditional ideal of the university as a haven from the winds of contentious social strife, a place where students could join with professors in forming a learning community in which objective truth could be pursued and discovered. The motto of the University of California, after all, is "let there be light" rather than "let there be heat." This old fashioned ideal may never have been closely approximated, but lip-service to it had been *de rigueur*. The younger professors, now tenured, envisioned quite a different environment, a "dissenting academy" one in which the university was no longer treated as a handmaiden to society, training experts to run the corporate machine, but as an agent for social change.[30]

The Berkeley case also illustrates that the emerging activists among the faculty had little practical understanding of social change nor much appreciation of the attitudes of ordinary taxpaying citizens, who did not see the same reality and chose to elect a conservative governor, Ronald Reagan, who clipped the wings of the unruly bird by slashing its budget and threatening it with "law and order." Although Reagan fired Kerr, the troubles at Berkeley would continue throughout the sixties, mutating from free speech to filthy speech and portentous revolutionary rhetoric. Berkeley would also serve as a beacon for radicals throughout the nation, some of whom came down the Ho Chi Minh Trail from Berkeley.[31]

4. From Protest to "Revolutionary Action"

The New Left came away from the Berkeley Free Speech movement with two firm beliefs: first, that there was a strong constituency to be recruited by stimulating student grievances, and second, that the university as an institution was ideally suited to serve as a catalyst for radical change. It was under the tenure of Carl Oglesby, president of SDS from 1965 to 1966, that the New Left moved beyond protest and reform to "revolutionary action."[32] Unlike most SDS activists, Oglesby came from a blue-collar background; he was the son of a South Carolina sharecropper who had moved to Akron, Ohio, to work in a rubber factory. Oglesby had gone to college in the 1950s, married, and fathered three children. After working for Bendix Aerospace Corporation in Ann Arbor, Michigan, as a technical writer, he became attracted to the allure of the counterculture and to radical political causes. He left his wife and children to do his own thing, which was to pull the New Left in a more radical direction. Under his one-year tenure, Oglesby helped create a Radical Education Project within SDS, a kind of research bureau setting firm ideological positions that could serve as a *point d'appui* for the growing number of SDS chapters throughout the nation. Between 1963 and 1965, SDS had grown from 23 to 125 chapters.[33] The Free Speech movement was one reason for its growth, but what really invigorated it was the war in Vietnam. In April 1965 SDS sponsored a national student march on Washington that attracted some twenty thousand students and catapulted SDS to national prominence. After the April march hundreds of campuses across the nation witnessed "teach-ins" or public forums in which professors and students denounced the Vietnam War. New waves of demonstrations, often spearheaded by SDS, hit the nation in the fall of 1965. The Berkeley Vietnam Day Committee, organized by Jerry Rubin and Professor Stephen Smale, staged demonstrations against the war in May and October, accompanied by efforts to disrupt troop trains in Oakland.

At a large protest rally against the war in November 1965, Oglesby blamed the war on American liberals, who, he claimed, had sold out to the corporate elite that was profiting from it. Oglesby praised the Vietcong leadership as a role model for would-be revolutionary leaders, and he also cast an adoring glance at other third world radicals, chiefly Fidel Castro and Che Guevara.

By 1966, SDS increasingly insinuated itself into the antiwar "carrier" movement, sponsoring protests in cooperation with other antiwar organizations. The war, as previously mentioned, brought together a broad, fluctuating, loose coalition of protesters from different political and philosophical positions, including religious pacifists, liberals, and a host of left-wing groups such as the Du Bois Clubs, the Young Socialist Alliance, the May 2nd Movement, the old socialist left, and the Communist Party. The Young Socialist Alliance was a Trotskyite student organization, the Du Bois Clubs were offshoots of the communist party, and the May 2nd Movement was sponsored by the Maoist Progressive Labor Party. A rage against the war was one of the few common bonds that could bring these splinter groups together. They all despised the war, opposed the draft, and wanted to revolutionize American society in their own image.

In May 1966, General Lewis Hershey, director of the Selective Service System, announced that students would no longer receive automatic draft deferments but would be judged for eligibility by their class standing (grades) or by their performance on a new Selective Service Qualification Test. The response from students as well as professors was predictable and almost immediate. The level of anxiety about being drafted had already risen sharply when Lyndon Johnson escalated the war in 1965. Students had counted on their automatic deferments, and the sudden threat of being sent to Vietnam galvanized them all over the nation in what can only be described as a frenzy of anger and moral outrage. Professors and administrators worried about giving the Selective Service System access to university records and letting the government use campus facilities to administer the Selective Service Qualification Test. Some professors had ethical qualms in giving low grades to male students out of fear that they might be responsible or coresponsible for their deaths in an unjust war. Sit-ins almost immediately erupted at dozens of universities, including Chicago, City College of New York, Wisconsin, Oberlin, and others. SDS advised its chapters to pressure campus administrators not to comply with the Selective Service. By hook or by crook, students from all sides of the political spectrum, including the conservative Young Americans for Freedom, opposed induction and did their best to find loopholes to evade it.

Just about the time the antiwar and antidraft protests gave SDS a strong momentum, the students made a fateful tactical move. At an SDS Convention in June 1965 at Kewadin, Michigan, the old guard lost overall control to less disciplined newcomers, many of whom had streamed into SDS after the antiwar march on Washington. Instead of being run by an intellectual elite from America's premier universities, SDS was to be run according to syndicalist lines without ties to its original founders. SDS chapters were to be autonomous on the local level and organize students along trade union lines, concentrating primarily on issues of local concern and relevance.[34] What was relevant to all students was gaining, maintaining, and expanding student power. Building on the Berkeley experience, the Young Turks just coming into SDS wanted to attract as many uncommitted students into the movement with the promise that they would be empowered to shape their own education. In practice, this meant breaking down the paternalistic, authoritarian wall of the corporate university and demanding a coequal, if not primary, share in university governance. Specifically, SDS activists demanded an end to all *in loco parentis* rules, the abolition of grades, smaller and more "relevant" classes, evaluation of professors, severing ties with military recruiters or defense-related corporations, and so forth. Conspicuously absent among such demands were higher entrance requirements, tighter standards, longer class hours, and more assignments.

In order to implement the new "student power" tactics, SDS formed teams of traveling organizers who were to assist local chapters in electing SDS candidates to student offices. By the fall of 1966 such strategies were being implemented at various campuses across the nation. SDS candidates, advocating student power, won elections for student body presidents and other student offices. Although grassroots organizing on the local level was consistent with what the students called participatory democracy, in practice it spelled fragmentation to the movement as a whole. Regional autonomy undermined party centralism and encouraged sectarian bickering and grandstanding. What held the movement together at this point were issues outside the academy—issues over which the students had little control such as the war in Vietnam, university ties to the government, the direction of the two-party system, and civil unrest in the nation's urban centers.

The students, however, imagined that they had genuine influence and potential control over these larger national issues. It was an illusion of control amounting almost to a fervent belief; and when that belief was tested by the hard reality of power, many radical students responded with ever more frantic, disruptive, and violent behavior. They turned from reformism to revolution. In December 1966 Berkeley once more took the lead in staging a massive sit-in after radical students were expelled from the Student Union when they tried to set up tables next to Navy recruiting tables. This issue of ties to the government and to war-related industries would play a prominent role at many campuses over the next three years. One month after the Berkeley sit-in, students at Brown protested the presence of Dow Chemical representatives on campus, accusing them of war crimes in the manufacturing of napalm and other chemical weapons of mass destruction. In the spring of 1967 protests against CIA recruiters erupted on many campuses, followed in the fall by militant anti-Dow protests.

Using the tactics of the civil rights movement, the students became increasingly more belligerent and intolerant. SDS delegates to the 1965 national convention, drunk with the illusion of power, had earlier proclaimed, "We have slogans which take the place of thought: 'There's a change gonna come' is our substitution for social theory. . . . What sociology, what psychology, what history do we need to know the answers?"[35] Unlike the more disciplined minds of the older guard, the new militants already knew all the answers and therefore did not need to listen to other views, let alone the other side. The left at Wisconsin, for example, had made it quite clear in 1966 that the right to free speech did not extend to anyone who supported Lyndon Johnson's side.[36] Government supporters were shouted down or prevented from speaking at many campuses. Harvard SDS militants ambushed Secretary McNamara's car and let him depart only after a lengthy session of cursing and jeering.

The year 1967 witnessed, among other events, the long hot summer of urban riots and militant black nationalism. Here again, radical students exploited these violent events. In 1967 SDS leaders became enamoured of black power radicals such as Stokely Carmichael, Eldridge Cleaver, H. "Rap" Brown, Huey Newton, and Bobby Seale. Pilgrimages to the holy lands of the Left—China, Vietnam, Cuba, Russia— became *de rigueur*. At one time or another, most New Left radicals journeyed to the communist holy places and returned, as Todd Gitlin later reported, with an exhilarated sense of rejuvenation, a kind of "NLF high."[37] They rationalized consorting with the enemy by saying that they "needed to feel that someone, somewhere in the world was fighting the good fight and winning."[38] What this meant was that the enemy was not communism but U.S. imperialism. In July 1965 a delegation of ten U.S. women met with high-ranking North Vietnamese women in Indonesia. During Christmas 1965 Tom Hayden, Professor Staughton Lynd of Yale, and communist theoretician Herbert Aptheker went on a "diplomatic trip" to Vietnam. In September 1967 Tom Hayden and the peace activist David Dellinger traveled to Bratislava, then in communist Czechoslovakia, to attend a meeting with high-ranking North Vietnamese delegates. Later Hayden and Rennie Davis went to Hanoi; Todd Gitlin went to Cuba; and in 1972 Jane Fonda, forever a brash publicity hound, went to Hanoi and consorted with the enemy by denouncing U.S. imperialism. Pictures showed the young actress sitting behind an antiaircraft artillery piece with its cross-sight and barrel pointed at the sky, where her nation's planes were expected to swoop down and attack a poor and defenseless country. She capped this photo-op by broadcasting from Hanoi radio denouncing the United States for wanton aggression, destruction, and violation of international agreements. Later in 1972 Fonda married Tom Hayden, symbolizing the close partnership between the radical left and fellow travelers in the entertainment industry.

The proliferating causes on the political left also enmeshed students in the political arena. Since 1966 SDS had been supporting "New Politics" candidates espousing radical ideas outside the two-party system. In September 1967 white leftists, including members of SDS, explored the possibility of forming a coalition with black militants by arranging a conference at the Palmer House in Chicago. Billed as a "New Politics Conference" more than two thousand delegates, representing two hundred organizations, met to discuss the formation of a radical third party that would challenge Lyndon Johnson in the 1968 election. The conference failed miserably because militant blacks, though representing only 15 percent of the delegates, demanded half of the convention votes. Thuggish behavior rather than reasonable discussion were the order of the day. H. Rap Brown refused to address the white delegates, the comedian Dick Gregory denounced Zionism, and SNCC members booed Martin Luther King's keynote address, chanting "Kill Whitey! Kill Whitey!"[39] The Palmer Conference proved, if proof was needed by late 1967, that a united left, black and white, was impossible, given the racial divisions between the bickering sectarian white left and the black militants. SDS elder Rennie Davis justified the shambles of Chicago by arguing that SDS was a movement with very different needs from those of the black radicals. But what were the needs of radical white students? To remain students within the castle walls of the university and fling insults at middle-class America and at the university itself? And what alliances had the students forged with groups in American society? Blue-collar workers showed no sympathy for the radicals, and SDS wrote the workers off as rednecks. Black militants went their own way, and so increasingly did feminists and other minority groups. Nor did SDS bother to make common bonds with their age peers in uniform, instead treating them with contempt and calling them baby killers and fascists.

5. Students at War with the Establishment

The big explosion of student protests, many of them instigated by the New Left, occurred in 1968, spilled over into 1969 following the election of Richard Nixon, and tapered off by the end of 1970. Student protest followed in the wake of domestic and international crises in 1968: the Tet Offensive in January, the announcement by Lyndon Johnson in March that he would not run for reelection, the assassination of

Martin Luther King in April, the assassination of Robert F. Kennedy in June, the chaos surrounding the Democratic Convention in Chicago in August, and the election of Richard Nixon in November. Between January and June 1968 the National Student Association counted 221 major demonstrations at 101 campuses, involving nearly 40,000 students.[40] SDS leaders at Columbia University provided the catalyst for the 1968 protests. The leader of the Columbia "revolutionary action" was Mark Rudd, an immature and arrogant young man with a penchant for street theater and publicity. Rudd came from upper-middle-class Jewish parents and enrolled at Columbia in 1966. By 1968 he had been picked to lead the SDS chapter at Columbia. Inspired by Marxist-Leninist philosophy and great admiration for Castro's Cuba, which he had visited for several weeks, Rudd wanted to "bring the war home" by stopping the wheels of the odious machinery at Columbia University. Although Rudd was not an anarchist, he greatly admired an outlandish New York group of anarchists who called themselves "Up the Wall, Motherfuckers." The group's reputation rested on trashing property, ridiculing liberals, and staging outrageous spectacles. Rudd had taken a page from the "Motherfuckers" when he hit a Selective Service official with a pie, an act that was warmly applauded by his followers and brought him to the attention of the ever news-hungry New York media.[41]

Columbia University was one of the most liberal institutions in American academia; its administrators and professors were overwhelmingly progressive on social issues and adamantly opposed to the war in Vietnam. The university, however, had pursued several policies the students strongly opposed, including severe limitations on student participation in academic governance, strong ties with the Pentagon through the Institute for Defense Analysis (IDA), a consortium of leading universities doing work for the government, and the university's decision to build a gymnasium in Morningside Park—the border between Harlem and the campus—without consulting the people living in Harlem, thousands of whom (blacks and Puerto Ricans) would be displaced by the new building.[42] Provoking a crisis over these issues, Rudd and his militant followers began a week-long seizure of buildings (April 23–30) during which Rudd confronted Grayson Kirk, the president of the university, saying, "Up the Wall, motherfucker, this is a stick-up."[43] The occupation, however, did not go well. The first building occupied by SDS and black militants from the Afro-American Society on campus was Hamilton Hall, where the black activists held three university officials hostage. The black militants, renaming the building Malcolm X Hall, then decided to expel the white SDS members from the building and demanded that the university abandon the Morningside project. In this demand the black students had strong support from Harlem officials, from black nationalists such as H. Rap Brown and Stokely Carmichael, and from New York intellectuals such as Susan Sontag, Norman Mailer, and Dwight McDonald. Mayor John Lindsay of New York was horrified by the prospect of a race riot, temporized with the black militants, and eventually got Columbia to abandon its building plans.

In the meantime, white SDS students expelled from Hamilton Hall proceeded to "liberate" Low Library, where they put up posters of Che, Lenin, and Malcolm X. When the police tried to clear Hamilton Hall, dozens of militant professors intervened and blocked the entrances. Kirk backed down and more buildings were occupied. Mathematics Hall was taken over by the "Motherfuckers." Oblivious to the serious consequences of their illegal actions, most students decided to have plenty of dope, sex, and music. The Grateful Dead and the folk singer Pete Seeger arrived and provided free concerts. Tom Hayden and Dwight McDonald also came to lend a helping hand. At Fayerweather Hall two students were married while others broke into faculty offices and destroyed the research work of politically incorrect professors. Mark Rudd and his cronies made themselves at home in Kirk's office, drinking his sherry, smoking his cigars, and rifling through his private papers.

The theatrical antics of the sit-in protests, especially as they were reported by the media, conveyed the false impression that the majority of students at Columbia supported the radical students. On the contrary, most students supported the efforts of Young Americans for Freedom to oust the protesters because they were disrupting the educational process and had no right to do so. The will of the majority of students also opposed SDS demands to ban Dow Chemical from the campus. The disruptive students left the university administration no choice but to put an end to the siege but there was considerable soul-searching about the way this should be done. Mayor Lindsay, fearing a black riot, negotiated a peaceful withdrawal of the African American students who had occupied Hamilton Hall. The radical white students, however, faced the wrath of the New York City police, whose blue-collar officers, enraged by the behavior of snooty and privileged college kids, decided to attack brutally and indiscriminately, further polarizing the campus community. When it was over, the university closed its doors early for the spring term. A minority of radical students had managed to bring a great university to its knees. The Columbia case, according to William O'Neill, was a sign of an "advanced national pathology,"[44] partly because it was allowed to happen so easily, partly because professors and leading intellectuals had pandered to the students by justifying their actions when they should have told them in no uncertain terms that a great university should be cherished rather than destroyed. In fairness to Herbert Marcuse, who went to Columbia to reason with the students, the German-Jewish professor showed respect for learning by telling the students that universities are worthwhile institutions of higher learning that needed to be reformed rather than wrecked. The students failed to appreciate his comments. They thought that they were making history and changing the world. As one exhilarated student later said: "we had done something that nobody else had done, and, who knows, maybe we we were going to *make the revolution* at Columbia. . . . Everybody believed that this university would never be the same, that society would be irrevocably changed, that there'd be a revolution in the United States within five years, and a whole new social order."[45]

All too many faculty members encouraged their students to believe in their own fantasies. Some administrators also pandered to the students, as did the New York intelligentsia, who cheered them on and praised them for their fun-loving revolutionary behavior. The literary critic Dwight McDonald, recapturing his old radical youth, showered praise on the students and reveled in the "joyous excitement" of the Columbia revolt. Many liberal critics felt that Grayson Kirk deserved what he got.

The playwright Eric Bentley dismissed Kirk as an out-of-touch old fogey who did not have a clue what students were really like since he had not spoken to anyone under thirty since he was under thirty.[46] Even today some academic historians sympathize with the radical students at Columbia, arguing that "Columbia was an appropriate target for student activism," that Kirk's administration was "repressive," and that most students sympathized with the radicals, except for some conservatives who were "mostly composed of athletes, fraternity men, business, or engineering majors."[47] Even if this were true, it would mean that a sizable number of students resisted the radicals.

The relative ease with which radical students had intimidated both faculty and administrators at Columbia was taken as proof positive that physical and verbal intimidation, combined with sit-ins, occupations of buildings, boycotts, and even the taking of hostages, was the most effective method of cowing pliable administrators into submission. What the students only gradually seemed to recognize was that universities are either publicly funded or privately endowed and are administered by Boards of Trustees who have an obligation to maintain an academic environment that fosters intellectual growth, free inquiry, unhampered research, and collegiality. Radical students were undermining these essential conditions of academic freedom, and faculty and staff acted more like willows than oak trees in bending to the prevailing winds.

By 1968, however, adult Americans were becoming sick and tired of student radicals, just as they were disgusted by the antics of hippies and war protesters. The country was polarizing itself to the breaking point, and there seemed no end in sight to the growing turmoil on campuses and on the streets of America. Radical students continued to fish in these troubled waters, pushing the movement into ever more confrontational and violent directions. Columbia was one more nail in the coffin for moderate liberalism, a belief system that radical students despised even more than conservatism on the right.

After Columbia, the dadaists on the countercultural left hatched a plan to wreck the Democratic Convention scheduled for the summer in Chicago. The brains behind the plans to subvert the convention were Jerry Rubin and Abbie Hoffman, two demented pranksters who took nothing seriously except nihilism. While high on drugs and alcohol on New Year's Day, the two subversive anarchists founded a new protest movement called Youth International Party, or Yippie, a party that would combine countercultural street theater with anarchist tactics.[48] Both Rubin and Hoffman had already built up long resumes of outlandish pranks and provocations designed to attract media attention. They delighted in using foul language and staging surreal "happenings." Their aim, they announced, was to convince people that they "should fuck all the time, anytime, whomever they want."[49] This preoccupation with fornication, of course, was a major concern of most radicals; their writings and subsequent autobiographical accounts abound in stories about loveless and infantile sexual misadventures. This was particularly true of male radicals, who were driven by their libido and largely regarded their women as sex objects. Many radical women either became complicit in such male-dominated sexuality or tried to usurp male roles by playacting fantasies of queen bees, Amazons, or women warriors who fought and loved side by side with their male heroes.

As shown in the previous chapter, the riots that wrecked the Democratic Convention in the summer of 1968 were blamed at the time on Mayor Daley's out-of-control police force. The fact is that long before the convention convened, Hoffman, Rubin, and dozens of SDS leaders had made it abundantly clear that they planned to go to Chicago to bait Daley's rednecks and force them into a violent confrontation on the streets of Chicago, with the ultimate aim of disrupting the Democratic Convention. Rubin and Hoffman saw themselves as stoned-out warriors of the Age of Aquarius, blending pot and politics and engaging in a theater of the absurd. In the winter of 1967 Hoffman had written to a friend that he expected at least 100,000 out of the expected 250,000 people who planned to attend the convention to be protesters who could be used to disrupt and subvert the convention.[50] Hoffman was living in a radical cuckoo land fantasizing about 100,000 radical protesters. Fewer than 10,000 actually showed up, but those 10,000 protesters, as we have seen, were enough to engage the police in such violent street battles that the American people were horrified by what they saw, horrified not so much by the actions of the police as by the actions of long-haired, bearded hippies and foul-mouthed radicals.

In retrospect, it appears that the radicals spent months in planting rumors, inuendos, and vague threats. They freely boasted that they would bring Chicago to its knees, putting LSD in the city's water supply, unleashing female hippies to seduce delegates, dressing up as Vietcong guerrillas, and so forth. No one could be sure whether this was just the politics of the put-on or whether it was deliberately inciting a riot. The Yippie provocateurs, the evidence suggests, clearly planned on stepping over the line from freedom to license and proudly proclaimed that free speech meant "the right to shout 'theater' in a crowded fire."[51] When later called to account for causing a riot, they alternatively whined and then managed to turn the trial into a theater of the absurd. It proved the Yippie proverb: "Don't grow up. Growing up means *giving up your dream.*"

The fact was that hippies, Yippies, radicals, and later yuppies, like Peter Pan, simply did not want to grow up and purposely prolonged their rootless adolescence out of fear that adult America would put an end to their fantasies and ego gratifications. In later years many former hippies or radicals refused to take responsibility for their actions and blamed the failure of the 1960s on Nixon, the radical right, Christian fundamentalists, and the military-industrial complex, proving that primary narcissism is incapable of honest self-reflection and objective insight.

It was not just the hippies or Yippies who planned to make a shambles of the Convention but also hard-core SDS members and assorted fringe groups on the left. They came not to support Democratic delegates but to sabotage the convention by staging disruptive demonstrations. Before going to Chicago, Tom Hayden and other SDS leaders had traveled to Czechoslovakia to meet with North Vietnamese communists and discuss ways and means of undermining the U.S. war effort. After returning refreshed from his experience in Bratislava, Hayden delivered a public threat to the Democrats by promising them that SDS would go to Chicago to "vomit on [Hubert Humphrey's] politics of joy."[52] He later added: "Let us make sure that if blood is going to flow, let it flow all over the city."[53] The radical faction within SDS, later known as the Weather Underground, or the Weathermen, had already puffed itself up psychologically at a June SDS convention by releasing an overwrought manifesto in which it threatened a political Armageddon in the form of urban guerrilla warfare. The Chicago police force and federal intelligence services were on tenterhooks, afraid of facing a potential disaster. Those who had read the underground papers picked up the same alarming message: Chicago was not going to be a festival of peace, love, and music.[54]

As soon as the Democratic Convention convened trouble began. About ten thousand hard-core protesters lined up to follow Hayden, Davis, Rubin, and Hoffman into a staged melodrama. Mayor Daley, an old-fashioned trade unionist and machine politician, wanted to show off his city in the best possible light and made it clear that he was not going to tolerate "hoodlums and communists" in Chicago. Daley was easy to bait: he was rotund, generally amiable, but also thin-skinned, a ward politician of the old Democratic Party whom the radicals had come to despise as a symbol of everything that was wrong with the Democratic Party. When Daley got wind of what the radicals were up to he gave his police force carte blanche to stop the protesters dead in their tracks if they engaged in illegal actions. But this was exactly what hard-core radicals and colorful hippies had come to Chicago for: to disrupt the convention and cause bedlam. What now began to unfold was part street action and part orchestrated incitement to violence. Rubin and a contingent of Yippies went to the city's Civic Center and nominated a pig called Pigasus for president. The squealing little pig ran on a "garbage platform" with the slogan "Why take half a hog when you can have the whole hog." Then things got more serious. Armed with helmets and improvised gas masks made of bandanas soaked in petroleum jelly, thousands of crazed protesters chanted obscene epithets at the police: "pigs", "cocksuckers," "motherfuckers," "fascists," taunting the police beyond the limits of the endurable and succeeding on several occasions in provoking the police into violent reaction. The protesters also succeeded in drawing innocent bystanders into the ensuing melee between them and the police. Their calculations about mass media involvement were also shrewd and accurate. The press reacted predictably and one-sidedly in condemning the police as out-of-control fascists beating innocent youngsters and bystanders to a bloody pulp. The images on TV showed Daley's cops completely out of control, which was one-sided and out of context; but there was enough truth to the charge that the Chicago police force had overreacted harshly and violently. All too many policemen had had enough and had decided to riot against the rioters. If the radicals shouted obscenities at the police, Daley's cops freely responded by excoriating the protesters and bystanders, including the press, with vile phrases such as "Kill the Commies," "Let's get those bastards," "*Newsweek* fuckers," and so forth. Tear gas permeated the convention site and tempers flared on the convention floor, where Mayor Daley glared in anger at accusing politicians and probing cameras.

The rioters had in many ways succeeded in raining on Hubert Humphrey's parade and befouling his nomination. As previously shown, it was a Pyrrhic victory for

Humphrey; his party was in total shambles. People asked how Humphrey could possibly restore law and order in America when he was unable to control his own party or maintain order at the convention. In retrospect the images of a war-torn Chicago were quite deceptive and exaggerated. Even Jerry Rubin said later that the violence in Chicago was primarily symbolic. Rubin prided himself on having scripted a superb street theater about America beating up its own children. The police, he said, obliged and played their part in the melodrama. He added defensively that compared to the violence abroad it wasn't such a big deal: "there were no permanent injuries, there were no deaths. People were clubbed, but the stitches healed."[55]

As the nation prepared for the fall 1968 election, students continued to stage protests at numerous colleges and universities. Protests were particularly intense at the State University of New York at Buffalo and at Kent State University in Ohio. At the University of Wisconsin student radicals fire-bombed South Hall, which housed the state headquarters of the Selective Service System. Students also disrupted speeches delivered by Richard Nixon and Hubert Humphrey, the Republican and Democratic candidates for the presidency. The 1968 campaign, however, clearly foreshadowed the coming conservative reaction to the violent demonstrations of the 1960s. This was particularly evident in the third-party candidacy of George Wallace, the feisty reactionary governor of Alabama who took his right-wing campaign to the fertile soil of blue-collar northern industrial states. Even among the students, especially right-wing YAF students, there was open opposition to some of the disruptive antics of the left. YAF staged counter sit-ins at the regional headquarters of SDS in New York and at headquarters of MOBE (the Mobilization Committee to End the War in Vietnam). They also picketed the Boston headquarters of a draft resistance movement, where they hoisted a South Vietnamese flag. At Purdue University, where there was little sympathy for disruptive demonstrations, YAF faced down SDS over the issue of CIA recruitment on campus. The students at Purdue actually mirrored the national mood far more accurately than the more radically inclined campuses. A Harris poll of September 1968 revealed that 80 percent of the American people believed that law and order had broken down in American society. The majority of white respondents blamed students, blacks, and antiwar Democrats for the violence. Clearly a conservative reaction was under way, and Nixon's victory in November confirmed it.

6. Revolutionary Terrorism and the Conservative Reaction

The election of Richard Nixon sent the hard-core radicals into a frenzy of violent actions. The first six months of 1969 witnessed nine thousand separate protests across the nation, including antiwar and antigovernment activities inside and outside the nation's colleges and universities.[56] SDS radicals had convinced themselves at this point that blowing up buildings was an effective and morally justifiable means of waging guerrilla war in America. Columbia SDS member Jane Alpert, seeing herself as a fearless Amazon, initiated a series of bombings against corporate-military buildings to express her rage against the repressive Nixon regime. Alpert came from an affluent Jewish family from Forest Hills, New York, and received her undergraduate degree from Swarthmore. One of her intellectual role models was Ayn Rand, the radical libertarian novelist and political pundit. Although Alpert rejected Rand's free-market ideas, she accepted her belief, expressed by the chief protagonist in her novel *Fountainhead*, that blowing up buildings was a legitimate means of expressing social protest.

Blowing up buildings or burning them to the ground preoccupied the nation's attention in February 1970 when radical students burned down the Bank of America in Isla Vista, a student community situated next to the University of California at Santa Barbara.[57] The violent events that unfolded at Santa Barbara serve as a convenient summary of violent student protests during the stormy 1960s. UC Santa Barbara had passed through all the various crises that afflicted institutions of higher learning during the sixties: explosive growth and overcrowding, antidraft demonstrations, protests and sit-ins against Dow chemical, threats and demands by black militants, seizure of the student center and establishment of a New Free University, and the bombing of the Faculty Club resulting in the death of a janitor. The university reeled from one crisis to another, some centered on purely local frustrations, others connected to the hysterical climate of the late 1960s, particularly the Vietnam War and the radicalization of civil rights by African American and Hispanic students.

Many UC Santa Barbara students lived in a student community called Isla Vista, located next to the university campus. This apparently idyllic community by the Pacific Ocean was actually a dense and overcrowded housing community that was badly served by the university and the county of Santa Barbara. Students had complained for years about landlord neglect and gouging, lack of municipal services and amenities, and benign neglect by university authorities. On campus, students steadily protested the war and searched for a catalyst to escalate their demands. The spark was provided by an unremarkable but popular anthropology professor, William Allen, who was denied tenure for lack of publications and for his countercultural approach to the classroom, which consisted of political harangues and easy grading practices. During the Allen controversy a radical Student Union had come into being that fueled the conflict and led to a series of violent demonstrations that had to be broken up by the police. The faculty refused to give in to student demands that the hiring and promotion of professors require student consent. The majority of the faculty insisted that faculty hiring, promotion, and firing should continue to reside in the hands of the faculty.[58]

On February 25, 1970, William Kunstler, the civil rights advocate and one of the defense attorneys for the Chicago 8, gave a speech in the campus stadium in which he denounced universities for destroying young minds and police forces for cracking their heads with night sticks. Resistance to police violence, he insinuated, was justified when those who resisted were fighting for civil rights. He then called on the students to go to the streets and protest. This is exactly what the students did after the speech. In fact, they went one better on Kunstler by rioting in the streets of Isla Vista. They overturned a police car and set it on fire and chased the small police contingent out of Isla Vista altogether, lustily chanting: "We have the pigs on the run."[59] In control of Isla Vista until the early morning of February 26, the students used this opportunity to burn down the Bank of America because it allegedly was a symbol of corporate oppression. The Bank of America, in point of fact, had been a generous supporter of student financial needs, providing loans to thousands of students and carrying their low-yielding checking and savings accounts. The bank burning set off several days of street warfare. The police often acted brutally and indiscriminately by breaking down apartment doors and roughing up students. Tear gas blanketed the community. The Bank of America was not cowed by the violence, and corporate headquarters decided to remain in Isla Vista by putting up a temporary trailer next to the charred remains of the old bank. When radical students decided to burn the trailer down, too, moderate students intervened before it could be firebombed. One of the defending moderate students, Kevin Moran, was shot when a policeman's rifle accidentally discharged. Moran died of massive bleeding on the scene.

For about a week, Isla Vista became a national media event that caused further hyperinflated rhetoric on all sides. Governor Ronald Reagan, who flew to Santa Barbara shortly after the bank burning, called the radicals "cowardly little bums," and suggested that outside agitators were responsible for the violence and destruction. Reagan was actually right: outside agitators like Kunstler had been partly responsible, and they continued to fuel the fire. When the university turned down Jerry Rubin as a guest speaker, his wife came in his place and proclaimed, among other things, that "property is theft." Stew Albert, a Berkeley radical who appeared with her, told the students to rip off the pigs (police).

When it was all over, about a thousand students had been arrested, but only a few activists were imprisoned. Many students were radicalized by their arrests or mistreatments, parents were shocked, politicians outraged, and professors shook their heads. It had been a surreal American melodrama, consisting of staged protests in which students battled police while sirens screamed, helicopters flew overhead, and tear gas was unleashed. The real victims were the serious students who wanted to learn.

The UC Santa Barbara upheavals came at the tail end of white student radicalism, because SDS had already imploded as a result of irreparable splits in 1969. By the spring of 1970 the bickering factions within SDS had destroyed the overall effectiveness of the student organization. One faction was the Progressive Labor (PL) group, a disciplined revolutionary cadre of committed communists, though for public purposes they concealed their communist pedigree. PL had been trying for some time to purge SDS by expelling undisciplined and fuzzy-minded countercultural types from the organization. A real revolution, the group insisted, could not be launched by undisciplined students who enjoyed playing revolution but really preferred sex, dope, and rock 'n' roll, with a bit of insurrectionary violence sandwiched in between. Furthermore, PL warned against bombing buildings and advised students to build bridges to white working people.

A second SDS faction was the Revolutionary Youth Movement I, called the Weather Underground, or the Weathermen. The name Weathermen came from the lyrics of a song by Bob Dylan: "You don't need a Weatherman to know which way the wind blows." The Weathermen faction was led by James Mellon, Mark Rudd, Bernardine Dohrn, Jeff Jones, Bill Ayers, Diana Oughton, Kathy Boudin, and Cathy Wilkerson. Undoubtedly the most interesting of the group was Bernardine Dohrn, who fancied herself a revolutionary Amazon.[60] Dohrn came from a modest middle-class family of mixed religious background. Her mother was a Christian Scientist and her father was Jewish credit manager in a furniture store in Whitefish Bay, Wisconsin. While in high school, Dohrn's father changed the family name from Ohrnstein to Dohrn because he wanted to avoid being accused by his customers of "Jewing" them out of their money.[61] Dohrn attended Miami University of Ohio, where she tried to get into one of the most exclusive sororities but was rejected because of her father's Jewish background. She then transferred to the University of Chicago in her junior year. This change of academic location sharpened her social awareness of inequality and racial discrimination. She participated in SDS community action programs and worked for Martin Luther King's SCLC to end segregation in northern suburbs. After completing both a bachelor's degree and a master's degree at Chicago, she enrolled in the school's law school and received her law degree in 1967. Dohrn was pretty, bright, and remarkably self-assertive, making full use of her sexual attraction to men. She often dressed in leather miniskirts, knee-high boots, black jackets, and tops adorned with political buttons proclaiming "Cunnilingus is Cool, Fellatio is Fun," managing to turn more than just radical male heads. David Horowitz and Peter Collier, in their retrospective on the destructive generation of the 1960s, described her as "somewhat of a radical pin-up during the years she scourged the nation for its racism at home and genocide abroad and warned that she and her comrades were 'crazy motherfuckers' dedicated to scaring the shit out of honky America." This kind of provocative language, designed to slap white middle-class America in the face, was very much a hallmark of Bernardine Dohrn. Despite three University of Chicago degrees, there was little intellectual substance in what she said or the way she said it. Shock value always trumped intellectual depth among the fringe elements of SDS. After Chicago, Dohrn moved to New York to work for the National Lawyers Guild, where she was active in draft resistance and was subsequently elected SDS national secretary, impressing initially skeptical activists when she took a firm stand by saying "I consider myself a revolutionary communist."[62]

Dohrn and her compatriots in the Revolutionary Youth Movement I called themselves revolutionary communists of the third world Marxist variety. They admired the Vietcong, Castro, and communist revolutionaries in Africa. The United States, in their minds, was an evil nation because it was inherently racist and imperialistic. Reforming American society, they believed, was like putting a Band-Aid on cancer. Only revolutionary change could redeem the nation's claim that it was a beacon to freedom and social equality. All middle-class values were simply expressions of full-blown bourgeois hypocrisy and decadence. Shocking the bourgeoisie was a favorite tactic of these radicals, especially in matters of sexuality, family values, drugs, or personal expression. The RYM-I favored "smashing monogamy" through enforced gay and straight group sex. One is tempted to speculate that this is how the group released its nihilistic energy, showering contempt on their privileged upbringing, and when their revolutionary fantasies were not fulfilled, throwing violent temper tantrums. Whatever the psychological reason for such behavior, these children of privilege were making a remarkable statement of defiance against their parents, schools, social institutions, and their country as a whole.

The third splinter group within the SDS was the Revolutionary Youth Movement II, which differed from RYM-I in little more than leadership. The group was led by Berkeley SDS member Bob Avakian, who admired Mao and wrote for the Black Panther newspaper, and by Mike Klonsky, another Californian who served as SDS national secretary. Both Avakian and Klonsky championed the cause of the proletariat as well as that of third world people. The RYM-II favored social disruptions but did not endorse bombing or assassinations. Avakian later founded the Maoist Revolutionary Communist Party, while Klonsky developed a rival communist group that followed Marxist-Leninist ideology and practice.

At a national convention held at the gloomy Chicago Coliseum in June 1969, all these factions, joined by representatives of the Black Panthers, gathered in a raucous free-for-all over the control of SDS. It was at this convention that the revolutionary Weathermen came officially into being and promptly purged SDS by expelling Progressive Labor. The coup was led by Bernardine Dohrn, who shrewdly recognized that her faction might be outvoted by the others (PL and RYM-II), called for a recess, and then took the rostrum, flanked by Rudd and Terry Robbins, and boldly announced that PL was expelled from SDS. Followed by her entourage, Dohrn marched out of the hall and proceeded to SDS headquarters, seizing its papers and assets. The Weathermen claimed that they now were SDS; so much for participatory democracy. The Weathermen also cut themselves loose from RYM-II, calling that group revisionist "running dogs." Richard Flacks, one of the original founders of SDS, could not believe what had happened to his organization, saying that SDS had turned into the very opposite of what its founders had intended:

> SDS had begun with the intention of avoiding dogma, doctrine, top-down discipline, factional warfare, and sectarian style and language. Its purpose was to create the basis for a left that could appeal broadly to the American people. By its final convention in 1969, SDS had not only fallen prey to all the supposed failures of the Old Left, it had become an incredible caricature of its worst excesses. Monolithic, slogan-chanting factions met in open combat over obscure points of dogma, beyond any hope of intelligibility.[63]

The new line was "revolutionary action," what nineteenth-century anarchists called "Propaganda by the Deed"—that is, the use of terror as a means of bringing down the system. The group's first violent action occurred in October 1969 in Chicago. Some five hundred Weathermen gathered in Chicago to teach the city a lesson for what it had done in August 1968 to the protesters at the Democratic National Convention. Dohrn's group had fortified itself by ingesting huge quantities of drugs and by arming itself with guns, pipes, knives, and so forth. They had also talked themselves into revolutionary wishful thinking that was oblivious to reality. A veil of unreality surrounded the group. Solidarity was reinforced by group sex and smashing monogamy on the grounds that sexual exclusivity promoted inequality. The motto was "People who fuck together stay together."[64] Male and female cadres were instructed "to make it with their own sex." Dohrn, however, held herself aloof from these sexual orgies; she was the queen bee who selected her own lovers, invariably the strongest leaders. One saying had it that "Bernardine's cunt goes wherever the power is."[65]

Not surprisingly, the four "Days of Rage" were a miserable failure. Although the Weathermen went into battle with the Chicago police force on several occasions, the disheveled horde of revolutionaries was easily subdued, though not before they had caused considerable damage to downtown Chicago businesses. In the end they were little more than juvenile delinquents, held in contempt not only by ordinary working people but also by the vast majority of American students, many of whom agreed with the common sentiment circulating on college campuses that "You don't need a rectal thermometer to know who the assholes are."

At a three-day "war council" in December 1969, the Weathermen decided to continue the armed struggle against corporate "Amerika." Dohrn exhorted the members present to be less wimpy and to move like heroic Black Panthers. She also commended the example of Charles Manson and his women groupies for the gruesome blood orgies in the Tate-LaBianca slayings. In a particularly vile comment, Dohrn said: "Dig it. First they killed those pigs, then they ate dinner in the same room with them, they even shoved a fork into a victim's stomach. Wild!" She held up three fingers in a Manson "fork salute."[66] The group later went to the nave of a Catholic church for group sex or "wargasms."

Hounded by the law, these outlaw revolutionaries then went underground and staged a series of bombings, which caused more public anxiety than it did serious damage. Major damage was self-inflicted. In March 1970 an accidental explosion devastated a New York townhouse that had been used by the Weathermen as a bomb factory. Three of the members—Ted Gold, Terry Robbins, and Diana Oughton—were torn to pieces by the bomb that accidentally detonated, while Kathy Boudin and Cathy Wilkerson miraculously survived, fleeing half-naked from the rubble. Living by their wits, along with generous financial help from radical lawyers, wealthy families and friends, the Weathermen gradually faded from the scene in the 1970s. All of them were eventually caught or gave themselves up, writing their self-serving autobiographies and becoming professors, social workers, private detectives, carpenters, or experts on meditation and stress.

In summarizing the destruction of SDS, one is tempted to place it in the larger cyclical development of student movements as a whole, which usually begin with euphoric expectations and end up in the depth of despair. In eight years, William O'Neill has pointed out, the New Left recapitulated practically the whole history of American radicalism before it decomposed into squabbling and self-defeating sects.[67] From open-minded and nonsectarian groups committed to participatory democracy, the New Left moved to conspiratorial cells of violent revolutionaries. What had happened to participatory democracy, love, peace, and brotherhood? The answer is that it was taken over by the lunatic fringe that was more interested in dope, sex, and violent action. As O'Neill has pointed out, one cannot make a successful revolution out of hedonistic self-indulgence and immature temper tantrums. There was the additional fact that the New Left was student-centered and inherently, if not always consciously, elitist. The students found no viable constituency outside their own narrow circle of student radicals. Even the proposed alliance with the Black Panthers came to nothing. In the end, there were only small sectarian terrorists that lashed out feebly and ineffectively against mainstream society.

Radical students had set themselves totally unrealistic goals, and they pursued them with self-righteous intensity. As one of them later admitted, "We were awash in the purity of the we-versus-them feeling on the streets,"[68] but "the fact was that we were living in a bubble, talking to ourselves, reading texts drawn from nineteenth century Germany or turn-of-the-century Russia."[69] Their perception that the American power structure, especially in comparison with other powers in the world, was inherently evil was also deeply flawed. If anything, the American power structure was inconsistently liberal, muddled, and ineffective. Perhaps one of the most flawed perceptions was a kind of autointoxication about what radicals called "the movement," a metaphor used by other past revolutionary movements, including the Nazi movement (*Bewegung*) of the 1930s. For radicals the term "movement" implied that those who joined it would be swept progressively forward by some mighty stream. Joining the movement was like getting on a freeway from different on-ramps such as student protests, civil rights, antiwar demonstrations, and so forth. Once being on the moving freeway, one would join millions in this mighty stream toward social and personal perfectibility. Movement was everything. Fixity or planning could wait. Radicals defined themselves in revolutionary and heroic action. What ultimately counted was collective action: sit-ins, be-ins, boot-ins, demonstrations, happenings, street theaters—all of them producing the illusion of social change, heightened, of course, by drug-induced euphoria.

7. Black Student Militancy

The unraveling of SDS did not spell the end of student upheavals in the late 1960s. Student protests continued because there was no end in sight to the Vietnam War and to the draft that dangled over the heads of young Americans. The fallout of the civil rights movement was also spreading to college campuses in the form of militant black nationalism. The vast majority of American institutions of higher learning had been almost exclusively white until the late 1960s. Minority students, especially black students, had been generally excluded from higher education either because of racial discrimination or lack of financial opportunities. This traditional pattern of restricting black students to underfunded black schools and universities was beginning to change when the Johnson administration tried, through "affirmative action" policies, to attract historically unrepresented blacks to the nation's white universities. Affirmative action as originally conceived simply meant recruiting qualified black students and giving them preferential treatment over similarly qualified white applicants in order to redress historical inequities. The policy of affirmative action, in essence, allowed skin color to be one of the criteria of admission to higher education, and thus it was bound to aggravate the tensions between black and white people in America. In practice, affirmative action became a quota system that often excluded white candidates who were as qualified as or more qualified than black applicants. Over time Johnson's innocuous policy of rectifying past racial injustices blossomed into a big government program of racial categorizing, racial preferences, racial entitlements, and racial sensitivity policies. These programs were conceived with the best of intentions, but in the hands of zealous advocates they would drive additional racial tensions and animosities into the already splintered social system of American society.

One immediate outcome of these liberal social policies was heightened tensions on American college campuses. All too many academically unprepared black students, feeling themselves empowered by the civil rights movement, arrived at major universities and found themselves uncomfortably marginalized by the prevailing white culture, with its inconsistent, annoying, and even infuriating attitudes of condescension and patronization. Although white students, faculty, and administrators did their best to welcome and accommodate black students, the tensions were palpable from the beginning. Out of a combination of self-defense and self-assertiveness, many black students formed black student unions and lobbied for black studies programs, the hiring of more black professors, and segregated facilities. When administrators voiced objections, claiming that one could not create new fields of study out of whole cloth or hire Ivy-League trained black professors overnight, the students bristled with resentment and increasingly staged disruptive activities that threatened the educational process at major American universities. According to one historian's estimate, black militancy comprised 59 percent of the 232 protests during the first six months of 1969, though most of these protests did not result in violence or property destruction.[70]

Three of the most disruptive demonstrations by black militants between 1969 and 1970 occurred at San Francisco State, Cornell, and Yale. San Francisco State was one of the larger state colleges in California's three-tier system of higher education: the top UC campuses, admitting the best high school graduates (12 percent), the less select state and polytechnic colleges, and the growing community colleges, operating on the basis of open and tuition-free admissions. The California master plan on which this educational division was based was envied throughout the nation for its overall excellence and inclusivity. By the late 1960s, however, the master plan was encountering financial, administrative, and educational challenges, not least of which was a conservative counterreaction against disruptive student activities on all educational levels. San Francisco State, one of the more innovative universities, was experiencing an influx of militant black students in the late 1960s who, supported by the New Left and other radical organizations on campus, demanded an independent black studies program, open and tuition-free admissions for blacks, and the hiring of twelve black professors acceptable to the students to teach in the black studies department.[71] As elsewhere in the nation, black militant students, threatening to resort to disruptive activities, demanded immediate action on their grievances because, as they put it, they were sick and tired of receiving a "white-washed" education. Barricading themselves behind the rhetoric of civil rights, they intimidated educators into believing that the tactics that had been employed against racial injustices in the South were equally justifiable against liberal-minded universities. All too many professors and administrators accepted this false extension of civil disobedience into the educational process. This led to a further and even more troubling confusion, namely, that civil disobedience leading to disruptive mob action was morally acceptable, but that resistance to such mob action by the authorities was immoral. In other words, students naively assumed that they could bring the educational process to a standstill with impunity, and when force was used to stop them from wrecking the university, they whined, grandstanded, and condemned what they called the mindless violence committed against them. Yet these tactics worked wonderfully well against liberal administrators, especially when threats were delivered by black students because the majority of white professors and administrators regarded black students as victims rather than ordinary students who should be treated like every other kind of student. San Francisco State quickly gave in to the Black Student Union's demand to establish a black studies program and promised to lower, but not waive, admissions standards for black students.

It was not very long before this black studies department became a hotbed of black militancy under the leadership of its chairman, Nathan Hare, who followed his radical students in confusing education with propaganda. The situation quickly spun out of control, with the Western Association of Schools and Colleges (WASC) the western regional accreditation organization, notifying San Francisco State that its accreditation might be withdrawn unless the school set its house in order. That house had actually been on fire since November 1968 when the radical students, black and white, had called a strike against the university. By January the strike turned ugly when black militants carrying arms on campus, threatened Professor John Bunzel, a political science professor and former aide to Robert F. Kennedy, by disrupting his lectures with obscenities and by planting a bomb outside his office.[72] Although Bunzel was not hurt, black militants beat up other "white racists," including the editor of the student newspaper because he had written a mildly critical piece on the boxer Muhammad Ali. The strike continued for over four months, and students who continued to attend class had to run the gauntlet every day while the radicals called them scabs, showered them with obscenities, and even roughed them up. Outsiders fed the chaos, as they always did in the 1960s, for as soon as demonstrations erupted anywhere, the usual agitators seemed to materialize almost immediately, e.g., Stokely Carmichael, H. Rap Brown, Eldridge Cleaver, Tom Hayden, and Todd Gitlin. President Robert R. Smith resigned and was replaced by the conservative semanticist S. I. Hayakawa, a feisty, independent-minded and combative scholar with strong academic credentials but no administrative experience. Nathan Hare was fired, but continued to stoke the fires of revolt from the sidelines. Hayakawa declared a state of emergency and prohibited campus demonstrations. When students defied his orders, he brought the police on the campus and had 450 students and a number of professors arrested and subsequently suspended from the university. Hayakawa also announced that students could not give speeches on campus using microphones. When that rule was also defied, Hayakawa donned his favorite Tam o' Shanter, marched out of his office, mounted the truck carrying the protesters' microphone, and ripped out the wires connected to the amplifier. The press photo showing Hayakawa's encounter with student protesters was widely applauded by ordinary Americans who were sick and tired of obnoxious students. Ronald Reagan purportedly remarked, "I think we have our man."[73] Although Hayakawa became an instant popular hero and later went into politics, the strike and the violence continued until both sides were exhausted and decided to negotiate. Hayakawa compromised by agreeing to expand the black studies program; waive admissions requirements for "third world" students, chiefly black, Latino, and Indian; and hire a black fiscal expert to oversee the programs and resources pertaining to black students. In return for these concessions, the university refused to drop the charges that had been brought against the protesters during the strike and also fired twenty-four professors who had participated in the demonstrations.

Apart from leaving bitter divisions on the campus, the strike at San Francisco State stimulated a sympathy strike at Berkeley and other schools. Across the bay from San Francisco State at Berkeley, radical third world students joined by SDS militants set fire to Wheeler Auditorium and blocked Sather Gate, one of the main entrances to UC Berkeley. From Berkeley, the turmoil spread to America's heartland—Kansas State University—where black militants tried to emulate their West Coast brothers by bringing the campus to its knees. Kansas State, however, was not a radicalized campus situated in a cosmopolitan liberal environment. Without a radical constituency, the militants were decisively rebuffed by a strong administration and faculty, though not before managing to firebomb Nichols Gymnasium and harassing the authorities, chanting, among other things, "San Francisco State, here we come."[74]

The most abject surrender to black radicals came at Cornell University, one of the most prestigious Ivy League schools in America.[75] Shortly after James Perkins had been appointed president of Cornell University in 1963, he formed a committee that was to recruit black students whose SAT scores were lower than those of white students admitted to Cornell. When Perkins became president, Cornell had 11,000 students; only 25 of these were black. These 25 students were easily assimilated into the mainstream, but by 1969, when the number of black students had risen to 225, Cornell, like many other universities, was confronted with a different, a far more intransigent type of black student.[76] In April 1969 many of the black students who had been recruited by Perkins from inner-city ghettos, denounced the university as a racist institution and demanded an autonomous black studies department and separate facilities. Perkins had already approved lower admissions requirements, the development of an Afro-American Society, and separate living quarters; but black demands steadily outran Perkins's ability to satisfy them. He had also given black students an assurance that the university would build a black center and establish a black studies program. The students, however, argued that this did not go far enough in the direction of black autonomy. What they wanted and demanded was a separate black degree-granting college within the university. This demand took the form of an ultimatum, which Perkins, the ever accommodating liberal, did not reject outright as a racist demand but was willing to consider seriously, though confessing that "it would involve a lot of rearranging of [his] own personality."[77] As events would reveal, that rearrangement proceeded quite satisfactorily under threats and intimidations. A Center for Afro-American Studies was established and a twenty-eight-year-old graduate student in sociology from Northwestern University was appointed to supervise it. For the first course in the program on "black ideology," a SNCC organizer without a bachelor's degree was hired to teach it. The faculty members who had hired the SNCC organizer justified their choice by admitting that it was done under pressure from the Afro-American Society, that they would never do it again, and that they did it to strengthen the hands of the moderate black students on campus.

These "moderates," however, quickly went berserk on the campus, setting fire to buildings, harassing teachers, students, and professors, trashing the library, and even grabbing Perkins and pulling him from a podium while at the same time chasing off the campus police chief, who had come to his aid. The "moderates" then crowned their radical actions by deliberately burning a cross on the lawn of a black women's dormitory, using this staged incident as an excuse for bringing guns on campus and essentially taking over the university.[78] Led by Thomas W. Jones, who would later become president of TIAA-CREF (the world's largest pension fund for college teachers),[79] the radicals barricaded themselves in a building and threatened to do worse if their demands were not met. Predictably, Perkins and the administration caved in and signed the surrender terms. TV cameras recorded the drama of rifle-toting militants, draped in ammunition belts, signing Perkins's surrender document in the presence of vice president Steven Muller.

The faculty toed the line just as easily, especially after Thomas Jones had gone on radio and threatened that "Cornell has only three hours to live," unless it accepted the surrender terms. Dissenting professors who did not accede to the demands would be "dealt with." The professors did not need much prodding. As Allan Bloom, then a philosophy professor at Cornell, pointed out: "a few students discovered that pompous teachers who catechized them about academic freedom could, with a little shove, be made into dancing bears."[80] We might add, "crocodile-tear" dancing bears, as illustrated by the dean of the College of Arts, who publicly confessed that he, like all white professors, was an institutional racist. Allan Bloom, who later left Cornell in disgust, said of James Perkins that he was always more interested in protecting himself and avoiding confrontations at all cost or giving in to the other side. He was made of the sort of moral stamp, Bloom said, that the appeasers in 1939 were made of, blaming Poland for starting World War II by resisting Hitler's invasion.[81] The irony was that Perkins and many liberal professors had made a career out of saying that German professors had acted cowardly in face of the violations of academic freedom under the Nazis, but now that the shoe was on the other foot, they looked distinctly like hypocrites. Perkins eventually had to resign but only after negative publicity compelled the Board of Trustees to ask for his resignation. As Walter Berns, who also left Cornell, said,

Perkins left his mark not only on Cornell but on American academia in general. By surrendering to students armed with guns he made it easier for those who came after him to surrender to students armed only with epithets ("racists," "sexists," "elitists," "homophobes"); by inaugurating a black studies program, Perkins paved the way for Latino studies programs, women's studies programs, and multicultural studies programs; by failing to support a professor's freedom to teach, he paved the way for speech codes and political correctness; and of course he pioneered the practice of affirmative action admissions and hiring.[82]

In the spring of 1970 Yale University, located in New Haven, Connecticut, became the center of media attention when twenty-one Black Panthers were being tried for killing a black radical, Alex Rackley, whom the Panthers mistook for an FBI informant. Rackley's corpse had been fished out of the Coginchaug River some twenty-five miles north of New Haven. The body was covered with bruises, cigarette burns, and wounds inflicted by an ice-pick.[83] Black and white militants, convinced that the Panthers were innocent, swore to wreck the trial of Bobby Seale, the head of the Panthers, who had allegedly ordered the execution of Rackley. The trouble began when the home of the New Haven judge who presided over the trial was bombed by Terry Robbins, one of the radical Weathermen. As previously mentioned, Robbins blew himself up accidentally just shortly afterwards in a New York townhouse. These violent events, however, did not prevent the trial from moving forward, though the judge further angered the militants when he jailed two Black Panthers who were sitting in the visitor's section for contempt of court for their disruptive behavior.

New Haven was only one focus of attention; the other was Yale University and its radical constituency among its administrators, faculty, and students.[84] The consensus of the politicized members of the Yale community—and that included President Kingman Brewster—was that the Panthers could not receive a fair trial in New Haven. President Brewster, in fact, made a statement to the press saying, "I am skeptical of the ability of black revolutionaries to achieve a fair trial anywhere in the U.S.,"[85] an opinion also echoed by William Sloane Coffin Jr., the university chaplain and widely known peace activist. Brewster and Coffin were hardly alone in their opposition to the Panther trial. The students felt the same way, especially those who were attending Yale Law School. One such law student who strongly supported the Panthers was Hillary Rodham, future wife of President Bill Clinton, who was also supportive of the Panthers. By the late 1960s Yale Law School harbored some of the more radical students on campus.

According to Judge Robert Bork, who was then a professor of law at Yale, the radicals had turned the Law School into an intellectual and pedagogical shambles.[86] Some professors openly sided with the radical students, the result being that turmoil was the order of the day in the form of strikes, arson in university buildings, classroom disruptions, rejection of rationality as a reactionary bourgeois practice, and harassment of students and professors who disagreed with the radicals. Judge Bork also points out that the ferocity of radical protest was proportional to the presence of mass media on campus.[87] The fervor of these radicals in the Yale Law School can still be gauged by reading the incendiary articles written for the student law journal called *Yale Review of Law and Social Action*. Among the journal's editors and contributors one can find some of America's future leaders such as Hillary Clinton, Robert Reich, and Mickey Kantor. One can also find interesting illustrations that depict the police as pigs and the Panthers as heroic freedom fighters who decapitate the heads of the pigs and leave their bleeding heads rolling in the sand. Roger Kimball has referred to these radical shenanigans as the "infantilizing of the American intelligentsia."[88]

This infantilizing was made easier by the threats and intimidations coming from the Black Panthers, who warned that "If Bobby dies, Yale fries." At one point the black Law School Union "summoned" the law professors to appear before them at the faculty lounge for some tongue-lashing, which some professors found morally uplifting, while others found it offensive and repulsive. President Brewster, the ever-accommodating appeaser, aggravated the already volatile atmosphere at Yale by inviting both the Panthers and SDS to a May Day protest rally, which was to involve a peaceful march from the campus to the New Haven courthouse.[89] Brewster's invitation, which involved an offer of free meals and lodging, attracted a large crowd of Panthers and their white supporters to Yale. To show their solidarity, the student senate voted to authorize a campus-wide strike in support of the Panthers. President Brewster thought that this was an excellent idea and recommended it for faculty approval. Some professors, however, were outraged that a university would involve itself so directly in a legal and political issue that was none of its concern. In good Orwellian language Brewster then slightly modified the statement supporting the strike by changing the phrase "suspension of normal academic function" to "modification of normal expectation." The proposal that faculty "should suspend their classes" was modified to read "should be free to suspend their classes."[90] These modifications were then overwhelmingly passed by a faculty that appeared oblivious to the possibility that it was compromising the neutrality of the university in response to radical intimidation. It was a recipe for trouble. The presence of thousands of radicals on campus, including the usual outside agitators, virtually guaranteed violent activities. Abbie Hoffman and Jerry Rubin lent their hands by staging a little street theater, chanting, "Fuck Brewster! Fuck Nixon!" William Kunstler, a classmate and friend of Brewster, hurried to Yale to speak at a Panther fundraiser. Tom Hayden called on the activists to act like real revolutionaries, which they did by bombing the Yale hockey rink and later blaming right-wing fascists for having done it. That opinion was seconded by Brewster who blamed right-wing extremists, a surprising judgment, according to Robert Bork, since no one knew of any right-wing terrorists being anywhere near New Haven or New England.[91] It was a sign of those bizarre times that many students and faculty assumed axiomatically that the police, prosecutors, and courts were evil.

Throughout the mayhem that led up to and included the May Day rally of 1970, few people were sensible enough to raise the real issue at hand, namely, that a man had been murdered and that the crime was most likely committed by the Black Panthers. As the *New York Times* commented in an editorial, "those students and faculty members at Yale who are trying to stop a murder trial by calling a strike against the university have plunged the campus into new depths of irrationality."[92] Fortunately for Yale, the May Day demonstration did not erupt into major violence, for the faculty, students, and the New Haven city police saw to it that the campus did not go up in flames. Classes resumed on Monday May 4, 1969. Kingman Brewster deserves no credit for his actions, and the judgment by one historian that he helped prevent liberals from turning into radicals through his appeasement methods is as empty as it is erroneous. By accommodating radicalism and just plain irrationality, Brewster had sacrificed academic integrity to the threat of violence. Such were the consequences of a great liberal university lending its reputation in support of illiberal thugs who had absolutely no commitment to learning and truth.

As to the Black Panthers who were tried in New Haven, the jury convicted one Panther of conspiracy to murder, two others pleaded guilty, and the jury deadlocked as to the charges of the others. Ericka Huggins, who boiled the water that was used to torture Rackley, was later elected to a California school board, while Warren Kimbro, who confessed to shooting Rackley in the head, won an affirmative action scholarship to Harvard and later became an assistant dean at Eastern Connecticut State College.[93]

Black militancy, followed by feminist, Latino, Indian, Asian, and gay-lesbian activism, continued to erupt periodically in the 1970s and after, but the powerful wave of student protests that had been fueled by civil rights and antiwar protests ran its course by the early 1970s. The passionate zeal that had animated civil rights burned itself out after the movement veered away from peaceful integration to black nationalism and separatism, while the furor of the antiwar protests died down after the Cambodian invasion and the tragedy at Kent State University. University students quickly lost interest in Vietnam after Nixon steadily reduced American troops in Vietnam and introduced a draft lottery that greatly diminished student anxieties about their draft status in any given year. Almost overnight, the majority of American college students switched from antiwar fervor to either stoic acceptance of their draft status or a collective sigh of relief for those who drew high lottery numbers and were thus assured of avoiding military service altogether.

8. The Student Right

Since the student left caused the greatest turmoil on U.S. campuses in the 1960s, historians have usually overlooked an important student movement on the other side of the political fence—the conservative Young Americans for Freedom (YAF).[94] The movement had its origin in the cold war atmosphere of the 1950s. In December 1959, Douglas Caddy, a student at Georgetown University and David Franke, a student at nearby George Washington University, established a student committee in support of loyalty oaths for all National Defense Education Loan recipients. Both Caddy and Franke were members of the Conservative Intercollegiate Studies Institute; both were also associated with Young Republicans, serving as catalysts for a stronger organizational framework that could unite young conservatives.

In September 1960 over one hundred delegates from forty-four colleges met at the family estate of William F. Buckley in Sharon, Connecticut. By that time Buckley had become a prominent spokesman for conservative causes. His book *God and Man at Yale* (1951) had explored a pervasive secularism and liberal bias at Yale, especially among the faculty—so much so, that Christian conservatives got the distinct feeling that their beliefs were not really wanted in the academy. Buckley used his charm, quick wit, and considerable forensic abilities to great effect in the public arena. His television program, *Firing Line*, was immensely popular, entertaining, and informative, often featuring exciting debates and interviews with prominent intellectuals on all sides of the political spectrum. In hosting the student meeting at his estate, Buckley threw his considerable weight behind the fledgling student group.

Just like the student left, which coincidentally also came into being in 1960, the conservative student right produced a mission statement called the Sharon Statement. The conservative students strongly committed themselves to what they called "eternal truths," including the belief in free will, political freedom, a strong national defense, and a free market economy. They singled out communism as the greatest threat to freedom and rejected the idea of peaceful coexistence in favor of defeating communism. There were some minor squabbles among the delegates relating to the insertion of the word "God" in the document, which proved objectionable to some libertarian advocates, and there was also considerable debate about the name of the new organization and the age limit on admission. At the time the ceiling on age was thirty-five, later extended to thirty-nine years.

One major difference between conservatives and members of the New Left was that the conservative students maintained a greater degree of continuity with the beliefs and mores of their parents. This was due, in large part, to the fact that the conservative students came from privileged backgrounds in the sense that their social pedigrees were traditional upper middle class, white, and Protestant. YAF was entirely white, and its values were a reflection of parental beliefs. Both parents and students despised Franklin Roosevelt because in their eyes he had undermined capitalism and fathered the welfare state. Both admired and read the books of Friedrich Hayek, Ludwig von Mises, Milton Friedman, Russell Kirk, Richard Weaver, and Barry Goldwater. Their favorite publications were Buckley's *National Review*, the *American Mercury*, the *Wall Street Journal*, and *Modern Age*. If conservative students had an intellectual hero it was the novelist and literary pundit Ayn Rand. Her unabashed libertarianism, anticommunism, and elitism held out immense appeal. The political hero of young conservatives was the independent-minded and outspoken senator from Arizona, Barry Goldwater, whose 1964 presidential campaign became a crucial event for young conservatives, who worked enthusiastically for the Goldwater campaign. They liked his anticommunist rhetoric, his focus on traditional American values of family, hard work, and success, and his challenge of the "Eastern Establishment." When Goldwater lost in 1964, YAF backed Nixon and later Ronald Reagan. Reagan would later become for Republicans what FDR had been for Democrats.

Although conservative students generally experienced only mild generational conflicts, they often displayed more opposition to their own peers either on the left or in the counterculture. Hippies were perceived as nasty, unpleasant, self-indulgent and self-destructive. YAF members accepted the 1950s popular culture as main-stream and therefore desirable. One YAF student, commenting on the 1960s, had this to say:

> It was a generally unpleasant time.... I thought the music was nasty; I thought people were nasty. They dressed horribly ... it was a time I'm glad is gone. I see no romance in it.... I loved the early sixties, you know, the Beach Boys, that sort of time.... But I was totally turned off [by the counterculture]. .... The potheads and this sort of thing I found a waste.[95]

The libertarian wing of YAF, however, empathized with some hippie values and lifestyles because they promoted individual freedom and hostility toward institutions. In reviewing the countercultural movie *Easy Rider*, the YAF monthly magazine, the *New Guard*, printed both pro and con opinions of the movie, with the traditionalists trashing it as subversive and corrupting, the libertarians praising it for its courageous stand on individual liberty and the right to be different in America. The libertarian wing of YAF also supported the legalization of prostitution, pornography, and narcotics, convictions which they shared with the vast majority of the counterculture.

Clearly both libertarians and traditionalists were greatly worried about their country, and they were not oblivious to the injustices still existing in it. Though opposed to both the New Left and the counterculture, students on the right also shared some common beliefs and lifestyles with their peers. Love of rock 'n' roll was common to all young people, and so was suspicion of authority, support for decentralized government, community control, and individual freedom. What accentuated the conflicts between student right and student left were profound differences over the role and function of government and the allocation of resources. Conservative students perceived the left as an assortment of subversive radicals who wanted to undermine the very foundation of America as a Christian, capitalist, and democratic nation, while left-wing students saw the conservatives as an assortment of white, privileged and reactionary fools wanting to maintain the status quo. Both sides talked past each other and polarized themselves more sharply than previous generations. They would ultimately extend this intragenerational split into the future.

By the mid 1960s, YAF had a membership of 20,000 and 250 chapters across the nation's campuses; in 1970 those numbers had doubled.[96] Furthermore, young conservatives had strong support from leading politicians and media celebrities—Ronald Reagan, Strom Thurmond, John Wayne, and William F. Buckley Jr. Although represented on the nation's campuses, the conservatives did not enjoy the media coverage given to their more disruptive peers on the left, whose antics resonated with the ever-hungry and sensationalistic press. Moreover, rather than engage in noisy demonstrations, YAF preferred to wage literary battles or launch legal challenges. This is not to say that YAF did not demonstrate on the nation's campuses, but their protests were almost always in reaction to SDS demonstrations. This pattern can be seen as early as the Free Speech movement at Berkeley, when YAF withdrew from the escalating demonstrations on December 2, 1964. In response to the FSM, conservatives at Berkeley organized University Students for Law and Order, condemning the disruptive demonstrations against the university and recommending legal rather than illegal actions. Flyers condemned FSM radicals for confusing means and ends, asking: "What victory will be gained by the destruction of our university?"[97] Later in the decade, when SDS protests proliferated, YAF staged some dramatic counter actions, especially at the University of Minnesota, Washington State University, and Purdue.

Despite having a small core constituency on many campuses, the student left far outnumbered the student right at almost any protest demonstration. YAF admitted that they were simply overwhelmed, marginalized, and ridiculed. One student conservative complained later, "You hear so much about the left in the sixties. You rarely hear much about the youngsters in the conservative movement then. There were thousands, thousands across the country on campuses all over. We never got the publicity and we weren't interested in that. . . . we were out canvassing the precincts, trying to identify young conservatives to run in the Republican precinct campaigns."[98] A law student at Harvard said, "We were regarded as being totally Neanderthal,"[99] while another student sadly remarked, "the word conservative was a curse word, almost like standing up and saying 'I'm an alcoholic.'"[100]

There are several obvious reasons why conservative students received so little publicity and support in the 1960s. In the first place, the sixties, following on the heels of the conservative and conformist 1950s, were a decade of liberal experimentation and radical protests. Conservatives were out of season and out of power, but that is not always a disadvantage. The liberal consensus was shattered in 1968, and so was the whole New Left movement, which was in utter ruin. In the meantime, conservatives had time to take stock of the shambles left by their adversaries. The majority of the American people were not enamored with the antics of the New Left and the outrageous behavior of hippies. As the conservative counterreaction set in, YAF would put as important a stamp on the future as did their counterparts on the Left. Many leaders of YAF would later go on to shape the New Right, including Howard Phillips, Richard Viguerie, and Connie Marshner. Many Reagan appointees were recruited from former YAF members; the same is true of conservative groups and foundations today.

Although SDS and YAF appeared to be polar opposites, they were in some way, as Rebecca Klatch reminds us, very much alike because they were both suspicious of authority and government control. Both groups were strongly committed to individual freedom, decentralization of power, and community control.[101] If SDS left an indelible mark on the 1960s, YAF made its voice heard in the 1980s and 1990s under President Ronald Reagan and President George Bush. Both groups shared the high degree of political zeal and arrogance so typical of the baby boom generation, but they also demonstrated that their political commitments were ill-defined and murky, resulting in internal fissures and open splits. Just as SDS splintered in the late 1960s, so did YAF. At the 1969 YAF convention an open split occurred between the social conservatives and the libertarians over social issues, the draft, and the Vietnam War. It was at this convention that social conservatives, including the movement's mentor, William F. Buckley Jr., gasped when the radical libertarian Dave Schumacher publicly burned his draft card.

9. Coda

Student protests in the 1960s attached themselves to two great carrier movements: the civil rights movement and the antiwar crusade. As these movements changed from peaceful to violent protests, so did the student contingents that participated in them. Moreover, student impatience and immaturity fueled additional irrational upheavals in American higher education, disruptions that went far beyond free speech or civil rights. The Free Speech movement, for example, had little to do with free speech but everything to do with student power.

Radical students wanted to wrest power from administrators, professors, and boards of trustees, but not by using the democratic process; they believed that they could get their way through mass demonstrations and intimidations rather than reasoned discussion or political action in the civil domain. All too many professors supported the students without being aware of the real stakes involved. Radicalized professors, wittingly or unwittingly, did not mind commiting academic treason by dumbing down the curriculum, assisting in the creation of dubious new programs and disciplines, undermining academic integrity by involving students in the evaluation of teachers, and using the university as an agent of social change.

The notion that professors should dedicate themselves to the ideal of agitating for political or social change in the academy is incompatible with the Western ideal of dispassionate and objective scholarship. The university, of course, was never a cloister in modern times, but that it should be transformed into a partisan instrument of political change runs counter to the ideal expected of the university. George Kennan warned that radical efforts of politicizing the university invited the establishment of one-dimensional and closed orthodoxies in higher education just as they did in the political arena.[102] The idea of a free forum of ideas was one of the noblest contribution of modern liberalism, and it is for this reason that it should have been defended against extremists on all sides of the political spectrum.

The so-called Free Speech movement set a terrible precedent because mass demonstrations short-circuited the democratic process, encouraging the notion that threats and intimidations were justifiable against a liberal institution. Berkeley was not the Deep South, and Clark Kerr was not Sheriff Bull Connor. It took an academic outsider, Ayn Rand, to point out this absurd and false equation of campus protests with black civil rights. Rand accused dithering academics of betraying democratic principles. The students at Berkeley, and later other universities, were fond of making a distinction between force and violence, arguing that the use of force to achieve moral goals was legitimate, but that resistance to such force was illegitimate and immoral. As Rand suggested, this is a grotesque moral inversion: to make the *initiation* of force moral and resistance to force immoral is to "obliterate the *right of self-defense.*"[103]

An even greater degree of damage than the Free Speech movement arose from special interest groups that demanded that the university bestow special privileges based on group or ethnic membership rather than individual merit. These protests were often delivered in the form of ultimatums. Blacks, Latinos, Indians, and feminists demanded special programs, admissions procedures, or independent facilities without any obligation or reservation on their part. Far from wanting to be academically assimilated, these radicalized groups wanted to be treated like a separate constituency rather than as independent and autonomous individuals. In later decades, their demands for special treatment were widely defended by both academics, politicians, and judges as socially necessary in a "multicultural" country. Universities and the federal government made it a priority to "protect" minorities through affirmative action policies and entitlement programs, even if these violated the rights of the majority. The ideals of common citizenship, the hallmark of democracy, were abandoned in favor of creating enclaves of special communities: black, Latino, Asian, gay and lesbian, feminist, and so forth.

Since the 1960s universities have pioneered the idea of proportional representation by setting aside specially allotted places for minorities and pandering to their ethnicities. Individual merit and high achievement were often abandoned in the process because it smacked of Western rationality and elitism. This is why a concerted attack against Western literary canons was launched by minority groups. The chant "Hey, hey, ho, ho Western civilization has got to go" illustrates the subversive nature of such radical demands. Group rights trump individual rights and merit is either undefinable or must be determined by the group that exercises judgment in individual cases. The ability to differentiate between right and wrong, good and bad, was rejected by radicals as a false Western construction based on social inequality. In order to safeguard this belief, radical theorists constructed elaborate ideologies such as deconstructionism, postmodernism, radical feminism, and historicism. Thanks to radical academics, such theories are now standard in the humanities and social sciences.

Looking back on the student upheavals in the 1960s, especially in regard to what they did to American higher education, the picture looks almost entirely grim and deeply troubling. Students, of course, did not wreck American institutions of higher learning, but they undermined standards of academic excellence and civilized rules of decorum, decency, and civility. This would not have happened if the students had not been able to draw upon the support of "treasonable clerks" in the academic community itself, fifth columnists in the form of spineless administrators and sympathetic professors who were complicit in defining moral excellence down to the lowest common denominator. Today's university reflects the fractured social divisions of the 1960s; it is a much weaker and less dedicated community of higher learning than it was before the 1960s. Even the much-vaunted educational reforms that came out of the 1960s—the proliferation of pseudo-academic courses, programs, and degrees; student evaluations of professors; "diversity" in the hiring process; affirmative action programs; ethnic, gender, and sexual studies; sexual harassment policies and speech codes—have all been double-edged swords of both reform and divisiveness.

In light of the overwrought rhetoric and violent actions of the 1960s, one cannot help but share Allan Bloom's sentiment that "about the sixties it is now fashionable to say that although there were indeed excesses, many good things resulted. But so far as the universities were concerned, I know of nothing positive coming from that period; it was an unmitigated disaster for them."[104] The claim that there was greater "openness," less "rigidity," or "freedom from authority," Bloom observed, has little relevance to what is wanted from a sound education in a democracy.[105] What is needed is higher standards, a uniformly rigorous curriculum, strong moral principles, and good educational role models. The 1960s subverted these essential qualities of higher education. It will take a different generation, probably functioning under extreme national peril, to level up the standards rather than to level them down, and to groom the meritocracy the university requires in order to function as an institution of "higher learning."

10

COUNTERCULTURAL PROTEST MOVEMENTS

1. Was There a Counterculture?

In the 1960s young people in America and western Europe seemed to rise almost spontaneously against the values and mores of their elders—so much so, that many historians referred to the emerging values of the young rebels as constituting a "counterculture" in contradistinction to the established mainstream culture of middle-class America. Historians at the time suspected that this youthful revolt was a symptom of widespread cultural change, and a flood of books attempted to fix its meaning and its long-range consequences. Since the late 1960s there has been considerable controversy about the nature, scope, and meaning of the counterculture, from Theodore Roszak's seminal *The Making of a Counter Culture* (1969), Charles Reich's euphoric *Greening of America* (1970), to Jean François Revel's equally hopeful *Without Marx or Jesus* (1970). These earlier accounts, written during the turbulent era of the sixties and seventies, claimed to identify the growth of a nascent culture-in-the-making that seemed to define itself largely by what it was rejecting: mind-numbing consumerism, the hypocrisy of middle-class adults, corporate greed, and the pervasive deceptions of public relations experts and image makers. In looking at youthful protests and its ethical presuppositions, Theodore Roszak thought he detected the "saving vision our endangered civilization requires";[1] he referred to this generational revolt as a "culture so radically disaffiliated from the mainstream assumptions of our society that it scarcely looks to many as a culture at all, but takes on the alarming appearance of a barbaric intrusion."[2] Roszak, however, was confident that a new and healthier culture would eventually emerge out of the decay of the old, provided, of course, that sound youthful instincts would not be perverted by the decadence and cynicism of the old culture. Clearly, Roszak and Reich saw young people as harbingers of regeneration, replacing the profit-hungry world of their elders with a cooperative, peaceful, and egalitarian alternative. Roszak subsequently tried to link the "new age" values of hip society with recurring romantic movements and their critiques of technological society in *Where the Wasteland Ends* (1972), *Unfinished Animal* (1975), and *Person/Planet* (1978).

Later works dismissed these claims that young people were like third-century Christians furnishing the building blocks of a new civilization. The sociologist Daniel Bell referred to the youth movement of the 1960s as a Children's Crusade that tried to eliminate the line between fantasy and reality, perpetuating adolescence indefinitely and demanding total liberation without constraints.[3] Other observers agreed that youthful protest was significant but only as a symptom of decay rather than regeneration. This view was held by conservatives as well as Marxists, except for different reasons, pointing to the breakdown of Judeo-Christian values and the disintegration of capitalism, respectively. Such notions of decay have been countered by other historians who stress the spiritual side of youthful seekers. Harvey Cox, for example, argued that hippie dropouts represented "the secular version of the historical American quest for a faith that warms the heart, a religion one can experience deeply and feel intensely."[4] Cox claimed to detect historical antecedents to hippie yearnings in nineteenth-century Methodist camp meetings and even in the life of St. Francis of Assisi. Such historical parallels have been noted by numerous other scholars who variously compared the 1960s counterculture to Hellenistic mystery cults, medieval heretics, Levellers or Diggers of seventeenth-century England, and nineteenth-century youth movements. The most common historical parallel drawn was that the counterculture of the 1960s was a continuation of previous romantic protests against overly rigid classical mainstream cultures. According to this view, countercultures are seen as romantic movements reacting against the anti-instinctual rigidity and classical order of mainstream cultures. In fact, the dynamic of Western civilization itself has been seen as a dialectical interplay between a dominating classical (Apollonian) and a recurring romantic (Dionysian) cross current. If this is so, the counterculture of the 1960s could be viewed as a recrudescence of past romantic movements, embodying a revitalized mode of life and consciousness.

According to some social historians, the counterculture's affinity with romanticism can only be understood as a reaction to modernization. What young protesters were really challenging was the whole way of bureaucratized life in corporate America. The German sociologist Max Weber had already predicted that modernization in the form of human mechanization, bureaucratization, and the rationalization of life would lead to "disenchantment of the world."[5] He suspected that there might be a widespread revolt against the "iron cage," the routinized way of life under capitalism, and that such a revolt would be organized under some neoromantic movement that affirmed spontaneity, charismatic leadership, and preconscious impulses. Weber did not live long enough to see that movement materialize in perverted Nazi form, but one could argue that the American response to the iron cage, taking place within a democratic setting, would take on a distinctive populist, youth-oriented coloration that was made possible only because socioeconomic circumstances in the post–World War II era were exceptionally favorable to such a response. The spectacular growth of the American economy after World War II not only spelled a shift from deprivation to abundance but also created the first generation in American history that took endless affluence and the satisfaction of material needs for granted. Being free of the fear of scarcity, the younger generation found little to admire in the way their parents lived and made a living. They also perceived that economic affluence was exacting too heavy a cost on individuals and their environment. In other words, young people asked themselves whether the mindless growth ethic was worth the cost, both in human and in environmental terms. Members of the hip movement certainly questioned the core values on which the American economic system was built. In opting out of the industrial system and rejecting the values that undergirded it, hippies potentially represented a real threat to that system; but what the young drop-outs failed to realize was that they were the children of affluence, which was based on the growth ethic, and that opting out meant having to live with scarcity, limitations, and renunciations. Such a hard bargain was unacceptable to all but the most committed countercultural types.

Since youthful protest has dissipated or has been absorbed by the classical mainstream, few historians today would argue that there ever was *a* counterculture at all. Arthur Marwick, for example, argued that the 1960s witnessed a large number of subcultures that expanded and interacted with each other, creating the pullulating flux which characterized that turbulent period. In Marwick's view, there was no unified, integrated counterculture, nor were there two sharply opposed cultures confronting each other. Instead, there were several countercultural movements that eventually altered the cultural mainstream, while at the same time being altered by it.[6] This argument has much to commend it. There were alternative cultural movements in the 1960s, but no single "counterculture." These alternative cultural movements never coalesced into one unified counterculture; instead, their development was either arrested or absorbed into the mainstream technocratic society.

Arnold Toynbee would probably have referred to these movements as aborted cultures because they faced too many economic or political challenges to become independent or full-blown cultures. Oswald Spengler, in turn, would have viewed these countercultural movements as pseudomorphic, comparing them with irregular or unclassifiable minerals that had the outward appearance of other minerals which they had replaced by chemical action. "By the term historical pseudomorphosis," Spengler said, "I propose to designate those cases in which an older or alien culture lies so massively over the land that a young culture, born of this land, cannot get its breath and fails not only to achieve pure and specific expression forms, but even to develop fully its own self consciousness."[7] The result is a distorted form whose inner structure contradicts its external shape. History is replete with antinomian movements that were ruthlessly destroyed, co-opted, or assimilated by the dominant civilizations in which they appeared. The same can be observed with the countercultural movements of the 1960s, which were deformed, co-opted, or channeled into the broad stream of American business civilization.

None of the adversarial movements of the 1960s constituted real cultures in the traditional sense of "high" cultures. The term "culture" comes from the Latin *cultivare,* or tilling the soil; it usually refers to the sum total of refined accomplishments in the life of a particular people, including its art, music, literature, religion, customs, and so forth. But in the twentieth century the term has been largely redefined anthropologically as "regularities in the behavior, internal and external, of the members of a society, excluding those regularities which are clearly hereditary in origin."[8] In other words, a society is comprised of people, and the way they behave, believe, and express themselves is their culture. The distinction between what is prized by the few (high brow) and what is preferred by the many (low brow) is no longer relevant to the collective life of industrialized consumer societies.[9] The rise of mass democracy and the need to cater to a mass audience have made cultural expressions, especially in the United States, popular (pop) and "no brow."

Since countercultural expressions of the 1960s came from disaffected young people who rejected middle-class values, the movement lacked a clear-cut substance and direction. In the end, it amounted to little more than a mood, a rebellious frame of mind, and a "lifestyle" choice. Although at the time the adversarial mood seemed like a tidal wave of generational change, in retrospect, that adversarial mood did not substantially change either the polity or the economic structure of American society. What it changed was the popular culture in the form of music, entertainment, lifestyles, and values. The white monochromatic culture of the 1950s, though cherished by conservative Americans today as a lost paradise, is a thing of the past, superseded by a freewheeling "multicultural" and multiethnic popular culture that encourages diversity rather than uniform standards. White middle-class values pertaining to ethics, work, fashion, and general decorum have also been denigrated as a consequence of countercultural movements.

2. The Myth of a Woodstock Nation

The most significant of these countercultural movements were the New Left, already described; hippiedom; militant ethnic groups, notably black nationalists, Latino irredentists, Native Americans; radical feminists; and radical ecologists. These movements followed essentially the same pattern and direction as the black civil rights movement. Their followers at first demanded the same rights that were enjoyed by their fellow Americans in the social mainstream; they wanted, above all, to be integrated into the mainstream as coequal citizens. The push toward integration, however, gave way to increasingly strident demands by radicals that the social mainstream either provide previously excluded groups with special or preferred treatment or make it possible for them to form semi-autonomous communities within the social mainstream. Integration thus gave way to separatism and strident demands that the mores and beliefs of minority groups not just be tolerated but officially legitimized and accepted as cultural norms. Of all these groups, it appeared that the hippies and their camp followers (weekend or lifestyle hippies) represented the greatest threat to middle-class Americans because these rebels were their children.[10] These young people formed an underground that spawned a host of adversarial groups: beatniks, hippies, yuppies, freaks, heads, communards, Diggers, crazies, and so forth. At one time or another, all of them were called hippies, a term that was coined by Michael Fallon, a San Francisco reporter who wrote an article about a coffee house, the Blue Unicorn, in the Haight-Ashbury district of San Francisco.[11] Fallon compared the young people congregating at the Blue Unicorn with the Beats of the 1950s, noting that the lifestyle of both groups was much the same: antiestablishment and nonconformist.[12] At the same time, there were obvious differences: the Beats were born during the Depression and had gone through war and postwar McCarthyism; their mood was pessimistic and their attitudes were those of vulnerable yet fiercely independent outsiders. By contrast, the hippies, as the diminutive implies, were "lite" Beats—that is, less gruff, heavy, and self-contained. Hippies had grown up in white middle-class affluence and had not been bruised by life. They were optimistic, full of their own self-importance, naive, and visibly impatient to change the world for the better.

The Beats, however, served as trailblazers, and their writings became for the hippies a vehicle of protest and liberation. The beat message was not a political one because most beat writing was self-referential; its literary aim was not merely to shock the bourgeoisie *(epater les bourgeois),* but to use literature as a vehicle of protest and total liberation. Beats wanted nothing more than to be left alone, and their political opinions spanned the whole spectrum from Kerouac's apolitical indifference to Ginsberg's romantic anarchism. The Beats had no political vision other than negative freedom—to be left alone to enjoy the moment rather than to prepare for the future. They had no awareness of common values, of educating children, maintaining traditions, or fighting evil. There was only the naked self out to lunch.

Hippies exuded a more optimistic and vibrant spirit, which could be seen, among other things, by the outrageous way they dressed and behaved. Around 1965 the world of dress and fashion changed abruptly. White middle-class preferences for suits, jackets, ties, elegant dresses, high heels, and white gloves gave way to an amazing and eclectic mixture of hip (colorful or outrageous), multiethnic, and just plain old-fashioned attire: colorful vests, leather jackets, workmen's overalls, T-shirts, dashikis, Old Mother Hubbard dresses, ankle-length madras skirts, headbands, cowboy hats, coonskin hats, gypsy cummerbunds, boots, and sandals. For young hippie men long hair, beards or mustaches were *de rigueur,* while young women favored natural hair over their mothers' permed hairdos. Diamonds were no longer a girl's best friend. Expensive jewelry was bourgeois decadence. "Flower children" preferred cheap love beads or primitive teeth necklaces. Since the hippie movement was in many ways a reversion to primitive tribalism, perceptive observers were not surprised by the proliferation of tattoos, ear and nose piercing, and other forms of body mutilations. In the same vein, the rage against Christian Western traditions manifested itself in the widespread preference for neopagan or Far Eastern necklaces, rings, bracelets, or amulets. Some hippies enjoyed mocking traditional Christian symbols by sporting occult or even satanic symbols. Not even the American flag or the military was safe from being mocked or parodied. Hippies ridiculed American superpatriots by wearing military garments, some of them, as worn by the protagonist in the movie *Easy Rider,* displaying the American flag on the backs of leather jackets.

Sociologically speaking, most hippies came from white middle-class backgrounds. They recruited primarily from the ranks of disaffected dropouts who envisioned a more meaningful way of life outside the cultural mainstream.[13] The hippie way of life, as it crystallized in the late 1960s, revolved basically around dope, rock 'n' roll music, liberated sexuality, and some form of communal living. A common bond, in addition to ethnicity, class, and age, was rock 'n' roll, the defining characteristic of the baby boomers. For many young people rock was simply fun because it celebrated raw adolescent feelings and emotions. At the same time, rock was often a form of escapism from adult reality of hard work and responsibility. Country Joe McDonald captured this flight from reality perfectly when he said: "You take drugs, you turn up the music very loud, you dance around, you build yourself a fantasy world where everything is beautiful."[14]

Between 1965 and the end of the decade millions of young people, influenced by the images they saw in the media and the risk-taking behavior of their own peers, experimented with some form of hippie life. At the heart of this youthful revolt was a generational identity crisis that stemmed from inconsistent parenting, fluctuating between permissive neglect and meddlesome control, and from a failure of adult institutions to moderate or accommodate the needs and frustrations of so many young people. The conformist mainstream culture allowed for few genuine outlets for youthful rebellion and idealism. There were also few compelling role models of the old generation that the young intrinsically trusted or admired. The death of John F. Kennedy, one of the last role models of the older generation that the young had trusted, removed the sort of leadership young people had been yearning for; the president's tragic death by an assassin's bullet, followed by years of paranoid speculation about the perpetrators, only widened the gap between the generations. Hippies asked what there was that one could emulate in corporate America. The pursuit of money? Supporting a senseless war? Praying in a fossilized church that showed contempt for fun, joy, or sexuality? Taking meaningless courses leading to meaningless degrees in bloated multiversities? Many young people felt that it was perhaps better to drop out, to "do one's own thing," to live in a hip commune of like-minded seekers. Dropping out of the mainstream, of course, was difficult in the long run because baby boomers lacked the intellectual and economic resources to invent their own world outside the adult mainstream. Within the adult world, however, they found some role models whose harsh criticisms of American society could, with some simplification, be used as an intellectual armory by rebellious young people. Hippies could draw on at least three sources for their rebellious opposition to mainstream America: the civil rights movement, which furnished the techniques of protest; the Beats, who supplied rebellious role models; and left liberal critics, who provided the intellectual weapons of dissent. Black protest and the music that accompanied it served as great inspiration to youthful rebels. The Beats, as previously mentioned, were subversive individualists who left behind them the cult of the rebel, which involved, among other things, a certain mood of opposition to the straight world of conformity, work, and responsibility. The lifestyle of the Beats—hanging out in coffee houses, sexual experimentation, drug usage, and spouting cool lingo—was the preserve of a few bohemian cliques in the 1950s. By adopting the beat lifestyle, the hippies democratized it by their sheer numbers.

In addition to the rebellious lifestyles of the Beats, hippies drew on a sizable literature of alienation and resistance. Socialist and anarchist writers had fabricated utopian visions for well over a hundred years. They had captured the hearts and minds of many oppressed and alienated people by trying to dismantle the kingdom of heaven with a new kingdom of earth, where there would be no more poverty, war, and injustice, where lions would lie down with lambs in perpetual and universal harmony. Novelists, too, had confabulated new and better worlds, as did Aldous Huxley in *Island*, B. F. Skinner in *Walden Two*, and Robert Heinlein in *Stranger in a Strange Land*. For those who found themselves boxed in a sterile "air-conditioned nightmare," as Henry Miller called it, science fiction writers such as Isaac Asimov, Arthur Clarke, C. S. Lewis, or J. R. R. Tolkien offered escape hatches into other worlds or different futures. Similarly, for those who found Western religion unbearably rigid or intellectually impoverished there were writers offering insights into Native American and Far Eastern religions. D. T. Suzuki, Gary Snyder, and Alan Watts popularized Buddhist beliefs to receptive Americans, while Carlos Castaneda tried to teach young white Americans to think like Castaneda's invented Native Americans in *The Teachings of Don Juan*. The German novelist Herman Hesse, who never dreamed that his writings would be avidly read by young Americans, provided a bridge of youthful rebellion that connected the interwar generation fighting totalitarianism in the 1930s with the post–World War II generation fighting its own battles against cold war institutions. A favorite guru of young hippies was Buckminster Fuller, whose many books and inventions, most notably the geodesic dome, stressed the use of benign technology in an effort to save the world's dwindling resources. Hippies could also draw on a vast literature of "alienation," a favorite term philosophers and psychologists had used to describe an existential predicament by which humans are estranged from their own essential nature as well as from the environment in which they live. Marx's early writings had been devoted to human alienation, a condition that he blamed on the capitalist system and its inherently exploitive nature. Those who had embraced the writings of the young romantic Marx, notably Erich Fromm, drew attention to those elements in Marx's thought that they considered more liberating in a humanistic sense than the spiteful and angry judgments the older Marx pronounced from his exile in London. The theme of alienation echoed through countless works by social critics, sociologists, psychologists, philosophers, and novelists, including such prominent writers as David Riesman, Vance Packard, Philip Slater, Norman Mailer, Joseph Heller, and Kurt Vonnegut. The ideas of some of these writers were beyond the intellectual comprehension of young hippie dropouts, but there was one book, though written with pretensions toward scholarly respectability, that many hippies had read and carried about with them, and that was Charles Reich's national bestseller *The Greening of America*. Using simplistic intellectual scaffolding, Reich had postulated the existence of two major forms of consciousness in American history, with a third one just emerging and poised to replace the first two. He labeled these cultural mentalities consciousness I, II, and III—the first being Puritanism, the second managerial liberalism, and the third the hippie lifestyle of the counterculture. Whereas the first two had been the product of guilt-ridden Puritans and corporate liberals, respectively, the third form of consciousness would green the sterile and oppressive landscape of corporate America and transform it into a blooming garden in which people could frolic without guilt or repression. The new cultural lifestyle, Reich predicted, would be permissive, egalitarian, and polymorphically perverse. The society of the future would be completely nonjudgmental; no one would judge anyone as being better or worse. The whole concept of excellence and comparative merit would have been eliminated. As Reich saw it, there would be no governing standards and no one would be rejected.[15] In discussing just how America would be greened, Reich insisted that it would occur not through political revolution but rather more organically through a change in the collective consciousness of the American people, particularly young Americans. By seceding from the corporate rat race and just being themselves, young hippie dropouts would eventually effect a complete change in the national character. This meant a revolution in consciousness, an utterly different form of social change, and the young were to be the instruments of that change. In fact, according to Reich, the revolution was already under way. If one wanted to describe it, one only had to look at the lives the young rebels were already living. The hippie lifestyle *was* the revolution. Hello Woodstock Nation! As Abbie Hoffman would later describe it during his 1969 trial for conspiring to riot:

Attorney Weinglass:	Would you state your name?
Witness:	My name is Abbie. I'm an orphan of America.
Attorney:	Where do you reside?
Witness:	Woodstock nation.
Attorney:	What state is that in?
Witness:	The state of mind. It's a nation of alienated young people which we carry in our minds, just as the Sioux Indians carried around the Sioux nation in their minds.[16]

That such intellectual platitudes were taken seriously not just by Hoffman or unreflective hippies but also by journalists and literary pundits illustrated just how shallow public conversation had become in America.[17] Young people, however, embraced Reich as a serious guru, just as they followed the siren song of Timothy Leary, Richard Alpert (Ram Dass), Allen Ginsberg, Ken Kesey, Mr. Zig-Zag, and Fritz the Cat.

What, then, was this Woodstock Nation, this new form of consciousness and way of life? By Woodstock, of course, Abbie Hoffman was referring to the August 1969 rock festival that attracted half a million hippies and gave the world a visual sense of the new lifestyle in action. The new lifestyle favored a combination of "doing one's own thing" and primitive tribal bonding. At the heart of this style was "feeling good" and living for the moment. In order to heighten this search for the ever higher "high," hippies saturated the senses with a cacophony of sounds and generous doses of mind-altering drugs. Rock music encouraged the importance of good feeling now; it had no use for either the past or the future. The line "Don't know nothin' 'bout history" reflected its primitive mentality, which always lacked historical perspective. The music celebrated being forever young, good vibrations, and ecstatic feelings. It stressed motion and energy, but without any particular aim or direction other than motion itself. To be young "You Gotta Move," and that movement had to be new and exciting. One former hippie recalled that her contemporaries felt "like birds seized by a migratory urge,"[18] moving to places that they thought were not only new or different but would change them forever.

As a metaphor, Woodstock, of course, stood not for a place but for a state of mind, perhaps even a new millennial age—the Age of Aquarius. Metaphysically, that age is said to occur when the constellation of Aquarius replaces the Age of Pisces, which has dominated the human race for the past two thousand years. The New Age, hippies believed, would usher in an eon of honesty, compassion, and love, replacing hate, war, and selfishness. The song "The Age of Aquarius" from the Broadway rock musical *Hair,* was seen as heralding a new age of sincerity and mystic revelations. Hippies saw themselves on the cusp of a new age, as harbingers of the next evolutionary step on the way toward planetary peace and love:

> When the Moon is in the Seventh House
> And Jupiter aligns with Mars
> Then peace will guide the planets
> And love will steer the stars.

Whether such longings could be labeled a new form of religiosity has been much debated.[19] It certainly was not a religion in the traditional sense because it lacked specific creeds, doctrines, and institutions. Probably the best way to describe its essential nonconformist and protean nature is to call it romantic pantheism, which is the belief in the sacredness of everything: rocks, trees, rivers, people, animals, planets, galaxies—in short, the sacredness of the cosmos itself. This vague and indistinct view has been criticized by some as a "garbage pail philosophy"[20] that indiscriminately mixes scraps of everything. In the words of one ardent hippie, "our emerging religion is not borrowed, but homegrown—and potentially planetary. Buddhism, Native American religion, various forms of psychotherapy (especially Gestalt and Jungian) Jewish, Christian, and Islamic mysticism, have all poured into it and fused into a new brew, alive, nameless, and endlessly mutating."[21] The new pantheism, of course, knows no hierarchy, but is a direct one-on-one communication with the sacred spirit world. Everyone is free to assemble his or her own beliefs, rituals, customs, or holidays. There is no need for churches, festivals, or denominations. You can call yourself what you want. The New Age seeker who said she picked eclectically from different traditions had no trouble with those who call themselves "Coyote Christians" or "Jewish Catholics."[22] If the term "God" is not an apt description for ultimate reality, one can always worship nature or the cosmos. In the same vein, if God in the traditional sense is too masculine, one can always worship the living earth goddess (Gaia).

The protean nature of these spiritual longings has now filtered into the cultural mainstream where they uneasily coexist with traditional beliefs. In the 1960s they seemed radical and subversive because they were associated with young protesters who threatened to tear down mainstream beliefs. This has not happened. What did happen, however, was the weakening of traditional religious traditions and their power over the cultural domain.[23] From a spiritual point of view, America is no longer a Christian but a pluralistically diverse society in which spirituality has been consumerized and can be readily identified under New Age labels at Borders or

Barnes and Noble. In other words, the Woodstock spirit, like so much else from the 1960s, has been mainstreamed by being commercialized. As such, its influence has been neither spiritually profound nor culturally subversive.

The same cannot be said of another Woodstock legacy: the widespread use of drugs. Jerry Rubin, one of the pied pipers of the counterculture, proclaimed that "drug use signifies the total end of the Protestant ethic: screw work, we want to know ourselves."[24] Such knowledge, he insisted, could be gained through psychedelic drugs, which would provide instant enlightenment. Rubin and his like-minded seekers were not the real discoverers of psychedelic drugs. The older generation of Beats and bohemian nonconformists had already shown the way to the gates of Eden. The word "psychedelic" was first used by the psychologist Humphrey Osmond in 1959. Along with the British novelist Aldous Huxley, he had already experimented with mescaline and LSD. Subsequently, Timothy Leary and Richard Alpert experimented with LSD at Harvard and became zealous apostles of drug usage. Nor had such drug experimentation been the exclusive practice of cultural nonconformists. Assorted cold warriors working for the CIA had experimented with mind-altering drugs on nonsuspecting Americans since the early 1950s. But what had been practiced in tiny enclaves of government researchers or bohemians began to spill out into the rest of America, with the young serving as guinea pigs of drug experimentation. When Leary experienced his epiphany after sampling magic psilocybin mushrooms in Mexico in 1960, he could hardly wait to tell the world the good news:

> Listen! Wake up! You are God! You have the divine plan engraved in cellular script within you. Listen! Take this sacrament! You'll see! You'll get the revelations! It will change your life. You'll be reborn![25]

While at Harvard, Leary violated his contract with the university by persuading students to take LSD in order to prove that the drug could produce mystical experiences; and when the university fired him, he transformed himself from a professional researcher into a popular drug guru, publishing his own journal, developing a network of like-minded believers, and lecturing college students all over America "to turn on, tune in, and drop out."[26] Leary's gospel spread through important contacts. While still at Harvard, Leary contacted the British novelist Aldous Huxley, an enthusiastic proponent of mescaline, who was at that time a visiting professor at M.I.T. Soon thereafter, Allen Ginsberg got wind of Leary's work at Harvard and traveled to Cambridge to visit Leary. It was in one of Leary's upstairs bedrooms that Ginsberg took the small pink LSD pills, removed his clothes, and, to the consternation of Leary's teenage daughters who fled to the third floor, proceeded to wander downstairs, proclaiming: "I'm the Messiah! I've come down to preach love to the world. We're going to walk through the streets and teach people to stop hating."[27] After being dissuaded from plunging naked into the street, Ginsberg phoned Kerouac and told him of the new miracle drug. Word then quickly spread through the avant garde of artists, writers, musicians, movie stars, and eventually rebellious young people that LSD and other forms of "good dope" (marijuana, mescaline, peyote, psilocybin, hashish) were good for body and soul.

Leary turned out to be a kind of Johnny Appleseed of drugs, dispensing pills to all and sundry because Ginsberg had persuaded him that drug usage should be democratized. The hippie ethos was that drugs, like bread, should be free; they were the manna from heaven to all the people. In order to persuade uninformed and repressed Americans that psychedelic drugs were the genuine article, Leary and his passionate followers left no stone unturned to find converts. The work of propaganda on behalf of psychedelics was made easier by the fact that little was known about these drugs by the public; in fact, until 1966 LSD was not illegal. But when the authorities got wind of its widespread usage, they staged a variety of high profile crackdowns, notably on a mansion at Millbrook, located on a four-thousand-acre estate up the Hudson River. It was here that Timothy Leary, thanks to a wealthy benefactor, had gathered like-minded drug enthusiasts to celebrate the coming Age of Aquarius. News of the weird goings-on at Millbrook quickly circulated through the neighborhood grapevine. In April 1966, a young ambitious Duchess County prosecutor, G. Gordon Liddy, staged a raid on Millbrook, and though the raiding party found LSD and marijuana, the case was subsequently tossed out because Liddy failed to give the Miranda warning.[28] Liddy, however, continued to harass Leary and his acolytes, forcing them to take their drug show to the West Coast; but wherever Leary went, the law continued to breathe down his neck. Leary's life increasingly spun out of control: broken marriage, the suicide of his daughter, constant arrests, and flights from the law. He spent his later life as a stand-up philosopher preaching such profundities as: "the key political issue of our time is that every individual is entitled complete and free access to his or her own brain." Before his death from prostate cancer in 1996, Leary requested that his remains be allowed to go on a final far-out trip into space. On April 2, 1997, a rocket carried his ashes into space, undoubtedly evoking in the minds of his followers the final exclamation of the dying Cleopatra: "I am fire and air; my other elements I give to baser life."

Those elements did make life a great deal baser as a result of Leary's crusading efforts on behalf of mind-altering drugs. The historian William L. O'Neill rightly referred to Leary and other drug pushers as false prophets leaving behind them a generational wasteland strewn with the victims of brain damage, overdose, and tragic deaths.[29] From Leary and the celebrity elites drug usage spread to the population at large, especially to rebellious young people. The novelist Ken Kesey, who had taken LSD as a volunteer in a psychological experiment at Menlo Park Veteran Hospital, gathered an outrageous band of acolytes, the Merry Pranksters, and took his drug show on the road in a psychedelically painted school bus. The conductor of this madhouse on wheels was none other than Neal Cassady, Jack Kerouac's frantic sidekick both in life and in his widely hailed novel *On the Road*. While the Pranksters were on the road to New York, where Kesey planned a party to celebrate his forthcoming book *Sometimes a Great Notion*, they took frequent "acid trips" and engaged in outrageous antics to mock and shock middle-class squares. Along the way through this drug haze and sexual romp, the Pranksters pulled up briefly at Leary's place at Millbrook but found the company too puffed up with their own sense of importance.

One of the most psychedelic communities in America was the Haight-Ashbury district in San Francisco, which had attracted thousands of young people in the mid to late 1960s.[30] In 1967 Scott McKenzie's song "San Francisco" beckoned young people to the city of the Golden Gate, reminding young travelers: "If you're going to San Francisco, Be sure to wear some flowers in your hair. All across the nation, such a strange vibration." The subtext of the song, of course, was that San Francisco welcomed free drug usage and the lifestyle associated with it. San Francisco had a long history of tolerating eccentrics, and the city's North Beach section had served as the congenial home of the Beats in the 1950s. The city was also becoming the home of acid-tinged rock music, featuring such bands as the Great Society, Charlatans, the Grateful Dead, Jefferson Airplane, Quicksilver Messenger Service, Moby Grape, and Big Brother and the Holding Company. From across the bay in Berkeley came Country Joe and the Fish. Psychedelic rock music was on tap at various music or dance halls such as Longshoremen's Hall, the Avalon Ballroom, and the Fillmore, not to mention smaller holes in the wall. Bands played ear-shattering rock 'n' roll, while strobelights further pummeled the senses of the gyrating young bodies on the dance floor. The image of mindless zombies, enveloped entirely in their own crazy musical world, was widely discussed at the time by startled observers in the press. Indeed, as Paul Kantner of the Jefferson Airplane later remarked; "If you can remember anything about the sixties, you weren't really there."[31]

Those who took the lead in tiptoeing through the fog were widely celebrated by those who naively followed behind. Drug suppliers, far from being demonized, were lionized by hippies. In San Francisco, the major drug supplier was a Berkeley student and grandson of a U.S. senator, Augustus Owsley (Stanley) III, who used part of his trust fund to manufacture millions of psychedelic (acid) pills, selling them for two dollars apiece. By the mid-1960s, Owsley was widely hailed as the Henry Ford of acid, Mr. LSD, and the LSD King. Owsley also supplied LSD to the Grateful Dead and helped finance the band's equipment. Another countercultural hero was Bill Graham, a German-Jewish immigrant who staged rock 'n' roll concerts at the Longshoremen's Hall, the Fillmore, Fillmore East in New York, and Winterland. Graham was instrumental in bringing together hip artists, musicians, and poets, ranging from the San Francisco Mime Troupe to well-known rock bands of the 1960s. At one time or another, Graham booked most of the major rock stars: Janis Joplin, Jimi Hendrix, Bob Dylan, the Who, the Rolling Stones, and many others. Graham was a free spirit, a brilliant impresario, and, as he put it in his autobiography, "he was *anti*. He was *anti*-everything . . . Anti-establishment all the way."[32]

The hippie gurus, drug suppliers, impresarios, and the ever-accommodating media promoted and widely publicized a series of national "happenings," be-ins, rock festivals, put-ons—the latest always trying to outdo the previous ones in shock value. The gathering of masses of young people, freely acting out their feelings in public, had been relatively rare before the mid-1960s. The "happenings" of the 1950s and early 1960s were largely uncoordinated and spontaneous events associated with avant-garde artists or college students. In January 1967, however, a more organized mass event occurred in San Francisco called a "Human Be-In" or "Gathering of the

Tribes," which brought together a large assortment of hippies in San Francisco's Golden Gate Park. The *San Francisco Oracle*, a psychedelic underground newspaper that promoted the event, estimated that over twenty thousand young people had gathered to celebrate a "Renaissance of compassion, awareness, and love in the revelation of the Unity of all Mankind."[33] The use of such pseudo-spiritual language that inflated personal feelings into planetary significance was quite common among hippies, avant-garde writers, and assorted New Age believers. The real purpose of the Human Be-In was coming together and "grooving," which meant taking drugs, exchanging flowers and poems, listening to music—by the Grateful Dead and the Jefferson Airplane, among others—and becoming "enlightened" by the words of such countercultural gurus as Timothy Leary and Allen Ginsberg.

The events in the summer of 1967 brought over a hundred thousand young people to the West Coast: the Summer of Love in San Francisco and the Monterey Pop Festival. Throughout the summer of 1967 young hippies took to the road, either hitchhiking or driving in rundown vehicles or vans decorated with psychedelic Day-Glo images; their destination was San Francisco, the City of Love.[34] They quickly formed makeshift friendships and shared each other's drugs, food, and sexual favors. Many of the young adolescents simply wanted to get away from school and parents, to enjoy, if only briefly, an ephemeral moment of exhilaration and personal freedom. Others, however, were more troubled and saw in this opportunity an escape from conventional middle-class life and perhaps a means of discovering a wholly different way of life.

The influx into San Francisco of so many young and inexperienced hippies put a serious strain on the city's social services, which were not able to cope with so many of them. The Haight-Ashbury district was flooded with disheveled, stoned-out hippies, who panhandled, spread diseases, and, not unexpectedly, attracted numerous predators who ripped them off and sexually assaulted them. For a brief moment, however, many experienced the illusion of love and communal sharing. The press, always more interested in reporting the sensational at the expense of the real, ignored the split message these young people were trying to convey. Their outrageous behavior captured the jaundiced imagination of reporters, who naturally highlighted the degenerate activities of the hippies without providing context and deeper probing into what was, after all, a major social dysfunction. Conductors on special tour buses took goggle-eyed tourists on a Haight-Ashbury district "Hippie-Hop Tour," advertising that this was "the only foreign tour within the continental limits of the United States."[35] Upon entering the Haight-Ashbury district the tour guide exclaimed: "We are now passing down Haight Street, the very nerve center of a city within a city. . . . Marijuana, of course, is a household staple here, enjoyed by the natives to stimulate their senses. . . . Among the favorite pastimes of the hippies, besides taking drugs, are parading and demonstrating, seminars and group discussions about what's wrong with the status quo; malingering; plus the ever-present preoccupation with the soul, reality and self-expression, such as strumming guitars, piping flutes and banging on bongo drums."[36]

For the media nothing so much succeeded as excess reduced to a light comedy.

Similarly, nothing succeeded better than to make money out of excess and merchandize it. It was also a measure of intergenerational alienation that the very existence of Haight-Ashbury and other countercultural slums like it were growing throughout the United States. Something had clearly gone wrong with the process of transmitting sound social values to young people and helping them to live by civilized rules of conduct. The fault lay squarely with poor parenting or no parenting at all. What was happening to America's children was a social catastrophe that few people wanted to understand. One of the few astute observers, Joan Didion, referred to what was happening in San Francisco and elsewhere as a social hemorrhaging of the most serious nature. Describing in stark and clinical detail what was really going on in the Haight—drug abuse, venereal disease, rape, arrests—Didion put her finger on the social dysfunction by pointing out the obvious, that "at some point between 1945 and 1967 we had somehow neglected to tell these children the rules of the game we happened to be playing. Maybe we had stopped believing in the rules ourselves, maybe we were having a failure of nerve about the game.... There were children who grew up cut loose from the web of cousins and great-aunts and family doctors and lifelong neighbors who had traditionally suggested and enforced society's values."[37] This is exactly what had happened, and the result was that young people were thrown back on their own devices, which failed to prepare them for a mature and stable social life. Looking at those drifting and unstable hippies, Didion sadly but correctly observed that "we were seeing the desperate attempt of a handful of pathetically unequipped children to create a community in a social vacuum."[38]

It is therefore important to realize that these mass gatherings of young people were not simply about having fun or listening to music, but experiencing a sense of community belonging without the presence of adults. Many of these young people hoped that out of such tribal meetings a real alternative way of life would somehow emerge, a way of life that was totally nonrepressive and pleasurable. That real community was based on instinctual renunciation was either ignored or postponed, for what counted was the present moment of being young, unencumbered, and self-indulgent.

In their ongoing search of rock, dope, and pleasure, young people streamed from one large event to another. In June 1967 many of the participants in the Summer of Love attended the Monterey Rock Festival (June 16–18), an event that signaled the beginning of the great rock festival years (1967–71) during which mass rock concerts were organized all over the United States.[39] The Monterey festival set the stage, attracting well over fifty thousand young people. The vast majority of those who attended the Monterey concert and those that followed were young whites under thirty years of age, typically between eighteen and twenty-five. Their interest was primarily in music; but as previously mentioned, forming relationships and sharing common experiences were also very important. Much to the chagrin of the New Left, politics was of little interest to those who attended rock concerts. This was especially true of hippies, who had dropped out of the mainstream, were uninterested in reforming institutions, and rejected political solutions to cultural problems as a waste of time. They believed in the power of the "Politics of Love,"[40] which required that one drop out of the hate-filled society, form core fellowships of love, and gradually allow that loving energy to subvert the power of the establishment. Such feel-good sentiments were present at all rock events, but the antics of tens of thousands of raucous fans often tested the limits of even hippie love and tolerance. At Monterey the sheer presence of over fifty thousand stoned-out hippies created a serious problem of crowd control for a small contingent of local law enforcement officials. The authorities were afraid that well-intentioned feelings of peace and love could easily be subverted by rowdy behavior, drug overdoses, damage to private property, and clashes with the police. That this did not happen at Monterey was the result of unusual good will on all sides. The police generally ignored drug usage because they could not have coped with the mass arrests that would have ensued, for how do you lock up fifty thousand people? Thus, the atmosphere at Monterey was light-hearted and peaceful. Those who attended were treated to three days packed with musical events, including a succession of bands and singers: the Byrds, Country Joe and the Fish, the Who, Simon and Garfunkel, Janis Joplin, Otis Redding, and Jimi Hendrix, among others. Three of the most popular rock acts—the Beatles, Rolling Stones, and Bob Dylan—were not performing at Monterey, but a real class act was: the master of the sitar, Ravi Shankar, who received one of the most enthusiastic rounds of applause at the festival.

Although the large crowd at Monterey was peaceful and law enforcement officials had no trouble in controlling it, the same would not always be true of subsequent rock festivals at Newport (June 20–22, 1969), Denver (June 27–28, 1969) and Altamont (December 6, 1969). It became quickly apparent that some young people came to these festivals looking for trouble, especially while being under the influence of psychedelic drugs. Often gate-crashing the event and destroying property, these hooligans disrupted performances and clashed with the police in violent encounters. Performers on stage also acted out wild and primitive spectacles, inciting the audience to react with uninhibited and unbridled emotions. Jimi Hendrix, for example, worked himself into a Dionysian frenzy during which he played his guitar behind his back, then rammed it through his legs, swinging and twirling the instrument, until, thoroughly exhausted he sank to his knees, dousing the guitar with lighter fluid and then setting it on fire. Such profusion of madness on stage would later become *de rigueur* with bands that incorporated violence on stage to connect emotionally with their audience. What an odd contrast between the peace/love elements in the counter-culture and the violence/destruction impulse enacted by freaked-out performers and their acolytes.

The year 1969 was the most important one for large-scale rock festivals. Over a million young people attended concerts at the Newport Jazz Festival, the Atlanta Pop Festival, the Seattle Pop Festival, the Atlantic City Pop Festival, Woodstock, New Orleans, the Texas International Pop Festival, the Second Annual Sky River Rock Festival, and Altamont. Of all these festivals, Woodstock clearly stands out, not only because it attracted over four hundred thousand fans but also because it created a generational myth that shows no sign so far of being demythologized.[41] The festival was held for three days in August (15–17) near Woodstock, New York. It was the home of Bob Dylan and was regarded by rock musicians as a real countercultural hotspot. The festival site was located on a nearby farm that lacked adequate facilities, for the promoters had no idea that they were going to accommodate over four hundred thousand pleasure seeking hippies. For days the roads leading to Woodstock were lined with weird vehicles of all sorts: VW bugs and buses, station wagons, vans, wildly painted school buses, and even hearses. With the influx of so many people, the promoters faced a logistical nightmare, made all the more ominous when the area was hit by a series of thunderstorms that turned the festival site into one vast mud pile. Many of the more seasoned hippies, stoned out of their minds by drugs, took things in stride and probably barely noticed the bad weather, but for many other young people the bad weather and the lack of basic facilities considerably dampened their enthusiasm. The spectacle of this big mud pile filled with disheveled young people, prompted the *New York Times* to ask "What kind of culture is it that can produce so colossal a mess?"[42] The young people who attended subsequently answered this question by elevating the festival to the position of a planetary event of love, peace, and music, for it turned out that despite the deplorable conditions, the vast majority of the participants not only endured the bad weather but had the time of their lives. Such positive nostalgic perceptions, however, should be qualified by mentioning that if it had not been for the help of mature adults—policemen, electricians, food suppliers, medical professionals—the festival would probably have collapsed into violent anarchy. Even the United States Army helped out by dispatching helicopters, forty-five doctors, and medical supplies.

Dozens of famous bands kept this immense countercultural city entertained for three ecstatic and trying days. Despite bitter complaints about "no water, no food, no medical supplies," there never was any shortage of drugs to heighten the illusion that the festival, in Allen Ginsberg's overblown phrase, was a "major planetary event." Some bands, like Sly and the Family Stone, openly urged the dancing and clapping crowd to get stoned, bellowing to the crowd: "I wanna take you higher," inviting them to join in the chanting of "Higher! Higher! Higher!" Stone worked the frenzied audience: "Say higher and throw up the peace sign. It'll do you no harm. Wanna take you higher." The crowd responded with "Higher! Way up on the hill higher. Higher! Higher! Higher!"[43] Hundreds of hippies went so high that they seriously overdosed. One died.

The country did not quite know what to make of this youthful revelry. Was it a portent of a new way of life? Was it a countercultural message to older Americans? Was it a symptom of massive cultural decline? Or was it simply a spontaneous gathering of youth seeking a temporary escape from adult responsibilities, including the heavy burden of having to go to war? To some extent, of course, it was all of these, excepting those hyper-inflated judgments on both sides of the cultural divide. Woodstock was not a "planetary event" that signaled a paradigm shift in the culture, nor was it a dangerous invasion of scummy young savages. *Time* magazine called Woodstock a "squalid freakout, a monstrous Dionysian revel, where a mob of crazies gathered to drop acid and groove to hours of amplified cacophony."[44] *Time*'s allusion to "Dionysian" contained a grain of truth, for what was on display at Woodstock was unbridled and irrational romanticism of the sort experienced by young people during the *Sturm und Drang* (Storm and Stress) period in late-eighteenth-century Germany. Culturally it implied youthful immaturity, rebellion, and the release of raw emotion without consideration of form and structure. In the context of the eighteenth century it was a sign of revitalization, but in the context of the 1960s it was symptomatic of a demotic culture in decline.

Few observers at the time noticed the deeper cultural significance of Woodstock. One critic who saw this phenomenon in a larger cultural context was Ayn Rand, whose provocative essay "Apollo and Dionysius" examines the Woodstock festival (the Dionysian) and contrasts it to the Apollo 11 Moon Landing (the Apollonian) that took place about a month previous to Woodstock.[45] Rand contrasted Woodstock with the thoughtful and civilized men and women, close to one million, who traveled to Cape Kennedy to watch the launching of Apollo 11. These people, she pointed out, were the salt of the earth; they were not a stampeding herd nor a manipulated mob; they did not wreck the Florida communities, . . . they did not throw themselves, like whining thugs, at the mercy of their victims; they did not create any victims."[46] Rand depicted the majority of the American people as Apollonian: reality-oriented, common sense-oriented, and technology-oriented. By contrast, the hippies and the intellectuals who pandered to them were emotion-oriented and tried to escape from the technological civilization because it was unresponsive to their feelings. Rand had collected some valuable pieces of the puzzle, but her indictment of the intellectual establishment and the degree of influence it allegedly exercised was not entirely satisfactory. Neither mainstream intellectuals nor mainstream journalists were in any sense "Dionysian"; if anything, they were desiccated Apollonians who probably envied the hippies for their unbridled hedonism. Apollo 11 was the healthy blend of humane technology and risk-taking romantic exploration. This was one of the few healthy cultural expressions of the 1960s, but Apollo 11 was a blip on the cultural screen. Today, few people remember the names of the astronauts, and fewer remember just when Americans landed on the moon. Rand's equation of Apollo 11 with a healthy Apollonian mainstream in American culture was quite off the mark. The culture of the 1960s was split between extreme Dionysian protest and a decaying form of Apollonian rationalism. At one end of the culture there was indeed what Max Weber referred to as "the iron cage," the extremes of bureaucratization, conformity, and the replacement of human needs with technological gadgets. At the other end were young people trying to break out of the cage by using ineffective and self-defeating tactics. People are unlikely to break out of the iron cage by smoking dope or shouting mystical incantations.

That the Age of Aquarius, the age of planetary peace and love, would not be fulfilled through rock 'n' roll super spectacles was indicated at the Altamont racetrack in Livermore, California, on December 6, 1969. The Altamont raceway, which no longer attracted real motor races but rather third-rate demolition derbies, was a rundown track surrounded by messy grounds that could only accommodate a midsize crowd of twenty thousand people. When some three hundred thousand rock fans showed up trouble could not be far behind, particularly since the promoters had hired about two hundred Hell's Angels to keep order at the concert. Given a long leash by the promoters and fortifying themselves with generous doses of drugs and alcohol, the Hell's Angels indiscriminately beat up spectators that they judged to be out of control. The star attraction of the concert was Mick Jagger and the Rolling Stones. By the time they appeared, the sun had already set and the atmosphere was tense and eerie. Violence was in the air. Jagger later said, "If Jesus had been there, he would have been crucified."[47] It did not help when the Stones launched into their song "Sympathy for the Devil," for halfway through the song, in plain view of Jagger and the band, several Hell's Angels pounced on a young black man, Meredith Hunter, and knifed him to death. Utter chaos surrounded the stage. Cries by Jagger to stop the violence did little good as the Hell's Angels, now in a wild frenzy, beat people at will. In order to prevent a large-scale riot, the Stones, after several interruptions, decided to play on and then quickly departed by helicopter. The devil had triumphed at Altamont, but mass rock festivals had suffered an irreversible setback with the public.

3. Back to Nature: The Commune Movement

If the real road to countercultural freedom could not be reached through music or politics, perhaps it could be achieved by escaping from the mainstream society altogether. The more seriously minded hippies discovered that "dropping out" by dropping acid and grooving at concerts was a cop-out, a totally ineffective response to the iron cage of industrial society because the response was temporary and hedonistic. Some hippies discovered that sooner or later, dropping out meant having to rebuild some viable form of community, for human beings are, after all, social animals rather than solipsistic hedonists. There was a great deal of discussion among disaffected hippie radicals and even intellectuals in the 1960s about constructing alternative societies outside the much despised middle-class mainstream.

The widely shared need by young people to find a different form of social organization revitalized the commune movement that had deep roots in American history. There had been numerous experiments in building alternative communities in nineteenth-century America that combined all sorts of social panaceas with utopian visions. Some of them were inspired by religious fervor, others by secular and socialistic calls for economic justice and personal self-fulfillment. Few communes lasted for more than a decade, but some, like Brook Farm (Massachusetts), Oneida (New York), Amana Society (Iowa), the Hutterites (South Dakota), and the Shakers (New York), had a long record of independent and self-sufficient living. If hippie dropouts had informed themselves about the history of these earlier communes, they could have avoided the fate of creating communities out of a cultural vacuum. The problem was that many hippies did not know anything beyond momentary impulses and often impulsively charged ahead without proper preparation or discipline. All they knew was that they did not want to live a suburban middle-class life, hoping that their instinctual needs could be satisfied in the company of like-minded peers. In order to give substance to these longings, thousands of hippies joined the "back to the land" movement and fanned out across the wide open spaces of America in search of a better way of life.[48] Those who joined this social secession were by no means all drug-crazed hippies; some were disenchanted artists, writers, Vietnam veterans, rebellious outsiders, women seeking liberation, and so forth. The majority of these communards were young whites in their twenties with some college education; their communes were generally small, consisting of perhaps a dozen people who occupied a few primitive buildings. In some parts of the country, however, the communards took over abandoned towns, as in Georgeville Trading Post, Minnesota, or developed their own villages as in Pandanaram, Indiana. A group of West Coast hippies built a commune in Tennessee called The Farm, while others established communes near Taos, New Mexico, or near the mountains of southern Colorado, notably Drop City, a postindustrial village of geodesic domes.

An important part of the "back to the land" movement was not just farming but communing with nature and expressing oneself in a completely "natural way" which meant uninhibited sensuality. One young female said about life in such a communal setting: "I like it here because I can stand nude on my front porch and yell, fuck."[49] The availability of "free love" undoubtedly attracted many lechers to such communities, but the purpose of dropping out of the mainstream went far beyond sex or drugs. Behind the impulse to escape middle-class society was a strong romantic longing for primitivism, for a way of life without property, rank, or social distinctions. These longings for social self-fulfillment in small and primitive communities were undoubtedly sincere, but many hippies failed to recognize just how difficult it would be to create islands of separatism within modern industrial America.

There were communards who tried to build their communities on avant-garde principles of psychology or Eastern religions. The community at Twin Oaks, Virginia, was modeled on the psychology outlined by B. F. Skinner in his novel *Walden Two*, while New Vrindaban in West Virginia was a Hare Krishna experiment. There were also fundamentalist Christian communes, notably the Children of God settlement on a farm near Brenham, Texas. Some communes featured a smorgasbord of beliefs and practices that their founders threw together higgledy-piggledy.

Although sharing and self-sacrifice were strongly encouraged in most communes, communards had difficulties in submitting to any discipline whatsoever. "Free Love" and drug usage were commonplace, as were bisexuality and group sex. Equality was a watchword on the assumption that all community activity was equal. In one notable exception, when it involved "women's work"—cooking, washing the dishes, or cleaning house—the men usually refused to do it. Sexual roles and stereotypes proved to be almost as resistant to change in the commune as they were in mainstream society. Except for Christian communes, where traditional gender roles were maintained, other communes at least made a pretense of encouraging "consciousness raising" for women, which prepared the way for new male-female roles.

Whether operating communes in the Santa Cruz mountains of California or the desert of New Mexico, communards believed in combining two ultimately irreconcilable needs: doing one's own thing while at the same time functioning as a community of equals. This split-mindedness is at the heart of all utopian experiments; it involves the counterfactual historical claim that humans can indulge in uninhibited narcissism and escape its destructive social consequences. Belief in the impossible, however, opened at least a window of opportunity for many communards. The initial gathering of like-minded believers produced a brief illusion of a new wonderful reality. But after a euphoric high, which involved genuine moments of love, dance, and fraternal feelings, came the awakening to reality. This took the form of bickering and bullying; male sexist prejudices; lack of experience with rural life; and hostility from the surrounding "straight" community. Living a primitive tribal existence proved impossible for many pampered and affluent young Americans. Since few young people had practical skills in managing a household or a farm, they tried to draw on their own meager experiences or turn to self-help books such as Stewart Brand's *Whole Earth Catalog* for support. Sometimes friendly farmers or neighbors lent a helping hand.

It is estimated that by the early 1970s several hundreds of thousands of young Americans lived in some communal setting, ranging from rural farms to urban crashpads.[50] These numbers seem to suggest to some historians that the communes "constituted an enormous social movement."[51] Although it would be foolish to underestimate the importance of communalism, its social significance within American society was relatively minor. Even if we grant that a quarter of a million young people experimented with communal "lifestyles," that number is not very impressive once we remember that seventy-six million baby boomers were born between 1946 and 1964. By 1970 roughly twenty-five million were old enough to participate in communal life, but more young people (eight million) went to college than to the communes. If these figures are any indication, less than 2 percent of young Americans participated in the communal movement. Since most communes ultimately failed, it is safe to say that only a tiny number of dedicated and seasoned communards succeeded in living this lifestyle over more than ten years. Taking into account what has happened since the 1960s it is obvious that the project of developing a competing culture through communes has failed.

The reasons for this failure reside in the fact that the children of a technological civilization could not take a flying leap backwards into tribal primitivism, except as a short-lived fad. Primitive communal life in the modern age cannot sustain a society of 275 million Americans, let alone a global population of six billion. Moreover, historical evidence has shown again and again that people who actually live in primitive and preindustrial areas of the world can hardly wait to escape from such poverty-ridden places and opt for the affluence that modern industrial societies provide. Beyond the obvious economic facts of life, however, what ultimately undermined the communal ideal was the essential narcissistic motives that characterized the behavior of many countercultural rebels. Dropping out of the social mainstream was easy as a temporary fad during unusually prosperous times, but dropping out and creating a viable long-range alternative proved far more difficult, if not impossible, for the pampered children of affluence. Community building beyond one's own generation requires strong religious beliefs, staunch discipline, intergenerational cooperation, and excellent survival skills. Most young people not only lacked such qualities but did not want them in the first place. "Doing one's own thing" is asocial and selfish; it does not build community but undermines it.

The hippie counterculture was essentially an expression of romantic anarchism; it was a heresy of self-love, and as such it was a reactionary phenomenon. But like all such reactionary movements, it was a portent, perhaps a real warning, that indicated that there was something seriously wrong with the spiritually exhausted soil of the cultural mainstream. When all too many young people were not just protesting against the social mainstream but actively trying to escape from it, one can say without exaggeration that the fabric of society was being torn apart. Few hippies succeeded in seceding, and those who did were later marginalized by the corporate mainstream. At the same time many cultural expressions of former countercultural protesters have carried over into the cultural mainstream for the simple reason that the baby boomers now control society. As it turned out, that society was far more tolerant than former radicals were willing to admit at the time, for what other country in the world was as open and tolerant in allowing so many young people to experiment with such radical lifestyles that tested the limits of the endurable?

This raises the question about what cultural elements have been carried over into the mainstream from the hip movement of the 1960s. In the first place, the hip culture of the 1960s was a youth-oriented culture that in many ways attacked maturity as an undesirable stage of life. The slogan "forever young" was intended to promote an unending worship of youth; by contrast, it implied hostility to old age and to the past. By glorifying youth, countercultural movements degraded old age and the collective wisdom of experiences that went along with it to the junkyard of obsolescence. Little Richard's First Law of Youth Culture was to please the kids by shocking the parents. Those who pandered to infantile attitudes—Beats, hippies, intellectuals, and ultimately business corporations—implicitly or explicitly affirmed the virtues of immaturity, instant gratification, self-centeredness, grandiosity, impulsivity, entitlement, and flights of fantasy. Give us anything, many hippies were saying, except bourgeois normality: routine, work, planning for the future, and, above all, rationality.

These countercultural attitudes have not only been carried forward but they have been institutionalized by the consumer society. Since many countercultural rebels have adjusted themselves to the world of work, they have managed to bend that world to their own needs; the business system, in turn, has made major concessions to the puerile attitudes of the baby boomers by accommodating them and turning a good profit in the bargain. Much of today's consumer culture, as Roger Kimball has pointed out, is "Dionysius with a credit card and a college education."[52] Is this what the young rebels meant by liberation? Thanks to the free-wheeling and affluent type of capitalism, young people felt empowered to act irresponsibly and selfishly forever. Was this the inevitable outcome of a special kind of amoral capitalism? In Roger Kimball's judgment, the cultural revolution of the 1960s was not so much anticapitalist as a "toxic by-product of capitalism's success."[53] This judgment is largely accurate, but Kimball does not draw the obvious corollary that the counterculture, in turn, made capitalism more toxic. Whether the counterculture amounted to a cultural revolution is still hotly debated by historians. Revolution involves affirmation as well as rejection. Youthful protest contained few genuine building blocks from which a viable industrial or even postindustrial community could be built. There were only utopian visions that ran counter to both history and human psychology. If there was a revolution, it was an aborted one that destroyed much and built little.

What the countercultural revolt managed to undermine, perhaps even subvert completely, was the Judeo-Christian moral system of the Western world. With its insistence on absolute moral standards and behavioral restraints, the Judeo-Christian morality was widely denounced as a moral straitjacket. Moral relativism was far more congenial to the counterculture because it allowed a maximum of self-indulgence without fear of moral censure. Intellectuals at the time referred to the new and more permissive ethics as "situational ethics," which tried to find ethical solutions within the context of each situation rather than acting on universal principles. In the past, such approaches had been rejected by the Christian mainstream as antinomian. Those who saw themselves as antinomian rejected Christian laws and tried to improvise a makeshift morality that spoke to their own subjective sense of what was right or proper. In many cases, antinomianism was a response to social crisis and the expectation of some impending doom. From a moral point of view, antinomianism has often served as an excuse for libertinism and other excesses, including financial ones. Young people of the 1960s carried this antinomian style forward and tried to institutionalize it. Our current cultural wars are a direct outcome of this 1960s neoromantic and antinomian style, which continues to operate in American culture.

Connected to the antinomian style was the rejection of Western rationality in favor of feelings, emotions, and intuitions. At some point in the 1960s Americans began saying "I feel" rather than "I think," an inversion of the Cartesian dictum "I think therefore I am" (*cogito, ergo sum*). Rousseau has triumphed over Descartes in the popular culture, while Descartes still validates the American illusion of technique. The result is what psychologists call cognitive dissonance: a culture that on the one hand affirms primitivism and feelings but on the other adheres to a counterfactual model of progress through rationality, science, and technology. The tribalism of Woodstock continues, albeit on a smaller screen, on MTV and on just about every level of popular culture. Side by side with such merchandized hedonism there is the iron cage that controls it. One could even argue that such merchandized hedonism is *in* the iron cage. The cultural dissonance is palpable, but most Americans bridge the cultural divide by holding contradictory beliefs in their intellectual worldview and accepting all of them. Whether a country can subscribe to incompatible beliefs indefinitely, can affirm cultural incoherence as well as faith in progress, is most unlikely.

If a youth culture is a cultural dead end, was there anything profound or morally uplifting about the hip culture of the 1960s? Its excesses, of course, are by now well documented, but was there something about youthful protest that transcended narcissistic self-concern? Although white counterculturalists did not create the civil rights movement, their support for social justice was genuine and heartfelt, as was their revulsion against racial prejudice and bigotry. Anyone who had any close relationship with hippies in the 1960s knows how accepting, kind, and almost childlike these young people behaved. They wanted to be treated on their own terms rather than to be judged by adult standards. In addition, what counterculturalists had to say about the dark underside of modern technological society—overcommercialization and overdevelopment—is still highly relevant today. This is why there is a strong connection between the hip movement and the emerging environmental movement. Both converged in their insistence that the planet had to be saved from the ravages of overdevelopment and its associated calamities—population explosion, pollution, destruction of nonrenewable resources, soil erosion, depletion of rain forests, and overcrowding. A deep concern with the environment permeates the music, poetry, and the art of the hip movement. Joni Mitchell's "They paved paradise and put up a parking lot" comes to mind. The flower children of the counterculture were ardent proselytizers for the values of deep ecology, which seeks to replace the destructive nature of unlimited growth with a more conservationist alternative.

There was, of course, a major difference between counterculture and the environmental movement. The difference was one of realism and scientific understanding. Rather than dreaming about ecological utopias such as envisioned in Ernest Callenbach's novel *Ecotopia*, according to which northern California and the Pacific northwest have been deindustrialized, given over to a sustainable economy, enabling its inhabitants to groove on pot, alcohol, and sex, modern environmentalists have approached the problem of postmodern society in a far more realistic way. Jettisoning escapist approaches in the form of realistic alternatives, most scientifically grounded environmentalists have tried to demonstrate that humans cannot escape from society into some romanticized state of nature or wilderness, but can, with some scientific ingenuity, live a far more balanced and wholesome way of life than the one that is now experienced in the industrialized West.

The youth culture displayed genuinely idealistic tendencies, but these were rarely guided by insight or wisdom, as one would expect from young people. If their hearts were often in the right place, their heads were not. In fact, their anti-intellectual attitudes undercut their capacity for both recognizing and preventing the predictable consequences that always seem to occur when feelings short-circuit rationality. Nor did it help to cut oneself loose from the wisdom of previous experience and generational ties. The resulting vacuum produced a great deal of cultural chaos from which no order has emerged so far.

4. It's the Music, Stupid!

In his splendid cultural history of the Western world, entitled *From Dawn to Decadence*, Jacques Barzun never mentions rock 'n' roll, the music that mesmerized more people in the Western world than any other music before or since. Barzun devoted the last section of his book to what he called "Demotic Life and Times," by which he meant the ethos of the period in decline, the ethos of what is "common" or "of the people."[54] What could be more common or of the people, especially young people, than rock 'n' roll music? Barzun's omission of rock 'n' roll is really puzzling in view of the fact that he has done considerable work on romanticism, which is one of the strains that can be detected in rock music. It may well be that Barzun, like other cultural critics, believes that rock is a perverse form of neoromantic modernism and therefore can be safely dismissed as a serious musical idiom. Such an interpretation, however, would be shortsighted on several accounts. In the first place, music is music, no matter how many or how few people listen to it. Since the mid-1950s rock has been the music of young people around the world, and for that reason it deserves serious attention. In the second place, the music of the 1960s is a cultural benchmark that reveals what was in the hearts and minds of young people not only in America but also in the Western world as a whole, including those parts of the world that were strongly influenced by the West: Latin America, Africa, India, and sizable portions of Southeast Asia. In the third place, rock 'n' roll was a rebellious kind of music because it broke down inhibitions and repressions, allowing people to regain their bodies and express feelings otherwise forbidden by conventional society. As such, rock was culturally subversive to any classical or Apollonian society, which explains, in part, the initial rage against it by mainstream critics. Rock musicians unlocked the Pandora's box of white civilization, releasing its quintessential fears of unbridled sexuality, unabashed vulgarity, the release of the primitive, and the breaking of all cultural taboos.[55]

It could have happened only in America precisely because its demotic way of life encouraged a multitude of popular and ever-mutating musical idioms: rhythm and blues, jazz, country western, and folk music. Moreover, these idioms were multicultural and ethnically diverse in contrast to the more homogeneous classical music of the West. What is particularly unique about the various strains that molded rock music is that they are part of the racial dynamics of American society. Many American musical idioms have been created by black people but have been subsequently appropriated by whites in both a warmly appreciative but also a coldly exploitive way. This crossover of black music into white society is one of the most fascinating cultural phenomena of the modern world, but its deeper psychological significance has usually been ignored by historians because that story involves what Martha Bayles calls the "racial blood-knot."[56] The term comes from a play by the South African writer Athol Fugard; it is the story of two half-brothers, one officially black and the other officially white, whose lives intertwine despite the racist segregationist policies of apartheid in South Africa. Blood-knot is an apt metaphor for the tangled web of sex and race that is at the heart of American culture. This is not the place to untie this tangled knot except to say in passing that rock music is the white man's adoption of black musical idioms. Cultural crossovers are always hybrids because they are imitations of form rather than substance. For white audiences, however, the mythology of black music became a "screen upon which to project a montage of the primitive for at least three hundred years."[57] The imitation of black musical idioms, first in America, then Europe, and now in most of the world, according to Robert Pattison, represents the biggest cultural crossover since Moses parted the Red Sea.[58]

What resonated through the music of the 1960s was a mood of rebellious opposition to authority on all levels. This oppositional stance, of course, was the leitmotif of the baby boom generation in general. It marked them distinctly from previous generations in both mood and style of expression. Like earlier popular musical idioms, rock began as a medium of sentimental love lyrics, but as it evolved under the influence of larger social forces such as the civil rights movement and the antiwar protests, the music took on a far more serious role. Young people began to express their alienation from American institutions and openly protested racial injustice and war. Popular critics, who hardly deigned to take this music seriously in the 1950s, began to notice that the popular music of the 1960s was an eclectic mixture of many musical traditions and instruments, and that its subject matter conveyed serious social issues such as racial injustice, drug experiences, sexual expression, interracial dating, war, and so forth.[59] A harsher world was impinging on the dream world of the 1950s changing the music beyond recognition.

This greater seriousness can be seen very early in the 1960s with the popular resurgence of folk music, which followed on the heels of the 1950s rock craze associated with Elvis Presley. The folk revival started on American campuses in the early 1960s and included Joan Baez; the Kingston Trio; Peter, Paul and Mary; the Limeliters; and the Chad Mitchell Trio. Some of these folksingers harked back to the 1930s and drew on populist themes sung by a previous generation of folksingers—Woody Guthrie, Jack Elliott, Pete Seeger, and the Weavers. This began to change when folksingers wrote their own songs rather than relying on traditional themes. The most compelling folk minstrel of the 1960s was Bob Dylan, who consciously modeled himself after Woody Guthrie while at the same time voicing the specific concerns of his own generation.[60] Such concerns are expressed in his songs "Blowin' in the Wind," "A Hard Rain's A-Gonna Fall," and the most famous 1960s countercultural song "The Times They Are A-Changin'." Dylan's artistic concerns parallel the concerns of young people in the 1960s: they start out with songs about the plight of the common man, racial injustice, and social exploitation, and mutate into preoccupation with personal obsessions about drugs, love relationships, and existential anxieties.

Although the music of the 1960s reflects the turbulence of the time, its general message is curiously apolitical. There is protest aplenty, but its mood reflects the personal alienation of the musician from what he perceives to be an unfriendly, even callous environment. Most musicians were young and white. Not surprisingly, their concerns were with their own fears and anxieties, though some white singers, notably Phil Ochs, Janis Joplin, and Frank Zappa, made genuine efforts to identify with the reality of black suffering in the south or in northern ghettos. Country Joe and the Fish warns: "But if you can't go to Harlem . . . Maybe you'll be lucky and Harlem will come to you,"[61] while Frank Zappa sadly admits, "You know something people, I ain't black but there's whole lots of times I wish I could say I'm not white."[62]

Such sympathetic references to the plight of blacks are relatively rare, as are the traditional concerns with exploited workers, labor leaders, scabs, and company spies. Young whites also withdrew from mainstream politics after the assassination of John F. Kennedy. The fallen hero of Camelot, of course, inspired more than one song, notably, "He Was a Friend of Mine." The same accolades were not accorded to John-

son or Nixon. Country Joe and the Fish spoke for their generation in mocking Johnson as a pathetic cowboy: "It's a bird, it's a plane, it's a man insane, it's my President
LBJ . . . come out Lyndon with your hands held high. Drop your guns, baby, and reach
for the sky . . . I've got you surrounded and you ain't got a chance. Send you back to
Texas, make you work on your ranch."[63]

The war in Vietnam caused a flood of musical protest. The most popular was P. F.
Sloan's "Eve of Destruction" (1965), in which the strident and angry singer cries out:
"You're old enough to kill, but not for votin'/And tell me over and over and over
again my friend/You don't believe we're on the eve of destruction."[64] Defiance of the
draft and refusal to carry a gun are themes in Buffy Sainte-Marie's "Universal Soldier" and Phil Ochs's "I Ain't a' Marchin' Anymore." One of the most poignant antiwar songs is by the Byrds, called "Draft Morning," in which a young man leaves his
warm bed to take up arms against "unknown faces," asking, "Why should it happen?"

The Vietnam War inspired many blistering antiwar songs but only one prowar
ballad, "The Ballad of the Green Berets." In "I-Feel-Like-I'm Fixin'-to-Die Rag,"
Country Joe McDonald mocks the sordid propaganda of Uncle Sam beckoning
young Americans to get him out of a jam in Vietnam:

Come on all you big strong men
Uncle Sam needs your help again
He's got himself in a terrible jam
Way down yonder in Vietnam
So put down your books and pick up a gun
We're gonna have a whole lot of fun!
And it's one, two, three
What are we fighting for
Don't ask me, I don't give a damn
Next stop is Viet Nam
And it's five, six, seven
Open up the Pearly Gates
There ain't no time to wonder why
Whoopie, we're all gonna die! . . .
Come on, Wall Street, don't be slow
Why, man, this war is au-go-go
There's plenty of money to be made
Supplyin' the army with the tools of the trade
Just hope and pray if they drop the Bomb
They drop it on the Viet Cong!
Come on, mothers, throughout the land
Pack your boys off to Viet Nam
Come on, fathers, don't hesitate
Send your sons off before it's too late
Be the first on your block
To have your boy come home in a box[65]

The fact that young people protested the war in both song and deed is understandable, since the Vietnam War was a real danger to the lives of those who were sent

to fight there. What is less understandable, even astounding, is that the music of the 1960s conveyed the conviction that American society and its institutions were so repressive that withdrawal, escapism, and revolution were the only meaningful response to such intolerable conditions. Coming from largely young whites who had enjoyed remarkable affluence, this perception of an ugly, repressive, and conformist America represents one of the most curious generational perceptions in history. Without assessing the relative merit or demerit of this negative image of American society, just listen to the complaints and indictments that came out of the music of that troubled decade.

The most common complaint one hears in the music of the 1960s is that American society stifles freedom and creativity by forcing people, especially young people, to conform to narrow middle-class rules pertaining to speech, dress, sexual activity, and public behavior. Young people saw themselves as victims of a mendacious older generation that was always down on young people: "Down on me, down on me/ Looks like everybody in this whole round world is down on me,"[66] sang Janis Joplin. Why is that? Is it because older Americans cannot tolerate differences and hate all those things young people like: long hair, beards, funky clothes, loud music? Well, said the young, "If it's too loud, you're too old."[67] You are also too old if you don't understand "a-wop-bob-a-loom-op-a-lop-bam boom" or "ah-ummm" or "da-doo-run-run-run, da-doo-run run."[68]

One of the great fears of young people was to be a tiny cog in the conformist machine. In "Mr. Blue," written by Tom Paxton, the Orwellian narrator tells the title character that he is always under surveillance by Big Brother, who wants him to fill a slot and love it or else he will break him. The chorus then breaks in menacingly by reminding Mr. Blue:

> What will it take to whip you into line
> A broken heart?
> A broken head?
> It can be arranged.[69]

The numbing vision that Henry Miller described in *The Air-conditioned Nightmare*, the prefabricated world of modern industrial America, is a recurring theme in the music of the 1960s. Having grown up in the tidy well-manicured environment of suburban Levittowns, young people disdainfully denounced their surroundings as little boxes made of ticky-tacky:

> Little boxes on the hillside,
> Little boxes made of ticky tacky
> Little boxes on the hillside
> Little boxes all the same;
> There's a green one and a pink one
> And a blue one and a yellow one
> And they're all made of ticky tacky
> And they all look just the same

And the people in the houses
All went to the university
Where they were put in boxes
And they came out all the same,
And there's doctors and lawyers,
And business executives,
And they're all made out of ticky tacky
And they all look just the same.

And they all play on the golf course
And drink their martinis dry
And they all have pretty children
And the children go to school
And the children go to summer camp
And then to the university,
Where they are put in boxes
And they come out all the same.

Little boxes on the hillside,
Little boxes made of ticky tacky
Little boxes on the hillside
Little boxes all the same;
And the boys go into business
And marry and raise a family
In boxes made of ticky tacky
And they all look just the same[70]

Many young people said no to the ideals of their parents—no to crew cuts, bow ties, skirts, make up, sexless dating, polite manners, Rodgers and Hammerstein songs. "The Times They Are A-Changin'" sang Bob Dylan; and in "Ballad of a Thin Man" he taunted Mr. Everyman: "Something is happening here/But you don't know what it is/Do you, Mister Jones?"[71] Young people did not want the tidy world that their parents were worshiping. In their complaints against middle-class life, there is usually some rejection of technology because it is a double-edged sword that protects as well as slays, provides comforts and destroys the environment. Jim Morrison of the Doors asked: "What have we done to the earth? What have we done to our fair sister? Ravished and plundered and nipped her and bit her. Stuck her with knives in the side of the dawn. And tied her with fences and dragged her down."[72]

Little boxes of ticky-tacky, plastic flowers, artificial scents and flavors—all of these are by-products of an artificial technocracy, raising fears among singers that modern America was becoming absurdly artificial, standardized, and conformist. Frank Zappa and the Mothers of Invention repeatedly warned that the United States is a plastic country run by a plastic Congress and a plastic president. In the song "Plastic People" the Mothers suggest that everyone, including the Mothers and their listeners, might be plastic—in short, artificial, which would make the whole world plastic. The ultimate horror, of course, is that even love might be plastic, especially in the

United States. In fact, in his autobiographical ramblings *The Real Frank Zappa Book*, Zappa said that he detested love lyrics because they do not tell the truth about love; they feed the illusion of plastic love called "making love," a "wussy word" no one uses in the real world.[73]

Like Dustin Hoffman playing Ben in the motion picture *The Graduate,* many young people were afraid of being ensnared in loveless marriages in which sex becomes an infrequent or perfunctory routine rather than a celebration of love and life. Singers expressed the fear of ending up like their parents, trapped in a middle-class marriage. Since most of the songs reflect white male attitudes about women, the songs of the 1960s criticize women for hanging on to their mothers' allegedly frigid attitudes. The Mothers of Invention accuse women of lying in bed and gritting their teeth, and the Sopwith Camel insist that "I don't want no woman wrapped in cellophane."[74]

Since young musicians believed that society was dominated by repressed old people who were trying to mold the young into their mental straitjacket, the song writers recommended various coping mechanisms: sex, drugs, or escape into communes of like-minded seekers. Live for the moment and be free; drugs are the gateway to such freedom. Take that journey to the center of your mind:

Come along if you can
Come along if you dare
Take a ride to the land inside of your mind
But please realize, you'll probably be surprised
For in the land unknown to man
Where fantasy is fact
So if you can, please understand
You might not come back[75]

Acid-tinged songs began to proliferate in the late sixties under the stresses of violence, war, and protest. From the Rolling Stones' early "Mother's Little Helper" to the Beatles' acid-dripping "Strawberry Fields Forever" and Dylan's "Rainy Day Women," the drug message is clear: run for the shelter of mother's little acid helper, live on the edge, and avoid, if at all possible, being forced into the straitjacket of adulthood. The great fear was growing old: "hope I die before I get old," exclaimed the Who. It is best, therefore, to "hold onto sixteen as long as you can." The baby boomer chorus added a triumphant exclamation point with the generational refrain:

We are the young,
Breaking all the walls,
Breaking all the rules.[76]

In the meantime, of course, there were still those old people trying to maintain the wall of bourgeois oppression. Another way of coping with this repressive society was to beat a retreat to the country. This theme figured prominently in Bob Dylan's *Nashville Skyline* and *New Morning* albums, Buffy Sainte-Marie's "I'm Gonna Be a

Country Girl Again," Canned Heat's "Goin' up the Country," and Creedence Clear-water Revival, which combined country, blues, and rock with a tinge of bayou.

The main rock themes of the 1960s, ranging from defying authority, longing for freedom, and smashing conventions, to protesting against war and injustice culminated in the most popular band of the decade—the Beatles.[77] When the four Liverpudlian mop-heads—John Lennon, Paul McCartney, George Harrison, and Ringo Starr—first appeared on the *Ed Sullivan Show* on November 9, 1964, it began the second pop explosion, the first being associated with Elvis Presley in the 1950s. This second explosion occurred not just in the United States but throughout the whole Western world. It is estimated that some seventy-three million viewers watched the Beatles on the *Ed Sullivan Show*.[78] By 1967 "Beatlemania" had spread around the world, prompting John Lennon to opine that the Beatles were more popular than Jesus Christ. How 1960s—all the fame with none of the pain. When the group's *Sgt. Pepper* album came out in the same year, one musical critic, Langdon Winner, announced that this event marked a red-letter day of global unity that had not been experienced since the Congress of Vienna in 1815.[79] What accounts for such extraordinary reactions to a small band of talented but not brilliant musicians from Liverpool?

Part of the answer to this mass media hyperventilating, which still shows no serious signs of diminishing, can be found in the yearning of young people for role models of their own, particularly since the assassination of John F. Kennedy had left a real void in genuine hero worship. Another piece of the puzzle was the power of mass media in transforming even modest talent and inflating it to the ranks of the great musical masters. Without the business genius of Brian Epstein, who gave the Beatles a modish-looking makeover, the band would have probably remained a purely local British oddity. If we add the aggressive merchandizing that churned out Beatle wigs, clothes, dolls, lunch boxes, and other assorted kitsch, then the behavior of hysterical fans begins to explain this curious postmodern spectacle. The final missing element however, was the creative contribution of the Beatles themselves. The band operated like a huge sponge, absorbing most of the musical idioms that had come before them. The Beatles were brilliant synthesizers who creatively recombined all sorts of musical elements from previous rock 'n' roll innovators. Their electric guitar riffs came from Chuck Berry and Buddy Holly, as did the importance of writing their own lyrics. Gospel and blues vocalists showed them how to mix harmony with rhythm, and to heighten the effects of their singing through a mid-tempo range.[80] The use of studio techniques came from Motown and Phil Spector, and "skiffle" music, a New Orleans type of black street music, taught the Beatles initially to stick to simple self-instrumentation rather than opt for elaborate studio arrangements. Black sounds and rhythms were the crucial ingredients that made Beatle music such a great success. As John Lennon later told *Rolling Stone* magazine, "It was the black music we dug . . . we felt that we had the message, which was 'Listen to the music.' When we came here . . . nobody was listening to rock and roll or to black music in America. We felt as though we were coming to the land of its origin, but nobody wanted to know about it."[81] Lennon was not exaggerating about the significance of black music in shaping rock 'n' roll. In black music white adolescents felt that they had discovered the key to passionate self-expression. Feeling themselves to be cultural outsiders, opposed to the stifling rules imposed on them by their parents, teenagers discovered in black music the sounds of protest they could use to validate their own generational opposition in the form of primitive and unbridled romanticism.

The history of Beatle music paralleled the social changes of the 1960s. Initially the Beatles turned out simple boy-meets-girl songs that were not overly threatening to adults. In fact, their light-hearted, witty, and often self-deprecating manners disarmed even their most skeptical critics. The band's early songs—"Love Me Do," "I Want to Hold Your Hand," "Please Please Me"—were quite innocent and sexually nonthreatening; they moved entirely within a restrained, even sanitized milieu of 1950s rock 'n' roll. By 1964, however, their music became far more varied, complex, and in some respects more subversive to traditional middle-class tastes. After meeting Bob Dylan, who introduced them to marijuana, the Beatles began to absorb drugs into their musical bloodstream. This preoccupation with drugs was on display in their second and third motion pictures—*Help* and *A Hard Day's Night*—as well as two of their best selling albums—*Rubber Soul* and *Revolver*. In their *Rubber Soul* album, which was a variation on a theme rather than a collection of singles, the Beatles struck a persistent sexual tone, while in *Revolver* the lyrics were tinged with acid, especially in the song "Dr. Roberts," where the sounds were played backwards, a technique that Lennon accidentally discovered while being under the influence of LSD.

Just about the time when American flower children were heading toward San Francisco to participate in the "Summer of Love," the Beatles came out with their *Sgt. Pepper's Lonely Hearts Club Band* album. This concept album, packed with brilliant lyrics and social commentary, represents the best but also some of the more troublesome expressions of the 1960s. The album was a triumph of audience manipulation, from the opening "It's wonderful to be here, we'd love to take you home with us," the invitation to "get high with a little help from my friends," "Lucy in the Sky with Diamonds" (the title reduces to the acronym LSD), mournful evocations of loneliness and spiritual emptiness, to New Age psychology of finding the truth within and saving the world through love. The album's cover, a mélange of images of popular icons, including Marx, Mae West, Marilyn Monroe, W. C. Fields, Marlon Brando, Bob Dylan, Gandhi, among others, was a typical and incoherent smorgasbord of countercultural perceptions of reality. The point of the music and its lyrics was to take the listeners into a split world in which fantasy and reality were blurred. Since the Beatles insisted that everything about this album had to be different, the band and the sound engineers pushed rock 'n' roll far beyond its traditional musical limits, resulting in bizarre experimentation with crowd noises, screeching tires, crowing roosters, barking dogs, the use of different keys and tempos, and even the reliance on massed orchestral instruments. As the recording engineer, Geoff Emerick, put it,

> everything was either distorted, limited, heavily compressed or treated with excessive equalization. We had microphones right down in the bells of the brass instruments and headphones turned into microphones attached to violins. We plastered vast amounts of echo onto vocals, and sent them through the circuitry of the revolving Leslie speaker

inside a Hammond organ. We used giant primitive oscillators to vary the speed of instruments and vocals and we had tapes chopped to pieces and stuck together upside down and the wrong way round.[82]

The result was a technological illusion of sounds and voices that perfectly captured the chaotic mood of the turbulent 1960s. That mood reflected the wishful thinking, anxieties, frustrations, and longings of young people with remarkable accuracy. Each song raised particular social concerns—that money could not buy love, teachers were not "cool," parents were selfish control freaks, the system did not work, and escape into a dream world of love and spiritual introspection was the only answer to the ills of the world.

Following the *Sgt. Pepper* album, the Beatles produced an unsuccessful television film, *Magical Mystery Tour,* which spelled the beginning of a gradual decline for the band. The psychedelic tour the Beatles wanted their fans to take was to such marvelous places as Strawberry Fields where nothing is real, "but nothing to get hung about." The Beatles, however, were beginning to get hung about drugs and "Transcendental Meditation," journeying to India with the Maharishi Mahesh Yogi, who was mass merchandising yogic techniques that promised practitioners that they did not have to deal with the harsh, external world but needed only to reach within themselves to unlock some reservoir of happiness and joy. The Beatles did not find that ultimate joy for themselves, though John Lennon exclaimed that he discovered at least two things he could believe in: himself and his Japanese girlfriend Yoko Ono. Lennon's new girlfriend, who hung around the recording studio too often, caused serious friction in the band, as did the increasingly competitive differences between Lennon and McCartney. Success and ever higher and higher expectations of the band by the public produced more tensions. In August 1967, Brian Epstein, the Beatles' brilliant manager, died of a drug overdose. Still the Beatles turned out several additional albums before they split up and went their separate ways. Their *White Album,* released in 1968 under their own Apple Record label, consisted of mostly solo vocals. The cartoon film *Yellow Submarine* produced by Czech designer Heinz Edelmann, turned out to be one of the last great Beatle successes, except for their highly popular single "Hey Jude," introduced on the *Ed Sullivan Show* in 1968. In 1969 the band tried to produce a *Get Back* album featuring a kind of movie soundtrack of dozens of Beatle songs going all the way back to their Hamburg years. The sessions revealed that serious problems were brewing; in fact, the session essentially recorded their breakup. The initial editing fell to Phil Spector, who put together a mélange of songs published in 1969 as *Get Back,* followed by a slightly altered version, *Let It Be* in the spring of 1970. The latter edition is essentially a movie soundtrack version, including an impromptu concert on the rooftop of the Apple Corporation headquarters building. Before *Let It Be* was finally released the Beatles had collaborated for the last time on an album in the spring and summer of 1969. *Abbey Road,* a kind of reconciliation album arranged by their manager George Martin, became their best-selling album, but it was their final hurrah. John Lennon announced that he wanted a divorce from the band and went his own way, accompanied by Yoko Ono. The others also went their own separate paths, opting for countercultural rebellion

(John Lennon), pop music (Paul McCartney), spiritual self-discovery (George Harrison) and all-around celebrity good guy (Ringo Starr).

The Beatles were an amplified echo of the turbulent sixties; they absorbed and exhibited every popular fashion, fad, and excess, but they did it with playful irreverence rather than subversive intent.[83] The same cannot be said of the invasion of other British rock bands who followed on the heels of the Beatles—the Who, Kinks, Animals, and Rolling Stones.

Of these British rock bands, it was the Rolling Stones who inspired the self-righteous contempt for middle-class culture that was imitated by so many other bands of the 1960s and beyond.[84] The Stones adopted the posture of social outlaws, and they heaped contempt on mainstream society by mocking its most cherished values. Lead singer Mick Jagger, supported by his friend and guitarist Keith Richards, had started the band in 1962, adding, along the way, blues guitarist Brian Jones, bassist Bill Wyman, and drummer Charlie Watts. Billing themselves as darker and grittier Beatles, they soon set the musical scene on fire with their wild antics and defiant provocations. Their music, generally considered to be of greater intensity, depth, and complexity than that of the Beatles, was a blend of amplified gospel, repetitive blues riffs, soulful background vocals, and dark, jagged rhythms. Bill Wyman and Charlie Watts provided the background beat, while Brian Jones and Keith Richards covered the middle ground. This left Mick Jagger to scream out the lyrics in a style that alternated between ecstatic self-love and willful defiance. Nothing was sacred to the Stones, no social taboo safe from mocking ridicule. Strutting about the stage like a bantam rooster, Jagger whined about "I can't get no satisfaction, I can't get no girl reaction," but that "Time Is on My Side," the "Little Red Rooster Is on the Prowl." Nothing so much offended middle-class sensibilities as reference to explicit sexuality. Americans, in particular, had a visceral fear of open sexuality, while at the same time tolerating the most obscene depiction of raw violence. The Rolling Stones delighted in lacing their lyrics with sexually suggestive language. When Ed Sullivan invited them on his show in 1967, the Stones had to change the title of one of their songs from "Let's Spend the Night Together" to "Let's Spend Some Time Together." Besides obsessing about sex, drugs, and violence, the music of the Rolling Stones took on a darker and darker hue, evoking troubling images of ghosts and demons, as in "Paint It Black," "Let It Bleed," and "Sympathy for the Devil." These were dark rhapsodies of lost innocence, loneliness, despair, and death. Given such preoccupations with nihilistic moods, it is not surprising that trouble shadowed the band wherever it went. Jagger, Richards, and Jones were arrested on drug possession charges; in July 1969 Brian Jones was found dead in his swimming pool, most likely the result of a drug overdose; and in August 1969 the Stones were embroiled in the Altamont tragedy, already described.

Not to put too fine a point on it, the Stones and similar acid bands of the late 1960s no longer played rock 'n' roll but raunch 'n' roll of the most decadent sort. This was perhaps only to be expected, for rock absorbed and refracted the turbulent social changes rather than helped to shape them.[85] The music's increasingly violent and nihilistic tone, however, significantly depressed the mood of many young people, which in turn, expressed itself in defiant attitudes and morbid preoccupation with the abnormal. In fact, rock music morphed into neoromantic perversity, a sickness of the soul long recognized by critics as the inevitable consequence of unbridled romanticism. In a demotic culture, such unbridled romanticism, luxuriating in primitivism, animalism, and vulgarity, infected the whole culture by the sheer numbers of its practitioners. The Rolling Stones and other bands reflected the feelings of millions of young people who felt like tearing the whole fabric of polite, refined, or "civilized" society to shreds and replacing it with a culture of democratic primitivism.

One of the most destructive bands of the 1960s, one that raised the nihilism and apocalyptic mood of the Rolling Stones to an even higher level, was a West Coast band called the Doors. Led by its deeply disturbed lead singer, Jim Morrison, a kind of man-child aspiring to be a poet like Blake, Rimbaud, or Baudelaire, the Doors specialized in shocking their audiences, giving them, in the words of one critic, the "psychological equivalence of the guillotine."[86] The term "Doors" actually referred to the poet Blake's belief that certain visionary powers could open the doors of perception and allow people to behold an infinite and purer reality. Aldous Huxley had also used the metaphor in his essay "Doors of Perception" (1954). Needless to say, far from opening the door to a "purer" world, the Doors found little more than violence, sexual perversity, nihilism, and death. Their *pièce de résistance* was the Oedipal song "End," in which a demented son commits the unspeakable taboo of killing his father and fucking his mother. In some live performances, the son graphically describes going down the family hallway, knocking on his father's bedroom door: "Father? Yes son? I want to kill you. Mother? I want to fuck you." After a sinister whine, followed by a crashing sound, the son's (Morrison's) hoarse voice could be heard chanting: "Kill! Kill! Kill! Fuck! Fuck! Fuck!" One contemporary musical critic called this song truly revolutionary, a term frequently used by puerile boosters of vulgarity, and referred to the Doors as the "finest performing musicians on the contemporary scene."[87] In the same breath, this critic dismissed Oswald Spengler's "unfounded anxieties" about cultural decline and asserted that such rock 'n' roll music had elevated popular tastes to "the summit of popular culture."[88] It is truly edifying to learn that incest and patricide are summits of popular taste.

Such pandering, puerile, and perverse judgments, however, are—well, so 1960s. Everything in the 1960s was grist for the same vulgar mill. A succession of weirder and wilder bands pulled the neoromantic cultural chains: the Velvet Underground, the Animals, Black Sabbath, Fleetwood Mac, Led Zeppelin, Steppenwolf, and so forth. Fortunes were quickly made and lost, fame proved ephemeral, and drugs took a heavy toll. Janis Joplin died of a drug overdose, so did Jim Morrison, Brian Jones, Jimi Hendrix, Brian Epstein, Gram Parsons, Dennis Wilson, Sid Vicious, Brian Cole, Tim Hardin, Keith Moon, Gary Thain, Danny Whitten, and others.[89]

At the very heart of the youth culture of the 1960s, then, was rock 'n' roll music, and what ultimately defined it was the mood it created for millions of baby boomers. This mood and the attitudes that stemmed from it were all about self-absorption, sexual self-expression, and defiance of middle-class values. The "rock star" was both worshiped and self-worshiping. Young pubescent boys and girls responded to the rock stars on stage by emitting ecstatic shrieks and erotic moans; they became a pack of primitive yahoos infatuated with the sensations the music aroused in their bodies. The sexual component was obvious, especially with young teenage girls, who moaned at the sight of young, horny, and well-hung male rockers. The "rock experience," especially in large concert settings, was a cultural regression to primitive tribalism; by going to a rock festival, as Herbert London put it, one felt as though one was participating in the rites of some obscure tribe.[90] But such tribal musical rituals were a white fantasy about black culture, whose mournful, hard-edge blues music and genuine sensuality came out of centuries of black suffering. When affluent white boys appropriated black music, they ultimately produced a counterfeit of make-believe primitivism and either ooooo-feeling so good about everything juvenile—girls, cars, game, sun, and surf—or ooooo-feeling so bad about the world. As the music absorbed the violence and decadence of the late 1960s, often hijacked by corporate greed, it increasingly became a social narcotic, a postmodern opium of the people. Moreover, in its many different forms and expressions, it almost completely displaced any other form of music in the Western world. Both classical music and jazz are essentially dead as demotic musical idioms because they require a high degree of musical proficiency and a mature aesthetic sensibility. With today's technology, even musical fools can make recordings. None of the members of Duran Duran knew how to play an instrument six months before the band became internationally famous.[91] Milli Vanilli, after receiving a Grammy award, admitted that they lip-synched their hits and actually never sang a note on their records—all of it being done electronically. It proved that one could make "records" without any live performance at all, composing everything from disconnected tracks of guitars, keyboards, drums, vocals, strings—all of it put through electronic blenders (synthesizers) in a recording studio.

Rock has indeed proved, with a mighty helping hand from corporate giants, that it is here to stay, but its original freshness in the early 1960s has been dissipated. It was the hard side of the youthful counterculture that undermined popular music, turning it into what Martha Bayles called perverse modernism, with its attack on the past, aesthetic standards, and its denial that there is a line between art and life.[92] This kind of decadent modernism also represented the white perversion of black music with a good helping hand from technological wizardry. As Robert Pattison observed, rock is a counterfeit because it

> celebrates pastoral and primitive utopias while swathing its stars in polyester jockstraps and arming itself with the latest devices of electronic technology. It chants the beauty of individuality to an audience that has become a howling mob. It extols the simple virtues of honest feelings from record and video studios created on the most greedy and ambitious frontiers of electronic capitalism.[93]

Left-wing critics, often joined by right-wing conservatives, have condemned rock music not only as a vulgar form of art but also as a social narcotic that alienates young people from social reality and thus turns them into pliant zombies of corporate capitalism. These accusations have never resonated with those who love rock 'n' roll, which today in its many protean varieties has completely triumphed in popular culture. Whether rock is good or bad, revolutionary, primitive, or vulgar is of no concern to those who love it; they love it because it is, as Aretha Franklin rightly put it, "all about feelings." And if rock is all about feelings, it is immune to intellectual criticism. It is good because the majority feels that it is good; therefore it is good. This, of course, is nonsense on stilts, but therein lies the meaning of the rock experience: it is the genuine demotic expression of Western civilization in decline. As Pattison put it, rock is the "democracy of instinct"; and as such, it transcends all traditional class distinctions.[94] As this is being written, rock music knows no class, ethnicity, religion, or nationality; it appeals to the educated and uneducated alike. In short, its absence of aesthetic standards and its appeal to feelings make it a global and demotic medium of popular moods and lifestyles.

Rock music has also blasted the traditional Western culture of refinement, good taste, and aesthetic self-limitation to smithereens. With the help of other postmodern movements, rock has given us the culture we deserve: a culture without cultivation.[95] In the *Republic* Plato alerted his readers to "mark the music" in a society because that would provide the most reliable means of taking its spiritual temperature. As readers of Plato know, the *Republic* includes strong strictures against rhythm and harmony, especially when combined with dance, because they are barbarous expressions of the soul. Plato knew that music was the medium of archaic primitivism and coarse sensuality; as such, it represented a threat to cultivation and refinement, which are the hallmarks of civilization. In Plato's view civilization implies the taming of the soul's raw passion, a theme that undergirded not only Greco-Roman (classical) but also Judeo-Christian civilization. In his book *Closing of the American Mind*, Allan Bloom worried not just about the moral effect of rock music—whether it leads to sex, violence, and drugs—but about what it does to education, especially the education of the senses. It is Bloom's contention that the music ruins the imagination of young people because it undermines real passion for learning and all other forms of spirituality.[96] Thus, by radically separating intellect from feeling, subordinating the former to the latter, rock music as a mode of being arouses passions and provides models that have no relation to the real life young educated people are expected to lead. A music that has become a "lifestyle," fixated entirely on the body and its needs, wants, and desires, is unlikely to inspire higher-order thinking, let alone genuine spirituality. Moreover, a culture that mass markets a flood of seductive images and sounds and sexualizes its young people before they can maturely handle their raw feelings, is toying with disaster. Sounds and images are more seductive than words; they produce pleasurable sensations that seem to speak a deeper truth than the mere rational babblings of parents or teachers. Hearing the enticing sounds of rock music sends shivers down the spines of pubescent teenagers. It makes them want to dance. By contrast, you cannot dance to Beethoven. The music is too refined and perhaps also too cerebral, requiring mature aesthetic sensibility. This is why classical music, associated with a pre-demotic past, has no salience in Western culture today. Rock music is, and for a long time will be, the music of mass democracy. At its very core, it consists of little more than puerile emotions and superficial sentiments. Extraordinary how potent cheap music is.

5. Counterculture into Consumer Culture

One of the most persistent myths that came out of rock music was the idea that authenticity meant uncompromising rebellion against the cultural mainstream, including rock music, which appeared to become too popular and was therefore no longer on the cutting edge of authenticity. When that stage had been reached, when musicians or artists became mainstream because more people enjoyed appreciating their art, they were often condemned by countercultural critics for having "sold out" to the corporate system. This explains the mania to discover new "alternative" styles of cultural rebellion, the latest always pushing further beyond the line of commonly held middle-class proprieties—until, at length, rebellion and excess themselves became the cultural benchmark. The evolution of rock music shows this line of "progression" toward the holy grail of rebellion, mutating from one style to another: classical rock, Doo Wop, pop rock, Beatle rock, folk rock, acid rock, heavy-metal rock, soul, Motown, punk, funk, disco, Reggae, schock, hip hop, rap, gangsta rap, progressive rock, industrial rock, techno rock, Euro-rock, art rock, etc., etc.

The myth that music, art, and literature must be oppositional to be authentic and that this require artistic independence from corporate control still exercises a seductive influence on the imagination of countercultural rebels. It is a mythic theme that is as old as the "art for art's sake" movement, a theme that expresses genuine fear of having to compromise one's artistic integrity by going mainstream and prostituting oneself to capitalist market forces. Such fear and loathing have given rise over the last one hundred years to a number of artistic strategies designed to insulate artistic authenticity from the corrupting influence of bourgeois capitalism, strategies that have ranged from escape into Elysian utopias, enchantments with primitive or exotic lands or people, defiant poses or attitudes (the dandy, bohemian, Beat, hippie), longing for the fraternal or spiritual community of like-minded outsiders, to the search for some charismatic leader with a redemptive ideology. A distinctive contribution of sixties rebels was the assumption that cultural protest and "consciousness-raising" by themselves could subvert the whole system of capitalist exploitation.

Countercultural rebellion, however, did not undermine consumer capitalism but actually strengthened it. What the young rebels failed to understand was that modern capitalism is a far more flexible system than their critiques suggested. As Joseph Heath and Andrew Potter have shown in their book *Nation of Rebels: Why Counterculture Became Consumer Culture* (2004), the countercultural critique of modern capitalism, which was really a sociological and psychological critique of "mass society," was not just misleading but positively counterproductive.[97] The theories advanced by sixties radicals, most of them stemming from Marxian and Freudian roots, rested on doctrines that misjudged the actual workings of modern capitalism and its acceptance by the vast majority of the American people.

In the first place, the countercultural critics accepted a whole nexus of false ideas from Karl Marx and his followers, notably the mistaken belief that working people, though claiming to support the system, were really victims of a collective illusion that capitalism could lift them out of poverty. Marx labeled this illusion "false consciousness," arguing that it was the bane of the working class because it prevented class solidarity and united action against bourgeois oppression. This critique, however, has turned out to be counterfactual on both psychological and economic grounds. Far from impoverishing a greater and greater number of workers, capitalism has lifted more people out of poverty than any other system in history, including what we now know to have been failed socialist and communist systems.

In the second place, having failed to prove that modern consumer capitalism has led to the increasing impoverishment of the working people (in the German the word for impoverishment is *Verelendung*, denoting both poverty and moral degradation), countercultural critics have retreated to the default position that capitalism was really an intolerably conformist and repressive system that stifled individual freedom. We have already seen that critics drew on a sizable literature of alienation and repression that assumed without empirical proof that Americans *had* to be repressed even if they claimed to be happy with their lives in modern America. The claim that Americans could be happy under capitalism was another sign of false consciousness, the critics insisted, demonstrating that working people had obviously internalized the repressive features of capitalism without being consciously aware of their alienation. This line of reasoning was based on the Freudian assumption that conscious awareness was governed by hidden forces in the unconscious, a postulate that is empirically unfalsifiable and therefore inherently suspect. The "false consciousness" theory also allowed countercultural radicals to dismiss people's beliefs or preferences as mere reflections of alienated expressions from the unconscious. Furthermore, the theory enabled elite intellectuals to legitimize themselves as psychological authorities who were entitled to tell the majority what was true and healthy. Based on these suspect theories, countercultural critics proceeded to spin yarns of social commentaries that had little, if anything, to do with how working people actually felt but everything to do with what intellectual critics wanted them to think and feel. And what the critics wanted them to think was that the SYSTEM—that interlocking set of bureaucratic institutions under capitalism—was oppressive and needed to be changed, if not by actual political revolution, then by a revolution in consciousness (Reich, Marcuse, Roszak, Brown).

Unlike the New Left, which wanted to force people to be free through revolution, young counterculturalists wanted to persuade people to free themselves from middle-class restraints by changing their consciousness, just as they themselves had already claimed to have done. It was just a matter of convincing deluded Americans that they were psychologically damaged by the system, to admit that they were in denial, and to undergo therapeutic reprogramming by way of communal living, forms of yogic meditation, drugs, and other countercultural lifestyles. Since the root of injustice was psychological rather than social, most countercultural rebels rejected liberal reforms as a waste of time. Reforming specific injustices was just putting a

Band-Aid on cancer; the whole system had to be changed. It was an all-or-nothing position.

A good illustration of this countercultural all-or-nothing ideology can be found in the writings of Theodore Roszak, who has kept the faith with his 1960s critique of what he calls the single-vision of modern technocracy. There is much in Roszak's critique of scientism that still holds up, but his romanticizing of primitivism, nature, and pre-logical forms of consciousness, together with his call for a "politics of eternity," the need for a new "rhapsodic intellect," and the formulations of new epistemologies (ecopsychology, Eupsychian vision)—all this has the ring of a countercultural voice that is singing completely out of tune. For Roszak, there can be no compromise with a technological world that is drunk with its own godlike pretensions. Shamanistic culture was better because it celebrated the sacredness of life and envisioned nature as spirit rather than machinelike matter in motion, devoid of meaning and purpose.[98] Western technocracy pays no attention to how animals, rocks, or trees feel when they are shot, crushed, or chopped down by insensitive, greedy, and violent white men. All efforts to synthesize the magical visions of pre-Western cultures with Western technocracy are bound either to fail or end up in dilettantish New Age experiments. The technological, patriarchal ego of Western culture, Roszak insisted, must be replaced with an entirely different type of consciousness that fosters a new ecological ego, receptive to magic, feminist spirituality, deep ecology, the recapturing of the primitive, and voluntary simplicity. These are romantic and anarchistic visions that have had little traction in the culture at large, although they are animated by a sincere desire to save the planet from the excesses of industrial civilization. So far, such radical countercultural projects have failed completely, though alienated intellectuals, mostly on the political left, are steadily churning out new critiques and utopian panaceas in portentous-sounding book titles such as *The Death of Nature* (Carolyn Merchant), *Ecological Imperialism* (Alfred Crosby), *Small Is Beautiful* (Ernst Schumacher), *Ecology and the Politics of Scarcity* (William Ophuls), *Ecotopia* (Ernest Callenbach), *The Gaia Hypothesis* (James Lovelock), *The End of Nature* (Bill McKibben), and so forth.

Utopian projections can serve as a liberating, perhaps even a revitalizing, force when societies have become rigidly conformist, but they can also serve as catalysts of intolerant ideologies furnishing the energy for political tyranny. Compared to the decadent direction Western societies have taken, these utopian longings are not to be sneered at because they reveal the darker side of Western civilization and provide us with a possible direction for the future. As a Spenglerian, however, I have to wonder whether these anguished voices and futuristic panaceas are not just a "toying with myths that no one really believes, a tasting of cults that it is hoped might fill the inner void."[99]

In the end, countercultural rejections of the modern world, especially consumer capitalism, have often been little more than intellectual fashions in a social vacuum. In fact, many countercultural rebellions have turned out to be one of the driving forces of entrepreneurial capitalism. The common complaint by left-wing critics that consumer capitalism "co-opted" rebellion by merchandizing it is not supported by the facts. The vast majority of countercultural rebels became avid producers and consumers of New Age merchandise and services—from funky clothes sold in boutiques, alternative medicine, and numerous psychological therapies to dabbling in spiritual practices such as astrology, witchcraft, tarot cards, I Ching, yoga, neopaganism, and so on. In short, cool things and values have become mainstream. As Heath and Potter point out, the United States is covered by "cool communities"— San Francisco, Minneapolis, Seattle, Boston, Denver—where entrepreneurs are saturating the market with funky cafés, vegetarian restaurants, musical scenes, New Age specialty stores, and so on.[100] Who can seriously argue today, as did Marcuse thirty years ago, that capitalism de-eroticizes human beings and forces them to conform to unremitting toil under capitalist domination? The opposite has turned out to be true: capitalism is the great modernizing force that thrives on creativity, innovation, and change. In the words of Heath and Potter, countercultural values have become the "very lifeblood of capitalism. Cool people like to see themselves as radicals, subversives, who refuse to conform to accepted ways of doing things. And this is exactly what drives capitalism."[101] The objection that we live in an Orwellian consumer culture that brainwashes gullible people by manipulating their unconscious desires or fears, as Vance Packard and other critics of consumer society have argued, is simply not borne out by empirical evidence. The argument uncritically assumes that humans are malleable automatons with few defenses against mass media appeals, particularly those deeply embedded in unconscious motivations. We now know far more about mental filters by which information is ignored, registered, or stamped into the brain; and while we may receive thousands of images daily, few of us remember any of them unless we are ready to accept their importance to our self-interest. The notion of a top-down, manipulated conformism bears little relation to how markets actually function in a free enterprise system.

This is not to deny the inherently manipulative nature of advertisers, nor the lies or deceptions of politicians, but to point out the seriously flawed assumptions by countercultural critics of economic institutions under capitalism. By rejecting specific remedies or reforms in favor of root-and-branch change of the whole system, countercultural critics have proved themselves singularly unhelpful in solving social problems in the modern world.

In retrospect, the bleating sheep referred to by radical critics of capitalism have not turned out to be the independent and self-reliant members of the middle class who have kept society functioning at high level of affluence, but unregenerate counterculturalists—former hippies, leftover lefties, extreme feminists, ethnic separatists, and environmental Luddites—all of them waging fierce rearguard actions against the despised corporate system. This would suggest that the "countercultural wars" are a continuation of the social divisions of the 1960s, and that they will most likely continue as long as the baby boomer pig keeps on moving through the digestive system of the python.

In answer to the question posed at the beginning of this chapter—Was there ever a counterculture?—the answer is that the very concept was the invention of certain intellectual critics, notably Theodore Roszak, who misleadingly saw in youthful protests against middle-class society a set of uniformly shared "counter" values without distinction of class, ethnicity, religion, or political affiliation. Even Roszak recently admitted that "when I coined the term 'counterculture,' I had a precise but far-too-narrow definition in mind. I meant the rebellion against certain essential elements of industrial society: the priesthood of technical expertise, the world view of mainstream science and the social dominance of the corporate community—the military-industrial complex, as Dwight Eisenhower called it."[102] Roszak went on to commend a more inclusive definition offered by Peter Braunstein and Michael William Doyle that referred to the counterculture as "an inherently unstable collection of attitudes, tendencies, postures, 'lifestyles,' ideals, visions, hedonistic pleasures, moralisms, negations and affirmations."[103] If the first definition by Roszak misses the mark, the second splits the term counterculture, like the atom, into infinite and undefinable pieces that make it impossible to explain the phenomenon in any comprehensive manner whatsoever. In short, if the counterculture was all the things mentioned by Braunstein and Doyle, it was everything and nothing, so protean as to be virtually undefinable at all.

Respect for historical clarity therefore compels me to state the obvious: a culture is not born full-blown from the head of Zeus; it is not instantaneously produced by student protests, journalists, or academics. The term "counter" thus begs the question because there was no culture that countered the cultural mainstream. There were intense protest movements, as we have seen, such as black civil rights, antiwar protests, New Left radicalism, hippie dropouts, feminism, gay and lesbian demands for equal civil rights, and Hispanic and Indian demands for greater self-determination. None of these movements amounted to a culture. Although they were inspired by some common themes—equal rights, cultural recognition, even cultural separatism—their inherent differences based on gender, class, or ethnicity made it impossible to forge a common center against the cultural mainstream. What these movements accomplished, however, was to shred a commonly shared culture in favor of pluralistic lifestyle choices that depended on different notions of "self-identity." No real culture can emerge from such pluralistic incoherence until the cultural fragments are reintegrated into the common core.

In short, there was no common "counterculture," and what Roszak saw as a culture-in-the-making was really an explosion of protests set in motion by the civil rights movement and the antiwar protests. As these two carrier movements swept across the country, a host of aggrieved constituencies grafted themselves onto these protests and demanded specific rights and recognition. Subsequently, the protests splintered; some of them were absorbed by the mainstream culture, others left dangling without resolution. No society can fulfill all the self-interests of so many constituencies without tearing itself apart at the cultural seams. That this did not happen in the 1960s or after was the result of an accommodating economic system and a liberal tradition that was receptive enough to accommodate protest through reform but not through revolution.

11

RIDING THE COATTAILS OF REVOLT

Neglected Minorities

1. Women's Liberation

The social rebellions of the counterculture extended far beyond antiwar protesters, New Left radicals, and hippies, stimulating a whole rash of revolts by other aggrieved groups and constituencies. Far more important in the long run than the somewhat ephemeral rebellion of hippies or Yippies was the feminist movement, which was powerfully reactivated in the 1960s. Historians, in fact, often talk about the 1960s as setting in motion a "third wave" of women's liberation struggles, the first wave referring to the Women's Rights Convention at Seneca Falls, New York in 1845 by female antislavery activists, and the second wave to the struggle and attainment of the franchise in 1920. A long history of civil rights struggles therefore preceded the 1960s, most of them centering on legal disabilities that had reduced women to the status of second-class citizens.

What proved revolutionary about the women's liberation movement of the 1960s and beyond was the changes it caused in areas of sexuality, interpersonal relationships, gender issues, lifestyles, career choices, and the structure of the traditional family. The marketing of the birth control pill in 1960 is often said to have set in motion the third wave of the women's liberation movement, but that would be the reverse order of how events actually unfolded. The pill by itself did not change generational attitudes; it was merely one of its technological side effects. In 1960 the vast majority of women in America still believed in the traditional role of women as homemakers rather than as autonomous individuals freely choosing how they planned to spend the rest of their lives. A generational change of attitudes, involving different conceptions of how women might live differently in America, had to occur before visible changes in social patterns could be detected. In retrospect, these changes can be dated to the early 1960s, when a great many American women became dissatisfied and frustrated with their traditional roles as homemakers.

In order to appease prominent women who complained that the Kennedy administration had no women in cabinet positions, Kennedy appointed Eleanor Roosevelt to chair the first President's Commission on the Status of Women. Although

Roosevelt played a minor role in its deliberations and died before the committee issued its findings in 1963, her appointment lent weight and credibility to the commission. When the commission reported its findings and offered its recommendations, it still did so with the traditional assumption that the fundamental responsibility of women was to serve as mothers and housewives. At the same time, the commission made reference to still existing inequalities and called for an end to job and legal discrimination along with the creation of day-care centers and paid maternity leaves.

That same year Betty Friedan published her seminal work, *The Feminine Mystique*, in which she alerted the nation to an alleged social problem that had no name, at least not until Friedan pointed it out. The problem, she claimed, had lain buried and unspoken in the minds of American women. Specifically, it was a problem of suburban women who found themselves deeply unfulfilled after they had done everything expected of them: made beds, shopped for groceries, matched slipcover material, ate peanut butter with their children, chauffered Cub Scouts and Brownies, lay beside their husbands at night, all the while wondering: "Is this all?"[1] The American mystique, being a male projection, gave the same reply: women could only find happiness in being mothers, wives, and homemakers. All other women—career women, single women, spinsters, lesbians—were by definition unfulfilled and robbed of their true nature. To Betty Friedan and an increasing number of educated women this answer was not good enough because they wanted something more than their husbands, children, and homes. Friedan suggested that there was an identity and a meaning for women that lay outside the traditional male image of the suburban housewife, though she did not specify precisely what that was because it depended on how individual women defined it for themselves. One thing was sure, according to Friedan, women needed to be emancipated from the mental cave of the feminine mystique, released from society's legal chains, and encouraged to search for genuine self-identity.

Friedan's critique of the feminine mystique stemmed in part from her own experiences with a lifestyle that did not suit her. Born into a rich Jewish family and educated at Smith College, an exclusive all-women's college in Massachusetts, she gave up a fellowship to do graduate work in psychology at the University of California at Berkeley when she married Carl Friedan. She then became a housewife and raised children in the suburbs. Such a routine and intellectually unfulfilling life, however, was deeply troubling to Friedan. The result was her best-selling book, which was based, she told her readers, on the latest research and theoretical developments in the biological and social sciences. In retrospect, of course, the book had little to do with science but everything with shifting patterns of generational needs in modern America. Just how many American women were deeply unhappy as suburban housewives cannot be determined with any degree of certainty; but judging by the success of Friedan's book, which struck a responsive cord with women all over the country, there is no doubt that many women identified themselves with Friedan's concerns. *McCall's*, the premier women's magazine of the day, published a short version of Friedan's book and was overwhelmed with letters thanking the author for putting their feelings into words.

Friedan was not a utopian dreamer but a practical activist who believed that women had to be financially independent or equal partners as breadwinners. By pursuing a career, she believed, women had a good chance in redefining their roles in American society. In 1966 Friedan helped found the National Organization for Women (NOW) and served as its first president. She also campaigned for the ratification of the Equal Rights Amendment to the United States Constitution and for specific attainable goals for women such as equal pay for equal work, greater educational opportunities, child care centers, abortion rights, and so forth.

In 1964 Congress passed the landmark Civil Rights Act which prohibited not only racial but also sex discrimination in employment. Title VII of the Civil Rights Act established the Equal Employment Opportunity Commission as a federal enforcement agency. NOW continued to support the traditional structure of the family, but worked hard to enlarge women's opportunities within that widely held framework.

2. Radical Feminism

A number of radical women on the left, however, steadily pushed beyond this traditional social framework, demanding not only greater opportunities for women but liberation from what they considered to be patriarchal oppression. Not surprisingly, most of these women came out of the Students for a Democratic Society (SDS) and similar organizations on the left. These were angry young women, angry with both traditional society and male-dominated radical groups that had marginalized and even ridiculed them. Whether as members of SDS or SNCC, they had never been accepted as equals by their male counterparts, which prompted them to launch out on their own in search of their own identity. Their numbers were small, but they were vocal and strident, at first limited to countercultural centers in major cities such as New York, Boston, Chicago, and San Francisco, but then spreading rapidly across the country in hundreds of local women's groups.[2] What they had learned from their participation in student or civil rights protests, including the whole range of provocational tactics—rallies, demonstrations, guerrilla theater, incendiary slogans—they unleashed on the public at large. By the late 1960s it was impossible to ignore their outrageous antics, thanks to the media blowing them all out of proportion to their actual political significance. One unique contribution of radical feminists, which subsequently spread across the cultural landscape in the 1970s, was the use of "consciousness-raising" techniques and sessions. The term "consciousness-raising" was apparently coined by Kathie Sarachild; its aim was to encourage women to share their innermost feelings, frustrations, pains, and fantasies, to disclose to their sisters what was really on their minds.[3] Group members would learn to empathize with each other, share experiences, and develop common goals. Those members who did not follow "groupthink," however, were eventually marginalized, shamed, disciplined, or expelled. The group did not encourage intellectual dialogue or opposition but demanded conformity. If someone presented different ideas, they were accused of suffering from "false consciousness," a technique that came straight from the

Marxist playbook. Although members felt liberated after undergoing consciousness-raising sessions, the whole process, as Richard Ellis pointed out, "seemed in practice and even in conception to be little better than a crude reeducation camp in which participants were guided to predetermined conclusions."[4]

The women who participated in these radical groups saw themselves as sisters-in-arms confronting a hostile male environment; and in sharing their experiences, they claimed to be energized, empowered, and ready for battle. There was nothing new in this, of course, because revolutionaries on the left had long experimented with "self-criticism" in the company of devout party members. There was also a venerable practice among American evangelicals that public confession or giving testimony was good for the soul.

Small groups of women radicals, isolating themselves from the cultural mainstream, wallowing in their own alleged victimhood and developing overarching utopias of liberation, often undermined their cause when they insisted that only their own visions of reality were true, and that the present system of social organization had to be completely reconstructed to fit their radical assumptions. Such attitudes were rampant among certain radical feminists in the late 1960s, women who hated their lives, their country, and men.

The younger and more radical feminists quickly clashed with the older traditional liberal groups associated with Betty Friedan and NOW. On October 17, 1967, Ti-Grace Atkinson, who had unsuccessfully tried to introduce her brand of "participatory democracy" into the New York NOW chapter, founded the "October 17th Movement," later renamed the Feminist movement. The brief history of this "movement" is highly instructive because it reveals how grandiose, inflated, doctrinaire, and ultimately self-defeating the radical women turned out to be. Instead of working through the established political and legal institutions of society, Atkinson's group tried to organize itself as a disciplined and revolutionary vanguard with strict membership and stifling rules. Members were required to attend regularly and to subordinate all of their activities, including family and work, to the group. Since married women were considered to be "hostages" or "prisoners" of their husbands, strict quotas on the number of married women were instituted. Furthermore, the group discouraged elitism in any form or shape, going to such lengths as to exclude women with superior writing or speaking abilities from holding office. Women with such skills were expected to recuse themselves in favor of those who wanted to cultivate skills. Even the loquacious Atkinson was not allowed to hog discussions. To achieve their egalitarian aims, the group instituted the "disc system," by which each participating discussion member received an even number of chips and had to surrender one each time she spoke.[5] If a member ran out of chips, she could no longer speak; but Atkinson spoke so much longer than anyone else, that it ultimately made little difference. The group's obsession with making all members equal, of course, violated the first rule of revolutionary vanguardism developed by Lenin: the revolutionary party, though practicing comradeship among its members, must be an elite organization led by its most talented individuals. In depriving itself of strong leadership, together with its stifling internal conformity, bickering, and personality clashes, the Feminists degenerated into a loony countercultural fringe group whose members cultivated their matriarchal roots with the help of support-group jargon, all the while convinced that women would eventually rule the world.

Within the developing circles of these radical feminists, two distinct positions about the plight of women competed for public attention. The first position was the Marxist view that inequality, whether it was based on gender or class, was the inevitable consequence of the unjust distribution of wealth under capitalism. The source of oppression, in other words, resided in the economic inequality that capitalism had spawned throughout the world. Black and white, men and women, were equally exploited. The answer, therefore, was self-evident: capitalism had to be replaced by a socialist commonwealth. The second group of feminists blamed men and patriarchy as the real cause of all historical suffering. For them the black box of evil was biological rather than economic; it was "sexism" promoted by a long succession of patriarchal systems that held the key to all the other forms of human oppression—feudalism, capitalism, fascism, racism. These women saw themselves as waging a gender war that was aimed at dismantling patriarchy and the traditional nuclear family. Their battle cry was total liberation from male dominance; but when it became clear that even the radical men in SDS ridiculed their ideas, the rejected females launched out on their own and developed a variety of cells such as the Women's Radical Action Project and the Westside Group in Chicago, Cell 16 in Boston, the New York Radical Women (NYRW), and so forth.

For whom did these women claim to speak? As it would turn out, they spoke largely for themselves, but their incendiary tactics and intellectual manifestos caused much public attention, most of it in the form of derision. The Redstockings Manifesto, issued by a radical feminist group in 1969, declared that "women are an oppressed class. Our oppression is total, affecting every facet of our lives. We are exploited as sex objects, breeders, domestic servants and cheap labor. . . . We identify the agents of our oppression as men. Male supremacy is the oldest, most basic form of domination. All other forms of exploitation and oppression (racism, capitalism, imperialism) are extensions of male supremacy. . . . *All men* have oppressed women."[6]

If these women really believed that men had robbed them of their lives, how were they to liberate themselves from their male oppressors? Liberation, they believed, meant separating from men and then forging independent communities for women, an idea that appealed particularly to lesbians. The lesbian case was forcefully articulated by Anne Koedt's "Myth of the Vaginal Orgasm" (1970), in which she debunked the widespread belief that vaginal orgasm was not only more sexually fulfilling but also more mature in both a physiological and a psychological sense. The reality, she avowed, was that the only satisfactory orgasm was clitoral because the clitoris had no other function than that of sexual pleasure. Since females were endowed with the equivalent of a penis as well as a vagina they had the best of all possible worlds and could do without males. As Koedt put it, "the position of the penis inside the vagina, while perfect for reproduction, does not necessary stimulate an orgasm in women because the clitoris is located externally and high up. . . . Lesbian sexuality could make an excellent case, based upon anatomical data, for the extinction of the male organ."[7] If these women wanted to get rid of the male organ, why not get rid of males as well? After all, men were just "an obsolete form of life." The next step would be sexual cleansing followed by extermination, as Betsy Warrior (her party name) recommended, saying that since men "constitute a social disease" they should be exterminated on ecological grounds.[8] How, then, would the human race reproduce? Some radical feminists suggested artificial insemination, others some form of parthenogenesis by which women breeders developed eggs that did not need fertilization. As Jill Johnston put it,

> the key to survival in the interests of a natural death (of the male) is the gradual extinction of the reproductive function as it is now still known and practiced. For it is by this function that the woman is so desperately deprived of herself. Lesbian or woman prime is *the* factor in advance of every projected solution for our embattled world. In her realization of herself as both sensually polymorphously and genitally orgasmic she experiences her original self reproduction or parthenogenetic recreation of herself apart from the intruding and disturbing and subjugating male.[9]

Although heterosexuality was predominant among radical feminists, a strident lesbian minority began to exercise a disproportionate influence on the movement. Lesbian feminists were the ones who insisted that heterosexuality reduced women to bondage to men and that marriage was essentially "legalized rape." These voices, however, found little resonance in the public at large until radical women began to stage a series of demonstrations, sit-ins, speak-outs, and lawsuits. In September 1968, members of the New York Radical Women protested what they considered the worst male chauvinist event: the Miss America Pageant, held that year in Atlantic City. Inside the hall, they unfurled a women's liberation banner when the winner was announced, while outside they crowned a sheep as Miss America, chanted slogans, and heaved into a trash can the "instruments of torture"—girdles, curlers, false eyelashes, cosmetics, wigs, *Cosmopolitan* and *Playboy* magazines, and bras.[10]

Mass media, as always in pursuit of drama, provided ample coverage and distortion. It was the media that largely manufactured the image of silly, hysterical women burning their bras in protest against male bondage. This being said, radical feminists played right into the media's desire to display freaks and freakish spectacles, especially after receiving unexpected coverage at Atlantic City. On Halloween 1968, a group that called itself WITCH (Women's International Terrorist Conspiracy from Hell) dressed as shamans, faerie queens, matriarchal old sorcerers, and guerrilla witches, tried to put a hex on the Federal Reserve Bank and the New York Stock Exchange, denouncing both as evil powers of the "Imperialist Phallic Society."[11]

Amidst the constant flurry of public street theater, most people were unaware of various incendiary intellectual contributions that feminist writers were making in their attempt to redefine the role of women in American society. The years 1968–72 witnessed the publication of numerous books, articles, and pamphlets that would influence feminist thought in the future. Most notable among these ideological works of feminist advocacy were: *Our Bodies, Ourselves: A Book for Women* by the Boston Women's Health Collective (1969), *The Black Woman* (1970) by Toni Cade Bambara; *The Female Eunuch* (1971) by Germaine Greer; *Dialectics of Sex* (1970) by

Sulamith Firestone; *Sisterhood Is Powerful* (1970) by Robin Morgan; and *Women Power* (1970) by Celestine Ware.

What these books had in common was the central conviction that sex rather than class lay coiled like a snake in the heart of human darkness. The snake, of course, was the male who had institutionalized his phallic oppression through patriarchy, most notably the institution of marriage. All women were socially crippled because they had to conform to their biological aggressors—men who had fashioned sexual role norms that oppressed and crippled all women. In describing the nature of their oppression, these radical feminists frequently invoked analogies from the black civil rights movement, claiming that their treatment was akin to the treatment meted out to blacks by racial bigots in the south. And just as radical black activists had called for separation from "whitey," some of the more strident feminists called for a separation from all men. Those who did so generally came from the demimonde of perpetually angry lesbians, for whom "the fall was from some primeval division into two sexes."[12] These women wanted to be free from the pain of childbirth, menial domestic chores, unwanted pregnancies, and the drudgery of raising children. They claimed that many women were feminists but all lesbians were feminists. Even love was purer and healthier when shared by lesbians because it was not based on oppression. Ultimate sexual satisfaction, too, required independence from the "phallic organ of invasion." It was one thing to demand sexual independence but quite another to hector the majority of American women to alter their whole being and support the demands of a tiny minority of strident women, many of whom were lesbians (Robin Morgan, Kate Millett, Sarah Holland, Rita Mae Brown). These were the kind of women who would later demand the purging of the English language of all sexist terms such as man, mankind, chairman, manhole, history, women, to be replaced with either gender neutral or self-serving epithets: person, humankind, chairperson, personhole cover, herstory, womyn, and so forth. Ensconced as professors in "women's studies" programs, they would revamp curricula, "trash" male professors, brainwash students, and construct a whole vocabulary of ideological terms by which to structure their mental universe:

Sensitivity	Standpoint Theory
Diversity	Liberated Zones
Narratives of Pain	Consciousness-raising
Inclusion	Cultural Pluralism
Empowerment	Safe spaces
Healing Therapies	Hate Free Zones
Androcentric	Gynocentric
Clitoral hermeneutics	Defense Guarding
Transformationalist	Building coalitions
Phallic Imperialism	Cybernetic Socialism

Women's liberation in the 1960s, according to one historian, should be understood as a "generational revolt against the ultra domesticity of that aberrant decade, the 1950s."[13] Calling a decade "aberrant" assumes some ideological measure of what is "normal," a position historians should avoid like the plague because it is ahistorical and tendentious. A more balanced assessment can be found in William O'Neill's analysis of the postwar domestic "pact" by which returning GIs tacitly agreed to serve as single breadwinners, providing their wives and children with the consumer goods considered to be essential for the enjoyment of the good life in suburbia.[14] Women, in return, accepted their role as mothers and homemakers, many of them dropping out of school to help their husbands through school. This postwar domestic contract worked for the World War II generation, but it did not for their rebellious offspring, who wanted to find fulfillment outside the home. Three major factors shifted familial patterns and the lifestyles associated with them: the demographics of the workforce, the civil rights movement, and baby boomer demands for liberation from traditional restraints. As in World War I, women found greater opportunities in the workforce during the Second World War, and many were reluctant to give them up following the war. Furthermore, many women entered the job market to help their husbands financially, thus providing the discretionary spending needed for new television sets, furniture, automobiles, clothes, and so forth. It is estimated that by 1960 a substantial number of women (30.5 percent) worked for wages.[15] The civil rights movement strongly reinvigorated the feminist movement by providing it with both a sense of mission and tactical, especially legal, strategies necessary to breach the wall of inequality.

At this point, from 1960 to about 1967, the women's liberation movement was still largely liberal and strongly intergenerational. This began to change when younger and radicalized women, who had cut their radical eye teeth in SDS, SNCC, and other left-wing movements, tried to wrench the feminist movement steadily to the extreme left; in so doing, they undermined not only their own cause, which was widely rejected by the majority of the American people, but also jeopardized further advances in progressive and liberal changes for women in general. What these radical women did was to shift the women's liberation movement from its liberal integrationist focus to a more separatist path.

In abandoning the universalist philosophy of the Enlightenment, radical women followed in the train of other minority groups that demanded quasi cultural and political communities in American society. The overwrought rhetoric of radical feminists was much like that of the Black Panthers, who blamed "whitey" for everything. Radical women blamed "phallic imperialism" for all the ills of the world. Just as black radicals found the master key to evil in "racism," radical feminists found it in "sexism." Again, like the Black Panthers or SDSers, radical feminists were true believers in "total" structural change, in sweeping away the whole liberal and middle-class system of life and culture. Intoxicated by their feelings of righteousness and their visions of liberation, these women actually believed—at least for a short period of time—that they were at the center of creation, where everything was possible. And what was possible to the most radical of these feminists was the creation of a New Woman, just as communists had called for the creation of New Soviet Man, or Nazi's for New Aryan Man. Such thinking creates its own defeat. By the early 1970s radical feminism was in disarray. The New York Radical Women dissolved in 1969, followed in 1970 by the Redstockings, in 1971 by the New York Radical Feminists, and in 1973 by Cell 16.[16]

Given the public antics of radical feminists, it is, of course, tempting to ridicule or trivialize their concerns, but this would be a grave mistake because their complaints exposed real inequalities in American society. If the women's liberation movement had remained cautiously reformist, it is unlikely that significant cultural changes would have occurred so rapidly. The majority of American women, however, did not respond favorably to radical feminism, but neither did they to the extreme conservative right, spearheaded in opposition to radical feminists by Phyllis Schlafly and a host of Christian groups. Public opinion polls have consistently shown that the majority of American women accept "equity" feminism—that is, the belief in an equal partnership between men and women. They decidedly reject "gender" feminism that seeks to redefine women as a special class whose interests are fundamentally opposed to those of men.[17] As with most of the legacies of the divisive sixties, women spoke in many different voices, some radical, others conservative, and still others liberal. And what continues to be true in the political arena in general is also true in gender politics: the hard minorities continue to hammer the soft majority with no consensus in sight.

3. Coming out of the Closet: Gay Men

It was not until the end of the 1960s that another aggrieved minority made its accumulated pain a nationwide concern. Shortly before midnight on June 27, 1969, police officers from Manhattan's Sixth Precinct raided the Stonewall Inn, a gay bar in the heart of Greenwich Village.[18] Having staged such gay-bashing raids many times before, the officers did not expect any trouble. They were dreadfully wrong. As the officers dragged away the Stonewall's bartender, bouncer, three drag queens, and a lesbian, to nearby patrol cars, an ugly crowd that had formed in front of the Stonewall Inn began to riot. The rioters threw beer cans, heaved cobblestones, and torched the bar. The riot continued throughout the night, with Puerto Rican transvestites and young people charging against a row of uniformed policemen and then withdrawing and regrouping for another onslaught. Nor was this the end of the riot. On June 28, graffiti appeared along Christopher Street, where the bar was located, proclaiming "Gay Power," and by evening a crowd estimated to be more than two thousand gays and sympathizers battled four hundred uniformed policemen.

Stonewall became both a battle cry and a myth in the men's liberation movement, sparking a nationwide grassroots liberation struggle. Within a month after the Stonewall incident, gay men and lesbians formed the Gay Liberation Front, proclaiming that they rejected the sexual roles society had tried to impose on them, and that they would live their lives without shame as homosexuals. Those who formed the Gay Liberation Front had also been active in left-wing movements, particularly SDS. This explains why the GLF consciously adopted New Left ideas and tactics. As previously shown, the New Left in 1968 was about to tear itself apart with its wild antics, shrill slogans, and sectarian bickering. It should, therefore, not be surprising that radical gay activists often behaved in a similar overwrought and over-the-edge manner, which was not about to commend them to ordinary Americans. Some gay liberationists, intoxicated by late 1960s rhetoric, baited "straights" with provocative slogans and camplike "performance art," attracting much media attention and shocking straightlaced squares. Like their women counterparts, they even called for revolution:

> We are a revolutionary group of men and women formed with the realization that complete sexual liberation for all people cannot come about unless existing social institutions are abolished. We reject society's attempt to impose sexual roles and definitions of our nature. We are stepping outside these roles and simplistic myths. We are going to be who we are. At the same time we are creating new social forms and relations, that is, relations based upon brotherhood, cooperation, human love, and uninhibited sexuality. Babylon has forced us to commit ourselves to one thing—revolution![19]

How was this revolution to be achieved? Some gays called for community building, others for a gay counterculture, still others for a coalition of all radical opponents of "Amerika" that would bring down a racist, bigoted, oppressive, and homophobic system. As with the radical feminist movement, these views did not represent the majority of homosexual men, who preferred more moderate and at the same time more effective methods of breaching the wall of legalized inequality. Gay men initiated a series of court cases challenging discriminatory statutes against gays all over the country. Another approach, which turned out to be far more effective with the sensitivities of the American people, was the simple technique of "coming out of the closet," which meant affirming one's sexual orientation openly and unashamedly. In the past, this had been accompanied by a combination of social ostracism and considerable danger to personal safety; but when large numbers of homosexuals, gays as well as lesbians, publicly and proudly revealed their sexual orientation, the nation took notice and, in many instances, acknowledged the injustice that had been perpetrated on homosexuals in America. The process of "coming out," of course, extended over the next decades; it did not begin all at once, nor did it involve—at least not initially—a great number of gay people. It started with a few risk-takers who tested the water, found out that it was not as ice cold as they expected, and beckoned the rest to follow them. Each case of "coming out" was hard, but it was also cathartic in the sense that it released years of pent-up fears and anxieties.

The big question for homosexuals was to what extent mainstream America would change its discriminatory institutions and accommodate gay people, both as individuals and as a group. In other words, what kind of legitimacy was mainstream America willing to grant homosexuals? And looking at it from the opposite side of the coin, how could a small minority pressure the majority into making concessions? As of this writing, these questions are still open. In the 1960s homosexuals were just beginning to organize on a large, nationwide scale; by 1973, according to one historian, almost eight hundred gay and lesbian groups had formed, reaching into the thousands by the end of the 1970s.[20] The majority of these groups were not composed of hard-core radicals who wanted to bring down the system, a pipe dream that died with the excesses of the New Left and the conservative reaction in 1968. Their aim was to whittle away at prejudices and legal inequalities. Gay organizations opened up a dialogue with liberal Christian denominations that were willing to accept gays as Christians in good standing. This was not an easy rapprochement because traditional hostility toward homosexuals had strong biblical roots, condemning the practice as an "abomination" to be punished by death (Leviticus 20:13), a "vile passion . . . against nature" (Romans 1:26-27). In Judeo-Christian communities homosexuality had traditionally been criminalized and demonized, though advanced industrial societies that had undergone democratization had become more tolerant by the mid-twentieth century. The National Council of Churches took up the issue of homosexuality in January 1966, reaching no definite conclusion but questioning the criminalization of homosexuality. Most Christian leaders in the 1960s still adhered to the notion that homosexuality was not only immoral but also illegal. Episcopal Bishop James Pike was one of the few Christian leaders who urged the repeal of laws against sexual behavior between consenting adults.

Gays had not only been condemned as immoral and criminal but also as "sick." The American Psychiatric Association had long labeled homosexuality a mental illness, a pathology, and a socially threatening disease. This view was still common in the 1960s. *Time* magazine, for example, declared in January 1966 that homosexuality "deserves no encouragement, no glamorization, no rationalization, no fake status as minority martyrdom, no sophistry about simple differences in taste—and above all, no pretense that it is anything but a pernicious sickness."[21] Yet three years later, following the Stonewall Inn riot, *Time* magazine, in an article entitled "The Homosexual: Newly Visible, Newly Understood," acknowledged that there was an emerging homosexual constituency; it even referred to a homosexual community.[22] Although still considering homosexuality a developmental maladjustment, most likely originating in childhood, the article leaned toward the view that homosexuals were an oppressed minority. On the question whether homosexuals were sick, *Time* consulted a variety of experts; only the psychoanalyst on the panel argued that homosexuality was a pathology, while the others suggested that it might be a socially constructed prejudice against gay people. The article clearly indicated that changes in social attitudes were taking place. To gay people, they seemed to move snail-paced but to others they seemed like a tidal wave.

In 1973 the American Psychiatric Association removed homosexuality from its list of mental illnesses in its official Diagnostic and Statistical Manual (DSM). By the mid-1970s half of the states had removed their sodomy statutes and the Civil Service Commission had eliminated its ban on the employment of homosexuals.

4. Brown Power

As the rumble of the civil rights movement reached historically unrepresented, under-represented, or neglected groups before the protests had burned themselves out, two important ethnic minorities seized their opportunities and presented their grievances to the American mainstream: Latinos and Native Americans. Both groups could show a long history of mistreatment at the hands of white Americans, particularly Indians, who had been, on the one hand, portrayed as savages delighting in war and on the other hand, glamorized as noble savages playing Tonto to the Lone Ranger.

The demands of Latinos, especially Mexican Americans, would carry with them momentous changes in how elite policy makers tried to reconfigure the nation's cultural self-identity. Debates over bilingual education, for example, which in the 1960s appeared innocuous to most Americans, involved much larger issues centering on immigration, cultural identity, and minority rights. Latino groups represented a potentially much larger voting block than blacks, while already having replaced all other immigrants by their sheer numbers. In discussing the emergence of Latinos, or "Hispanics," it is important to be clear about terminology. The term "Hispanic" which is now widely used, is really a linguistic construction by the United States government, particularly the U.S. Census Bureau. It refers to Americans of Spanish descent or immigrant groups who came from Spanish-speaking countries, including Mexico, Central American republics, Latin American nations, Caribbean nations (Puerto Rico, Dominican Republic, Cuba), and, of course, Spain. Being a U.S. government classification, the term "Hispanic" is of little use in a historical, ethnic, or even linguistic context. For this reason, I shall employ the term "Latino," now common in academic usage, when referring to Spanish-speaking groups, the most important being Mexican Americans. In the 1960s Mexican activists referred to themselves as Chicanos, but the term is now rarely used in public discourse, except in specialized academic circles. The two most important Latino groups were Mexicans and Puerto Ricans, but the following discussion centers largely on Mexican Americans because they became the torchbearers of "Brown Power."

Historically, Mexico was one of Spain's conduits in carrying out its imperial and colonial mission, and when Mexico became independent in 1821 Mexico's territories would occupy that huge southwestern corner of North America that now includes California, Nevada, Arizona, parts of Colorado, New Mexico, and Texas. Those territories were lost by Mexico in the Mexican–American war of 1846, and rapid Anglo-Americanization followed in its wake. Marginalized and discriminated against since the war with Mexico, deprived of their lands by rapacious Anglo real estate contractors, most Mexican Americans, especially those at the bottom of the social ladder, found themselves excluded from significant positions in the Anglo world. Mexicans and Anglos lived parallel lives that generally intersected only on the economic level, though often the two ethnic communities came to blows when racial incidents sparked violence. Mexicans were seen as a particularly repugnant group in Texas, an attitude that was the consequence of a long history of ethnic hostilities dating back to the 1820s. What set Mexicans apart in Texas and the rest of the Southwest was their ethnicity, low economic status, high degree of illiteracy, distinct folkways, large families, and, of course, their Catholic religion. Yet they performed the hard "stoop labor" without which the Southwest could not have been turned into one of the richest agricultural and later industrial areas of the country.

Mexican Americans, of course, shared in the nation's growing prosperity, but progress and upward mobility proved to be slow and frustrating, especially for immigrants who arrived in America before World War II. Most of these immigrants came to America as either contract laborers or illegals looking for work in agriculture, mining, or the railroad industry. Labor shortages in these fields encouraged open recruitment, supported by state and federal authorities; but when the number of Mexicans exceeded the required needs, causing considerable strain on already inadequate social services, the authorities responded with stricter immigration policies and forced deportations. Mistreatment by Anglo employers, who provided low wages and inadequate facilities, contributed to a growing sense of resentment, frustration, and hostility toward the dominant society. Wartime labor shortages (1941–45) brought a huge influx of additional Mexicans to the Southwest. Under the government-sponsored "bracero" program, Mexicans came to America as "contract workers" or hired hands—the term "bracero" deriving from the Spanish word *brazo*, meaning "arm." The program was largely seasonal, and most Mexican workers were expected to return home after having fulfilled the terms of their contracts. Started in 1942, the program actually lasted until 1964, though the wartime phase has usually received greater attention. It was during the second phase of the "bracero program" (1946–64), however, that more Mexicans came to the United States than ever before. It is estimated that some 4.5 million Mexicans came to the United States during the second phase, compared to only 200,000 during the first phase.

United States agricultural employers and labor contractors found a veritable gold mine in these hardworking and reliable immigrants, paying them low wages and providing them with inadequate facilities. Whether working on the railroads, in construction, or in the fields picking vegetables or fruits, these Mexican workers were often shamefully exploited and mistreated by their greedy employers. Moreover, American employers generally did not care whether Mexican workers were in the country legally or illegally, as contract workers in the bracero program, or resident aliens. Those who came to America illegally were called *morjados* or "wetbacks" because presumably they had entered the United States by swimming across the Rio Grande. "Wetback" quickly became a derogatory term that bolstered the stereotype of Mexican Americans as dirty, illiterate, and uncouth aliens.[23]

Given such a background of discrimination and mandated segregation in many areas of the Southwest, it should not be surprising that Mexicans and other Latinos, especially younger people, should be galvanized by the civil rights movement of the 1960s. Although Latinos as a whole had not experienced the vicious forms of slavery that blacks had endured, Latino activists would frequently employ the analogy of black oppression and black suffering. In the 1960s Mexican Americans, indeed all Latinos, became more acutely conscious of their ethnic identity and their potential power in American politics. Before the 1960s the vast majority of Mexican Americans did not vote, either because many of them had not become naturalized or because the indifference of Anglo politicians toward Mexican Americans made them indifferent to American politics. John F. Kennedy, a Catholic known to be sympathetic to Latino minorities, inspired enthusiastic support among Spanish-speaking Americans who formed "Viva Kennedy" clubs throughout the Southwest. The president's brother, Robert Kennedy, inspired even more support from Latinos, especially in California, where he was idolized and cheered by huge throngs wherever he campaigned.

It was young activist Mexican Americans who politicized their communities as never before. Some of these activists, especially those who were involved in the Cesar Chavez crusade for socioeconomic justice and those who tried to work through the Democratic Party, which Latinos regarded as more responsive to their concerns than the Republicans, were pragmatic reformers and integrationists. Other Latino activists however, followed the path of black nationalists and New Left radicals, demanding not just equal rights but separation from the hated American mainstream. Among this group were to be found resentful irredentists and their intellectual spokesmen, who were just about to establish beachheads in academia, especially in "Chicano studies" programs, where they attempted to indoctrinate a new generation in resentful attitudes and separatist ideologies. Their aim was to encourage open borders and unlimited immigration, cultural nationalism, and the election of Latinos to public office. In this way, and over time, the ideologues reasoned, most of the Southwest would eventually revert back to Mexico or become an independent state (Aztlan). Although this nationalistic philosophy did not gain much ground among Latinos, it did contribute to the steady balkanization of America into a tangle of race-conscious minorities who were increasingly turning their backs on the notion of one common people, language, and culture.

It was not until the 1960s that Mexican American activists succeeded in developing the programs and organizations necessary to deal with the socioeconomic problems that Mexicans were facing in the United States. Until the 1960s problems and issues pertaining to Mexican concerns had been dealt with on local community levels whether in rural areas or urban *barrios*. This began to change during the civil rights era, which provided Mexican activists, as it had other minority groups, with the tactics required for social change. A number of Mexican American activists rose to the challenge, some of them speaking the language of Gandhian nonviolence, others a more strident language of revolution and separatism.

Notable among the more peaceful, nonviolent activists was Cesar Chavez, who helped organize the United Farm Workers (UFW) in California.[24] Born to migrant farm workers and only receiving an eighth-grade education, he spent much of his youth working with his parents in the fields in California. A gentle and deeply religious man with a strong belief in nonviolent approaches to reform, Chavez was widely accepted by most Mexican Americans as the Latino counterpart to Martin Luther King Jr. In 1966 Chavez became the first president of the National Farm Workers Association, chartered by the AFL-CIO and subsequently renamed United Farm Workers. Between 1966 and 1970 Chavez successfully used a number of nonviolent strikes against California farm owners who, in Chavez's view, had exploited Mexican American workers by paying them low wages, providing them with substandard housing, exposing them to pesticides, and feeding them bad food. With the help of other activists such as Dolores Huerta, Chavez developed a grassroots mass movement that quickly caught the attention of politicians, mass media, and ordinary

Americans. In 1968 Chavez mounted a national boycott of California table grapes that received national attention and brought Chavez support from the United Auto Workers and leading politicians. Robert Kennedy, who had worked on the Migratory Labor Subcommittee of the Senate, had taken a special interest in the wretched conditions among itinerant farm workers and publicly embraced *La Causa*.[25] The senator and the migrant farm organizer made an odd pair, but they did share a Catholic background and a fierce determination to achieve social justice through peaceful methods. The table grape boycott, which had started on a small scale with the Delano strike of 1965, involved boycotts against grape growers all over the state of California. Despite intense resistance by the grape owners, a three-year labor contract between the two parties was signed in 1970, but when the contract expired the growers signed with the Teamsters Union, which worked against Chavez's UFW. When Chavez then proceeded to organize lettuce pickers in the Salinas Valley, he once more encountered the Teamsters Union there and failed to unionize the farm workers under the banner of UFW. By that time, Chavez was not just encountering the Teamsters, but internal divisions in his own ranks and the anti-union climate of the late 1970s. Chavez was never willing or able to move beyond local Latino issues and create a national organization similar to Martin Luther King's SCLC or even A. Philip Randolph's Brotherhood of Sleeping Car Porters, organizations that had exerted considerable pressure on local as well as federal authorities.

While Cesar Chavez was organizing Mexican American farm workers in California, a feisty and spellbinding activist, Reies López Tijerina, galvanized a group of militant followers in New Mexico with the avowed purpose of reclaiming ancestral lands that had allegedly been stolen from Mexicans by Anglo Americans in the 1840s. Tijerina, like Chavez, came from a dirt-poor family of agricultural migrants, a fact that accounts for his lack of formal schooling. As a young man, he left the Catholic Church and converted to a fundamentalist Protestant sect, attended an Assembly of God Bible School, and went to California to preach. He also spent time in Mexico researching Spanish land grants in Texas and the southwest, which convinced him that all of the problems of "New Mexicans" derived from being uprooted from their rightful lands.[26] In 1963 Tijerina organized the Alianza Federal de Mercedes (Federal Alliance of Land Grants), whose mission was to reclaim lost territories and transform them into a confederation of free city-states independent of the United States. This secessionist program resonated with young Mexican American nationalists who had been absorbing nationalistic doctrines that were very much in the air in the late 1960s.

Supported by his followers, Tijerina staged a number of demonstrations and provocative actions, starting with a demand that the federal government return millions of acres that had allegedly belonged to Mexican villagers according to the Treaty of Guadalupe Hidalgo (1848). In 1966 Alianza activists attempted to take over Kit Carson National Forest, and one year later a group of Tijerina's supporters broke into a courthouse in Tierra Amarillo, a small town in northwestern New Mexico, and attempted to free members of the Alianza who had been jailed there for unlawful assembly. Shooting two policemen and escaping with two hostages, the *aliancistas* fled into the wilderness. It took a massive manhunt that included helicopters, two tanks, state troopers, and the National Guard to capture Tijerina and other Alianza members. The courthouse raid made Tijerina a national figure and a hero to militant "chicanos"; while out on bail, the messianic Alianza leader spoke to young activists at colleges, participated in Martin Luther King's Poor People's March on Washington, and even contemplated running for governor of New Mexico. In the end, Tijerina was convicted on both state and federal charges stemming from the Kit Carson National Forest and Tierra Amarillo incidents. In 1971, however, he was released from prison with the proviso that he agree not to serve in the Alianza.

Tijerina had clearly tapped a highly emotional vein among disenchanted Mexican Americans, many of whom found increasing strength in numbers. They also found their self-identity as Chicanos or Latinos rather than Americans, dreaming about reclaiming the loss of Mexican territories and creating a Chicano nation of Aztlan in the southwest. The man who helped to formulate "El Plan Espiritual de Aztlan" was Rodolfo "Corky" Gonzales, a Chicano activist, boxer, and poet.[27] Like Tijerina, Gonzales was a Mexican American nationalist and separatist, who had given up his position as an official in Lyndon Johnson's antipoverty program in order to create a Chicano society based on humanistic principles. In 1966, in Denver, Colorado, he founded the Crusade for Justice, aimed at securing civil rights and socioeconomic justice for Chicanos. Three years later, Gonzales organized a Chicano Youth Conference in Denver that attracted fifteen hundred delegates representing over one hundred Mexican American and associated Latino organizations. The delegates drew up a secessionist plan for a national homeland in the southwest to be called Aztlan. One way of bringing this about involved Gonzales's proposal to appeal to the United Nations for a plebiscite to be conducted in the Southwest to determine whether members of *la raza* (the race) wanted to secede from the United States.[28] Although nothing came of this dream of reviving the legendary Aztec homeland of Aztlan, Gonzales's nationalistic vision is still propagated in Chicano studies programs today, programs that foster Chicano self-identity and political self-determination. From a practical point of view, this ideal of ethnic self-identity took on flesh and blood in 1970 when José Angel Gutiérrez founded a new political party called La Raza Unida in Crystal City, Texas, also known as the "Spinach Capital of the World." With the support of La Raza Unida, Gutiérrez and two other Mexican Americans were elected to the city council and then to the presidency of the school board. In this capacity he instituted bicultural and bilingual changes that inspired other La Raza Unida candidates in nearby towns. At the same time, these aggressive tactics inspired fierce reactions by Anglo politicians, who labeled La Raza programs reverse racism and condemned them as un-American.

In 1966 Latino leaders pressured the federal government to recognize their language and culture, a demand that prompted the Johnson administration to appoint a task force on problems relating to "Spanish-surnamed Americans." The task force's recommendations called for bilingual programs and asserted that Spanish-speaking Americans had a "legitimate claim to identification with a distinctive culture."[29] Here was one of the first of several government proposals and later legislative acts that encouraged "group rights" and the maintenance and even cultivation of cultural patterns of distinct immigrant groups. Bilingual programs, however, did not find enthusiastic support among all Latino leaders because they were said to delay rapid assimilation into the mainstream of American society.

Latino leaders also demanded that the federal government recognize their grievances in the same way in which it had embraced black demands. In 1965 and 1966 the White House held two conferences on the problems of black Americans, prompting vocal protests from Latino organizations demanding a special conference for Mexican American problems. The president turned down the demand by Mexican activists, but when these militants scheduled a conference in Los Angeles under the theme "Brown Power" and invited Johnson officials, the administration agreed to meet more moderate Mexican American leaders in Texas. The setting for this occasion was provided in October 1967, when the president delivered a speech in El Paso as part of hearings that had been held there by the Inter-Agency Committee on Mexican-American Affairs, chaired by the new EEOC commissioner Vicente Ximenes. The president's speech was more of a defense of his civil rights record than it was a specific plan of action about improving conditions for Mexican Americans. Help would be forthcoming, Johnson promised his audience, but it would have to be carefully tailored to the unique needs of Latinos.

By the fall of 1967 the press had picked up growing signs of discontent among Mexican American students, especially in California, where radical students began calling themselves "Chicanos." John Skrentny correctly described this phenomenon as the beginning of an "inchoate identity politics," promoted at the time by such student groups as the United Mexican American Students, the Mexican American Student Association, and MEChA (Movimiento Estudiante Chicano de Aztlan).[30] The students, taking a leaf from black nationalists, demanded Chicano studies courses and programs that were expected to instill ethnic pride and prepare Mexican American students to live independently from Anglo Americans. Students staged disruptions, chanted slogans, made "non-negotiable" demands, published "Brown Power" newspapers, and so forth. Compared to the more coordinated protests by black organizations, Latino protests were largely local and usually in response to specific local problems, not all of them being separatist in nature.

Although Latino activists claimed that their interests had always been ignored by the liberal establishment, their protests did not go unnoticed, as the president's reaction showed, nor was the president alone in responding. In 1966 the National Education Association (NEA) published a report entitled "The Invisible Minority," referring to neglected and "alienated" Mexican Americans. The report was a projection of liberal guilt about forcing Latinos to undergo the trauma of sudden immersion into an alien culture, as though such a practice of assimilation was somehow unjust. Few countries in the world at that time had made it an official government practice to encourage large groups of immigrants to form anti-nations within mainstream nations. From the beginning of the Republic, immigrants to America, including this author, were expected to learn the English language, to acquire the necessary skills for citizenship, to respect mainstream cultural norms, and to pledge allegiance to the flag. What some of the radical Latino students and their leaders were actually protesting against were not segregated schools but overly integrated schools.[31] Their aim was to cultivate cultural enclaves, consisting of their own Spanish-speaking teachers and students, both of them subject to Mexican American control.

Politicians who courted Latino voters often gave in to such ethnic demands. On January 2, 1968, Johnson signed the Bilingual Education Act, which was designed "to meet the special needs of the large numbers of children of limited English speaking ability in the United States." The Act specifically singled out Limited English Proficiency (LEP) students who came from impoverished families who would benefit from instruction in their own language, history, and culture. Critics have called this a monumental error not just in educational pedagogy but also in the exercise of national self-interest. Blind-sided by a combination of guilt, good will, and pressure by vocal Latino groups, the Johnson and later the Nixon administrations continued to support and expand these measures of ethnic self-identity and minority rights. As subsequent events would demonstrate, entirely new curricula, teaching methods, and textbooks had to be designed in order to promote untested programs, which, in the end, failed to teach Spanish-speaking students how to master the English language, while at the same time reinforcing ideologically driven values that were calculated to alienate rather than to integrate students into the mainstream of American society.

In supporting these dubious policies, government officials and educators began using psychological and educational terminology that would become the vogue in the 1970s: "self-esteem," "bilingual education," "language maintenance," "affirmative action," respecting the culture of the "deprived child," "culturally biased intelligence tests," "language accommodation," and so forth. Politicians were unprincipled pragmatists, while educators were true believers; both committed themselves to splintering the whole by pandering to the parts. To many educators "language rights" meant belief in the notion that immigrant children learn better if they are taught in their own native language until they are ready to be "transitioned" into the mainstream. Some educators believed that this would bolster children's self-esteem and reinforce their cultural self-identity. The ideal was to produce a multicultural society in which everyone was bilingual, though for most educators bilingualism meant English and Spanish rather than English and French, Chinese, Russian, German, Yiddish, Serbo-Croatian, Japanese, etc.

Were these educators or politicians unaware of the nation's past traditions of a common language and a common culture? Did they know that they were about to abandon the nation's commitment to the idea that a country's unity is to be found in a common language? Given the divisive atmosphere of the late 1960s, the answers to these questions are difficult to ascertain; but it is undeniable that a substantial number of elite politicians and educators were beginning to question the traditional American project of the "melting pot," favoring a variety of "multicultural" projects that would later tear at the seams of national unity. That such approaches would be championed by Mexican irredentists or black nationalists goes without saying, but that the federal government would engage in such potentially divisive measures is a truly remarkable example of cultural "failure of nerve." During Senate hearings for bilingual education, government officials dismissed the melting pot metaphor as an "anachronism" and Harold Howe, the U.S. commissioner of education, stated that the term "mosaic" was a better term because "the melting pot idea carries with it a kind of homogenization concept, which can be destructive."[32]

5. Red Power

At a time when black secessionists demanded a black nation to be carved out of southern states, Latino militants threatened to reclaim the southwest and rename it the nation of Aztlan, radical feminists proclaimed the death of the male organ, could it possibly get any worse? It did. American Indians, too, harbored dreams about reclaiming their ancestral lands and achieving full independence from white society. Before Indian activists started rattling white people's guilt chains, the vast majority of Euro-Americans possessed only a dim awareness that in pre-Columbian days, long before there was a United States of America, North America was occupied by at least seven and possibly eighteen million Native Americans.[33] By the 1960s their numbers had dwindled to slightly below one million, but these Indians lived their own quasi-independent lives; they were divided into some 315 tribal groups in 26 states ranging from larger tribes like the Navajo, whose 132,000 people lived on 16 million acres of land, to the tiny Mission Creek Indians of California, whose 15 people lived on a small parcel of property.[34] These tribal groups considered themselves "sovereign nations" under treaty status with the United States government. For most Euro-Americans, however, these Indians had long been declared "vanishing Americans" as though, in the words of one historian, the Indians were as "natural and untamable as the wild animals with which they share the wilderness." Most Europeans thought that the Indians had been simply unable to adapt in the struggle with a more advanced white civilization, thus being doomed "to melt away like snow before the sun."[35] In Euro-American folklore, Native Americans were the fly in the Edenic ointment, to be Christianized, ghettoized, or driven into "vacant" territory—swampy, barren, and infertile. The heroic Puritan pioneers had "settled" rather than "invaded" the New World, and the westward movement was called "expansion" rather than "conquest."[36] When the European settlers arrived in the New World, they found a virgin country ready to be "developed"—that is, transformed from its unproductive state into a fully commercialized Western society. What resided between the two shining seas, the Atlantic and the Pacific, was basically wasted space. As late as the turn of the twentieth century, President Theodore Roosevelt referred to western expansion as the spread of the English-speaking peoples over the "world's waste space" as the most striking feature of human history, adding that "only a warped, perverse, and silly morality" would condemn the American conquest of the West.[37] Teddy Roosevelt's condemnation of namby-pamby moralists decrying war and conquest resonated with white Americans, who constructed American history as a heroic tale of triumphant white people conquering and developing a great continent.

This triumphalist narrative, like so much else that Anglo Americans had cherished, did not survive the 1960s. Indians or Red Americans, piggy-backing on the black civil rights movement, demanded redress of long-standing grievances and recognition as an independent people. A new generation of impatient American Indians planned to take full advantage of the minority rights movement that was unfolding in the 1960s. The major lobbying organization for Native Americans had been the National Congress of American Indians, a pan-Indian group founded in 1944. Its major concern was to challenge the government's "termination" policies of dissolving Indian tribes, the heart and soul of Indian self-identity, thereby accelerating full assimilation. The intent of termination actually was to free Native Americans from federal supervision and control so that they could become full citizens enjoying equal rights with all other Americans. To the Indians, however, "termination" meant being wiped out or killed off.[38] What they wanted was full sovereignty rather than being permanent wards of the government and subject to the corrupt or indifferent bureaucrats of the Bureau of Indian Affairs. By the 1960s thousands of tribes had already been terminated, a process dating back to the Dawes Severalty Act of 1887, which dissolved numerous tribes as legal entities, wiped out ownership of land, and promised individual families 160 acres of land if they transitioned into white society. The act came at a time of intensive efforts to "christianize" Native Americans, and to stamp out superstitious practices like the "Ghost Dance" that had spread throughout the Dakotas and culminated in the infamous massacre of four hundred Indian men, women, and children by the U.S. cavalry at Wounded Knee, Dakota Territory, in 1890.

Two events, barely noticed by most Americans, marked the beginning of Native American protests in the early 1960s. In August 1960 ten Indian university students founded the National Indian Youth Council in Gallup, New Mexico. Speaking for the younger generation of American Indians, these students opposed the government's termination policy, called for Indian unity, greater self-determination, and the cultivation of ethnic pride and culture. Two of these students were Navajos; the rest came from different tribes: Crow, Ute, Mohawk, Powhatan, Ponca, Shoshone-Bannock, and Tuscarora. For the future of the Indian movement it was significant that these college students and those who followed them identified themselves, first and foremost, as "Indians" rather than as members of particular tribes, and underscoring this nationalistic spirit by later using such slogans as "Red Nationalism" or "Red Power."

The resurgent spirit of Indian self-identity also manifested itself in 1961 when the National Congress of American Indians held an Indian Congress in Chicago. Attended by 420 members representing 76 tribes, the congress issued a remarkable pan-Indian declaration which asserted, "We, the Indian people, must be governed by high principles and laws in a democratic manner, with a right to choose our own way of life. Since our Indian culture is slowly being absorbed by the American society, we believe we have the responsibility of preserving our precious heritage."[39] The document, however, was not a call for resistance but a reassertion that the Indian way of life must be protected from the encroachment of white America, especially in the form of termination policies by the federal government. This was a curious paradox because Native Americans sought autonomy from white America by evading termination policies, while at the same time they opposed the government's intention to withdraw all financial and legislative support of Indian tribes under the provision of termination policies.

The old "Uncle Tomahawks," as they were called by the younger and more radical Indians, were not ready to cross the Rubicon, burning all their bridges behind them and seceding completely from the American mainstream, and certainly not when it came to turning their backs on financial support from Washington. Generations of Indians had been treated as wards of the government and its patronizing paternalism. It was difficult to shed such long-standing dependencies, but a number of frustrated Indian radicals left Chicago with the firm belief that the conference had not gone far enough in the direction of Indian autonomy. Throughout the sixties these younger and more radical Indians not only opposed white society but also their own "red apple" (red on the outside, white on the inside) tribal elders and leaders.[40] In the words of Clyde Warrior, president of the National Indian Youth Council, their elders had succeeded in conveying the rich legacy of a once free way of life, but they had too readily adapted to a life of dependency, which fostered a strong sense of unworthiness.

> If there is one thing that characterizes Indian life today, it is poverty of the spirit. We still have human passions and depth of feeling . . . but we are poor in spirit because we are not free—free in the most basic sense of the word . . . our choices are made for us; we are the poor. For those of us who live on reservations these choices and decisions are made by federal administrators, bureaucrats, and their "yes men" euphemistically called tribal governments. Those of us who live in non-reservation areas have our lives controlled by local white power elites. We have many rules. They are called social workers, "cops," school teachers, churches, etc, and now OEO employers.[41]

Clyde Warrior's reference to OEO employers determining the lives of American Indians was a jab against the soldiers in Johnson's army fighting the war on poverty. The elders of tribes welcomed the war on poverty, but it was the younger activists who brought strong pressure on the Johnson administration to make Native Americans eligible for assistance under the New Economic Opportunity Act.[42] It was their rhetoric that made Johnson promise to put "first Americans first" and include them, despite strong opposition from the Bureau of Indian Affairs, under the mantle of the war on poverty. As it would turn out, Johnson did not put first Americans first, spending a niggardly sum of money on Indian poverty and then forgetting all about them. Johnson's autobiography is silent on American Indians; the same is true of Johnson's biographers. It should therefore not be surprising that young Indian activists had strong misgivings about the war on poverty, seeing it as a double-edged sword, perhaps even a back door termination, for in return for greater government financial aid came an army of white poverty officials deciding what was good for Native Americans. How could Indian leaders justify an even closer entanglement with the federal government with the promise they had made to their people to free them from "all federal supervision and control"? Here, again, it was young activists who perceived the danger more clearly than their elders and alerted their communities to the cultural threat this posed to the Indian way of life, a threat that lay concealed behind the paternalism of Washington.

Native American activism came to the attention of the public in the late 1960s when young activists of the Indian Youth Council focused their efforts on tribal fishing rights in the northwestern states of Oregon, Washington, and Idaho. The issues of tribal fishing rights dated back to 1957 when Robert Satiacum, a Native American, had been arrested for fishing steelhead trout out of season with fixed gill nets in Washington. This set off the "fish-in" movements of the 1960s because the Indians insisted that they had treaty rights to fish in the waters of the Nisqually, Columbia, and other rivers of the Pacific Northwest.[43] The "fish-in" disputes eventually reached the Supreme Court, which ruled in favor of the Indians. During the course of these "fish-ins" Indians found supportive allies throughout America, including high-profile celebrities such as Marlon Brando and the black comedian Dick Gregory.

The National Indian Youth Council campaign over fishing rights greatly invigorated the Native American rights movement. The press began to refer to some of the young Indian activists as "New Indians" distinguishing them from their more cautious elders. Among these New Indians were Clyde Warrior, president of NIYC; Vine Deloria, executive director of NIYC and author of *Custer Died for Your Sins* (1969) and *God Is Red* (1973); Dennis Banks, cofounder along with George Mitchell and Mary Jane Wilson of the American Indian Movement (AIM); Leonard Peltier, who became the leader of AIM in 1970 and pushed the movement into violent confrontations with the federal government; and Russell Means, another activist in AIM who played a prominent role in several confrontations with government officials. It was these young Indians, college educated and militant, who began using the term "Red Power" and engaging in deliberately provocative actions in order to highlight Indian grievances, notably fighting corruption in the Bureau of Prisons, restoring "sacred lands," stressing treaty rights, and revitalizing the traditional Indian way of life. In November 1969, a contingent of seventy-eight Native Americans led by irate students who protested the lack of opportunities to study and practice their own culture, occupied the abandoned island of Alcatraz, site of the infamous federal prison, and "reclaimed" it in the name "of all American Indians by right of discovery."[44] In their proclamation, which was not without its humorous elements, the Indians suggested that they would be willing to purchase Alcatraz for $24 in glass beads and red cloth, a precedent set by the white man's purchase of Manhattan Island three hundred years ago. For nineteen months the occupiers issued proclamations, held news conferences and powwows, and negotiated with increasingly addled federal officials. The unrealistic aim of the protesters was to use the island as a cultural center of pan-Indian unity, featuring a college, religious site, ecological center, and training school. In June 1971, after negotiations had hopelessly deadlocked, federal marshals finally repossessed the island.

The occupation of Alcatraz was followed by a decade of occupations of federal properties around the country: at Fort Lawton and Fort Lewis in Washington state; Ellis Island in New York; Twin Cites Naval Air Base in Minneapolis; and various former Nike missile sites. Militant Indians also established a number of protest sites, notably at Mount Rushmore and the Badlands National Monument. Government buildings also became sites of protest and occupation. In 1971 and again in 1972 militants occupied the Bureau of Indian Affairs in Washington D.C. The second occupation of the BIA came at the end of the march on Washington that had followed the "Trail of Broken Treaties"—the Cherokee Trail of Tears (1838) and the site of the infamous massacre at of Sioux Indians Wounded Knee (1890). In 1973 some two hundred Sioux, led by members of AIM, notably Dennis Banks and Russell Means, occupied the town of Wounded Knee, South Dakota.[45] Wounded Knee was located on the Pine Ridge reservation, a place of rolling prairie and spectacular skies, but also grinding poverty that one observer called distinctly unnerving.[46] It was also a place of ugly infighting and corruption, pitting the chairman of the tribal council, Dick Wilson, who was supported by Bureau of Indian Affairs officials, against tribal activists. An effort by dissidents to remove Wilson from his post resulted in a split of the Sioux community into two armed camps who battled each other for almost three months. The conflict pitted Wilson's tribal government, supported by BIA officials and federal marshals, and 150 activists from AIM, notably Russell Means, Dennis Banks, and assorted black, Chicano, and Euro-American radicals. Entrenched in the village of Wounded Knee, the militant Indians fought pitched battles, carried on negotiations with the government; and, after their complaints had been rejected, proclaimed a new Independent Oglala Nation. Officials of the Nixon administration flatly refused to negotiate with the dissenters and informed them that the days of treaty making with Indians had ended over a hundred years ago. In the end, the militants agreed to leave the village in return for a pledge that the government would not retaliate against them, and that federal officials would continue discussing their grievances.

The events centering on Wounded Knee attracted extraordinary attention by the mass media, both in the United States and abroad; it also caused renewed national debate about the plight of Indians and their place in modern America. The occupation of Wounded Knee was the highwater mark of Indian activism that had begun with the "fish-ins," the occupation of Alcatraz, the events of the "Trail of Broken Treaties" and a host of other protests and demonstrations. Cumulatively, these events forced the federal government to make significant concessions to Indian demands. On July 8, 1970, President Richard Nixon sent a message to Congress in which he acknowledged the Indians' right to self-determination and denounced the government's long-standing policy of paternalism and termination. Although the message was only a statement of intent, it shifted the direction of federal policy, eventually ending forced termination in a series of bills that involved the restoration of land to the Taos Pueblos (Blue Lake), the land settlements with Alaskan Natives, and the restoration of lands to tribes in Oregon and Arizona. The most important of these acts was the Indian Self-Determination and Education Act, which gave the tribes a far greater degree of autonomy by decentralizing services and placing greater control in the hands of the tribes rather than in the traditional tightly controlled Bureau of Indian Affairs. The Self-Determination Act, however, did not resolve Indian co-dependency, nor did it lay to rest the bitter legacy of prejudice, hate, and distrust that had characterized white and red relationships.

One positive outcome of the 1960s red power activism, however, was that it put an end to the traditional white image of the American Indian of folklore and Hollywood movies. A sudden outburst of revisionist books, most of them written by Indian activists, tried to correct the traditional white stereotype of either a noble savage or just plain savage; but in attempting to correct the record, many of these works—and some motion pictures (*Dances with Wolves*)—created new and troublesome confusions. In seeking to write a different record of the American Indian, some revisionists created new mythologies about a pre-white paradise that was lost when the white man committed genocide against the Indians. Christopher Columbus and his minions, these revisionists argued, brought nothing but conquest and brutal subjugation, teaching the Indians to hate themselves, and to think of Europe as the real source of civilization. The European conquerors saw themselves as agents of God, sent to the New World in order to christianize the savages. The reality, the revisionists claimed, was that American Indians were peaceful people living in harmony with their environment and practicing profoundly satisfying spiritual beliefs. Not only were the Indians deep ecologists but they also helped shape the democracy of the founding fathers. The reality was that Indians frequently engaged in ferocious wars and committed brutal and unspeakable acts of cruelty.

Such self-serving and European-bashing views fit perfectly into the radical mood of the late 1960s and early 1970s. But did these views in fact help Native Americans to come to grips with their ambiguous feelings about the past, their own tribal differences and their relationship with an increasingly pluralistic America? Those who defined themselves as "New Indians" were just beginning to wrestle with these issues, but they did not always succeed in rising above radical rhetoric or ideology. They often failed to cure concrete problems such as getting their people off the welfare rolls, providing them with economic opportunities, and educating them to the realities of the modern world. One thing they all agreed upon: creating a revitalized Indian world within the United States.[47] They did not want to be assimilated into the cultural mainstream; they did not want government officials to tell them what it means to be an Indian—or an American, for that matter. Yet most Indians did not want "termination" either of their tribes or their financial dependence on the U.S. government. Only a few "born again" Indians believed in the feasibility of complete autonomy; the rest realized the facts of political life—that Indian communities resided in the United States and were, therefore, subject to its superior power. The question raised by Fergus Bordewich in *Killing the White Man's Indian* (1996) still cry out for an answer: "Are Indians so fundamentally different from other Americans, so historically and culturally unique, that they occupy a special category over which conventional American values, laws, and criteria of ethics should not apply?"[48] Or are Native Americans simply one more American ethnic group with special pleadings and demands, contributing to the balkanization of America? Should Indians be mainstreamed, inviting cries of racism? Are Indian reservations precious national resources, to be preserved or developed? Is tribal self-determination a form of self-perpetuating segregation, or is it the only way of preserving the Indian way of life? To this day, none of these questions has been conclusively settled, either by Native Americans or by the Euro-American majority.

6. The Minority Rights Problem:
More Pluribus than Unum?

Both parties, Republicans and Democrats, attempted to respond to the legitimate grievances of previously neglected minorities. However, they also, either by design or by default, encouraged the left-liberal project of corporate "minority rights." In retrospect, this minority rights project was a double-edged sword: it addressed genuine past injustices through reform and accommodation, while at the same time pursuing divisive strategies of interest-group politics that would cause much resentment and anger over the next few decades. Politicians were easily swayed by militant minority activists and by disruptive demonstrations; they all too often accommodated grievances without thinking through long-term consequence; and by doing so, discovered new electoral constituencies. At the same time they wove anger and discontent into the fabric of American society by supporting affirmative action, bilingual education, cultural pluralism, minority capitalism, and so forth. John Skrentny has characterized the process by which policy makers responded to minority protests as "anticipatory" rather than "participatory" politics because politicians did not follow the wishes of the majority but the demands of strident minorities. They "anticipated" what minorities wanted and then reached into their "new rights policies like an archer reaches for arrows in a quiver."[49] If the target group could be analogized as black, then policy makers, congressional staff members, and bureaucrats would rush to devise rules and regulations that sounded virtuous, cost relatively little money, appeased some, and angered many.

In the 1960s few politicians foresaw the social cost of pursuing minority rights at the expense of the rights of the majority, assuming—often rightly—that granting rights to minorities was simply extending rights already enjoyed by the majority. Sooner or later, however, the black metaphor, which was used as justification of redressing historical injustices, would become inappropriate when applied to women, homosexuals, the disabled, the mentally ill, the disadvantaged, and so on. The analogy to black suffering quickly breaks down when extended to any other group except American Indians. Privileging some groups over others would become a spoils system that would be deeply unpopular with the Euro-American mainstream, but that majority was generally uninformed and, as subsequent decades would show, was gradually but steadily shrinking. According to estimates based on patterns of immigration, the Euro-American majority will end by 2050. Fundamental changes in immigration, dating to the 1965 Immigration Act, which eliminated quotas in favor of Europeans, is only partly responsible for this estimated reconfiguration of the U.S. population in the second half of the twenty-first century. Declining fertility rates among whites and massive waves of immigrants from Mexico, Latin America, and Asia are equally important factors in changing the ethnic, cultural, linguistic and political map of the United States.

The debate about historical injustices that have been meted out to women, gays and lesbians, Latinos, and Native Americans was ultimately a heated conversation about what it means to be American and whether that question could even be answered considering the presence of so many groups which endlessly harped on their differences rather than their similarities. Some intellectuals who were concerned about the nation's common center were beginning to wonder by the end of the decade whether the United States was not tearing itself apart and entering a period of rapid decline. Andrew Hacker, for example, in a provocative book, *The End of the American Era* (1968), warned that national self-identity and love of country had been replaced by so many divisive forces that the country was in danger of imminent disintegration. Hacker predicted that a willingness to sacrifice was no longer in the American character, and that "the conviction that this country's beliefs and institutions merit global diffusion is in decline." Looking at the state of the American union, he added that "what was once a nation has become simply an agglomeration of self-concerned individuals; men and women who were once citizens are now merely residents of bounded terrain, where birth happens to have placed them."[50]

Hacker attributed the malaise to the rise of large corporations which produced half of the country's goods and whose executives wielded such extraordinary powers that they were virtually immune from the reach of the law. The great conglomerates, he said, were "elephants dancing among the chickens";[51] they administered prices, determined salaries, generated growth in one location and terminated it in another, shaped educational institutions, encouraged nomadic and rootless lifestyles, spent their corporate wealth on corporate whims, including big salaries for their CEOs; and made life-altering decisions without democratic consent. Hacker's criticism of the divisive and undemocratic behavior of multinational corporations was subsequently developed at greater length by Christopher Lasch in his critique of the corporate elite betraying democracy.[52] Although these criticisms carry considerable weight, historians have not paid enough attention to the fragmentation of America that was caused by such policies as group identity and multicultural agendas. The danger to national unity that these strategies, most of them dating back to the 1960s, presented was pointed out in no uncertain terms by Arthur M. Schlesinger, the eminent American historian. Schlesinger warned that strident ethnic ideologies, now embodied in school curricula, government programs, and ethnic studies departments at American institutions of higher learning, are threatening to "reverse the historic theory of America as one people.... The multiethnic dogma abandons historic purposes, replacing assimilation by fragmentation, integration by separation. It belittles unum and glorifies pluribus."[53] Schlesinger forcefully argued that multicultural programs such as Afrocentricity, the cult of ethnicity, and bilingualism were elitist rather than popular movements, spearheaded primarily by ethnic zealots and their followers in academia.[54] Although Schlesinger remains optimistic that America's forces driving toward "one people" are still powerful, the present forces that are pulling toward "disuniting" America are putting such optimism into serious doubt.

Immigration patterns and policies reinforce the pessimistic side. The immigration policies of the U.S. government shifted dramatically in the 1960s, abandoning national origins quotas that favored immigrants who shared the ethnic and cultural heritage of Europe.[55] The 1965 Immigration and Nationality Act Amendments abolished the principle of national origins and replaced it with "hemispheric" ceilings; it also established priorities for professionals and highly trained technical workers and made provisions for "family reunifications."

Although the liberal leaders in Congress, notably Edward Kennedy, assured the public that the Immigration Act would not significantly change ethnic patterns of immigration, such assurances were a deliberate deception.[56] The new policies actually encouraged immigration from Asia, Africa, and the Americas; by the end of the 1970s fewer than 18 percent of the new immigrants came from Europe. The rest came from Mexico, the Caribbean, and the poorer states of South America. Together with wide open borders, which encouraged millions of illegals to enter the United States, the country was inundated not only by immigrants, legal and illegal, but also by newcomers who did not share the nation's core cultural roots. It had been hard enough to assimilate the many European nationalities, but it would prove even more difficult to integrate non-Europeans who came from different civilizations. Assimilation was made difficult also by liberal elites who claimed to promote bilingualism, which did not, as it would turn out, foster mastery of foreign languages, but was designed to encourage multiculturalism. They also sponsored "affirmative action" programs, which discriminated against white Americans and devalued the nature of citizenship by extending government support and services to alien residents or even illegals.[57]

John Lukacs has argued that government and politicians stood idly by while the idea and practice of American nationality were being steadily diluted, so that over time large portions of the United States resembled third world countries.[58] The result was that the original Anglo-American core, already shrinking in the twentieth century, was not only being overwhelmed demographically, but was steadily declining in its ability to exercise leadership. Lukacs is one of a tiny group of historians who have recognized that immigration and assimilation patterns have radically changed—so radically, in fact, that the consequences could point to a complete reconfiguration of American life and culture. The fault lines identified in chapter 2 relating to ethnic fissures and American self-identity have considerably widened since the 1960s, and the great challenge that lies ahead consists in assimilating newcomers, immersing them in the English language, and persuading them to make a sincere commitment to the democratic ideals and institutions of the United States.

12

PEERING INTO THE HISTORICAL LOOKING GLASS

1. Fault Lines Revisited

The 1960s left a legacy of social divisions and cultural polarizations. Not since the Civil War have Americans been so divided against each other. Historians who have tried to capture the mood of the sixties have given us variations on this theme of conflict and division by labeling the period as the *Unraveling of America, The Troubles, America Divided, The Overheated Decade, Coming Apart, The Politics of Rage, The End of the American Era, The End of Victory Culture, The Dust of Death, The Death of a Nation, Years of Discord*, and so forth. Titles are suggestive but never conclusive; they illuminate the contours of an era without necessarily providing a deeper understanding of its antecedents or its consequences. I therefore invite the reader to recall the fault lines in American history that erupted into earthquakes (protests, demonstrations, riots, generational rifts) and to explore, if only briefly, the long-range aftershocks they have caused since the 1960s.

The mythology of American exceptionalism suffered a serious setback in the wake of sixties upheavals, especially the war in Vietnam. For almost a generation few Americans evinced a strong commitment to the messianic sense that America was God's country, or God's anything else; but since the cold war continued, and evil empires still had to be slain, the nation continued, if somewhat inconsistently, to pursue the crusading mission. The perfectionist impulse still drives the nation into foreign policy crusades to redeem the world, if not from communism, then from global terrorism.

Such global missions, however, have been seriously impeded by a problem of national self-identity that has grown more acute since the 1960s. The focus on racial, ethnic, gender, class, and cultural differences, celebrated by the elites as "multiculturalism," has made it difficult, if not impossible, to unite the nation behind the traditional civic values of the past. The question: "What does it mean to be an American in the 21st century?" has largely been deconstructed as meaningless because it assumes a belief in cultural consensus, which philosophers have discounted because they have abandoned monism in favor of pluralism, being in favor of becoming. Elite intellectual thought in America since the 1960s has rejected traditional American policies of assimilation and the ideal of the melting pot in favor of preserving and encouraging cultural and ethnic differences. The metaphor of the melting pot in such circles has given way to that of the "salad bowl," or the "glorious mosaic." What this has done, however, is to weaken the concept of American nationality and self-identity; but what is a culture if not a common set of values and a common vision of reality? If unmeltable ethnics or immigrant groups refuse to assimilate, they will eventually fracture the very spine of nationality, the bonds that make a common social life possible.

By the end of the 1960s integration gave way to racial and ethnic segregation—the very evil Martin Luther King Jr. and the older generation of civil rights leaders had attempted to eliminate. The 1965 immigration law, which flung the door wide open to previously underrepresented groups, brought larger numbers of new immigrants to the United States who were no longer expected to assimilate into society the way earlier immigrants had been obliged to do. National unity and pride are unlikely to be fostered when a national government encourages cultural differences without furnishing a unifying ideology or creed that transcends these differences. Hard multiculturalists believe that the whole concept of American nationality must be exposed as inherently destructive, while hard American nationalists, especially of the conservative (Reagan, Bush) variety, have tried to revitalize Americanism or the creed that Americans are the last hope on earth and that their civil religion should be disseminated around the world. Neither hard multiculturalism nor a warmed-over version of Americanism has succeeded in gaining the cultural upper hand. A third and the most unpalatable alternative may well emerge in the near future, for if left-liberals continue to consolidate the welfare state and right-wing Republicans continue to beat the drum for nationalism, the outcome may well be an American version of national socialism. It may come under the guise of democratic populism headed by a demagogic leader who promises a domestic welfare state and a nationalistic warfare state battling international enemies in perpetuity.[1]

In fracturing the ideal of nationality and encouraging a postmodern kind of tribalism, countercultural activists on the left and their followers in academia and government have unwittingly managed to stir the embers of ethnic and racial animosities. When a government or a university traffics in racial categorizing, racial remediation, or racial-ethnic set-asides, quotas, or special considerations, if only to correct past injustices, it becomes complicit in racial discrimination. What exactly is a "protected minority"? And by what constitutional and democratic principle is government justified in treating one group differently from another? These questions were frequently raised after the 1960s upheavals when the federal government, by judicial and regulatory rather than by democratic means, involved itself in such controversial issues as forced busing, affirmative action programs in higher education, and special consideration in hiring procedures in business. Paradoxically, while implementing policies designed to rectify past inequities and to mainstream historically marginalized groups, government and academic elites at the same time encouraged minority groups to "celebrate" and maintain their unique differences. The result was not what the government elites expected: far from bringing groups together under a common American tent, they not only drifted apart but stridently clung to pan-ethnic ideologies of Afrocentrism, brown power, red power, and so forth. Feelings of ethnic solidarity definitely replaced class solidarity in the 1960s and they are continuing to tear at the fabric of national solidarity, the sort of solidarity that has been transmitted from one generation of Americans to another since the beginning of the Republic. By the end of the 1960s, ethnic separatism was on the rise, especially among black and Latino nationalists, who favored segregation from, rather than integration into, the Anglo mainstream.

In 1999 a poll conducted by Hamilton College under the aegis of the NAACP and the polling firm of Zogby International revealed that about 50 percent of young white adults believed that the separation of the races in America was acceptable as long as all races enjoyed equal opportunities. The poll seemed to indicate an ominous trend, namely, that young Americans do not object to the idea of a segregated society. More disturbing still was the poll data that 40 percent of African Americans also believed that separate but equal was an acceptable social goal.[2] Judging from the way in which black and white students have segregated themselves on the nation's college campuses, one might conclude that color lines, far from fading, are becoming rigid once more. This is certainly how Andrew Hacker perceived it in his best-selling book *Two Nations: Black and White, Separate, Hostile, Unequal.* Hacker's view, however, is unduly pessimistic and minimizes the remarkable emancipation of black people from the shackles of legalized inequality. Even on the economic front, there has been much progress in empowering a significant segment of the black population, as Stephan and Abigail Thernstrom have shown in their rebuttal to Hacker, claiming that America may still be a nation in white and black, but that it is also one nation, indivisible. Some polls give credence to the Thernstrom claim. Since the 1960s the perceptions white Americans have held about blacks have definitely changed for the better. In 1991, for example, only 13 percent of whites polled said that they had generally unfavorable opinions about blacks.[3] If this is compared to similar perceptions of majority ethnic groups toward minority ethnics in other countries, the United States ranks higher on the tolerance scale than any of the others surveyed by the Times Mirror Center for the People and the Press.[4] In surveying black perceptions, it turns out that 40 percent of the nation's black citizens consider themselves members of the middle class, a further indication that, subjectively and objectively, black people have come a long way and that the 1960s were instrumental in improving their condition. Having said this, it is widely admitted that black people still have not been fully integrated into the American mainstream. The fact that the majority of black people still live in separate communities in America's inner cities confirms the existence of an active racial fault line. Despite the Civil Rights Act of 1964, the Voting Rights Act of 1965, the Fair Housing Act of 1968, the Equal Credit Opportunity Act of 1974, the Home Mortgage Disclaimer Act of 1975, forced busing, and affirmative action programs, there is still a much higher level of racial segregation between whites and blacks than there is between whites and Latinos or Asians.[5]

Why is it that America has not been able to solve its racial problem? What else must be done? No unanimity exists on these questions. Some see the black and white issue in socioeconomic terms, going so far as to call for a racial Marshall Plan, while others see it as a biological issue with strong psychological overtones. Nathan Glazer, for example, has drawn attention to the fact that black and white marriages are still relatively rare because blacks marry largely within their own racial group, but this is not true of whites, who intermarry with other ethnic groups—Latino or Asian. A remarkably high percentage of black women (98.7 percent) marry other blacks.[6] If government-forced integration policies have failed to integrate black and white, what will integrate them, assuming that both sides continue to work toward this goal? Perhaps Jefferson was right in the end: only miscegenation can cut the Gordian blood-knot. Such a solution, however, lies in a postethnic future, one in which ethnicity is no longer a determinant of social standing.

2. Consumer Culture Is Boomer Culture

The "revolutionary" sixties did not bring down the government, nor did they change the economic order that safeguarded and helped to expand it. Corporate capitalism ultimately spoke a language that the majority of the American people could understand and support. That language was embodied in the theory and practice of consumerism, the only "ism," as Gary Cross reminds us, that triumphed and defeated all the other isms of the twentieth century—communism, fascism, liberalism, conservatism, existentialism and so forth. The message of consumerism is now a global one; it holds that the good life resides in unbounded consumption and that individual self-identity is derived from the consumption of goods and services. People find meaning primarily in the goods they consume—that is, what they consume, where they consume, and how much they consume. As Gary Cross put it, "visions of political community of stable, shared values and active citizenship have given way to a dynamic and seemingly passive society of consumption in America"; and he adds that the reason why it has is because it expressed the cardinal political ideals of the twentieth century—liberty and democracy—better and in a less self-destructive way than the revolutionary ideals of political ideologies.[7]

It could have happened only in America because it was here that the "free market" held sway more strongly than in any other country; here traditions of restraint and rituals of self-abnegation were weakest. Furthermore, America's abundant resources and the uninhibited way in which they were exploited gave rise to a philosophical creed of avarice, self-interest, and greed that eventually undermined traditional Christian values of self-restraint, altruism, and guilt. Expectations of indefinite economic growth and affluence also made social conflict far less acute than it was in the class-ridden countries of the old world. If everyone believed that he could become rich, there was no compelling reason to promote class warfare. Already in the later nineteenth century the well-known German sociologist Werner Sombart, asked the question: "*Wieso gibt es keinen Sozialismus in Amerika*—Why is there no socialism in America?" He answered by saying that "roast beef and apple pie," abundant food, land and opportunities, made socialism a quaint concept in America.

Indeed, liberal America strongly believed that economic and material solutions were the most effective means of solving social problems and satisfying spiritual needs. Shopping became a secular religion in America, even on Sunday, a day previously reserved for religious worship. The suburban shopping mall with its greatly expanded floor space and free parking made its appearance in the 1960s, superseding the urban supermarkets and department stores. For some Americans the mall became a therapeutic release from boredom and alienation; it provided a counterfeit for spiritual self-worth or meaning. Kenneth Clark has referred to this Western delight in materialistic pursuits as "heroic materialism" because for all its excesses it has transformed the natural environment into an artificial and mechanical system of mass production for mass consumption. Clark asks us to imagine an immensely speeded up movie of Manhattan Island during the last hundred years. Watching that film we would have a ringside view of the almost demonic energy, the suffering, and the brutality that have gone into the development of the greatest commercial city in the Western world.[8] New York expresses the quintessential spirit of the New World, where nothing succeeds like excess, the lubricant that runs the engine of consumption.

Preoccupation with consumerism has also invaded people's private lives, intruding and insinuating itself into every nook and cranny. It has become increasingly difficult to fence off time and space from constant commercial intrusions on our privacy. Home, school, and work have all been staked out by advertisers. Far from respecting the privacy and sanctuary of the family, and leaving it alone from commercial intrusion, advertisers now refer to the family and its individual members as "market terminals." They willfully breach the wall of privacy and encourage family members to become private consumers who do not need to interact much with each other. Family members can consume goods, entertainment, or fantasy wholly in private. It would be an exaggeration, of course, to blame consumerism for every spiritual or civic failing, but that does not make its influence any less powerful, especially since the culture seems to offer no moral equivalent to the world of consumption.[9] Unfettered consumerism subverts, divides, and trivializes by turning everything— sex, love, religion, politics—into a commodity. Nothing is sacred: Kosher hot dogs tap into the Jewish market, nuns and monks are seen endorsing products, God himself lends his good name to a brand product. Women are divided into eight "consumer clusters"; forty different "lifestyle groups" are identified and saturated with advertisements, commercials, phone calls, e-mail messages, and faxes, while "ethnic marketing" or child marketing reaches every other member of society not already targeted.

In short, uncontrolled consumerism can be a menace to culture because it subverts self-discovery, invades our private sphere and reduces everything to a materialistic flatland. It also coopts genuine protest by seducing it with material comforts or desires. As previously shown, the consumer culture trumped the counterculture by turning it into a "market terminal." Western consumerism has also brought down communism, a system that collapsed because it failed to provide the materialistic satisfactions the Russian people desired. Although Soviet communism was based on the notion of "dialectical materialism," the belief in organizing material reality so that it could be shared equally, the Soviets went about implementing it unsuccessfully by using totalitarian means. It is well in this connection to remember the famous "kitchen debate" between Vice President Nixon and the Soviet leader Nikita Khrushchev in Moscow in 1959.[10] The "kitchen debate" involved the opening of an American National Exhibition, featuring the latest American technological inventions. As Khrushchev and Nixon walked through the exhibition, bantering and needling each other, they arrived at the most controversial attraction, a full-size model of a middle-class American home priced at $14,000. The Soviet press later referred to the model as a "Taj Majal," doubting that any American worker could possibly afford to own it. The modern kitchen, replete with the latest conveniences, set off Khrushchev's insecurities. The Soviet premier blustered that Soviet houses would have the same conveniences, that it was just a matter of time. Earlier he had asked Nixon: "How long has America existed?" Nixon replied that it was 180 years. "Well then," said Khrushchev, "we will say America has been in existence for one hundred and eighty years and this is the level she has reached. . . . We have existed not quite forty-two years and in another seven years we will be on the same level as America." By the same level, the Soviet premier meant materialistic level, the only level that communist ideology recognized. Under communism, individuals were treated as mere factors of production, objects to be controlled by a totalitarian regime. What neither Nixon nor Krushchev understood was that both capitalism and communism were based on a materialistic view of reality, except that capitalism, to be functional, required freedom as one of its essential elements.

Yet what happened in the twentieth century was that capitalism developed a culture of consumerism that began to detach itself from the larger ethical and religious framework of Western culture. In fact, consumption as an ideology and a way of life without control by a higher ethical power has become not just an American but a global goal. These observations are not intended as a critique or rejection of free enterprise, which is the basis of freedom and a democratic way of life, but a critique of the amorality and depersonalization that accompany the pursuit of consumer goods as an end in itself, the sine qua non of self-identity and spiritual fulfillment. If one's worth is measured by what one consumes, one is robbed of one's spiritual freedom, and thus becomes a slave to desire. The possession of goods or the desire for a better way of life is not a bad thing, but to elevate these aims to the level of the absolute, which consumerism does, amounts to the denial of any higher form of human freedom.

3. The Great Cultural Implosion

Consumerism without a moral framework subordinates higher spiritual values to individual selfishness and pleasure. That this has been the thrust of American society since the 1950s is commonly recognized, but that it has become a global aspiration is not usually understood by most Americans. Close to two billion people worldwide now belong to the consuming classes—that is, people who follow a diet of highly processed food, desire big houses, want more and bigger cars, incur higher levels of debt, and follow lifestyles devoted to the accumulation of nonessential products or the satisfaction of simulated needs.[11] Nearly half of these consuming classes come from developing countries, notably China and India. The resulting environmental problems stemming from high energy wastage, pollution, and planned obsolescence will wreak greater and greater damage on the world's ecosystems. There is, however, another and equally important consequence of following a purely sensate goal, and that is its impact on the cultural life of a society.

Consumerism clearly predated the 1960s, but it capitalized on the countercultural mores and lifestyles that developed during that decade. Consumerism not only made money out of the libertine manners of the 1960s; it normalized them. As previously stated, business culture and counterculture, though developing separately, have meshed since the 1960s, producing what James Twitchell has called a "carnival culture," a voyeuristic peekaboo world in which "hip" sells. As a result of the convergence of consumer culture and boomer culture, high culture has largely vanished from the public square. This transition from highbrow to lowbrow was greatly facilitated by the rise and triumph of electronic media, catering to popular tastes and gratifications. The traditional literary media, consisting of books and serious magazines and newspapers has been declining steadily. The growth of democracy and commercial capitalism had already marginalized the more intellectually demanding ideas of a small cultural elite. Electronic mass media has made nearly all cultural expressions popular rather than highbrow. What this has meant to the quality of cultural expressions has been much debated by historians, but what has been rarely mentioned is that the triumph of visual as opposed to abstract thought has also undermined contextual knowledge, rationality, and coherency. Higher-order thought is difficult when the content of consciousness consists largely of disparate bits of visual images derived from television.[12] Mass media has been deeply implicated in "the rising tide of illiteracy" that swept across American society following World War II. When people no longer said "have you read" but "have you seen," high culture gave way to popular visual culture, and that popular culture, as Marshall McLuhan pointed out in his book *Understanding Media* (1964), undermined the old intellectual and aesthetic standards. The medium is the message, McLuhan said. What counts is not content but people's experiences in seeing images.

Images and sound bites undermine thought and reflection, while entertainment tends to trump instruction and edification. The 1960s were a crucial turning point in this respect. In a consumer and advertising culture, it was image rather than intellectual substance that counted in persuading people whether they should choose Pepsi or Coke. The same was true of politics, for what counted was not so much what a candidate was really like but what the candidate appeared to be. The role of television in shaping public perception had been recognized in the 1950s, but it was not until the televised presidential debates between Nixon and Kennedy in 1960 that television came into its own as the major instrument of mass persuasion. Before the first televised debate, Nixon was the acknowledged front-runner because of his experience as vice president under Eisenhower. Kennedy had several liabilities, not least of which was his Roman Catholicism and his reputation as an inexperienced, privileged scion of a wealthy family. Television changed that perception. The screen revealed a glamorous, handsome, charming, and vibrant figure who took to the camera like a fish to water. By contrast, Nixon looked haggard and shifty-eyed, affecting a heavy solemnity that was more appropriate to an undertaker than a politician. He was also blustering, sarcastic, and abrasive. Those who listened to the debate on radio, following ideas rather than seeing images, thought that Nixon had won the debate. The television audiences, however, gave the edge to Kennedy, who appeared far more suave, trustworthy, and knowledgeable than Nixon. Despite a dark underside to Kennedy's character, as we have seen, which was carefully concealed from the public, the production of the Kennedy mystique quickly shifted into high gear and persuaded the American people into believing that the Kennedys were touched by some special magic and grace. The reality, as we now know, was otherwise, but one would not have known this from television, which traffics in simplistic and unexamined images. The Kennedy legend has withstood criticism to this day, and Thomas Reeves's judgment that the Kennedys belong in the pantheon of movie or television stars is as true now as it was then.[13] It was not only politics but the quality of culture itself that was unalterably changed by television and other mass media providers. Since mass consumption and mass entertainment drive the electronic media, advertisers of products and producers of programs primarily follow their own commercial interests. Catering as they do to a mass audience, their aim is to manipulate and please mass tastes, no matter how vulgar. Moreover, programs and messages must be pitched to short attention spans and audience demands for instant thrills or gratifications. Programmers initially started out with relatively high expectations, hoping to inform as well as entertain. The bland programming of the 1950s, which was a sign of a timid, cautious, and security-conscious age, quickly gave way in the 1960s to a far more freewheeling, unrestrained, and tasteless wave of electronic exhibitionism. Media moguls began to exploit the worst instincts in their viewers on the assumption that the viewing public wanted to be fed a steady dose of sensationalism, violent conflict, the normalization of the abnormal, the thrill of seeing freaks, the emphasis on colossal spectacles, and scandalous exposés. Television and motion pictures increasingly featured a bizarre reality populated by vulgar people with jaded opinions and greedy appetites. Journalists and newscasters fell all over themselves to dig up the worst muck, acting on the perverse modernist assumptions that goodness or normality cannot be real but must conceal ulterior motives of greed and corruption. This "act of digging-to-uncover," as Jacques Barzun has aptly called it, always tells its own accusatory tale and reveals once more that there is no dignity, decorum, or honesty in the world.[14] The cumulative effect of mass media, in other words, has been subversive to the quality of American culture as well as to its mental health. This is especially true of the deluge of news, most of it negative, that has been unleashed on unsuspecting Americans since the 1960s. On September 2, 1963 CBS expanded its evening news broadcast from fifteen to thirty minutes. The result over the next decade was an explosion of "news," most of it in short sound bites and images—disjointed, out of context, sensational, incoherent, bizarre, and menacing. Historians generally agree that this deluge of news, most of it accentuating the negative, shifted the public mood from optimism to pessimism.[15] News stories in the 1950s tended to be upbeat; after 1963 this was no longer true.

Mass media, of course, function as both mirror and lamp in the sense that they both reflect what is going on and actively shape public consciousness. The 1960s was a violent decade and television reflected that reality. At the same time, television and motion pictures also exacerbated the situation by normalizing it. As James Twitchell has observed, "the carnival now controls the show"[16] because the mass audience has marginalized the elite tastes of high culture. The 1960s removed the gatekeepers of taste and urged everyone to define his or her own taste of what is beautiful or ugly, proper or improper, good or bad. Public discourse since the 1960s has increasingly taken the form of entertainment. As Neil Postman put it, "our politics, religion, news, athletics, education and commerce have been transformed into congenial adjuncts of show business."[17]

Out of the protest movements of the 1960s also emerged new forms of uninhibited exhibitionism that shattered centuries of civility and decorum. This was accompanied by the disappearance of cultural gatekeepers who had tried to uphold high ethical or literary standards. The countercultural critics of the 1960s, in fact, did their utmost to subvert the whole canon of bourgeois taste and manners. The construction of anticanons of vulgarities, as Twitchell calls it, arose out of the counterculture, perverse modernism, cultural relativism, and academic theories of deconstructionism. From divergent sources a collective resentment against Western values built up among radical critics, who proceeded to mock, ridicule, defame everything Western civilization pretended to be: rationalistic, creative, progressive, and humane. The critics, of course, had a point, because in practice Western civilization had undermined its own ideals by tolerating ugly habits of racial, class, or national prejudices that had led to world wars, the Holocaust, and the atomic bomb.

Young people saw through the cultural pretensions of their elders and decided to storm the gates of civilization and level them to the ground. As we have seen, the young were supported by older intellectual radicals who provided some of the theoretical battering rams in the form of postmodernism, Marxist philosophy, and deconstructionism. Many young people were taught that middle-class culture was not only morally corrupt but that its tastes and values, previously assumed to be timeless and absolute, were merely ephemeral reflections of decadent bourgeois capitalism. Scientific canons that supposedly revealed the methods by which objective truth could be discovered were held to be equally tenuous. Truth did not exist, and neither did facts; they were merely transitive functions of power and social conditions. Postmodern critics taught that truth was relative and entirely in the eye of the beholder. It followed that humans could never discover objective truths because every perceiver sees and therefore interprets reality from his or her own egocentric perspective. Since every individual is the ultimate arbiter of truth, beauty, and goodness, no one can ultimately judge one way or the other. The only thing that matters is the usefulness or pleasure of an action to the person who experiences that action.

William James, one of the precursors of intellectual modernism, had already asserted a hundred years ago that "it is useful because it is true" is exactly the same as saying that "it is true because it is useful."[18] Americans today strongly believe that change is constant and that fixity is an illusion. From this perception that everything is flux, that "whirl is king," as the Greek philosopher Heraclitus pointed out, it follows that there can be no transcendental truths, no absolute moral commandments, but only pragmatic adjustments to change and corresponding formulations of makeshift moralities.

In the past, such attitudes would have been decisively rejected, but not so in the morally thin air of the 1960s. An alarming number of people were unable to distinguish between the psychological factors that led someone to hold a certain belief and the logical reasons that warranted one to hold it. The logic of knowing was subordinated to the psychology of knowing, so that if something felt good, it had to be good in practice. It was in this way that the motto "if it feels good, do it," became paradigmatic of American morality. If pragmatic or psychological factors become the only source of knowledge or behavior, normative judgments based on reason must be decisively rejected. In other words, if there is no cognitive standard of truth—truth having been reduced to being a function of subjective judgment or "feelings"—there is no normative right or wrong at all. Right or wrong depend on the subjective vision of the perceiver. How, then, do we sort out differences or adjust conflicts when individual perceptions clash? William James and other liberal thinkers had a simple answer: universal toleration and diversity of opinion. Thus, whenever opinions, perceptions, beliefs, or values collide, the best strategy is to tolerate them all unless they do demonstrable harm. In essence, this generous but intellectually and morally flabby answer has become the emerging American creed: since nothing can be proved one way or the other, people are entitled to believe whatever they want to believe, which amounts to a fundamental betrayal of the Western classical, Christian, and scientific tradition and its belief in an objectively knowable world. Expecting young people to find spiritual nourishment in such relativistic ideologies was courting disaster. If you stare at the abyss long enough, Nietzsche said, the abyss stares back at you. Harold Bloom recounts the remark of a colleague at Cornell who said that his educational goal was to knock down all of the students' prejudices (certainties) like tenpins; but having done so, the professor did not know what the opposite of prejudice was nor what one should do once all certainties had been eradicated.[19] The educators had no answers to these existential questions, other than the evasive mantra that all beliefs are subjective, and that no objective criteria exist by which one can judge that one belief is better or truer than another. Confused students might thus be pardoned if they felt that there was something missing in an education that deprived them of all reasonable standards, as did one student who said:

> If I had been brought up in Nazi Germany—supposing I wasn't Jewish—I think I would have had an absolute set of values, that is to say, Naziism, to believe in. In modern American society, particularly in the upper-middle class, a very liberal group, where I'm given no religious background, where my parents always said to me "If you

want to go to Sunday School, you *can*." Or "If you want to take music lessons, you *can*," but "It's up to *you*," where they never did force any arbitrary system of values on me— what I find is that with so much freedom, I'm left with no value system, and in certain ways I wish I had a value system forced on me, so that I could have something to believe in.[20]

This is not the place to trace the subsequent degeneration of character and morality that resulted from such attitudes, but to point out a related corollary of such sixties attitudes regarding truth and knowledge. An increasing number of young people, especially those who had joined radical movements, rejected Christian middle-class values as historically obsolete and therefore invalid. As Christopher Lasch pointed out, this rejection followed from the pragmatic view of knowledge and its claim that there is no stock of accumulated wisdom or inherited values because technological or economic change constantly make received knowledge obsolete and therefore nontransferable from one generation to another.[21] In practice, this false doctrine implied that the young could not learn anything from the old-fashioned values or beliefs of their elders because that sort of knowledge, being old, was ipso facto obsolete.

It took several decades for this sort of nihilism to play itself out in the culture at large. Such doctrines, as Edmund Burke warned long ago, severed the chains of intergenerational continuity, set one generation against another, elevated the present to the status of the absolute, and reduced human beings to little more than "flies of a summer."[22] Such attitudes, we might add, also foreclosed any commitment to the future. Why should the older generation pass on anything to the young if there was nothing of a lasting nature to be passed on. Moreover, since the old generation no longer thinks of itself as living on in the next, as Christopher Lasch pointed out, it will not give way graciously to the young but cling tenaciously to its power in society.[23]

Such intellectual attitudes, cross-fertilizing with various developments in the popular culture, produced a radical shift in cultural norms and behaviors. One consequence was a cheerful toleration and acceptance of cultural incoherence. The other was the youthful protest against traditional cultural norms or canons. The rejection of high literary artistic or musical standards, together with an easy-going toleration of all forms of artistic expression, produced a curious acceptance of cultural pluralism. By the end of the 1960s, as Morris Dickstein points out, many Americans would embrace both Shakespeare and Ginsberg, literature and movies, Beethoven and rock.[24] It was not culture but cultural smorgasbord, a table laden with hundreds of goodies to be consumed indiscriminately. Elvis Presley next to Beethoven, Jacqueline Susann next to Dickens, Jesus next to Anton LaVey and the Satanic Bible, Freud next to Norman Vincent Peale or Billy Graham. An endless array of cultural products, undigested, out of context, all seemingly equal in this bazaar of cultural incoherence. And this was long before the Internet atomized the culture to the vanishing point. Was this cultural liberation or liberation from culture? The truth is that Americans were learning to live without past cultural references and adapted quickly to the technological changes and innovations that had inundated them.

Young people instinctively felt that Western middle-class culture had become deformed by overemphasizing the classical virtues of decorum, restraint, moderation, and publicly repressing joy or ecstasy. They searched for a less demanding and uninhibited culture that ratified instinctual desires. Theirs was a revolt against technical rationality, capitalist greed, and what they conceived to be repressive middle-class values. They longed for uninhibited self-expression and authentic self-identity; they wanted to subordinate technical rationality to poetic modes of expression and to forge a healthier relationship with nature than their middle-class parents had allegedly done. Linking with the romantic tradition, countercultural critics searched for a more holistic vision of mother earth, a new sensitivity to the environment that would include a greater willingness to protect the land and its resources from spoliation. They also favored community-based strategies to build a civic culture based on cooperation, modesty, and thrift rather than competition, greed, and selfishness. These were all wholesome and laudable objectives, as Theodor Roszak pointed out long ago in his book *The Making of the Counterculture* (1969), but why these objectives could not be met within the framework of middle-class culture was never seriously entertained by radical critics.

Contrary to Roszak's belief, there was no real counterculture but only a series of amorphous subcultures consisting of rebellious young people who were going through a collective identity crisis, blamed the culture for their problems, and demanded a more caring, therapeutic culture that would minister to their innermost longings. As Freud noted long ago, a nonrepressive culture that enhances and fulfills all the instinctual needs and desires of its members is a self-contradiction, an oxymoron.[25] Cultures are inherently repressive; it is just a matter of degree. Yet the neo-gnostic heretics of the 1960s continued to dream about a more perfect culture in which poverty, war, disease, and hatred would be eliminated. The reality turned out differently. The revolution of consciousness that would "green" America, as Charles Reich predicted, has not happened and neither has the arrival of Theodore Roszak's "Rhapsodic Intellect" and "Visionary Commonwealth," Herbert Marcuse's Marxist Utopia, or Norman O. Brown's Body Mysticism. The youthful followers of these intellectual critics lacked the self-discipline and ideological commitment to translate the amorphous and insubstantial ideas of their mentors into practice. They were too inexperienced, immature, and self-indulgent, too steeped in the mainstream culture that they supposedly rejected, to mount a serious countercultural revolt that could have seriously threatened what they called corporate capitalism.

What they did, however, was to force a real redefinition of the permissible range of moral and cultural self-expression. Every society has a line of permissible actions, specifying what individuals are allowed to do and what society is allowed to stop them from doing. Some societies draw this line overwhelmingly in favor of collective or authoritarian habits. As a result of the 1960s the United States has veered in the opposite direction, jettisoning ancient prohibitions, moral conventions, and aesthetic standards in favor of extreme permissiveness. What would once have appeared intolerable has now been tolerated to the limits of the endurable and beyond.

4. The End of Shame and Guilt

Ordinary middle-class Americans in the 1960s felt that these cultural excesses were particularly disturbing when it came to music and personal lifestyles. The music of the 1950s was bland and sentimental. After the big bands faded away in the early 1950s, popular music centered largely on pop vocalists who turned out slick formulaic songs—bland, inoffensive, and sentimental. Some of these vocalists, like Frank Sinatra, were very good, others eminently forgettable. Young people found little excitement in listening to Patti Page's "Doggie in the Window" or similar schmaltzy songs belched out by such popular crooners as Doris Day, Perry Como, Dean Martin, Kay Starr, Rosemary Clooney, Vic Damone, or the Lennon Sisters.

Whites, as we have seen, had looked beyond their own musical idioms from the moment they found themselves living in a multiracial society. They had warmly embraced but also coldly exploited black music.[26] Rhythm and blues and jazz were unique inventions of black people, but whites often appropriated and exploited them as their own. What attracted whites in the black experience, not just music, was its primitive, unpretentious, and emotionally rich timber. Blacks, it was said, were more primitive in relation to life, partly because they were attached to a simpler culture and partly because they were not immersed in white puritanical America, thus retaining a more vivid, sensuous relation to life and expressing it in music, art, manner, and everyday living.

This exemption from white cultural repression is what white people envied and resented in black people. As previously shown, Martha Bayles attributed this to the "blood-knot" in American culture,[27] that tangled web of sex and race that permeates American society. Black music and other elements of black culture seemed to promise liberation from instinctual restraints, accompanied by uninhibited joy and sensuality. Sam Phillips, a white entrepreneur who recorded black singers in the South, once told his assistant "if I could find a white man with a Negro sound I could make a billion dollars."[28] That white man, as everyone knows, was Elvis Presley, the "King of Rock 'n' Roll," the white conduit through which a series of mostly black musical idioms—blues, jazz, gospel—found their way into a whole generation of young whites and significantly shaped their lifestyles. This is not the place to trace that sad and even tragic transformation of the youthful, exuberant, and innocent Presley into the corrupt and decadent pop star, except to indicate that Presley's transformation was emblematic of the music he helped to shape. The pink Cadillac corrupted the king of rock 'n' roll: in mass culture America, as Greil Marcus has pointed out, "Elvis would lose his talent in its reward."[29] The same, as we have seen, was true of the music itself after the youthful revolt went sour and attracted people less interested in music than in exploiting it for commercial success.

In the early 1960s both folk music and rock 'n' roll had served a truly integrative function in the sense that the songs they produced were interracial. Moreover, they contained a genuine populist quality that dated back to Woody Guthrie and was passed on to Pete Seeger and Bob Dylan. In the increasingly popular musical festivals, culminating in Woodstock, there was also a real generational solidarity as audiences moved and surged in unison to a proliferation of rock bands. The invasion of the Brits, most notably the Beatles and the Rolling Stones, revitalized a wave of popular enthusiasm.

If popular music had a star who remained true to himself it was Bob Dylan, who bridged the gap between protest folk music and rock 'n' roll, revolutionized the genre by "going electric" at the Newport Folk Festival, and served as a cultural weather vane with lyrics like "The Times they Are A-Changin'," "Blowin' in the Wind," "Ballad of a Thin Man," "Masters of War," and "Hard Rain's A-Gonna Fall."

In the interplay of tunes and moods of the Beatles and the Rolling Stones, as previously shown, we can already hear the future. The Beatles were joyful, exuberant, fresh and vibrant, whereas the Rolling Stones were moved by hostility, anger, and nihilism. The future would belong to the Stones and the dark underworld of musical idioms—dreary acid-tinged lyrics, sexual preoccupations, suicidal themes, escapism, incest, and demonic obsessions. What started as a liberal romantic movement of protest and self-expression turned into a dark spectacle that Mario Praz has called in another context the "Romantic Agony"[30] with its inverted aesthetic values of delight in cruelty, sexual lust, and the seduction and perversion of goodness. As an antidote to parental preaching and schoolroom discipline, rock stars, now elevated into cultural icons, offered young people the seductive alternative of sex, speed, youth, and rock music. As the sounds became more frantic and violent, so did the reality of frequent overdoses and suicides. The rock stars showed the way. Janis Joplin, Jimi Hendrix, Brian Jones of the Rolling Stones, Jim Morrison of the Doors all died of drug-related causes between 1969 and 1971. By that time, rock artists generally followed the dark mood of the times, gave up fresh and innocent themes, and wallowed in self-indulgence, perversity, nihilism, and despair. They also infected a whole generation with essentially life-denying and ugly attitudes and thus further poisoned a culture already tainted by perverse modernism. In other words, music blended with postmodernism in an effort to smash the idols of middle-class culture and in its place enthrone the orthodoxy of shock, sensationalism, and narcissistic self-expression.

Rock 'n' roll was not just music but a whole lifestyle for many young people in the 1960s. The music broke down sexual inhibitions by encouraging its listeners to synchronize their bodies with the rhythmic beat of the music, which allegedly helped many white people in reclaiming their bodies from the repressive control of puritanical taboos. But at a certain point the music went sour and so did the lyrics. Black music, as Martha Bayles has pointed out, always aimed beyond just sheer lust to spiritual ecstasy, physical exuberance, and emotional catharsis.[31] Although there was a considerable and healthy crossover between black and white musical culture, white rock 'n' roll pushed steadily in the direction of perverse modernism, especially after the youthful "counterculture" degenerated into enclaves of deviant sexuality and drug usage. The harbingers were the Rolling Stones, the Doors, Frank Zappa, and the Velvet Underground. From innocent songs about love, the music moved to acid-tinged lyrics glamorizing uninhibited drug use and sexual promiscuity. "My music," Janis Joplin once said, "isn't supposed to make you riot; it is supposed to make you fuck,"[32] which was, at best, a half truth because the basic components of rock were protest, uninhibited expression, drugs, and sometimes radical politics. And the tone counted.

What a quick descent from "Young girl, get out of my mind . . . You're much too young girl . . . I'm afraid we'll go too far . . . hurry home to your mama"—to the many songs that went over the line, as did the young protesters who mixed music and radical politics. Extending the metaphor, it could be argued that a whole generation went over the line in the realm of personal morality and justified doing so by embracing a public morality based on love, peace, and liberal humanitarianism. The assumption behind the behavior of baby boomers seems to have been that public do-goodism expiated or even validated private excesses, and that what one did in one's private life had no moral bearing on the public domain as long as one kept the two separate spheres of morality in their proper place. Yet, does not one affect the other? The way we live our private lives, the sort of habits and lifestyles we choose significantly shapes our public behavior as well. Moreover, a generation's choice in personal lifestyles is also its ethical signature. The baby boom generation, it has been argued, has now groomed a new generation in over-the-line morality, and we do not have to belabor the consequences because they are all around us in the form of crime, drug use, welfare dependency, sexual permissiveness, and the degradation of popular entertainment.

Go back to your mama has now become:

I won't tell your mama if you don't tell your dad, I know he'll be disgusted when he sees your pussy busted. ("Me so Horny," *As Nasty as They Wanna Be*, 2 Live Crew)[33]

Elvis Presley:
Love me Tender, love me true, all my dreams fulfilled. For my darlin', I love you, and I always will.

NWA, "Findum, Fuckum, and Flee":
When the pussy holes are open, ready to fuck until my dick is raw . . . So come here, bitch, and lick up the, lick up the, lick up the dick![34]

Rock and drugs complement each other. Americans have always had a strong fascination for drugs and the magical potencies that they allegedly contained. Nineteenth-century America has often been called a "Dope Fiend's Paradise."[35] Physicians dispensed opiates directly to their patients, drugstores and grocery stores sold them over the counter, and users could order them through the mail. Morphine was legally manufactured from imported opium, and opium poppies were legally grown. Coca Cola, it will be recalled, originally contained cocaine. A country that had committed itself to the gospel of furthering individual happiness and the elimination of pain and suffering intermittently took a tolerant view of drug use, seeing drugs as a means of alleviating pain, inducing happiness, and perhaps even as a pathway to enlightenment. This attitude, however, was at odds with another powerful strain in American culture—Puritan sobriety, which accounts for the fact that Americans have sharply alternated between alcoholic or narcotic excess and stern prohibitionism. The parents of the baby boomers had experienced a strong whiff of sobriety dating back to the Prohibition era (1919–1934), but otherwise followed a far more permissive path when it came to alcohol, tobacco, or all sorts of prescription drugs, excepting marijuana, heroin, and hallucinogens. Alcohol, tobacco, and a variety of prescription drugs were widely used—so much so, that one could make a compelling case that baby boom parents had been hooked and brainwashed by the government, mass media, and even the medical-chemical establishment into believing that licit drugs could immeasurably improve the quality of their lives. In 1965 in the United States, for example, 123 million prescriptions were written for tranquilizers and 24 million for amphetamines.[36]

The profusion of illicit drugs, therefore, did not fall on Americans out of a blue sky; it stemmed from the easy acceptance of drugs by the older generation. The younger generation merely upped the ante and became even more addicted than their parents. Hippies associated drugs with a sense of liberation from the repressive society in which they lived; they viewed drugs as a springboard to heavenly enlightenment. Drugs, in other words, became a short-cut to peace, freedom, happiness, and enlightenment, not to speak of sexual pleasure. As shown in chapter 10, the drug guru of the 1960s was Timothy Leary, a former Harvard drug researcher who had a mystical epiphany informing him that hallucinogenic drugs (LSD) could lead to enlightenment and ecstatic happiness. Along with his colleague Richard Alpert, who later changed his name to Baba Ram Dass, Leary became a strident advocate for LSD and urged young Americans to "turn on, tune in, and drop out." He lectured to college students all over the country and tried to disseminate a drug philosophy that praised LSD, marijuana, and other drugs as personally fulfilling and socially liberating. Drug use, these gurus taught, heightened spiritual awareness and led to the profoundest mystical or religious insights. Drugs, they claimed, did not confuse people or cloud their minds. The term "getting stoned," they insisted, was misleading. What really happened was not confusion but enlightenment. Charles Reich, in his bestselling book *The Greening of America*, argued that drugs sharpened perception, so that when somebody smoked grass the effect was like what happened when a person with fuzzy vision put on glasses.[37] Smoking grass, Reich said, is a subtle and delicate experience, an educated experience, one of the most important means for restoring dulled consciousness.[38]

These drug gurus were false prophets because they taught a destructive and misleading message of easy enlightenment through quick drug fixes rather than spiritual discipline requiring a lifelong commitment. In a remarkably candid self-portrait one youthful protester observed: "Everything about us stresses instantaneousness of gratifications of wants. We can travel anywhere in a matter of hours or days. We can communicate instantly, etc.... Is it any wonder that young people living in this climate want instant spiritual fulfillment, instant physical gratification, instant change in the political and social system? Not only do these people not have the capacity. . . . for hard work towards rational goals but they do not even have the patience for the serious meditation of the Indian mystic and they take LSD as a seeming short-cut."[39]

The problem with such short-cuts, of course, is that LSD and other drugs suppress the normal discriminatory functions of the mind, making it virtually impossible to distinguish between the relative importance of certain sounds, sights, tastes, and smells. This, in turn, produces the illusion that all stimuli and sensory perceptions are equally valid. Rather than seeing the world as a structural or coherent holism, a drug "trip" breaks down structure or hierarchy and produces the illusion that we are experiencing reality in its raw detail without any rational hierarchy whatsoever. A "trip" gives the user a sense of vivid and almost childlike perception, unencumbered by rational judgment. It also fosters a sense of connectedness to all phenomena, even a sense of oneness with the universe. The feeling that all is one and one is all reinforced the countercultural ethos of love and bonding.

Although drug use to some extent reinforced primitive love or bonding and even evoked a sense of revulsion to violence or war, its side effects were psychologically debilitating and physically life-threatening. In fact, many "brains were fried," as they used to say, and many lives were shattered. Yet the revolution through acid spread rapidly throughout the stormy 1960s. Leary, Alpert, and Ken Kesey and his Merry Pranksters found many imitations: San Francisco hippies congregating in the Haight-Ashbury district, New York East Village types, college students on many campuses, and scores of dropouts. "Bad trips" were commonplace and had devastating consequences: psychotic episodes, personality changes, suicides, and lethal overdoses. Art Linkletter's daughter, purportedly thinking that she could fly, jumped out of her high-rise apartment and plunged to her death. Thousands overdosed, suffered serious and lasting brain damage, passed on their addiction to their children, or died prematurely.

Combined with rock music, drugs promoted uninhibited and unsafe sex and extremely antisocial behavior that would have been inconceivable on such a scale to earlier generations. Inhibitions melted away under the influence of these drugs, and so did the traditional values of Judeo-Christian culture that were based on shame, guilt, discipline, hard work, and postponement of gratifications.

Historians who have taken a critical look at the 1960s generally argue that many people in the 1960s luxuriated in extreme lifestyles without perceiving the corrosive impact this had on the culture. This, of course, is a matter of perception. Where one observer sees a soft generation, kind and generous, liberal, tolerant, and naively uninhibited, another observer could argue with equal plausibility that many young people had stepped over the line and "let it all hang out," and what they hung out was not always so beautiful or loving. The countercultural mind-set of "doing your own thing," of being "groovy," and of not judging anyone or anything, produced at best amiable hedonists, at worst callous manipulators and inauthentic charlatans of the stripe of Jerry Rubin or Abbie Hoffman. Yet, in a way, the hippies were merely living a parallel world of hedonistic indulgence that resembled the corporate mainstream. Hugh Heffner is the obverse of the same hedonistic coin. His slick magazine *Playboy*, featuring a titillating array of nude Playboy "bunnies" endowed with gigantic breasts, together with his chain of Playboy Clubs throughout the country, offered well-heeled corporate types an entree to the new Eden, replete with seductive women, booze, expensive clothes, and technological gadgets.

Heffner's *Playboy* magazine was emblematic of the so-called liberated sexuality of the 1960s, cutting across all age groups and ethnicities, though focusing its appeal primarily on those who were benefiting from corporate America. Whether there actually was a real revolution in sexuality in the 1960s has been much debated, but one thing is clear: people felt far more open than ever before in expressing a whole range of sexual behaviors. They also displayed an open and uninhibited manner that would have mortified earlier generations. Group sex and orgies became more commonplace; instant gratification replaced lengthy courtship or "harmless" dating. Pornography was out in the open and widely available, at least in metropolitan areas. The seeds of sexual freedom could be found in a variety of sources: the music, the pill, *Playboy* magazine, the Kinsey and later the Masters and Johnson studies on human sexuality, widespread drug use, and the ineffectiveness of traditional gatekeepers. The result was no-holds-barred experimentation, including group sex, lesbian and homosexual sex, premarital and intermarital (spouse swapping) sex, fetish, bondage—all in as many imaginative positions as possible.

What was the impact of this free-flowing erotic energy? Obsessed but not enlightened by sex, boomers have been telling us that white America was at last liberated from stifling Puritan taboos and from a whole range of repressive rules that had made sexuality a shameful activity. Although they were hardly the first generation in history to open up the range of sexual freedom, they certainly did so on a far larger scale. There was a lot of "making it," "getting it on," "doing it," but there was not a great deal that aimed at genuine love or bonding, certainly not among young males, who were fixated almost entirely on orgasm. "There are a lot of young girls," one Haight-Ashbury observer said, "who are coming in from the suburbs who really want to get laid and be liked and be loved. And they're getting fucked but they're not getting loved. And that's because the young males have their own hang-ups. They can't love everybody . . . I know a couple of communal places . . . that have more and more meth-heads going all the time, and girls are getting stoned on meth and get fucked for a couple of days until they freak out. But that's not sexual freedom, that's sexual compulsion."[40]

Did this greater sexual openness actually improve the quality of American life and institutions? The evidence so far is not too encouraging. Sexual permissiveness went far beyond personal lifestyles to the very heart and soul of American family life. It led to an increase in divorce, illegitimacy and single-mother families, sexually transmitted diseases, and greater poverty among teenagers and poor minorities. In 1972 more than one million children were affected by divorces; just four years later, three times as many children were involved in divorce as had been twenty years earlier.[41] One tragic byproduct was the emergence of a lot of single-parent families, most of them headed by women, because baby boomers rejected the custom of saving a marriage "for the sake of the children" as hopelessly old-fashioned. The most devastating blow fell on the black families. By the late 1970s fewer than half of black pre-school children were living with their natural parents, compared to 87 percent of white preschool children.[42] This dismal picture was made even worse by government welfare regulations that discouraged black women from living with their spouses, thus financially rewarding single-parent families.

The pain, guilt, and mental anguish that millions of children have experienced as a result of this mounting tide of divorce has been widely discussed in recent years, particularly since children of baby boomers have often translated their inner hurts into orgies of violent public rages. Being self-centered rather than child-centered, baby boomers have all too often looked upon their children as inconvenient nuisances who might run them off center stage. By regarding marriage and children as an exploitive and restrictive bourgeois institutions, some boomers may have deliberately and ignorantly closed themselves to the joy and personal growth that come through the hard work and sacrifice involved in bringing up children. It was particularly the well-educated men and women of upper-middle-class backgrounds who regarded marriage and children as an impediment to self-indulgence. In other words, if children are seen as a nuisance or an obstacle to careers and ego gratification, what sort of children would the boomers leave behind them to carry on the work of civilization? Little thought was given to these problems in the 1960s. All too many members of the "Now Generation" had no great desire to have children, and easy access to contraceptives reduced the risk of having children in the first place. The first birth control pill was approved as safe for use by the FDA in 1960. Until 1973 access to abortion was illegal in most states, except when the life of the mother was at risk. After intense battles, the Supreme Court ruled in the case of *Roe v. Wade* (1973) that states could not pass laws interfering with a woman's right to an abortion in the early months of pregnancy. Armed with the pill and liberalized abortion laws, boomers faced much smaller risks of having unwanted children and could therefore completely alter traditional patterns of courtship and marriage. In Landon Jones's view, the boomers proceeded to do just that and in the process "came precariously close to balkanizing our basic unit of cultural transmission: the family." Today, we have a whole new vocabulary for transitory relationships in which children are, at best, an afterthought: blended families, cohabitants, reconstituted families.

The new sexuality, far from producing intimacy, love, joy, or happy children, more often promoted promiscuity, sexually transmitted diseases, and broken families. Like so many other liberation movements, it exacted as heavy, if not a heavier, toll than the alleged restrictions, repressions, or authorities it tried to replace.

5. The Indigestible Sixties

Since the python is still digesting the pig, it may be too early to deliver definitive judgments about the impact of the baby boom generation on American life and culture. Yet several judgments, both positive and negative, can be made about the transformation of American society since the 1960s. On a positive note, the 1960s protests, especially the countercultural protests, reawakened, if only briefly, the romantic sensibility in Western culture. Those protests also questioned the dominant technocratic society's overemphasis on material affluence, greed, and mindless hedonism. The counterculture tried to focus on the spiritual needs of human beings that could not be satisfied through affluence or consumption. It also opposed the mainstream culture's belief in the mystique of scientific infallibility, the worship of bigness, and unrestrained urban-industrial expansion. In the end, the counter-culture knew what it did not want better than what it wanted. Youthful protesters insisted that they wanted absolute liberty of self-expression, no matter how eccentric or unorthodox. They also wanted to flee urban America and revert to a more organic way of life associated with the soil and more primitive soil-bound occupations. Following E. F. Schumacher, many endorsed the motto "small is beautiful,"[43] and tried to live it on various communes that sprang up in response to these romantic longings. Yet, being children of the technocracy, reared in affluence and craving the goods of the consumer culture, few youthful protesters were willing to give up their automobiles, stereos, and other technological pacifiers. The mainstream technological culture sat too heavily on these youthful longings and in the end squashed what was genuinely valuable and fresh. The corporate system deflected and absorbed the protest by merchandising it for profits. Artists and musicians were bought off with money and the celebrity status that flows from it in a sensate culture. Protesters were eventually integrated into the mainstream because they had to make a living and take responsibility for adult decisions such as getting married, raising children, taking care of elderly parents, and simply coping with the many pressures of ordinary life.

Although radicalism burned itself out and was apparently co-opted, it also succeeded in profoundly altering American society. In the first place, the great upheavals in civil rights have transformed America from a white Anglo-Saxon culture into a far more diverse ethnic culture in which the formerly dominant white power establishment was forced to include other ethnic groups, perhaps not on a coequal basis but certainly on a far more equitable and "shared" basis than ever before. This was a positive contribution of the stormy 1960s. Unfortunately, the rhetoric of integration and inclusivity, as previously mentioned, was not translated into social practice. By the end of the 1960s integration had given way to ethnic separatism and the politics of the spoils system, making it difficult to forge a common civic culture. The same tendency toward separatism took place in the cultural domain. The 1960s protests splintered a relatively homogeneous culture and made manifest a tendency that was always latent in American society: its shift toward a centrifugal kind of multi-culturalism. Far from integrating Americans of diverse creeds or ethnicities, the 1960s protests ended up dividing Americans from each other. As Arthur Schlesinger has observed, the multiethnic dogma that reigns supreme in influential political circles today threatens to reverse the theory of America as one people, and he rightly adds that exactly that theory has so far managed to keep American society whole.[44]

The social direction since and because of the 1960s has been toward fragmentation. Radical feminists advocated a separate women's culture based on allegedly unique female experiences; their anti-male ideology caused serious divisions and tensions between men and women in America. Black activists and other minority leaders have also promoted separatism rather than racial integration. As a result, many black people have re-ghettoized themselves under the cover of Afrocentric creeds, which may promote a temporary sense of self-esteem but is doomed to sever black people from the good life that only a common culture can provide.

Another divisive outcome of the 1960s has been the tendency to protest against unjust institutions and to demand instant compensation for being an alleged victim. It is safe to say that victimhood has become a favorite preoccupation in modern America, and it is also safe to argue, as Charles J. Sykes has done in his book *A Nation of Victims*, that the result has been detrimental to the American character. Therapeutic culture has turned all too many people into victims who deserve special privileges in the form of quotas, entitlements, and financial compensation. This is the degeneration of the civil rights movement, its transformation from righting genuine racial or legal wrongs to jumping onto the entitlement bandwagon. The premier legal tactic to promote entitlements consists in twisting the Constitution into an egalitarian rather than a libertarian document that can be used as a blueprint of discovery for an endless series of individual rights. As a result of the 1960s, radical egalitarians have dreamed up new rights on demand for everybody and everything. In the absence of legislation, litigation has become the method of choice for radical egalitarians who demand redress of endless grievances on the part of allegedly victimized individuals or groups.

As a result of decades of protest, dissent, and deconstructionism there is today no common center, not even a public opinion that speaks for all Americans. The balkanization of opinion, as Christopher Lasch has shown, is the inevitable consequence of the physical segregation of the population into self-enclosed, racially homogeneous enclaves. Each group tries to barricade itself behind its own dogma and its own ghetto walls.[45] The evening news reports what is taking place not in America's communities but in the "black," "gay," "Latino," "Korean," "Chinese," or "Jewish" community. Putting a shiny veneer of "multiculturalism" or diversity on the centrifugal forces tearing apart the cultural center merely hides the problem. Those who imagine a multicultural future, as Theodore Dalrymple put it, seem to restrict the term largely to food: "you can eat Thai on Monday, Italian on Tuesday, Szechuan on Wednesday, Hungarian on Thursday, and so forth. . . . Under multiculturalism, a man might turn towards Mecca in the morning, sacrifice a chicken in the afternoon, and go to Mass in the evening without ever becoming a Muslim, an animist, or a Catholic."[46] Even if "diversity" is a demographic fact, it hardly follows that all cultural practices are coequal or that they should become a new morality. As Lasch has pointed out, more often than not diversity has legitimized a new form of dogmatism in which rival groups take shelter and curse civilization from behind varying sets of beliefs impervious to rational discussion.[47]

The great American experiment in a common culture seems to have failed as a result of the turbulent 1960s. The idea that all races, creeds, and religions would be assimilated into the "melting pot" and emerge as homogeneous values in the "Great Society" has been discredited and replaced by heterogeneous pluralism. In its ideal form, this pluralism accepts all races, creeds, and religions and permits them to flourish in their individual cultural expressions, while at the same time expecting a point of homogeneity, specifically in the economic and political manifestation of the American ideals embodied in the "sacred" documents that form the cornerstone of American democracy. Time will tell if this new experiment with diversity within unity will succeed in creating a cohesive society, one in which multicultural expressions are consistent with a unitary civic style.

If the 1960s have taught anything, it is that protest without universal affirmation and consensus building undermines a people's common democracy. This is essentially what the protest movements of the 1960s have done. Although originally limited to civil rights, the antiwar opposition, the New Left, and the counterculture, the protest movements cross-fertilized, and they significantly expanded beyond these groups to the population at large and turned protest into a corrosive cultural style. Traditionalists smugly assumed that the end of widespread public protests in the 1970s also meant the end of the socioeconomic or cultural reasons that had produced them. While it is true that the protests splintered, that the end of the Vietnam War and the draft stopped the antiwar protests, that the New Left disintegrated, and that many countercultural hippies turned into corporate yuppies driving BMWs, the underlying cultural and political factors that fueled the protests have continued to operate below the surface, profoundly altering the face of American society.

The 1960s began as a moral reformation period in American history, as America tried to redeem its lofty creeds from past injustices. What started as a moral crusade for the heart and soul of the nation's noblest dreams, gradually derailed from its moral path and degenerated into mutual recrimination and self-centered ideologies. Young people had really subscribed to the notion of American exceptionalism and the utopian belief associated with it—namely, that, unlike any other nation on earth, America was blessed by infinite goodness, perfection, and plenitude. They sincerely endorsed the liberal credo that evil and injustice are the result of social or environmental causes, and that these causes—bad parenting, poor education, poverty, bigotry, war—were susceptible to social change. All that was required to change the world, many seemed to believe, was to change the prevailing mode of consciousness. But if consciousness is dulled by drugs, poor education, and hedonistic lifestyles, the world is unlikely to change for the better.

In the meantime, there was still the corporate-technological machine, Max Weber's Iron Cage that had to be administered, and it goes without saying that corporate capitalism, increasingly global and impersonal, did not conform to youthful expectations of a world of love, peace, and universal happiness. The hopes and expectations embodied in many of the 1960s protests quickly crashed when they encountered the reality of cynical men with cold hearts and greedy appetites. Unlike the Greeks and other people who incorporated tragedy into their cultural styles, Americans refused to acknowledge the existence of the Gap of Tragedy—the inevitable failure that always occurs when lofty ideals fall short of their full attainment. There will always be a gap between the perfection we conceptualize and the reality we can attain. What the Greeks accepted as a tragic, unalterable fact of life,

Americans have viewed as a mere accident of history that did not apply to them. Consequently, they believed that there was nothing they could not do or accomplish, even if it meant splitting the heavens by wiping out poverty, war, disease, and ignorance within a lifetime.

Such lofty ideals, as we have seen, were more fervently held by young people. When that generation of young people embarked on its search for both social perfection and personal fulfillment, it quickly came face to face with the same intractable obstacles experienced by other generations before it. The difference was that the sixties generation regarded itself as historically unique, the apex of the accumulated riches and wisdom of past generations. The youthful protesters of the 1960s expected to succeed where all earlier generations had failed; they fully expected to finish the circle of American exceptionalism by purging it at the same time of all moral imperfections.

Failure to reach the highest expectations is bound to result in the most bitter disappointments leading to cynicism and despair. Indeed, in addition to the social and cultural divisions of the 1960s, there was also a change in the public mood. In fact, the shift in mood from roseate hope withered to despair. The cultural exhaustion that followed and the splintering of the national style that ensued cannot be understood without plotting this swing in mood. Until the mid-1960s the public mood in America was essentially optimistic, as it had been throughout American history. Americans had always structured their narrative history in a distinctly hopeful and progressive manner. Their history was a mighty drama in which the forces of good, associated with the white, Protestant American way of life, would inevitably triumph over the forces of evil. The story of American history was emplotted in a unitary and dramatic form; it was a victory culture immune from the tragic effects of history.

The 1960s changed this long-standing belief in exceptional American dispensation from the laws of history, particularly after the defeat in Vietnam. The public mood shifted toward pessimism, and so did the way in which Americans have framed their history, which has become a tale no longer colored in black and white but in gray. Largely as a result of the divisive forces of the 1960s, American society is going through a "form-free period, a kind of hiatus that lies between a fading and a rising cultural style.

If there is a way out of this wilderness, it lies in the recovery of a common democracy and a civic way of life that includes core values and stronger restraints for those who refuse to restrain themselves. It will be difficult to reclaim such a common civic culture with a unique American identity because the nation's leadership, especially those who control the flow of money and information, has no loyalty to middle America. As Lasch has shown, the nation's elite has betrayed democracy; it has no loyalty to country, only to money and global markets.[48] Moreover, today's corporate elite lives in a simulated reality of abstract money manipulations and technological gadgetry. Having no commitment beyond its own self-enrichment, it shows contempt for ordinary Americans, especially for those who envision a different kind of America than the MacDonaldized America in which standardized bigness is always better and people have been reduced to obedient consumers and gullible voters.

Exercising a virtual stranglehold on the nation's polity, as well as the corporate establishment that bankrolls it, the new technological elite dispenses bread and circuses through vulgar mass entertainment and super spectacles, co-opts potential protest by either denying it access to mass media or corrupting it with money, and tries to banish subversive thought by reducing cultural literacy in the educational system. These disturbing signs do not necessarily point to some orchestrated conspiracy by the corporate leadership but a synchronicity of interests that feed on the nation's resources and cultural patrimony for their own financial gain. And in order to cover up its shameless greed, the new corporate elite hides behind advertising slogans and recruits the best politicians money can buy. By tolerating the dumbing down of the American people, the corporate leadership frequently escapes criticism because fewer and fewer Americans are able to penetrate the deceptions that it circulates through the mass media. One of its biggest lies, which is based on clever pandering to the vanity of the populace, is that never before in history have people been so free, so well informed, and so highly educated. Under the benign influence of technology more and more people will be able to access unfiltered information and make rational choices leading to greater and greater self-empowerment. Not too many people realize that the apparent multiplicity of news and information sources does not mean that consumers have real diversity because the same corporate few control both the quantity and the quality of information, disguising their monopolistic practices under a smokescreen of choice and diversity.

In the meantime, the cultural and intellectual deterioration of educational standards, codes of civility, and common decencies continues throughout the Western world. The well of faith has seemingly dried up. If current trends going back to the 1960s continue, fewer and fewer people will be culturally literate. Most will have been brainwashed by the mass media and its manipulators into believing whatever conforms to current thinking. Numbers and images will most likely replace the vocabulary of Shakespeare, Milton, Jefferson, Locke, and Kant.

It is at this point that people need to ask themselves whether the Consumer Republic, as Lizabeth Cohen calls it, is compatible with the Democratic Republic they have inherited from their founders. In other words, to what extent is mass production for private mass consumption compatible with the democratic ideal that the common good is more important than the private good when the latter undermines the former? Another implication of the uncontested reign of the Consumer Republic concerns the role of citizenship: Is consuming more important than citizenship? Or, putting it another way, is consuming a duty of citizenship? These are not idle questions, as Cohen reminds us, because citizenship and consumption have become increasingly interlinked.[49] Such a linkage threatens to displace the civic energy needed for social justice and the maintenance of the public sector.

One could argue, in fact, that the Democratic Republic seems to have been on a leave of absence since the 1960s. For all its excesses, the decade of the 1960s was a democratic reform period; it was civic-minded and receptive to needed social changes. Unfortunately, liberal reformers set themselves unrealistic goals, confused their own utopian visions with reality, and thereby lost support with the American people. The high hopes of many young people were dashed quickly when the Democratic Republic refused to ratify their desires on demand. By the end of the 1960s disenchantment with the democratic process was widespread among young people, and every election since then has witnessed a steady decrease in voter participation by the young.

Such widespread disenchantment with politics among the young was due to the naive belief that politics saved or redeemed people from every social or existential ill. Expectations outran realities; and when they did, the flight from politics began. Of particularly crushing disappointment was the demise of the liberal dream of achieving justice by legislating perfect fairness, a dream that paradoxically rested on a lot of liberal self-deception. Liberals ranked social justice higher than the truth, while radicals ranked utopian untruth higher than reality. The dialectical tension between liberals and radicals has resulted in a forty-five year reaction against perfect liberal reform as well as social perfection through revolution. In the absence of strong spiritual commitments, what remains is the Consumer Republic; but human beings demand more out of life than consumption; they crave genuine love and affection along with higher spiritual satisfactions. In this connection, one thing that this author has learned about America long ago is that the American people are a strongly religious people. The religious impulse, even among the baby boomers, may yet provide a strong counterpoise to the Consumer Republic, revitalizing the barren soil of materialism and centering the perfectionist impulse on where it really belongs: the spiritual plane. Such issues, however, exceed the limits of historical inquiry; in fact, as John Lukacs has pointed out, it is the task of the historian to tell the truth with the understanding that he cannot tell the perfect truth, but what he can do is to "pursue the truth through the reduction of ignorance."[50]

In retrospect, the 1960s illustrate that the pursuit of "perfect" justice without a sense of historical reality is a self-defeating enterprise. At the same time, this author, growing to maturity during the 1960s, has taken away a strong belief from *his* 1960s experiences that human beings have a spiritual duty to ameliorate injustice in the same way that they have a duty to enhance the truth by reducing ignorance. Except for civil rights, most of the 1960s protests were unrealistic, at best exchanging the iron cage with a gilded cage. If it is genuine existential protests Americans are seeking, it would require a humanization of the industrial system, a radical change in which politicians are selected rather than packaged and sold, and a reawakening of religious sensibility. If such changes have any chance of succeeding, future reformers will have to go beyond youthful idealism, build strong bridges to ordinary Americans, and choose wiser and more ethically grounded leaders. Perhaps then the better parts of the 1960s could be used as a foundation for a better American polity and a more meaningful way of life.

NOTES

Chapter 1: Introduction

1. Quoted in Vance Packard, *The Waste Makers* (New York: David McKay, 1960), p. 28.

2. Harvey Cox, *The Secular City* (New York: Macmillan, 1965), pp. 192–216.

3. Tom Mathews, "The Sixties Complex," *Newsweek*, September 5, 1988, p. 18

4. Ibid.

5. Terry Anderson, *The Sixties* (New York: Longman, 1999), p. 8.

6. *Life Magazine*, July 4, 1955.

7. Connie Shepard, "'Good Morning, Teacher' Is Ancient History," *Los Angeles Times*, April 18, 2003.

8. Martin Gross, *The End of Sanity: Social and Cultural Madness in America* (New York: Avon Books, 1997), p. 18

9. Ibid., p. 120.

10. Robert Hughes, *The Culture of Complaint: The Fraying of America* (New York: Oxford University Press, 1993), p. 10.

11. Michael Medved, *Hollywood vs. America* (New York: HarperCollins, 1992), p. 26.

12. Ibid.

13. Ibid., p. 262.

14. Ibid., p. 303.

15. On the baby boomers and their significance in American history, see Landon Y. Jones, *Great Expectations: America and the Baby Boom Generation* (New York: Ballantine Books, 1980); Lewis S. Feuer, *The Conflict of Generations: The Character and Significance of Student Movements* (New York: Basic Books, 1969); Henry Malcolm, *The Generation of Narcissus* (Boston: Little, Brown, 1971); Christopher Lasch, *The Culture of Narcissism* (New York: Warner Books, 1979); Richard A. Easterlin, *Birth and Fortune: The Impact of Numbers on Personal Welfare* (Chicago: University of Chicago Press, 1980); Michael X. Delli, *Stability and Change in American Politics: The Coming of Age of the Generation of the 1960s* (New York: New York University Press, 1986).

16. Two good collections containing a variety of historical perspectives are Stephen Macedo, ed., *Reassessing the Sixties: Debating the Political and Cultural Legacy* (New York: Norton, 1997); and Gerald Howard, ed., *The Sixties* (New York: Washington Square Press, 1982). Of the many general studies of the 1960s, written from different ideological perspectives, the following are especially noteworthy: William L. O'Neill, *Coming Apart: An Informal History of America in the 1960s* (New York: Quadrangle, 1976); Allen J. Matusow, *The Unravelling of America: A History of Liberalism in the 1960s* (New York: Harper and Row, 1984); David Burner, *Making Peace with the 60s* (Princeton, N.J.: Princeton University Press, 1996); Godfrey Hodgson, *America in Our Time* (New York: Vintage, 1976); Todd Gitlin, *The Sixties: Years of Hope, Days of Rage* (New York: Bantam, 1987); Morris Dickstein, *Gates of Eden: American Culture in the Sixties* (Cambridge, Mass.: Harvard University Press, 1997); Edward P. Morgan, *The Sixties Experience: Hard Lessons about Modern America* (Philadelphia: Temple University Press, 1991); Terry Anderson, *The Movement and the Sixties: Protest in America from Greensboro to Wounded Knee* (New York: Oxford University Press, 1995); Joseph Conlin, *The Troubles: A Jaundiced Glance Back at the Movement of the Sixties* (New York:

Franklin Watts, 1982); Herbert I. London, *The Overheated Decade* (New York: New York University Press, 1976); Ronald Berman, *America in the Sixties: An Intellectual History* (New York: Free Press, 1968); John Morton Blum, *Years of Discord: American Politics and Society, 1961–1974* (New York: W. W. Norton, 1991); and Arthur Marwick, *The Sixties: Cultural Revolution in Britain, France, Italy, and the United States, c. 1958–1974* (New York: Oxford University Press, 1998).

17. Two major books explored this change in cultural consciousness in the early 1970s: Theodore Roszak, *The Making of a Counter Culture* (New York: Anchor, 1969) and Charles A. Reich, *The Greening of America* (New York: Bantam Books, 1971). Although a national best-seller, Reich's work quickly faded from public consciousness after being savagely attacked by the critics, but Roszak, a far more acute writer, continued drawing reference to the importance of countercultural forces in the modern world in a series of interesting books, notably *Where the Wasteland Ends* (New York: Anchor, 1973); *Unfinished Animal: The Aquarian Frontier and the Evolution of Consciousness* (New York: Harper & Row, 1975); and *Person/Planet: The Creative Disintegration of Industrial Society* (New York: Doubleday, 1979).

18. The historical antecedents of countercultural protests are explored by Roszak, *Making of a Counter Culture*; Nathan Adler, *The Underground Stream: New Life Styles and the Antinomian Personality* (New York: Harper & Row, 1972); Paul Zweig, *The Heresy of Self-Love: A Study of Subversive Individualism* (New York: Harper & Row, 1968); and J. Milton Yinger, *Countercultures: The Promise and the Peril of a World Turned Upside Down* (New York: Free Press, 1982).

19. Adler, *Underground Stream*, pp. 20–54.

Chapter 2: Fault Lines in a Land of Perfection

1. Hector St. John de Crevecoeur, *Letters from an American Farmer*, quoted in Arthur Schlesinger, *The Disuniting of America* (New York: Norton, 1992), p. 12

2. Quoted in Schlesinger, *Disuniting of America*, p. 32.

3. Ibid., p. 33.

4. Theodore Roosevelt, *Works* (New York, 1923–26), chap. XX, p. 456.

5. The term is generally associated with Arthur Schlesinger's work *The Vital Center: The Politics of Freedom* (Boston: Houghton Mifflin Company, 1949).

6. Morris R. Cohen, *The Faith of a Liberal* (New York: Henry Holt, 1946), p. 452.

7. Bertrand Russell quoted in William Ebenstein, *Today's Isms* (New York: Prentice Hall, 1961), p. 129.

8. Gordon Allport, *The Nature of Prejudice* (New York: Anchor Books, 1958), p. 403.

9. Richard Hofstadter, *The Paranoid Style in American Politics* (New York: Vintage, 1967). In fairness to Hofstadter, he is generally careful in limiting the term "paranoid" to the political lunatic fringe—the Know-Nothings, the Ku Klux Klan, the Illuminati.

10. Quoted in John Lukacs, *A New Republic: A History of the United States in the Twentieth Century* (New Haven, Conn.: Yale University Press, 2004), p. 5.

11. Quoted in Reinhold Niebuhr, *The Irony of American History* (New York: Scribner's, 1962), p. 27. Niebuhr's analysis of America's idealism and its lack of knowledge of the use and abuse of power still stands up half a century after the publication of his book.

12. Lukacs, *New Republic*, pp. 306, 318, 422.

13. I owe the terms "beacon" and "crusader" to Henry Kissinger's broad-ranging work *Diplomacy* (New York: Simon & Schuster, 1994), p. 18.

14. George Kennan, *Memoirs, 1925–1952* (Boston: Little, Brown and Company, 1967), p. 322.

15. Quoted in Lukacs, *New Republic*, p. 318.

16. Kennan, *Memoirs*, p. 323.

17. Lukacs, *New Republic*, p. 242.

18. Ibid., p. 241.

19. *Congressional Record*, 80th Congress, 1st session, p. 1981 (March 12, 1947). The Truman

doctrine was formally embodied in a National Security Council document (NSC-68), which served as the official statement of U.S. cold war strategy.

20. Kennan, *Memoirs*, p. 321.

21. William L. O'Neill, *American High: The Years of Confidence, 1945–1960* (New York: Free Press, 1986), p. 69.

22. Quoted in Kissinger, *Diplomacy*, p. 34.

23. For British social-imperial thought, see Bernard Semmel, *Imperialism and Social Reform* (New York: Doubleday, 1968).

24. Lukacs, *New Republic*, p. 242.

25. For the Jefferson Hemings controversy, see Annette Gordon-Reed, *Thomas Jefferson and Sally Hemings: An American Controversy* (Charlottesville, Va.: University of Virginia Press, 1997).

26. Quoted in Gordon-Reed, *Thomas Jefferson and Sally Hemings*, p. 61.

27. I owe this story to David K. Shipler, *A Country of Strangers: Blacks and Whites in America* (New York: Knopf, 1997), pp. 169–75.

28. Ibid., p. 171.

29. S. T. Jashi, ed., *Documents of American Prejudice* (New York: Basic Books, 1999), p. 11.

30. Ibid.

31. C. Vann Woodward, *The Strange Career of Jim Crow* (New York: Oxford University Press, 1966), p. 17.

32. Alexis de Tocqueville, *Democracy in America* (New York: HarperCollins, 1988), p. 343.

33. Quoted in Woodward, *Strange Career of Jim Crow*, p. 21.

34. David Herbert Donald, *Lincoln* (London: Jonathan Cape, 1995), p. 167. On Lincoln's stand regarding colonization for blacks, see Michael Vorenberg, "Abraham Lincoln and the Politics of Black Colonization," *Journal of the Abraham Lincoln Association* 14 (Summer 1993): 1–21.

35. Lerone Bennett Jr., for example, has argued that Lincoln was a racist and white supremacist (*Forced into Glory: Abraham Lincoln's White Dream* [Chicago: Johnson, 2000]; also the same author's article in *Ebony Magazine*, "Was Abe Lincoln a White Supremacist?" [1968]).

36. Woodward, *Strange Career of Jim Crow*, pp. 84–85.

37. Ibid., pp. 97–102.

38. Quoted in Harvard Sitkoff, *The Struggle for Black Equality, 1954–1992* (New York: Hill and Wang, 1993), p. 30.

39. Woodward, *Strange Career of Jim Crow*, p. 169.

Chapter 3: The Pig in the Python

1. Landon Y. Jones, *Great Expectations: America and the Baby Boom Generation* (New York: Ballantine Books, 1980), p. 10.

2. Ibid., pp. 4–7.

3. José Ortega y Gasset, *Man and Crisis* (New York: Norton, 1962), chapters 3 and 4.

4. Ibid., pp. 44–45.

5. Samuel Beers, "Memoirs of a Political Junkie," *Harvard Magazine* (September-October, 1984): pp. 165–70.

6. William H. Whyte, *The Organization Man* (New York: Simon & Schuster, 1965).

7. See Tom Brokaw, *The Greatest Generation* (New York: Random House, 1998).

8. "For Adults, Today's Youth Are Always the Worst," *Los Angeles Times,* Opinion Section, November 21, 1999. The article is based on Males's book *Framing Youth: Ten Myths about the Next Generation* (Monroe, Me.: Common Courage Press, 1999).

9. Males, *Framing Youth,* pp. 1–27.

10. *New York Times,* October 26, 1949, p. 36.

11. Robert M. Collins, *More: The Politics of Economic Growth in Postwar America* (New York: Oxford University Press, 2000), p. 22.

12. David Halberstam, *The Fifties* (New York: Fawcett Columbine, 1993), p. 140.

13. John Lukacs, *A New Republic: A History of the United States in the Twentieth Century* (New Haven, Conn.: Yale University Press, 2004), pp. 419–20.

14. On the evolution and growth of American cities, especially social problems, see Fred Siegel, *Tales of the City: The Future Once Happened Here* (New York: Free Press, 1997).

15. Quoted in Halberstam, *The Fifties*, p. 141.

16. William L. O'Neill, *American High: The Years of Confidence, 1945–1960* (New York: Free Press, 1986), p. 19.

17. Elaine Tyler May, *Homeward Bound: American Families in the Cold War Era* (New York: Basic Books, 1999), p. xxi.

18. Ibid., p. 105.

19. Quoted in Michael Barson and Steven Heller, *Teenage Confidential: An Illustrated History of the American Teen* (San Francisco: Chronicle Books, 1998), p. 101.

20. Gary Cross, *An All-Consuming Century: Why Commercialism Won in Modern America* (New York: Columbia University Press, 2000), p. 84.

21. Steve Gillon, *Boomer Nation: The Largest and Richest Generation Ever and How It Changed America* (New York: Free Press, 2004), p. 2; John Huizinga, *America*, trans. Herbert H. Rowen (New York: Harper & Row, 1972), p. 9.

22. Gillon, *Boomer Nation*, p. 21.

23. Dwight McDonald quoted in Kenneth J. Heineman, *Put Your Bodies upon the Wheels: Student Revolt in the 1960s* (Chicago: Ivan R. Dee, 2001), p. 93.

24. The *New Yorker*, November 1958; see also Tom Engelhardt, *The End of Victory Culture* (New York: Basic Books, 1995), p. 134.

25. Joseph Conlin, *The Troubles: A Jaundiced Glance Back at the Movement of the Sixties* (New York: Franklin Watts, 1982), p. 77.

26. Grace Palladino, *Teenagers: An American History* (New York: Basic Books, 1996), pp. 109–10.

27. "A Caste, A Culture, A Market," *New Yorker*, November 1958.

28. Halberstam, *The Fifties*, p. 473.

29. Landon Y. Jones, *Great Expectations: America and the Baby Boom Generation* (New York: Ballantine Books, 1980), p. 72.

30. Edgar Morin, "The Case of James Dean," in James B. Hall and Barry Ulanov, eds., *Modern Culture and the Arts* (New York: McGraw-Hill, 1967), pp. 456–64.

31. William Burroughs's self-confession in *Junkie* (New York: Penguin, 1977), p. xix. See also Jill Jonnes, *Hep-Cats, Narcs, and Pipe Dreams: A History of America's Romance with Drugs* (Baltimore: Johns Hopkins University Press, 1996), p. 208.

32. Ibid., p. 209.

33. Jack Kerouac, *On the Road* (1953; repr., New York: Penguin Books, 1976), pp. 5–6.

34. Ibid., p. 152.

35. Ibid., p. 212.

36. Neil A. Hamilton, ed., *The 1960s Counterculture in America* (Santa Barbara, Calif.: ABC Clio Press, 1997), p. 54.

37. Norman Mailer, "The White Negro: Superficial Reflections on the Hipster," in *Advertisements for Myself* (New York: Putnam, 1959), pp. 337–58.

38. Norman Mailer, "Superman Comes to the Supermarket," in *Smiling through the Apocalypse: Esquire's History of the Sixties* (New York: McCall Publishing Company, 1969), pp. 16–17.

Chapter 4: John F. Kennedy and the Camelot Image

1. For Clinton's account, see *My Life* (New York: Knopf, 2004), p. 62

2. Quoted in Joan Morrison and Robert Morrison, eds., *From Camelot to Kent State: The Sixties Experience in the Words of Those Who Lived It* (New York: Times Books, 1987), p. 10.

3. Philip Caputo, *A Rumor of War* (New York: Henry Holt), p. xiv.

4. David M. Lubin, *Shooting Kennedy: JFK and the Culture of Images* (Los Angeles: University of California Press, 2003), p. 3.

5. On belonging to generations and generational cycles, see José Ortega y Gasset, *Man and Crisis* (New York: Norton, 1958); Karl Mannheim, "The Problem of Generations," in Paul Kecskemeti, ed., *Essays on the Sociology of Knowledge* (New York: Oxford University Press, 1952); and William Strauss and Neil Howe's suggestive work, *Generations: The History of America's Future, 1584 to 2069* (New York: Morrow, 1971).

6. Thomas Reeves, *A Question of Character: A Life of John F. Kennedy* (Rocklin, Calif.: Prima, 1992), pp. 1–2.

7. Ibid., pp. 11–12.

8. Ibid., p. 32; see also Nigel Hamilton, *J.F.K.: Reckless Youth* (New York: Random House, 1992), pp. 690–91.

9. Peter Collier and David Horowitz, *The Kennedys: An American Drama* (New York: Summit Books, 1984), p. 162.

10. Sorensen strongly takes Kennedy's side in rejecting the notion that the book was ghost-written (*Kennedy* [New York: Bantam, 1966], pp. 68–70). Rumors that *Profiles in Courage* was ghostwritten were made public by the columnist Drew Pearson on the ABC *Mike Wallace Show* (December 7, 1957). In a confrontation with ABC executives, Sorensen signed a statement that he was not the author of *Profiles in Courage*. Kennedy family attorneys put enough pressure on Drew Pearson that he publicly recanted his charge that Kennedy had not written *Profiles in Courage*. The rumors and charges, however, persisted. Thomas Reeves, following the research of Herbert Parmet on the origins of *Profiles in Courage*, argues that Kennedy's handwritten notes constitute an incoherent and disorganized melange taken from secondary sources. In his judgment, and the judgment of other historians, Kennedy merely transmitted his thoughts and roughly written notes to Sorensen and a team of researchers that included such well-known historians as Jules David, Arthur Schlesinger Jr., James McGregor Burns, and Allan Nevins. These Kennedy loyalists gave full credit to Kennedy for having written the book.

11. Reeves, *Question of Character*, pp. 156–57.

12. Joan and Clay Blair, *The Search for JFK* (New York: Berkeley Books), pp. 238, 243–44. For the original embellishment and creation of the *PT 109* myth, see John Hershey, A Reporter at Large, "Survival," *New Yorker* (June 17, 1944), pp. 31–43. For the best deconstruction of the myth, see John Hellmann, *The Kennedy Obsession: The American Myth of JFK* (New York: Columbia University Press, 1997), pp. 37–61.

13. For the rumors in the late 1950s about an impending divorce between Jack and Jackie and Joseph Kennedy's role in keeping the marriage afloat, see C. David Heymann, *A Woman Named Jackie* (New York: Lyle Stuart, 1989), pp. 192–94. Peter Lawford's mother, whose son had married Patricia Kennedy, claimed in her autobiography (Lady Mary Sommerville Lawford, *Bitch! The Autobiography of Lady Lawford* [Brookline, Mass.: Brandon, 1986], p. 77) that "Old Joe Kennedy offered his daughter-in-law a check. The check was for one million dollars! The payoff: to remain married to Jack. Jackie Kennedy was a clever girl; such a good businesswoman. She said, 'make it tax free and it's a deal.'"

14. Thomas Reeves's judgment that the "Kennedys belonged in the pantheon of movie stars and television stars" would be hard to contest. Moreover, the literature of adulation that Kennedy's death set off is unprecedented in American history. The sheer volume of sentimental gush far exceeded what Americans had expressed about Lincoln in the nineteenth century. That historians were swept up in this wave of adulation should not be surprising, given the fact that most American historians were liberal in their political orientation. The first decade after JFK's death produced an outpouring of "Camelot" books, of which the following are worth reading: Arthur M. Schlesinger, *A Thousand Days: John F. Kennedy in the White House* (Boston: Houghton Mifflin, 1965); Theodore White, *The Making of the President 1960* (New York: Atheneum, 1961); Sorensen, *Kennedy*; William Manchester, *The Death of a President* (New York: Harper & Row, 1967); Hugh

Sidey, *John F. Kennedy, President* (New York: Atheneum, 1964). These works, written shortly after Kennedy's death, were regarded as standard for a whole generation. The only critical work written about Kennedy in the 1960s was by Victor Lasky, *J.F.K* (New York: Macmillan, 1963), but in the wake of the president's tragic death it was all but forgotten. It was not until the 1990s that more critical works about Kennedy began to appear, the most important being Nigel Hamilton, *J.F.K: Reckless Youth*; Seymour Hersh, *The Dark Side of Camelot* (Boston: Little, Brown, 1997); Richard Reeves, *President Kennedy: Profile of Power* (New York: Simon & Schuster, 1993); and Thomas Reeves, *Question of Character*. The most balanced recent biography of Kennedy is Robert Dallek, *An Unfinished Life: John F. Kennedy, 1917–1963* (Boston: Little, Brown, 2003).

15. Reeves, *Question of Character*, p. 136.

16. Dallek, *Unfinished Life*, p. 308.

17. John F. Kennedy, "Yale University Commencement Speech," *New York Times*, June 12, 1962, p. 20.

18. Robert S. McNamara, *The Essence of Security* (New York: Harper & Row, 1968), pp. 109–10.

19. Pierre Salinger, *With Kennedy* (New York: Doubleday, 1966), pp. 73, 139–44; also Reeves, *Question of Character*, p. 250.

20. On Melbourne's influence on Kennedy, see Hellmann, *Kennedy Obsession*, pp. 29–32.

21. Paul B. Fay Jr., *The Pleasure of His Company* (New York: Harper & Row, 1966), p. 102.

22. David Halberstam, *The Best and the Brightest* (1969; repr., New York: Ballantine Books, 1993), p. 40.

23. Dallek, *Unfinished Life*, p. 484.

24. Ibid., p. 380.

25. Ibid., p. 384.

26. Ibid., p. 492.

27. Ibid., chapter 12.

28. Reeves, *Question of Character*, p. 284.

29. Hugh Sidey, quoted in Hersh, *Dark Side of Camelot*, p. 253.

30. Quoted in Richard Reeves, *Kennedy: Profile of Power*, p. 186.

31. Ibid., p. 22.

32. Schlesinger, *Thousand Days*, p. 252.

33. On the Bay of Pigs operation, see Haynes Johnson, *The Bay of Pigs* (New York: Norton, 1964); Peter Kornbluth, ed., *Bay of Pigs Declassified: The Secret CIA Report on the Invasion of Cuba* (New York: New Press, 1998); and Peter Wyden, *The Bay of Pigs: The Untold Story* (New York: Simon & Schuster, 1979).

34. Schlesinger, *Thousand Days*, p. 267.

35. On the Soviet missile crisis, see Michael Beschloss, *The Crisis Years: Kennedy and Khrushchev, 1960–1963* (New York: HarperCollins, 1991); Dino Brugioni, *Eyeball to Eyeball: The Inside Story of the Cuban Missile Crisis* (New York: Random House, 1991); Aleksandr Fursenko and Timothy Naftali, eds., *"One Hell of a Gamble": Khrushchev, Castro, and Kennedy* (New York: Norton, 1997); Robert F. Kennedy, *Thirteen Days: A Memoir of the Cuban Missile Crisis* (New York: Norton, 1969); Ernest R. May and Philip Zelikow, eds., *The Kennedy Tapes: Inside the White House during the Cuban Missile Crisis* (Cambridge, Mass.: Harvard University Press, 1997); James Nathan, ed., *The Cuban Missile Crisis Revisited* (New York: St. Martin's Press, 1992); and Philip Zelikow and Ernest May, eds., *The Presidential Recordings* (New York: Norton, 2001).

36. Paul Johnson, *A History of the American People* (New York: HarperCollins, 1998), p. 864.

37. Dallek, *Unfinished Life*, pp. 691–92.

38. Ibid., p. 693.

39. Gerald Posner, *Case Closed: Lee Harvey Oswald and the Assassination of JFK* (New York: Anchor Books, 2003), 217–18.

40. Ibid., 214–15.

41. On Oswald, see Edward J. Epstein, *Legend: The Secret World of Lee Harvey Oswald* (New York: Ballantine, 1978); Gerald R. Ford and John R. Stiles, *Portrait of the Assassin* (New York: Simon

& Schuster, 1965); Priscilla Johnson McMillan, *Marina and Lee* (New York: Harper & Row, 1977); Norman Mailer, *Oswald's Tale: An American Mystery* (New York: Random House, 1995); and Robert L. Oswald, *Lee: A Portrait of Lee Harvey Oswald* (New York: Coward-McCann, 1967).

42. Quoted in Epstein, *Legend*, p. 111.

43. Henry Hurt, *Reasonable Doubt: An Investigation into the Assassination of John F. Kennedy* (New York: Holt, Rinehart & Winston, 1985), p. 254.

44. Posner, *Case Closed*, pp. 114–15.

45. Epstein, *Legend*, p. 243.

46. Quoted in Lubin, *Shooting Kennedy*, p. 223. Also Epstein, *Legend*, p. 245.

47. Quoted in C. David Heymann, *A Woman Named Jackie* (Secaucus, N.J.: Carol Communications, 1989), p. 408.

48. Testimony of Jack Ruby, *The Warren Commission*, vol. 5:200; also Posner, *Case Closed*, p. 395.

49. Ibid.

50. On Ruby, see Seth Kantor, *Who Was Jack Ruby?* (New York: Everest House, 1978).

51. On Robert Kennedy's reaction, or lack of it, to the Warren Commission, see Arthur M. Schlesinger Jr., *Robert Kennedy and His Times* (Boston: Houghton Mifflin, 1978), 2:641–44; Ronald Steel, *In Love with Night: The American Romance with Robert Kennedy* (New York: Simon & Schuster, 2000), chapter 9; Harris Wofford, *Of Kennedys and Kings* (Pittsburgh: University of Pittsburgh Press, 1992), pp. 411–12.

52. Posner, *Case Closed*, p. 293.

53. *New York Times*, November 22, 1966; also Ed Cray, *Chief Justice: A Biography of Earl Warren* (New York: Simon & Schuster, 1997), p. 422.

54. Posner, *Case Closed*, chapter 18.

55. Ibid., pp. 473–74.

56. Ibid., p. 474.

57. On the real Garrison, see Milton E. Brener, *The Garrison Case: A Study in the Abuse of Power* (New York: Clarkson N. Potter, 1969); Edward Jay Epstein, *Counterplot* (New York: Viking, 1968); James Kirkwood, *American Grotesque: An Account of the Clay Shaw–Jim Garrison Affair in New Orleans* (New York: Simon & Schuster 1970); and James Phelan, *Scandals, Scamps and Scoundrels: The Casebook of an Investigative Reporter* (New York: Random House, 1982)

58. Posner, *Case Closed*, p. 470.

59. Heymann, *Woman Named Jackie*, chapter 24.

60. Reeves, *Question of Character*, p. 4.

61. George Bernard Shaw, *Man and Superman: The Revolutionist's Handbook & Companion* (Norwalk, Conn.: Heritage Press, 990), p. 47.

62. On Carlyle and hero worship, see Eric Bentley, *A Century of Hero Worship* (Boston: Beacon Press, 1957).

63. Thomas Maier, *The Kennedys: America's Emerald Kings* (New York: Basic Books, 2003), p. 371.

64. Quoted in W. J. Rorabaugh, *Kennedy and the Promise of the Sixties* (New York: Cambridge University Press, 2002), 224.

65. Garry Wills, *The Kennedy Imprisonment: A Meditation on Power* (Boston: Little, Brown, 1981), p. 188.

66. Dallek, *Unfinished Life*, p. 307.

67. Sorensen, *Kennedy*, p. 281.

68. Reeves, *President Kennedy*, p. 23.

69. Wills, *Kennedy Imprisonment*, pp. 168–69.

70. Halberstam, *Best and the Brightest*, p. 60.

71. Arthur M. Schlesinger claimed that had Kennedy lived, "we would have avoided a good deal of the turmoil of the 1960s. I think a lot of the sense of alienation that the young people had was due to the assassination" (Robert MacNeil, *The Way We Were: 1963 The Year Kennedy Was Shot* (New York: Carroll and Graf, 1988), p. 248.

72. Sidey, *John F. Kennedy*, p. 122.

73. Wills, *Kennedy Imprisonment*, p. 149.

Chapter 5: Searching for the Promised Land

1. Harvard Sitkoff, *The Struggle for Black Equality, 1954–1992* (New York: Hill & Wang, 1993), p. 45.

2. On Martin Luther King Jr., see Taylor Branch, *Parting the Waters: America in the King Years, 1954–1963* (New York: Simon & Schuster, 1988), and the same author's *Pillar of Fire: America in the King Years, 1963–65* (New York: Simon & Schuster, 1998); Adam Fairclough, *To Redeem the Soul of America: The Southern Christian Leadership Conference and Martin Luther King Jr.* (Athens: University of Georgia Press, 1987); David Garrow, *Bearing the Cross: Martin Luther King Jr. and the Southern Christian Leadership Conference* (New York: William Morrow, 1986); David L. Lewis, *King: A Critical Biography* (New York: Praeger, 1970); Stephen Oates, *Let the Trumpet Sound: The Life of Martin Luther King Jr.* (New York: Harper & Row, 1982); and Flip Schulke, ed., *Martin Luther King Jr. A Documentary—Montgomery to Memphis* (New York: W. W. Norton, 1986).

3. On Niebuhr and King, see Garrow, *Bearing the Cross*, pp. 42–47.

4. On the role of the churches in the civil rights movement, see Adam Fairclough, "The Southern Christian Leadership Conference and the Second Reconstruction, 1957–1973, *South Atlantic Quarterly* 80 (Spring 1981): 177–94; James F. Findley, *Church People in the Struggle: The National Council of Churches and the Black Freedom Movement, 1950–1970* (New York: Oxford University Press, 1993); David Garrow "Black Ministerial Protest Leadership," in Samuel S. Hill, ed., *Encyclopedia of Religion in the South* (Macon, Ga.: Mercer University Press, 1984), pp. 106–108; and Philip A. Rahming, "The Church and the Civil Rights Movement in the Thought of Martin Luther King Jr." (Th.M. thesis, Southern Baptist Theological Seminary, 1971).

5. A splendid recent book on these idealistic students who served as the footsoldiers of civil rights is David Halberstam, *The Children* (New York: Ballantine, 1998).

6. On the Greensboro sit-in, see William F. Chafe, *Civilities and Civil Rights: Greensboro, North Carolina, and the Black Struggle for Freedom* (New York: Oxford University Press, 1980); and Miles Wolff, *Lunch at the Five and Ten: The Greensboro Sit-ins, A Contemporary History* (New York: Stein and Day, 1970).

7. Quoted in Sitkoff, *The Struggle for Black Equality*, p. 62.

8. Ibid., p. 63.

9. James Farmer has left two revealing autobiographical accounts of the freedom rides, *Freedom—When?* (New York: Random House, 1965), and *Lay Bare the Heart: An Autobiography of the Civil Rights Movement* (New York: Arbor House, 1986).

10. For John Lewis's account, see John Lewis and Michael D'Orso, *Walking with the Wind* (New York: Simon & Schuster, 1999), pp. 158–60.

11. Sitkoff, *Struggle for Black Equality*, pp. 94–95; Robert Weisbrot, *Freedom Bound: A History of America's Civil Rights Movement* (New York: Norton, 1990), pp. 59–60.

12. On law enforcement involving state and federal authorities, see Michael R. Belknap, *Federal Law and Southern Order: Racial Violence and Constitutional Conflict in the post-Brown South* (Athens: University of Georgia Press, 1987)

13. Allen Matusow, *The Unraveling of America: A History: A History of Liberalism in the 1960s* (New York: Harper & Row, 1984), pp. 66–67.

14. Quoted in David Burner, *Making Peace with the 60s* (Princeton, N.J.: Princeton University Press, 1996), p. 41.

15. On Hoover's animus toward King, see David J. Garrow, *The FBI and Martin Luther King Jr.* (New York: Norton, 1981); and Kenneth O'Reilly, *Racial Matters: The FBI's Secret File on Black America, 1960–1972* (New York: Free Press, 1989).

16. On Bob Moses, see Eric Burner, *And Gently He Shall Lead Them: Robert Parris Moses and Civil Rights in Mississippi* (New York: New York University Press, 1994).

17. Wyatt Walker, quoted in David L. Lewis *King: A Biography* (Urbana: University of Illinois Press, 1978), p. 173.

18. Martin Luther King Jr., "Letter from Birmingham Jail," April 16, 1963, in Carson Clayborne, ed., *The Autobiography of Martin Luther King Jr.* (New York: Time Warner Books, 1998), pp. 188–89.

19. Martin Luther King Jr., "Letter from Birmingham Jail," in Irwin Unger and Debi Unger, eds., *The Times Were a Changin': The Sixties Reader* (New York: Three Rivers Press, 1998), p. 130.

20. On this eye-opening meeting between Robert Kennedy and Baldwin's entourage, see Arthur M. Schlesinger Jr., *Robert Kennedy and His Times* (Boston: Houghton Mifflin, 1978), 2:344–48.

21. Carl Brauer, *John F. Kennedy and the Second Reconstruction* (New York: Columbia University Press, 1978), p. 247.

22. Quoted in Sitkoff, *Struggle for Black Equality*, p. 146.

23. On the March on Washington, see Branch, *Parting the Waters*, chapter 22.

24. Ibid., p. 882.

25. Quoted in Garrow, *Bearing the Cross*, pp. 283–84.

26. Sitkoff, *Struggle for Black Equality*, pp. 139–40.

27. Quoted in Sitkoff, *Struggle for Black Equality*, p. 163.

28. On Fannie Lou Hamer, see Kay Mills, *This Little Light of Mine: A Life of Fannie Lou Hamer* (New York: Dutton, 1993), and Fannie Lou Hamer's autobiography, entitled *To Praise Our Bridges: An Autobiography of Mrs. Fannie Lou Hamer* (Jackson, Miss.: KIPCO, 1967).

29. Branch, *Pillars of Fire*, pp. 526ff.

30. Lewis and D'Orso, *Walking with the Wind*, pp. 327–29.

31. Quoted in Sitkoff, *Struggle for Black Equality*, pp. 181–82.

32. For the best account of the Watts riots, see Robert Conot, *Rivers of Blood, Years of Darkness* (New York: Morrow, 1968). There is also a good collection containing the voices of Watts residents in Paul Bullock, ed., *Watts: The Aftermath by the People of Watts* (New York: Grove Press, 1969).

33. *Report of the National Advisory Commission on Civil Disorders* (New York: Bantam, 1968), pp. 1–2.

34. See Gareth Davies, *From Opportunity to Entitlement: The Transformation and Decline of Great Society Liberalism* (Lawrence: University of Kansas Press, 1996), pp. 203–6; and Irwin Unger and Debi Unger, *Turning Point, 1968* (New York: Scribner, 1988), p. 184.

35. Davies, *From Opportunity to Entitlement*, p. 204.

36. Sitkoff, *Struggle for Black Equality*, p. 155.

37. On black power, it is best to sample the writings of the believers themselves, starting with the man who coined the term, Stokely Carmichael, *Stokely Speaks: Black Power to Pan-Africanism* (New York: Random House, 1971). Besides Carmichael, the most important black nationalist was Malcolm X. For a survey of his views, a good start is his autobiography, entitled *The Autobiography of Malcolm X* (New York: Ballantine, 1993; originally published in 1965). There are also a number of collections containing his speeches, including George Breitman, ed., *Malcolm X Speaks: Selected Speeches and Statements* (New York: Merit Publishers, 1965); George Breitman, ed., *By Any Means Necessary: Speeches, Interviews, and a Letter by Malcolm X* (New York: Pathfinder, 1970); and Bruce Perry, ed., *Malcolm X: The Last Speeches* (New York: Pathfinder, 1989). For other statements by black power advocates, see Bobby Seale, *Seize the Time: The Story of the Black Panther Party and Huey P. Newton* (New York: Random House, 1970); Eldridge Cleaver, *Soul on Ice* (New York: McGraw-Hill, 1968); Angela Davis, *Angela Davis: An Autobiography* (New York: Random House, 1974); H. Rap Brown, *Die, Nigger, Die!* (New York: Dial Press, 1969); and Huey Newton, *Revolutionary Suicide* (New York: Harcourt Brace Jovanovich, 1973) and *To Die for the People: The Writings of Huey P. Newton* (New York: Vintage, 1973).

38. Burner, *Making Peace with the 60s*, p. 50.

39. Malcolm X, *Autobiography of Malcolm X*, p. 3.

40. Ibid., p. 38.

41. On the Nation of Islam, see H. Eric Lincoln, *The Black Muslims in America* (Boston: Beacon Press, 1973).

42. Malcolm X, *Autobiography of Malcolm X*, p. 250.

43. Quoted in Sitkoff, *Struggle for Black Equality*, p. 199.

44. Speech given at the Conference of the Organization of Latin American Solidarity. See, *Stokely Carmichael Speaks: Black Power to Pan-Africanism* (New York: Random House, 1971), p. 101.

45. Joseph Conlin, *The Troubles* (New York: Franklin Watts, 1982), p. 150.

46. Cleaver, *Soul on Ice*, p. 26.

47. Ibid., p. 10.

48. Ibid., p. 9

49. Quoted in Roger Kimball, *The Long March* (San Francisco: Encounter Books, 2000), p. 220.

50. Tom Wolf, *Radical Chic & Mau-Mauing the Flak Catchers* (New York: Farrar, Straus & Giroux, 1970).

51. Quoted in Robert Dallek, *Flawed Giant: Lyndon Johnson and His Times, 1961–1973* (New York: Oxford University Press, 1998), p. 223.

52. Unger and Unger, *Turning Point*, p. 175.

53. Garrow, *Bearing the Cross*, pp. 595–96.

54. Ibid., pp. 620–21.

Chapter 6: Liberalism at High Tide under Lyndon Johnson

1. Paul Johnson, *A History of the American People* (New York: HarperCollins, 1998), p. 871.

2. Robert Dallek, *Flawed Giant: Lyndon Johnson and His Times, 1961–1973* (New York: Oxford University Press, 1998), p. 10.

3. Doris Kearns, *Lyndon Johnson and the American Dream* (Norwalk, Conn.: Easton Press, 1987), pp. 26–27.

4. Ibid., pp. 42–44.

5. On Johnson's voracious sexual desires, see Johnson, *History of the American People*, pp. 872–73; Dallek, *Flawed Giant*, pp. 186–87.

6. Quoted in Paul Johnson, *History of the American People*, p. 872.

7. Ibid., p. xxxi.

8. Ibid., p. 287.

9. Ibid., pp. 16ff., 272–75, 285–86.

10. Quoted in David Halberstam, *The Best and the Brightest* (New York: Random House, 1972), p. 434.

11. Quoted in Dallek, *Flawed Giant*, p. 44.

12. Quoted in Kearns, *Lyndon Johnson*, p. 177.

13. Lyndon B. Johnson, *The Vantage Point: Perspectives of the Presidency, 1963–1969* (New York: Holt, Rinehart & Winston, 1971), p. 95.

14. On Goldwater, see Peter Iverson, *Barry Goldwater: Native Arizonan* (Norman: University of Oklahoma Press, 1997); Edwin McDowell, *Barry Goldwater: Portrait of an American* (Chicago: Henry Regnery, 1964); and Goldwater's own book, *The Conscience of a Conservative* (New York: McFadden-Bartell, 1961).

15. *Time*, September 4, 1964.

16. Reproduced in Joseph R. Conlin, *The American Past* (Belmont, Calif.: Wadsworth, 2004), p. 708).

17. Quoted in Kearns, *Lyndon Johnson*, pp. 236–37.

18. Dallek, *Flawed Giant*, p. 64.

19. Quoted in Kearns, *Lyndon Johnson*, p. 163.

20. Irwin Unger and Debi Unger, *The Best of Intentions: The Triumph and Failure of the Great Society under Kennedy, Johnson, and Nixon* (New York: Doubleday, 1996), p. 79.

21. Edward Berkowitz, "Losing Ground: The Great Society in Historical Perspective," in *The Columbia Guide to America in the 1960s* (New York: Columbia University Press, 2001), p. 98.

22. Robert M. Collins, *More: The Politics of Economic Growth in Postwar America* (New York: Oxford University Press, 2000), p. 53.

23. Irving Bernstein, *Guns or Butter: The Presidency of Lyndon Johnson* (New York: Oxford University Press, 1996), p. 84.

24. Johnson, *Vantage Point*, p. 71.

25. Ibid, p. 74.

26. Frances Fox Piven and Richard A. Cloward, "A Strategy to End Poverty," *Nation* (May 2, 1966); and the same authors' *Regulating the Poor: The Function of Public Welfare* (New York: Pantheon, 1971); also Irvin and Debi Unger, *Turning Point, 1968* (New York: Scribner's, 1988), p. 43.

27. Allen J. Matusow, *The Unraveling of America: A History of Liberalism in the 1960s* (New York: Harper & Row, 1984), p. 220.

28. Bernstein, *Guns or Butter*, p. 102.

29. Johnson, *Vantage Point*, p. 79.

30. Richard Goodwin, *Remembering America: A Voice from the Sixties* (Boston: Little, Brown, 1988), p. 258.

31. Doris Kearns lists the lengthy shopping list of benefits Johnson promised to the American people (*Lyndon Johnson*, p. 226). It must be read to be believed.

32. For a fair and nuanced discussion of this issue, see Daniel P. Moynihan, *Maximum Feasible Misunderstanding* (New York: Free Press, 1969) and Unger and Unger, *The Best of Intentions*.

33. Quoted in Matusow, *Unraveling of America*, p. 270.

34. Unger and Unger, *Best of Intentions*, p. 156.

35. Matusow, *Unraveling of America*, p. 245.

36. Fred Siegel, *The Future Once Happened Here: New York, D.C., L.A., and the Fate of America's Big Cities* (New York: Free Press, 1997), p. 11.

37. Matusow, *Unraveling of America*, p. 259; also Conlin, *Troubles*, p. 183.

38. Unger and Unger, *Turning Point*, p. 40.

39. Ibid., p. 42.

40. Ibid., p. 36.

41. Matusow, *Unraveling of America*, p. 267.

42. Ibid., p. 268.

43. Lyndon B. Johnson, *Public Papers, 1965*, pp. 813–14.

44. Berkowitz, "Losing Ground," *Columbia Guide*, p. 104.

45. Moynihan, *Maximum Feasible Misunderstanding*, p. 25.

46. Quoted in Gareth Davies, *From Opportunity to Entitlement: The Transformation and Decline of Great Society Liberalism* (Lawrence: University of Kansas Press, 1996), p. 144.

47. Michael Harrington, *The Other America* (Baltimore: Penguin Books, 1962), pp. 9, 171–86. What made matters worse was that Harrington insisted that poverty should also be defined psychologically because those who suffer from structural poverty are "progress-immune"; they are internal exiles who suffer from attitudes of defeat and pessimism (p. 175). Admittedly, poverty is a state of mind as well as of body, but Harrington's inflated figures and shifting definitions make it sometimes difficult to follow the logic of his argument, though the moral cause he is making is a compelling one.

48. Collins, *More: The Politics of Economic Growth*, p. 41.

49. Charles Murray, *Losing Ground: American Social Policy, 1950–1980* (New York: Basic Books, 1984), p. 59.

50. Johnson, *Vantage Point*, p. 87.

51. For a good analysis of the failure of the Great Society, see Matusow, *Unraveling of America*, pp. 217–21.

52. Moynihan, *Maximum Feasible Misunderstanding*, p. 168.

53. Ibid., p. 193.

54. Ibid., p. 179.

55. Matusow, *Unraveling of America*, p. 240.

56. Bernstein, *Guns and Butter,* p. 533.

57. Unger and Unger, *Best of Intentions*, p. 202.

58. Bernstein, *Guns or Butter*, p. 378.

59. Quoted in Davies, *From Opportunity to Entitlement*, pp. 185–86.

60. Dallek, *Flawed Giant*, p. 83.

61. Murray, *Losing Ground*, p. 8.

62. Ibid., p. 9.

63. Unger and Unger, *Best of Intentions*, p. 202.

64. On the Warren Court, see Alexander M. Bickel, *Politics and the Warren Court* (New York: Harper & Row, 1965); Archibald Cox, *The Warren Court: Constitutional Decision as an Instrument of Reform* (Cambridge, Mass.: Harvard University Press, 1968); Morton J. Horowitz, *The Warren Court and the Pursuit of Justice* (New York: Hill & Wang, 1998); Bernard Schwartz, ed., *The Warren Court: A Retrospective* (New York: Oxford University Press, 1996); and Mark Tushnet, ed., *The Warren Court in Historical Perspective* (Charlottesville, Va.: University of Virginia Press, 1993).

65. Horowitz, *Warren Court,* p. 42.

66. Ibid., p. 43.

67. John Morton Blum, *Years of Discord: American Politics and Society, 1961–1974* (New York: Norton, 1991), p. 188. Blum's discussion of the politics of the Supreme Court is the most succinct and even-handed to be found anywhere.

68. Quoted in Blum, *Years of Discord*, p. 194.

69. Kermit L. Hall, ed., *The Oxford Guide to United States Supreme Court Decisions* (New York: Oxford University Press, 1999), pp. 115–18.

70. Horowitz, *Warren Court,* p. 108.

71. Hall, *Oxford Guide*, p. 269.

72. Quoted in Horowitz, *Warren Court,* p. 100.

73. Ibid., p. 101.

74. Hall, *Oxford Guide*, pp. 188–89.

75. Ibid., pp. 19–20.

76. On Earl Warren, see Ed Cray, *Chief Justice: A Biography of Earl Warren* (New York: Simon & Schuster, 1997); Bernard Schwartz, *Super Chief: Earl Warren and His Supreme Court* (New York: New York University Press, 1983); Earl Warren's own *Memoirs* (New York: Doubleday, 1977); and Edward G. White, *Earl Warren: A Public Life* (New York: Oxford University Press, 1982).

77. Quoted in Cray, *Chief Justice*, p. 462.

78. Quoted in Hall, *Oxford Guide*, pp. 193–94.

79. On figures for the Vietnam War, see David L. Anderson, ed., *The Columbia Guide to the Vietnam War* (New York: Columbia University Press, 2000), p. 287. For social spending, see Unger and Unger, *Best of Intentions*, p. 344.

80. Godfrey Hodgson, *America in Our Time* (New York: Vintage, 1976), p. 488.

Chapter 7: Vietnam and Protest

1. Paul Hendrickson, *The Living: Robert McNamara and Five Lives of a Lost War* (New York: Random House, 1996), p. 9. I owe this revealing vignette to Hendrickson's remarkable book about five lives that were wrenchingly changed by the Vietnam War.

2. Ibid., p. 8.

3. Ibid.

4. Ibid.

5. Joan Morrison and Robert K. Morrison, *From Camelot to Kent State* (New York: Random House, 1987), pp. 161–70.

6. Quoted in *Breaking the Chains: Documents on the Vietnamese Revolution of August 1945* (Hanoi: Foreign Languages Publishing House, 1960), pp. 94–97.

7. The literature on the Vietnam War has been growing steadily and it has become more contentious over time. Among the most readable and reliable general studies, the following merit special attention: George C. Herring, *America's Longest War: The United States and Vietnam, 1950–1975* (New York: McGraw-Hill, 1996); A. J. Langguth, *Our Vietnam: The War, 1954–1975* (New York: Simon & Schuster, 2001); Stanley Karnow, *Vietnam: A History* (New York: Penguin, 1984). There are three helpful guides to the conflicting interpretations of the war: Lester Brune and Richard Dean Burns, eds., *America and the Indochina Wars, 1945–1990: A Bibliographic Guide* (Claremont, Calif.: Regina Press, 1992), Gary R. Hess, "The Unending Debate: Historians and the Vietnam War," *Diplomatic History* 18 (Spring 1994): 239–264; and Stanley I. Kutler, ed., *Encyclopedia of the Vietnam War* (New York: Scribner's, 1996). Of the various interpretations about what went wrong or right, see James C. Thomson, "How Could Vietnam Happen: An Autopsy," *Atlantic Monthly* 221 (April 1968): 47–53; Arthur M. Schlesinger, *The Bitter Heritage: Vietnam and American Democracy* (Boston: Houghton Mifflin, 1966); Ward Just, *To What End?* (Boston: Houghton Mifflin, 1968); Leslie H. Gelb and Richard K. Betts, *The Irony of Vietnam: The System Worked* (Washington, D.C.: Brookings Institution, 1978); Guenter Lewy, *America in Vietnam* (New York: Oxford University Press, 1978); Norman Podhoretz, *Why We Were in Vietnam* (New York: Simon & Schuster, 1982); and Michael Lind, *Vietnam: The Necessary War* (New York: Simon & Schuster, 1999).

8. On Ho Chi Minh, see Jean Lacouture, *Ho Chi Minh: A Political Biography*, trans. Peter Wiles (New York: Random House, 1968); David Halberstam, *Ho* (New York: McGraw-Hill, 1993); and William J. Duiker, *Ho Chi Minh* (New York: Hyperion, 2000).

9. Duiker, *Ho Chi Minh*, pp. 414–21, 569–73.

10. For the Franco-American role in Indochina, see Ronald E. M. Irving, *The First Indochina War: French and American Policy, 1945–54* (London: C. Helm, 1975); Lloyd C. Gardner, *Approaching Vietnam: From World War II through Dienbienphu* (New York: Norton, 1988); Irwin M. Wall, *The United States and the Making of Postwar France, 1945–1954* (New York: Cambridge University Press, 1991), and David L. Anderson, *Trapped by Success: The Eisenhower Administration and Vietnam, 1953–1961* (New York: Columbia University Press, 1991).

11. U.S. House Committee on Armed Services, *United States–Vietnam Relations, 1945–1967*, vol. 9, *The Eisenhower Administration, 1953–1960* (Washington D.C.: Government Printing Office, 1971), p. 675.

12. On Geneva, the French perspective can be found in François Joyaux, *La Chine et le règlement du premier conflit d'Indochine* (Paris: Sorbonne, 1969) and the standard American in Robert F. Randle, *Geneva 1954: The Settlement of the Indochinese War* (Princeton, N.J.: Princeton University Press, 1969).

13. Herring, *America's Longest War*, p. 50.

14. Ibid., p. 51.

15. Ngo Dinh Diem has not inspired a great many biographies, but two older works shed important light on this complex leader: Denis Warner, *The Last Confucian* (New York: Macmillan, 1963); and Anthony Bouscaren, *The Last of the Mandarins: Diem of Vietnam* (Pittsburgh: Duquesne University Press, 1965).

16. Herring, *America's Longest War*, p. 64.

17. Kennedy interview with Walter Cronkite, in Walter Cronkite, *A Reporter's Life* (New York: Knopf, 1996), p. 243.

18. Quoted in Walter Capps, ed., *The Vietnam Reader* (New York: Routledge, 1991), p. 139.

19. William J. Duiker, *The Communist Road to Power in Vietnam* (Boulder, Colo.: Westview Press, 1981), p. 198.

20. Lewis R. Ward, "Vietnam: Insurgency or War?" *Military Review* 69 (January 1989), p. 17.

21. North Vietnamese atrocities, labeled by some observers as "genocidal," have been long ignored by the Western media, which has been more zealous in digging up American wrongdoing than in covering the brutal mass executions committed by North Vietnamese communists. For a correction of the record, there are two studies worth mentioning: Edwin E. Moise, *Land Reform in China and North Vietnam: Consolidating the Revolution* (Chapel Hill: University of North Carolina Press); and Bernard Fall, *The Two Vietnams* (New York: Praeger, 1963).

22. Karnow, *Vietnam: A History*, pp. 229–39.

23. *New York Times Magazine*, October 4, 1970.

24. United States Government, *Public Papers of the Presidents of the United States: Dwight D. Eisenhower, 1954* (Washington, D.C.: Government Printing Press, 1958), pp. 381–90. The occasion was the press conference of April 7, 1954.

25. William Appleman Williams et al., eds., *America in Vietnam: Documentary History* (New York: Norton, 1985), p. 200.

26. The *New York Times*, Editorial, November 3, 1963.

27. On the lack of expertise on Southeast Asia, see Thomson, "How Could Vietnam Happen?" pp. 48–49; Herring, *America's Longest War*, p. 79; and Karnow, *Vietnam: A History*, especially pp. 271–73, dealing with the quantrophelia mentality of U.S. policy makers.

28. On the Kennedy team, see David Halberstam, *The Best and the Brightest* (New York: Ballantine Books, 1968; repr., 1992). A more recent and more scholarly work on the Kennedy and Johnson involvement in Vietnam is David Kaiser, *American Tragedy: Kennedy, Johnson and the Origins of the Vietnam War* (Cambridge, Mass.: Harvard University Press, 2000).

29. John F. Kennedy, State of the Union Address, January 30, 1961, *John F. Kennedy: Public Papers, 1961* (Washington, D.C., 1962).

30. Herring, *America's Longest War*, p. 84.

31. Ibid., p. 90.

32. Chester Bowles, *Promises to Keep* (New York: Harper & Row, 1971), p. 409.

33. Roger Hilsman, *To Move a Nation* (Garden City, N.Y.: Doubleday, 1957), p. 432.

34. Karnow, *Vietnam: A History*, p. 274.

35. Herring, *America's Longest War*, p. 95.

36. The term "rattle-assing around the country" comes from Richard Tregaski's *Vietnam Diary* (New York: Holt, Rinehart and Winston, 1963), p. 155.

37. All three wrote incisive books about the Vietnam conflict: Malcolm Browne, *The New Face of War* (Indianapolis: Bobbs-Merrill, 1965); David Halberstam, *The Making of a Quagmire* (New York: Random House, 1964); and Neil Sheehan, *A Bright Shining Lie* (New York: Vintage, 1989).

38. Herring, *America's Longest War*, p. 105.

39. Richard Reeves, *President Kennedy: Profile of Power* (New York: Simon & Schuster, 1993), p. 565.

40. Ibid., p. 567.

41. Karnow, *Vietnam: A History*, p. 316.

42. On Johnson's involvement in Vietnam, David Kaiser, *American Tragedy: Kennedy, Johnson, and the Origins of the Vietnam War* (Cambridge, Massachusetts: Harvard University Press, 2000); George C. Herring, *LBJ and Vietnam: A Different Kind of War* (Austin, Texas: University of Texas Press, 1994); Larry Berman, *Lyndon Johnson's War* (New York: Norton, 1989); Wallace J. Thies, *When Governments Collide: Coercion and Diplomacy in the Vietnam Conflict, 1964–1968* (Berkeley, California: University of California Press, 1980); and Brian VanDeMark, *Into the Quagmire: Lyndon Johnson and the Escalation of the Vietnam War* (New York: Oxford University Press, 1991).

43. Quoted in Tom Wicker, "The Wrong Rubicon," in Robert Manning and Michael Janeway, eds., *Who We Are: An Atlantic Chronicle in the United States and Vietnam* (Boston: Little, Brown, 1969), p. 216.

44. Doris Kearns, *Lyndon Johnson and the American Dream* (Norwalk, Conn.:Easton Press, 1987), pp. 278–79.

45. Quoted in Karnow, *Vietnam: A History*, p. 337.

46. National Security Council Action Memorandum 273, *The Pentagon Papers: The Senator Gravel Edition*, 4. vols. (Boston: Beacon Press, 1971), 3:17–20.

47. Karnow, *Vietnam: A History*, p. 350.

48. Ibid., p. 356.

49. On the Gulf of Tonkin and the Resolution that followed, see John Galloway, *The Gulf of Tonkin Resolution* (Rutherford, N.J.: Farleigh Dickinson University Press, 1970); Karnow, *Vietnam: A History*, pp. 380–90; Herring, *America's Longest War*, 133–37; "The Phantom Battle that Led to War," *US News & World Report*, July 23, 1984, pp. 56–67; and Edwin E. Moise, *Tonkin Gulf and the Escalation of the Vietnam War* (Chapel Hill: University of North Carolina Press, 1996).

50. For McNamara'a account, see *In Retrospect: The Tragedy and Lessons of Vietnam* (New York: Random House, 1995), pp. 128–43. For a slightly different and more critical account, see H. R. McMaster, *Dereliction of Duty: Lyndon Johnson, Robert McNamara, The Joint Chiefs of Staff, and the Lies that Led to Vietnam* (New York: HarperCollins, 1997), chapter 6.

51. U.S. Congress, Senate, "To Promote the Maintenance of Peace and Security in Southeast Asia," 88th Congress, 2nd session, *Congressional Record*, Vol. 110, part 14 (August 4–12, 1964), p. 18132.

52. Herring, *America's Longest War*, p. 136.

53. Ibid., p. 137.

54. Brian VanDeMark, *Into the Quagmire: Lyndon Johnson and the Escalation of the Vietnam War* (New York: Oxford University Press, 1991), p. 207.

55. George McGovern, *Grassroots* (New York: Random House, 1977), pp. 104–5; also Herring, *America's Longest War, p. 156.*

56. Quoted in Herring, *America's Longest War*, p. 159.

57. Karnow, *Vietnam: A History*, 431–32.

58. Herring, *America's Longest War*, p. 163.

59. Karnow, *Vietnam: A History,* p. 452. For an excellent and disturbing book on America's zeal of fighting "technowar," see James William Gibson, *The Perfect War: Technowar in Vietnam* (New York: Atlantic Monthly Press, 2000).

60. Karnow, *Vietnam,* p. 431.

61. Philip Caputo, *A Rumor of War* (New York: Henry Holt, 1986), p. xix.

62. Ibid., p. xx.

63. Herring, *America's Longest War*, p. 174.

64. Quoted in Herring, *America's Longest War*, p. 180.

65. Ibid., p. 184.

66. Adam Garfinkle, *Telltale Hearts: The Origin and Impact of the Vietnam Antiwar Movement* (New York: St. Martin's Press, 1995), p. 34.

67. Ibid., p. 45.

68. On the American academy and the Vietnam War, see Lewis Feuer, *The Conflict of Generations: The Character and Significance of Student Movements* (New York: Basic Books, 1969); Ronald Fraser, ed., *1968: A Student Generation in Revolt* (New York: Pantheon, 1988); Patrick Lloyd Hatcher, *Suicide of an Elite: American Internationalists and Vietnam* (Stanford, Calif.: Stanford University Press, 1990); Roger Kimball, *Tenured Radicals* (New York: Harper & Row, 1990); and the same author's *The Long March: How the Cultural Revolution of the 1960s Changed America* (San Francisco: Encounter Books, 2000); Seymour Lipset, *Rebellion in the University* (Chicago: University of Chicago Press, 1983); William Rorabough, *Berkeley at War: The 1960s* (New York: Oxford University Press, 1989); and Theodor Roszak, ed., *The Dissenting Academy* (New York: Pantheon, 1968).

69. On draft resistance, see Sherrie Gottlieb, *Hell No, We Won't Go: Resisting the Draft during the Vietnam War* (New York: Viking, 1991).

70. Garfinkle, *Telltale Hearts*, p. 67.

71. This annoying self-contradictory premise has been exposed at length by Paul Berman, "The Fog of Political Correctness," *Tikkun* 7, no. 1 (January-February 1992): 53.

72. Garfinkle, *Telltale Hearts*, p. 71.

73. On SDS, see Alan Adelson, *SDS* (New York: Scribner's, 1972); Edward J. Bacciocco, *The New Left in America: Reform to Revolution, 1950–1970* (Stanford, Calif.: Hoover Institute Press, 1974); John Bunzel, *New Force on the Left: Tom Hayden and the Campaign against Corporate America* (Stanford, Calif.: Hoover Institute Press, 1983); Todd Gitlin, *The Sixties: Years of Hope, Days of Rage* (New York: Bantam, 1987); James Miller, *Democracy in the Streets: From Port Huron to the Siege of Chicago* (New York: Simon & Schuster, 1987); David R. Myers, ed., *Toward a History of the New Left: Essays from within the Movement* (New York: Carlson, 1989); and Kirkpatrick Sale, *SDS* (New York: Random House, 1973).

74. On Jerry Rubin and the antics of revolutionary theater, see Jerry Rubin, *Do It! Scenarios of the Revolution* (New York: Simon & Schuster, 1970); and Abbie Hoffman, *Revolution for the Hell of It* (New York: Dial, 1968).

75. The idea of "street theater" was actually adopted by Rubin from the San Francisco Diggers, who emerged originally from a mime group, borrowing the name Digger from seventeenth-century English radicals who protested the ownership of the land by the rich, claimed common ownership of all land, began digging their own land, and were promptly arrested by the authorities.

76. Garfinkle, *Telltale Hearts*, pp. 96–97.

77. Quoted in Garfinkle, *Telltale Hearts*, p. 112.

78. William L. O'Neill, *Coming Apart: An Informal History of America in the 1960s* (New York: Quadrangle, 1976), p. 288; also Garfinkle, *Telltale Hearts*, p. 114.

79. Norman Mailer, *The Armies of the Night: History as a Novel/The Novel as History* (New York: Penguin, 1968; repr. 1994), p. 130.

80. Herring, *America's Longest War*, 189–90.

81. Ibid., p. 191.

82. Quoted in Herring, *America's Longest War*, p. 193.

83. David Halberstam, *Best and the Brightest* (New York: Random House, 1972), p. 564.

84. Ibid., p. 198.

85. On the communist Tet Offensive, see Don Oberdorfer, *Tet!* (Garden City, N.Y.: Doubleday, 1971); Ronald H. Spector, *After Tet: The Bloodiest Year in Vietnam* (New York: Free Press, 1993); and James J. Wirtz, *The Tet Offensive: Intelligence Failure in War* (Ithaca: Cornell University Press, 1991).

86. Karnow, *Vietnam: A History*, pp. 538–43.

87. Quoted in Oberdorfer, *Tet!*, p. 158; also Herring, *America's Longest War*, p. 209.

88. Along with the Buddhist monk who burned himself to death in June 1963 and the picture of the nude little girl, crying in agony after having been napalmed, this photo of South Vietnam's police chief, General Nguyen Ngoc Loan, executing a young Vietcong suspect, was commonly used by the media to indict the American war effort as evil. Pictures, however, do not always tell the truth. Before the film was taken some of General Loan's relatives—men, women, and children— were gunned down by the Vietcong in his own home. The picture was taken by Eddie Adams, an AP photographer, and the film, subsequently shown around the world, was taken by Vo Suu, a cameraman working for NBC news. It goes without saying that no pictures of Vietcong atrocities were taken by North Vietnamese cameramen and shown to the North Vietnamese public. Historians should ask, however, why the American people were not shown the evils perpetrated by the communists.

89. Cronkite, *Reporter's Life*, pp. 257–58.

90. Dallek, *Flawed Giant*, p. 515.

91. For Johnson's account of why he chose not to run again, see Lyndon Johnson, *The Vantage Point: Perspectives of the Presidency, 1963–1969* (New York: Holt, Rinehart and Winston, 1971), chapter 18.

92. On Nixon and his team, see Stephen E. Ambrose, *Nixon*, 3 vols. (New York: Simon & Schuster, 1987–92); Garry Wills, *Nixon Agonistes* (New York: New American Library, 1970); Richard Nixon, *RN: The Memoirs of Richard Nixon* (New York: Grossett & Dunlap, 1978); Henry Kissinger, *White House Years* (Boston: Little, Brown, 1979) and *Years of Upheaval* (Boston: Little, Brown,

1982); Walter Isaacson, *Kissinger: A Biography* (New York: Simon & Schuster, 1992); H. R. Haldeman, *The Haldeman Diaries* (New York: G. P. Putnam, 1994).

93. Quoted in Karnow, *Vietnam: A History*, p. 597.

94. Herring, *America's Longest War*, p. 248.

95. For Nixon's account, see *Memoirs*, pp. 401–14.

96. Karnow, *Vietnam: A History*, p. 613.

97. Herring, *America's Longest War*, p. 253.

98. Nixon, *Memoirs,* p. 452.

99. On the Cambodian tragedy, see William Shawcross, *Sideshow: Kissinger, Nixon and the Destruction of Cambodia* (New York: Simon & Schuster, 1979); Michael Haas, *Genocide by Proxy: Cambodian Pawn on a Superpower Chessboard* (New York: Praeger, 1991); Karl D. Jackson, *Cambodia, 1975–78: Rendezvous with Death* (Princeton, N.J.: Princeton University Press, 1989); and Samantha Power, *A Problem from Hell: America in the Age of Genocide* (New York: Basic Books, 2003).

100. Herring, *America's Longest War*, p. 263. For Nixon's post hoc rationalization, see *Memoirs,* pp. 469–75.

101. On My Lai, see William R. Peers, *Report of the Department of the Army Review of the Preliminary Investigation into the My Lai Incident* (Washington D.C., March 14, 1970); Seymour Hersh, *My Lai: A Report on the Massacre and Its Aftermath* (New York: Random House, 1970); Martin Gershen, *Destroy or Die: The True Story of My Lai* (New Rochelle, N.Y.: Arlington House, 1971); Richard Hammer, *The Court Martial of Lt. Calley* (New York: Coward, McCann & Geoghegan, 1971); John Sack, *Lieutenant Calley: His Own Story* (New York: Viking, 1971); and David L. Anderson, ed., *Facing My Lai: Moving Beyond the Massacre* (Lawrence: University of Kansas Press, 1998).

102. On the Pentagon Papers, see George C. Herring, ed., *The Secret Diplomacy of the Vietnam War: The Negotiating Volumes of the Pentagon Papers* (Austin: University of Texas Press, 1983); *The Pentagon Papers: The Defense Department History of the United States Decision-Making on Vietnam*, 4 vols (Boston: Beacon Press, 1971) and the abbreviated version by the The New York Times, *The Pentagon Papers: The Secret History of the Vietnam War* (New York: Bantam, 1971); and Daniel Ellsberg, *Secrets: A Memoir of Vietnam and the Pentagon Papers* (New York: Viking, 2002).

103. Quoted in Karnow, *Vietnam: A History*, p. 658.

104. Herring, *America's Longest War*, p. 280.

105. Quoted in Paul Berman, *No Peace, No Honor: Nixon, Kissinger and Betrayal in Vietnam* (New York: Simon & Schuster, 2001), pp. 4–5.

106. Quoted in Capps, *Vietnam Reader*, p. 173.

107. United States Senate, Committee on Foreign Relations, *Legislative Proposals Relating to the War in Southeast Asia Hearing* (Washington D.C.: Government Printing Office), pp. 180–210.

108. Tom Engelhardt, *The End of Victory Culture: Cold War America and the Disillusioning of a Generation* (New York: Basic Books, 1995), p. 296.

109. Michael Herr, *Dispatches* (New York: Knopf, 1977), p. 20.

110. Caputo, *Rumor of War*, p. xiv.

111. Ibid., p. 6.

112. John McNaughton, "Memorandum for General Goodpaster," *Pentagon Papers*, 4:292.

113. Quoted in Gelb and Betts, *Irony of Vietnam*, pp. 135–36.

114. Quoted in Capps, *Vietnam Reader*, p. 60.

115. Ibid., p. 33.

116. Ibid., p. 84.

117. Ibid., pp. 85–86.

Chapter 8: The Crisis of 1968

1. Robert M. Collins, *More: The Politics of Economic Growth in Postwar America* (New York: Oxford University Press, 2000), p. 70.

2. Ibid., p. 72.

3. Robert Dallek, *Flawed Giant: Lyndon Johnson and His Times, 1961–1973* (New York: Oxford University Press, 1998), p. 460.

4. Ibid., p. 515.

5. Quoted in Collins, *More: The Politics of Economic Growth in Postwar America*, p. 94.

6. Eric F. Goldman, *The Tragedy of Lyndon Johnson* (New York: Knopf, 1969), p. 521.

7. Irving Bernstein, *Guns or Butter: The Presidency of Lyndon Johnson* (New York: Oxford University Press, 1996), p. 527.

8. Collins, *More: The Politics of Economic Growth in Postwar America,* p. 97.

9. Frank Kusch, *Battleground Chicago: The Police and the 1968 Democratic National Convention* (Westport, Conn.: Praeger, 2004), p. 34.

10. "Take Everything You Need Baby," *Newsweek* (April 15, 1968), p. 31.

11. Lyndon B. Johnson, *The Vantage Point: Perspectives of the Presidency, 1963–1969* (New York: Holt, Rinehart & Winston, 1971), p. 538.

12. James Q. Wilson and Richard J. Herrnstein, *Crime and Human Nature* (New York: Simon & Schuster, 1986), p. 409.

13. Michael W. Flamm, *Law and Order: Street Crime, Civil Unrest, and the Crisis of Liberalism in the 1960s* (New York: Columbia University Press, 2005), p. 5.

14. Thomas Edsall and Mary Edsall, *Chain Reaction: The Impact of Race, Rights, and Taxes on American Politics* (New York: Norton, 1991), p. 8.

15. Flamm, *Law and Order*, p. 34.

16. Quoted in Flamm, *Law and Order*, p. 26.

17. Ibid., p. 55.

18. *Los Angeles Times*, April 20, 1966.

19. Michael Dorman, "The Killing of Kitty Genovese," *Newsday.com.*, p. 1. Also A. M. Rosenthal, *Thirty-Eight Witnesses* (New York: McGraw-Hill, 1964), p. 33.

20. Ibid.

21. Mark Gado, "All about Kitty Genovese," *Crimelibrary.com.*, p. 3.

22. Dorman, "Killing of Kitty Genovese," p. 2.

23. *New York Times*, March 20, 1964.

24. Flamm, *Law and Order*, pp. 84–85.

25. Fred Siegel, *The Future Once Happened Here: New York, D.C., L.A., and the Fate of America's Big Cities* (New York: Free Press, 1997), p. 3.

26. Ibid., p. 9.

27. Flamm, *Law and Order*, p. 94.

28. Quoted in Flamm, *Law and Order*, p. 108.

29. Arthur M. Schlesinger Jr., *Robert Kennedy and His Times* (Boston: Houghton Mifflin, 1978), 2:861–62.

30. Quoted in Jack Newfield, *Robert Kennedy: A Memoir* (New York: Dutton, 1969), p. 186.

31. Eugene McCarthy, *1968* (Red Wing, Minn.: Lone Oak Press, 2000), p. 49.

32. Dallek, *Flawed Giant*, p. 525.

33. Dominic Sandbrook, *Eugene McCarthy: The Rise and Fall of Postwar American Liberalism* (New York: Knopf, 2004), pp. 7–10.

34. Albert Eisele, *Almost to the Presidency: A Biography of two American Politicians* (Blue Earth, Minn.: Piper Company), p. 39.

35. Sandbrook, *Eugene McCarthy*, p. 79.

36. Ibid., p. 116.

37. Ibid., p. 149.

38. Quoted in Walter LaFeber, *Deadly Bet: LBJ, Vietnam, and the 1968 Election* (New York: Rowman and Littlefield, 2005), p. 38.

39. Sandbrook, *Eugene McCarthy*, p. 176.

40. Ibid., p. 173.

41. Dallek, *Flawed Giant,* p. 526.

42. Quoted in Paul R. Henggeler, *In His Steps: Lyndon Johnson and the Kennedy Mystique* (Chicago: Ivan R. Dee, 1991), pp. 235–36.

43. Quoted in C. David Heymann, *RFK: A Candid Biography of Robert F. Kennedy* (New York: Dutton, 1998), p. 454.

44. Doris Kearns, *Lyndon Johnson and the American Dream* (Norwalk, Conn.: Easton Press, 1987), p. 359.

45. Schlesinger, *Robert Kennedy,* 2:899.

46. Sandbrook, *Eugene McCarthy,* pp. 192–93.

47. Quoted in Heymann, *RFK,* pp. 461–62.

48. Charles Kaiser, *1968 in America* (New York: Grove Press, 1988), p. 168.

49. Carl Solberg, *Hubert Humphrey: A Biography* (New York: Norton, 1984), p. 12.

50. Hubert Humphrey, *The Education of a Public Man* (Garden City, N.Y.: Doubleday, 1976), p. 66.

51. Quoted in Lewis Chester et al., *An American Melodrama: The Presidential Campaign of 1968* (New York: Viking, 1968), pp. 162–63.

52. For Humphrey's account of this episode, see *Education of a Public Man,* chapter 34.

53. Johnson, *Vantage Point,* p. 548.

54. Irwin Unger and Debi Unger, *Turning Point, 1968* (New York: Scribner, 1988), p. 473.

55. Sandbrook, *Eugene McCarthy,* p. 205.

56. Schlesinger, *Robert Kennedy,* vol. 2, chapter 35.

57. Mark Kurlansky, *1968: The Year that Rocked the World* (New York: Ballantine, 2004), p. 140.

58. Quoted in Sandbook, *Eugene McCarthy,* p. 207.

59. Schlesinger, *Robert Kennedy,* 2:972–73.

60. Garry Wills, *The Kennedy Imprisonment: A Meditation on Power* (Boston: Little, Brown, 1981), p. 210.

61. *Newsweek,* June 17, 1968.

62. Heymann, *RFK,* p. 511.

63. Newfield, *Robert Kennedy,* p. 304.

64. On Wallace, see Dan Carter, *The Politics of Rage: George Wallace, the Origin of the New Conservatism, and the Transformation of American Politics* (New York: Simon & Schuster, 1995); and Marshall Frady, *Wallace* (New York: Random House, 1996; orig. published in 1968).

65. Quoted in Matusow, *The Unraveling of America,* pp. 433–34.

66. On Nixon, see Jonathan Aitken, *Nixon: A Life* (Washington D.C.: Regnery, 1993); Stephen Ambrose, *Nixon.* 3 vols. (New York: Simon & Schuster, 1987–92); Fawn Brody, *Richard Nixon: The Shaping of His Character* (Cambridge, Mass.: Harvard University Press, 1983); Bruce Mazlish, *In Search of Nixon: A Psychohistorical Inquiry* (Baltimore: Penguin Books, 1973); Herbert Parmet, *Richard Nixon and His America* (Boston: Little, Brown, 1990); and Garry Wills, *Nixon Agonistes: The Crisis of the Self-Made Man* (Boston: Houghton Mifflin, 1970).

67. *Los Angeles Times,* November 8, 1962.

68. Wills, *Nixon Agonistes,* pp. 161–77.

69. Quoted in David Halberstam, *The Fifties* (New York: Fawcett Columbine, 1993), p. 324.

70. Aitken, *Nixon,* p. 184.

71. Ibid., p. 178.

72. Wills, *Nixon Agonistes,* pp. 122–23.

73. Quoted in Unger and Unger, *Turning Point, 1968,* p. 451.

74. Ibid., p. 458.

75. Wills, *Nixon Agonistes,* p. 89.

76. Unger and Unger, *Turning Point, 1968,* p. 455.

77. Quoted in Jules Witcover, *The Resurrection of Richard Nixon* (New York: Putnam's, 1970), p. 25.

78. *Newsweek,* August 19, 1968.

79. Lewis L. Gould, *1968: The Election that Changed America* (Chicago: Ivan R. Dee, 1993), pp. 68–69.

80. Dallek, *Flawed Giant*, pp. 556–68.

81. Quoted in Arthur M. Schlesinger, ed., *The Election of 1968 and the Administration of Richard Nixon* (Philadelphia: Mason Crest Publishers, 2003), p. 44.

82. Kusch, *Battleground Chicago*, pp. 52–53; also Adam Cohen and Elizabeth Taylor, *American Pharaoh: Mayor Richard J. Daley. His Battle for Chicago and the Nation* (Boston: Little, Brown, 2000), pp. 462–63.

83. Cohen and Taylor, *American Pharaoh*, p. 462.

84. David Farber, *Chicago '68* (Chicago: University of Chicago Press, 1988).

85. Quoted in Flamm, *Law and Order*, pp. 158–59.

86. *Time* magazine, September 6, 1968.

87. Flamm, *Law and Order*, p. 159.

88. Kusch, *Battleground Chicago*, p. 155.

89. Ibid., p. 151.

90. *Time* magazine, August 26, 1968; also Kusch, *Law and Order*, p. 154.

91. Ibid., p.108.

92. Ibid.

93. Quoted in Flamm, *Law and Order*, p. 160.

94. Kaiser, *1968 in America*, p. 249.

95. Joe McGinniss, *The Selling of the President* (New York: Penguin Books, 1988; orig. published in 1969), p. 37.

96. Ibid.

97. Dallek, *Flawed Giant*, p. 586.

98. Ibid.

99. Gould, *1968: The Election That Changed America*, pp. 156–60; also Walter LaFeber, *The Deadly Bet: LBJ, Vietnam, and the 1968 Election* (New York: Rowman & Littlefield, 2005), pp. 163–64.

100. Dallek, *Flawed Giant*, pp. 591–92; also Humphrey, *Education of a Public Man*, pp. 8–9.

101. Gould, *1968: The Election That Changed America*, p. 161.

Chapter 9: A Young Generation in Revolt

1. For a general survey of young people in American history, see Louis Filler, *Vanguards and Followers: Youth in the American Tradition* (Chicago, 1996); Harvey J. Graff, *Conflicting Paths: Growing up in America* (Cambridge, Mass.: Harvard University Press, 1995); Landon Y. Jones, *Great Expectations: America and the Baby Boom Generation* (New York: Coward, McCann, Geoghegan, 1980); and Thomas Hine, *The Rise and Fall of the American Teenager* (New York: Avon, 1999).

2. See Kenneth J. Heineman, *Put Your Bodies upon the Wheels: Student Revolt in the 1960s* (Chicago: Ivan R. Dee, 2001), pp. 64–68; Lewis S. Feuer, *The Conflict of Generations: The Character and Significance of Student Movements* (New York: Basic Books, 1969), pp. 423–31; and Stanley Rothman and S. Robert Lichter, *Roots of Radicalism: Jew, Christians and the New Left* (New York: Oxford University Press, 1982).

3. Many of these radical students have left their personal accounts. The more noteworthy are Todd Gitlin, *The Sixties: Years of Hope, Days of Rage* (New York: Bantam, 1987); Tom Hayden, *Reunion: A Memoir* (New York: Random House, 1988); David Horowitz and Peter Collier, *Destructive Generation: Second Thoughts about the 1960s* (New York: Simon & Schuster, 1989); David Horowitz, *Radical Son: A Generational Odyssey* (New York: Touchstone, 1998); Paul Krassner, *Confessions of a Raving, Unconfirmed Nut* (New York: Simon & Schuster, 1993); Jane Alpert, *Growing Up Underground* (New York: 1981); Susan Stern, *With the Weathermen: The Personal Journey of a Revolutionary Woman* (New York: Doubleday, 1975); and Ronald Radosh, *Commies: A Journey through the Old Left, the New Left, and the Leftover Left* (San Francisco: Encounter Books, 2001).

4. Feuer, *Conflict of Generations*, p. 8.

5. Ibid., p. 11.

6. Ibid, p. 20.

7. Friedrich Heer, *Challenge of Youth*, trans. Geoffrey Skelton (London: George Weidenfeld, 1974), p. 7.

8. Ibid., p. 173.

9. Feuer, *Conflict of Generations*, p. 318.

10. Roland Stromberg, *After Everything: Western Intellectual History since 1945* (New York: St. Martin's Press, 1975), pp. 56–57.

11. For a good view of the SAT, see Nicholas Lemann, *The Big Test: The Secret History of the American Meritocracy* (New York: Farrar, Straus, and Giroux, 1999).

12. *Advisory Panel on the Scholastic Aptitude Test Score Decline: On Further Examination* (New York: College Entrance Examination Board, 1977), including the same panel's *Appendixes to On Further Examination.*

13. One has to tread carefully in assessing the New Left because most accounts have been written by former leftists who have tried to ennoble the movement after its demise. Although a really balanced history has not yet been written, there are some fairly reliable accounts, notably Edward Bacciocca, *The New Left in America: Reform to Revolution, 1956–1970* (Stanford, Calif.: Hoover Institution, 1974); John Diggins, *The Rise and Fall of the American Left* (New York: Norton, 1992); James Miller, *Democracy in the Streets: From Port Huron to the Siege of Chicago* (New York: Simon & Schuster, 1987); Gitlin, *Sixties*; Maurice Isserman, *If I Had a Hammer: The Death of the Old Left and the Birth of the New Left* (New York: Basic Books, 1987); Irwin Unger, *The Movement: A History of the American Left, 1959–1972* (1974; reprint, Lanham, Maryland: University Press of America, 1988); and Terry Anderson, *The Movement and the Sixties: From Greensboro to Wounded Knee* (New York: Oxford University Press, 1996).

14. C. Wright Mills, "The New Left," *New Left Review* (October 1960).

15. Gitlin, *Sixties*, p. 26.

16. *Port Huron Statement* (Chicago: Students for a Democratic Society, 1966), p. 6.

17. For ERAP and other community action programs, see Wini Breines, *Community and Organization in the New Left, 1962–1968: The Great Refusal* (New Brunswick, N.J.: Rutgers University Press, 1989).

18. Irwin Unger and Debi Unger, *Turning Point, 1968* (New York: Scribner's, 1988), p. 37.

19. William O'Neill, *Coming Apart: An Informal History of the America in the 1960s* (New York: Quadrangle), p. 279.

20. Ibid.

21. On Berkeley, see Feuer, *Conflict of Generations*, pp. 436–500; W. J. Rorabaugh, *Berkeley at War* (New York: Oxford University Press, 1989); Clark Kerr, *The Uses of the University* (Cambridge, Mass.: Harvard University Press, 1963); Henry May, "Living with Crisis," *American Scholar* 38 (1969): pp. 588–605; Seymour M. Lipset and Sheldon S. Wolin, eds., *The Berkeley Student Revolt* (Garden City, N.Y.: Doubleday, 1965); and John R. Searle, *The Campus War* (New York: Penguin, 1972).

22. Rorabaugh, *Berkeley at War*, p. 12.

23. Jones, *Great Expectations*, p. 98.

24. Quoted in Rorabaugh, *Berkeley at War*, p. 31.

25. Ibid., p. 46.

26. Feuer (*Conflict of Generations*, p. 384) estimates that the radical core at Berkeley, including several faculty members, fluctuated between twenty-five and fifty students.

27. Ibid., pp. 24–25.

28. Heineman, *Put Your Bodies upon the Wheels*, p. 62; also Rorabaugh, *Berkeley at War*, p. 34.

29. Heineman, *Put Your Bodies upon the Wheels*, p. 20.

30. For the views of these "dissenting" members of the academy, see Theodore Roszak, ed., *The Dissenting Academy* (New York: Vintage Books, 1968).

31. I owe this telling phrase to Robert Bork, who owed it to a scholarly acquaintance (Robert Bork, *Slouching toward Gomorrah* [New York: HarperCollins, 1999], p. 36).

32. Bacciocca, *New Left in America*, p. 169.

33. Ibid., pp. 63–65.

34. *The Skolnik Report to the National Commission on the Causes and Prevention of Violence: The Politics of Protest* (New York: Ballantine Books, 1969), pp. 96–97; Also, Gitlin, *Sixties*, pp. 189–91; and Anderson, *Movement and the Sixties*, p. 148.

35. Quoted in Heineman, *Put Your Bodies upon the Wheels*, p. 116.

36. Ibid., p. 119.

37. Gitlin, *Sixties*, p. 264.

38. Ibid., p. 262.

39. Heineman, *Put Your Bodies upon the Wheels*, pp. 121–22.

40. O'Neill, *Coming Apart*, p. 289.

41. For the specifics on the Columbia crisis, there is a fact-finding report, headed by Archibald Cox, entitled *Crisis at Columbia: Report of the Fact-Finding Commission Appointed to Investigate the Disturbances at Columbia University in April and May 1968* (New York: Vintage, 1968). Another factual account is Robert Friedman, ed., *Up against the Ivy Wall: A History of the Columbia Crisis* (New York: Atheneum, 1969). The student side of the story can be found in James Simon Kunen's colorful and distorted *The Strawberry Statement: Notes of a College Revolutionary* (New York: Random House, 1969). The title comes from a flippant remark by Grayson Kirk, who allegedly said: "Whether students vote 'yes' or 'no' on a given issue means as much to me as if they were to tell me that they like strawberries" (Friedman, *Up against the Ivy Wall*, pp. 119–20).

42. On the Morningside Heights issue, see Roger Kahn, *The Battle for Morningside Heights: Why Students Rebel* (New York: Morrow, 1970).

43. Heineman, *Put Your Bodies upon the Wheels*, p. 139.

44. O'Neill, *Coming Apart*, p. 291.

45. Joan Morrison and Robert Morrison, eds., *From Camelot to Kent State: The Sixties Experience in the Words of Those Who Lived It* (New York: Times Books, 1987), p. 273.

46. Charles Kaiser, *1968 in America* (New York: Grove Press, 1988), p. 157.

47. Anderson, *Movement and the Sixties*, pp. 194–97.

48. For the mentality of blending pot and politics, see Abbie Hoffman, *Revolution for the Hell of It* (New York: Dial, 1968) and Jerry Rubin *Do It: Scenarios of the Revolution* (New York: Simon & Schuster, 1970).

49. Heineman, *Put Your Bodies upon the Wheels*, p. 142

50. Ibid., pp. 142–43.

51. Anderson, *Movement and the Sixties*, p. 219. Anderson's account is overly partisan in favoring the protesters, especially the nihilistic Yippies. Part of the problem is that many accounts of the 1960s have been written by former radicals, now turned tenured professors, and by camp followers inside and outside the academy who find meaning in their youthful excesses. As Heineman points out in his book *Put Your Bodies upon the Wheels* (pp. 143–43), scholarly accounts of the Chicago convention put SDS in a favorable light, while condemning Daley and his police force as having incited the violence against peaceful protesters. This portrait was also drawn by a popular PBS documentary, (*Chicago 1968*), which showed Daley in the most unflattering light as a bloated and ugly party boss. The historian David Farber has written a spirited book in which he recreated the voices of those who participated in the demonstrations at Chicago, but his account strongly favors the side of the demonstrators. The same is true of Norman Mailer's history as novel and the novel as history approach in *Miami and the Siege of Chicago: An Informal History of the Republican and Democratic Conventions of 1968* (New York: New American Library, 1968).

52. Heineman, *Put Your Bodies upon the Wheels*, p. 144.

53. Ibid.

54. Abe Peck, *Uncovering the Sixties: The Life and Times of the Underground Press* (New York:

Citadel Press, 1991), pp. 99–119. Peck was an underground writer and editor who provides a very one-sided account of America in the 1960s that strongly favors protesters and hippies. Many 1960s radicals later became teachers or journalists in the nation's mainstream press. For that reason their descriptions tend to be self-serving and misleading. Peck, for example, believes that the Chicago police wanted to wage class war, gang war, and style war, all rolled into one. Charles Kaiser, a well-known reporter, seems to think that "America in 1968 was more like the 'police state' radicals had alleged than most people suspected" (*1968 in America*, p. 233). Such pundits need to read accounts of real police states such as Nazi Germany or the Soviet Union to be disabused of such silliness.

55. Morrison and Morrison, eds., *From Camelot to Kent State*, p. 288; also Peck, *Uncovering the Sixties*, p. 118.

56. Heineman, *Put Your Bodies Upon the Wheels*, p. 153.

57. For the events of the student riots at UC Santa Barbara, see Robert A. Potter and James J. Sullivan, *The Campus by the Sea Where the Bank Burned Down: A Report on the Disturbances at UCSB and Isla Vista, 1968–70* (Santa Barbara, 1970); and Robert Kelley, *Transformations: UC Santa Barbara, 1909–1979* (UC Santa Barbara: Associated Students, 1981). There is also a revealing follow-up of some of the radical students who participated in these upheavals by Jack Whalen and Richard Flacks, *Beyond the Barricades: The Sixties Generation Grows Up* (Philadelphia: Temple University Press, 1989). If the authors are serious about what they mean by growing up, we can confidently look forward to the emergence of a new enlightened intelligentsia with a deeper moral outlook and a greater commitment to peace, environmental protectionism, a revitalized labor movement, and gender and class equality. Moreover, according to the authors, the radicals of the sixties have served as the vanguard of a new intellectual class that is about to replace the industrial proletariat, a new intelligentsia that is "occupationally engaged in the creation, production, distribution, and inculcation of culture" (p. 279). What culture?

58. Kelley, *Transformations*, p. 46.

59. Personal observation by the author, who decidedly did not participate in the riot.

60. There is a telling and entirely creditable profile of Dohrn in David Horowitz and Peter Collier, *Destructive Generation: Second Thought about the Sixties* (New York: Summit Books, 1990), chapter 2.

61. Ibid., *p. 77.*

62. Ibid., *p. 74.*

63. Richard Flacks, "Making History vs. Making Life: Dilemmas of an American Left," *Working Papers* 2, no. 2 (1972), p. 68.

64. Collier and Horowitz, *Destructive Generation*, pp. 86–87.

65. Ibid., p. 88.

66. Ibid., p. 96.

67. O'Neill, *Coming Apart*, p. 298; also Bacciocca, *New Left in America*, p. 249.

68. Gitlin, *Sixties*, p. 335.

69. Ibid., p. 337.

70. O'Neill, *Coming Apart*, p. 190.

71. On the problems at San Francisco State, see William H. Orrick Jr., *Shut it Down! A College in Crisis: San Francisco State College, October 1968–April 1969, A Report to the National Commission on the Causes and Prevention of Violence* (Washington D.C.: United States Government Printing Office, 1969).

72. John Bunzel's retrospective, which still makes the hairs on the back of the neck stand on end, can be found in "Liberal in the Middle," in *Political Passages: Journeys of Change through Two Decades, 1968–1988*, ed. John H. Bunzel (New York: Free Press, 1988), pp. 132–61. The book is a collection of critical essays by disenchanted liberals and radicals of the 1960s; it is a worthy successor to *The God That Failed* essays of the 1950s.

73. Anderson, *Movement and the Sixties*, p. 297.

74. Heineman, *Put Your Bodies upon the Wheels*, p. 164.

75. On the Cornell crisis, see Donald Alexander Downs, *Cornell '69: Liberalism and the Crisis of the American University* (Ithaca, N.Y.: Cornell University Press, 1999).

76. Walter Berns, "The Assault on the Universities: Then and Now," in Stephen Macedo, ed., *Reassessing the Sixties* (New York: W. W. Norton, 1997), pp. 164–65.

77. Quoted in Berns, "Assault on the Universities," p. 158.

78. Ibid., p. 159.

79. As Roger Kimball points out, college teachers who participate in TIAA-CREF can breathe a sigh of relief that Jones is no longer president of the nation's largest college teacher's retirement program. He has moved on to other financial ventures (Kimball, *The Long March: How the Cultural Revolution of the 1960s Changed America* [San Francisco: Encounter Books, 2000], p. 118).

80. Allan Bloom, *The Closing of the American Mind* (New York: Simon & Schuster, 1987), p. 315.

81. Ibid., p. 316.

82. Berns, "Assault on the Universities," p. 163.

83. For the background of the Yale upheavals, see John Taft, *Mayday at Yale: A Case Study in Student Radicalism* (Boulder, Colo.: Westview Press, 1976), pp. 5–10.

84. On the Yale crisis in May 1970, see John Taft, *Mayday at Yale*.

85. Ibid., p. 32; see also Geoffrey Kabaservice, *The Guardians: Kingman Brewster, His Circle, and the Rise of the Liberal Establishment* (New York: Henry Holt, 2004), p. 407; Laura Kalman, "The Dark Ages," in Anthony T. Kronman, ed., *History of the Yale Law School* (New Haven, Conn.: Yale University Press, 2004), p. 189.

86. Bork, *Slouching towards Gomorrah*, p. 37.

87. Ibid.

88. Kimball, *Long March*, p. 120.

89. Kabaservice, *Guardians*, p. 405.

90. Taft, *Mayday at Yale*, p. 92; also Kabaservice, *Guardians*, p. 408; Kalman, "Dark Ages," pp. 188–89.

91. Bork, *Slouching towards Gomorrah*, p. 42.

92. Quoted in Taft, *Mayday at Yale*, p. 102.

93. Kimball, *Long March*, p. 121.

94. On the political right, see John A. Andrew III, *The Other Side of the Sixties: Young Americans for Freedom and the Rise of Conservative Politics* (New Brunswick, N.J.: Rutgers University Press, 1997); Robert H. Bork, *Slouching towards Gomorrah: Modern Liberalism and American Decline* (New York: HarperCollins, 1996); Mary C. Brennan, *Turning Right in the Sixties: The Conservative Capture of the GOP* (Chapel Hill: University of North Carolina Press, 1995); Rebecca E. Klatch, *Generation Divided: The New Left, the New Right, and the 1960s* (Berkeley: University of California Press, 1999); and Ayn Rand, *The New Left: The Anti-Industrial Revolution* (New York: New American Library, 1971).

95. Klatch, *Generation Divided*, p. 145.

96. Anderson, *Movement and the Sixties*, p. 109.

97. Ibid., p. 108.

98. Klatch, *Generation Divided*, p. 85.

99. Ibid., p. 19.

100. Ibid., p. 108.

101. Ibid., p. 332.

102. George Kennan, "Rebels without a Program," *The New York Times Magazine*, January 21, 1968.

103. Rand, *New Left*, p. 40.

104. Bloom, *Closing of the American Mind*, p. 320.

105. Ibid.

Chapter 10: Countercultural Protest Movements

1. Theodore Roszak, *The Making of a Counter Culture* (New York: Anchor, 1969), p. 1.

2. Ibid., p. 42.

3. Daniel Bell, *The Cultural Contradictions of Capitalism* (New York: Basic Books, 1976), pp. 81, 144.

4. Harvey Cox, "God and the Hippies," *Playboy* 15, no. 1 (January, 1968): p. 94.

5. H. H. Gerth and C. Wright Mills, *From Max Weber: Essays in Sociology* (New York: Oxford University Press, 1958), pp. 148, 155.

6. Arthur Marwick, *The Sixties: Cultural Revolution in Britain, France, Italy, and the United States, c.1958–c.1974* (New York: Oxford University Press, 1998), pp. 11–13. Although Roszak claims to have coined the word "counterculture," the term was used much earlier. Talcott Parsons, for example used the term in 1951 in connection with deviant groups such as delinquent gangs (*The Social System* [New York: Free Press, 1951], p. 522).

7. Oswald Spengler, *The Decline of the West*, 2 vols. (New York: Knopf, 1926), 2:189.

8. Philip Bagby, *Culture and History: Prolegomena to the Comparative Study of Civilizations* (Berkeley: University of California Press, 1963), p. 84.

9. The distinction between highbrow, middlebrow, and lowbrow was made by Van Wyck Brooks in 1915. Brooks reacted against the intellectual and moral vulgarization he saw emerging from modern magazines, but he equally disdained the pretentious tone of so-called magazines of intellectual refinement (John Lukacs, *A New Republic: A History of the United States in the Twentieth Century* [New Haven, Conn.: Yale University Press, 2004], p. 306).

10. For two colorful accounts of America's children and their generational protests, see Nicholas von Hoffman, *We Are the People Our Parents Warned Us Against* (Chicago: Ivan R. Dee, 1969); and Joan Didion, *Slouching towards Bethlehem* (New York: Farrar, Straus and Giroux, 1968).

11. On the hippie phenomenon, see Timothy Miller, *The Hippies and American Values* (Knoxville: University of Tennessee Press, 1991); Leonard Wolf, *Voice from the Love Generation* (Boston: Little, Brown, 1968); and Lewis Yablonsky, *The Hippy Trip* (New York: Bobbs-Merrill, 1968).

12. Neil A. Hamilton, ed., *The ABC-CLIO Companion to the 1960s Counterculture in America* (Santa Barbara: ABC Clio Press, 1997), pp. 148–51.

13. For a statistical analysis of hippy attitudes and beliefs, see Yablonsky, *Hippy Trip*, pp. 340–66.

14. Quoted in Terry Anderson, *The Movement and the Sixties: Protest in America from Greensboro to Wounded Knee* (New York: Oxford University Press, 1995), p. 247.

15. A sample of Reichian profundity: "the individual self is the only true reality" (p. 242); "consciousness III rejects the whole concept of excellence and comparative merit" (p. 283); "each individual is truly protean" (p. 253); "the new clothes express truly democratic values" (p. 256); consciousness III is deeply suspicious of logic, rationality, analysis, and of principles" (p. 278); "grass is a subtle and delicate experience, an educated experience" (p. 280); "excellence rests on someone else's degradation" (p. 310).

16. Quoted in Hamilton, *1960s Counterculture in America*, p. 151.

17. The reader is invited to sample the collection of articles in Philip Nobile, ed., *The Con III Controversy: Critics Look at the Greening of America* (New York: Pocket Books, 1971) in which, according to the book's cover, "more than thirty social critics discuss the *revolutionary book of our times* (italics mine).

18. Annie Gottlieb, *Do You Believe in Magic? The Second Coming of the 60s Generation* (New York: Times Books, 1987), p. 40.

19. On religion and spirituality, see Wade Clark Roof, *Spiritual Marketplace: Baby Boomers and the Remaking of American Religion* (Princeton, N.J.: Princeton University Press, 1999); and Robert Wuthnow, *After Heaven: Spirituality in America since the 1950s* (Los Angeles: University of California Press, 1998).

20. Robert Pattison, *The Triumph of Vulgarity: Rock Music in the Mirror of Romanticism* (New York: Oxford University Press, 1987), p. 123.

21. Gottlieb, *Do You Believe in Magic?* p. 209.

22. Ibid., p 219.

23. For the most astute analysis of this de-christianizing tendency of the counterculture, see Os Guiness, *The Dust of Death: The Sixties Counterculture and How It Changed America Forever* (Wheaton, Ill.: Crossway Books, 1994).

24. Quoted in Jill Jonnes, *Hep-Cats, Narcs, and Pipe Dreams: A History of America's Romance with Drugs* (Baltimore: Johns Hopkins University Press, 1996), p. 239.

25. Ibid., p. 218.

26. On Leary's experiences at Harvard, see Jay Stevens, *Storming Heaven: LSD and the American Dream* (New York: Grove Press, 1987), chapter 12.

27. Ibid., p. 219.

28. On the goings-on at Millbrook, see Art Kleps, *Millbrook* (Oakland: Bench Press, 1975).

29. William L. O'Neill, *Coming Apart: An Informal History of America in the 1960s* (New York: Quadrangle, 1976), pp. 238–40.

30. On the Haight-Ashbury scene, see Charles Perry, *The Haight-Ashbury: A History* (New York: Random House, 1984); Stephen Gaskin, *Haight-Ashbury Flashbacks* (Berkeley: Ronin, 1990); Didion, *Slouching towards Bethlehem*; and von Hoffman, *We Are the People They Warned Us Against*.

31. This statement, variously attributed to Paul Kantner of the Jefferson Airplane and John Lennon of the Beatles, is an apt description of freaked-out hippies and rock musicians in the 1960s.

32. Hamilton, *1960s Counterculture in America*, p. 124.

33. Ibid., p. 26.

34. For the Summer of Love, see Gene Anthony, *The Summer of Love: Haight-Ashbury at Its Height* (Milbrae, Calif.: Celestial Arts, 1980); Perry, *Haight-Ashbury*; von Hoffman *We Are the People Our Parents Warned Us Against*; and Joel Selvin, *Summer of Love* (New York: Cooper Square Press, 1999).

35. Perry, *Haight-Ashbury*, p. 171.

36. Quoted in Stevens, *Storming Heaven*, p. xiii; *Saturday Review*, August 1967, p. 52.

37. Didion, *Slouching Towards Bethlehem*, p. 123.

38. Ibid., p. 122.

39. On the rock festival years, see Robert Santelli, *Aquarius Rising: The Rock Festival Years* (New York: Dell, 1980).

40. The slogan the "Politics of Love" came from an essay by Tuli Kupferberg, a member of the Fugs and a peace activist, in the *East Village Other* (May 1967).

41. As is to be expected, those who attended Woodstock remember it fondly and without regrets, still spinning it as "a planetary event of love and peace." Since Woodstock was not a cerebral event—no countercultural event ever was—the best approach is to watch films taken of the event, notably Michael Wadleigh, ed., *Woodstock* (1970). Among the noteworthy accounts of the event, see Jack Curry, *Woodstock: The Summer of Our Lives* (New York: Widenfeld and Nicolson, 1989); Joel Makower, *Woodstock: The Oral History* (New York: Doubleday, 1989); Bob Spitz, *Barefoot in Babylon: The Creation of the Woodstock Music Festival* (New York: Viking, 1979); and Jean Young and Michael Lang, *Woodstock Festival Remembered* (New York: Ballantine, 1979).

42. *New York Times*, August 18, 1969.

43. Quoted in Santelli, *Aquarius Rising*, p. 141.

44. *Time Magazine*, August 29, 1969.

45. Ayn Rand, *The New Left: The Anti-Industrial Revolution* (New York: New American Library, 1970), pp. 57–81).

46. Ibid., pp. 59–60.

47. Quoted in Santelli, *Aquarius Rising*, p. 155.

48. On the commune movement, see Timothy Miller, *The 60s Communes: Hippies and Beyond* (Syracuse: Syracuse University Press, 1999).

49. Ibid., p. 25.

50. Ibid., p. xviii.

51. Ibid., p. xx.

52. Kimball, *Long March*, p. 248.

53. Ibid., p. 249.

54. Jacques Barzun, *From Dawn to Decadence* (New York: HarperCollins, 2000), pp. 773–802.

55. This is essentially the argument of Robert Pattison in his hard-hitting but far-ranging book, *The Triumph of Vulgarity*.

56. Martha Bayles, *Hole in our Soul: The Loss of Beauty and Meaning in American Popular Music* (Chicago: University of Chicago Press, 1994), pp. 68–72.

57. Pattison, *Triumph of Vulgarity*, p. 42.

58. Ibid., p. 33.

59. Robert A. Rosenstone, "The Times They Are A-Changin': The Music of Protest," *The Annals of the American Academy of Political and Social Science* (March 1969), pp. 132–34.

60. On Bob Dylan, see Anthony Scaduto, *Bob Dylan* (New York: Grosset and Dunlap, 1971); Robert Shelton, *No Direction Home: The Life and Music of Bob Dylan* (New York: Morrow, 1986); Clinton Heylin, *Bob Dylan: Behind the Shades* (New York: Summit, 1991); Patrick Humphries, *Absolute Dylan* (New York: Viking Studio, 1991); Tim Riley, *Hard Rain: A Dylan Commentary* (New York: Knopf, 1992). Besides listening to Dylan's music, two works by Dylan are worth reading: *Bob Dylan in His Own Words* (New York: Omnibus, 1993) and *Chronicles* (New York: Simon & Schuster, 2004).

61. Country Joe and the Fish, "The Harlem Song," *Together* (1969).

62. Frank Zappa and the Mothers of Invention, "Trouble Coming Every Day," *Freak Out* (1966). Zappa wrote that song during the Watts riot of 1965.

63. Quoted in Rosenstone, "Times They Are A-Changin'," p. 135.

64. Quoted in Scott Buchanan, ed., *Rock 'n' Roll: The Famous Lyrics* (New York: Harper Perennial, 1994), p. 189.

65. Ibid., pp. 70–71.

66. Ibid., p. 63.

67. Ted Nugent, who coined this cultural truism, also staged the "Noble Savage" act, loincloth and all.

68. David Pichaske, *A Generation in Motion: Popular Music and Culture in the Sixties* (Peoria, Ill.: Ellis Press, 1989), p. 43.

69. Rosenstone, "Times They Are A-Changin'," p. 137.

70. Pichaske, *Generation in Motion*, pp. 13–14.

71. Buchanan, *Famous Lyrics*, p. 100.

72. Quoted in Rosenstone, "The Times They Are A-Changin'," p. 138.

73. Frank Zappa, *The Real Frank Zappa Book* (New York: Poseidon Press, 1989), pp. 89–90.

74. Quoted in Rosenstone, "Times They Are A-Changin'," p. 139.

75. Buchanan, *Famous Lyrics*, p. 17

76. Dan Hartman, "We are the Young" (MCA, 1984).

77. John Lennon may have been arrogant and blasphemous in his remark about the Beatles being more popular than Jesus Christ, but looking at the sheer volume of information about the Beatles, he did have a point. Using any of the major search engines on the Internet, there are literally millions of entries (hits) about the Beatles. The best way to get to know the Beatles or remember them is to listen to their music. In the late 1980s, Capitol Records released all the Beatle albums on CD, including the original British title, track listing and configuration (*The Rolling Stone Illustrated History of Rock 'n' Roll* [New York: Random House, 1992], p. 222). Among the more reliable works on the Beatles, see Philip Norman, *Shout! The Beatles in Their Generation* (New York: Simon & Schuster, 1981); Peter Brown and Steven Gaines, *The Love You Make: An Insider's Story of the Beatles* (New York: McGraw-Hill, 1983); Bill Harry, *The Ultimate Beatles Encyclopedia* (New York: Hyperion, 1992); and Hunter Davies, *The Beatles: The Only Authorized Biography* (London: Arrow, 1993).

78. Bayles, *Hole in Our Soul*, p. 170.

79. *Rolling Stone Illustrated History of Rock 'n' Roll*, p. 216.

80. Bayles, *Hole in Our Soul*, p. 171.

81. Quoted in Charles Kaiser, *1968 in America* (New York: Grove Press, 1988), pp. 198–99.

82. Quoted in *Sgt. Pepper's Lonely Hearts Club Band* attachment to the compact disc (EME Records Ltd., 1987), p. 4.

83. Glenn C. Altschuler argues that the Beatles may not have been consciously subversive but in actual practice they were perceived to be that way by middle-class traditionalists (*All Shook Up: How Rock 'n' Roll Changed America* [New York: Oxford University Press, 2003], p. 183).

84. On the Rolling Stones, the best musical collection is a two-CD set *The Rolling Stones: Hot Rocks 1964–1971* (Abko). Most books or articles on the Stones, as well as other rock bands, are anecdotal, uncritical, and campy. Among the more interesting ones, provided the reader reads between the lines, are Stanley Booth, *Dance with the Devil: The Rolling Stones and Their Times* (New York: Random House, 1984) and the same author's *The True Adventures of the Rolling Stones* (New York: Vintage, 1985); Philip Norman, *Sympathy for the Devil: The Rolling Stones Story* (New York: Simon & Schuster, 1984); and Tony Sanchez, *Up and Down with the Rolling Stones* (New York: American Library, 1979).

85. London, *Closing the Circle*, p. 11.

86. Ibid., p. 32.

87. Albert Goldman, "The Emergence of Rock," in Gerald Howard, ed., *The Sixties* (New York: Washington Square Press, 1982), p. 363.

88. Ibid., p. 360.

89. For the untimely death of many rock stars, see Gary J. Katz, *Death by Rock & Roll* (New York: Citadel, 1995).

90. London, *Closing the Circle*, p. 23.

91. Pattison, *Triumph of Vulgarity*, p. 136.

92. Bayles, *Holes in Our Soul*, pp. 385–91.

93. Pattison, *Triumph of Vulgarity*, p. 127.

94. Ibid., p. 154.

95. See the profound remarks in this connection by Jacques Barzun in *The Culture We Deserve* (Middletown, Conn.: Wesleyan University Press, 1989) pp. 3–22.

96. Bloom, *Closing of the American Mind*, pp. 71–73.

97. Joseph Heath and Andrew Potter, *Nation of Rebels: Why Counterculture Became Consumer Culture* (New York: HarperCollins, 2004), pp. 8, 86–87.

98. Theodore Roszak, *The Making of a Counter Culture* (New York: Anchor, 1969), chapter 8.

99. Spengler, *Decline of the West*, 2:310.

100. Heath and Potter, *Nation of Rebels*, p. 174; also Marwick, *Sixties*, 13ff.

101. Ibid., 206ff.

102. Book review, *San Francisco Chronicle*, December 23, 2001.

103. Peter Braunstein and Michael William Doyle, eds., *Imagine Nation* (New York: Routledge, 2002), p. 10.

Chapter 11: Riding the Coattails of Revolt

1. Betty Friedan, *The Feminine Mystique* (New York: Norton, 1963), p. 11.

2. John D'Emilio and Estelle Freedman, *Intimate Matters: A History of Sexuality in America* (Chicago: University of Chicago Press, 1988), p. 311.

3. Richard J. Ellis, *The Dark Side of the Left: Illiberal Egalitarianism in America* (Lawrence: University of Kansas Press, 1998), p. 200.

4. Ibid.

5. For a telling account of such in-group fanaticism, see Ellis, *Dark Side of the Left*, pp. 198–99.

6. Robin Morgan, ed., *Sisterhood Is Powerful: An Anthology of Writings from the Women's Liberation Movement* (New York: Doubleday, 1970), pp. 598–602.

7. Anne Koedt, "The Myth of the Vaginal Orgasm, " in Jeffrey Escoffier, ed., *Sexual Revolution* (New York: Thunder's Mouth Press, 2003), p. 108.

8. Irwin Unger and Debi Unger, *Turning Point, 1968* (New York: Scribner's 1988), p. 441.

9. Jill Johnston, "The Myth of the Myth of the Vaginal Orgasm," in Escoffier, *Sexual Revolution*, p. 512.

10. Ruth Rosen, *The World Split Open: How the Modern Women's Movement Changed America* (New York: Viking, 2000), p. 160.

11. Unger and Unger, *Turning Point*, p. 445.

12. Johnston, "Myth of the Myth of the Vaginal Orgasm," p. 511.

13. Alice Echols, "Nothing Distant about It: Women's Liberation and Sixties Radicalism," in David Farber, ed., *The Sixties: From Memory to History* (Chapel Hill: University of North Carolina Press, 1994), p. 152.

14. William L. O'Neill, *American High: The Years of Confidence, 1945–1960* (New York: Free Press, 1986), p. 41.

15. Echols, "Nothing Distant about It," pp. 152–53.

16. Ellis, *Dark Side of the Left*, p. 206.

17. The most sensible account of this subject of equity and gender feminism is by Christina Hoff Sommers, *Who Stole Feminism? How Women Have Betrayed Women* (New York: Simon & Schuster, 1994).

18. On the Stonewall incident, see Martin Duberman. *Stonewall* (New York: Dutton, 1993).

19. Quoted in John D'Emilio and Freedman, *Sexual Politics, Sexual Communities* (Chicago: University of Chicago Press, 1983), p. 234.

20. D'Emilio, *Intimate Matters*, p. 323.

21. *Time*, January 21, 1966, p. 41.

22. *Time*, October 1969.

23. Matt S. Meier and Feliciano Rivera, *The Chicanos: A History of Mexican Americans* (New York: Hill and Wang, 1972), pp. 210–11.

24. On Cesar Chavez, see Richard A. Garcia, "Cesar Chavez: A Personal and Historical Testament," *Pacific Historical Review* 63, no. 2 (May 1994): 225–33; Griswald del Castillo and Richard Garcia, *Cesar Chavez: A Triumph of Spirit* (Norman: University of Oklahoma Press, 1995); David Goodwin, *Cesar Chavez Hope for the People* (New York: Fawcett Columbine, 1991); Craig Jenkins, *The Politics of Insurgency: The Farm Workers Movement in the 1960s* (New York: Columbia University Press, 1985); Jacques Levy, *Cesar Chavez: Autobiography of la Causa* (New York: Norton, 1974); Joan London and Henry Anderson, *So Shall Ye Reap: The Story of Cesar Chavez and the Farm Workers Movement* (New York: Crowell, 1971); Jean M. Pitrone, *Chavez: Man of the Migrants* (New York: Piramid, 1972).

25. Arthur M. Schlesinger Jr., *Robert Kennedy and His Times*, 2 vols. (Boston: Houghton Mifflin, 1978), 2:825–26.

26. On the issue of land grants, which is mired in ideology, see Richard Gardner, *Grito! Reies Tijerina and the New Mexico Land Grant War of 1967* (New York: Harper & Row, 1970).

27. On the colorful Corky Gonzales, see Stan Steiner, "Epilogue: The Poet in the Boxing Ring," in *La Raza: The Mexican Americans* (New York: Harper & Row, 1969).

28. Meier and Rivera, *Chicanos*, p. 275.

29. John D. Skrentny, *The Minority Rights Revolution* (Cambridge, Mass.: Harvard University Press, 2002), p. 197.

30. Ibid., p. 200.

31. Ibid., pp. 202–3.

32. Ibid., pp. 194–95.

33. James Wilson, *The Earth Shall Weep: A History of Native America* (New York: Atlantic Monthly Press, 1998), p. 20.

34. Alvin M. Josephy and and Joane Nagel, eds., *Red Power: The American Indians' Fight for Freedom* (Lincoln: University of Nebraska Press, 1999), p. 29.

35. Wilson, *Earth Shall Weep*, p. xxii.

36. For how Euro-Americans began shifting their perceptions of the colonization of the New World as a result of 1960s radicalism, readers should turn to Francis Jennings's book, *The Invasion of America: Indians, Colonialism, and the Cant of Conquest* (New York: Norton, 1976).

37. Roosevelt quoted in Richard Hofstadter, *The American Political Tradition and the Men Who Made It* (New York: Vintage, n.d.; originally published by Knopf, 1948), p. 212.

38. Wilson, *Earth Shall Weep*, p. 377.

39. Josephy and Nagel, *Red Power*, p. 13.

40. Ibid., p. 16.

41. Ibid., p. 17.

42. Wilson, *Earth Shall Weep*, p. 381.

43. For the fish-in movement, see Daniel Boxberger, *To Fish in Common* (Lincoln: University of Nebraska Press, 1989; and Fay G. Cohen, *Treaties on Trial: The Continuing Controversy over Northwest Indian Fishing Rights* (Seattle: University of Washington Press, 1986).

44. On the Alcatraz occupation, see Adam Fortunate Eagle, *Alcatraz! Alcatraz! The Indian Occupation, 1969–71* (San Francisco: Heyday, 1992); Troy Johnson, *The Occupation of Alcatraz Island: Indian Self-Determination and the Rise of Indian Activism* (Urbana: University of Illinois Press, 1996); and Paul Chaat Smith and Robert Allen Warrior, *Like a Hurricane: The Indian Movement from Alcatraz to Wounded Knee* (New York: Free Press, 1996).

45. On Wounded Knee, see Richard Jensen, Eli Paul, and John Carter, *Eyewitness at Wounded Knee* (Lincoln: University of Nebraska Press, 1992); Peter Mathiessen, *In the Spirit of Crazy Horse* (New York: Viking, 1983); and Smith and Warrior, *Like a Hurricane*.

46. Fergus M. Bordewich, *Killing the White Man's Indian: Reinventing Native Americans at the End of the Twentieth Century* (New York: Anchor Books, 1997), p. 15.

47. Ibid., p. 12.

48. Ibid., p. 16.

49. Skrentny, *Minority Rights Revolution*, pp. 328–30.

50. Andrew Hacker, *The End of the American Era* (New York: Grove Press, 1969), p. 226.

51. Ibid., p. 73.

52. Christopher Lasch, *The Revolt of the Elites and the Betrayal of Democracy* (New York: Norton, 1996).

53. Arthur Schlesinger, *The Disuniting of America* (New York: Norton, 1992), pp. 16–17.

54. Ibid., p. 110.

55. It took an Englishman who became a U.S. citizen to sound the alarm on these disturbing changes in immigration policy. See Peter Brimelow, *Alien Nation: Common Sense about America's Immigration Disaster* (New York: Random House, 1995).

56. Ibid., p. 97.

57. Ibid., p. 219.

58. John Lukacs, *A New Republic: A History of the United States in the Twentieth Century* (New Haven, Conn.: Yale University Press, 2004), p. 156.

Chapter 12: Peering into the Historical Looking Glass

1. John Lukacs has drawn attention to this ominous possibility in several of his works, notably *Democracy and Populism: Fear and Hatred* (New Haven: Yale University Press, 2005), p. 140.

2. *Los Angeles Times*, August 17, 1999.

3. Stephan Thernstrom and Abigail Thernstrom, *America in Black and White: One Nation, Indivisible* (New York: Simon & Schuster, 1997), pp. 530–31.

4. Ibid., p. 533.

5. Nathan Glazer, *We Are All Multiculturalists Now* (Cambridge, Mass.: Harvard University Press, 1997), p. 131.

6. Ibid., p. 129.

7. Gary Cross, *An All-Consuming Century: Why Commercialism Won in Modern America* (New York: Columbia University Press, 2000), pp. 1–2.

8. Kenneth Clark, *Civilisation* (New York: Harper & Row, 1969), p. 321.

9. Cross, *An All-Consuming Century*, p. 6.

10. For Nixon's account of the episode, see *RN: The Memoirs of Richard Nixon*, pp. 208–9.

11. Hillary Mayell, "As Consumerism Spreads, Earth Suffers," *National Geographic News*, January 12, 2004.

12. For one of the most acute criticisms of modern mass media, see William Ophuls, *Requiem for Modern Politics: The Tragedy of the Enlightenment and the Challenge of the New Millennium* (Boulder, Colo.: Westview Press, 1997), especially chapter 2 (Electronic Barbarism).

13. Thomas Reeves, *A Question of Character: A Life of John F. Kennedy* (Rocklin, Calif.: Prima, 1992), p. 2.

14. Jacques Barzun, *The Culture We Deserve* (Middletown, Conn.: Wesleyan University Press, 1989), pp. 165–66.

15. Godfrey Hodgson, *America in Our Time* (New York: Vintage, 1976), p. 146.

16. Twitchell, *Carnival Culture*, p. 28.

17. Neil Postman, *Amusing Ourselves to Death: Public Discourse in the Age of Show Business* (New York: Viking, 1985), p. 3.

18. William James, *Pragmatism* (New York: Meridian Books, 1967), p. 135.

19. Allan Bloom, *The Closing of the American Mind* (New York: Simon & Schuster, 1987), p. 42.

20. *New York Times Magazine*, October 22, 1967. Also London, *Closing the Circle*, p. 108.

21. Christopher Lasch, *The Culture of Narcissism: American Life in an Age of Diminishing Expectations* (New York:Warner Books, 1979), pp. 360–61.

22. Edmund Burke, *Appeal from the New to the Old Whigs*, in *Works*, vol. 5 (London, 1954–57), p. 94.

23. Lasch, *Culture of Narcissism*, p. 361.

24. Morris Dickstein, *Gates of Eden: American Culture in the Sixties* (Cambridge, Mass.: Harvard University Press, 1997), p. 5.

25. The meaning of Freud on the subject of culture was hotly debated in the 1960s, as right-wing and left-wing Freudians argued whether Freud had propounded either a deep therapeutic pessimism or a more hopeful message of instinctual fulfillment in a nonrepressive culture. Those who identified themselves with the counterculture preferred to listen to the Freudian left wing, notably Norman O. Brown, *Life against Death: The Psychoanalytical Meaning of History* (New York: Vintage, 1959) and Herbert Marcuse, *Eros and Civilization: A Philosophical Inquiry into Freud* (New York: Vintage, 1955). The debate highlighted a cultural issue that went far beyond Freud, and that was the disintegration of traditional moral beliefs associated largely with preindustrial and religiously-oriented societies. It is clear that since the sixties, the United States has been going through a "form-free" period that lies between a dying and a rising moral style. The old culture of denial, appropriate to an age of scarcity, gave way in the sixties to a culture of permissiveness and self-gratification. In such a culture, repression also gave way, as Philip Rieff pointed out in his book on the uses of faith after Freud (*Triumph of the Therapeutic* [New York: Harper & Row, 1966]), to therapeutic intervention; but this is hardly a cheerful prospect because it substitutes faith in therapeutic technique for faith in the transcendent. Putting it simplistically, it replaces Jesus with Freud or B. F. Skinner.

26. Martha Bayles, *Hole in Our Soul: The Loss of Beauty and Meaning in American Popular Music* (Chicago: University of Chicago Press, 1994), p. 11.

27. Ibid., p. 11.

28. Greil Marcus, *Mystery Train: Images of America in Rock 'n' Roll Music* (New York: Penguin, 1997), p. 11.

29. Ibid., p. 158.

30. Mario Praz, *The Romantic Agony* (New York: Meridian Books, 1967).

31. Bayles, *Hole in Our Soul*, pp. 69–72.

32. Quoted in Hodgson, *America in our Time*, p. 341.

33. Quoted in Michael Medved, *Hollywood vs. America* (New York: HarperCollins, 1993), pp. 99–100.

34. Ibid., p. 105.

35. Edward M. Brecher and the Editors of Consumer Reports, *Licit and Illicit Drugs* (Boston: Little, Brown, 1972), pp. 3–7.

36. Jay Stevens, *Storming Heaven: LSD and the American Dream* (New York: Grove Press, 1987), p. 306.

37. Charles A. Reich, *The Greening of America* (New York: Bantam Books, 1971), p. 280.

38. Ibid.

39. Quoted in Joseph Conlin, *The Troubles: A Jaundiced Glance Back at the Movement of the Sixties* (New York: Franklin Watts, 1982), p. 276.

40. Quoted in Leonard Wolf, *Voices from the Love Generation* (Boston: Little, Brown, 1968), p. 71.

41. Landon Y. Jones, *Great Expectations: America and the Baby Boom Generation* (New York: Ballantine Books, 1980), p. 246.

42. Ibid., p. 247.

43. E. F. Schumacher, *Small Is Beautiful: Economics as if People Mattered* (New York: Harper & Row, 1973).

44. Arthur Schlesinger, *The Disuniting of America* (New York: Norton, 1992), p. 16.

45. Christopher Lasch, *The Revolt of the Elites and the Betrayal of Democracy* (New York: Norton, 1995), p. 17.

46. Theodore Dalrymple, *Life at the Bottom* (Chicago: Ivan R. Dee, 2001), p. 26.

47. Ibid.

48. Ibid., chapter 2.

49. Lizabeth Cohen, *A Consumers' Republic: The Politics of Mass Consumption in Postwar America* (New York: Vintage, 2003), p. 409.

50. John Lukacs, *At the End of an Age* (New Haven, Conn.: Yale University Press, 2002), p. 77.

BIBLIOGRAPHY

Documents and Collections

Beschloss, Michael R. *Taking Charge: The Lyndon Johnson White House Tapes, 1963–1964*. New York: Simon & Schuster, 1997.

Breines, Wini, and Alexander Bloom, eds. *"Takin' It to the Streets": A Sixties Reader*. New York: Oxford University Press, 1997.

Gallup, George H. *The Gallup Poll: Public Opinion, 1935–1971*. New York: Random House, 1972.

Gibbons, William Conrad, ed. *The US Government and the Vietnam War: Executive and Legislative Roles and Relationships*. 4 vols. Princeton, N.J.: Princeton University Press, 1986–95.

Herring, George C. *The Secret Diplomacy of the Vietnam War: The Negotiating Volumes of the Pentagon Papers*. Austin: University of Texas Press, 1983.

Kennedy, John F. *Published Papers*. Washington D.C.: U.S. Government Printing Office, 1963.

Kerner Report: The 1968 Report of the Nation's Advisory Commission on Civil Disorders. New York: Pantheon, 1968; rev. ed., 1988.

Kutler, Stanley I. *Abuse of Power: The New Nixon Tapes*. New York: Free Press, 1997.

Massimo, Teodori, ed. *The New Left: A Documentary History*. New York: Bobbs-Merrill, 1969.

May, Ernest R., and Philip D. Zelikow, eds. *The Kennedy Tapes: Inside the White House during the Cuban Missile Crisis*. Cambridge, Mass.: Harvard University Press, 1997.

Morgan, Robin, ed. *Sisterhood Is Powerful: The Women's Anthology for a New Millennium*. New York: Washington Square Press, 2003.

Naftali, Timothy, et al., eds. *The Presidential Recordings: John F. Kennedy*. 3 vols. New York: Norton, 2001.

Orrick, William H., Jr. *Shut It Down! A College in Crisis: San Francisco State College, October 1968– April 1969*. Report to the National Commission on the Causes and Prevention of Violence. Washington D.C.: U.S. Government Printing Office, 1969.

Peers, William R. *Report of the Department of the Army Review of the Preliminary Investigation into the My Lai Incident*. Washington D.C., 1970.

Pentagon Papers: The Senate Gravel Edition. 4 vols. Boston: Beacon Press, 1971.

Public Papers of the Presidents of the United State: John F. Kennedy, 1961–1963. Washington D.C.: U.S. Government Printing Office, 1962–64.

Public Papers of the Presidents of the United States: Lyndon B. Johnson. 10 vols. Washington D.C.: U.S. Government Printing Office, 1965–70.

Report of the Warren Commission on the Assassination of John F. Kennedy. New York: New York Times Company, 1964.

Sheehan, Neil, et al., eds. *The Pentagon Papers as Published by the New York Times*. Chicago: Quadrangle, 1971.

Skolnick Report to the National Commission on the Causes and Prevention of Violence: Black Militants, Student Riots, Anti-War Demonstrations. New York: Ballantine Books, 1969.

Unger, Irwin, and Debi Unger, eds. *The Times Were a Changin': The Sixties Reader*. New York: Three Rivers Press, 1998.

US House Committee on Armed Services, United States-Vietnam Relations, 1945–1967. Washington D.C.: U.S. Government Printing Office, 1971.

United States Senate, Committee on Foreign Relations: Legislative Proposals Relating to the War in Southeast Asia Hearing. Washington D.C.: U.S. Government Printing Office, March 14, 1970.

United States. Department of State. *Foreign Relations of the United States, 1961–1963*. Washington D.C.: U.S. Government Printing Office, 1992.

———. *Foreign Relations of the United States, 1964–1968*. Washington D.C.: U.S. Government Printing Office, 1992.

———. President's Commission on Campus Unrest. *Report of the President's Commission on Campus Unrest*. Washington D.C.: U.S. Government Printing Office, 1970.

Williams, Appleman, et al., eds. *America in Vietnam: A Documentary History*. New York: Norton, 1985.

Autobiographies and Diaries

Abernathy, Ralph David. *And the Walls Came Tumbling Down: An Autobiography*. New York: Harper, 1990.

Baez, Joan. *And a Voice to Sing With: A Memoir*. New York: Summit, 1987.

Ball, George W. *The Past Has Another Pattern: Memoirs*. New York: Norton, 1982.

Brown, Elaine. *A Taste of Power: A Black Woman's Story*. New York: Pantheon, 1962.

Brown, H. Rap. *Die, Nigger, Die!* New York: Dial Press, 1969.

Caputo, Philip. *A Rumor of War*. New York: Holt, Rinehart and Winston, 1977.

Cleaver, Eldridge. *Soul on Ice*. New York: McGraw Hill, 1968.

Cronkite, Walter. *A Reporter's Life*. New York: Knopf, 1996.

Davis, Angela. *An Autobiography*. New York: Random House, 1974.

Dean, John. *Blind Ambition*. New York: Simon & Schuster, 1976.

Dellinger, David. *From Yale to Jail*. New York: Random House, 1963.

Farmer, James. *Lay Bare the Heart: An Autobiography of the Civil Rights Movement*. New York: American Library, 1985.

Galbraith, John Kenneth. *A Life in Our Times*. Boston: Houghton Mifflin, 1981.

Goldwater, Barry. *The Conscience of a Conservative*. New York: McFadden-Bartell, 1961.

Haldeman, H. R. *The End of Power*. New York: Time Books, 1978.

Harris, David. *Dreams Die Hard*. New York: St. Martin's Press, 1982.

Hayden, Tom. *Rebel: A Personal History of the 1960s*. Los Angeles: Red Hen Press, 2003.

———. *Reunion: A Memoir*. New York: Random House, 1988.

Hoffman, Abbie. *Revolution for the Hell of It*. New York: Dial Press, 1968.

Horowitz, David. *Radical Son: A Generational Odyssey*. New York: Free Press, 1997.

Humphrey, Hubert. *The Education of a Public Man: My Life and Politics*. Garden City, N.Y.: Doubleday, 1976.

Johnson, Lyndon B. *The Vantage Point: Perspectives of the Presidency, 1963–1969*. New York: Holt, Rinehart and Winston, 1971.

King, Martin Luther, Jr. *Strength by Love*. New York: Harper & Row, 1963.

King, Mary. *Freedom Song: A Personal Story of the 1960s Civil Rights Movement*. New York: Morrow, 1989.

Kissinger, Henry. *Years of Upheaval*. Boston: Little, Brown, 1982.

———. *White House Years*. Boston: Little, Brown, 1979.

Kovic, Ron. *Born on the Fourth of July*. New York: McGraw-Hill, 1976.

Kunen, James Simon. *The Strawberry Statement: Notes of a College Revolutionary*. New York: Random House, 1969.

Kunstler, William. *Deep in my Heart*. New York: Morrow, 1963.

Leary, Timothy. *Flashbacks: An Autobiography*. Los Angeles: J. P. Torcher, 1983.

———. *The Politics of Ecstasy*. New York: Putnam, 1968.

Lester, Julius. *Look Out Whitey! Black Power's Gon' Get Your Mama*. New York: Grove Press, 1968.

Lewis, John, and Michael D'Orso. *Walking with the Wind: A Memoir of the Movement*. New York: Simon & Schuster, 1998.

McCarthy, Eugene. *The Year of the People*. New York: Doubleday, 1969.

Nixon, Richard M. *RN: The Memoirs of Richard Nixon*. New York: Grosset & Dunlap, 1974.

Rusk, Dean. *As I Saw It: The Memoirs of Dean Rusk*. New York: Norton, 1990.

Seale, Bobby. *A Lonely Rage: The Autobiography of Bobby Seale*. New York: Times, 1978.

———. *Seize the Time: The Story of the Black Panther Party and Huey P. Newton*. New York: Random House, 1970.

Twiggy. *Twiggy: An Autobiography*. London: Hart-Davis, MacGibbon, 1975.

Vidal, Gore. *Palimpset: A Memoir*. New York: Random House, 1995.

Watts, Allan. *In My Own Way: An Autobiography*. New York: Pantheon, 1972.

X, Malcolm. *Autobiography of Malcolm X*. New York: Grove Press, 1965.

Zappa, Frank. *The Real Frank Zappa Book*. New York: Poseidon Press, 1989.

Significant Works of the 1960s

Baldwin, James. *Another Country*. New York: Dial, 1962.

Bell, David. *The End of Ideology. On the Exhaustion of Political Ideas in the Fifties*. New York: Collier Books, 1961.

Brand, Stewart, ed. *The Whole Earth Catalog*. New York: Random House, 1971.

Brown, Helen Gurley. *Sex and the Single Girl*. New York: Pocket, 1962.

Capote, Truman. *In Cold Blood*. New York: Random House, 1965.

Carson, Rachel, *Silent Spring*. Boston: Houghton Mifflin, 1962.

Castaneda, Carlos. *The Teachings of Don Juan: A Yaqui Way of Knowledge*. Berkeley: University of California Press, 1968.

Didion, Joan. *Slouching Towards Bethlehem*. New York: Farrar, Straus & Giroux, 1968.

Deloria, Vine, Jr. *Custer Died for Your Sins: An Indian Manifesto*. New York: Macmillan, 1968.

Ellison, Ralph. *Invisible Man*. New York: Random House, 1947.

Fanon, Frantz. *The Wretched of the Earth*. Translated by Constance Farrington. New York: Ballantine, 1963.

Firestone, Shulamith. *The Dialectics of Sex: The Case for Feminist Revolution*. New York: Morrow, 1970.

Friedan, Betty. *The Feminine Mystique*. New York: Norton, 1963.

Galbraith, John Kenneth. *The Affluent Society*. Boston: Houghton Mifflin, 1958.

———. *The New Industrial State*. New York: American Library, 1967.

Ginsberg, Allen. *The Fall of America*. San Francisco: City Lights Books, 1972.

———. *Howl and Other Poems*. San Francisco: City Lights Books, 1956.

———. *Planet News*. San Francisco: City Lights Books, 1968.

———. *Reality Sandwiches*. San Francisco: City Lights Books, 1963.

Goodman, Paul. *Growing Up Absurd*. New York: Random House, 1960.

Griffin, John Howard. *Black Like Me*. New York: American Library, 1960.

Harrington, Michael. *The Other America: Poverty in the United States*. Baltimore: Penguin Books, 1962.

Hesse, Hermann. *Steppenwolf*. Translated by Basil Creighton. New York: Modern Library, 1963.

Kerouac, Jack. *On the Road*. New York: Viking, 1957.

Kesey, Ken. *One Flew over the Cuckoo's Nest*. New York: New American Library, 1962.
———. *Sometimes a Great Notion*. New York: Penguin, 1964.
King, Martin Luther, Jr. *Stride toward Freedom: The Montgomery Story*. New York: Harper & Row, 1968.
———. *Where Do We Go from Here: Chaos or Community?* New York: Harper & Row, 1967.
———. *Why We Can't Wait*. New York: Harper & Row, 1964.
Le Carré, John. *The Spy Who Came in from the Cold*. New York: Coward-McCann, 1964.
Mailer, Norman. *The Armies of the Night: History as a Novel/The Novel as History*. New York: American Library, 1968.
———. *Miami and the Siege of Chicago*. New York: American Library, 1968.
———. *Of a Fire on the Moon*. Boston: Little, Brown, 1970.
McLuhan, Marshall. *Understanding Media*. New York: McGraw-Hill, 1964.
Millett, Kate. *Sexual Politics*. New York: Doubleday, 1970.
Mills, C. Wright. *The Power Elite*. New York: Oxford University Press, 1956.
Nader, Ralph. *Unsafe at Any Speed: The Designed-In Dangers of the American Automobile*. New York: Grossman, 1965.
Philips, Kevin. *The Emerging Republican Majority*. New Rochelle, N.Y.: Arlington House, 1969.
Thompson, Hunter S. *Fear and Loathing in Las Vegas: A Savage Journey to the Heart of the American Dream*. New York: Random House, 1972.
Watts, Allan. *Beat Zen, Square Zen, and Zen*. San Francisco: City Light Books, 1959.
———. *Psychotherapy: East and West*. New York: Pantheon, 1961.
———. *The Way of Zen*. New York: Pantheon, 1957.
Wolfe, Tom. *The Electric Kool-Aid Acid Test*. New York: Bantam, 1968.
———. *Radical Chic and Mau-Mauing the Flak Catchers*. New York: Farrar, Straus & Giroux, 1970.

Bibliographic Aids

Anderson, David L., ed. *The Columbia Guide to the Vietnam War*. New York: Columbia University Press, 2002.
Buchanan, Scott, ed. *Rock 'n' Roll: The Famous Lyrics*. New York: HarperCollins, 1994.
Brune, Lester, and Richard Dean Burns, eds. *America and the Indochina Wars, 1945–1990: A Bibliographic Guide*. Claremont, Calif.: Regina Press, 1992.
Farber, David, and Beth Baily, eds. *The Columbia Guide to America in the 1960s*. New York: Columbia University Press, 2001.
Hamilton, Neil A., ed. *The ABC-CLIO Companion to the 1960s Counterculture in America*. Santa Barbara: ABC-Clio Press, 1997.
Hess, Gary R. "The Unending Debate: Historians and the Vietnam War," *Diplomatic History* 18 (Spring 1994), pp. 239–64.
Jackson, Rebecca. *The 1960s: An Annotated Bibliography of Social and Political Movements in the United States*. Westport, Conn.: Greenwood Press, 1992.
Keniston, Kenneth. *Radicals and Militants: An Annotated Bibliography of Empirical Research on Campus Unrest*. Lexington, Mass.: Heath, 1973.
Kutler, Stanley I., ed. *Encyclopedia of the Vietnam War*. New York: Scribner's, 1996.
Meier, Matt S. *Notable Latino Americans: A Biographical Dictionary*. Westport, Conn.: Greenwood Press, 1997.
Olson, James S. *Historical Dictionary of the 1960s*. Westport, Conn.: Greenwood Press, 1999.
———. *The Vietnam War Handbook of Literature and Research*. Westport, Conn.: Greenwood Press, 1993.
Rolling Stone Encyclopedia of Rock and Roll. New York: Rolling Stone Press, 2001.
Rolling Stone Illustrated History of Rock & Roll. New York: Pantheon, 1992.

General Works and Interpretations of the 1960s

Anderson, Terry. *The Movement and the Sixties: Protest in America from Greensboro to Wounded Knee.* New York: Oxford University Press, 1995.

———. *The Sixties.* New York: Longman, 1999.

Barzun, Jacques. *The Culture We Deserve.* Middletown, Conn.: Wesleyan University Press, 1989.

Bloom, Allan. *The Closing of the American Mind.* New York: Simon & Schuster, 1987.

Blum, John Morton. *Years of Discord: American Politics and Society, 1961–1974.* New York: Norton, 1991.

Burner, David. *Making Peace with the 60s.* Princeton, N.J.: Princeton University Press, 1996.

Cavello, Dominick. *A Fiction of the Past: The Sixties in American History.* New York: St. Martin's Press, 1999.

Cohen, Lizabeth. *A Consumers' Republic: The Politics of Mass Consumption in Postwar America.* New York: Vintage, 2004.

Collins, Robert M. *More: The Politics of Economic Growth in Postwar America.* New York: Oxford University Press, 2000.

Cross, Gary. *An All-Consuming Century: Why Commercialism Won in Modern America.* New York: Columbia University Press, 2000.

Conlin, Joseph. *The Troubles: A Jaundiced Glance Back at the Movement of the Sixties.* New York: Franklin Watts, 1982.

Dickstein, Morris. *Gates of Eden: American Culture in the Sixties.* Cambridge, Mass.: Harvard University Press, 1977; repr., 1997.

Engelhardt, Tom. *The End of Victory Culture: Cold War America and the Disillusioning of a Generation.* New York: Basic Books, 1995.

Farber, David. *Age of Great Dreams.* New York: Hill and Wang, 1994.

———, ed. *The Sixties: From History to Memory.* Chapel Hill: University of North Carolina, 1994.

Gitlin, Todd. *The Sixties: Years of Hope, Days of Rage.* New York: Bantam, 1987.

Halberstam, David. *The Fifties.* New York: Ballantine, 1993.

Hodgson, Godfrey. *America in Our Time.* New York: Vintage, 1976.

Howard, Gerald, ed. *The Sixties.* New York: Washington Square Press, 1982.

Isserman, Maurice, and Michael Kazin. *America Divided: The Civil War of the 1960s.* New York: Oxford University Press, 2000.

Kimball, Roger. *The Long March: How the Cultural Revolution of the 1960s Changed America.* San Francisco: Encounter Books, 2000.

Lasch, Christopher. *The Culture of Narcissism: American Life in an Age of Diminished Expectations.* New York: Warner Books, 1979.

———. *The Revolt of the Elites and the Betrayal of Democracy.* New York: Norton, 1996.

London, Herbert I. *The Overheated Decade.* New York: New York University Press, 1976.

Lukacs, John. *A New Republic: A History of the United States in the Twentieth Century.* New Haven, Conn.: Yale University Press, 2004; orig. published in 1984.

Lyons, Paul. *New Left, New Right, and the Legacy of the Sixties.* Philadelphia: Temple University Press, 1996.

Macedo, Stephen, ed. *Reassessing the Sixties: Debating the Political and Cultural Legacy.* New York: Norton, 1997.

Magnet, Myron. *The Dream and the Nightmare: The Sixties' Legacy to the Underclass.* New York: Morrow, 1993.

Margolis, J. *The Last Innocent Year: America in 1964, The Beginning of the Sixties.* New York: Morrow, 1999.

Marwick, Arthur. *The Sixties: Cultural Revolution in Britain, France, Italy, and the United States.* New York: Oxford University Press, 1998.

Matusow, Allen J. *The Unraveling of America: A History of Liberalism in the 1960s*. New York: Harper & Row, 1984.

McQuaid, Kim. *The Anxious Years: America and the Vietnam-Watergate Era*. New York: Basic Books, 1989.

Morgan, Edward P. *The Sixties Experience: Hard Lessons about Modern America*. Philadelphia: Temple University Press, 1991.

Morris, Charles. *A Time of Passion: America, 1960–1980*. New York: Harper & Row, 1984.

O'Neill, William L. *Coming Apart: An Informal History of America in the 1960s*. New York: Quadrangle, 1976.

Patterson, James T. *Grand Expectations: The United States, 1945–1974*. New York: Oxford University Press, 1996.

Steigerwald, David. *The Sixties and the End of Modern America*. New York: St. Martin's Press, 1995.

Unger, Irwin, and Debi Unger, eds. *The Times Were A Changin'*. New York: Three Rivers Press, 1998.

The Kennedy Administration

Bernstein, Irving. *Promises Kept: John F. Kennedy's New Frontier*. New York: Oxford University Press, 1991.

Beschloss, Michael R. *The Crisis Years: Kennedy and Khrushchev, 1960–1963*. New York: HarperCollins, 1991.

Bishop, Jim. *A Day in the Life of President Kennedy*. New York: Random House, 1964.

———. *The Day Kennedy Was Shot*. New York: Funk and Wagnalls, 1968.

Blair, Joan, and Clay Blair. *The Search for J.F.K.* New York: Berkeley Books, 1976.

Brown, Thomas. *JFK: History of an Image*. Bloomington: Indiana University Press, 1988.

Burner, David. *John F. Kennedy and a New Generation*. Boston: Little, Brown, 1988.

Burner, David, and Thomas R. West. *The Torch Is Passed: The Kennedy Brothers and American Liberalism*. New York: Atheneum, 1984.

Collier, Peter, and David Horowitz. *The Kennedys: An American Drama*. New York: Summit Books, 1984.

Dallek, Robert. *An Unfinished Life: John F. Kennedy, 1917–1963*. Boston: Little, Brown, 2003.

Davis, John H. *The Kennedys: Dynasty and Disaster, 1848–1983*. New York: McGraw-Hill, 1984.

Epstein, Edward J. *Inquest*. New York: Viking, 1966.

Fairly, Henry. *The Kennedy Promise: The Politics of Expectation*. Garden City, N.Y.: Doubleday, 1973.

Fay, Paul. *The Pleasure of His Company*. New York: Harper & Row, 1966.

Fischer, Fritz. *Making Them Like Us: Peace Corps Volunteers in the 1960s*. Washington D.C.: Smithsonian Institution Press, 1998.

Frankel, Max. *High Noon in the Cold War: Kennedy, Khrushchev and the Cuban Missile Crisis*. New York: Ballantine, 2004.

Fursenko, A.V. *"One Hell of a Gamble": Khrushchev, Castro, and Kennedy, 1958–64*. New York: Norton, 1997.

Giglio, James N. *The Presidency of John F. Kennedy*. Lawrence: University of Kansas Press, 1991.

Goodwin, Doris Kearns. *The Fitzgeralds and the Kennedys*. New York: Simon & Schuster, 1987.

Halberstam, David. *The Best and the Brightest*. New York: Random House, 1972.

Hamilton, Nigel. *J.F.K.: Reckless Youth*. New York: Random House, 1992.

Hellmann, John. *The Kennedy Obsession: The American Myth of JFK*. New York: Columbia University Press, 1993.

Henggeler, Paul. *The Kennedy Persuasion: The Politics of Style since JFK*. Chicago: Ivan R. Dee, 1995.

Hersh, Seymour. *The Dark Side of Camelot*. Boston: Little, Brown, 1997.

Kennedy, John F. *Profiles in Courage*. New York: Harper & Row, 1956.

Kennedy, Robert F. *Thirteen Days: A Memoir of the Cuban Missile Crisis.* New York: Norton, 1969.

Lasky, Victor. *JFK: The Man and the Myth.* New York: Macmillan, 1964.

Lincoln, Evelyn. *My Twelve Years with John F. Kennedy.* New York: David McKay, 1965.

Lubin, David M. *Shooting Kennedy: JFK and the Culture of Images.* Berkeley: University of California Press, 2003.

Mahoney, Richard D. *Sons and Brothers: The Days of Jack and Bobby Kennedy.* New York: Arcade Publishing, 1999.

Maier, Thomas. *The Kennedys: America's Emerald Kings.* New York: Basic Books, 2003.

Manchester, William.*The Death of a President.* New York: Harper & Row, 1967.

———. *Portrait of a President.* New York: Macfadden, 1964.

Matthews, Christopher. *Kennedy & Nixon: A Rivalry that Shaped Postwar America.* New York: Simon & Schuster, 1996.

Nathan, James, ed. *The Cuban Missile Crisis Revisited.* New York: St. Martin's Press, 1992.

Navasky, Victor. *Kennedy Justice.* New York: Atheneum, 1971.

O'Donnell, Kenneth P., and David Powers. *Johnny, We Hardly Knew Ye.* New York: Pocket Books, 1973.

Parmet, Herbert. *Jack: The Struggles of John F. Kennedy.* New York: Dial, 1980.

———. *JFK: The Presidency of John F. Kennedy.* New York: Penguin Books, 1984.

Posner, Gerald. *Case Closed: Lee Harvey Oswald and the Assassination of JFK.* New York: Random House, 1993.

Quirk, Lawrence J. *The Kennedys in Hollywood.* New York: Cooper Square Press, 2004.

Reeves, Richard. *President Kennedy: Profile of Power.* New York: Simon & Schuster, 1993.

Reeves, Thomas. *A Question of Character: A Life of John F. Kennedy.* Rocklin, Calif.: Prima, 1992.

Rorabaugh, W. J. *Kennedy and the Promise of the Sixties.* New York: Cambridge University Press, 2002.

Salinger, Pierre. *With Kennedy.* New York: Doubleday, 1966.

Schlesinger, Arthur, Jr. *Robert Kennedy and His Times.* Boston: Houghton Mifflin, 1978.

———. *A Thousand Days.* New York: Doubleday, 1966.

Sidey, Hugh. *John F. Kennedy, President.* New York: Atheneum, 1964.

Sorensen, Theodore C. *Kennedy.* New York: Bantam Books, 1966.

———. *The Kennedy Legacy.* New York: Macmillan, 1969.

White, Theodore. *The Making of the President, 1960.* New York: Atheneum, 1961.

Wills, Garry. *The Kennedy Imprisonment: A Meditation on Power.* Boston: Little, Brown, 1981.

Wofford, Harris. *Of Kennedys and Kings.* Pittsburgh: University of Pittsburgh Press, 1992.

The Struggle for Black Civil Rights

Bloom, Jack. M. *Class, Race and the Civil Rights Movement.* Bloomington: Indiana University Press, 1987.

Branch, Taylor. *Parting the Waters: America in the King Years, 1954–1963.* New York: Simon & Schuster, 1988.

———. *Pillar of Fire: America in the King Years, 1963–65.* New York: Simon & Schuster, 1998.

Breitman, George, ed. *Malcolm X Speaks: Selected Speeches and Statements.* New York: Grove Press, 1990.

Brooks, Thomas R. *Walls Came Tumbling Down: A History of the Civil Rights Movement, 1940–1970.* Englewood Cliffs, N.J.: Prentice Hall, 1974.

Burner, Eric. *And Gently He Shall Lead Them: Robert Parris Moses and Civil Rights in Mississippi.* New York: New York University Press, 1994.

Cagin, Seth, and Philip Dray. *We Are Not Afraid: The Story of Goodman, Schwerner, and Chaney and the Civil Rights Campaign for Mississippi.* New York: Macmillan, 1988.

Carson, Clayborn. *In Struggle: SNCC and the Black Awakening of the 1960s.* Cambridge, Mass.: Harvard University Press, 1981.

Chafe, William H. *Civilities and Civil Rights: Greensboro, North Carolina and the Black Struggle for Freedom.* New York: Oxford University Press, 1980.

Conot, Robert. *Rivers of Blood, Years of Darkness.* New York: Morrow, 1967.

Dittmer, John. *Local People: The Struggle for Civil Rights in Mississippi.* Urbana: University of Illinois Press, 1994.

Fager, Charles E. *Selma, 1965: The March the Changed the South.* Boston: Beacon Press, 1985.

Fairclough, Adam. *Race and Democracy: The Civil Rights Struggle in Louisiana.* Athens: University of Georgia. 1995.

―――. *To Redeem the Soul of America: The Southern Christian Leadership Conference and Martin Luther King Jr.* Athens: University of Georgia Press, 1987.

Garrow, David. *Bearing the Cross: Martin Luther King Jr. and the Southern Christian Leadership Conference.* New York: Morrow, 1986.

―――. *The FBI and Martin Luther King Jr.: From "Solo" to Memphis.* New York: Norton, 1981.

―――. *Protest at Selma: Martin Luther King Jr. and the Voting Rights Act of 1965.* New Haven, Conn.: Yale University Press, 1978.

―――. *Ready for Revolution: The Life and Struggle of Stokely Carmichael.* New York: Scribner's, 2004.

Gerstle, Gary. *American Crucible: Race and Nation in the Twentieth Century.* Princeton, N.J.: Princeton University Press, 2001.

Graham, Hugh Davis. *The Civil Rights Era: Origins and Development of National Policy, 1960–1972.* New York: Oxford University Press, 1990.

Haines, Herbert. *Black Radicals and the Civil Rights Mainstream, 1954–1970.* Knoxville: University of Tennessee Press, 1988.

Jacobs, Ronald N. *Race, Media, and the Crisis of Civil Society: From the Watts Riots to Rodney King.* New York: Cambridge University Press, 2000.

Kluger, Richard. *Simple Justice.* New York: Vintage Books, 1977.

Kotz, Nick. *Judgment Days: Lyndon Baines Johnson, Martin Luther King Jr., and the Laws That Changed America.* Boston: Houghton Mifflin, 2005.

Lawson, Steven. *Black Ballots: Voting Rights in the South, 1944–1969.* New York: Columbia University Press, 1976.

Lewis, David L. *King: A Biography.* Urbana: University of Illinois Press, 1978.

McAdam, Douglas. *Freedom Summer.* New York: Oxford University Press, 1988.

Meier, August, and Elliott Rudwick. *CORE: A Study in the Civil Rights Movement.* New York: Free Press, 1984.

Mills, Kay. *This Little Light of Mine: The Life of Fannie Lou Hamer.* New York: Plume, 1993.

Morris, Aldon D. *The Origins of the Civil Rights Movement.* New York: Free Press, 1984.

Oates, Stephen B. *Let the Trumpets Sound: The Life of Martin Luther King Jr.* New York: Harper & Row, 1982.

O'Reilly, Kenneth. *"Racial Matters": The FBI's Secret File on Black America, 1960–1972.* New York: Free Press, 1989.

Pearson, Hugh. *Shadow of the Panther: Huey Newton and the Price of Black Power in America.* Reading, Mass.: Addison-Wesley, 1994.

Robnett, Belinda. *How Long? How Long? African-American Women in the Struggle for Civil Rights.* New York: Oxford University Press, 1997.

Raines, Howell, ed. *My Soul Is Rested: Movement Days in the Deep South Remembered.* New York: Penguin, 1983.

Sitkoff, Harvard. *The Struggle for Black Equality, 1954–1992.* New York: Hill and Wang, 1993.

Thernstrom, Stephan, and Abigail Thernstrom. *America in Black and White: One Nation, Indivisible.* New York: Simon & Schuster, 1997.

Van Deburg, William. *New Day in Babylon: The Black Power Movement and American Culture, 1965–1975*. Chicago: University of Chicago Press, 1992.

Weisbrot, Robert. *Freedom Bound: A History of America's Civil Rights Movement*. New York: Norton, 1990.

Wolff, Miles. *Lunch at the Five and Ten: The Greensboro Sit-Ins, A Contemporary History*. New York: Stein and Day, 1970.

Woodward, C. Vann. *The Strange Career of Jim Crow*. New York: Oxford University, 1978.

The Johnson Years

Andrew, John A. *Lyndon Johnson and the Great Society*. Chicago: Ivan R. Dee, 1998.

Berkowitz, Edward. *America's Welfare State: From Roosevelt to Reagan*. Baltimore: Johns Hopkins University Press, 1991.

Bernstein, Irving. *Guns or Butter: The Presidency of Lyndon Johnson*. New York: Oxford University Press, 1996.

Beschloss, Michael R. *Taking Charge: The Johnson White House Tapes, 1963–64*. New York: Simon & Schuster, 1997.

Bornet, Vaughn Davis. *The Presidency of Lyndon Johnson*. Lawrence: University of Kansas Press, 1983.

Califano, Joseph. *The Triumph and Tragedy of Lyndon Johnson: The White House Years*. New York: Simon & Schuster, 1991.

Caro, Robert A. *The Years of Lyndon Johnson: Means of Ascent*. New York: Knopf, 1990.

———. *The Years of Lyndon Johnson: The Path to Power*. New York: Knopf, 1982.

Conkin, Paul. *Big Daddy from the Pedernales*. Boston: Twayne, 1986.

Dallek, Robert. *Flawed Giant: Lyndon Johnson and His Times, 1960–1973*. New York: Oxford University Press, 1998.

———. *Lone Star Rising: Lyndon Johnson and His Times, 1908–1960*. New York: Oxford University Press, 1991.

Davies, Gareth. *From Opportunity to Entitlement: The Transformation and Decline of Great Society Liberalism*. Lawrence: University of Kansas Press, 1996.

Divine, Robert A., ed. *The Johnson Years*. 3 vols. Lawrence: University of Kansas Press, 1981–94.

Gillette, Michael. *Launching the War on Poverty: An Oral History*. Boston: Twayne, 1996.

Goldman, Eric F. *The Tragedy of Lyndon Johnson*. New York: Knopf, 1969.

Graff, Henry F. *The Tuesday Cabinet: Deliberation and Decision on Peace and War under Lyndon B. Johnson*. Englewood Cliffs, N.J.: Prentice Hall, 1970.

Henggeler, Paul R. *In His Steps: Lyndon Johnson and the Kennedy Mystique*. Chicago: Ivan R. Dee, 1991.

Kaplan, Marshall, and Peggy Cucity, eds. *The Great Society and Its Legacy: Twenty Years of US Social Policy*. Durham, N.C.: Duke University Press, 1986.

Katz, Michael, ed. *The "Underclass" Debate: Views from History*. Princeton, N.J.: Princeton University Press, 1993.

———. *The Undeserving Poor*. New York: Pantheon, 1989.

Kearns, Doris. *Lyndon Johnson and the American Dream*. New York: Harper & Row, 1976.

Miller, Merle. *Lyndon: An Oral Biography*. New York, 1980.

Moynihan Daniel Patrick. *Maximum Feasible Misunderstanding: Community Action in the War on Poverty*. New York: Free Press, 1969.

Murray, Charles. *Losing Ground: American Social Policy, 1950–1980*. New York: Basic Books, 1984.

O'Connor, Alice. *Poverty Knowledge: Social Science, Social Policy, and the Poor in the Twentieth Century*. Princeton, N.J.: Princeton University Press, 2001.

Patterson, James. *America's Struggle against Poverty, 1900–1994.* Cambridge, Mass.: Harvard University Press, 1995.

Reedy, George. *Lyndon B. Johnson: A Memoir.* New York: Andrews and Michael, 1982.

Schandler, Herbert Y. *The Unmaking of a President: Lyndon Johnson and Vietnam.* Princeton, N.J.: Princeton University Press, 1977.

Schulman, Bruce. *Lyndon Johnson and American Liberalism.* New York: St. Martin's Press, 1995.

Shesol, Jeff. *Mutual Contempt: Lyndon Johnson, Robert Kennedy, and the Feud That Defined a Decade.* New York: Norton, 1997.

Turner, Kathleen. *Lyndon Johnson's Dual War.* Chicago: University of Chicago Press, 1985.

Unger Irwin, and Debi Unger. *The Best of Intentions: The Triumph and Failure of the Great Society under Kennedy, Johnson, and Nixon.* New York: Doubleday, 1996.

———. *LBJ: A Life.* New York, 1999.

Valenti, Jack. *A Very Human President.* New York: Norton, 1975.

Other Political Leaders of the 1960s

Aitken, Jonathan. *Nixon: A Life.* Washington D.C.: Regnery, 1993.

Ambrose, Stephen. *Nixon: The Education of a Politician, 1913–1962.* New York: Simon & Schuster, 1987.

———. *Nixon: The Triumph of a Politician, 1962–1972.* New York: Simon & Schuster, 1989.

———. *Nixon: Ruin and Recovery, 1973–1990.* New York: Simon & Schuster, 1992.

Beran, Michael Knox. *The Last Patrician: Bobby Kennedy and the End of American Aristocracy.* New York: St. Martin's Press, 1998.

Berman, Edgar. *Hubert: The Triumph and Tragedy of the Humphrey I Knew.* New York: Putnam, 1979.

Bernstein, Carl, and Bob Woodward. *All the President's Men.* New York: Simon & Schuster, 1974.

———. *The Final Days.* New York: Simon & Schuster, 1976.

Brody, Fawn M. *Richard Nixon: The Shaping of His Character.* Cambridge, Mass.: Harvard University Press, 1983.

Cannon, Lou. *Governor Reagan: His Rise to Power.* New York: Public Affairs, 2003.

———. *Reagan.* New York: Putnam, 1982.

Carter, Dan. *The Politics of Rage: George Wallace, the Origin of the New Conservatism, and the Transformation of American Politics.* New York: Simon & Schuster, 1995.

Cohen, Adam, and Elizabeth Taylor. *American Pharaoh: Mayor Richard J. Daley; His Battle for Chicago and the Nation.* Boston: Little, Brown, 2002.

Dean John. *Blind Ambition.* New York: Simon & Schuster, 1976.

Ehrlichman, John. *Witness to Power: The Nixon Years.* New York: Simon & Schuster, 1982.

Frady, Marshall. *Wallace.* New York: World, 1968.

Genovese, Michael A. *The Nixon Presidency: Power and Politics in Turbulent Times.* New York: Greenwood, 1990.

Goldberg, Robert Alan. *Barry Goldwater.* New Haven, Conn.: Yale University Press, 1995.

Guthman, Edwin O. *We Band of Brothers.* New York: Harper & Row, 1971.

Guthman, Edwin O., and Jeffrey Shulman, eds. *Robert Kennedy: In His Own Words.* New York: Bantam, 1988.

Halberstam, David. *The Unfinished Odyssey of Robert Kennedy.* New York: Random House, 1968.

Haldeman, H. R. *The Ends of Power.* New York: Times Books, 1978.

Heymann, C. David. *RFK: A Candid Biography of Robert F. Kennedy.* New York: Dutton, 1998.

Hilty, James W. *Robert Kennedy: Brother Protector.* Philadelphia: Temple University Press, 1997.

Hoff, Joan. *Nixon Reconsidered.* New York: Basic Books, 1994.

Isaacson, Walter. *Kissinger: A Biography*. New York: Simon & Schuster, 1992.

Iverson, Peter. *Barry Goldwater: Native Arizonan*. Norman: University of Oklahoma Press, 1997.

Lesher, Stephan. *George Wallace: American Populist*. Reading, Mass.: Addison-Wesley, 1994.

Mazlish, Bruce. *In Search of Nixon: A Psychohistorical Inquiry*. Baltimore: Penguin Books, 1973.

Morris, Edmund. *Dutch: A Memoir of Ronald Reagan*. New York: Random House, 1999.

Newfield, Jack. *Robert Kennedy: A Memoir*. New York: Dutton, 1969.

Parmet, Herbert. *Richard Nixon and His America*. Boston: Little, Brown, 1990.

Royko, Mike. *Boss: Richard J. Daley of Chicago*. New York: Penguin, 1988.

Safire, William. *Before the Fall*. Garden City, N.Y.: Doubleday, 1975.

Sandbrook, Dominic. *Eugene McCarthy: The Rise and Fall of Postwar American Liberalism*. New York: Knopf, 2004.

Schlesinger, Arthur M. *Robert Kennedy and His Times*. 2 vols. Boston: Houghton Mifflin, 1978.

Schudson, Michael. *Watergate in American Memory: How We Remember, Forget, and Reconstruct the Past*. New York: Basic Books, 1992.

Shesol, Jeff. *Mutual Contempt: Lyndon Johnson, Robert Kennedy, and the Feud that Defined a Decade*. New York: Norton, 1997.

Solberg, Carl. *Hubert Humphrey: A Biography*. New York: Norton, 1984.

Steel, Ronald. *In Love with Night: The American Romance with Robert Kennedy*. New York: Simon & Schuster, 2000.

Strobes, Gerald S., and Deborah H. Strobes. *Nixon: An Oral History of his Presidency*. New York: HarperCollins, 1994.

Thomas, Evan. *Robert Kennedy: His Life*. New York: Simon & Schuster, 2002.

White, Theodore. *Breach of Faith: The Fall of Richard Nixon*. New York: Dell, 1975.

Wills, Garry. *Nixon Agonistes: The Crisis of the Self-Made Man*. Boston: Houghton Mifflin, 1970.

Witcover, Jules. *85 Days: The Last Campaign of Robert Kennedy*. New York: Putnam, 1969.

———. *The Resurrection of Richard Nixon*. New York: Putnam's, 1970.

Vietnam

Anderson, David L., ed. *Shadow in the White House: Presidents and the Vietnam War, 1945–1975*. Lawrence: University of Kansas Press, 1993.

Appy, Christian J. *Working Class War: American Combat Soldiers and the Vietnam War*. Chapel Hill: University of North Carolina Press,

Baker, Mark. *Nam*. New York: Cooper Square Press, 1981.

Barrett, David M. *Uncertain Warriors: Lyndon Johnson and His Vietnam Advisers*. Lawrence: University of Kansas Press, 1993.

Berman, Larry. *Lyndon Johnson's War*. New York: Norton, 1989.

———. *Planning a Tragedy*. New York: Norton, 1982.

Berman, Paul. *No Peace, No Honor: Nixon, Kissinger and Betrayal in Vietnam*. New York: Simon & Schuster, 2001.

Capps, Walter. *The Unfinished War: Vietnam and the American Conscience*. Revised Edition. Boston: Beacon Press, 1990.

———, ed. *The Vietnam Reader*. New York: Routledge, 1990

Clodfelter, Michael. *The Limits of Air Power: The Bombing of North Vietnam*. New York: Free Press, 1989.

———. *Vietnam in Military Statistics: A History of the Indochina Wars, 1772–1991*. Jefferson, N.C.: McFarland, 1995.

Cooper, Chester. *The Lost Crusade: America in Vietnam*. New York: Dodd, Mead, 1970.

DeBenedetti, Charles, and Charles Chatfield. *An American Ordeal: The Antiwar Movement of the Vietnam Era*. Syracuse, N.Y.: Syracuse University Press, 1990.

DeGroot, Gerald J. *A Noble Cause? America and the Vietnam War*. London: Longman, 1999.

Duiker, William J. *The Communist Road to Power in Vietnam*. Boulder, Colo.: Westview Press, 1981.

———. *Ho Chi Minh*. New York: Hyperion, 2000.

Ellsberg, Daniel. *Papers on the War*. New York: Simon & Schuster, 1972.

Emerson, Gloria. *Winners and Losers: Battles, Retreats, Gains, Losses, and Ruins from a long War*. New York: Random House, 1977.

Fall, Bernard B. *Last Reflections on a War*. Garden City, N.Y.: Doubleday, 1967.

———. *The Two Vietnams: A Political and Military Analysis*. New York: Praeger, 1963.

———. *Vietnam Witness, 1953–1966*. New York: Praeger, 1966.

Fitzgerald, Frances. *Fire in the Lake: The Vietnamese and the Americans in Vietnam*. Boston: Little, Brown, 1972.

Garfinckle, Adam. *Telltale Hearts: The Origin and Impact of the Vietnam Antiwar Movement*. New York: St. Martin's Press, 1995.

Gelb, Lester, and Richard K. Betts. *The Irony of Vietnam: The System Worked*. Washington D.C.: Brookings Institution, 1978.

Gibson, James William. *The Perfect War: Technowar in Vietnam*. New York: Atlantic Monthly Press, 2000.

Gottlieb, Sherrie. *Hell No, We Won't Go: Resisting the Draft during the Vietnam War*. New York: Viking, 1991.

Halberstam, David. *The Making of a Quagmire*. New York: Random House, 1966.

Hendrickson, Paul. *The Living: Robert McNamara and Five Lives of a Lost War*. New York: Random House, 1996.

Herr, Michael. *Dispatches*. New York: Knopf, 1977.

Herring, George C. "American Strategy in Vietnam: The Postwar Debate," *Military Affairs* 46 (April 1982): 57–63.

———. *America's Longest War: The United States and Vietnam, 1950–1975*. New York: McGraw-Hill, 1996.

———. *LBJ and Vietnam: A Different Kind of War*. Austin: University of Texas Press, 1994.

Hess, Gary R. *Vietnam and the United States: Origins and Legacy of a War*. Boston: Twayne, 1991.

Kaiser, David. *American Tragedy: Kennedy, Johnson and the Origins of the Vietnam War*. Cambridge, Mass.: Harvard University Press, 2000.

Karnow, Stanley. *Vietnam: A History*. New York: Viking, 1983.

Kolko, Gabriel. *Anatomy of a War: Vietnam, the United States, and the Modern Historical Experience*. New York: Pantheon, 1985.

Lacouture, Jean. *Ho Chi Minh: A Political Biography*. Translated by Peter Wiles. New York: Random House, 1964.

Langguth, A.J. *Our Vietnam: The War, 1954–1975*. New York: Simon & Schuster, 2001.

Lewy, Guenter. *America in Vietnam*. New York: Oxford University Press, 1978.

Lind, Michael. *Vietnam: The Necessary War*. New York: Simon & Schuster, 1999.

McMaster, H. R. *Dereliction of Duty: Lyndon Johnson, Robert McNamara, the Joint Chiefs of Staff, and the Lies the Led to Vietnam*. New York: HarperCollins, 1997.

Newman, John M. *JFK and Vietnam*. New York: Warner, 1992.

Oberdorfer, Don. *Tet!* New York: Doubleday, 1971.

O'Nan, Stewart, ed. *The Vietnam Reader: The Definitive Collection of American Fiction and Nonfiction on the War*. New York: Doubleday, 1998.

Palmer, Bruce. *The 25 Year War*. Lexington: University Press of Kentucky, 1984.

Podhoretz, Norman. *Why We Were in Vietnam*. New York: Simon & Schuster, 1999.

Schlesinger, Arthur M., Jr. *The Bitter Heritage: Vietnam and American Democracy*. Boston: Houghton Mifflin, 1966.

Sheehan, Neil. *A Bright Shining Lie: John Paul Vann and America in Vietnam*. New York: Random House, 1989.

Showcross, William. *Sideshow: Kissinger, Nixon and the Destruction of Cambodia.* New York: Simon & Schuster, 1979.

Shultz, Richard H. *The Secret War against Hanoi: Kennedy's and Johnson's Use of Spies, Saboteurs, and Covert Warriors in North Vietnam.* New York: HarperCollins, 1999.

Smith, R. B. *An International History of the Vietnam War.* 3 vols. New York: St. Martin's Press, 1986.

Spector, Ronald. *After Tet: The Bloodshed Years in Vietnam.* New York: Free Press, 1993.

Thies, Wallace J. *When Governments Collide: Coercion and Diplomacy in the Vietnam Conflict, 1964–1968.* Berkeley: University of California Press, 1980.

Thomson, James. "How Could Vietnam Happen? An Autopsy," *Atlantic Monthly* 221 (April 1960): 47–53.

Turner, Robert F. *Vietnam Communism: Its Origin and Development.* Stanford, Calif.: Hoover Institute Press, 1975.

Warner, Denis. *The Last Confucian.* New York: Macmillan, 1963.

Wirtz, James J. *The Tet Offensive: Intelligence Failure in War.* Ithaca, N.Y.: Cornell University Press, 1991.

The Crisis of 1968

Caute, David. *The Year of the Barricades: A Journey through 1968.* New York: Harper & Row, 1988.

Chester, Lewis, et al. *An American Melodrama: The Presidential Campaign of 1968.* New York: Viking, 1968.

English, David. *Divided They Stand.* Englewood Cliffs, N.J.: Prentice-Hall, 1969.

Farber, David. *Chicago '68.* Chicago: University of Chicago Press, 1988.

Flamm, Michael W. *Law and Order: Street Crime, Civil Unrest, and the Crisis of Liberalism in the 1960s.* New York: Columbia University Press, 2005.

Gould, Lewis L. *1968: The Election That Changed America.* Chicago: Ivan R. Dee, 1993.

Hastings, Max. *America's Year of Crisis.* New York: Taplinger, 1969.

Kaiser, Charles. *1968 in America: Music, Politics, Chaos, Counterculture and the Shaping of a Generation.* New York: Grove Press, 1988.

Knappman, Edward W., ed. *Presidential Election, 1968.* New York: Facts on File, 1970.

Kurlansky, Mark. *1968: The Year That Rocked the World.* New York: Ballantine, 2004.

Kusch, Frank. *Battleground Chicago: The Police and the 1968 Democratic National Convention.* Westport, Conn.: Greenwood Press, 2004.

LaFeber, Walter. *The Deadly Bet: LBJ, Vietnam, and the 1968 Election.* New York: Rowman & Littlefield, 2005.

McCarthy, Eugene. *1968: War & Democracy.* Red Wing, Minn.: Lone Oak Press, 2000.

McGinniss, Joe. *The Selling of the President.* New York: Penguin Books, 1988; originally published in 1969.

Scammon, Richard M., and Ben J. Wattenberg. *The Real Majority.* New York: Coward-McCann, 1970.

Schlesinger, Arthur M., ed. *The Election of 1968.* Philadelphia: Mason Crest Publishers, 2003.

Unger, Irwin, and Debi Unger. *Turning Point, 1968.* New York: Scribner's, 1988.

White, Theodore H. *The Making of the President, 1968.* New York: Atheneum, 1969.

Witcover, Jules. *The Year the Dream Died.* New York: Warner Books, 1997.

Political Movements: Right, Left, and Center

Addison, Adam M. *SDS.* New York: Scribner's, 1972.

Alinsky, Saul D. *Rules for Radicals.* New York: Random House, 1971.

Andrews, John A. *The Other Side of the Sixties: Young Americans for Freedom and the Rise of Conservative Politics.* New Brunswick, N.J.: Rutgers University Press, 1997.

Bacciocca, Edward, Jr. *The New Left in America: Reform to Revolution, 1956–1970.* Stanford, Calif.: Hoover Institution, 1974.

Brennan, Mary C. *Turning Right in the Sixties: The Conservative Capture of the GOP.* Chapel Hill: University of North Carolina Press, 1980.

Chafe, William H. *Never Stop Running: Allard Lowenstein and the Struggle to Save American Liberalism.* New York: Basic Books, 1993.

Collier, Peter, and David Horowitz, eds. *Second Thoughts: Former Radicals Look Back at the 60s.* Lanham, Md.: Madison Books, 1989.

Crawford, Alan. *Thunder on the Right: The "New Right" and the Politics of Resentment.* New York: Pantheon, 1980.

Diggins, John. *The Rise and Fall of the American Left.* New York: Norton, 1992.

Downs, Donald Alexander. *Cornell '69: Liberalism and the Crisis of the American University.* Ithaca, N.Y.: Cornell University Press, 1999.

Ellis, Richard J. *The Dark Side of the Left: Illiberal Egalitarianism in America.* Lawrence: University of Kansas Press, 1998.

Flacks, Richard. *Making History: The American Left and the American Mind.* New York: Columbia University Press, 1980.

Heineman, Kenneth J. *Put Your Bodies upon the Wheels: Student Revolt in the 1960s.* Chicago: Ivan R. Dee, 2001.

Isserman, Maurice. *If I Had a Hammer: The Death of the Old Left and the Birth of the New Left.* New York: Basic Books, 1987.

Keniston, Kenneth. *The Uncommitted: Alienated Youth in American Society.* New York: Harcourt, Brace and World, 1965.

Klatch, Rebecca E. *Women of the New Right.* Philadelphia: Temple University Press, 1987.

————————————. *Generation Divided: The New Left, the New Right, and the 1960s.* Berkeley: University of California Press, 1999.

Kolkay, Jonathan M. *The New Right: 1960–1968: With Apologies, 1964–1980.* Washington D.C.: University Press of America, 1983.

Levy, Peter B. *The New Left and Labor in the 1960s.* Urbana: University of Illinois Press, 1993.

Lipset, Seymour Martin, and Sheldon S. Wolin, eds. *The Berkeley Student Revolt: Facts and Interpretations.* New York: Anchor, 1965.

Miller, James. *Democracy in the Streets: From Port Huron to the Siege of Chicago.* New York: Simon & Schuster, 1987.

Miles, Michael W. *The Radical Probe: The Logic of Student Rebellion.* New York: Atheneum, 1971.

Mills, C. Wright. "The New Left," *New Left Review* (October 1960).

Radosh, Ronald. *Commies: A Journey through the Old Left, the New Left and the Leftover Left.* San Francisco: Encounter Books, 2001.

Rorabaugh, W. J. *Berkeley at War: The 1960s.* New York: Oxford University Press, 1989.

Rothman, Stanley, and S. Robert Lichter. *Roots of Radicalism: Jews, Christians and the New Left.* New York: Oxford University Press, 1982.

Sale, Kirkpatrick. *SDS.* New York: Random House, 1973.

Schneider, Gregory L. *Cadres for Conservatism: Young Americans for Freedom and the Rise of the Contemporary Right.* New York: New York University Press, 1999.

Taft, John. *Mayday at Yale: A Case Study in Student Radicalism.* Boulder, Colo.: Westview Press, 1976.

Unger, Irwin. *The Movement: A History of the American New Left.* New York: Harper & Row, 1974.

Vickers, George R. *The Formation of the New Left.* Lexington, Mass.: Heath, 1975.

Viorst, Milton. *Fire in the Streets: America in the 1960s.* New York: Simon & Schuster, 1979.

Countercultural Protest Movements

Adler, Nathan. *The Underground Stream: New Life Styles and the Antinomian Personality.* New York: Harper & Row, 1972.

Altschuler, Glenn C. *All Shook Up: How Rock 'n' Roll Changed America.* New York: Oxford University Press, 2003.

Anthony, Gene. *The Summer of Love: Haight-Ashbury at Its Height.* Milbrae, Calif.: Celestial Arts, 1980

Barzun, Jacques. *From Dawn to Decadence: 500 Years of Western Cultural Life, 1500 to the Present.* New York: HarperCollins, 2000.

Bayles, Martha. *Hole in Our Soul: The Loss of Beauty and Meaning in American Popular Music.* Chicago: University of Chicago Press, 1994.

Booth, Stanley. *Dance with the Devil: The Rolling Stones and Their Times.* New York: Random House, 1984.

Brown, Norman O. *Life against Death: The Psychoanalytic Meaning of History.* New York: Vintage, 1959.

———. *Love's Body.* New York: Vintage, 1966.

Brownstein, Peter, and Michael William Doyle, eds. *Imagine Nation: The American Counterculture of the 1960s and 1970s.* New York: Routledge, 2002.

Curry, Jack. *Woodstock: The Summer of Our Lives.* New York: Weidenfeld and Nicolson, 1989.

Davies, Hunter. *The Beatles: The Only Authorized Biography.* London: Arrow, 1993.

Decter, Midge. *Liberal Parents, Radical Children.* New York: Coward, McCann and Geoghegan, 1975.

Didion, Joan. *Slouching Towards Bethlehem.* New York: Farrar, Straus & Giroux, 1968.

Draper, Robert. *Rolling Stone Magazine: The Uncensored History.* New York: Doubleday, 1990.

Feuer, Lewis S. *The Conflict of Generations: Character and Significance of Student Movements.* New York: Basic Books, 1969.

Frank, Thomas. *The Conquest of Cool: Business Culture, Counterculture, and the Rise of Hip Consumerism.* Chicago: University of Chicago Press, 1997.

Gaskin, Stephen. *Haight-Asbury Flashbacks.* Berkeley, Calif.: Ronin, 1990.

Gottlieb, Annie. *Do You Believe in Magic? The Second Coming of the 60s Generation.* New York: Times Books, 1987.

Guiness, Os. *The Dust of Death: The Sixties Counterculture and How It Changed America Forever.* Wheaton, Ill.: Crossway Books, 1994.

Heath, Joseph, and Andrew Potter. *Nation of Rebels: Why Counterculture Became Consumer Culture.* New York: HarperBusiness, 2004.

Heylin, Clinton. *Bob Dylan: Behind the Shades.* New York: Summit, 1991.

Hoffman, Nicholas von. *We Are the People Our Parents Warned Us Against.* Chicago: Ivan R. Dee, 1968.

Jonnes, Jill. *Hep-Cats, Narcs, and Pipe Dreams: A History of America's Romance with Drugs.* Baltimore: Johns Hopkins University Press, 1996.

Makower, Joel. *Woodstock: The Oral History.* New York: Doubleday, 1989.

Malcolm, Henry. *The Generation of Narcissus.* Boston: Little, Brown, 1971.

Marcus, Greil. *Like a Rolling Stone: Bob Dylan at the Crossroad.* New York: Public Affairs, 2005.

———. *Mystery Train: Images of America in Rock 'n' Roll.* New York: E. P. Dutton, 1982.

Marcuse, Herbert. *Eros and Civilization: A Philosophical Inquiry into Freud.* Boston: Beacon Press, 1955.

———. *An Essay on Liberation.* Boston: Beacon Press, 1969.

———. *One Dimensional Man.* Boston: Beacon Press, 1964.

Miller, Timothy. *The Hippies and American Values.* Knoxville: University of Tennessee Press, 1991.

———. *The Sixties Communes: Hippies and Beyond.* Syracuse, N.Y.: Syracuse University Press, 1999.

Nobile, Philip, ed. *The Con-III Controversy: Critics Look at the Greening of America.* New York: Pocket Books, 1971.

Pattison, Robert. *The Triumph of Vulgarity: Rock Music in the Mirror of Romanticism.* New York: Oxford University Press, 1987.

Peck, Abe. *Uncovering the Sixties: The Life and Times of the Underground Press.* New York: Pantheon, 1985.

Perry, Charles. *The Haight-Ashbury.* New York: Vintage, 1983.

Pichaske, David. *A Generation in Motion: Popular Music and Culture in the Sixties.* Granite Falls, Minn.: Ellis Press, 1989.

Pollock, Bruce. *When the Music Mattered: Rock in the 1960s.* New York: Holt, Rinehart, and Winston, 1983.

Reich, Charles A. *The Greening of America.* New York: Bantam, 1971.

Roszak, Theodore. *The Making of a Counterculture.* New York: Anchor, 1969.

———. *Unfinished Animal: The Aquarian Frontier and the Evolution of Consciousness.* New York: Harper & Row, 1975.

———. *Where the Wasteland Ends.* New York: Anchor, 1973.

Santelli, Robert. *Aquarius Rising: The Rock Festival Years.* New York: Dell, 1980.

Selvin, Joel. *Summer of Love.* New York: Cooper Square Press, 1999.

Slater, Paul. *The Pursuit of Loneliness: American Culture at the Breaking Point.* Boston: Beacon Press, 1970.

Spitz, Bob. *Barefoot in Babylon: The Creation of the Woodstock Music Festival.* New York: Viking, 1979.

Stevens, Jay. *Storming Heaven: LSD and the American Dream.* New York: Harper & Row, 1987.

Tipton, Steven M. *Getting Saved from the Sixties: Moral Meaning in Conversion and Cultural Change.* Berkeley: University of California Press, 1982.

Wolf, Leonard. *Voice from the Love Generation.* Boston: Little, Brown, 1968.

Yablonsky, Lewis. *The Hippie Trip.* New York: Pegasus, 1968.

Yinger, J. Milton. *Countercultures: The Promise and Peril of a World Turned Upside Down.* New York: Free Press, 1982.

Young, Jean, and Michael Lang. *Woodstock Festival Remembered.* New York: Ballantine, 1979.

Zweig, Paul. *The Heresy of Self-Love: A Study of Subversive Individualism.* New York: Harper & Row, 1968.

Riding the Coattails: Aggrieved Minorities

Acuna, Rodolfo. *Occupied America: A History of Chicanos.* New York: Harper & Row, 1981.

Adam, Barry. *The Rise of a Gay and Lesbian Movement.* Boston: Twayne, 1987.

Bailey, Beth. *Sex in the Heartland.* Cambridge, Mass.: Harvard University Press, 1999.

Blue Cloud, Peter. *Alcatraz Is Not an Island.* Berkeley, Calif.: Wingbow Press, 1972.

Bordewich, Fergus M. *Killing the White Man's Indian: Reinventing Native Americans at the End of the Twentieth Century.* New York: Anchor Books, 1996.

Burnette, Robert, and John Koster. *The Road to Wounded Knee.* New York: Bantam, 1974.

Cornell, Stephen. *The Return of the Native: American Indian Political Resurgence.* New York: Oxford University Press, 1988.

Deloria, Vine, Jr. *American Indian Policy in the Twentieth Century.* Norman, Oklahoma: University of Oklahoma Press, 1985.

———. *Behind the Trail of Broken Treaties: An Indian Declaration of Independence.* Austin, Texas: University of Texas Press, 1985.

———. *We Talk, You Listen: New Tribes, New Turf.* New York: Dell, 1970.

Deloria, Vine, Jr., and Clifford M. Lytle. *American Indians, American Justice.* Austin: University of Texas Press, 1983.

———. *The Nations Within: The Past and Future of American Indian Sovereignty.* New York: Pantheon, 1984.

D'Emilio, John. *Making Trouble: Essays on Gay History, Politics, and the University.* New York: Routledge, 1992.

———. *Sexual Politics, Sexual Communities: The Making of a Homosexual Minority in the United States, 1940–1970.* Chicago: University of Chicago Press, 1983.

D'Emilio, John, and Estelle B. Freedman. *Intimate Matters: A History of Sexuality in America.* Chicago: University of Chicago Press, 1988.

Duberman, Martin. *Stonewall.* New York: Dutton, 1993.

Echols, Alice. *Daring to Be Bad: Feminism in America, 1967–1975.* Minneapolis: University of Minnesota Press, 1989.

Escoffier, Jeffrey, ed. *Sexual Revolution.* New York: Thunder's Mouth Press, 2003.

Evans, Sara. *Personal Politics: The Roots of Women's Liberation in the Civil Rights Movement and the New Left.* New York: Vintage, 1980.

———. *Tidal Wave: How Women Changed America at Century's End.* New York: Free Press, 2003.

Firestone, Shulamith. *The Dialectics of Sex: The Case for Feminist Revolution.* New York: Morrow, 1970.

Fixico, Donald. *Termination and Relocation.* Albuquerque: University of New Mexico Press, 1986.

Friedan, Betty. *The Feminine Mystique.* New York: Norton, 1963.

Garcia, F. Chris. *La Causa Politica: A Chicano Politics Reader.* Notre Dame, Ind.: University of Notre Dame Press, 1975.

Garcia, Ignacio. *Chicanismo: The Forging of a Militant Ethos among Mexican-Americans.* Tucson: University of Arizona Press, 1997.

Greer, Germaine. *The Female Eunuch.* New York: McGraw-Hill, 1972.

Griswold del Castillo, Richard, and Richard Garcia. *Cesar Chavez: A Triumph of Spirit.* Norman: University of Oklahoma Press, 1995.

Hammerback, John C., et al. *A War of Words: Chicano Protests in the 1960s and 1970s.* Westport, Conn.: Greenwood Press, 1985.

Hertzberg, Hazel W. *The Search for an American Indian Identity: Modern Pan-Indian Movements.* Syracuse, N.Y.: Syracuse University Press, 1971.

Humphrey, Laud. *Out of the Closets: The Sociology of Homosexual Liberation.* Englewood Cliffs, N.J.: Prentice Hall, 1972.

Jenkins, Craig. *The Politics of Insurgency: The Farm Workers Movement in the 1960s.* New York: Columbia University Press, 1985.

Jennings, Francis. *The Invasion of America: Indians, Colonialism, and the Cant of Conquest.* New York: Norton, 1976.

Josephy, Alvin M., and Joane Nagel, eds. *Red Power: The American Indians' Fight for Freedom.* Lincoln: University of Nebraska Press, 1999.

Koedt, Ann, Ellen Divine, and Anita Rapone, eds. *Radical Feminism.* New York: Quadrangle Books, 1973.

Lasch-Quinn, Elizabeth. *Race Experts.* New York: Norton, 2001.

Linden-Ward, Blanche, and Carol Hurd Green. *Changing the Future: American Women in the 1960s.* New York: Twayne, 1993.

Marcus, Eric. *Making History: The Struggle for Gay and Lesbian Equal Rights.* New York: HarperCollins, 1992.

Mathiessen, Peter. *In the Spirit of Crazy Horse*. New York: Viking, 1983.

Meier, Matt S., and Feliciano Rivera. *The Chicanos: A History of Mexican Americans*. New York: Hill and Wang, 1972.

Millett, Kate. *Sexual Politics*. Garden City, N.Y.: Doubleday, 1970.

Morgan, Robin, ed. *Sisterhood Is Powerful*. New York: Random House, 1970.

Rosales, F. Arturo. *Chicanos: A History of the Mexican-American Civil Rights Movement*. Houston: Arte Publico Press, 1997.

Rosen, Ruth. *The World Split Open: How the Modern Women's Movement Changed America*. New York: Viking, 2000.

Skerry, Peter. *Mexican Americans: The Ambivalent Minority*. Cambridge, Mass.: Harvard University Press, 1993.

Skrentny, John D. *The Minority Rights Revolution*. Cambridge, Mass.: Harvard University Press, 2002.

Smith, Paul C., and Robert Allen Warrior. *Like a Hurricane: The Indian Movement from Alcatraz to Wounded Knee*. New York: New Press, 1996.

Sommers, Christina Hoff. *Who Stole Feminism? How Women Have Betrayed Women*. New York: Simon & Schuster, 1994.

Sowell, Thomas. *Ethnic America: A History*. New York: Basic Books, 1981.

Wilson, James. *The Earth Shall Weep: A History of Native America*. New York: Atlantic Monthly Press, 1998.

Peering into the Historical Looking Glass

Berman, Marshall. *All That Is Solid Melts into Air: The Experience of Modernity*. New York: Penguin, 1988.

Berman, Morris. *The Twilight of American Culture*. London: Duckworth, 2000.

Brimelow, Peter. *Alien Nation: Common Sense about America's Immigration Disaster*. New York: Random House, 1995.

Dalrymple, Theodore. *Our Culture, Or What's Left of It*. Chicago: Ivan R. Dee, 2005.

DeLeon, David. *The American Anarchist: Reflections on an Indigenous Radicalism*. Baltimore: John Hopkins University, 1978.

Diamond, Jared. *Collapse: How Societies Choose to Fail or Succeed*. New York: Viking, 2005.

Freud, Sigmund. *Civilization and Its Discontents*. New York: Norton, 1962.

Fukuyama, Francis. *The End of History and the Last Man*. New York: Free Press, 1992.

Hacker, Andrew. *Two Nations: Black and White, Separate, Hostile, Unequal*. New York: Scribner's, 1992.

Hayek, F. A. *The Road to Serfdom*. Chicago: University of Chicago Press, 1944.

Herman, Arthur. *The Idea of Decline in Western History*. New York: Free Press, 1997.

Herrnstein, Richard J., and Charles Murray. *The Bell Curve*. New York: Free Press, 1994.

Howard, Philip K. *The Death of Common Sense: How Law Is Suffocating America*. New York: Time Warner, 1996.

Hughes, Robert. *The Culture of Complaint: The Fraying of America*. New York: Oxford University Press, 1993.

Hunter, James David. *Culture Wars: The Struggle to Define America*. New York: Basic Books, 1991.

Huntington, Samuel P. *The Clash of Civilizations and the Remaking of the World Order*. New York: Simon & Schuster, 1996.

———. *Who Are We? The Challenge to America's Identity*. New York: Simon & Schuster, 2004.

Jencks, Christopher. *Rethinking Social Policy: Race, Poverty and the Underclass*. New York: Harper-Collins, 1993.

Kennedy, Paul. *The Rise and Fall of the Great Powers.* New York: Random House, 1988.

Lipset, Seymour M. *American Exceptionalism: A Double Edged Sword.* New York: Norton, 1996.

Lukacs, John. *At the End of an Age.* New Haven, Conn.: Yale University Press, 2002.

———. *Democracy and Populism: Fear and Hatred.* New Haven, Connecticut: Yale University Press, 2005.

Marx, Leo. *The Machine in the Garden: Technology and the Pastoral Ideal in America.* New York: Oxford University Press, 1964.

Noble, David W. *Death of a Nation: American Culture and the End of Exceptionalism.* Minneapolis: University of Minnesota Press, 2002.

Ophuls, William. *Ecology and the Politics of Scarcity: Prologue to a Political Theory of the Steady State.* San Francisco: W. H. Freeman, 1977.

———. *Requiem for Modern Politics: The Tragedy of the Enlightenment and the Challenge of the New Millennium.* Boulder, Colo.: Westview Press, 1997.

Ortega y Gasset, José. *The Revolt of the Masses.* New York: Norton, 1957.

Peterson, Wallace C. *Silent Depression: The Fate of the American Dream.* New York: Norton, 1994.

Phillips, Kevin. *Wealth and Democracy.* New York: Broadway Books, 2002.

Postman, Neil. *Amusing Ourselves to Death: Public Discourse in the Age of Show Business.* New York: Viking, 1985.

———. *Technopoly: The Surrender of Culture to Technology.* New York: Random House, 1992.

Samuelson, Robert J. *The Good Life and Its Discontents: The American Dream in the Age of Entitlement, 1945–1995.* New York: Times Books, 1995.

Sorokin, P. A. *The Crisis of Our Age.* New York: Dutton, 1941.

Sowell, Thomas. *Conflict of Visions: Ideological Origins of Political Struggles.* New York: Morrow, 1987.

Spengler, Oswald. *The Decline of the West.* 2 vols. New York: Knopf, 1926.

Steele, Shelby. *The Content of Our Character: A New Vision of Race in America.* New York: St. Martin's Press, 1990.

Sykes, Charles J. *A Nation of Victims: The Degeneration of the American Character.* New York:

Tainter, Joseph A. *The Collapse of Complex Societies.* Cambridge, England: Cambridge University Press, 1990.

Thernstrom, Stephan, and Abigail Thernstrom. *America in Black and White: One Nation, Indivisible.* New York: Simon & Schuster, 1997.

Thompson, William Irwin. *Pacific Shift.* San Francisco: Sierra Club, 1985.

Toynbee, Arnold. *A Study of History.* 2 vols. Abridged by D. C. Sumervell. Oxford: Oxford University Press, 1957.

Twitchell, James B. *Carnival Culture: The Trashing of Taste in America.* New York: Columbia University Press, 1992.

Wagar, Warren W. *The Three Futures: Paradigms of Things to Come.* New York: Praeger, 1991.

William, Julius Wilson. *The Truly Disadvantaged: : The Inner City, the Underclass, and Public Policy.* Chicago: University of Chicago Press, 1987.

Index